Eleventh Edition

Washington Real Estate Fundamentals

Kathryn J. Haupt
David L. Rockwell
David L. Jarman
Megan Dorsey
Jennifer Gotanda

Rockwell Institute

Table of Contents

Chapter 4: Encumbrances **63**

Chapter 5: Public Restrictions on Land **79**

Chapter 6: Contract Law **95**

The Nature of Real Property

Chapter Overview

Real estate agents are concerned not just with the sale of land and houses, but with the sale of real property. Real property includes the land and improvements, and it also encompasses the rights that go along with ownership of land. The first part of this chapter explains those rights, which are known as appurtenances. It also explains natural attachments and fixtures, which are sold as part of the land, and the distinction between fixtures and personal property, which ordinarily is not transferred with the land. The second part of this chapter explains methods of legal description—the different ways in which a parcel of land may be identified in legal documents to prevent confusion about its boundaries or ownership.

What is Real Property?

There are two types of property: real property (realty) and personal property (personalty). Real property is commonly described as land, anything affixed to the land, and anything incidental or appurtenant to the land. Sometimes it is referred to as "that which is immovable." Personal property, on the other hand, is usually movable. A car, a sofa, and a hat are simple examples of personal property.

The distinction between real and personal property is very important in real estate transactions. When a piece of land is sold, anything that is considered part of the real property is transferred to the buyer along with the land, unless otherwise agreed. But if an item is considered personal property, the sellers can take it with them when they leave.

Of course, the principal component of real property is land. But real property is more than just the surface of the earth. It also includes everything beneath the surface down to the center of the earth, and everything above the surface, to the upper reaches of the sky.

A parcel of real property can be imagined as an inverted pyramid, with its tip at the center of the globe and its base above the earth's surface. The landowner owns not only the earth's surface within the boundaries of the parcel, but also everything under or over the surface.

The rights and privileges associated with land ownership are also considered part of the real property. Think of real property as the land plus a bundle of rights. The owner's

Fig.1.1 The inverted pyramid

bundle of rights includes the right to possess, use, enjoy, encumber, will, sell, or do nothing at all with the land.

Appurtenances

In addition to the basic bundle of ownership rights, a landowner has appurtenant rights. An appurtenance is a right or interest that goes along with or pertains to a piece of land. A landowner's property may include any or all of these appurtenances:

- air rights,
- water rights,
- solid mineral rights,
- oil and gas rights, and
- support rights.

Appurtenances are ordinarily transferred along with the land, but the landowner can sell certain appurtenant rights separately from the land. For example, the owner may keep the land but sell his or her mineral rights to a mining company.

Air Rights

In theory, a landowner's rights extend to the upper limits of the sky. In practice, however, this is no longer true. Congress gave the federal government complete control over the nation's airspace. A landowner still has the exclusive right to use the lower reaches of airspace over his or her property, but may do nothing that would interfere with normal air traffic.

On the other hand, sometimes air traffic interferes with a property owner's right to the normal use of his or her land. If aircraft overflights cause substantial damage to a landowner, he or she may sue the government for some form of reimbursement. The classic example is an airport built next door to a chicken farm. The noise and vibrations from overflights are so severe that the chickens no longer lay eggs. If the land cannot be used for any other reasonable purpose, the value of the land is significantly diminished. The landowner may be able to force the government to condemn the property and compensate him or her for its fair market value.

Water Rights

Water is found both on the surface of the earth and beneath the surface. Surface water may be confined to a channel or basin, or it may be unconfined water, such as run-off or flood water. The water beneath the surface may also be "confined" in the sense that it runs in recognizable underground streams, or it may collect in porous ground layers called aquifers.

In regard to confined surface waters, there are two types of property rights:

1. riparian rights, and
2. appropriative rights.

Riparian Rights. Riparian rights are the water rights of a landowner with respect to water that flows through or adjacent to his or her property. Such a landowner, called a riparian landowner, has a right to make reasonable use of the stream's natural flow. A riparian landowner also has the right to use stream water for domestic uses, such as drinking, bathing, and watering a personal-use produce garden. Upstream landowners are prevented from substantially diminishing the flow in quantity, quality, or velocity.

Whether a riparian owner also owns the land under the stream depends on whether the stream is considered navigable or not. A waterway is generally considered navigable if it is large enough to be used in commerce. If a stream is not navigable, the riparian owner owns the land under the water to the midpoint of the streambed. If a stream is navigable, the government owns the land under the water and the riparian landowner only owns the land to the mean high water mark of the streambed. The general public has the right to use navigable waterways for transportation and recreation.

Property located beside a lake, as opposed to a river or stream, is called **littoral** property. The owner of littoral property is entitled to have the lake maintained at its natural level, and to use the lake for fishing or recreation. The owner is also entitled to have the natural purity of the lake's waters maintained. If the lake is non-navigable, each littoral owner owns a portion of the lake bed adjacent to his or her property.

There is one important restriction on a riparian or littoral owner's water rights. A riparian or littoral owner may never divert water from a stream or lake for use on non-riparian land—that is, land that does not adjoin the stream or lake from which the water is taken.

> **Example:** Brown is a riparian landowner. She owns Parcel C, property that borders Swiftwater River. She also owns Parcel D, property that is about 300 feet inland. She cannot divert water from Swiftwater River to feed the livestock that graze on her non-riparian property. (See Figure 1.2.)

In Washington, the riparian water rights system has been superceded by the appropriative rights system (discussed below). Thus, all riparian and littoral owners were required to register their water rights with the Department of Ecology by June 30, 1974. Any unregistered riparian or littoral rights were extinguished after that date.

Appropriative Rights. Riparian and littoral rights are tied to ownership of land beside a body of water. The second major type of water rights, appropriative rights, does not depend on land ownership. Instead, appropriative rights are based on a permit system called the prior appropriation system.

Fig.1.2 Riparian and non-riparian property

To establish an appropriative right, someone who wants to use water from a particular lake or stream applies to the state government (in Washington, the Department of Ecology) for a permit. It is not necessary for the applicant to own land beside the body of water. Water taken by a permit holder does not have to be used on property adjacent to the water source.

The prior appropriation system is primarily used in the western United States, where water resources are often scarce and therefore carefully controlled. If someone with an appropriative right fails to use the water for a certain period of time, he or she will lose the appropriative right. Another person can apply for a permit to use the water.

Ground Water. Landowners have **overlying rights** in regard to the ground water in aquifers beneath their property. Overlying rights are similar to riparian rights; the landowner is allowed to make reasonable use of the ground water, but not to transport the water for use on land outside the ground water basin from which it was removed. The prior appropriation system may also be applied to ground water.

Solid Mineral Rights

A landowner owns all the solid minerals within the "inverted pyramid" under the surface of his or her property. These minerals are considered to be real property until they are extracted from the earth, at which point they become personal property.

Remember that a landowner can sell his or her mineral rights separately from the rest of the property. When rights to a particular mineral are sold, the purchaser automatically acquires an implied easement—the right to enter the land in order to extract the minerals.

Oil and Gas Rights

Ownership of oil and gas is not as straightforward as ownership of solid minerals. In their natural state, oil and gas lie trapped beneath the surface in porous layers of earth. However, once an oil or gas reservoir has been tapped, the oil and gas begin to flow toward the point where the reservoir has been pierced by the well. A well on one parcel of land can attract all the oil and gas from the surrounding properties.

Ownership of oil and gas is governed by the "rule of capture." That is, a landowner owns all of the oil and gas produced from wells on his or her property. The oil and gas become the personal property of the landowner once they are brought to the surface. The rule of capture has the effect of stimulating oil and gas production, since the only way for a landowner to protect his or her interest in the underlying gas and oil is to drill an offset well to keep the oil and gas from migrating to the neighbor's wells.

Other Appurtenant Rights

In addition to rights concerning air, water, minerals, and oil and gas, there are some other important appurtenant rights.

A piece of land is supported by the other land that surrounds it. A landowner has **support rights**—the right to the natural support provided by the land beside and beneath his or her property. **Lateral support** is support from adjacent land, which may be disturbed by construction or excavations on the adjacent property. **Subjacent support**—support from the underlying earth—may become an issue when a landowner sells his or her mineral rights.

Easements and restrictive covenants also create appurtenant rights. These are discussed in detail in Chapter 4.

Attachments

You have seen that the land and appurtenances are considered part of the real property. The third element of real property is attachments. There are two types of attachments:

1. natural, and
2. man-made.

Natural Attachments

Natural attachments are things attached to the earth by roots, such as trees, shrubs, and crops. This includes plants that grow spontaneously, without the help of humans; these are almost always classified as real property. Natural attachments also include plantings cultivated by people, which are also a part of the real property. However, crops from cultivated plantings are treated as personal property. Thus, a cultivated apple orchard would be realty, but the apples themselves would be personalty.

A special rule, called the **doctrine of emblements**, applies to crops planted by a tenant farmer. If the tenancy is for an indefinite period of time and the tenancy is terminated through no fault of the tenant before the crops are ready for harvest, he or she has the right to re-enter the land and harvest the first crop that matures after the tenancy is terminated.

Man-made Attachments: Fixtures

Articles attached to the land by people are called **fixtures**. Houses, fences, and cement patios are all examples of fixtures. Fixtures are considered part of the real property.

Fixtures always start out as personal property—for example, lumber is personal property, but it becomes a fixture when it's used to build a fence. So it is sometimes difficult to determine whether a particular item has become a fixture or is still personal property. If the item remains personal property, the owner can remove it from the property when the land is sold. But if the item is a fixture, it's transferred to the buyer along with the land unless otherwise agreed.

Distinguishing Fixtures from Personal Property

Buyers and sellers often disagree as to exactly what has been purchased and sold. For instance, is the heirloom chandelier installed by the seller real property that's transferred to the buyer, or can the seller remove it when he moves out?

The easiest way to avoid such a controversy is to put the intentions of the parties in writing. If there is a written agreement between a buyer and seller (or a landlord and tenant, or a lender and borrower) stipulating how a particular item shall be treated—as part of the real estate or as personal property—then the court will respect and enforce that agreement. The stipulation between a buyer and seller would ordinarily be found in their purchase and sale agreement. For example, if a seller plans to take certain shrubs from the property before the transaction closes, a statement to that effect ought to be included in the purchase and sale agreement, since shrubs are usually considered part of the real property.

Similarly, if the seller intends to transfer personal property, such as a couch, to the buyer, that should also be stated in the purchase agreement. In addition to the deed conveying title to the real property, a separate document called a **bill of sale** will be needed. A bill of sale conveys title to personal property.

In the absence of a written agreement, courts apply a series of tests to classify the item in dispute. These tests include:

- the method of attachment,
- adaptation of the item to the realty,
- the intention of the annexor, and
- the relationship of the parties.

Method of Attachment. As a general rule, any item a person permanently attaches to the land becomes a part of the real estate. A permanent attachment occurs when the item is:

- annexed to the land by roots, as with trees and shrubs;
- embedded in the earth, like sewer lines or septic tanks;
- permanently resting on the land, like certain types of buildings; or
- attached by any other enduring method, such as by cement, plaster, nails, bolts, or screws.

It isn't absolutely necessary for an item to be physically attached to the real property in order to be considered a fixture. Often there is physical annexation even without actual attachment. The force of gravity alone may be sufficient, as in the case of a building with no foundation. Also, an article enclosed within a building may be considered annexed to the real property if it cannot be removed without dismantling it or tearing down part of the building.

Even easily movable articles may be considered "attached" to the real property, if they are essential parts of other fixtures. For example, the key to the front door of a house is a fixture. Also, fixtures that have been temporarily removed for servicing or repair remain legally attached to the real property. For example, a built-in dishwasher that has been sent to the repair shop is still considered to be a part of the house that it is ordinarily attached to.

Adaptation of the Item to the Realty. If an unattached article was designed or adapted specifically for use on a particular property, it is probably a fixture. Examples include the pews in a church, and storm windows made for a particular building.

Intention of the Annexor. The method of attachment was once regarded as the most important test in determining whether an item was a fixture, but over time the courts decided that test was too rigid. It did not allow for special situations where something permanently affixed would be more justly classified as personal property. Now, the intention of the annexor is considered a more important test. Courts try to determine what the person who annexed the item to the property intended. Did he or she intend the item to

Fig.1.3 Fixture tests

> **Fixture Tests**
>
> • Method of attachment
> • Adaptation to the property
> • Intention of the annexor
> • Relationship of the parties

become part of the realty or to remain personal property? Each of the other tests (including method of attachment) is viewed as objective evidence of this intention. For instance, permanently imbedding a birdbath in concrete indicates an intention to make the item a permanent fixture, while just setting a birdbath out in the yard does not.

Relationship of the Parties. Intent is also indicated by the relationship between the parties: landlord/tenant, buyer/seller, borrower/lender. For example, it is generally held that a tenant who installs an item, such as new lighting, probably does so with the intention of removing it at the expiration of the lease. On the other hand, it's assumed that an owner making the same alteration is trying to improve the property and does not intend to remove the item. So an item that would be considered personal property if installed by a tenant might be considered a fixture if installed by an owner.

Items installed by a tenant so he or she can carry on a trade or business are called **trade fixtures**. Trade fixtures may be removed unless there is a contrary provision in the lease, or the fixtures have become an integral part of the land or improvements. In the latter case, if the tenant still wants to remove the fixtures, it is his or her responsibility to either restore the property to its original condition, or compensate the landlord for any physical damage resulting from the removal. Trade fixtures that are not removed by the tenant become the property of the landlord.

Mobile Homes as Fixtures

The distinction between fixtures and personal property has special significance in connection with mobile homes. Mobile homes have developed from trailers in parks to modern manufactured homes: large structures that can be set permanently on a full-sized lot.

A manufactured home is personal property until it is permanently attached to land by removing the wheels and mounting the unit on a concrete pad or other foundation. When it is still personal property, a manufactured home can be sold by a dealer without a real estate license, and the sale is subject to sales tax.

Once a manufactured home is permanently attached to the land, it will be taxed as real property. Its sale is no different from the sale of a site-built home, so an agent who lists or sells a mobile home must have a real estate license.

Methods of Legal Description

When real property is transferred from one party to another, an accurate description of the land being conveyed is essential. An ambiguous or uncertain land description could make a contract or a deed invalid, and confusion over exactly what land was transferred could cause problems not only for the parties involved in the current transaction, but also for the parties in future transactions.

There are three major methods used to describe land in legal documents:

- the metes and bounds method,
- the government survey, and
- platting.

Metes and Bounds

The metes and bounds method describes a parcel by establishing its boundaries. The boundaries are described by reference to three things:

- monuments, which may be natural objects such as rivers or trees, or man-made objects such as roads or survey markers;
- directions or courses, in the form of compass readings; and
- distances, measured in any convenient units of length.

Point of Beginning. A metes and bounds description begins at a convenient and well-defined point along the boundary of a tract of land (called the point of beginning). It then sets out directions that would allow a surveyor to trace the

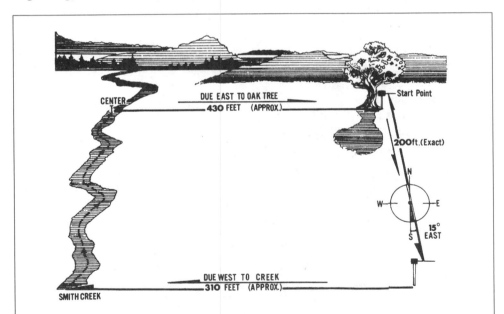

Fig.1.4 Metes and bounds description
"A tract of land, located in Smith County and described as follows: Beginning at the old oak tree, thence south 15° east, 200 feet, thence north 90° west, 310 feet more or less to the centerline of Smith Creek, thence northwesterly along the centerline of Smith Creek to a point directly west of the old oak tree, thence north 90° east, 430 feet more or less to the point of beginning."

boundaries of the tract all the way back to the point of beginning. The point of beginning will always be described by reference to a monument, such as "the SW corner of the intersection of Front and Cherry," or "200 feet north of the old barn." Notice that the point of beginning does not have to be a monument itself, but can be described by referring to a monument.

Tracing Boundaries by Course and Distance. The point of beginning is established, then courses and distances are given. For example, "north, 100 feet" is a course and distance. Both the course and the distance may be described in terms of a monument; for example, "northerly along the eastern edge of Front Street 100 feet" or "north, 100 feet more or less, to the centerline of Smith Creek."

If there is a discrepancy between a monument and a course or distance, the monument will take precedence. In the examples above, the first boundary would be along the edge of Front Street, even if that edge does not run due north, and the second boundary would extend to the center of Smith Creek even if the actual distance to that point is not 100 feet.

A metes and bounds description continues with a series of courses and distances, until the parcel's boundaries have been described all the way around, back to the point of beginning. A metes and bounds description must end at the point of beginning, or else it does not describe a totally enclosed tract.

Metes and bounds descriptions tend to be quite lengthy, and they are often confusing. Furthermore, monuments and reference points do not always maintain their exact locations over the years. An actual survey of the property is usually necessary when dealing with a metes and bounds description.

Conflicting Directions. As noted above, discrepancies may occur between the various elements of a metes and bounds description. In resolving them, the order of priority is as follows:

1. natural monuments,
2. then man-made monuments,
3. then courses,
4. then distances,
5. then names (e.g., "Smith Farm"),
6. then areas (e.g., "40 acres").

If any two of these elements conflict, the one with higher priority will prevail.

Compass Bearings. Directions or courses in metes and bounds descriptions are given in a peculiar fashion. A direction is described by reference to its deviation from either north or south, whichever is closer. Thus, northwest or 315° is written as north 45° west, since it is a deviation of 45° to the west of north. Similarly, south southeast or 157½° is written south 22½° east, since it is a deviation of 22½° to the east of south. East and west are both written relative to north: north 90° east, north 90° west, respectively.

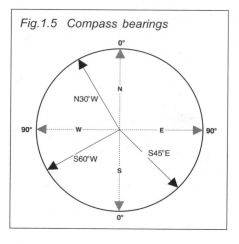

Fig.1.5 Compass bearings

Government Survey

The government survey system, also called the rectangular survey system, describes land by reference to a series of grids. This system of land description was established after many of the northeastern states were already surveyed. Thus, it is mainly used west of the Mississippi River.

The grids and terms used in the government survey system may seem confusing at first, and we recommend that you study the accompanying diagrams closely.

The grids are composed of two sets of lines, one set running north/south, the other east/west. Each grid is identified by a **principal meridian**, which is the original north/south line established in that grid, and by a **base line**, which is the original east/west line. (See Figure 1.6.) In Washington, the principal meridian is the Willamette Meridian.

Grid lines run parallel to the principal meridian and the base line at intervals of six miles. The east/west lines are called **township lines**, and they divide the land into rows or tiers called **township tiers**. The north/south lines, called **range lines**, divide the land into columns called **ranges**. Every fourth range line is a **guide meridian**. (See Figure 1.8.)

A particular area of land that is located at the intersection of a range and a township tier is called a **township**, and it is identified by its position relative to the principal meridian and base line. For example, the township that is located in the fourth tier north of the base line and the third range east of the principal meridian is called "Township 4 North Range 3 East." (See Figure 1.8.) This is often abbreviated "T4N, R3E."

Grid systems are identical across the country, so it is necessary to include in the description the name of the principal meridian that is being used as a reference. (Since each principal meridian has its own base line, it is not necessary to specify the base line.) It's also a good practice to mention the county and state where the land is situated, to avoid any possible confusion. Thus, for example, a complete description of a township might be T4N, R3E of the Willamette Meridian, Clark County, State of Washington.

Each township measures 36 square miles and contains 36 sections. Each section is one square mile, or 640 acres. (See Figure 1.9.) These sections are numbered in a special way, starting with the northeast corner and moving west, then down a row and eastward, snaking back and forth and ending with the southeast corner.

Smaller parcels of land can be identified by reference to sections and partial sections, as illustrated in Figure 1.10.

Government Lots. A government lot is a section of land of irregular shape or size that is referred to by a lot number. Because of the curvature of the earth, range lines converge, so it is impossible to keep all sections exactly one mile square. As a result, the sections along the north and west boundaries of each township are irregular in size. The quarter sections along the north and west boundaries of these sections are used to take up the excess or shortage. The quarter-quarter sections, then, along the north and west boundaries of a township are given government lot numbers.

Another situation in which government lots occur is when a body of water or some other obstacle makes it impossible to survey a square-mile section. The irregularly shaped sections are assigned government lot numbers.

Fig.1.6 Principal meridians and baselines

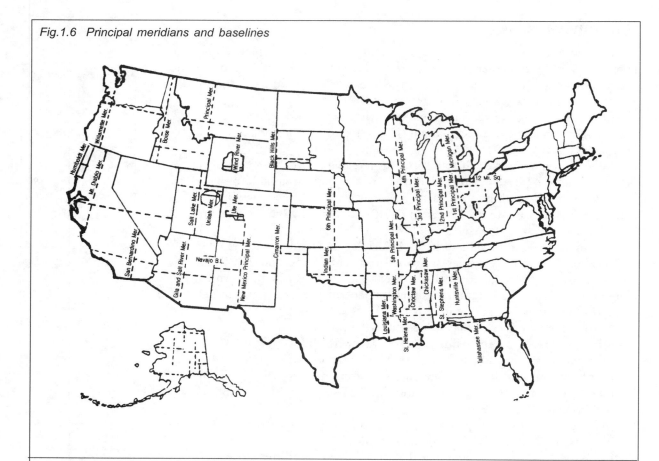

Fig.1.7 Units of land measurement

UNITS OF MEASUREMENT FOR LAND	
UNITS OF AREA	1 Tract = 24 mi. x 24 mi. (576 sq. mi) = 16 townships 1 Township = 6 mi. x 6 mi. (36 sq. mi) = 36 sections 1 Section* = 1 mi. x 1 mi. (1 sq. mi) = 640 acres 1 Acre = 43,560 sq. ft. = 160 sq. rods 1 Square Acre = 208.71 ft. x 208.71 ft.
UNITS OF LENGTH	1 Mile = 5,280 ft. = 320 rods = 80 chains 1 Rod = 16½ ft. 1 Chain = 66 ft. = 4 rods

* Note: To determine the area of partial sections, simply multiply the fraction of the section by 640. For example,

1 half-section = ½ x 640 = 320 acres
1 quarter-section = ¼ x 640 = 160 acres
1 quarter-quarter section = ¼ x ¼ x 640 = 40 acres

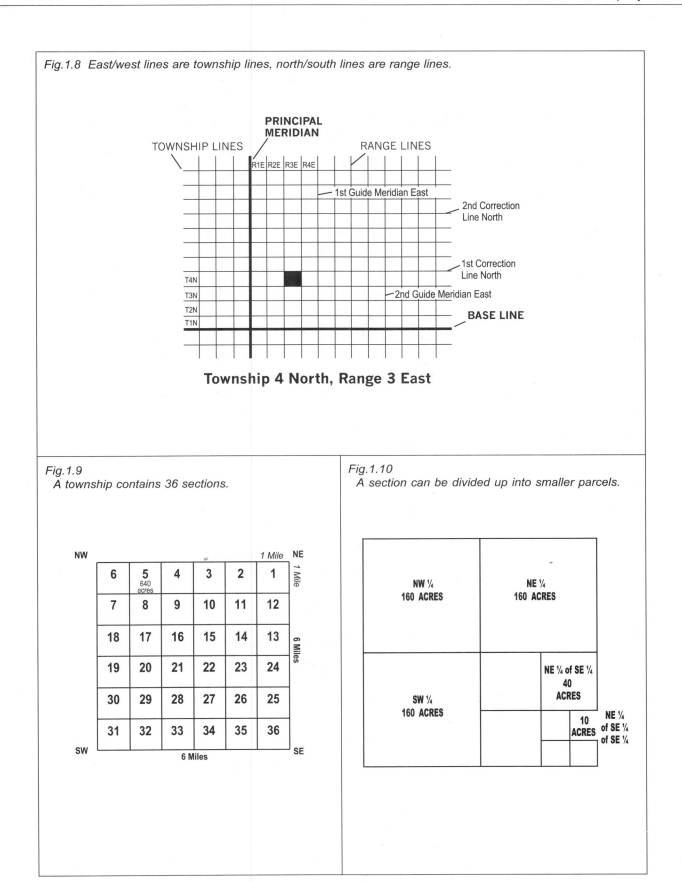

Fig.1.8 East/west lines are township lines, north/south lines are range lines.

PRINCIPAL MERIDIAN

TOWNSHIP LINES

RANGE LINES

R1E R2E R3E R4E

1st Guide Meridian East

2nd Correction Line North

1st Correction Line North

2nd Guide Meridian East

BASE LINE

T4N
T3N
T2N
T1N

Township 4 North, Range 3 East

Fig.1.9
A township contains 36 sections.

6	5 640 acres	4	3	2	1
7	8	9	10	11	12
18	17	16	15	14	13
19	20	21	22	23	24
30	29	28	27	26	25
31	32	33	34	35	36

NW   1 Mile   NE
1 Mile
6 Miles
SW   6 Miles   SE

Fig.1.10
A section can be divided up into smaller parcels.

NW ¼
160 ACRES

NE ¼
160 ACRES

SW ¼
160 ACRES

NE ¼ of SE ¼
40 ACRES

10 ACRES

NE ¼ of SE ¼ of SE ¼

Fig. 1.11 Plat map

Lot and Block

The lot and block method is sometimes referred to as the platting method or the maps and plats system. When land is subdivided, lots and blocks (groups of lots surrounded by streets) are mapped out by a surveyor on a subdivision map called a **plat**. The plat is then recorded in the county where the land is located.

After the plat has been recorded, a reference to one of the lot numbers on the specified plat is a sufficient legal description of the lot. Since a detailed description of the lot is already on file in the county recorder's office, that description may be incorporated into any legal document simply by reference to the lot number and subdivision plat.

To find the precise location and dimensions of the parcel, you would look in the map book at the county recorder's office. Here is an example of a lot and block description:

> Lot 2, Block 4 of Tract number 455, in the City of Vancouver, County of Clark, State of Washington, as per map recorded in Book 25, page 92, of maps, in the office of the recorder of said county.

Plat maps frequently contain a considerable amount of useful information beyond a detailed description of lot boundaries. For example, they may include area measurements, the locations of various easements, right-of-way dimensions, the location of survey markers, and a list of use restrictions applying to the land.

Other Methods of Land Description

There are other methods of describing land besides the three major systems discussed above. When an adequate description of property is already a matter of public record—contained in a recorded document—then a simple reference to that earlier document serves as an adequate property description in a new document. (For example, "All that land described in the grant deed recorded under recording number 92122401503 in Skagit County, Washington.") Also, generalized descriptions such as "all my lands" or "Smith Farm" can be adequate, as long as they make it possible to determine exactly what property is being described. But it's always best to use the least ambiguous description possible, to prevent future problems. It should be noted that a property's street address is usually not an adequate legal description.

Air Lots. Not every parcel of real property can be described simply in terms of its position on the face of the earth. Some forms of real property (e.g., condominiums) require description in terms of elevation above the ground as well. These descriptions are made by reference to an established plane of elevation, called a **datum**. Most large cities have their own official datum, and frequently subsidiary reference points, called bench marks, are also established. A **bench mark** is a point whose position relative to a datum has been accurately measured. Thereafter, surveyors can use the bench mark as a reference when it is more convenient than the datum.

Chapter Summary

1. There are two types of property: real property and personal property. Real property is the land, anything affixed to the land, and anything appurtenant to the land. Movable items, such as furniture, are usually personal property.

2. Appurtenances to land include air rights, water rights, mineral rights, oil and gas rights, and support rights.

3. Attachments may be natural (growing plants) or man-made (fixtures). In the absence of a written agreement, the tests used to distinguish fixtures from personal property include: the method of attachment, the adaptation of the item to the realty, the intention of the annexor, and the relationship of the parties.

4. Before property can be transferred, it must be adequately described. There are three major methods of legal description: metes and bounds, government survey, and lot and block.

🔑 Key Terms

Real property—Land, attachments, and appurtenances.

Personal property—Anything that is not real property; its main characteristic is movability.

Appurtenance—A right incidental to the land that is transferred with it.

Emblements—Crops, such as wheat, produced annually through the labor of the cultivator.

Trade fixtures—Personal property attached to real property by a tenant for use in his or her trade or business. Trade fixtures are removable by the tenant.

Riparian rights—The water rights of a landowner whose land borders on a stream or other surface water. Riparian rights allow only reasonable use of the water.

Littoral land—Land bordered by a stationary body of water, such as a lake or pond.

Appropriative rights—Water rights established by obtaining a government permit, and not based on ownership of land beside a body of water.

Lateral support—The support that a piece of land receives from the surrounding land.

Subjacent support—The support that a piece of land receives from the underlying earth.

Metes and bounds—A system of land description in which the boundaries of a parcel of land are described by reference to monuments, courses, and distances.

Monument—A visible marker (natural or artificial) used in a survey or a metes and bounds description to establish the boundaries of a piece of property.

Point of beginning—The starting point in a metes and bounds description; a monument or a point described by reference to a monument.

Course—In a metes and bounds description, a direction, stated in terms of a compass bearing.

Distance—In a metes and bounds description, the length of a boundary, measured in any convenient unit of length.

Government survey—A system of land description in which the land is divided into squares called townships, and each township is, in turn, divided up into 36 sections, each one square mile.

Principal meridian—In the government survey system, the main north-south line in a particular grid, used as the starting point in numbering the ranges and township tiers.

Range—In the government survey system, a strip of land six miles wide, running north and south.

Township—The intersection of a range and a township tier in the government survey system. It is a parcel of land that is six miles square and contains 36 sections.

Section—One square mile of land, containing 640 acres. There are 36 sections in a township.

Government lot—In the government survey system, a parcel of land that is not a regular section.

Lot and block—The system of description used for subdivided land. The properties within a subdivision are assigned lot numbers on a plat map, which is then recorded; the location and dimensions of a particular lot can be determined by consulting the recorded plat.

Air lot—A parcel of property above the surface of the earth, not containing any land: for example, a condominium unit on the third floor.

Chapter Quiz

1. Real property is equivalent to:

   a) land
   b) personal property
    c) land, attachments, and appurtenances
   d) land and water

2. The most important consideration in determining whether an article is a fixture is:

    a) physical attachment
   b) the annexor's intention
   c) adaptation of the article to the realty
   d) intended use of article

3. Articles installed in or on realty by tenants for use in a business are called:

   a) personalty
    b) trade fixtures
   c) emblements
   d) easements

4. A right that goes with or pertains to real property is called:

   a) an attachment
    b) an appurtenance
   c) personal property
   d) a fixture

5. A landowner's rights regarding water in a stream flowing through his or her land are called:

    a) riparian rights
   b) littoral rights
   c) appropriative rights
   d) easement rights

6. Minerals become personal property when they are:

   a) surveyed
    b) extracted from the land
   c) taken to a refinery
   d) claimed

7. Rights to oil and gas are determined by:

    a) the rule of capture
   b) offset wells
   c) the Bureau of Land Management
   d) the Department of the Interior

8. Whether land borders on a lake or stream is irrelevant under the system of:

   a) riparian rights
    b) capture rights
   c) littoral rights
   d) appropriative rights

9. Ted's property is damaged by sinkholes caused by old coal mining tunnels beneath his land. The rights implicated in this situation are:

   a) riparian rights
    b) subjacent support rights
   c) proximate support rights
   d) lateral support rights

10. Which of the following is most likely to be considered part of the real property?

    a) Piano
     b) Dining room table
    c) Living room drapes
    d) Kitchen sink

11. Which of the following benefits tenant farmers?

    a) Doctrine of emblements
     b) Rule of capture
    c) Overlying rights
    d) Method of attachment test

12. A section of a township contains the following number of acres:

    a) 360
     b) 580
    c) 640
    d) 560

13. A parcel that measures $\frac{1}{4}$ of a mile by $\frac{1}{4}$ of a mile is:

a) $\frac{1}{4}$ of a section
b) $\frac{1}{8}$ of a section
c) $\frac{1}{16}$ of a section
d) $\frac{1}{36}$ of a section

14. The distance between the east and west boundary lines of a township is:

a) one mile
b) two miles
c) six miles
d) ten miles

15. A township contains 36 sections that are numbered consecutively 1 through 36. The last section in the township is located in the:

a) southeast corner
b) southwest corner
c) northeast corner
d) northwest corner

Answer Key

1. c) Real property is made up of land, everything that is attached to the land (e.g., fixtures), and everything that is appurtenant to the land (e.g., water rights).

2. b) The intention of the party who attached the item is the primary consideration in determining whether it is a fixture. The other tests provide evidence of the party's intention.

3. b) An article installed by a tenant for use in a business is called a trade fixture, and it remains the tenant's personal property.

4. b) An appurtenance is a right or interest that goes with the property. Riparian rights are an example.

5. a) Riparian rights include the right to reasonable use of the water that flows through a property owner's land.

6. b) When minerals are extracted from the land, they become personal property.

7. a) The rule of capture determines ownership of oil and gas. This rule provides that the landowner owns all the oil and gas removed from a well on his or her property, even if the oil or gas was originally beneath someone else's property.

8. d) To obtain a water appropriation permit, it is not necessary to own riparian or littoral land.

9. b) Subjacent support rights involve support from the underlying earth.

10. d) Unlike the other items listed, the kitchen sink is a fixture, and therefore part of the real property.

11. a) The doctrine of emblements allows a tenant farmer to return and harvest crops after the lease expires.

12. c) In the government survey system of land description, one section contains 640 acres.

13. c) A section is one mile on each side, a quarter section is ½ mile on each side, and a quarter of a quarter section is ¼ mile on each side.

14. c) A township measures six miles by six miles.

15. a) Section 36 is always in the southeast corner of a township.

Estates in Land and Methods of Holding Title

I. Estates
    A. Freehold estates
        1. fee simple estate
        2. qualified fee estate
        3. life estate
    B. Leasehold estates
        1. estate for years
        2. periodic estate
        3. estate at will
        4. tenancy at sufferance
II. Methods of Holding Title
    A. In severalty
    B. Concurrently
        1. tenancy in common
        2. joint tenancy
        3. community property
    C. Forms of business ownership
        1. partnerships
        2. corporations
        3. limited liability companies
        4. joint ventures
        5. real estate investment trusts
    D. Condominiums and cooperatives

Chapter Overview

Real property ownership can take many different forms. An owner typically has full title to the property and full possession of it, but that isn't necessarily the case. An owner may have a more limited interest instead of full title, or may allow someone else (a tenant) to take possession of the property without taking title. In addition, a property may be owned by more than one person at the same time, which is called concurrent ownership. The first part of this chapter explains the various types of ownership interests, and also the types of interests that tenants may have. The second part of this chapter explains concurrent ownership and the different ways co-owners may hold title.

Estates

The word "estate" refers to an interest in land that is or may become possessory. In other words, someone has now, or may have in the future, the right to possess the property—the right to exclusively occupy and use it.

The different types of estates are distinguished by two features: the duration (how long the estate holder has the right of possession); and the time of possession (whether the estate holder has the right to possess the property right now, or not until sometime in the future). There is a different name for each type of estate.

It is important to note that while all estates are interests in land, not every interest in land is an estate. Interests that are not estates are called non-possessory interests. For example, a mortgage gives a lender a financial interest in the property (a lien), but this interest is not an estate, because it is not a possessory interest. Non-possessory interests are covered in Chapter 4.

Estates fall into two categories:

1. freehold estates, and
2. leasehold (less-than-freehold) estates.

A freehold estate is an interest in real property that has an indeterminable (not fixed or certain) duration. The holder of such an estate is usually referred to as an owner. All other possessory interests are leasehold (less-than-freehold) estates. A leasehold estate has a limited duration (a one-year lease is an example). The holder of a leasehold estate is referred to as a tenant; a tenant has possession of the property but not title.

Freehold Estates

The freehold estate got its name back in the Middle Ages—it originally referred to the holdings of a freeman under the English feudal system. Freehold estates can be subdivided into fee simple estates and life estates.

Fee Simple Estates. The fee simple estate (also called the "fee," the "fee simple," or the "fee simple absolute") is the greatest estate that can exist in land, the highest and most complete form of ownership. It is of potentially infinite duration and represents the whole "bundle of rights."

A fee simple estate is freely transferable and inheritable, so it is sometimes referred to as the **estate of inheritance**. A fee simple estate has no set termination point, and theoretically can be owned forever by the titleholder and his or her heirs. When a fee simple owner transfers title by deed, it is presumed that the grantee (the new owner) receives a fee simple absolute estate, unless the deed includes language that indicates an intent to confer a lesser estate (such as a life estate, described below).

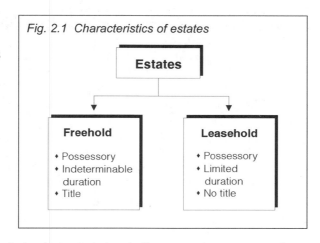

Fig. 2.1 Characteristics of estates

Estates

Freehold
- Possessory
- Indeterminable duration
- Title

Leasehold
- Possessory
- Limited duration
- No title

Qualified Fee Estates. A fee simple estate may be qualified when it is transferred from one owner to another. For example, in a deed, the grantor may specify that the grantee's estate will continue only as long as a certain condition is met, or until a certain event occurs.

> **Example:** Able conveys a parcel of land to "Barney and his heirs so long as it is used for church purposes, and if it is no longer used for church purposes it shall revert back to Able or his heirs."

This type of qualification creates a qualified fee estate (also known as a "defeasible fee," "base fee," or "conditional fee"). The owner of a qualified fee holds the same interest as the owner of a fee simple estate, but the qualified fee holder's interest is subject to termination.

There are two types of qualified fees: fee simple determinable, and fee simple subject to a condition subsequent. A **fee simple determinable** ends automatically if the condition is violated; the property reverts back to the grantor without legal action by the grantor. Language in a deed creating a fee simple determinable includes a phrase such as "so long as," "during," or "until." A **fee simple subject to a condition subsequent** doesn't end automatically when the condition is breached. The grantor must take some action to terminate the estate. This type of estate is created by the words "if" or "on the condition that."

Life Estates. An estate for life is a freehold estate whose duration is limited to the lifetime of a specified person or persons.

> **Example:** Noel gives a parcel of property to Beatrice for her lifetime, calling for a reversion of title to Noel upon Beatrice's death. Beatrice is the life tenant (holder of the life estate), and the duration of the life estate is measured by her lifetime.

The measuring life may be that of the life tenant (as in the example above, where Beatrice's life is the measuring life) or it may be the life of another person. Suppose, for example, Angie gives a parcel of property to Howard for the life of Charlie. Howard has a life estate which will end when Charlie dies. The fee simple estate is a perpetual estate; the life estate is a lesser estate because it is limited in duration. In granting a life estate, a fee simple owner transfers only part of what he or she owns, so there must be something left over after the life estate terminates. What remains is either an estate in reversion or an estate in remainder. These are known as future interests.

Estate in Reversion. If the grantor stipulates that the property will revert back to the grantor at the end of the measuring life, the grantor holds an estate in reversion. The grantor has a future possessory interest in the property. Upon the death of the person whose life the estate is measured by, the property will revert to the grantor or his or her heirs.

Estate in Remainder. If the grantor stipulates that the property should go to a person other than the grantor upon the death of the life tenant, that other person has an estate in remainder and is called the **remainderman**. The only difference between reversion and remainder estates is that the former is held by the grantor and the latter by a third party. (If the grantor doesn't name a remainderman, an estate in reversion is created.) The interest that will pass to the designated party on the death of the life tenant is a fee simple estate.

Rights and Duties of Life Tenants. A life tenant has the same rights as a fee simple absolute owner, including the right to profits or rents, and the right to lease or mortgage the property. And a life tenant has the same duties as a fee simple owner: to pay taxes, assessments, and liens. A life tenant also has certain additional duties, because someone else has a future interest in the property:

- A life tenant must not commit **waste**, which means that the life tenant must not engage in acts that will permanently damage the property and harm the interests of the reversionary or remainder estate.
- A life tenant must also allow for the reasonable inspection of the property by the remainderman, who is permitted to check the property for possible waste.

The life tenant may transfer or lease his or her interest in the property. But it should be noted that the life tenant can give, sell, or lease only that which he or

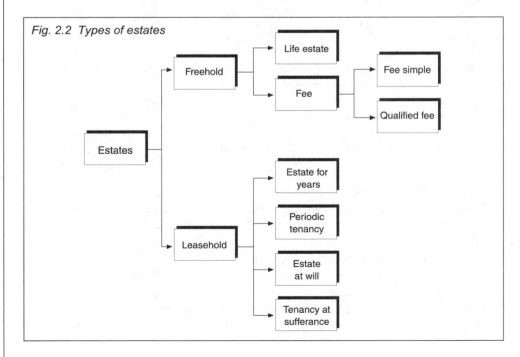

Fig. 2.2 Types of estates

she has. In other words, a lease given by a life tenant will terminate upon the death of the person designated as the measuring life. The lease need not be honored by a remainderman. Similarly, a mortgage on a life estate loses its status as a valid lien upon the death of the person named as the measuring life.

Leasehold Estates

Less-than-freehold estates are more commonly called **leasehold estates**. The holder of a leasehold estate is the tenant, who does not own the property, but rather has a right to exclusive possession of the property for a specified period.

The leasehold is created with a **lease**. The parties to a lease are the **landlord (lessor)**, who is the owner of the property, and the **tenant (lessee)**, the party with the right of possession. The lease creates the relationship of landlord and tenant. It grants the tenant the right of exclusive possession, with a reversion of the possessory rights to the landlord at the end of the rental period. The lease is a contract and its provisions are interpreted under contract law.

There are four types of leasehold estates:

1. the estate for years (tenancy for years),
2. the periodic estate (periodic tenancy),
3. the estate at will (tenancy at will), and
4. the tenancy at sufferance.

Estate for Years. The estate for years is a tenancy for a fixed term. Its name is misleading in the sense that the duration need not be for a year or a period of years; it must only be for some fixed term.

> **Example:** Bob rents a cabin in the mountains from Clark for a period from June 1 through September 15. Bob has an estate for years because the rental term is fixed.

An estate for years can be created only by express agreement. It terminates automatically when the agreed term expires; neither party has to give notice of termination. If either the landlord or the tenant wants to terminate an estate for years before the end of the lease period, he or she may do so only if the other party consents. Termination of a lease by mutual consent is called **surrender**.

Unless the lease includes a no-assignment clause, an estate for years is assignable—that is, the tenant can assign his or her interest to another person.

Periodic Estate. A periodic estate, more commonly called a periodic tenancy, has no fixed termination date. It lasts for a specific period (for example, one year, one month, or one week) and continues for successive similar periods (another year, month, or week) until either party gives the other proper notice of termination. Unlike an estate for years, which terminates automatically, a periodic tenancy automatically renews itself at the end of each period, unless one of the parties gives notice. Failure to give proper notice of termination results in the automatic extension of the lease for an additional period.

Like an estate for years, a periodic tenancy is assignable unless assignment is prohibited by the terms of the lease agreement.

Estate at Will. An estate at will is usually created after a periodic tenancy or estate for years has terminated. This estate is created with the agreement of both parties and can be terminated at the will of either. An estate at will often arises when a lease has expired and the parties are in the process of negotiating the terms of a new lease. The term of the tenancy is indefinite; it will continue until either party gives proper notice of termination. Note, however, that unlike an estate for years or periodic tenancy, which are not affected by the death of the landlord or tenant, an estate at will automatically expires upon the death of either the landlord or the tenant. Also, an estate at will is not assignable.

Tenancy at Sufferance. The tenancy at sufferance is the lowest type of estate; in fact, though it's sometimes called an "estate at sufferance," technically it isn't an estate at all. In a tenancy at sufferance, a tenant who came into possession of the property lawfully, under a valid lease, holds over after the lease has expired. The tenant continues in possession of the premises, but without the consent of the landlord.

> **Example:** Joe has a one-year lease with Landlord Sam. At the end of the term, Joe refuses to move out. Joe initially obtained possession of the property legally (under a valid lease), but he is remaining on the property without Sam's consent.

Tenancy at sufferance is simply a way to distinguish between someone who entered into possession of the property legally but no longer has a right to possession, and a trespasser, who never had permission to enter the land in the first place. Because a tenant at sufferance does not hold an estate (a possessory interest in the property), the landlord is not required to give the tenant notice of termination. Even so, the tenant cannot simply be forced off the property; the landlord must follow proper legal procedures for eviction.

Methods of Holding Title

Title to real property may be held by one person, which is ownership in severalty, or it may be held by two or more persons at the same time, which is concurrent ownership.

Ownership in Severalty

When one person holds title to property individually, the property is owned in severalty. The term is derived from the word "sever," which means to keep separate or apart. A sole owner is free to dispose of the property at will. Real property may be owned in severalty by a natural person (a human being) or an artificial person (such as a corporation, a city, or a state).

Concurrent Ownership

Concurrent ownership (also called co-ownership) exists where two or more people simultaneously share title to a piece of property. There are several forms of concurrent ownership, each with distinctive legal characteristics. Under Washington law, three forms of concurrent ownership are recognized:

- tenancy in common,
- joint tenancy, and
- community property.

Tenancy in Common. Tenancy in common is the most basic form of concurrent ownership. In a tenancy in common, two or more individuals each have an **undivided interest** in a single piece of property. This means that each tenant in common has a right to share possession of the whole property, not just a specified part of it. This is referred to as unity of possession.

Tenants in common may have equal or unequal interests. For example, if three people own property as tenants in common, they might each have a one-third interest in the property, or one of them might have a one-half interest in the property and each of the other two a one-quarter interest. But no matter how small a tenant in common's ownership interest is, he or she is still entitled to share possession of the whole property.

A tenant in common may deed his or her interest to someone else, without obtaining the consent of the other co-tenants. A tenant in common may also mortgage his or her interest without the others' consent. At death, a tenant in common's interest is transferred according to the terms of his or her will, or to the legal heirs.

Termination of Tenancy in Common. A tenancy in common may be terminated by a **partition suit**, a legal action that divides the interests in the property and destroys the unity of possession. If possible, a court will actually divide the land into separate parcels. If the property cannot be divided fairly, the court will order the property to be sold and the proceeds divided among the tenants in accordance with their fractional interests.

Joint Tenancy. The second form of concurrent ownership is joint tenancy. In a joint tenancy, two or more individuals are joint and equal owners of the property. The key feature that distinguishes joint tenancy from tenancy in common is the **right of survivorship**: on the death of one of the joint tenants, his or her interest automatically passes by operation of law to the other joint tenant(s). To create a joint tenancy, the "four unities of title" must exist. These unities are:

- unity of interest,
- unity of title,
- unity of time, and
- unity of possession.

These four unities signify that each joint tenant has an equal interest in the property (unity of interest), that each received title through the same deed or will (unity of title), which was executed and delivered at a single time (unity of time), and that each is entitled to undivided possession of the property (unity of possession). If any one of these unities does not exist when the tenancy is created, a joint tenancy is not established.

Since title passes directly to the other joint tenant(s) upon the death of one joint tenant (because of the right of survivorship), property held in joint tenancy can't be willed. The heirs of a deceased joint tenant have no interest in the joint tenancy property.

Example: Jim, Sue, and Bill own property as joint tenants. Jim dies. Sue and Bill now own the entire property fifty-fifty. Jim's heirs cannot make any legal claim to the property. On his death, it ceased to be a part of his estate. Accordingly, the property is not subject to probate and could not have been willed by Jim.

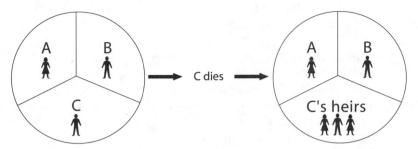

Fig. 2.3 Tenancy in common vs. joint tenancy: death of a co-owner

A, B, and C owned property as tenants in common. Then C died, and his heirs inherited his share of the property. Now the property is owned by A, B, and C's heirs as tenants in common.

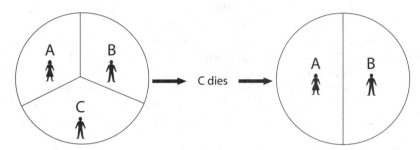

A, B, and C owned property as joint tenants, each with a 1/3 interest. Then C died. Now, by the right of survivorship, A and B own the property as joint tenants, each with a 1/2 interest.

Avoiding the delay and cost of probate proceedings is one of the primary advantages of joint tenancy. Also, the survivors hold the property free from the claims of the deceased tenant's creditors and from any liens against his or her interest. The main disadvantage is that a joint tenant gives up the right to dispose of his or her property by will.

Termination of Joint Tenancy. Like a tenancy in common, a joint tenancy can be terminated through a partition suit. But a joint tenancy also terminates automatically if any one of the four unities is destroyed. A joint tenant is free to convey his or her interest in the property to someone else. However, a conveyance destroys the unities of time and title. This terminates the joint tenancy with respect to the ownership of the conveying joint tenant.

> **Example:** Aaron, Bob, and Caroline own a piece of property as joint tenants. If Aaron conveys his interest to Alice, that terminates the joint tenancy with respect to that one-third interest. Since Alice did not receive title through the same deed or at the same time as Bob and Caroline, Alice can't be a joint tenant. Bob and Caroline are still joint tenants in relation to one another, but Alice holds title as a tenant in common.

Community Property. The community property system of ownership is of Spanish origin; for historical reasons, it is used in several western states, including Washington. In those states, all the property owned by a married couple is classified either as the separate property of one spouse or as the community property of husband and wife.

A spouse's separate property is the property he or she owned before the marriage, and any property he or she acquires during the marriage by inheritance, will, or gift. All other property the husband or wife acquires during the marriage is community property. For example, property purchased with wages earned by either spouse during the marriage is community property. Each spouse has an undivided one-half interest in the community property.

The separate property of either spouse is free from the interests and claims of the other spouse; it may be transferred or encumbered without the approval or interference of the other spouse. Any conveyance or encumbrance of community property, however, requires the approval of both spouses.

In some states that do not have a community property system, married couples may hold title to property as tenants by the entireties. A **tenancy by the entireties** is quite similar to a joint tenancy, but there are some differences. A tenancy by the entireties can only be created by a married couple, and (unlike a joint tenant) a tenant by the entireties cannot convey his or her interest without the other tenant's consent. Tenancy by the entireties is not recognized in community property states such as Washington, and it has been abolished in a number of other states as well.

Forms of Business Ownership

The discussion so far has focused on real property ownership by individuals, whether in severalty or concurrently. Real property can also be owned by business entities.

A **syndicate** is a group of individuals who come together and pool their resources to carry out an enterprise. The syndicate, as such, is not a recognized legal entity. A syndicate may be a business association or a non-profit organization, and it may be organized as a:

- partnership,
- corporation,
- limited liability company,
- joint venture, or
- trust.

The parties who create a syndicate usually decide which form of organization to use based on tax consequences and other considerations, such as the members' personal liability for the syndicate's debts. The form of organization affects how a syndicate holds title to real property.

Partnerships. A partnership is generally defined as an association of two or more persons, to carry on, as co-owners, a business for profit. There are two types of partnerships: general and limited.

A **general partnership** is formed by a contract. Although the agreement need not be in writing, it is wise to spell out all the terms in a written agreement. If the agreement is not in writing, the partnership will be governed by the terms of Washington's Uniform Partnership Act. If the agreement is in writing, the terms of the written agreement will govern, instead of the terms of the Uniform Partnership Act.

The partners in a general partnership all share in the profits and management of the partnership. Unless otherwise agreed, each one has an equal share of the profits and losses, and each has an equal voice in management and control of the business. Each partner can be held personally liable for the debts of the partnership.

Also, each partner is both a principal for and an agent of the general partnership for business purposes. Thus, the authorized acts of one partner (including the execution of legal documents) are binding on the partnership. A partnership is a fiduciary relationship; all the partners have a duty to act with utmost good faith toward one another. (See Chapter 7 for a discussion of agency.)

In general, property acquired for the partnership's business is **partnership property**. Title to partnership property may be held in the partnership's name. Alternatively, it may be held in the name of one or more of the partners, as long as the deed makes reference to the partnership.

Unless otherwise agreed, each partner has an equal right to possess and use all partnership property for partnership purposes. However, a partner is not a co-owner of the partnership property and has no transferable interest in it.

When title to partnership property is held in the partnership's name, it must also be conveyed in the partnership's name. Since each partner is an agent for the partnership, any authorized partner can sign the deed.

A **limited partnership** is a partnership with one or more general partners and one or more limited partners. Limited partnerships must strictly conform to the statutory requirements of the Uniform Limited Partnership Act, and there must be a written limited partnership agreement.

The general partners in a limited partnership have unlimited liability for the partnership's debts and obligations, and they have the exclusive right to manage the business. By contrast, the limited partners have limited liability (that is, they cannot be held personally liable for the partnership's debts and obligations), and they have no voice in management. In fact, if a limited partner took part in the day-to-day control of the business, he or she could be held liable to the same extent as a general partner.

Corporations. A corporation is owned by its shareholders, individuals who purchase shares of stock in the company as an investment. But the corporation is legally a separate entity from its shareholders. In the eyes of the law, a corporation is an "artificial person." It can enter into contracts, own property, and incur debts and liabilities, just like a natural person (a human individual).

Shares in a corporation are **securities**. A security is an ownership interest that represents only an investment in an enterprise, without managerial control over it. Securities are regulated by the federal government through the Securities and Exchange Commission.

A corporation is capable of perpetual existence; the death of a shareholder does not affect its operation. Corporate property is owned by the corporation in severalty, not by the shareholders. The shareholders own only a right to share in the profits of the business. Their liability is limited.

The main drawback to the corporate form of organization is double taxation. First the corporation must pay income taxes on any profits it generates. Then if the profits are distributed to the shareholders as dividends, the same money is taxed again as the personal income of the shareholders. Business investors can avoid double taxation by choosing a different form of organization, such as a partnership or a trust.

A corporation formed under the laws of Washington is called a **domestic corporation**. All other corporations, incorporated in other states or foreign countries, are called foreign corporations. Foreign corporations may conduct business in Washington, but they must obtain a certificate of qualification from the Secretary of State and abide by any conditions or limitations imposed.

Note that a corporation cannot co-own property in joint tenancy. Since a corporation has a potentially perpetual existence, the other joint tenant could not really have a right of survivorship. Thus, when a corporation co-owns real property with another entity or person, they hold title as tenants in common.

Limited Liability Companies. In the eyes of many business experts, a limited liability company (LLC) is the best of both worlds. It combines many of the advantages of a corporation with many of the advantages of a partnership.

An LLC is easily created. Any two business owners (called members) draw up an LLC agreement and file a certificate of formation with the state. LLC agreements can be quite flexible: members can choose virtually any manner of allocating income, losses, or appreciation among themselves. Once the LLC is created, annual reports must be filed with the state and an annual fee must be paid.

LLC members have the flexibility of a general partnership when it comes to managing the business. Certain members may be appointed to manage the company, or all of the members may manage the company. All managing members can bind the LLC with their actions. However, unlike the general partnership, all managing members are not personally liable for the company's contractual liabilities. LLC members have the same type of limited liability enjoyed by corporate stockholders or limited partners. Regardless of their level of participation in the company, LLC members risk only their initial investment in the company.

As noted earlier, a major disadvantage of the corporate form of ownership is the double taxation imposed on corporations and their stockholders. Income earned by an LLC, on the other hand, is taxed at only one level—the member level. LLC income is taxed as the personal income of each member, in the same manner as partnership income.

Joint Ventures. A joint venture is similar to a partnership, except that it is created for a single business transaction or for a series of individual transactions. It is not intended to be an ongoing business of indefinite duration. Joint ventures are generally governed by the same rules as partnerships. An example of a joint venture would be a property owner, an architect, and a building contractor joining together to design and construct a particular building.

Real Estate Investment Trusts. In a trust, one or more trustees manage property for the benefit of others (the **beneficiaries**). A trust instrument vests title to the property in the trustees, who have only the powers expressly granted in the instrument.

A real estate investment trust is an unincorporated syndicate created by investors to finance large real estate projects. The Internal Revenue Code offers tax benefits to real estate investors who organize their syndicate as a real estate investment trust. An REIT must have at least 100 investors, and must invest exclusively in real estate and real estate mortgages. Shares in an REIT are securities, subject to federal regulation.

Because an REIT is unincorporated, it avoids double taxation. As long as at least 95% of its income is distributed to the shareholders, the trust pays taxes only on the earnings it retains. Yet the investors, like corporate shareholders, are shielded from liability for the REIT's debts.

Condominiums and Cooperatives

Condominiums and cooperatives provide alternatives to ownership of a traditional single-family home. In a sense, they combine aspects of individual ownership with aspects of concurrent ownership.

Condominiums. In Washington, the development and management of condominium properties are governed by a state statute called the Condominium Act.

Someone who buys a unit in a condominium owns the unit itself in severalty, but shares ownership of the common elements with other unit owners as tenants in common. **Common elements** (also called common areas) are aspects of the condominium property that all of the unit owners have the right to use, such as the driveway or the elevator.

Some features may be designated as **limited common elements**, which are reserved for the owners of certain units. For example, an assigned parking space would be a limited common element. A feature such as a balcony, which is designed for use with a particular unit but is outside of the unit itself, would also be a limited common element.

Each unit owner obtains separate financing to buy his or her unit, receives an individual property tax bill, and may acquire a title insurance policy for the unit. A lien can attach to a single unit, so that the unit can be foreclosed on separately, without affecting the other units in the condominium.

An elected governing board usually manages the condominium, and monthly assessments are made to cover maintenance costs for the common elements. The sale of a unit ordinarily doesn't require the approval of the other unit owners. The seller's interest in the common elements passes to the buyer.

A condominium usually involves one or more multi-family residential buildings, but commercial and industrial properties can also be developed as condominiums. To establish a condominium, the developer must record a condominium plan and declaration. A large condominium project may be regulated as a subdivision.

Sometimes the owner of an apartment complex will find it profitable to change the complex into a condominium. This process, called **conversion**, is regulated to protect renters who will be displaced.

Cooperatives. In a cooperative, ownership of the property is vested in a single entity—usually a corporation. The residents of the cooperative building own shares in the corporation, rather than owning the property itself. They are tenants with long-term proprietary leases on their units; they do not hold title to their units.

To establish a cooperative, the corporation gets a mortgage loan to buy or construct the building, and other funds are raised by selling shares in the corporation to prospective tenants. The rent that each tenant pays to the corporation is a pro rata share of the mortgage, taxes, operating expenses, and other debts for the whole property. The cooperative corporation is managed by an elected board of directors.

In many cooperatives, a tenant cannot transfer stock or assign his or her proprietary lease without the consent of the governing board or a majority of the members. This approval process is used to screen out undesirable tenants; however, discrimination in violation of fair housing laws is not allowed (see Chapter 15).

Differences Between Condominiums and Cooperatives. In a condominium, each unit is owned individually. In a cooperative, a corporation owns the whole project; the tenants own shares in the corporation and have proprietary leases on their units.

In a condominium, each unit owner secures individual financing to buy the unit. In a cooperative, the corporation takes out one blanket loan for the entire project. One advantage of condominiums over cooperatives is that a condominium owner is not responsible for any default on another unit owner's loan. In a cooperative, if one tenant defaults on his or her share of the mortgage payments, the other tenants must cure the default or risk having the mortgage on the entire project foreclosed. This is also true for tax assessments and other liens.

A condominium owner can usually sell his or her unit to anyone who can pay for it. In a cooperative, the corporation usually must approve of the proposed tenant.

📖 Chapter Summary

1. An estate is a possessory interest in real property. Someone who has a freehold estate has title to the property and is considered an owner. Someone who has a leasehold (less-than-freehold) estate has possession of the property, but does not have title.

2. Freehold estates include the fee simple absolute, the qualified fee, and the life estate. A life estate lasts only as long as a specified person is alive; then the property either reverts to the grantor or else passes to the remainderman. Leasehold estates include the estate for years, the periodic estate, and the estate at will. (The tenancy at sufferance, which arises when a tenant holds over without the landlord's permission, is not really an estate.)

3. Title to real property can be held in severalty or concurrently. In Washington, the methods of concurrent ownership are joint tenancy, tenancy in common, and community property. The distinguishing feature of joint tenancy is the right of survivorship.

4. Real property can be owned by a syndicate, which may be organized as a general or limited partnership, a corporation, a limited liability company, a joint venture, or a real estate investment trust.

5. In a condominium, each unit is separately owned, and all the unit owners own the common elements as tenants in common. A cooperative is owned by a corporation; a resident owns shares in the corporation, and has a proprietary lease for a particular unit.

🔑 Key Terms

Estate—An interest in land that is or may become possessory.

Freehold estate—A possessory interest that has an indeterminable duration.

Less-than-freehold (leasehold) estate—A possessory interest that has a limited duration.

Fee simple absolute—The highest and most complete form of ownership, which is of potentially infinite duration.

Qualified fee—A fee simple estate that carries a qualification, so that ownership may revert to the grantor if a specified event occurs or a condition is not met. Also called a defeasible fee.

Life estate—A freehold estate whose duration is measured by the lifetime of one or more persons.

Waste—Permanent damage to real property caused by the party in possession, harming the interests of other estate holders.

Estate for years—A leasehold estate with a fixed term.

Periodic estate—A leasehold estate that is renewed at the end of each period unless one party gives notice of termination. Also called a periodic tenancy.

Estate at will—A leasehold estate that may arise after a periodic tenancy or an estate for years terminates. Also called a tenancy at will.

Ownership in severalty—Sole ownership of property.

Tenancy in common—Joint ownership where there is no right of survivorship.

Joint tenancy—Joint ownership with right of survivorship.

Right of survivorship—The right by which the surviving joint tenant(s) acquire a joint tenant's interest in the property upon his or her death.

Community property—Property owned jointly by husband and wife (in Washington and other community property states).

Corporation—An artificial person; a legal entity separate from its shareholders.

Limited liability company—A form of business entity that offers limited liability and tax benefits.

Real estate investment trust—An unincorporated trust that invests exclusively in real estate and real estate mortgages.

Condominium—A property that has been developed so that individual unit owners have separate title to their own units, but share ownership of the common elements as tenants in common.

Cooperative—A property that is owned by a corporation and tenanted by shareholders in the corporation who have proprietary leases for their units.

◯◯ Chapter Quiz

1. A fee simple title in real estate is of indefinite duration, and can be:

   a) freely transferred
   b) encumbered
   c) inherited
   d) All of the above

2. A conveyance of title with the condition that the land shall not be used for the sale of intoxicating beverages creates:

   a) a less-than-freehold estate
   b) a qualified fee
   c) a life estate
   d) a reservation

3. Lewis was given real property for the term of his natural life. Which of the following statements is incorrect?

   a) Lewis has a freehold estate
   b) Lewis has a fee simple estate
   c) Lewis is the life tenant
   d) If Lewis leases the property to someone else, the lease will terminate if Lewis dies during its term

4. Baker sold a property to Lane, but reserved a life estate for himself and remained in possession. Later Baker sells his life estate to Clark and surrenders possession to Clark. Lane then demands immediate possession as fee owner. Which of the following is true?

   a) Lane is entitled to possession
   b) Clark should sue Baker for return of the purchase price
   c) Baker is liable for damages
   d) Clark can retain possession during Baker's lifetime

5. Cobb owns a property in fee simple; he deeds it to Smith for the life of Jones. Which of the following is true?

   a) Jones holds a life estate; Smith holds an estate in reversion
   b) Smith holds a life estate; Cobb holds an estate in remainder
   c) Smith holds a fee simple estate; Jones holds a life estate
   d) Smith holds a life estate; Cobb holds an estate in reversion

6. Johnston, a life tenant, decides to cut down all the trees on the ten-acre property and sell them for timber. Mendez, the remainderman, can stop Johnston's actions because:

   a) a life tenant is never permitted to cut down any trees on the property for any reason
   b) a life tenant cannot commit waste
   c) Mendez's interest is superior to Johnston's, since it is a possessory estate
   d) None of the above; Mendez has no legal grounds for stopping Johnston

7. Jones and Adams signed an agreement for the use and possession of real estate, for a period of 120 days. This is:

   a) an estate for years
   b) an estate at sufferance
   c) a periodic tenancy
   d) an estate at will

8. The four unities of title, time, interest, and possession are necessary for a:

   a) tenancy in common
   b) partnership
   c) mortgage
   d) joint tenancy

A C D

9. Which of the following is incorrect? Joint tenants always have:

   a) equal rights to possession of the property
   b) the right to will good title to heirs
   c) the right of survivorship
   d) equal interests in the property

10. A, B, and C own property as joint tenants. C dies and B sells her interest in the property to D. The property is now owned:

   a) as joint tenants by A, D, and C's widow E, his sole heir
   b) by A and D as joint tenants
   c) by A and D as tenants in common
   d) None of the above

11. Asher and Blake own real property together. Asher has a one-third interest and Blake has a two-thirds interest. How do they hold title?

   a) Community property
   b) Tenancy at will
   c) Joint tenancy
   d) Tenancy in common

12. All of the following statements about a corporation are true, except:

   a) A corporation has a potentially perpetual existence
   b) Each shareholder is individually liable for the corporation's acts
   c) Corporations are subject to double taxation
   d) A corporation can enter into contracts in essentially the same way as an individual person

13. A real estate investment trust is required to:

   a) invest exclusively in real estate and mortgages
   b) have at least 150 participating investors
   c) have investors accept liability for the trust's acts
   d) be incorporated in the state in which it does business

14. In a condominium:

   a) individual units are owned in severalty, while common elements are owned in joint tenancy
   b) individual units are owned in joint tenancy, while common elements are owned in severalty
   c) individual units are owned in severalty, while common elements are owned in tenancy in common
   d) the entire building is owned in tenancy in common, with residents owning shares

15. A unit in a cooperative is owned:

   a) in severalty by its resident
   b) by the corporation that owns the building, in which the resident owns shares
   c) in tenancy in common among all residents of the building
   d) in partnership among all residents of the building

☞ Answer Key

1. d) A fee simple owner has the full bundle of rights.

2. b) A qualified fee (or defeasible fee) is an estate that will fail if a certain event occurs.

3. b) Although a life estate is a freehold estate, it is not a fee simple estate.

4. d) Baker was entitled to sell his life estate to Clark. Clark can retain possession during Baker's lifetime.

5. d) Smith has possession of the property for the duration of Jones's life, so Smith has a life estate. Cobb has an estate in reversion, because the property will revert to Cobb after Jones's death.

6. b) A life tenant cannot commit waste, which means that the life tenant cannot damage the property or harm the interests of the remainderman.

7. a) An estate for years has a set termination date.

8. d) A valid joint tenancy requires all four unities: title, time, interest, possession.

9. b) A joint tenant cannot will his or her interest in the property. The right of survivorship means the surviving joint tenants acquire the deceased tenant's title.

10. c) When C dies, his interest in the property goes to the other joint tenants, A and B. When B sells her interest to D, the joint tenancy is terminated and a tenancy in common is created between A and D.

11. d) Because their interests in the property are unequal, Asher and Blake must be tenants in common.

12. b) A corporation's shareholders have limited liability for the corporation's actions.

13. a) A real estate investment trust is restricted to investment in real estate and real estate mortgages. The minimum number of investors is 100, not 150.

14. c) In a condominium, residents own their individual units in severalty, but own the common elements as tenants in common.

15. b) A cooperative is owned by a business entity, usually a corporation. Residents purchase shares in the corporation and receive long-term leases, rather than title to their units.

Transfer of Real Property

Chapter Overview

A property owner may transfer property to someone else by choice, as when an owner deeds property to a buyer or wills it to a friend. Property may also be transferred involuntarily, as in a foreclosure sale or a condemnation. This chapter describes the various types of transfers, voluntary and involuntary. It also discusses how and why deeds and other documents are recorded, and how title insurance works.

Alienation

The process of transferring ownership of real property from one party to another is called **alienation**. Alienation may be either voluntary or involuntary. Voluntary alienation includes transferring property by deed or will. Involuntary alienation, a transfer of property without any action by the owner, can be the result of rules of law, accession, or occupancy (adverse possession).

Voluntary Alienation

Patents

Title to all real property originates with the sovereign government. The government holds absolute title to all the land within its boundaries, except what it grants to various other entities or persons. Title to land passes from the government to a private party by a document known as a **patent**. The patent is the ultimate source of title for all the land under private ownership.

Deeds

The most common form of voluntary alienation is transfer by deed. With a deed, the owner of real property, called the **grantor**, conveys all or part of his or her interest in the property to another party, called the **grantee**. The process of transferring real property by deed is known as conveyance. A grantor conveys real property to a grantee by means of a deed.

Types of Deeds. There are many different types of deeds. The ones used most often in Washington are the warranty deed, special warranty deed, quitclaim deed, trustee's deed, and deed executed under court order.

Warranty Deed. The warranty deed (also known as the general warranty deed) gives the greatest protection to a real estate buyer. Under a warranty deed, the grantor makes five basic promises, or covenants, to the grantee. These covenants warrant against defects in the title that arose either before or during the grantor's period of ownership (tenure). When a statutory warranty deed form is used, the covenants are implied; they do not have to be expressly stated in the deed.

The first covenant is called the **covenant of seisin**. Seisin means peaceable possession under color of title. Color of title means a good faith belief in ownership. So the covenant of seisin promises that the grantor actually owns the property interest he or she is transferring to the grantee.

The second covenant is the **covenant of right to convey**. The grantor promises that he or she has the power to make the conveyance. In other words, the grantor either has title to the interest, or is an agent of the owner with the authority to transfer the interest.

The **covenant against encumbrances** warrants that the property is not burdened by any easement, mortgage, lien, or other right of a third party. If such encumbrances do exist, they must be listed in the deed.

The fourth covenant is the **covenant of quiet enjoyment**. This covenant promises that the grantee's possession of the property will not be threatened by any lawful claim made by a third party. It does not protect the grantee from claims that have no legal basis, called spurious claims.

The final covenant in the warranty deed is the **covenant of warranty**. This is a promise that the grantor will defend the grantee's title against any claims superior to the grantee's that exist when the conveyance is made.

Special Warranty Deed. The special warranty deed contains the same covenants found in the general warranty deed, but the scope of the covenants is limited to defects that arose during the grantor's tenure. The grantor makes no assurances regarding defects that may have existed before he or she obtained title. This type of deed is most often used by entities such as corporations, which do not have the authority to make more extensive warranties.

A warranty deed (general or special) conveys the "after-acquired title" of the grantor. This means that if the grantor's title was defective at the time of transfer, but the grantor later acquires a more perfect title, the additional interest passes automatically to the grantee under the original deed.

> **Example:** Warner conveyed her property to Meyers on June 1, by a warranty deed. However, Warner did not have valid title to the property on June 1 because she held title under a forged deed. On August 12, Warner received good title to the property under a properly executed deed. Meyers automatically acquired good title to the property on August 12.

Quitclaim Deed. The quitclaim deed contains no warranties of any sort, and it does not convey after-acquired title. It conveys only the interest the grantor has when the deed is delivered. It conveys nothing at all if the grantor has no interest at that time. But if the grantor does have an interest in the property, the quitclaim deed will convey it just as well as any other type of deed.

The usual reason for using a quitclaim deed is to cure "clouds" on the title; in such situations, a quitclaim deed may be referred to as a **reformation deed**. A cloud is a title defect, often the result of a technical flaw in an earlier conveyance. Perhaps one of the parties' names was misspelled, or the land was inaccurately described. A quitclaim deed is also used when the grantor is unsure of the validity of his or her title and wishes to avoid giving any warranties.

> **Example:** Smith holds title by virtue of an inheritance that is being challenged in probate court. If Smith wants to transfer the property, she will probably use a quitclaim deed, because she is not sure that her title is valid.

In a quitclaim deed, words such as "grant" or "convey" should be avoided. The use of these words may imply that the grantor is warranting the title. A

Fig. 3.1 Warranty deed

AFTER RECORDING MAIL TO:
Joseph and Hannah Shapiro
3406 N.W. 66th St.
Anytown 99999

Filed for Record at Request of
Acme Escrow Co.
Escrow Number: 001021SHA

Statutory Warranty Deed

Grantor(s): Alan S. Matsumoto

Grantee(s): Joseph R. Shapiro, Hannah L. Shapiro

Abbreviated Legal: Lot 12, Block 8, Jasperson Add., Vol. 10, p. 94

Additional Legal(s) on page: N/A

Assessor's Tax Parcel Number(s): 117600-0720-05

THE GRANTOR   Alan S. Matsumoto

for and in consideration of   TEN DOLLARS AND OTHER GOOD AND VALUABLE CONSIDERATION

in hand paid, conveys and warrants to   Joseph R. Shapiro and Hannah L. Shapiro, a married couple

the following described real estate, situated in the County of Thurston , State of Washington:

LOT 12, BLOCK 8, JASPERSON ADDITION TO THE CITY OF ANYTOWN, ACCORDING TO THE PLAT THEREOF RECORDED IN VOLUME 10 OF PLATS, PAGE 94, RECORDS OF THURSTON COUNTY, WASHINGTON.

0110210094

Dated this _21st_ day of ___October___, 20_01_

By _Alan S. Matsumoto_   By _____
   Alan S. Matsumoto

By _____   By _____

STATE OF _WASHINGTON_____ } **SS:**

County of _THURSTON_____ }

I certify that I know or have satisfactory evidence that _____ALAN S. MATSUMOTO_____

_IS_ the person(s) who appeared before me, and said person(s) acknowledged that _HE_ signed this instrument and acknowledged it to be _HIS_ free and voluntary act for the uses and purposes mentioned in this instrument.

Dated: _OCTOBER 21, 2001_____   *Claire M. Vincent*_____
                                        CLAIRE M. VINCENT

                                        Notary Public in and for the State of ___WASHINGTON___

                                        Residing at _FIFE_____

                                        My appointment expires: _01-16-02_____

CLAIRE M. VINCENT
STATE OF WASHINGTON
NOTARY--|--PUBLIC
MY COMMISSION EXPIRES 1-16-02

quitclaim deed should use only terms such as "release," "remise," or "quit-claim" to describe the transfer.

Trustee's Deed. When property is foreclosed under a deed of trust, the trustee conveys the property to the buyer at the foreclosure sale with a trustee's deed. The trustee's deed states that the conveyance is in accordance with the trustee's powers and responsibilities under the deed of trust. (Deeds of trust are discussed in Chapter 10.)

Deeds Executed by Court Order. Court-ordered deeds are used after a court-ordered sale of property. A common example is the sheriff's deed used to transfer property to the highest bidder at a court-ordered foreclosure sale (see Chapter 10). Court-ordered deeds usually state the exact amount of the purchase price approved by the court, and carry no warranties of title.

Requisites of a Valid Deed. A deed will transfer title only if it meets the requirements for validity. To be valid, a deed must:

- be in writing,
- identify the parties,
- be signed by a competent grantor,
- have a living grantee,
- contain words of conveyance (the granting clause), and
- include an adequate description of the property.

In Writing. The statute of frauds is a state law that requires certain contracts and other legal transactions to be in writing. With only a few minor exceptions, the statute of frauds applies to any transfer of an interest in real property. An unwritten deed cannot transfer title; it has no legal effect.

Identification of the Parties. Both the grantor and the grantee must be identified in the deed. The name of the grantee is not required, as long as an adequate description is given; for example, "John T. Smith's only sister."

Signed by a Competent Grantor. The grantor must sign the deed. In addition to requiring a deed to be in writing, the statute of frauds also requires that the deed must be signed by the party to be bound by the transfer.

If the grantor can't sign his or her full name (due to disability or illiteracy), he or she may sign by making a mark. But a signature by mark must be accompanied by the signatures of witnesses who can attest to the grantor's execution of the deed.

A deed can also be signed by the grantor's **attorney in fact**. The attorney in fact (not necessarily a lawyer) is someone the grantor has appointed to act on his or her behalf in a document called a **power of attorney**. The power of attorney must specifically authorize the attorney in fact to convey the property, and it must be recorded in the county where the property is located.

Deeds from corporations are usually signed by an authorized officer of the corporation, and the signature must be accompanied by the corporate seal.

If there is more than one grantor, all of the grantors must sign the deed. If a prior deed named several grantees, all of them must sign as grantors of a new deed. The signatures of both the husband and the wife are required to convey community property (see Chapter 2). For this reason, it is a good idea (although not required) to state the grantor's marital status in the deed and to obtain the spouse's signature if the grantor is married, even if the property is not community property.

A grantor must be legally competent when he or she signs the deed. This means that the grantor must be an adult (at least 18 years old) and sane. If the grantor is not competent, the deed is not valid.

Living Grantee. The grantee does not have to be competent in order for the deed to be valid. It is only necessary for the grantee to be alive (or, if the grantee is a corporation, legally in existence) and identifiable when the deed is executed.

Words of Conveyance. The requirement of words of conveyance, the granting clause, is easily satisfied. The single word "grant" or a similar word is sufficient. Additional technical language usually does more harm than good, and should be avoided since it adds nothing to the validity of the deed.

Description of the Property. A valid deed must contain an adequate description of the property to be conveyed. A legal description of the property should always be included. (Land description is discussed in Chapter 1.)

Acknowledgment, Delivery, and Acceptance. To successfully convey real property, more than a valid deed is necessary; a proper conveyance also requires acknowledgment, delivery, and acceptance.

Acknowledgment occurs when the grantor swears before a notary public or other official witness that his or her signature is genuine and voluntary. The witness cannot be a person who has an interest in the transfer. For example, if Grandma deeds her property to Granddaughter, who is a notary public, Granddaughter should not be the one to notarize the deed.

Technically, a deed may be considered valid even if the grantor's signature is not acknowledged. However, an unacknowledged deed cannot be recorded.

A valid deed becomes effective, so that title is transferred, when the deed is **delivered** to the grantee. Delivery must occur while the grantor is alive.

> **Example:** When Sam Wiggins died, a deed was found in his safe deposit box. The deed transferred his property to his nephew, Frank Wiggins. The deed was void because it was not delivered during Sam's lifetime.

Delivery is more than the mere physical transfer of the document; the grantor's intent is a key element of delivery. The grantor must have the intention of immediately transferring title to the grantee. The conveyance is completed when the grantee accepts delivery of the deed. The grantee may accept delivery of the deed through an agent.

> **Example:** Clark deeds his property to Martinez. Clark hands the deed to Martinez's attorney, with the intention of immediately transferring ownership to Martinez. This is considered delivery to an agent of the grantee, and the deed is valid.

Because delivery of a deed involves some complicated legal issues, a real estate lawyer should be consulted when there is a question concerning delivery.

Non-essential Terms. There are some elements that should be included in a deed, even though they aren't required. A deed should include a **habendum clause** (also called a "to have and to hold" clause), which states the nature of the interest the grantor is conveying. Is the grantor conveying a fee simple absolute or a life estate? Unless otherwise specified, the grantor's entire interest is presumed to pass to the grantee. If there is more than one grantee, the deed should say how they will hold title: is this a tenancy in common or a joint tenancy?

Many deeds have an **exclusions and reservations clause**, which is a list of any encumbrances (easements, private restrictions, or liens) that the grantee will be taking title subject to. However, valid encumbrances usually remain in force even if they aren't listed in the deed.

A recital of the purchase price is helpful because it indicates that the transfer is a purchase instead of a gift. (If the transfer were a gift, the grantee might be vulnerable to the claims of the grantor's creditors.) The recital of consideration usually says something like, "for $1.00 and other valuable consideration."

The date of conveyance is standard, but not legally required. Other non-essential items include the grantor's seal, warranties, and technical terminology. "I hereby grant Greenacres Farm to Harry Carter. (signed) Sam Smith" is a valid deed, assuming that Sam Smith is legally competent. Note that the grantee does not ordinarily sign the deed.

Wills

The will (or testament) is another method of voluntary alienation. In general, a will must be:

1. in writing,
2. signed by the person making it (the testator), and
3. attested to by at least two competent witnesses.

The will must be signed by the testator in the presence of the witnesses. The witnesses must also sign an acknowledgment that the testator declared the document to be his or her will.

Although ordinarily a will must be in writing to be valid, under certain circumstances Washington will recognize an oral (**nuncupative**) will. The oral will may be valid if spoken while the testator is on his or her deathbed with two witnesses present. But if the testator recovers, the oral will is no longer valid. An oral will can transfer only personal property worth less than $1,000. Real estate can never be transferred by an oral will, since all transfers involving real property must be in writing.

Some states recognize handwritten, or **holographic**, wills. A holographic will is an unwitnessed will written entirely in the testator's own handwriting. Wash-ington law does not recognize holographic wills. A holographic will can be valid in Washington only if the testator executed it in a state where holographic wills are valid, then later moves to Washington and does not make out a new will.

Terminology. The person who makes a will is referred to as the **testator**. A testator **bequeaths** personal property to **legatees** and **devises** real property to **devisees**. An amendment to a will is called a **codicil**. The directions contained in the will

---

Fig. 3.2 Will terminology

Will Terminology

Testator: One who makes a will.

Bequeath: To transfer personal property by will.

Devise: To transfer real property by will.

Executor: Appointed by the testator to carry out the instructions in the will.

Administrator: Appointed by the court if no executor named.

Probate: Procedure to prove a will's validity.

are carried out by an **executor** named in the will, under the supervision of the probate court (in Washington, the superior court). **Probate** is the procedure by which a will is proved valid and the testator's directions are carried out. If no executor is named in the will, the court will appoint an **administrator** to manage and distribute the estate.

Probate Procedures. A will does not convey any interest until the testator has died and the will has been probated. Depending on the procedures followed, all conveyances of real property under the will may have to be approved by the probate court. The court also approves any brokerage commissions pertaining to such conveyances.

Involuntary Alienation

The patent, the deed, and the will are the three most common methods of transferring property voluntarily. We will now look at the different ways interests in real property can be conveyed without any voluntary action on the part of the owner.

Involuntary alienation of real property can be the result of rule of law, adverse possession, or accession. Alienation by rule of law includes dedication, intestate succession and escheat, condemnation, and court decisions regarding real property.

Dedication

When a private owner gives real property to the public, it is called dedication. While dedication may be voluntary, most often it is required in exchange for a benefit from a public entity.

> **Example:** The county requires a land developer to dedicate land within a new subdivision for public streets. Otherwise, the county will deny permission to subdivide.

This type of dedication is called **statutory dedication** because it involves compliance with relevant statutory procedures. In the example above, the subdivision statutes require that land for streets and utilities must be dedicated before a parcel can be subdivided.

A second type of dedication is called **common law dedication**. The usual requirement for common law dedication is the owner's acquiescence in the public's use of his or her property for a prolonged period of time. If property has been used by the public for long enough, a government entity can pass an ordinance accepting a common law dedication. The dedication may be treated as a transfer of ownership, or it may only establish a public easement, depending on the circumstances.

> **Example:** Barker owns some lakefront property. For many years, people from town have walked across a corner of his lot to gain access to the lake, and Barker has done nothing to prevent this. Barker's acquiescence to this public use would probably be considered a common law dedication.

Intestate Succession and Escheat

When a person dies without leaving a will, he or she is said to have died intestate. The law provides for the division of his or her property by a process called **intestate succession**. The procedure varies from state to state, but in general the property passes first to the surviving spouse, then to any surviving children, then to various other relatives.

Persons who take property by intestate succession are called **heirs**. Those who receive property by intestate succession are said to have received property by **descent**, rather than by devise or bequest. Intestate succession is supervised by the probate court. The court appoints an administrator, who is responsible for distributing the property in the manner required by the intestate succession statutes.

If a person dies intestate and the probate court is unable to locate any heirs, then the intestate person's property will pass back to the state according to the law of **escheat**. Since the state is the ultimate source of title to property, it is also the ultimate heir when there are no intervening interested parties. The state may also take ownership of abandoned property through escheat.

Condemnation

The government has the constitutional power to take private property for public use, as long as it pays just compensation to the owner of the condemned property. The government's power to condemn (take) property is called the power of **eminent domain**. Before the power of eminent domain can be exercised, the following requirements must be met:

- The use must be a **public use**—that is, it must benefit the public. Taking property for a public park would qualify as a public use. In cases of mixed public and private benefit the question is more diffi-cult, but generally there is no authority for the government to take one person's land for the sole purpose of turning it over to another person.
- The condemning entity must pay **just compensation** to the owner. As a general rule, just compensation is the fair market value of the property.

The power of eminent domain may be exercised by any government entity, and also by some semi-public entities, such as utility companies.

Inverse Condemnation. If a property owner feels that his or her property has been taken or damaged by a public entity, he or she may file a lawsuit called an inverse condemnation action to force the government to pay the fair market value of the taken or damaged property.

Court Decisions

Title to property can also be conveyed by court order in accordance with state statutes and the precedents of the common law. The most common forms of court action affecting title to property are the quiet title action, the suit for partition, and foreclosure.

Quiet Title. The quiet title action is used to remove a cloud on the title when the title cannot be cleared by the more peaceful means of an agreement and a quitclaim deed. In a quiet title action, the court decides questions of property ownership. The result is a binding determination of the various parties' interests in a particular piece of real estate.

> **Example:** A seller has found a potential buyer for his property. However, a title search uncovers a gap in the title: the public record doesn't indicate who owned the property for a certain time period.
>
> The seller brings a quiet title action. The defendants in the action are all persons who have a potential interest in the seller's property. This includes whoever the mystery person was who held title during the gap, even though his or her name is unknown.
>
> The seller asks the court to declare his title valid, thereby "quieting title" to the land. If no defendants appear to challenge the seller's title, the court will grant the seller's request. The buyer can then safely rely on the court's decision and consummate the sale.

Suit for Partition. A suit for partition is a means of dividing property held by more than one person when the co-owners cannot agree on how to divide it. For example, joint tenants may wish to end their joint tenancy but be unable to decide among themselves who gets what portion of the property. The court divides the property for them, and the owners are then bound by the court's decision. In many cases, the court will order the property sold and the proceeds divided among the co-owners.

> **Example:** Green and Black are joint tenants. The joint tenancy property is a vacation home in the mountains. After a serious argument, Green and Black decide they want to terminate their joint tenancy. However, they can't agree on how to divide the property. Green wants to put the property up for sale and divide the proceeds. Black wants to buy out Green's interest and keep the vacation home for himself, but Green says Black isn't offering him enough money.
>
> Finally, Green files a suit for partition. The court orders the vacation home sold and divides the proceeds between Green and Black. Black must abide by this decision, even though he doesn't like it.

Foreclosure Actions. Persons holding liens against real property may force the sale of the property if the debts secured by their liens are not paid. Foreclosure is available for any type of lien that attaches to real property, including mortgages, deeds of trust, construction liens, and judgment liens. (See Chapter 10 for further discussion of foreclosure.)

Adverse Possession

Adverse possession, another form of involuntary alienation, is the process by which the possession and use of property can mature into title. The law of adverse possession encourages the fullest and most productive use of land. It provides that someone who actually uses property may eventually attain a greater interest in that property than the owner who does not use it. The precise requirements for obtaining title by adverse possession vary from state to state. These requirements are often highly technical, and they must be followed exactly in order to obtain title. Legal counsel should be obtained in transactions where title may be affected by adverse possession.

Requirements. In Washington, there are five basic requirements for adverse possession. Possession of the land must be:

1. actual,
2. open and notorious,
3. hostile to the owner's interest,
4. exclusive, and
5. continuous and uninterrupted for a specific period of time.

Actual. Actual possession means occupation and use of the property in a manner appropriate to the type of property. It does not require residence on the property unless residence is the appropriate use. Thus, actual possession of farmland may be achieved by fencing the land and planting crops, while actual possession of urban property would require a residential or commercial use of the property.

Open and Notorious. The requirement of "open and notorious" possession means that the possession must put the true owner on notice that his or her interest in the property is being threatened. This requirement overlaps with the actual possession requirement. Actual possession generally constitutes reasonable notice to the world that the adverse possessor is occupying the property.

Hostile. The adverse possessor must intend to claim ownership of the property and defend that claim against all parties. Hostile intent is proven by the adverse possessor's actions. If the adverse possessor uses the property in the same fashion as an owner would use it, then hostile intent exists. Hostile intent can also be proven by color of title. An example of an adverse possessor with color of title is one who takes possession under an invalid deed, with a good faith but mistaken belief that he or she is the owner of the land. Note that the hostility requirement cannot be satisfied if the possession is with the permission of the actual owner.

Exclusive. An adverse possessor must have exclusive possession of the property; in other words, the true owner must be excluded from possession. Someone who is sharing use of the property with the true owner (even without the owner's knowledge) cannot acquire title by adverse possession.

Continuous. An adverse possessor is required to have continuous and uninterrupted possession of the property for the length of time prescribed by state statute. In Washington, possession generally must be continuous and uninterrupted for ten years.

In some cases, intermittent use of the property may be enough to fulfill the continuity requirement. This is true if the property is a type that an owner would ordinarily use only at certain times of year, such as seasonal farmland or summer resort property. However, the continuity requirement is not met if the adverse possessor fails

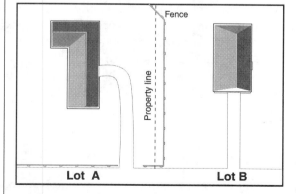

Fence

Property line

Lot A

Lot B

Fig. 3.3 Adverse possession
Use of property (here, the strip between Lot A's fence and the true property line) can mature into title by the process of adverse possession.

to use the property for a significant period when it would ordinarily be used, or if the true owner interrupts the period of exclusive possession.

Successive adverse possessors can add together their periods of possession to equal the statutory time period; this is called **tacking**.

> **Example:** Brown adversely possesses property for seven years, and then transfers possession to White, who possesses the property for five years. White can claim title because the total period of adverse possession is more than ten years.

Note that title to government property can never be acquired by adverse possession.

Perfecting Title. Since the adverse possessor's interest is not recorded, he or she must take additional steps to acquire marketable title. Unless the true owner is willing to provide a quitclaim deed, the adverse possessor has to file a quiet title action.

Accession

Accession is any addition to real property from natural or artificial causes. It can result in involuntary alienation. Accession includes:

- accretion,
- reliction, and
- avulsion.

Accretion. When riparian or littoral land is slowly enlarged by waterborne soil deposits (called alluvion or alluvium), the riparian or littoral owner acquires title to the new land. A key feature of accretion is that the build-up of soil must be so gradual that the process is virtually imperceptible.

Reliction. When riparian or littoral land is enlarged by the gradual retreat of the body of water, the landowner acquires title to the newly exposed land. Like accretion, reliction must be very gradual. Reliction is also called dereliction.

Avulsion. Accretion and reliction are both gradual processes. By contrast, avulsion occurs when land is violently torn away by flowing water or waves and deposited somewhere else, or when land is exposed by a sudden change in a watercourse. Unlike accretion and reliction, avulsion does not necessarily result in involuntary alienation of the land that has been moved or exposed. The original owner still has title to that land, if there is some way to claim it. If unclaimed, it eventually becomes part of the property it is now attached to.

Recording

Once an interest in property has been transferred (voluntarily or involuntarily), the new owner protects his or her interest by recording the document of conveyance with the county clerk. Recording is a way to provide convenient access to information regarding ownership of a property to anyone who's interested.

The Recording Process

Recording is accomplished by filing a copy of the deed or other document at the county clerk's office in the county where the property is located. The recorder catalogs, or **indexes**, the document twice, once under the grantor's last name and once under the grantee's last name. Sometimes a document will also be indexed according to tract, so that all documents affecting a particular property are listed together.

These indexes serve as the basis for **title searches**. A purchaser can search the grantor index to determine if the seller has already conveyed the interest to another party. The purchaser can also search the grantee index to discover the source of the seller's title, and trace the title back through a **chain of title** (successive grantors and grantees) that is long enough to ensure the validity of the seller's title.

Almost any document affecting title to land may be recorded: a deed, a mortgage, an abstract of judgment, a lis pendens (a notice of pending legal proceedings that may affect property), and so on. A deed or other document of conveyance must be acknowledged before it can be recorded, mainly to protect against forgeries. Also, the Federal Fair Housing Act prohibits the recording of any deed that contains a racially restrictive covenant (see Chapter 15).

The Effect of Recording

Recording has two significant consequences. Most importantly, it gives **constructive notice** of recorded interests to "the world." In other words, anyone who later acquires an interest in the property is held to know about all the other recorded interests, even if he or she does not check the record.

Example: Jones owns Haystack Farm. She sells the farm to Chin, who immediately records his deed. One week later, Jones sells Haystack Farm to Brown. Jones pretends she still owns the farm, and Brown simply takes her word for it; he doesn't do a title search. When Brown tries to record his deed, he discovers that Jones did not have title to Haystack Farm when she sold it to him.

Although Brown didn't actually know about the conveyance from Jones to Chin, he had constructive notice of that conveyance. He could have found out about it by checking the public record. As a result, he has no claim to the property. Chin owns Haystack Farm. Brown could sue Jones to get his money back, but she has probably left town by now.

A grantee who fails to record his or her deed can lose title to a subsequent good faith purchaser who did not have notice of the earlier conveyance. In a conflict between two purchasers, the one who records his or her deed first has good title to the property—even if the other purchaser's deed was executed first.

Example: Jones sells Haystack Farm to Chin, but Chin does not record his deed. One week later, Jones sells the same property to Brown. No one tells Brown about the previous conveyance to Chin.

Since Chin's deed isn't recorded, Brown doesn't have constructive notice of Chin's interest in the property. Even if Brown does a title search, there's nothing in the public record to indicate that Jones no longer owns the property.

Brown qualifies as a subsequent good faith purchaser without notice. If he records his deed before Chin records his, Brown has good title to the property.

In addition to providing constructive notice, recording also creates a presumption that the recorded instrument is valid and effective. Recording will not serve to validate an otherwise invalid deed, nor will it protect against interests that arise by operation of law, such as adverse possession.

Wild Deeds. Because of the grantor/grantee system of indexing, it is possible for a deed to be recorded in such a way that a title search would not discover it.

> **Example:** Suppose Smith sells property to Montgomery, who fails to record her deed. Not long thereafter, Montgomery conveys the property to Klein, who promptly records his deed.
> If Smith then makes another conveyance of the same property to Walker, Walker will not be able to discover Klein's interest because Klein is not in Smith's chain of title. There is a break in the chain of title between Smith and Klein because the connecting deed was not recorded.

The general rule in these situations is that the subsequent purchaser (in the example above, Walker) is not charged with constructive notice of a deed that is not in the chain of title. A deed outside the chain of title is called a wild deed.

Title Insurance

Given the complexity of real property law and the high cost of real estate, it's natural that a prospective buyer will want to do everything possible to protect his or her interest. One means of accomplishing this is to obtain warranties of title from the seller, but warranties aren't very valuable if the seller is financially unable to back them up.

The buyer could also obtain a complete history of all the recorded interests in the property (called a **chain of title**) or a condensed history of those interests (called an **abstract of title**), and then have the history examined by an attorney who could render an opinion on the condition of the title. But the buyer would still have no protection against latent or undiscovered defects in the title. Therefore, most buyers will protect their interests with a title insurance policy.

In a title insurance policy, the title insurance company agrees to indemnify (reimburse) the policy holder against any loss caused by defects in the title, except for any defects specifically excluded from coverage. The title company will also handle the legal defense of any claims covered by the policy.

Obtaining Title Insurance

There are two steps to getting a title insurance policy. First, the buyer (or the seller) pays a fee to the title company to cover the cost of a title search. Most title companies have their own sets of records (called title plants), so they do not have to search the files in the recorder's office.

After the title search is completed, the title company issues a **title report** describing the condition of the title. The report lists all defects and encumbrances of record; these items will be excluded from the policy coverage. If the buyer is satisfied with the report, he or she purchases an insurance policy by paying the required premium; one payment covers the entire life of the policy.

Limits on Coverage

Title insurance policies may be limited in a number of ways. As mentioned above, all defects and encumbrances of record are listed in the policy and excluded from coverage. In addition, the liability of the title company cannot exceed the face value of the policy. The extent of protection also varies according to the nature of the policy. The two most common types of policies are the standard coverage policy and the extended coverage policy.

The **standard coverage** policy is used to insure the owner against defects in title, including hidden risks such as forgery. It does not insure against the interests of a person in actual possession of the property (such as an adverse possessor), nor against interests that would be disclosed by an inspection of the premises (such as an encroachment).

The **extended coverage** policy insures against all matters covered by the standard policy, plus matters not of public record, such as the rights of parties in possession of the property, unrecorded construction liens, and encroachments. Extended coverage is most often purchased by the buyer to insure his or her lender; this is known as a mortgagee's policy.

A buyer may want to obtain coverage for a specific item not included in the standard policy. He or she can do so by purchasing an endorsement to cover the particular item.

Title insurance never protects a landowner from losses due to governmental action such as condemnation or zoning changes.

Title insurance coverage is also limited to losses resulting from defects in the particular interest covered. Thus, an owner's policy covers only defects in title, a mortgagee's policy only insures the lender's lien priority, and a leaseholder's policy only insures the validity of a lease.

Fig. 3.4 Title insurance coverage	
Standard Coverage	**Extended Coverage**

• Marketable title
• Latent defects in title
    forged deed
    incompetent grantor
• Right of access
	• Marketable title
	• Latent defects in title
	    forged deed
	    incompetent grantor
	• Right of access
	• Parties in possession
	    tenants
	    adverse possessors
	• Matters discovered by survey
	    boundary lines
	    encroachments
	    area
	• Unrecorded construction liens
	• Tax liens

Chapter Summary

1. A transfer of ownership of property from one person to another is called alienation. Alienation may be either voluntary or involuntary.

2. Property may be transferred voluntarily by patent, deed, or will. The deed is the most common way of voluntarily transferring property. To be valid, a deed must be in writing, identify the parties, be signed by a competent grantor, have a living grantee, contain words of conveyance, and include an adequate description of the property. For property to be successfully conveyed, there must be delivery and acceptance as well as a valid deed. Once the deed is delivered and accepted, it should be recorded to protect the new owner's interest.

3. When a person dies, his or her real property is transferred to devisees under a will, or to heirs by the rules of intestate succession. A person who dies without a will is said to have died intestate. Property from an estate is distributed under the jurisdiction of the probate court. If a person dies without a valid will and without heirs, the property escheats to the state.

4. In addition to intestate succession and escheat, there are several other methods of involuntary alienation, including dedication, condemnation, court decisions, and adverse possession. When someone uses property openly and continuously without the owner's permission for ten years, he or she may acquire title by adverse possession.

5. Ownership of property may be transferred by accession. Accession refers to an addition to real property by various natural means, including accretion, reliction, and avulsion.

6. Documents affecting real property are recorded to provide constructive notice of their contents to anyone interested in the property. Recording also creates a presumption that a document is valid.

7. To protect a newly acquired interest in real property, the owner usually obtains a title insurance policy. The title insurance company will reimburse the owner for any loss caused by defects in title, and will defend the title against the legal claims of others.

🔑 Key Terms

Alienation—The transfer of title, ownership, or an interest in property from one person to another. Alienation may be voluntary or involuntary.

Deed—A written instrument that, when properly executed, delivered, and accepted, conveys title or ownership of real property from the grantor to the grantee.

Warranty deed—The deed that provides the greatest protection to a purchaser of real property, because it contains five basic covenants against defects in the title.

Quitclaim deed—A deed that conveys and releases any interest in a piece of real property that the grantor may have. It contains no warranties of any kind, but does transfer any right, title, or interest the grantor has at the time the deed is executed.

Acknowledgment—A formal declaration made before an authorized official, such as a notary public or county clerk, by a person who has signed a document; he or she states that the signature is genuine and voluntary.

Will—The written declaration of an individual that designates how his or her estate will be disposed of after death.

Intestate—When a person dies without leaving a valid will, he or she dies intestate.

Escheat—The reversion of property to the state when a person dies without leaving a will and without heirs entitled to the property.

Adverse possession—A means by which a person may acquire title to property by using it openly and continuously without the owner's permission for the required statutory period.

Dedication—When a private owner voluntarily or involuntarily gives real property to the public.

Eminent domain—The power of the government to take (condemn) private property for public use, upon payment of just compensation to the owner.

Condemnation—The act of taking private property for public use under the power of eminent domain.

Accession—Any addition to real property from natural or artificial causes.

Constructive notice—Notice of a fact that a person is held by law to have (as opposed to actual notice); he or she had the opportunity to discover the fact in question by searching the public record.

Title search—An inspection of the public record to determine all rights to a piece of property.

Chain of title—A complete history of all the recorded interests in a piece of real property.

Abstract of title—A condensed history of the recorded interests in a piece of real property.

Title report—A report issued after a title search by a title insurance company, listing all defects and encumbrances of record.

Wild deed—A recorded deed that cannot be located under the grantor-grantee system of indexing.

Chapter Quiz

1. The process of transferring real property is called:

   a) avulsion
   b) quitclaim
   c) alienation
   d) dereliction

2. The government transfers title to private parties by means of a:

   a) patent
   b) deed
   c) quitclaim
   d) escheat

3. In a deed, the promise that the grantor owns the property is called the covenant:

   a) of quiet enjoyment
   b) against encumbrances
   c) of seisin
   d) of warranty

4. Clouds on title are usually cleared by:

   a) a suit for partition
   b) title insurance
   c) adverse possession
   d) a quitclaim deed

5. A valid deed must refer to a grantee who is:

   a) competent
   b) over 21 years old
   c) identifiable
   d) intestate

6. Conveyance requires a valid deed, plus:

   a) recording
   b) delivery
   c) acceptance
   d) Both b) and c)

7. A person who makes a will is called:

   a) a grantor
   b) an executor
   c) a testator
   d) an escheat

8. An unwitnessed, handwritten will is called:

   a) a witnessed will
   b) a holographic will
   c) a nuncupative will
   d) None of the above

9. The process by which possession of property can result in ownership of the property is called:

   a) fee simple
   b) succession
   c) adverse possession
   d) reliction

10. A quitclaim deed conveys:

   a) whatever interest the grantor has
   b) only a portion of the interest held by the grantor
   c) only property acquired by adverse possession
   d) None of the above

11. A nuncupative will:

   a) must be entirely handwritten
   b) is invalid in Washington
   c) is an oral will
   d) is only valid for sailors and merchant marines

12. The five basic promises made by a grantor
    through a warranty deed include all of the
    following, except:

    a) covenant of right to convey
    b) covenant of quiet enjoyment
    c) covenant of habitability
    d) covenant of warranty

13. When a cloud on the title cannot be cleared
    with a quitclaim deed, this judicial proceeding
    decides ownership:

    a) quiet title action
    b) suit for partition
    c) interpleader action
    d) reformation action

14. All of the following are requirements for
    adverse possession, except:

    a) open and notorious possession
    b) exclusive possession
    c) hostile possession
    d) recorded claim of possession

15. A standard title insurance policy would protect
    against:

    a) adverse possession
    b) encroachments
    c) a forged deed
    d) condemnation

☞ **Answer Key**

1. c) The general term for a transfer of ownership of real property from one party to another is alienation.

2. a) The government transfers title to property with a patent.

3. c) The covenant of seisin is a promise that the grantor actually owns the interest that is being conveyed.

4. d) A quitclaim deed is commonly used to clear clouds on title.

5. c) The grantee is only required to be identifiable. He or she need not be competent.

6. d) To successfully convey title, the deed must be delivered and accepted.

7. c) A testator is the person who makes a will.

8. b) A holographic will is one that is handwritten by the testator and not witnessed. Generally, holographic wills are not valid in Washington.

9. c) Adverse possession encourages the full use of land by providing a means by which a user may acquire ownership rights.

10. a) A quitclaim deed transfers whatever interest the grantor has. If the grantor has good title, it conveys good title. If the grantor has no interest in the property, it conveys nothing at all.

11. c) A nuncupative is an oral will; it is valid in Washington under limited circumstances.

12. c) A warranty deed carries no promise that the property is habitable or otherwise suitable for the buyer.

13. a) A quiet title action provides a binding determination of the parties' interests in a piece of real estate.

14. d) All of these are among the requirements for adverse possession, except recording a claim. Although an adverse possessor may perfect title by recording a quitclaim deed after the statutory period ends, that isn't a requirement for adverse possession.

15. c) Standard title insurance coverage insures only against defects of title (such as a forged deed), not matters that are not part of the public record.

Encumbrances

▲▫▲▫ Chapter Overview

An interest in real property may be held by someone other than the property owner or a tenant; such an interest is called an encumbrance. Nearly every property has encumbrances against it. Some encumbrances represent another person's financial interest in the property. Other encumbrances involve another person's right to make use of the property or to restrict how the owner uses it.

The first part of this chapter explains financial encumbrances, including mortgages and other types of liens. The second part of this chapter covers the non-financial encumbrances, including easements and private restrictions, and some related concepts.

Encumbrances

An encumbrance is a non-possessory right or interest in real property held by someone other than the property owner. The interest can be financial or non-financial in nature. A financial encumbrance only affects title; a non-financial encumbrance also affects the use or physical condition of the property.

Financial Encumbrances (Liens)

Financial encumbrances are more commonly called **liens**. A lien is a security interest in property; it is held by a creditor of the property owner. If the owner doesn't pay off the debt owed to the creditor, the security interest allows the creditor to force the property to be sold, so that the creditor can collect the debt out of the sale proceeds. This is called **foreclosure**. The most familiar example of a lien is a mortgage.

A creditor who has a lien against (a security interest in) the debtor's property is called a **secured creditor**. The lien does not prevent the debtor from transferring the property, but the new owner takes title subject to the lien. The creditor can still foreclose if the debt is not repaid.

Liens may be voluntary or involuntary. A **voluntary lien** is one the debtor voluntarily gives to the creditor, usually as security for a loan. The two types of voluntary liens are mortgages and deeds of trust. **Involuntary liens** (sometimes called statutory liens) are given to creditors without the property owner's consent, by operation of law. Examples of involuntary liens are property tax liens and judgment liens.

Example: Dunn sues Bronson for injuries sustained in a car crash and wins a $125,000 judgment. The judgment can become a lien against Bronson's property.

Liens may also be general or specific. A **general lien** attaches to all of the debtor's property. For instance, the judgment lien in the example is a general lien. Any property owned by Bronson could be encumbered by the judgment lien. On the other hand, a **specific lien** attaches only to a particular piece of property. A mortgage is an example of a specific lien. It is a lien against only the particular piece of property offered as security for the loan.

Types of Liens

The most common types of liens against real property include mortgages, deeds of trust, construction liens, judgment liens, attachment liens, and tax and assessment liens.

Mortgages. A mortgage is a specific, voluntary lien created by a contract between the property owner (the **mortgagor**) and the creditor (the **mortgagee**). The mortgagee is usually a lender, who will not loan money unless the borrower gives a lien as security for repayment.

Deeds of Trust. A deed of trust (also called a trust deed) is used for the same purpose as a mortgage. However, there are three parties to a trust deed rather than the two found in a mortgage transaction. The borrower is called a **trustor**; the lender or creditor is called the **beneficiary**; and there is an independent third party (often an attorney or title insurance company) called the **trustee**. The most significant difference between mortgages and deeds of trust is in the foreclosure process. Mortgages and deeds of trust are discussed in more detail in Chapter 10.

Construction Liens. A person who provides labor, materials, or professional services for the improvement of real property may be entitled to claim a construction lien against the property. For example, if a plumber who is involved in remodeling a bathroom isn't paid, he or she can claim a lien against the property for the amount owed. Eventually, if necessary, the plumber could foreclose on the lien, forcing the property to be sold to pay the debt.

A construction lien is a specific, involuntary lien, attaching only to the property where work was performed or materials were supplied. Construction liens are often called **mechanic's liens**, and a construction lien claimed by someone who provides materials (as opposed to labor) is sometimes called a **materialman's lien**.

Many improvement projects involve a complex hierarchy of contractors, subcontractors, laborers, and materials suppliers, all of whom may be entitled to claim construction liens. In certain cases, a potential construction lien claimant is required to give the property owner a notice of right to claim a lien (also called a "pre-lien notice") within a certain time after he or she begins providing services or materials. This is not necessary when the claimant has a contract directly with the owner, however.

A claim of lien must be recorded no later than 90 days after the claimant has stopped working on or providing materials for the project. A potential claimant who misses this deadline loses the right to a construction lien. He or she is still entitled to be paid for services rendered, but does not have a security interest in the debtor's property.

Fig. 4.1 Lien classifications

	Voluntary	**Involuntary**
Specific	Mortgages Deeds of trust	Property taxes Special assessments Construction liens
General		Judgment liens IRS liens

To foreclose on a construction lien, the lienholder must file a court action within eight months after the claim of lien was recorded.

Judgment Liens. Judgment liens are involuntary, general liens. If a lawsuit results in a money judgment against the loser, the winner (the judgment creditor) may obtain a lien against the loser's (the judgment debtor's) property. The lien attaches to all the property owned by the debtor in the county where the judgment was entered, and also attaches to any property acquired by the debtor during the lien period (the length of time the judgment creditor has to take action on the lien). The judgment lien may also be recorded in other counties in the state, if the debtor owns property in other counties.

Once a judgment lien has attached, the debtor must pay the judgment to free the property from the lien. If it's not paid, the property can be sold by a designated official to satisfy the judgment. To do this, the court issues a **writ of execution**.

Attachment Liens. When someone files a lawsuit, there is a danger that by the time a judgment is entered, the **defendant** (the party sued) will have sold his or her property and disappeared, leaving the other party with little more than a piece of paper. To prevent this, the **plaintiff** (the person who started the lawsuit) can ask the court to issue a writ of attachment. A **writ of attachment** directs the sheriff to seize enough of the defendant's property to satisfy the judgment the plaintiff is seeking. The writ of attachment is recorded and creates a lien on the defendant's real property.

Also, when a lawsuit that may affect title to real property is pending, the plaintiff may record a document called a **lis pendens**, which is Latin for "action pending." While a lis pendens is not a lien, anyone who purchases the property identified in the lis pendens has constructive notice of the pending lawsuit and therefore is bound by any judgment that results from the suit.

Property Tax Liens. Property is assessed (appraised for tax purposes) and taxed according to its value (ad valorem). When property taxes are levied, a lien attaches to the property until they are paid. Property tax liens are involuntary, specific liens. (Property taxation is discussed in more detail in Chapter 5.)

Special Assessments. Special assessments result from local improvements, such as road paving or sewer lines, that benefit some, but not all, property owners within the county. The properties that have benefited from the improvement are assessed for their share of the cost of the improvement. The assessment creates an involuntary, specific lien against the property. (Special assessments are also discussed in Chapter 5.)

Other Tax Liens. Many other taxes, such as federal income taxes, estate or inheritance taxes, and gift taxes, can result in liens against property.

Lien Priority

It is not at all unusual for a piece of property to have more than one lien against it. In fact, the dollar amount of all the liens may add up to more than the property will bring at a foreclosure sale. When this happens, the sale proceeds are not allocated among all the lienholders in a pro rata fashion (proportionate distribution). Instead, the liens are paid according to their priority. This means that the lien with the highest priority is paid first. If any money is left over, the lien with the second highest priority is paid, and so forth.

As a general rule, lien priority is determined by the date a lien was recorded. The lien that was recorded first will be paid first, even though another lien may have been created first.

> **Example:** Suppose Bakerman borrows money from two banks—$5,000 from National Bank on March 17, and $5,000 from State Bank on May 5 of the same year. Bakerman gives mortgages to both banks when the loan funds are received. If National Bank does not record its mortgage until July 14, but State Bank records its mortgage promptly on May 5, State Bank's lien will be paid before National Bank's in the event of foreclosure.

While "first in time (to record), first in right" is the general rule, there are some exceptions; some types of liens are given special priority. In Washington, special priority is given to property tax and special assessment liens; they have priority over all other liens. Construction liens are another exception. Their priority is determined by the date the claimant began working on the project, even though the claim of lien was recorded later on.

The Homestead Law

Homestead laws are state laws that give homeowners limited protection against lien foreclosure. In Washington, the homestead law offers protection only against general judgment liens. It does not apply to mortgages, deeds of trust, construction liens, liens for child support or spousal maintenance, or liens imposed by a condominium or homeowners association.

A **homestead** is an owner-occupied dwelling, together with any appurtenant buildings and land. Homestead protection is automatic; beginning as soon as the owner starts residing on the property.

An owner can obtain homestead protection in advance, for property he or she is planning to reside on, by recording a Declaration of Homestead for that property. However, a person may have only one homestead at a time.

Exemption. Homestead protection consists of a limited exemption from judgment liens and foreclosure. In Washington, the exemption amount is $40,000.

A judgment creditor cannot foreclose unless the net value of the property is greater than the $40,000 exemption amount. The net value is the property's market value, minus all liens that are senior to the lien being foreclosed on.

> **Example:** The Crenshaws own and occupy a home worth $175,000. The liens against the home, in order of priority, are a $1,500 property tax lien, a $125,000 mortgage, and a $7,000 judgment lien. The judgment creditor wants to foreclose on the judgment lien.
>
> The net value of the home is $48,500 ($175,000 − $126,500 = $48,500). Because the net value is greater than the $40,000 exemption amount, the judgment creditor will be permitted to foreclose.

When the proceeds of the foreclosure sale are distributed, first the exemption amount is paid to the homeowner, then the remaining proceeds are paid to the lienholders in order of priority. For up to one year after foreclosure, money paid to the former homeowner as a result of the homestead exemption is protected from creditors (just as it was protected while it was invested in the homestead). The former homeowner can reinvest the funds in a new homestead.

Termination. Homestead protection terminates automatically when the owner sells the property. However, out of the sale proceeds, the exemption amount is still protected from the claims of general creditors for one year following the sale. This allows the owner time in which to reinvest the exempt funds in a new home, which will then become his or her new homestead.

Non-Financial Encumbrances

While financial encumbrances affect only title to property, non-financial encumbrances affect the physical use or condition of the property itself. Thus, a property owner can find the use of his or her land limited by a right or interest held by someone else. Non-financial encumbrances include easements, profits, and private restrictions. We'll also cover licenses, encroachments, and nuisances in this section; they too involve someone using another's property or affecting the owner's use of it, although they aren't actually interests in real property.

Easements

An easement is a right to use another person's land for a particular purpose. It is a non-possessory interest in land. That means that the easement holder has a right to use the land, but has no title or right of possession. An easement is not an estate.

> **Example:** A landowner has an easement across her neighbor's lot for access to the public road. She has a right to make reasonable use of that easement to get to and from her property. However, she does not have the right to build a shed on the easement, or to use the easement in any way other than as a driveway.

Types of Easements. There are two main types of easements: easements appurtenant and easements in gross.

Easements Appurtenant. An easement appurtenant burdens one parcel of land for the benefit of another parcel of land. The parcel with the benefit is called the **dominant tenement**; the one with the burden is called the **servient tenement**. The owner of the dominant tenement is called the **dominant tenant**; the owner of the servient tenement is the **servient tenant**. Do not confuse the term "tenement," which is the land, with "tenant," which is the landowner.

Probably the most common example of an easement appurtenant is a driveway easement providing access across one

Fig. 4.2 *Types of encumbrances*	
Financial Encumbrances	**Non-Financial Encumbrances**
• Mortgages • Deeds of trust • Construction liens • Judgment liens • Attachment liens • Property tax liens • Other tax liens	• Easements • Profits • Private restrictions

parcel of land to another. (A driveway easement is often called an easement for **ingress and egress**, which means entering and exiting.) In Figure 4.3, Lot B has an easement appurtenant across Lot A. The easement provides access to a public road. Lot B is the dominant tenement. Lot A is the servient tenement.

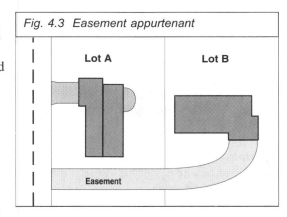

Fig. 4.3 Easement appurtenant

Lot A   Lot B

Easement

An easement appurtenant passes with or "runs" with the land. This means that if either the dominant or servient tenement is transferred to a new owner, the new owner also acquires the benefit or the burden of the easement. Refer to Figure 4.3 again. If Lot B were sold, the new owner would still have an easement across Lot A. If Lot A were sold, the new owner would still bear the burden of allowing the owner of Lot B to use the easement.

An easement that benefits a parcel of land is called an easement appurtenant because it goes along with ownership of the land like other appurtenances (air rights, for example). The easement is appurtenant to the dominant tenement.

Easements in Gross. An easement in gross benefits a person (a dominant tenant) rather than a parcel of land. When someone has an easement in gross, there is no dominant tenement, only a servient tenement.

> **Example:** Wilson has the right to enter Able's land and fish in Able's stream. Wilson is a dominant tenant with an easement in gross over Able's land (the servient tenement). The easement serves Wilson, not a parcel of land.

Since an easement in gross belongs to an individual, and not a parcel of land, it is a personal right that is extinguished on the death of the dominant tenant. In the example above, when Wilson dies, the easement will disappear. A personal easement in gross may not be assigned by its owner to a third party.

Most easements in gross are commercial easements. The most common example is the easement held by a utility company, which allows company employees to enter property to install and service the lines. Because commercial easements in gross are considered more substantial interests than personal easements, they can be assigned from one utility company to another.

Creating an Easement. Easements (whether appurtenant or in gross) can be created in any of the following ways:

- express grant,
- express reservation,
- implication,
- prescription,
- dedication, or
- condemnation.

Express Grant. An easement is created by express grant when a property owner grants someone else the right to use the property. The grant must be put into writing and comply with all the other requirements for conveyance of an interest in land (see Chapter 3).

Express Reservation. A landowner who is conveying a portion of his or her property may reserve an easement in that parcel to benefit the parcel of land that is retained. Like an express grant, an express reservation must be in writing.

Example: Carmichael owns 100 acres bordering on a state highway. She sells 40 acres, including all the highway frontage. In the deed, she reserves to herself an easement across the conveyed land so that she will have access to her remaining 60 acres.

Implication. An easement by implication (sometimes called an easement by necessity) can be either an implied grant or an implied reservation. This type of easement can arise only when a property is divided into more than one lot, and the grantor neglects to grant or reserve an easement on one lot for the benefit of the other. There are two requirements for an easement to be created by implication:

1. it must be reasonably necessary for the enjoyment of the property, and
2. there must have been apparent prior use.

The second requirement is fulfilled if the use was established before the property was divided, and would have been apparent from an inspection of the property.

Prescription. An easement by prescription is created through long-term use of land without the permission of the landowner. Acquiring an easement by prescription is similar to acquiring ownership through adverse possession. Here are the requirements for an easement by prescription:

- the use must be **open and notorious** (apparent to the landowner);
- the use must be **hostile** (without the permission of the landowner);
- the use must be **reasonably continuous** for a statutory period of time (in Washington, ten years).

Note that although an adverse possessor's use of the property must be exclusive, that isn't a requirement for a prescriptive easement. A prescriptive easement may be created even if the landowner is also using the property.

Dedication. A private landowner may grant an easement to the public to use some portion of his or her property for a public purpose, such as a sidewalk. The dedication may be expressly stated or implied.

Condemnation. The government may exercise its power of eminent domain and condemn private property to gain an easement for a public purpose, such as a road. This power may also be exercised by private companies that serve the public, such as railroad and power companies.

Terminating an Easement. An easement can be terminated in any of the following ways:

- release,
- merger,
- failure of purpose,
- abandonment, or
- prescription.

Release. The holder of the easement may release his or her rights in the servient tenement. This would be done by a written document, usually a quit-claim deed to the owner of the servient tenement.

Merger. Since an easement is, by definition, the right to make some use of another person's land, if the dominant and servient tenements come to be owned by the same person, the easement is no longer necessary and therefore is terminated. This is called merger; ownership of the dominant and servient tenements has merged.

Failure of Purpose. If the purpose for which the easement was created ceases, then the easement terminates. For example, if an easement were created for a railroad and the railroad company removed the rails and discontinued its use, the easement would be terminated through failure of purpose.

Abandonment. An easement is also terminated if the easement holder abandons it. This requires acts by the holder indicating an intent to abandon the easement. Mere non-use is not abandonment.

Example: If the dominant tenant were to build a fence that blocked any further use of an easement that had been used for ingress and egress, it would be reasonable for the servient tenant to conclude that the easement had been abandoned.

Prescription. An easement is extinguished if the servient tenant prevents the dominant tenant from using the easement for the statutory period (ten years).

Example: The servient tenant builds a brick wall around his property. The dominant tenant can no longer use his easement for ingress and egress. If the wall remains undisturbed for ten years, the easement will be terminated.

Profits

A profit is the right to take something from land belonging to someone else. For example, it might be the right to take timber, peat, or gravel from someone else's land. The difference between a profit and an easement is that the easement is just a right to use another's land, but a profit allows the removal of something from the land. A profit must be created in writing or by prescription.

Licenses

Like an easement, a license gives someone the right to make some use of another person's land. However, easements and licenses are different in many ways. An easement is created in writing or through action of law. Ordinarily, a license is just verbal permission to cross, hunt, fish on, or make some other use of a landowner's property. An easement is irrevocable, but a license can be revoked at the will of the landowner. In general, easements are permanent and licenses are temporary. A license is a personal right that does not run with or pass with the land. It cannot be assigned. Since the license is revocable at the will of the landowner, it is not actually considered an encumbrance or an interest in the property.

Encroachments

An encroachment is a physical object that is wholly or partially on someone else's property, such as a fence or garage built partially over the property line onto the neighbor's land (see Figure 4.4). Most encroachments are unintentional, resulting from a mistake concerning the exact location of the property line.

Fig. 4.4 Encroachments

TOOL SHED
ENCROACHMENT

Lot A

OVERHANGING TREE LIMBS

Lot B

Lot C

Lot D
PATIO BUILT OVER PROPERTY LINE

An encroachment may be a **trespass** if it violates the neighboring owner's right to possession. A court can order an encroachment to be removed through a judicial action called an **ejectment**, or if the cost of the removal would be too high, order the encroacher to pay damages to the neighbor.

Technically, an encroachment is not an encumbrance because it is not a right or interest held by the encroacher. However, if ignored for the statutory period, the encroachment could ripen into a prescriptive easement or even title by adverse possession.

Nuisances

A nuisance is an activity or a condition on neighboring property that interferes with a property owner's reasonable use or enjoyment of his or her own property. Common examples include odors, noises, and interference with communication signals. Like an encroachment, a nuisance isn't truly an encumbrance, but rather a violation of an owner's possessory rights.

A private nuisance affects only a few surrounding people. For example, rotting garbage in a neighbor's back yard would be a private nuisance. A public nuisance affects a larger community's health or welfare; jet noise and industrial emissions are examples. A property owner may ask a court for an injunction against a private or public nuisance, or may sue for damages.

A related concept is the **attractive nuisance** doctrine. The owner of a property with a feature that is dangerous and attractive to children, such as an unfenced swimming pool or construction site, will be held liable for any harm resulting from failure to keep out trespassing children.

Private Restrictions

Private restrictions (also known as deed restrictions) are restrictions on the use of a property that were imposed by some previous owner. For example, when selling a house long ago, a previous owner might have stated in the deed that the poplar trees in the front yard must not be cut down. Like easements, private restrictions can "run with the land," binding all subsequent owners of the property.

As long as a private restriction isn't unconstitutional, in violation of a law, or contrary to a judicial determination of public policy, it can be enforced in court. (An example of an unenforceable restriction is one prohibiting the sale of property to non-white buyers; see Chapter 15.)

Most subdivision developers impose a list of restrictions on all lots within the subdivision, before they begin selling individual lots. This is called a declaration of restrictions, or **CC&Rs** (covenants, conditions, and restrictions). The CC&Rs typically include rules limiting all the lots to single-family residential use, requiring property maintenance, and preventing activities that would bother the neighbors. The rules are intended to ensure that the subdivision will remain a desirable place to live.

Covenants vs. Conditions. A private restriction is either a covenant or a condition. A **covenant** is a promise to do or not do something, as in a contract. A property owner who violates a covenant may be sued, leading to an injunction (a court order directing the owner to comply with the covenant) or payment of damages for failure to comply. Violation of a **condition** can have more serious consequences. A condition in a deed makes the grantee's title conditional, so that he or she owns a qualified fee (rather than a fee simple absolute; see Chapter 2). Breach of the condition could result in forfeiture of title.

Whether a particular restriction is a covenant or a condition depends on the wording in the deed. Courts try to avoid forfeitures, so they will usually interpret a restriction as a covenant rather than a condition, if there is any ambiguity. (CC&Rs are virtually always covenants, even though the term includes the word "conditions.")

Termination of Restrictions. It is up to the property owners within a subdivision to enforce the CC&Rs. If the residents have failed to enforce a particular restriction in the past, they may no longer be able to enforce it.

> **Example:** The subdivision's CC&Rs state that recreational vehicles may not be parked within view of the street. Over the years, however, many homeowners have broken this rule and their neighbors haven't complained. If someone tries to start enforcing the parking restriction now, a court might rule that it has been abandoned and is no longer enforceable.

A private restriction will also terminate if its purpose can no longer be achieved. For example, this might occur because zoning changes and other factors have dramatically altered the character of the neighborhood. If there is a private restriction limiting a property to single-family residential use, but most of the surrounding properties are now used for light industry, the restriction is probably no longer enforceable.

Chapter Summary

1. An encumbrance is a non-possessory right or interest in real property held by someone other than the property owner. Encumbrances may be financial or non-financial.

2. A financial encumbrance (a lien) affects title to property. It gives a creditor the right to foreclose and use the sale proceeds to pay off the debt. A lien may be voluntary or involuntary, general or specific. The most common types of liens include mortgages, deeds of trust, construction liens, tax liens, and judgment liens.

3. A non-financial encumbrance affects the use or condition of the property. Non-financial encumbrances include easements, profits, and private restrictions.

4. An easement gives the easement holder the right to use a portion of someone else's property for a specified purpose. An easement runs with the land, affecting the title of subsequent owners of the property or properties in question.

5. An easement appurtenant burdens one parcel of land (the servient tenement) for the benefit of another parcel (the dominant tenement). An easement in gross burdens a parcel of land for the benefit of a person, not another parcel of land.

6. Licenses, encroachments, and nuisances may also affect the use or condition of property. They are not classified as encumbrances, however, because they are not interests in real property.

7. Private restrictions affect how an owner may use his or her own property. Like easements, private restrictions run with the land. A declaration of CC&Rs recorded by a subdivision developer is binding on the future owners of the subdivision lots.

🔑 Key Terms

Encumbrance—An interest in real property held by someone other than the property owner.

Voluntary lien—A security interest given to a creditor voluntarily.

Involuntary lien—A security interest given to a creditor by operation of law.

General lien—A lien that attaches to all of a debtor's property.

Specific lien—A lien that attaches only to one particular piece of property.

Construction lien—A lien on property in favor of someone who provided labor or materials to improve it; also called a mechanic's lien or materialman's lien.

Judgment lien—A lien held by someone who has won a judgment in a lawsuit, attaching to property owned by the person who lost the lawsuit.

Easement—The right to use another's land for a particular purpose.

Easement appurtenant—An easement that burdens one parcel of land (the servient tenement) for the benefit of another parcel (the dominant tenement).

Easement in gross—An easement that benefits a person rather than a parcel of land.

Easement by implication—An easement created automatically because it is necessary for the enjoyment of the benefited land.

Prescriptive easement—An easement created by continuous use for the statutory period, without the landowner's permission.

Merger—When both the dominant and servient tenements are acquired by one owner, resulting in termination of the easement.

Abandonment—A way in which an easement may terminate; it requires action by the easement holder, not simply non-use.

Profit—The right to take something (such as timber) from another's land.

License—Revocable permission to enter another's land, which does not create an interest in the property.

Encroachment—A physical object that intrudes onto another's property, such as a tree branch or a fence.

Nuisance—An activity or condition on nearby property that interferes with a property owner's reasonable use and enjoyment of his or her property.

CC&Rs—Covenants, conditions, and restrictions; private restrictions imposed by a subdivision developer.

Condition—A restriction on the use of land, the violation of which may result in forfeiture of title.

Covenant—A promise by a landowner to refrain from using his or her land in a particular manner.

Chapter Quiz

1. Real estate property taxes are:

   a) general, involuntary liens
   b) general, voluntary liens
   c) specific, voluntary liens
   d) specific, involuntary liens

2. A lawsuit against Thatcher is pending. The court rules that a lien should be placed on his farm, holding it as security in case of a negative judgment. This is:

   a) adverse possession
   b) prescription
   c) attachment
   d) appurtenance

3. A recorded document that informs potential buyers that the property may become subject to a judgment in a lawsuit is a:

   a) lis pendens
   b) writ of execution
   c) writ of attachment
   d) habendum clause

4. Which of the following has priority over a mortgage that has already been recorded?

   a) A deed of trust
   b) A judgment lien
   c) A property tax lien
   d) None of the above

5. If there were two deeds of trust against the same property and you needed to know which one had higher priority, you could find this information at the county recorder's office. The priority is usually established by:

   a) the printed trust deed forms, which have the words "first deed of trust" and "second deed of trust" on their face
   b) the date and time of recording
   c) the county auditor's stamp, which says "first trust deed" or "second trust deed"
   d) the execution date of each document

6. When there's an easement appurtenant, the dominant tenement:

   a) can be used only for purposes of ingress and egress
   b) is burdened by the easement
   c) receives the benefit of the easement
   d) cannot be sold

7. You have the right to cross another's land to get to your house. You probably own:

   a) a dominant tenement
   b) a servient tenement
   c) Both of the above
   d) Neither of the above

8. An easement in gross benefits:

   a) a dominant tenement
   b) a servient tenement
   c) Both of the above
   d) Neither of the above

9. Unlike a personal easement in gross, a commercial easement in gross:

   a) is not an encumbrance
   b) is considered a possessory interest in real property
   c) can be assigned to another party
   d) can be revoked by the owner of the servient tenement

10. Which of the following is not a method of creating an easement?

    a) Implication
    b) Express grant in a deed
    c) Dedication
    d) Spoken grant

11. The creation of an easement by prescription is similar to acquiring ownership of property by:

  a) adverse possession
  b) escheat
  c) alluvium
  d) intestate succession

12. A has an easement over B's property. If A buys B's property, the easement:

  a) goes with the land
  b) is terminated
  c) is unaffected
  d) None of the above

13. A porch or balcony that hangs over the established boundary line of a parcel of land is called:

  a) an easement in gross
  b) an encroachment
  c) an easement appurtenant
  d) a license

14. All of the following would be considered nuisances, except:

  a) fumes from a paper mill
  b) a house with regular drug-dealing activity
  c) radiation from a microwave tower
  d) a garage built on top of the property line

15. The private restrictions in a subdivision's CC&Rs:

  a) do not run with the land
  b) were imposed by the developer
  c) can terminate only with the approval of a majority of the lot owners
  d) create a lien against the property

👉 Answer Key

1. d) Property tax liens are specific (they attach only to the taxed property) and involuntary.

2. c) In an attachment, a lien is created against the defendant's property, pending the outcome of the lawsuit.

3. a) A lis pendens provides constructive notice of a pending lawsuit that may affect the property described in the document.

4. c) Property tax liens always have priority over other liens.

5. b) The date of recording governs lien priority, rather than the date of execution of the documents.

6. c) The dominant tenement is benefited by the easement; the servient tenement is burdened by the easement. An easement appurtenant is not necessarily an easement for ingress and egress.

7. a) Since you have the right to use another's property to reach your own, you probably own a dominant tenement.

8. d) An easement in gross benefits an individual (the dominant tenant) rather than any parcel of land.

9. c) A commercial easement in gross can be assigned to another party, but a personal easement in gross cannot be.

10. d) Like any other interest in land, an easement must be granted in writing, unless it is created by operation of law.

11. a) An easement by prescription is obtained in much the same way as ownership by adverse possession: the use must be open and notorious, hostile, and continuous for ten years. It does not have to be exclusive, however.

12. b) Merger occurs when one person acquires ownership of both the dominant tenement and the servient tenement. Merger terminates the easement.

13. b) An overhanging porch or balcony is an encroachment.

14. d) A structure built on the property line is an encroachment, not a nuisance. A nuisance is an activity or condition on neighboring property that negatively affects an owner's use and enjoyment of his or her property.

15. b) CC&Rs are usually imposed by the developer. They run with the land, which means that subsequent owners of the subdivision lots must abide by them.

Public Restrictions on Land

I. Land Use Controls
   A. Comprehensive planning
   B. Zoning
      1. nonconforming uses
      2. variances
      3. conditional uses
      4. rezones
   C. Building codes
   D. Subdivision regulations
      1. physical regulations
      2. consumer protection laws
   E. Environmental laws
      1. Shoreline Management Act
      2. NEPA
      3. SEPA
      4. CERCLA
      5. air and water pollution control laws

II. Eminent Domain

III. Taxation
   A. General real estate taxes
   B. Special assessments
   C. Real estate excise tax

▣▣▣ Chapter Overview

Although a property owner has many rights in regard to his or her property, those rights are limited by certain powers of the federal, state, and local governments. This chapter examines the ways in which governmental powers affect property ownership most directly. The first part of the chapter explains planning, zoning, and other public restrictions on land use, and the second part discusses the government's power to tax property.

Land Use Controls

In the United States, the powers of government are determined by the federal and state constitutions. Thus, efforts by the federal, state, and local governments to control the use of private property raise constitutional issues. When a property owner objects to a land use law, the central question is often whether the law is constitutional—whether the Constitution gives the government the power to interfere with private property rights in this way.

The constitutional basis for land use control laws is the **police power**. This is the power vested in a state to adopt and enforce laws and regulations necessary for the protection of the public's health, safety, morals, and general welfare. A state may delegate its police power to local governmental bodies.

It is the police power that allows state and local governments to regulate a private individual's use of his or her property. The Constitution does not give the federal government a general power to regulate for the public health, safety, morals, and welfare. But the federal government does have authority to use its other powers (such as the power to regulate interstate commerce) to advance police power objectives.

Exercises of the police power must meet constitutional limitations. As a general rule, a land use law or regulation will be considered constitutional if it meets these four criteria:

1. It is reasonably related to the protection of the public health, safety, morals, or general welfare.
2. It applies in the same manner to all property owners who are similarly situated (it is not discriminatory).
3. It does not reduce a property's value so much that the regulation amounts to a confiscation.
4. It benefits the public by preventing harm that would be caused by the prohibited use of the property.

Government land use controls take a variety of forms: comprehensive plans, zoning ordinances, building codes, subdivision regulations, and environmental laws. All of these are intended to protect the public from problems that unrestricted use of private property can cause.

Comprehensive Planning

To alleviate the problems caused by haphazard, unplanned growth, many states require cities and counties to have a planning agency, usually called a planning commission.

The planning commission is responsible for designing and adopting a comprehensive, long-term plan for all the development within the city or county. This is often called the "master plan" or "general plan." The purpose of the general plan is to outline the community's development goals and design an overall physical layout to achieve those goals. Once the general plan has been adopted, all development and all land use regulations (such as zoning laws) must conform to it.

The government uses both its police power and its power of eminent domain (discussed later) to implement the planning commission's general plan.

In Washington, land use planning and administration changed dramatically with the passage of the **Growth Management Act** in 1990 and its later amendments. The Growth Management Act has four major goals:

1. To change Washington's previous patterns of urban and suburban sprawl by concentrating new development in already existing urban growth areas.
2. To ensure adequate public facilities are available to serve all new development by requiring thorough infrastructure planning.
3. To protect critical areas from environmentally harmful activities, and to protect natural resource lands from incompatible development.
4. To encourage regional responsibility by coordinating the plans and regulations of neighboring communities.

Under the terms of the Growth Management Act, new development is to be concentrated in compact urban growth areas that are contiguous with presently urbanized areas.

Zoning

Zoning ordinances divide a community into areas (or zones) that are set aside for specific types of uses, such as agricultural, residential, commercial, or industrial use. Each of these basic classifications may be further divided. For instance, an industrial district may be divided into a light industrial zone and a heavy industrial zone. Keeping various uses in separate zones helps ensure that only compatible uses are located in the same area. In addition, areas zoned for incompatible uses may be separated by undeveloped areas called **buffers**.

Zoning ordinances regulate the height, size, and shape of buildings, as well as their use. The laws also usually include setback and side yard requirements, which prescribe the minimum distance between a building and the property lines. These regulations control population density, provide aesthetic guidelines, and help preserve adequate open space and access to air and daylight.

Fig. 5.1 Setbacks and side yards

Zoning Exceptions and Amendments. Complications inevitably arise when zoning regulations are administered and enforced. So zoning ordinances provide for certain exceptions and changes to their rules, including:

- nonconforming uses,
- variances,
- conditional uses, and
- rezones.

Nonconforming Uses. A **nonconforming use** can arise when an area is zoned for the first time, or when a zoning ordinance is amended. Certain established uses that were lawful before may not conform to the rules laid down in the new ordinance. These nonconforming uses will be permitted to continue.

> **Example:** Smith has been lawfully operating a bakery for seven months when his property is rezoned for single-family residential use. Smith's bakery will be allowed to continue as a nonconforming use.

Even though nonconforming uses are allowed to remain, the local government wants all uses to conform to the current zoning laws at some point. Consequently, the owners of a nonconforming use property are often prohibited from enlarging the use, rebuilding if the property is destroyed, or resuming the use after abandoning it.

> **Example:** Smith's bakery burns to the ground in a terrible fire. The zoning authority will not allow him to rebuild the bakery in this residential zone. He will have to sell the property and use the insurance proceeds to buy a suitable property located in a commercial zone.

Variances. In some cases, if a zoning law were strictly enforced, the property owner's injury would far outweigh the benefit of enforcing the zoning requirement. Under these circumstances, a **variance** may be available. A variance is authorization to build or maintain a structure or use that is prohibited by the zoning ordinance. For example, a variance might authorize construction of a house even though the topography of the lot makes it virtually impossible to comply with normal setback requirements. In most communities, the property owner applies to the local zoning authority for a variance.

A variance usually will not be granted unless the property owner faces severe practical difficulties or undue hardship (not created by the property owner him or herself) as a result of the zoning. The owner is generally required to prove that the zoning prevents any reasonable use of the land, not merely the most profitable use.

> **Example:** Corelli owns a piece of property that would make a perfect site for a convenience store, but it is in a residential zone. Corelli will not be able to get a variance by claiming that she could make much more money by building a convenience store than she could by building a single-family home.

Most variances authorize only minor deviations from the zoning law. A variance should not change the essential character of the neighborhood or conflict with the community's general plan.

Conditional Uses. Various special uses, such as schools, hospitals, and churches, don't fit into the ordinary zoning categories. These uses are necessary to the community, yet they may have adverse effects on neighboring properties. So in most communities the zoning authority can issue **conditional use permits** (also called special exception permits), allowing a limited number of these uses to operate in compliance with specified conditions. For example, a property owner might be given a conditional use permit to build a private school in a residential neighborhood, as long as the school meets certain requirements for parking, security, and so on.

Rezones. If a property owner believes that his or her property has been zoned improperly, he or she may petition the local appeals board for a **rezone** (sometimes called a zoning amendment). Usually, notice must be given to surrounding landowners and a hearing must be held before any decision is made on a petition.

When an area is rezoned to a more restrictive use (for example, a change from multiple-family dwellings to single-family dwellings), it is referred to as **downzoning**.

Building Codes

The enactment of building codes is another exercise of the police power. Building codes protect the public from unsafe or unworkmanlike construction. They are generally divided into specialized codes, such as a fire code, an electrical code, and a plumbing code. The codes set standards for construction methods and materials. A structure that was built before a new, stricter standard is enacted may still be required to meet the new standard.

Enforcement of building codes is usually accomplished through the building permit system. A property owner must obtain a permit from the city or county before constructing a new building or repairing, improving, or altering an existing building. For example, it is usually necessary to have a building permit in order to add on to a home, to convert a carport into a garage, or even to build a fence. The permit requirement allows officials to inspect the building plans to verify that building codes and zoning ordinances have been satisfied. Once the completed building has been inspected and found satisfactory, a **certificate of occupancy** is issued.

Subdivision Regulations

Another way in which state and local governments control land use is by regulating subdivisions. A subdivision is a division of one parcel of land into two or more parcels.

There are two basic types of subdivision regulations in Washington. The first type establishes requirements concerning the physical aspects of subdivisions, such as access roads, utilities, lot size, and so on. The second type is embodied in the state's Land Development Act. This is actually a consumer protection law rather than a land use control law; it requires subdivision developers to disclose certain information to prospective lot purchasers.

Physical Regulations. Regulations concerning the physical aspects of subdivisions are adopted and administered by each county in Washington. Although the regulations vary from county to county, the procedures for compliance are fairly uniform throughout the state. Someone who wants to subdivide a parcel of land must first notify county officials by submitting a plat map. The plat shows the boundaries of the proposed lots and provides information about provisions for utilities and other public services. If the property is within city limits or within one mile of a city, the plat map must also be submitted to the proper city officials (usually the planning commission).

There are three essential elements for a subdivision plat. First, the plat must include the legal description of the land to be subdivided. The plat must also include a statement of the landowner's consent to the subdivision. And the plat must provide for any dedications that the county or city requires, such as dedication of land within the subdivision for public streets. (Dedication is the transfer of property from private to public ownership; see Chapter 3.)

The county or city may approve the plat as submitted, or may require amendments. It is illegal for the subdivider to sell any lots until the plat has been approved.

Washington Land Development Act. The Land Development Act applies to anyone selling or advertising 26 or more unimproved lots to the general public in Washington as part of a common promotional plan. It applies even when the subdivision is located in another state, if it is promoted in this state.

Under the act, a subdivision developer must prepare a public offering statement, providing information about the development. The statement includes disclosures concerning liens against the subdivision, the physical condition of the land, compliance with land use laws, and warranties that apply to the purchase of a lot.

The developer should give a public offering statement to each lot buyer before the buyer signs a purchase contract. Otherwise, the buyer has a right to back out of the transaction (rescind the contract) within two days after receiving the statement. If the developer fails to give the buyer a statement before the transaction closes, the buyer can sue for damages.

The Land Development Act has a number of exemptions. It doesn't apply to a subdivision with fewer than 26 lots, or to one in which each lot is at least five acres. It doesn't apply if all the lots have buildings on them, or if the developer intends to build on the lots within two years. It doesn't apply when lots are sold to builders for development, or when all the lots are sold to one purchaser. And a subdivision that is entirely within city limits is not subject to the act.

ILSFDA. The **Interstate Land Sales Full Disclosure Act** (ILSFDA) is a federal consumer protection law concerning subdivisions offered for sale or lease in interstate commerce. It requires developers to register their projects with a division of the Department of Housing and Urban Development (HUD), and to disclose information to buyers. The law generally applies to subdivisions containing 25 or more vacant lots, although there are numerous exemptions.

Environmental Laws

The federal and state governments have enacted a number of laws aimed at preserving and protecting the physical environment, and many local governments have additional environmental regulations. These laws can have a substantial impact on the ways in which a property owner is allowed to use his or her land.

Shoreline Management Act. The purpose of this law is to protect Washington's shorelines by regulating development within 200 feet of the high water mark. It applies to coastal shorelines, and to the shores of larger lakes and streams.

National Environmental Policy Act (NEPA). NEPA is a federal law that requires federal agencies to prepare an **environmental impact statement** (EIS) for any governmental action that would have a significant impact on the environment. NEPA also applies to private uses or developments that require the approval of a federal agency.

State Environmental Policy Act (SEPA). Washington's SEPA is similar to NEPA in that it requires an environmental impact statement to be prepared in connection with all actions of state and local agencies that may have a significant effect on the environment. The act also applies to private uses and developments that require the approval of the state, county, or city. Thus, SEPA procedures must be followed before a city or county approves rezones, conditional use permits, variances, or building permits.

CERCLA. The Comprehensive Environmental Response, Compensation, and Liability Act, a federal law, concerns liability for environmental cleanup costs. In some cases, the current owners of contaminated property may be required to pay for cleanup, even if they did not cause the contamination.

Pollution Control Laws. Federal legislation sets national standards for air and water quality and requires the states to implement these objectives. Permits are required for the discharge of pollutants into the air or water.

Eminent Domain

As you've seen, the government can regulate the use of private property with a variety of laws—zoning ordinances, building codes, and so on. These laws are based on the police power, the government's power to regulate for the public health, safety, morals, and general welfare. Another governmental power that can be used to control land use is the power of **eminent domain**.

The power of eminent domain is the federal or state government's power to take private property for a public purpose upon payment of **just compensation** to the owner. A state government may delegate the power of eminent domain to local governments, and to private entities that serve the public, such as utility companies and railroads.

Condemnation is the process by which the government exercises its power of eminent domain. When a particular property is needed for a public purpose, the government first offers to buy it from the owner. If the owner refuses to sell for the price offered, the government files a condemnation lawsuit. The court will order the property to be transferred to the government. The owner's only grounds for objection are that the intended use of the property is not a public use, or that the price offered is not just compensation. (Just compensation is usually defined as the fair market value of the property.)

A local government can use the power of eminent domain to implement its general plan. For example, to fulfill the plan's open space goals, several pieces of private property might be condemned for use as public parks.

It is important to understand the distinction between eminent domain and the police power. Eminent domain involves taking property away from the private owner, and the Constitution requires the government to pay the owner compensation. In an exercise of the police power, private property is regulated, but not taken away from the owner. The government is not required to compensate the owner for a proper exercise of the police power, even though the action (such as a zoning change) may significantly reduce the value of the property.

Taxation

Real property taxes affect property ownership. The taxes create liens, and if the property owner fails to pay the taxes, the government can sell the property to collect them. Real property taxation has always been a popular method of raising revenue because land has a fixed location, is relatively indestructible, and is essentially impossible to conceal. Thus, there is a high degree of certainty that the taxes will be collected.

In this section, we will discuss these three types of taxes on real property:

- general real estate taxes (also called ad valorem taxes),
- special assessments (also called improvement taxes), and
- the real estate excise tax (also called the transfer tax).

General Real Estate Taxes

General real estate taxes are levied to support the general operation and services of government. Public schools and police and fire protection are examples of government services paid for with general real estate tax revenues. These taxes are levied by a number of governmental agencies, such as cities, counties, school districts, and water districts. Thus, a single property can be situated in five or six taxing districts.

Assessment. General real estate taxes are **ad valorem taxes**. That means the amount of tax owed depends on the value of the property. The valuation of property for purposes of taxation is called **assessment**. In Washington, all real property must be assessed at 100% of its "true and fair value" unless otherwise provided by law. True and fair value means market value: the most probable price that the property would sell for under normal market conditions.

Real property is assessed each year on January 1, although a physical examination of the property has to be performed only once every four years. In each county, a Board of Equalization hears appeals of property tax assessments from taxpayers.

Collection of Taxes. Tax bills are mailed to property owners each year in mid-February. Payment of half the taxes is due on April 30, and the balance is due on October 31.

General real estate taxes become a lien on January 1 of the year in which they are levied. Taxes are levied in October of each year and payable the following year.

The county can foreclose on a property when the taxes have been delinquent for three years. The owner can redeem the property before the sale by paying the amount of delinquent taxes, interest, and any other accumulated costs.

Exemptions. All real property in Washington is taxed unless it is exempt, but there are numerous exemptions. For example, general real estate taxes are not levied against publicly owned property, property used for church purposes, cemeteries, or non-profit hospitals and schools.

There are also some exemptions available to individual property owners. For example, there is a partial exemption for low-income homeowners who are 61 or older, or retired because of physical disability. In some cases, these owners may also be allowed to defer payment of the partial taxes they owe until their property is sold.

Open Space. Washington has a special rule for taxation of open space, which shows how the power to tax can be used for land use control. Certain land that qualifies as open space is eligible to be assessed not at its market value (which might mean how much it would be worth if developed) but at its value as it is currently being used. This results in a lower assessment, and therefore in lower taxes, providing an incentive to preserve the property as open space instead of developing it. To have property assessed in this way, the owner must agree that if the property is developed or sold for development, additional taxes will be paid at that point.

Special Assessments

Special assessments, also called local improvement taxes, are levied to pay for improvements that benefit particular properties, such as the installation of street lights or the widening of a street. Only the properties that benefit from the improvement are taxed, on the theory that the value of those properties is increased by the improvement. A special assessment is usually a one-time tax, although the property owners may be allowed to pay the assessment off in installments.

Like general real estate taxes, special assessments create liens against the taxed properties. If an owner fails to pay the assessment, the government can foreclose on the property.

Here is a summary of the distinctions between general real estate taxes and special assessments:

1. General real estate taxes are levied to pay for ongoing government services, such as police protection. A special assessment is levied to pay for a specific improvement, such as adding sidewalks to a section of street.
2. General real estate taxes are levied against all taxable real property within a taxing district, for the benefit of the entire community. A special assessment, on the other hand, is levied against only those properties that benefit from the improvement in question.

3. General real estate taxes are levied every year. A special assessment is a one-time tax, levied only when a property is benefited by a public improvement.

Real Estate Excise Tax

An excise tax is levied on each sale of real property in Washington. The tax is based on the property's selling price. The state's share of the tax is 1.28% of the selling price, and an additional amount (up to 0.77% of the price) is owed to the city or county government.

The excise tax is ordinarily collected when the buyer's deed is recorded; the recorder's office will not accept a deed for recording unless the tax is paid and a real estate excise tax affidavit is executed. By law, the seller is liable for payment of the excise tax. Yet the tax creates a lien against the transferred property (now owned by the buyer). Thus, even though payment is the seller's responsibility, a buyer should always make sure the excise tax is paid, so that the deed can be recorded and lien foreclosure avoided.

Chapter Summary

1. The police power—the government's power to adopt and enforce laws for the protection of the public health, safety, morals, and general welfare—is the constitutional basis for land use control laws.

2. Many communities have a general plan—a comprehensive, long-term plan for development—and some counties and cities are required by law to have one. A local government implements its general plan with zoning ordinances and other laws.

3. Zoning ordinances provide for certain exceptions to their rules: non-conforming uses, variances, and conditional uses. They also have procedures for rezones.

4. Building codes set standards for construction materials and practices, to protect the public. The codes are enforced through the building permit system.

5. Someone who subdivides land must submit a plat map to the county and comply with local subdivision regulations. In some cases a developer will also be required to comply with consumer protection laws regulating the sale of subdivision lots.

6. A number of important federal and state environmental laws affect land use, including the Shoreline Management Act, NEPA, SEPA, and CERCLA.

7. A government entity can use the power of eminent domain to implement its general plan. When property is taken under the power of eminent domain, the government must pay just compensation to the owner. (Compensation is not required when property is merely regulated under the police power.)

8. The government's power to tax also affects property ownership. General real estate taxes are levied each year to pay for ongoing government services. Special assessments are levied to pay for improvements that benefit specific properties. The real estate excise tax must be paid on every sale of real property in Washington.

Key Terms

Police power—The power of state governments to regulate for the protection of the public health, safety, morals, and general welfare.

General plan—A comprehensive, long-term plan of development for a community, which is implemented by zoning and other laws.

Zoning—A method of controlling land use by dividing a community into zones for different types of uses.

Nonconforming use—A formerly legal use that does not conform to a new zoning ordinance, but is nonetheless allowed to continue.

Variance—An authorization to deviate from the rules in a zoning ordinance, granted because strict enforcement would cause undue hardship for the property owner.

Conditional use permit—A permit that allows a special use, such as a school or hospital, to operate in a neighborhood where it would otherwise be prohibited by the zoning.

Rezone—An amendment to a zoning ordinance; a property owner who feels his or her property has been zoned improperly may apply for a rezone.

Building codes—Regulations that set minimum standards for construction methods and materials.

Eminent domain—The government's power to take private property for public use, upon payment of just compensation to the owner.

Condemnation—The process of taking property pursuant to the power of eminent domain.

General real estate taxes—Taxes levied against real property annually to pay for general government services; based on the value of the property taxed (ad valorem).

Special assessment—A tax levied against property that benefits from a local improvement project, to pay for the project.

Real estate excise tax—A tax levied when a piece of real property is sold; based on the selling price of the property.

Chapter Quiz

1. The police power is the government's power to:

   a) take private property for public use
   b) enact laws for the protection of the public health, safety, morals, and general welfare
   c) tax property to pay for police protection
   d) None of the above

2. Which of the following is likely to be controlled by a zoning ordinance?

   a) Use of the property
   b) Building height
   c) Placement of a building on a lot
   d) All of the above

3. Which of the following is NOT likely to be one of the goals of a land use control law?

   a) Ensuring that properties are put to their most profitable use
   b) Controlling growth and population density
   c) Ensuring that neighboring uses are compatible
   d) Preserving access to light and air

4. As a general rule, when a new zoning ordinance goes into effect, nonconforming uses:

   a) must comply with the new law within 90 days
   b) must shut down within 90 days
   c) will be granted conditional use permits
   d) are allowed to continue, but not to expand

5. An owner who feels that his or her property was improperly zoned should apply for a:

   a) conditional use permit
   b) variance
   c) rezone
   d) nonconforming use permit

6. A property owner is generally required to show undue hardship in order to obtain a:

   a) nonconforming use permit
   b) special exception permit
   c) rezone
   d) variance

7. Which of these is an example of a variance?

   a) Authorizing a hospital to be built in a residential zone
   b) Authorizing a structure to be built only 12 feet from the lot's boundary, although the zoning ordinance requires 15-foot setbacks
   c) Allowing a grocery store to continue in operation after the neighborhood is zoned residential
   d) Approving the subdivision of a parcel of land into two or more lots

8. Which of these is NOT an exercise of the police power?

   a) Condemnation
   b) Building code
   c) Zoning ordinance
   d) Subdivision regulations

9. Eminent domain differs from the police power in that:

   a) the government is required to compensate the property owner
   b) it can be exercised only by the state government, not a city or county government
   c) it affects only the use of the property, not the title
   d) the property must be unimproved

10. The Hancocks are planning to add a room onto their house. Before construction begins, they are probably required to:

   a) request a zoning inspection
   b) submit a proposal to the planning commission
   c) obtain a building permit
   d) All of the above

11. A special assessment is the same thing as:

   a) a general real estate tax
   b) an improvement tax
   c) a real estate excise tax
   d) an ad valorem tax

12. General real estate taxes are:

   a) used to support the general operation and services of government
   b) levied annually
   c) based on the value of the taxed property
   d) All of the above

13. Which of these is a state law that requires an environmental impact statement to be prepared in certain circumstances?

   a) ILSFDA
   b) CERCLA
   c) SEPA
   d) None of the above

14. The real estate excise tax is based on the property's:

   a) selling price
   b) fair market value
   c) current use
   d) highest and best use

15. Under the State Environmental Policy Act (SEPA):

   a) every building project must submit an environmental impact statement
   b) environmental impact statements are only required for state or federal projects
   c) an environmental impact statement is required for all actions of state agencies that may have a significant impact on the environment
   d) None of the above

👉 Answer Key

1. b) The police power is the government's power to pass laws (such as zoning ordinances) for the protection of the public health, safety, morals, and general welfare.

2. d) Zoning ordinances typically control the height and placement of buildings as well as type of use.

3. a) Land use controls are not aimed at encouraging the most profitable use of particular properties. In some cases they prohibit more profitable uses that would be detrimental to the public health, safety, or welfare.

4. d) A nonconforming use (a use established before new zoning rules go into effect, which does not comply with those rules) is ordinarily allowed to continue, but the use cannot be expanded, rebuilt after destruction, or resumed after abandonment.

5. c) A rezone is an amendment to the zoning ordinance, giving a particular area a new zoning designation.

6. d) A variance is granted when the property owner shows that strict enforcement of the zoning law would result in undue hardship.

7. b) A variance authorizes the improvement of property in a manner not ordinarily allowed by the zoning ordinance. Most variances permit only minor deviations from the rules.

8. a) Condemnation is an exercise of the power of eminent domain, not the police power.

9. a) When a government body takes property under the power of eminent domain, it is required to pay compensation to the owner. Compensation is not required if a property loses value due to regulation under the police power.

10. c) A building permit is generally required before an addition or remodeling project is begun, to ensure that the structure will comply with the building codes and zoning.

11. b) A special assessment is also called an improvement tax; it is levied to pay for a particular public improvement.

12. d) All of these statements concerning general real estate taxes are true.

13. c) SEPA is the State Environmental Policy Act. (CERCLA is a federal environmental law, and ILSFDA is a federal subdivision law.)

14. a) The real estate excise tax is levied only when title to property is transferred, and it is based on the selling price.

15. c) An EIS is required for all actions by state agencies that may have a significant impact on the environment.

Contract Law

I. Legal Classifications of Contracts
   A. Express vs. implied
   B. Unilateral vs. bilateral
   C. Executory vs. executed
II. Elements of a Valid Contract
   A. Capacity
   B. Mutual consent
   C. Lawful objective
   D. Consideration
   E. Writing requirement
III. Legal Status of Contracts
   A. Void
   B. Voidable
   C. Unenforceable
   D. Valid
IV. Discharging a Contract
   A. Full performance
   B. Agreement between the parties
V. Breach of Contract
   A. Rescission
   B. Liquidated damages
   C. Damages
   D. Specific performance
VI. Tender
VII. Types of Real Estate Contracts
   A. Listing agreements
   B. Purchase and sale agreements
   C. Land contracts
   D. Leases
   E. Escrow instructions
   F. Option agreements

Chapter Overview

Contracts are a significant part of the real estate business. Almost everyone has a basic understanding of what a contract is, but real estate agents need more than that. This chapter explains the requirements that must be met in order for a contract to be valid and binding; how a contract can be terminated; what is considered a breach of contract; and what remedies are available when a breach occurs.

Introduction

Real estate licensees deal with contracts on a daily basis: listing agreements, purchase and sale agreements, option agreements, and leases are all contracts. Thus, it is essential for a licensee to understand the basic legal requirements and effects of contracts.

Keep in mind, however, that a real estate licensee may not draft the original language for a contract. Anyone other than a lawyer who drafts a contract for someone else may be charged with the unauthorized practice of law.

Here is a general definition of a contract: an agreement between two or more competent persons to do or not do certain things in exchange for consideration. An agreement to sell a car, deliver lumber, or rent an apartment is a contract. And if it meets minimum legal requirements, it can be enforced in court.

Legal Classifications of Contracts

There are certain basic classifications that apply to any contract, no matter what type it is. Every contract is either express or implied, either unilateral or bilateral, and either executory or executed.

Express vs. Implied

An **express** contract is one that has been put into words. It may be written or oral. Each party to the contract has stated what he or she is willing to do and has been told what to expect from the other party. Most contracts are express. On the other hand, an **implied** contract, or contract by implication, is created by the actions of the parties, not by express agreement.

> **Example:** A written lease agreement expires, but the tenant continues to make payments and the landlord continues to accept them. Both parties have implied their consent to a new lease contract.

Unilateral vs. Bilateral

A contract is **unilateral** if only one of the contracting parties is legally obligated to perform. That party has promised to do a particular thing if the other party does something else; but the other party has not promised to do anything, and is not legally obligated to do anything.

Fig. 6.1 Contract classifications

Express *Written or oral*	OR	Implied *Actions of the parties*
Unilateral *One promise*	OR	Bilateral *Two promises*
Executory *Not yet fully performed*	OR	Executed *Fully performed*

Example: In an open listing agreement, a seller promises to pay a real estate broker a commission if the broker finds a buyer for the property. The broker does not promise to try to find a buyer, but if he or she does, the seller is obligated to pay. An open listing agreement is a unilateral contract.

A **bilateral** contract is formed when each party promises to do something, so that both parties are legally obligated to perform. Most contracts are bilateral.

Example: In a purchase and sale agreement, the seller promises to transfer title to the buyer, and the buyer promises to pay the agreed price to the seller. This is a bilateral contract. Each party has made a promise, and both are obligated to perform.

Executory vs. Executed

An **executory** contract is one that has not yet been performed, or is in the process of being performed. An **executed** contract has been fully performed. With respect to contracts, the terms "executed" and "performed" mean the same thing.

Elements of a Valid Contract

Four elements are needed for a valid and binding contract that will be enforced by a court:

1. legal capacity to contract,
2. mutual consent,
3. a lawful objective, and
4. consideration.

Capacity

The first requirement for a valid contract is that the parties have the legal capacity to enter into a contract. A person must be at least 18 years old to enter into a valid contract, and he or she must also be competent.

Age Eighteen. Eighteen years of age is sometimes referred to as the age of majority. Minors (those under the age of 18) do not have capacity to contract. If a minor signs a contract, it is voidable by the minor; that is, it cannot be enforced against him or her.

> **Example:** A 16-year-old signs a purchase and sale agreement, agreeing to buy a house. The seller cannot enforce the contract against the minor, although the minor could compel the seller to honor the terms of the agreement.

The purpose of this rule is to prevent people from entering into legally binding agreements when they may be too young to understand the consequences.

Competent. A person must also be mentally competent to have capacity to contract. If a person has been declared incompetent by a court, any contract he or she signs is void. If a court declares someone incompetent after a contract is signed, but the party was probably incompetent when the contract was signed, the contract is voidable at the discretion of the court-appointed guardian.

Contracts entered into by a person who is temporarily incompetent (for example, under the influence of alcohol or drugs) may be voidable if he or she takes legal action within a reasonable time after regaining mental competency.

Representing Another. Often, one person has the capacity to represent another person or entity in a contract negotiation. For instance, the affairs of minors and incompetent persons are handled by parents or court-appointed guardians; corporations are represented by properly authorized officers; partnerships are represented by individual partners; deceased persons are represented by executors or administrators; and a competent adult can appoint another competent adult to act on his or her behalf through a power of attorney. In each of these cases, the authorized representative can enter into a contract on behalf of the person represented.

Mutual Consent

Mutual consent is the second requirement for a valid contract. Each party must consent to the agreement. Once someone has signed a contract, consent is presumed, so no contract should be signed until its contents are fully understood. A person can't use failure or inability to read an agreement as an excuse for nonperformance. An illiterate person should have a contract explained thoroughly by someone who is concerned with his or her welfare.

Mutual consent is sometimes called mutual assent, mutuality, or "a meeting of the minds." It is achieved through the process of **offer and acceptance**.

Offer. A contract offer shows the willingness of the person making it (the **offeror**) to enter into a contract under the stated terms. To be valid, an offer must meet two requirements:

1. It must express a willingness to contract. Whatever words make up the offer, they must clearly indicate that the offeror intends to enter into a contract.
2. It must be definite and certain in its terms. A vague offer that does not clearly state what the offeror is proposing is said to be illusory, and any agreement reached as a result is unenforceable.

Note that an advertisement that lists a property's price is not considered a contract offer; it is merely an invitation to negotiate.

Terminating an Offer. Sometimes circumstances change after an offer has been made, or perhaps the offeror has had a change of heart. If an offer terminates before it is accepted, no contract is formed. There are many things that can terminate an offer before it is accepted, including:

- revocation by the offeror,
- lapse of time,
- death or incompetency of the offeror,
- rejection of the offer, or
- a counteroffer.

The offeror can **revoke** the offer at any time until he or she is notified that the offer has been accepted. To effect a proper "offer and acceptance," the accepting party must not only accept the offer, but must also communicate that acceptance to the offeror before the offer is revoked. (See the discussion of acceptance, below.)

Many offers include a deadline for acceptance. If a deadline is set and acceptance is not communicated within the time allotted, the offer terminates automatically. If a time limit is not stated in the offer, a reasonable amount of time is allowed. What is reasonable is determined by the court if a dispute arises.

If the offeror dies or is declared incompetent before the offer is accepted, it is terminated.

A **rejection** also terminates an offer. Once the **offeree** (the person to whom the offer was made) rejects the offer, he or she cannot go back later and create a contract by accepting the offer.

> **Example:** Howard offers to purchase Maria's house for $235,000. Maria rejects the offer the next day. The following week, Maria changes her mind and decides to accept Howard's offer. But her acceptance at this point does not create a contract, because the offer terminated with her rejection.

A **counteroffer** is sometimes called a qualified acceptance. It is actually a rejection of the offer and a tender of a new offer. Instead of either accepting or rejecting the offer outright, the offeree "accepts" with certain modifications. This happens when some, but not all, of the original terms are unacceptable to the offeree. When there is a counteroffer, the roles of the parties are reversed: the original offeror becomes the offeree and can accept or reject the revised offer. If he or she chooses to accept the counteroffer, there is a binding contract. If the counteroffer is rejected, the party making the counteroffer cannot go back and accept the original offer. The original offer was terminated by the counteroffer.

> **Example:** Palmer offers to buy Harrison's property under the following conditions: the purchase price is $150,000, the closing date is January 15, and the downpayment is $15,000. Harrison agrees to all the terms but the closing date, which she wants to be February 15. By changing one of the terms, Harrison has rejected Palmer's initial offer and made a counteroffer. Now it is up to Palmer to either accept or reject Harrison's counteroffer.

Acceptance. An offer can be revoked at any time until acceptance has been communicated to the offeror. To create a binding contract, the offeree must

Fig. 6.2 Mutual consent is achieved through the process of offer and acceptance.

Offer

• Willingness to contract
• Definite and certain terms

Termination (No Mutual Consent)

• Revocation
• Lapse of time
• Death or incompetency of the offeror
• Rejection of the offer
• Counteroffer

Acceptance (Mutual Consent)

• By offeree
• Communicated to the offeror
• In specified manner
• Doesn't vary terms

communicate acceptance to the offeror in the manner and within the time limit stated in the offer (or before the offer is revoked). If no time or manner of acceptance is stated in the offer, a reasonable time and manner is implied.

The offeree's acceptance must also be free of any negative influences, such as fraud, undue influence, or duress. If an offer or acceptance is influenced by any of these negative forces, the contract is voidable by the injured party.

Fraud is misrepresentation of a material fact to another person who relies on the misrepresentation as the truth in deciding to enter into a transaction.

• **Actual fraud** occurs when the person making the statement either knows the statement is false and makes it with an intent to deceive, or doesn't know whether or not the statement is true but makes it anyway. For example, a seller who paints over cracks in the basement and then tells the buyer that the foundation is completely sound is committing actual fraud.
• **Constructive fraud** occurs when a person who occupies a position of confidence and trust, or who has superior knowledge of the subject matter, makes a false statement with no intent to deceive. For example, if a seller innocently points out incorrect lot boundaries, it may be constructive fraud.

Undue influence is using one's influence to pressure a person into making a contract, or taking advantage of another's distress or weakness of mind to induce him or her to enter into a contract.

Duress is compelling someone to do something—such as enter into a contract—against his or her will, with the use of force or constraint or the threat of force or constraint.

Lawful Objective

The third requirement for a valid contract is a lawful objective. Both the purpose of the contract and the consideration for the contract (discussed below) must be lawful. Examples of contracts with unlawful objectives are a contract requiring payment of an interest rate in excess of the state's usury limit, or a contract relating to unlawful gambling. If a contract does not have a lawful objective, it is void.

Sometimes contracts contain some lawful provisions and some unlawful provisions. In these situations, it may be possible to sever the unlawful portions of the contract and enforce the lawful portions.

> **Example:** Callahan and Baker enter into a contract for the purchase and sale of an apartment house. A clause in the contract prohibits the buyer from renting the apartments to persons of a certain race. The contract concerning the sale of the property would probably be enforceable, but the racially restrictive clause would be void because it is unlawful.

Consideration

The fourth element of a valid contract is **consideration**. Consideration is something of value exchanged by the contracting parties. It might be money, goods, or services, or a promise to provide money, goods, or services. Whatever form it takes, the consideration must be either a benefit to the party receiving it or a detriment to the party offering it. The typical real estate purchase and sale contract involves a promise by the purchaser to pay a certain amount of money to the seller at a certain time, and a promise by the seller to convey title to the purchaser when the price has been paid. Both parties have given and received consideration.

While consideration is usually the promise to do a particular act, it can also be a promise to not do a particular act. For example, Aunt Martha might promise to pay her nephew Charles $1,000 if he promises to stop smoking.

As a general rule, a contract is enforceable as long as the consideration has value, even though the value of the consideration exchanged is unequal. A contract to sell a piece of property worth $120,000 for $105,000 is enforceable. However, in cases where the disparity in value is quite large (for example, a contract to sell a piece of property worth $185,000 for $55,000), a court may refuse to enforce the contract. This is particularly likely to happen if the parties have unequal bargaining power (such as if the buyer is a real estate developer and the seller is elderly, uneducated, and inexperienced in business).

The Writing Requirement

For most contracts used in real estate transactions, there is a fifth requirement: they must be put into writing, as required by the statute of frauds.

The **statute of frauds** is a state law that requires certain types of contracts to be in writing and signed. Only the types of contracts covered by the statute of frauds have to be in writing; other contracts may be oral.

Each state has its own statute of frauds, and the requirements vary slightly from state to state. As a general rule, however, almost all of the contracts typically used in a real

Fig. 6.3 Real estate contract requirements

A Valid Real Estate Contract

- Capacity
- Mutual consent
- Lawful objective
- Consideration
- In writing

estate transaction are covered by the statute of frauds. In Washington, the statute of frauds applies to:

- any agreement to convey an interest in real property (such as a purchase and sale agreement);
- any agreement to assume the debts of another (such as the assumption of a mortgage); and
- any agreement to employ an agent for compensation to sell, buy, lease, or exchange real property (a listing agreement).

The "writing" required by the statute of frauds does not have to be in any particular form, nor does it have to be contained entirely in one document. A note or memorandum about the agreement or a series of letters will suffice, as long as the writing:

1. identifies the subject matter of the contract,
2. indicates an agreement between the parties and its essential terms, and
3. is signed by the parties to be bound.

If the parties fail to put a contract that falls under the statute of frauds in writing, the contract is usually void. However, occasionally a court will enforce an unwritten agreement. This might occur if there is evidence that the contract exists and evidence of its terms, and if the party trying to enforce the contract has completely or substantially performed his or her contractual obligations. This is a relatively rare occurrence; the safest course is to put a contract in writing.

Legal Status of Contracts

Four terms are used to describe the legal status of a contract: a contract is void, voidable, unenforceable, or valid. These terms have already been used in our discussion, and now we'll look more closely at what each one means.

Void

A void contract is no contract at all; it has no legal effect. This most often occurs because one of the essential elements, such as mutual consent or consideration, is completely lacking.

Example: Talbot signed a contract promising to deed some property to Worth, but Worth did not offer any consideration in exchange for Talbot's promise. Since the contract is not supported by consideration, it is void.

A void contract may be disregarded. Neither party is required to take legal action to withdraw from the agreement.

Voidable

A voidable contract appears on its face to be valid, but has some defect giving one or both of the parties the power to withdraw from the agreement. Contracts entered into by minors or as a result of fraud are normally voidable by the injured party (the minor or the one defrauded).

It is important to note that action must be taken to rescind a voidable contract. Unlike a contract that is void from the outset, a voidable contract cannot simply be ignored. Failure to take action within a reasonable time may result in a court declaring that the contract was ratified. Alternatively, the injured party may decide to continue with the agreement; in that case, he or she may expressly ratify it.

Unenforceable

An unenforceable contract is one that cannot be enforced in court for one of the following reasons:

1. its contents cannot be proved,
2. the other party has a voidable contract, or
3. the statute of limitations has expired.

Contents Cannot Be Proved. This is most often a problem associated with oral agreements. Even if the law does not require a certain kind of contract to be written, it is a good idea to put it in writing because it avoids confusion and misunderstanding. Furthermore, even if a contract is in writing, the written agreement must clearly state all of the contract terms. Vaguely worded contracts are considered illusory and unenforceable.

One Party Has a Voidable Contract. If one party has a voidable contract, the other is left with an unenforceable contract. (Note that the party who has the voidable contract can enforce the contract against the other party.)

Statute of Limitations Expired. A statute of limitations is a law that sets a deadline for filing a lawsuit. Unless an injured party files suit before the deadline set by the applicable statute of limitations, his or her legal claim is lost forever. The purpose of a statute of limitations is to prevent one person from suing another too many years after an event, when memories have faded and evidence has been lost.

Every state has a statute of limitations for contracts. If one of the parties to a contract fails to perform his or her obligations (breaches the contract), the other party has to sue within a certain number of years after the breach.

Fig. 6.4 Legal status of contracts

Type of Contract	Legal Effect	Example
Void	No contract at all	An agreement for which there is no consideration
Voidable	Valid until rescinded by one party	A contract with a minor
Unenforceable	One or both parties cannot sue to enforce	A contract after the limitations period expires
Valid	Binding and enforceable	An agreement that meets all the legal requirements

Otherwise, the statute of limitations will run out and the contract will become unenforceable.

In Washington, the statute of limitations generally requires lawsuits concerning written contracts to be filed within six years after their breach, and lawsuits concerning oral contracts to be filed within three years after their breach.

Valid

If an agreement contains all of the essential elements, its contents can be proved in court, and it is free of any negative influences, it is a valid contract and can be enforced in a court of law.

Discharging a Contract

Once there is a valid, enforceable contract, it may be discharged by:

1. full performance, or
2. agreement between the parties.

Full Performance

Full performance means that the parties have performed all their obligations; the contract is executed. For example, once the deed to the property has been transferred to the buyer, and the seller has received the purchase price, the purchase and sale agreement has been discharged by full performance.

Agreement Between the Parties

The parties to a contract can agree to discharge the contract in any of the following ways:

- rescission,
- cancellation,
- assignment, or
- novation.

Rescission. Sometimes the parties to a contract agree that they would be better off if the contract had never been signed. In such a case, they may decide to rescind the contract. A rescission is occasionally referred to as a "contract to destroy a contract."

The buyer and seller sign an agreement that terminates their previous agreement and puts them as nearly as possible back in the positions they were in before entering into the agreement. If any money or other consideration has changed hands, it will be returned.

In certain circumstances, a contract can be rescinded by court order (rather than by agreement between the parties). Court-ordered rescission is discussed later in this chapter.

Cancellation. A cancellation does not go as far as a rescission. The parties agree to terminate the contract, but previous acts are unaffected. For example, money that was paid prior to the cancellation is not returned.

When contracting to purchase real property, a buyer generally gives the seller a deposit to show that he or she is acting in good faith and intends to fulfill the terms of their agreement. This is called an **earnest money deposit**, and the seller is entitled to keep it if the buyer defaults on the contract. If the buyer and seller agree to terminate the contract and the seller refunds the earnest money deposit to the buyer, the contract has been rescinded. If the seller keeps the deposit, the contract has been cancelled.

Assignment. Sometimes one of the parties to a contract wants to withdraw by assigning his or her interest in the contract to another person. As a general rule, a contract can be assigned to another unless a clause in the contract prohibits assignment. Technically, assignment does not discharge the contract. The new party (the assignee) assumes primary liability for the contractual obligations, but the withdrawing party (the assignor) is still secondarily liable.

> **Example:** A buyer is purchasing a home on a land contract over a 15-year period. In the absence of any prohibitive language, she can sell the home, accept a cash downpayment, and assign her contract rights and liabilities to the new buyer. The new buyer would assume primary liability for the contract debt, but the original buyer would retain secondary liability.

One exception to the rule that a contract can be assigned unless otherwise agreed: a personal services contract can't be assigned without the other party's consent.

> **Example:** A nightclub has a contract with a singer for several performances. The singer cannot assign her contract to another singer, because it is a personal services contract. The nightclub management has a right to choose who will be singing in their establishment.

Novation. The term "novation" has two generally accepted meanings. One type of novation is the substitution of a new party into an existing obligation. If a buyer under a real estate contract is released by the seller in favor of a new buyer under the same contract, there has been a novation. The first buyer is relieved of all liability connected with the contract.

Novation may also be the substitution of a new obligation for an old one. If a landlord and tenant agree to tear up a three-year lease in favor of a new ten-year lease, it is a novation.

Assignment vs. Novation. The difference between assignment and novation concerns the withdrawing party's liability. When a contract is assigned, there is continuing liability for the assignor. In a novation, on the other hand, the withdrawing party is released from liability, because he or she was replaced with an individual who was approved by the other party. Novation, unlike assignment, always requires the other party's consent.

Breach of Contract

A breach of contract occurs when one of the parties fails, without legal excuse, to perform any of the promises contained in the agreement. The injured party can seek a remedy in court only if the breach is a **material breach**. A breach is material when the promise that has not been fulfilled is an important part of the contract.

Many standard contract forms state that **"time is of the essence."** That phrase is used to warn the parties that timely performance is crucial and failure to meet a deadline would be a material breach. If one party misses a deadline, the other party may choose whether to proceed with the contract or use the time is of the essence clause as the basis for ending it.

When a breach occurs, there are four possible remedies available to the injured party:

- rescission,
- liquidated damages,
- damages, or
- specific performance.

Rescission

As previously explained, a rescission is a termination of the contract in which the parties are returned to their original positions. In the case of a purchase and sale agreement, the seller refunds the buyer's earnest money deposit and the buyer gives up his or her equitable interest in the property. The rescission can be by agreement, or it can be ordered by a court at the request of one party when the other party has breached the contract.

Liquidated Damages

The parties to a contract sometimes agree in advance to an amount that will serve as full compensation to be paid in the event that one of the parties defaults. This sum is called liquidated damages.

Example: Able agrees to buy 25,000 hinges from Baker. They agree that if Baker cannot deliver the hinges to Able on time, Baker will pay Able $3,000 as full compensation. If Baker fails to deliver the hinges on time, Able will only receive $3,000 from Baker; she could not sue for any additional amount, even if her actual damages were greater than $3,000.

In a real estate transaction, the buyer's earnest money deposit is often treated as liquidated damages. If the seller keeps the deposit and releases the buyer from the contract, the agreement is canceled.

Damages

A damages award is an amount of money that the court orders the breaching party to pay the other party. Damages are generally intended to put the non-breaching party in the financial position he or she would have been in if the breaching party had fulfilled the terms of the contract.

Example: Suppose Able and Baker (from the example above) did not agree to any liquidated damages. Baker fails to deliver the hinges on time, and Able suffers $7,000 in damages because she must quickly purchase the hinges from another supplier at a higher price. Able can sue Baker for the $7,000 in damages.

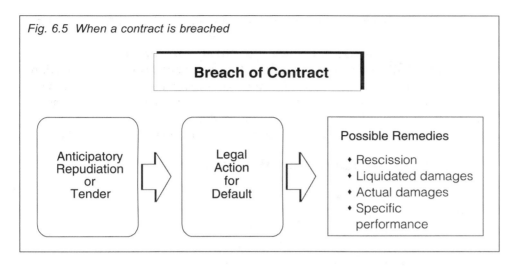

Fig. 6.5 When a contract is breached

Suppose a home seller breaches a purchase and sale agreement. The buyer has no earnest money deposit to keep as liquidated damages, so he or she may choose to sue the seller for monetary compensation for any losses that resulted from the breach of contract.

Specific Performance

Specific performance is a legal action designed to compel a defaulting party to perform under the terms of the contract. For example, a court can order a seller to sign and deliver a deed to a buyer to complete a purchase.

Specific performance is usually only available as a remedy when monetary damages are not sufficient compensation. For example, when the purchase of real property is involved, the court might order specific performance because there is no other property that is just like the one the seller agreed to sell. Payment of damages would not enable the buyer to purchase another property just like it.

Tender

A tender is an unconditional offer by one of the contract parties to perform his or her part of the agreement. It is frequently referred to as "an offer to make an offer good." A tender is usually made when it appears that the other party is going to default; it is necessary before legal action can be taken to remedy the breach of contract.

Example: A seller suspects that the buyer does not plan to complete the purchase, and he intends to sue the buyer if this happens. The seller must attempt to deliver the deed to the buyer as promised in the purchase and sale agreement. When the tender is made, if the buyer refuses to pay the agreed price and accept the deed, the buyer is placed in default and the seller may then file a lawsuit.

If a buyer has reason to believe the seller does not plan to complete the sale, the buyer tenders by attempting to deliver the full amount promised in the purchase and sale agreement to the seller. When the seller refuses to accept the money and deliver the deed, he or she is in default.

Sometimes there is an **anticipatory repudiation** by one of the parties. An anticipatory repudiation is a positive statement by the defaulting party indicating that he or she will not or cannot perform according to the terms of the agreement. When this happens, no tender is necessary as a basis for a legal action.

Types of Real Estate Contracts

This section provides a brief overview of some of the contracts a real estate agent should be familiar with: listing agreements, purchase and sale agreements, land contracts, leases, escrow instructions, and options. Each of these except the option is discussed in more detail in a later chapter, as noted below.

Listing Agreements

The listing agreement is a written employment contract between a property owner and a real estate broker. The owner employs the broker to find a buyer or tenant who is ready, willing, and able to buy or lease on the owner's terms.

In Washington and many other states, a broker can't sue to collect a commission unless he or she has a written listing agreement with the property owner. What the broker must do in order to earn the commission depends on what type of listing he or she has—open, exclusive agency, or exclusive right to sell—and on the terms of the contract. Listing agreements are discussed in more detail in Chapter 8.

Purchase and Sale Agreements

The purchase and sale agreement is a written contract between a buyer and a seller, stating the terms on which a piece of real property is going to be sold. It should spell out the details of the sale (such as price, possession and closing dates, any liens or encumbrances to be assumed, and any contingencies) and it must be signed by both parties.

In most cases, the purchase and sale agreement serves three functions:

- First, it is the buyer's receipt for the earnest money deposit that the buyer gives the seller when making an offer to purchase.
- Second, it becomes the contract of sale after it has been properly signed by both parties.
- Third, it protects the seller's broker, because the acceptance section of the document (where the seller accepts the buyer's offer) usually provides for the payment of a brokerage fee by the seller. Thus, the seller cannot accept the buyer's offer without also making a written promise to pay the broker's commission.

Once the agreement has been signed by both parties it is a binding contract, assuming that all the requirements for a valid contract have been met. The terms cannot be modified unless both parties agree and sign a written amendment to the original contract. Purchase and sale agreements are discussed in more detail in Chapter 9.

Land Contracts

Under a land contract (also called a real estate contract, installment sales contract, or contract for deed), the buyer purchases the seller's property on an installment basis. The parties to the contract are called the **vendor** (seller) and the **vendee** (buyer). Periodic payments towards the purchase price are made over a span of years, and during that time the vendor retains legal title to the property. The deed is not delivered to the vendee until the full purchase price is paid. In the meantime, the vendee has **equitable title** to the property, which is the right to possess and enjoy the property while paying off the purchase price.

> **Example:** Bender agrees to buy Jones's farm for $250,000, to be paid at the rate of $25,000 per year, plus 9% interest, for ten years. Jones allows Bender to take possession of the farm, and she promises to convey legal title to Bender when he's paid the full purchase price. Bender and Jones have entered into a land contract.

Land contracts are discussed in more detail in Chapter 10.

Leases

A lease is an agreement that transfers the right of possession and use of real property from the landlord (the property owner) to the tenant. A lease is both a conveyance and a contract. As a conveyance, the lease transfers the right of possession. As a contract, it sets forth the terms of the occupancy: the amount of rent, the rights and responsibilities of the parties, and the duration of the tenancy.

Leases are categorized according to their duration and manner of termination. Many of the terms of a residential lease are governed by the Washington Landlord-Tenant Act. Leases are discussed in more detail in Chapter 16.

Escrow Instructions

Escrow instructions authorize an escrow agent to close a transaction. They set forth the obligations of the parties and the conditions that must be fulfilled before a sale can be finalized. The buyer and the seller may each execute separate escrow instructions, or they may use joint escrow instructions. Escrow instructions are discussed in more detail in Chapter 13.

Option Agreements

An option agreement is essentially a contract to make a contract; it is an agreement that creates a right to buy, sell, or lease property for a fixed price within a set period of time. The parties to an option agreement are the **optionor** (the property owner who grants the option) and the **optionee** (the one who has the option right). In an option to purchase, the optionor is the seller and the optionee is the buyer.

> **Example:** Jensen is offering to sell his property for $240,000. Conners isn't yet sure that he wants to buy the property, but he doesn't want to lose the opportunity to do so. Jensen agrees to give him a three-week option to purchase. They execute a written option agreement, and Conners pays Jensen $1,000 as consideration for the option. The option gives Conners the right to buy the property at the stated price during the next three weeks, but does not in any way obligate him to buy it.

The optionor is bound to keep the offer open for the period specified in the option agreement. He or she is not allowed to sell or lease the property to anyone other than the optionee until the option expires.

If the optionee decides to exercise the option (that is, to buy or lease the property on the stated terms), he or she must give written notice of acceptance to the optionor. If the optionee fails to exercise the option within the specified time, the option expires automatically.

An option agreement may be considered a unilateral contract, because the optionee is not obligated to exercise the option. However, when the option is exercised, it becomes a bilateral contract.

Requirements. Because an option is a contract, it must have all the necessary elements of a contract, including consideration. The consideration may be a nominal amount—there's no set minimum. But some consideration must, in fact, pass from the optionee to the optionor; a mere statement of consideration in the agreement is not sufficient. (There is an exception to this rule for lease/option agreements: the provisions of the lease are treated as sufficient consideration to support the option.)

An option contract must be in writing; oral options are unenforceable. Furthermore, since an option to purchase anticipates that a sale may take place, the underlying terms of the sale (price, financing, etc.) should be spelled out in the option agreement.

Contract Rights. An option agreement gives the optionee a contract right, but does not create an interest in real property. An option is not a lien, and it also cannot be used as security for a mortgage or a deed of trust.

If the optionor dies during the option period, that will not affect the rights of the optionee, who may still exercise the right to purchase or lease. The option contract is binding on the heirs and assignees of the optionor.

An option can be assigned, unless the agreement includes a provision prohibiting assignment. One exception is when the consideration paid by the optionee is in the form of an unsecured promissory note. In that case, the optionee must obtain the optionor's written permission before the option may be assigned.

Recording. An option agreement may be recorded to give third parties constructive notice of the option. In that case, if the optionee exercises the option, his or her interest in the property will relate back to the date the option was recorded, taking priority over the rights of intervening third parties.

A recorded option that is not exercised creates a cloud on the optionor's title. The optionor should obtain a release from the optionee, and record the release to remove the cloud.

Right of First Refusal. An option should not be confused with a right of first refusal, which gives a person the first opportunity to purchase or lease real property when it becomes available. For instance, a lease might give the tenant a right of first refusal to purchase the property if the landlord decides to sell it.

Once the property owner offers the property for sale or receives an offer to buy from a third party, the holder of the right of first refusal must be given a chance to match the offer. If the right-holder does not want the property or is unwilling to match the offer, the property may be sold to the third party.

Chapter Summary

1. A contract is an agreement between two or more competent persons to do or not do certain things for consideration. Every contract is either express or implied, either unilateral or bilateral, and either executory or executed.

2. For a contract to be valid and binding, the parties must have the legal capacity to contract, and there must be mutual consent (offer and acceptance), a lawful objective, and consideration. The statute of frauds requires real estate contracts to be in writing.

3. A contract may be void, voidable, unenforceable, or valid.

4. An existing contract can be discharged by full performance or by agreement between the parties. The parties can agree to terminate the contract by rescission or cancellation, or there can be an assignment, or a novation.

5. A breach of contract occurs when a party fails, without legal excuse, to perform any material promise contained in the agreement. When a breach occurs, the four possible remedies are rescission, liquidated damages, damages, or specific performance.

6. In an option to purchase, the optionee has a right to buy the property at a specified price, but is under no obligation to buy. The optionor is not allowed to sell the property to anyone other than the optionee during the option period.

🔑 Key Terms

Contract—An agreement between two or more competent persons to do or not do certain things for consideration.

Capacity—A person must be mentally competent and at least 18 years of age to have the capacity to contract.

Mutual consent—The agreement of both parties to the terms of the contract, effected by offer and acceptance.

Offer—A communication that shows the willingness of the person making it (the offeror) to enter into a contract, and that has definite and certain terms.

Acceptance—A communication showing the willingness of the offeree to be bound by the terms of the offer.

Counteroffer—A qualified acceptance; technically a rejection of the offer, with a new offer made on slightly different terms.

Fraud—The misrepresentation of a material fact to someone who relies on the misrepresentation as the truth in deciding whether to enter into a contract.

Undue influence—Pressuring someone or taking advantage of his or her distress to induce him or her to enter into a contract.

Duress—Compelling someone to enter into a contract with the use or threat of force or constraint.

Consideration—Something of value exchanged by the parties to a contract; either a benefit to the party receiving it or a detriment to the party offering it.

Statute of frauds—A state law that requires certain types of contracts (including most contracts related to real estate transactions) to be in writing and signed.

Valid—When a contract contains all of the required elements and is enforceable in court.

Void—When a contract lacks an essential element, so that it has no legal force or effect.

Voidable—When one of the parties can choose to rescind the contract, because of lack of capacity, fraud, etc.

Unenforceable—When a contract cannot be enforced in a court of law because its contents cannot be proved, or it is voidable by the other party, or the statute of limitations has expired.

Rescission—When a contract is terminated and any consideration given is returned, putting the parties as nearly as possible back into the position they were in prior to entering into the contract.

Cancellation—When a contract is terminated but previous contractual acts are unaffected.

Assignment—When one party transfers his or her rights and obligations under the contract to another party, but remains secondarily liable.

Novation—When one party is completely replaced with another, or one contract is completely replaced with another, and all liability under the original contract ends.

Liquidated damages—An amount that the parties agree in advance will serve as full compensation if one of them defaults.

Specific performance—A remedy for breach of contract in which the court orders the defaulting party to perform as agreed in the contract.

Tender—An unconditional offer by one of the parties to perform his or her part of the agreement, made when it appears that the other party is going to default.

Option agreement—An agreement that gives one party the right to buy or lease property at a set price within a certain period of time.

🔁 Chapter Quiz

1. A contract can be valid and binding even though:

   a) it is not supported by consideration
   b) it does not have a lawful objective
   c) it is not put into writing
   d) there was no offer and acceptance

2. To have legal capacity to contract, a person must have:

   a) reached the age of majority
   b) been declared competent by a court
   c) a high school diploma or general equivalency certificate
   d) All of the above

3. An offer to purchase property would be terminated by any of the following, except:

   a) failure to communicate acceptance of the offer within the prescribed period
   b) revocation after acceptance has been communicated
   c) a qualified acceptance of the offer by the offeree
   d) death or insanity of the offeror

4. A counteroffer:

   a) terminates the original offer
   b) will result in a valid contract if accepted by the other party
   c) Both of the above
   d) None of the above

5. Tucker sends Johnson a letter offering to buy his property for $20,000 in cash, with the transaction to close in 60 days. Johnson sends Tucker a letter that says, "I accept your offer; however, the closing will take place in 90 days." Which of the following is true?

   a) Johnson's statement is not a valid acceptance
   b) Johnson's statement is a counteroffer
   c) There is no contract unless Tucker accepts the counteroffer
   d) All of the above

6. Which of these could be consideration for a contract?

   a) $63,000
   b) A promise to convey title
   c) A promise to not sell property during the next 30 days
   d) All of the above

7. An executory contract is one that:

   a) is made by the executor of an estate for the sale of probate property
   b) has not yet been performed
   c) has been completely performed
   d) has been proposed but not accepted by either party

8. A void contract is one that:

   a) lacks an essential contract element
   b) needs to be rescinded by the injured party
   c) can be rescinded by agreement
   d) can no longer be enforced because the deadline set by the statute of limitations has passed

9. A voidable contract is:

   a) not enforceable by either party
   b) enforceable unless action is taken to rescind it
   c) void unless action is taken to rescind it
   d) None of the above

10. The statute of frauds is a law that requires:

   a) all contracts to be supported by consideration
   b) unlawful provisions to be severed from a contract
   c) certain contracts to be unilateral
   d) certain contracts to be in writing and signed

11. A contract can be discharged by all of the following except:

   a) novation
   b) performance
   c) cancellation
   d) breach

12. Brown and Murdock have a five-year contract. After two years, they agree to tear up that contract and replace it with a new ten-year contract. This is an example of:

   a) novation
   b) rescission
   c) duress
   d) specific performance

13. Graves and Chung are parties to a contract that doesn't prohibit assignment. If Chung assigns his interest in the contract to Stewart:

   a) Graves is not required to fulfill the contract
   b) Graves can sue for anticipatory repudiation
   c) Chung remains secondarily liable to Graves
   d) Chung is relieved of all further liability under the contract

14. A clause in the contract provides that if one party breaches, the other party will be entitled to $3,500 and cannot sue for more than that. This is a:

   a) just compensation provision
   b) compensation cap
   c) satisfaction clause
   d) liquidated damages provision

15. The McClures agreed to sell their house to Jacobsen, but then they breached the contract by refusing to go through with the sale. If Jacobsen wants a court order requiring the McClures to convey the house to her as agreed, she should sue for:

   a) damages
   b) specific performance
   c) liquidated damages
   d) rescission

☞ Answer Key

1. c) Only certain types of contracts are required to be in writing, but all contracts require consideration, a lawful objective, and offer and acceptance.

2. a) A person has capacity to contract if he or she has reached the age of majority (in Washington, age 18) and is mentally competent. It isn't necessary to be declared competent by a court, however.

3. b) If the offeree accepts the offer before the offeror revokes it, a binding contract is formed.

4. c) A counteroffer terminates the original offer (operating as a rejection), but if the counteroffer is then accepted, a valid contract is formed.

5. d) All of the options are true statements.

6. d) Consideration is almost anything of value: money, goods, services, or a promise to do or not do something.

7. b) An executory contract has not yet been performed; an executed contract is one that has been fully performed.

8. a) A contract that lacks an essential element (such as consideration) is void. It has no legal force or effect, so there is nothing to rescind.

9. b) A voidable contract can be rescinded by the injured party, but unless it is rescinded it will be enforceable.

10. d) The statute of frauds requires certain contracts to be in writing and signed by the party or parties to be bound.

11. d) Performance, cancellation, and novation are all ways of discharging a contract. Breach does not discharge the contract; the breaching party is liable to the other party.

12. a) Novation is the replacement of an existing contract with a new contract, or the replacement of a party to a contract with a new party.

13. c) A contract can be assigned unless otherwise agreed, but the assignor remains secondarily liable to the other party.

14. d) Liquidated damages is an amount the contracting parties agree in advance will be paid as full compensation if one of them breaches the contract.

15. b) If the court granted Jacobsen specific performance, the McClures would be ordered to convey the house as agreed in the contract (not merely to pay Jacobsen damages as compensation).

Real Estate Agency Law

Chapter Overview

Agency is a special legal relationship that involves certain duties and liabilities. The law of agency governs many aspects of a real estate agent's relationships with clients and customers. The first part of this chapter explains what an agency relationship is and how one is created, then discusses real estate agency duties and liabilities. The second part of this chapter describes the various types of agency relationships that are possible under Washington's real estate agency law. Agency disclosure requirements and the broker/salesperson relationship are also covered.

Introduction to Agency

We'll begin our discussion of real estate agency with some basic definitions and some information about the framework of agency law.

The Agency Relationship

An agency relationship arises when one person authorizes another to represent him or her, subject to his or her control, in dealings with third parties. The parties in an agency relationship are the **agent**, the person authorized to represent another, and the **principal**, the party who authorizes and controls the actions of the agent. Persons outside the agency relationship who seek to deal with the principal through the agent are called **third parties**.

There is usually an agency relationship between a property seller and the real estate broker that he or she has listed the property with. The seller is the principal, who employs the broker to act as his or her agent. The broker/agent represents the seller/principal's interests in negotiations with potential buyers/third parties. The seller/principal is referred to as the broker's client.

A buyer is also likely to have an agency relationship with a broker. As a general rule, when a real estate broker works with a buyer—for example, by showing the buyer homes, preparing offers to purchase, and negotiating on the buyer's behalf—then that broker becomes the agent of the buyer, and the buyer is that broker's principal and client. A broker's principal is the person who has authorized the broker to act on his or her behalf.

There is also an agency relationship between a broker and the salespersons who work for the broker. In other words, a salesperson is his or her broker's agent. To the broker's principal (the seller or the buyer), a salesperson representing the broker would be a **subagent**—an agent of an agent.

Agency Law

An agency relationship has significant legal implications. For a third party, dealing with the agent can be the legal equivalent of dealing with the principal. For instance, when an agent who is authorized to do so signs a document or makes a promise, it's as if the principal signed or promised. And in some cases, if the agent does something wrong, the principal may be held liable to third parties for harm resulting from the agent's actions.

Those rules are part of general agency law, a body of law that applies to agency relationships in nearly any context. For example, it governs the relationship between lawyer and client, or between trustee and beneficiary. Traditionally, general agency law has also governed the relationship between a real estate broker and his or her client. In Washington, however, real estate agency relationships are now subject to the Real Estate Brokerage Relationships Act, which went into effect in 1997. This statute grew out of general agency law, but made important changes to address agency problems that were specific to the real estate field.

We will cover both general agency law and the Washington real estate agency statute, since both are tested on the state licensing examination. General agency law questions appear on the national portion of the exam, while questions concerning Washington's Real Estate Brokerage Relationships Act and agency disclosure rules appear on the state portion of the exam.

Creating an Agency Relationship

No particular formalities are required to create an agency relationship; the only requirement is the consent of both parties. Under general agency law, an agency relationship may be formed in four ways: by express agreement, by ratification, by estoppel, or by implication.

Express Agreement

Most agencies are created by express agreement: the principal appoints someone to act as his or her agent, and the agent accepts the appointment. The agreement does not need to be in writing in order to create a valid agency relationship.

The agency agreement also does not have to be supported by consideration. Agency rights, responsibilities, and liabilities arise even when the principal has no contractual obligation to compensate the agent for the services rendered.

For example, if a broker doesn't have a written listing agreement with a seller, the broker cannot sue the seller for compensation. Yet even without a written agreement, the broker still may be the seller's agent, with all of the duties and liabilities that agency entails.

Ratification

An agency is created by ratification when the principal gives approval after the fact to acts performed by:

- a person who is without authority to act for the principal, or
- an agent whose actions exceed the authority granted by the principal.

The principal may ratify unauthorized acts expressly, or by accepting the benefits of the acts. For example, if the principal accepts a contract offer negotiated by someone who wasn't authorized to negotiate on his or her behalf, the principal has ratified the agency.

Estoppel

Under the legal doctrine of estoppel, a person is not allowed to take a position that contradicts his or her previous conduct, if someone else has relied on the previous conduct. An agency can be created by estoppel when it would be unfair to a third party to deny the agent's authority, because the principal has allowed the third party to believe there was an agency relationship.

Implication

An agency may be created by implication when one person behaves toward another in a way that suggests or implies that he or she is acting as that other person's agent. If the other person reasonably believes that there is an agency relationship, and the supposed agent fails to correct that impression, he or she may owe the other person agency duties.

Although agency by implication resembles agency by estoppel, there's a significant difference between them. An agency by estoppel requires the principal to acknowledge that an agency relationship exists, to protect the interests of a third party. An agency by implication requires the agent to acknowledge that an agency relationship exists, to protect the principal's interests.

Creating a Real Estate Agency

In Washington, the Real Estate Brokerage Relationships Act imposed new rules concerning how agency relationships are created in real estate transactions. Under the statute, an agency relationship between a real estate licensee and a client begins when the licensee undertakes to provide real estate services for the client.

An agency relationship with a seller ordinarily begins with the execution of a written listing agreement. On the other hand, an agency relationship with a buyer begins automatically when a licensee performs real estate brokerage services for the buyer.

> **Example:** Booth, a prospective buyer, walks into Thompson Realty and is greeted by Salesperson Dickerson. Booth tells Dickerson that she wants to buy a home. She tells him her general price range and the kind of house she wants. Dickerson goes to his computer and enters in some information, then prints out a list of homes that Booth may be interested in. After making some phone calls, Dickerson and Booth go and look at three of the homes.
>
> Under the real estate agency statute, Dickerson and his broker, Thompson, are Booth's agents. This agency relationship is created automatically, without a written agreement, because Dickerson is performing brokerage services for Booth.

There is an important exception to this rule concerning buyer agency. A licensee working with a buyer does not automatically become the buyer's agent if there's a written agreement to the contrary. This might be a listing agreement with the seller, a written dual agency agreement with both parties, a written subagency agreement with the seller, or a written non-agency agreement.

> **Example:** To return to the previous scenario, suppose Dickerson shows Booth one of his own listings. Because Thompson Realty already has a written agreement with the seller, Dickerson and Thompson won't be representing Booth if she decides to buy this house. They'll be acting as the seller's agents, not the buyer's.

The Legal Effects of Agency

Once an agency relationship has been established, the principal is bound by acts of the agent that are within the scope of the agent's actual or apparent authority. Under general agency law, the principal may be held liable for harm caused by the agent's negligent or wrongful acts. In addition, the principal may be held to know information that is known to the agent. We will examine each of these legal effects of agency in turn.

Scope of Authority

The extent to which the principal can be bound by the agent's actions depends first of all on the scope of authority granted to the agent. There are three basic types of agents:

- universal agents,
- general agents, and
- special agents.

A **universal agent** is authorized to do anything that can be lawfully delegated to a representative. This type of agent has the greatest degree of authority.

A **general agent** is authorized to handle all of the principal's affairs in one or more specified areas. He or she has the authority to conduct a wide range of activities on an ongoing basis on behalf of the principal. For example, a business manager who has the authority to handle personnel matters, enter into contracts, and manage the day-to-day operations of the business is considered to be a general agent.

A **special agent** has limited authority to do a specific thing or conduct a specific transaction. For instance, an attorney who is hired to litigate a specific legal matter, such as a person's divorce, is a special agent.

In most cases, a real estate broker is a special agent, because the broker has only limited authority. A seller hires a broker to find a buyer for a particular piece of property, and the broker is only authorized to negotiate with third parties, not to sign a contract on the seller's behalf. A real estate broker can be granted broader powers, but usually is not.

Actual vs. Apparent Authority

An agent may have actual authority to perform an action on the principal's behalf, or else may have only apparent authority.

Actual authority is authority granted to the agent by the principal, either expressly or by implication. Express actual authority is communicated to the agent in express terms, either orally or in writing. Implied actual authority is the authority to do what is necessary to carry out actions that were expressly authorized.

Example: When a seller lists property with a broker, the broker is given express actual authority to find a buyer for the property. Based on custom in the real estate industry, the broker also has the implied actual authority to delegate certain tasks to a licensed salesperson. In contrast, the authority granted to the broker does not imply the power to enter into a contract or execute a deed on the seller's behalf.

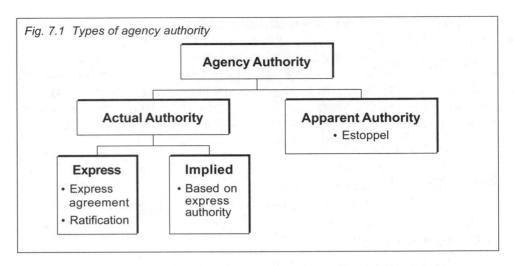

Fig. 7.1 Types of agency authority

A person has **apparent authority** when he or she has no actual authority to act, but the principal negligently or deliberately allows it to appear that the person's actions are authorized. In other words, the principal's words or conduct lead a third party to believe that this person (the **apparent agent** or **ostensible agent**) has authority to act on behalf of the principal. This type of authority corresponds to an agency created by estoppel, which was explained earlier.

A principal is bound by acts performed within the scope of an ostensible agent's apparent authority. However, declarations of the agent alone cannot establish apparent authority; the principal must be aware of the declarations or acts and make no effort to deny that they are authorized.

A third party has a duty, when dealing with an agent, to make a reasonable effort to discover the scope of the agent's authority. The third party will not be able to hold the principal liable when an agent acts beyond the scope of his or her actual authority and the principal's conduct does not indicate approval of those acts. Especially when a contract between the principal and a third party limits the agent's authority to make representations, the third party is on notice that any representations made by the agent beyond the written terms of the agreement are unauthorized and not binding on the principal.

Vicarious Liability

A **tort** is a negligent or intentional wrongful act involving breach of a duty imposed by law (as opposed to breach of a contractual duty). It is a mistake, accident, or misconduct that results in an injury or financial harm to another person. For example, negligent driving that results in an accident and injures another driver is a tort. Someone who commits a tort may be sued by the injured party and required to compensate him or her.

Under general agency law, a principal may be held liable for his or her agent's negligent or wrongful acts. This is referred to as **vicarious liability**. The Washington Real Estate Brokerage Relationships Act provides that, as a general rule, there is no longer vicarious liability between a real estate agent and his or her principal. This means that a seller or buyer is ordinarily not liable for any act, error, or omission by his or her broker, a salesperson working for the broker, or another subagent.

There are two exceptions to this exclusion from liability. The principal may be liable for his or her real estate agent's actions if:

1. the principal participated in or authorized the act, error, or omission; or
2. the principal benefited from the act, error, or omission, and a court determines that it is highly probable that the injured party would be unable to enforce a judgment against the agent or subagent.

Likewise, under the Washington law, an agent is not liable for an act, error, or omission of a subagent, unless the agent participated in or authorized the act, error, or omission. Note that a broker may still be held liable for the actions of his or her affiliated licensees, however.

Imputed Knowledge

Under general agency law, a principal is considered to have notice of information that the agent has, even if the agent never actually tells the principal. In other words, the agent's knowledge is automatically imputed to the principal. As a result, the principal could be held liable for failing to disclose a problem to a third party, even if the agent never informed the principal of the problem.

However, under Washington's real estate agency statute, the imputed knowledge rule no longer applies in the real estate context. A principal in a real estate transaction is not automatically held to have notice of facts known by his or her real estate agent.

Duties in an Agency Relationship

An agency relationship is a **fiduciary** relationship. A fiduciary is a person who stands in a special position of trust and confidence in relation to someone else. Under general agency law, an agent owes fiduciary duties to his or her principal. These include the duty of reasonable skill and care, obedience and utmost good faith, accounting, loyalty, and disclosure of material facts. By contrast, an agent's duties to third parties are much more limited.

Washington's real estate agency statute has modified agency duties for real estate licensees. While a licensee still owes special duties to his or her principal, the licensee's duties to third parties have been expanded.

The Licensee's Duties in General

In Washington, a real estate licensee owes certain duties to any party to whom he or she renders services, whether it is the licensee's principal or a third party. These duties include:

*   reasonable skill and care,
*   honesty and good faith,
*   presenting all written communications,
*   disclosure of material facts,
*   accounting for trust funds,
*   providing an agency law pamphlet, and
*   making an agency disclosure.

Reasonable Skill and Care. A licensee has a duty to use reasonable skill and care in the performance of his or her duties. If a licensee claims to possess certain skills or abilities, the licensee must act as a competent person having those skills and abilities would act. In other words, a person who holds him or herself out as a real estate broker must exercise the skill and care that a competent broker would bring to the transaction. If the licensee causes a party harm due to carelessness or incompetence, the licensee will be liable to that party.

Honesty and Good Faith. A licensee must act toward any party with honesty and good faith. He or she must avoid inaccuracies in statements to prospective buyers or sellers. As was explained in Chapter 6, any intentional misrepresentation may constitute actual fraud, and even an unintentional misrepresentation may be considered constructive fraud. In either case, the party to whom the misrepresentation was made would have the right to rescind the transaction and/or sue for damages.

Misrepresentations, which may give rise to a lawsuit, should not be confused with mere opinions, predictions, or puffing. These are nonfactual or exaggerated statements that a party should realize he or she can't rely on. Since it isn't reasonable to rely on them, opinions, predictions, and puffing generally can't be the basis of a lawsuit.

> **Examples:**
>
> Opinion: "*I think this is the best buy on the market.*"
>
> Prediction: "*The properties in this neighborhood could double in value over the next ten years.*"
>
> Puffing: "*This is a dream house; it has a fabulous view.*"

Present Written Communications. A licensee is obligated to present all types of written communications to and from either party in a timely manner. Written communications include written offers.

A real estate licensee must present all offers and counteroffers to the parties, regardless of how unacceptable a particular offer may appear to be. The party, not the licensee, decides whether or not to accept a particular offer or counteroffer. A licensee should never hesitate to inform a party of an offer, even if its acceptance would mean a smaller commission for the licensee.

This duty to present all offers continues even after the property is subject to an existing contract, or when the buyer is already a party to an existing contract.

> **Example:** Seller Howard has just accepted an offer from Buyer Carmichael. Trent, a real estate licensee, receives another written offer for the same property. Trent has a duty to present this offer to Howard, even though Howard has already accepted Carmichael's offer.

Disclosure of Material Facts. A licensee must disclose any material fact he or she knows to the appropriate party, if the fact is not apparent or readily ascertainable by the party. A **material fact** is defined by Washington's real estate agency law as information that has a substantial negative effect on the value of the property or on a party's ability to perform his or her contractual duties, or that defeats the purpose of the transaction.

For example, the property's true value is considered a material fact that a licensee should disclose to his or her principal. Misleading the principal as to the value of the property or withholding information that affects its value would be a breach of the licensee's duty to disclose material facts.

Latent property defects are material facts. A **latent defect** is one that is not discoverable by ordinary inspection. A licensee must disclose any known latent defects to the parties. A seller also has this duty to prospective buyers.

The law does not require certain types of information to be disclosed. It is not considered a material fact if the property was or may have been the site of any crime, suicide, gang-related activity, political or religious activity, or other occurrence that doesn't adversely affect the physical condition of or title to the property.

While some states have gone so far as to require real estate licensees to physically inspect the property and report all findings to the buyer, Washington's real estate agency law states that licensees do not have the duty to investigate any matters they have not specifically agreed to investigate. A licensee has no duty to inspect the property, investigate either party's financial position, or independently verify the seller's statements.

Washington does require sellers of residential property to give their buyers a disclosure statement. The purpose of the statement is to disclose the seller's knowledge regarding the condition of the property, including the condition of the buildings and utilities, the existence of any easements and encumbrances, and other material information. The statement is for disclosure purposes only, and is not to be considered a part of the sales agreement. Property disclosure statements are discussed in more detail in Chapter 9.

Accounting. A licensee must account for any funds or other valuable items he or she receives on behalf of a party to a transaction. The licensee is required to report to the party on the status of those funds (called **trust funds**) and avoid mixing (**commingling**) them with his or her own money. In most states, a real estate broker is required to deposit all trust funds in a special trust or escrow account in order to prevent improper use of the funds. Washington's trust fund requirements are discussed in Chapter 17.

Real Estate Agency Law Pamphlet. A licensee must give an agency law pamphlet to each party he or she renders services to. The pamphlet sets forth the provisions of the Real Estate Brokerage Relationships Act. Each party must receive the pamphlet before signing an agency agreement with the licensee, before signing an offer in a transaction handled by the licensee, before consenting to a dual agency, or before waiving any agency rights, whichever of these events comes first.

Agency Disclosure. Before a party signs an offer in a real estate transaction handled by a licensee, the licensee must disclose in writing to that party whether the licensee represents the buyer, the seller, both, or neither. The purpose of this disclosure is to avoid some of the confusion regarding who is representing whom. The specific disclosure requirements are discussed later in this chapter.

Agent's Duties to the Principal

In addition to the general duties owed by a licensee to any party to whom the licensee renders services, there are specific duties that licensees owe to the parties they represent. If the licensee represents the seller, these duties are owed to the seller. If the licensee represents the buyer, these duties are owed to the buyer. If the licensee is acting as a dual agent, these duties are owed to both the seller and the buyer.

Loyalty. Loyalty is essential to an agency relationship. The agent must place the principal's interests above the interests of a third party. For instance, the seller's agent must try to negotiate with the buyer to get the highest possible price for the seller, because the agent's loyalty is owed to the seller.

The agent must also place the principal's interests above his or her own interests. This means that the agent must not make any **secret profits** from the agency. A secret profit is a financial benefit that an agent receives without the principal's consent, such as a kickback for referring the principal's business to a contractor.

Conflicts of Interest. A licensee must disclose to the principal any conflicts of interest. For instance, a seller's agent must inform the seller if there is any relationship between the agent and a prospective buyer—before the seller decides whether to accept the buyer's offer. If the buyer is a friend, relative, or business associate of the agent, or a company in which the agent has an interest, there may be a conflict of interest. The seller has the right to have this information when making his or her decision.

Of course, a seller's agent must also let the seller know if the agent is buying the property him or herself. It would be a gross breach of duty for a broker to list a property for less than it is worth, secretly buy it through an intermediary, and then sell it for a profit. This is sometimes called **self-dealing**.

Confidentiality. An agent may not disclose any confidential information about the principal, even after the termination of the agency relationship. **Confidential information** is defined in Washington's real estate agency law as information from or concerning a principal that:

1. was acquired by the licensee during the course of an agency relationship with the principal;
2. the principal reasonably expects to be kept confidential;
3. the principal has not disclosed or authorized to be disclosed to third parties;
4. would, if disclosed, operate to the detriment of the principal; and
5. the principal personally would not be obligated to disclose to the other party.

The last item on this list puts an important limitation on the principal's right to confidentiality. For instance, information about a latent defect known to the agent must be disclosed to a third party no matter how "confidential" the principal may consider it, because the principal (as well as the agent) is legally obligated to disclose latent defects. On the other hand, the principal's need to sell the property quickly would be considered confidential information that must not be disclosed.

Expert Advice. A licensee must advise the principal to seek expert advice on any matters relating to the transaction that are beyond the agent's expertise. For instance, if the principal has questions about the property's structural soundness, the agent should advise the principal to contact a home inspector.

Good Faith and Continuous Effort. In general, real estate licensees have a duty to make a good faith and continuous effort to fulfill the terms of their agency agreement. This means that a seller's agent must make a good faith and continuous effort to find a buyer for the property. A buyer's agent must make a good faith and continuous effort to find a suitable property for the buyer to purchase.

Once the seller's agent finds a buyer and a purchase and sale agreement is signed, the seller's agent does not have to seek additional offers to purchase as long as the property remains subject to that contract. Similarly, the buyer's agent doesn't have to seek additional properties while the buyer is a party to an existing contract.

Breach of Duty

If a licensee breaches any duties owed to either a principal or a third party, it is considered a tort. (A tort, as we explained earlier, is a wrongful act resulting from a breach of a duty imposed by law.) The party injured by the tort, whether it is the principal or a third party, is then entitled to sue for redress.

The most common remedy in a tort suit is compensatory damages. A court will order the licensee to compensate the injured party for the value of the loss that the injured party suffered. This might include repaying any commission collected in a transaction.

Most breaches of duty by a licensee are also violations of the real estate license law. The Department of Licensing may take disciplinary action against the licensee even if the injured party does not pursue a lawsuit. Disciplinary action may include fines as well as suspension or revocation of the licensee's real estate license.

Terminating an Agency

Once an agency relationship has terminated, the agent is no longer authorized to represent the principal. Under general agency law, an agency may be terminated either by acts of the parties or by operation of law.

Termination by the Acts of the Parties

The ways in which the parties can terminate an agency relationship include:

- mutual agreement,
- revocation by the principal, and
- renunciation by the agent.

Mutual Agreement. The parties may terminate the agency by mutual agreement at any time. If the original agreement was in writing, the termination agreement should also be in writing.

Principal Revokes. The principal may revoke the agency by firing the agent whenever he or she wishes. (Remember that an agency relationship requires the consent of both parties.) However, in some cases revoking an agency breaches

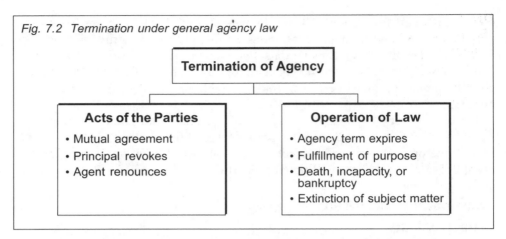

Fig. 7.2 Termination under general agency law

a contractual agreement, and the principal may be liable for any damages suffered by the agent because of the breach.

An **agency coupled with an interest** cannot be revoked. An agency is coupled with an interest if the agent has a financial interest in the subject matter of the agency. For instance, if a real estate licensee co-owns a property with other people, and they've authorized him to represent them in selling the property, it's an agency coupled with an interest. The co-owners can't revoke it.

Agent Renounces. An agent can renounce the agency at any time. Like revocation, renunciation may be a breach of contract, in which case the agent could be liable for the principal's damages resulting from the breach. But since an agency contract is a personal services contract (the agent has agreed to provide personal services to the principal), the principal could not demand specific performance as a remedy. The courts will not force a person to perform personal services, because that would violate the constitutional prohibition against involuntary servitude.

Termination by Operation of Law

Several events terminate an agency relationship automatically, without action by either party. These events include:

- expiration of the agency term,
- fulfillment of the purpose of the agency,
- the death, incapacity, or bankruptcy of either party, and
- extinction of the subject matter.

Expiration of Agency Term. An agency terminates automatically when its term expires. If the agency agreement did not include an expiration date, it is deemed to expire within a reasonable time (which would vary, depending on the type of agency in question). If there is no expiration date, either party may terminate the agency without liability for damages, although the other party might be able to demand reimbursement for expenses incurred before the termination.

Fulfillment of Purpose. An agency relationship terminates when its purpose has been fulfilled. For example, if a broker is hired to sell the principal's property and the broker does so, the agency is terminated by fulfillment.

Death, Incapacity, or Bankruptcy. An agency is terminated before it expires if either the agent or the principal dies. Most states provide that the agency also terminates if either party becomes mentally incompetent. Generally, the agent has no authority to act after the death or incompetence of the principal, even if the agent is unaware of the principal's death or incompetence. An agency is also terminated by the bankruptcy of either party.

Extinction of Subject Matter. The subject matter of a real estate agency is the property in question. If the property is in any way extinguished (e.g., sold or destroyed), the agency automatically terminates.

Terminating a Real Estate Agency

Under the terms of Washington's real estate agency law, a real estate agency relationship commences when the licensee undertakes to provide real estate brokerage services to a principal and continues until the earliest of the following:

1. Completion of performance by the licensee (the terms of the agency agreement are fulfilled).
2. Expiration of the agency term as agreed by the parties. (Note that an exclusive listing agreement should always specify a termination date. That is a legal requirement in some states, although it is not yet required in Washington.)
3. Termination of the relationship by mutual consent.
4. Notification from one party to the other that the agency is terminated.

When an agency relationship has terminated, the agent can no longer represent the principal. However, the agent still owes two statutory duties to the principal after the relationship terminates:

1. The agent must account for all money and property received during the relationship.
2. The agent must not disclose confidential information about the principal that was learned during the agency relationship.

Real Estate Agency Relationships

Washington's real estate agency statute fundamentally changed how agency relationships work in real estate transactions. Before discussing real estate agency relationships under the current law, we're going to examine how they used to work. This historical perspective will help you understand why the law developed as it did. We'll start by describing a typical residential transaction and reviewing some terminology.

Agents in a Typical Transaction

A typical residential real estate transaction is likely to involve more than one real estate agent. Someone who wants to find a home in a particular area contacts a real estate broker's office in that area. One of the salespersons who work for that broker will interview the prospective buyer to find out what kind of a home he or she wants and can afford, and then will show the buyer various suitable properties. Most brokers belong to a multiple listing service, so the salesperson will show the buyer not only homes that are listed directly with his or her own broker, but also homes that are listed with other MLS members. If the buyer becomes interested in a particular home, negotiations for the purchase of that home will involve the listing agent as well as the salesperson who has been showing properties to the buyer.

Meanwhile, other real estate agents may be showing the same house to other prospective buyers. By the time the transaction closes, it may involve a listing broker, a listing salesperson, a selling broker, and a selling salesperson, in addition to other cooperating agents who showed the home to buyers who didn't want it or didn't offer enough for it.

Understanding the agency relationships in this transaction means understanding which party each of these real estate licensees is representing. As a first step, you should be familiar with all of the following terms.

- **Real estate agent:** Real estate agent is the generic term used to refer to real estate licensees. Real estate brokers are the only real estate agents who are authorized to represent a buyer or a seller directly; real estate salespersons act on behalf of their real estate brokers.

- **Client:** A client is the person who has engaged the services of an agent. A client may be a real estate seller, buyer, landlord, or tenant.

- **Customer:** In transactions where the agent is representing a seller or a landlord, third parties are generally referred to as customers. A customer may be a buyer or a tenant.

- **Listing agent:** Either the listing salesperson or the listing broker may be referred to as the listing agent. The listing salesperson is the salesperson who takes the listing on a home. (He or she may or may not be the one who eventually procures a buyer for the listed home.) The listing broker is the broker that the listing salesperson works for.

- **Selling agent:** Either the selling salesperson or the selling broker may be referred to as the selling agent. The selling salesperson is the salesperson who procures a buyer for a property. (He or she may or may not have taken the listing for the property sold.) The selling broker is the broker that the selling salesperson works for.

- **Cooperating agent:** A cooperating agent is a licensee who did not take the listing on the property and who attempts to find a buyer. (The cooperating agent who succeeds in procuring a buyer is then the selling agent.)

Agency Relationships: a Historical Perspective

In the 1980s, various organizations, including the Federal Trade Commission, the National Association of Realtors, and the Association of Real Estate License Law Officials, conducted studies of agency representation in real estate transactions. Those organizations concluded that many real estate buyers and sellers were confused about which party the real estate agent represented. Buyers, in particular, appeared bewildered by the rules of real estate agency. They often thought the real estate agent that they were working with was representing them, when in fact the agent was almost always representing the seller.

Unilateral Offer of Subagency. This confusion was based on a standard provision found in most listing agreements. This provision stated that any member of the multiple listing service who found a buyer for a listed property automatically represented the seller. In other words, the selling agent was considered to be a subagent of the seller. This listing provision was referred to as a "unilateral offer of subagency."

As long as this provision remained in listing agreements, it was difficult to enter into a buyer agency relationship. In order to represent a buyer in a particular MLS transaction, a licensee had to reject the offer of subagency in a timely fashion and then enter into a separate written agreement with the buyer. Thus, nearly all licensees represented the seller.

Inadvertent Dual Agency. Under these circumstances, it was easy for a buyer to mistakenly believe that the selling agent was acting as the buyer's agent, not the seller's. After all, the selling agent was working with the buyer on a continuous and usually friendly basis. The agent would often encourage the buyer's loyalty by going out of his or her way to meet the buyer's needs. As a result, the buyer often told the selling agent confidential information. Yet because the selling agent was representing the seller, he or she had a duty to pass along that confidential information to the seller. If the agent fulfilled that responsibility, the buyer might well be surprised and dismayed. But in many cases the selling agent would let his or her natural desire to help the buyer interfere with the fiduciary duties owed to the seller. This confusion caused trouble for everyone, and sometimes resulted in the creation of an inadvertent dual agency.

> **Example:** Martinson was a salesperson working for Baker Realty. Over the course of several weeks, she showed the Greens many homes. Martinson enjoyed the Greens and worked very hard to find them a house they liked. She gave them advice about purchasing a home and discussed their financial situation with them. Understandably, the Greens believed that Martinson was their agent. But Martinson did not have an agency agreement with the Greens, and that meant (under the traditional presumption) that she was acting in the capacity of a seller's agent.
>
> The Greens decided to make an offer on a house listed by Broker Rush. They were very excited about the house, and they told Martinson that they were willing to pay full price for it. Nevertheless, they wanted to start out with an offer that was $5,000 less than the listing price.
>
> If Martinson failed to disclose to the seller that the Greens were willing to pay the full listing price, it would be a breach of her duty of loyalty to the seller. However, her conduct had caused the Greens to believe that she was representing them. Thus, if Martinson did disclose this information to the seller, the Greens could claim that she had breached her duty of loyalty to them. And because she was inadvertently acting as agent for both parties, both could claim that she acted as a dual agent without their consent.

Offer of Cooperation. In the 1990s, as new legal requirements and various other considerations made real estate transactions more complex, buyers became more interested in having their own agents to represent them. In response to the growing popularity of buyer agency, many multiple listing services replaced the unilateral offer of subagency in their listing agreements with an "offer of cooperation." Under the terms of this provision, other members of the MLS acted only as cooperating agents, not as subagents. A cooperating agent was simply any member of the MLS who attempted to find a buyer;

the listing agreement did not set any type of agency relationship for a cooperating agent. It became up to each individual cooperating agent to decide whether he or she would represent the seller or the buyer in a given transaction.

While the elimination of the unilateral offer of subagency from the listing agreement made buyer agency a little easier, many cooperating agents continued to act as the seller's agent almost by default. They did not offer to represent the buyer and they did not enter into an agency agreement with the buyer, so the traditional presumption that they were representing the seller continued.

Real Estate Agency Statute. In an effort to clear up the confusion over who was representing whom, many states (including Washington) passed agency disclosure laws. These laws require real estate agents to disclose to both the buyer and the seller, in writing, the identity of the party they represent. However, the Washington State Legislature decided that an agency disclosure law was not enough, and so it passed the Real Estate Brokerage Relationships Act.

As we discussed earlier, under the terms of this legislation a real estate licensee who works with a buyer is presumed to be the buyer's agent, unless there is a written agreement to the contrary. This rule has two important benefits. First, it turns the buyer's natural assumption—that the licensee the buyer is working with is acting as his or her agent—into reality. Second, it significantly reduces the danger of inadvertent, undisclosed dual agency. Because a licensee represents the buyer he or she is working with, there is no conflict between the licensee's desire to help the buyer and the licensee's agency duties.

It's important to remember that some states still follow the old rules for real estate agency, under which a cooperating agent is presumed to be a subagent of the seller. You may encounter a question based on that traditional presumption on the national portion of your state licensing exam.

Types of Agency Relationships

Under the Real Estate Brokerage Relationships Act, there are four types of real estate agency relationships:

- seller agency,
- buyer agency,
- dual agency, and
- non-agency.

Seller Agency. Whereas traditionally real estate agents nearly always represented the seller, under the Washington statute the only licensees who represent the seller are the listing broker and listing salesperson. The listing agreement creates a seller agency relationship.

Under the terms of the listing agreement, the primary task of a seller's agent is to find a buyer for the seller's property at a price that is acceptable to the seller. To accomplish this, the seller's agent advises the seller about preparing the property for sale, helps the seller decide on the listing price, markets the property to advantage, and negotiates on the seller's behalf with selling agents and buyers.

Seller's Agents and Buyers. Throughout a transaction, a seller's agent must use his or her best efforts to promote the interests of the seller. Yet the seller's

Fig. 7.3 Types of real estate agency relationships

agent may also provide some services to a prospective buyer. For example, the seller's agent may help a buyer who doesn't have his or her own agent fill out a purchase offer form and apply for financing. These services are considered to be in the best interests of the seller, and thus do not violate the agent's duties to the seller. Of course, the seller's agent must disclose to the buyer that he or she is acting as the seller's agent.

A seller's agent must be very careful to treat the buyer fairly, but the agent must not act as if he or she is representing the buyer. In other words, the agent must fully disclose all known material facts and answer the buyer's questions honestly. However, the agent should not give the buyer advice, such as suggesting how much to offer for the listed property.

> **Example:** Harrison, who works for Broker Yates, recently listed Tilden's house. The listing price is $315,000, but Harrison has reason to believe that Tilden would accept an offer of $308,000. Harrison shows the listed house to Markham, who asks Harrison, "How low do you think the seller will go?" Harrison should make it clear to Markham that he is representing Tilden and cannot divulge confidential information to Markham. If he were to do so, Tilden could sue Harrison's broker for breach of agency duties.

In some cases the seller's agent has had a previous agency relationship with the buyer. In this situation it may be difficult for the agent to represent the seller's interests without feeling some loyalty to the buyer as well.

> **Example:** Suppose Tilden listed his home with Harrison and liked him so well that he wanted Harrison to help him find another home. Harrison shows Tilden one of his own listings.
>
> Under these circumstances, it would be easy for Tilden to think that Harrison is acting as his agent. However, because of the listing agreement, Harrison is the seller's agent, and he should emphasize this fact to Tilden. Tilden should be reminded that Harrison is obligated to disclose any material information Tilden tells him to the seller, and that in all negotiations Harrison will be representing the seller's best interests.
>
> However, a real estate agent is not permitted to disclose confidential information about a principal even after the termination of the agency relationship. Thus, Harrison cannot disclose to the seller any confidential information about Tilden that he learned during his agency relationship with Tilden.

In transactions like the one in the example, where the listing salesperson is also the selling salesperson, a seller's agent may still come up against the problem of inadvertent dual agency. But aside from that situation, a seller's agent will rarely face that problem under current law.

Buyer Agency. Even before passage of Washington's real estate agency law, buyers were beginning to realize the benefits of having their own agent, and taking the trouble to find someone to represent them. Now that a buyer is automatically represented by the agent he or she is working with (unless there is a written agreement to the contrary), the majority of buyers are able to benefit from buyer agency. The advantages of buyer agency include confidentiality and loyalty, objective advice, help with negotiations, and access to more homes.

Confidentiality and Loyalty. A buyer's agent owes agency duties to the buyer, including the duties of confidentiality and loyalty. For many buyers, these two duties make up the most important advantage of buyer agency.

> **Example:** Broker Mendez is helping Buyer Jackson find a home. He shows Jackson many houses, and there are two that interest her. One is a large fixer-upper selling for $245,000. The other is a small, newer house in mint condition that is selling for $236,000. Because Mendez must put Jackson's interests before his own, he advises her to purchase the smaller house because it better suits her needs. He does so even though he would earn a bigger commission if she bought the more expensive house.
>
> Mendez advises Jackson to offer $229,900 for the $236,000 house. Jackson agrees to, although she tells Mendez that she is willing to pay the full listing price. Because Mendez is Jackson's agent, he is obligated to keep that confidential. If he were the seller's agent, he would have been required to disclose that information to the seller.

Objective Advice. A buyer's agent can be relied upon to give the buyer objective advice about the pros and cons of purchasing a particular home. He or she will point out various issues the buyer should be aware of, such as energy costs, the need for future repairs, and property value trends. By contrast, a seller's agent will present the property in the most positive light and may use expert sales techniques to convince the buyer to sign on the dotted line.

Help with Negotiating. Buyers often feel uncomfortable negotiating for a property, especially one they really want to buy. They may be afraid to make a mistake through ignorance, or they may feel pressured to make a high offer quickly before someone else snaps up the property. A buyer's agent can use his or her negotiating skills and intimate knowledge of the real estate market to help the buyer get the property on the best possible terms.

Access to More Properties. A buyer's agent may arrange to be compensated if the buyer purchases any home, even one that isn't listed with a broker. So a buyer's agent may pursue less traditional means of searching for properties, and show the buyer properties that are for sale by owner, properties with open listings, and properties in foreclosure or probate proceedings.

Creation of Buyer Agency. Although buyer agency relationships are created automatically under the terms of the real estate agency law, a buyer and his or her broker may also enter into a written **representation agreement**. (An example is shown in Figure 7.4.) While the terms of buyer representation agreements vary, they generally include the following:

- the duration of the agency;
- the general characteristics of the property the buyer wants;
- the price range;
- the conditions under which a fee will be earned;
- who will pay the fee; and
- a description of the broker's duties.

Fig. 7.4 Buyer representation agreement

NWMLS Form No. 41A
Buyer's Agency Agreement
Rev. 04/01
Page 1 of 1

© Copyright 2001
Northwest Multiple Listing Service
ALL RIGHTS RESERVED

BUYER'S AGENCY AGREEMENT

This Buyer's Agency Agreement is made this _____ day of _____ , 200 _____ between   1

_____ ("Buyer")   2

and _____ ("Broker").   3

1. **AGENCY RELATION CREATED.** Buyer authorizes Broker to appoint _____ ("Agent") to repre-   4
sent Buyer. This Agreement creates an agency relationship between Buyer, Agent, and Agent's Broker, Designated Broker, or Branch Manager. This Agreement   5
does not create an agency relationship or responsibilities between Buyer and any other broker or salesperson licensed with the company named above; pro-   6
vided Buyer authorizes Broker to appoint other salespersons affiliated with Broker as subagents to act on Buyer's behalf as and when needed, at Broker's dis-   7
cretion.   Any other broker or salesperson licensed to the company named above will not be representing the Buyer and may represent the Seller. Accordingly,   8
for purposes of this Agreement, the term "Broker" means Agent including any subagents and Agent's Broker, Designated Broker, or Branch Manager, unless   9
expressly stated otherwise. Buyer acknowledges receipt of the pamphlet entitled "The Law of Real Estate Agency."   10

2. **BROKER'S LISTINGS/AGENT'S OWN LISTINGS/DUAL AGENCY.** Buyer agrees that if Broker locates a property that is listed by one of Broker's salesper-   11
sons other than Agent, then Buyer consents to Broker acting as a dual agent. Buyer further agrees that if Broker locates a property listed by Agent then Buyer   12
consents to Agent and Broker acting as dual agents. Buyer agrees that different salespersons affiliated with Broker may represent different buyers in competing   13
transactions involving the same property and that this shall not be considered action by Broker that is adverse or detrimental to the interests of either buyer, nor .   14
shall it be considered a conflict of interest on the part of Broker.   15

3. **TERM OF AGREEMENT.** This Agreement will expire _____ (120 days from signing if not filled in) or by prior written notice by either party. Buyer shall be   16
under no obligation to Broker except for those obligations existing at the time of termination.   17

4. **NO WARRANTIES OR REPRESENTATIONS.** Broker makes no warranties or representations regarding the value of or the suitability of any property for   18
Buyer's purposes. Buyer agrees to be responsible for making all inspections and investigations necessary to satisfy Buyer as to the property's suitability and   19
value.   20

5. **INSPECTIONS RECOMMENDED.** Broker recommends that any offer to purchase a property be conditioned on Buyer's inspection of the property and its   21
improvements. Buyer acknowledges that Broker and Agent have no expertise on these matters and that Buyer is solely responsible for interviewing and   22
selecting all inspectors.   23

6. **COMPENSATION.** Buyer shall pay Broker compensation as follows: 24

_____   25

_____   26

_____   27

Buyer understands and acknowledges that Broker will utilize a Multiple Listing service to locate properties and that MLS rules may require the Seller to compen-   28
sate Broker by apportioning a commission between the Listing Agent and Broker. Broker will disclose any such commission or bonuses offered by Seller prior   29
to preparing any offer. Buyer will be credited with any commission or bonus so payable to Broker. In the event that said commission and any bonus is less than   30
the compensation provided in this Agreement, Buyer agrees to pay the difference at the time of closing. In the event that said commission and any bonus is   31
equal to or greater than the compensation provided for by this Agreement, no compensation is due Broker. If Broker acts as a dual agent, then Broker shall   32
receive the listing and selling commission paid by Seller plus any additional compensation Broker may have negotiated with the Seller. All such compensation   33
shall be credited toward the fee specified above.   34

If Buyer shall, during the course of or within six (6) months after the expiration or termination of this Agreement, purchase a property that was first brought to the   35
attention of Buyer by the efforts or actions of Broker, or through information secured directly or indirectly from or through Broker, then Buyer shall pay to Broker   36
the compensation provided for herein.   37

7. **V.A. TRANSACTIONS.** Buyer agrees that due to VA regulations, VA financed transactions shall be conditioned upon the full commission being paid by Seller.   38

8. **ATTORNEYS' FEES.** In the event of suit concerning this Agreement, including claims pursuant to the Washington Consumer Protection Act, the prevailing party is   39
entitled to court costs and a reasonable attorney's fee. The venue of any suit shall be the county in which the property is located.   40

9. **OTHER AGREEMENTS (none if not filled in).**   41

_____   42

_____   43

_____   44

_____   45

Buyer has read and approves this Agreement and hereby acknowledges receipt of a copy.   46

    47

_____   _____   _____
Buyer   Date   Broker (Company)   48

_____   _____   _____
Buyer   Date   By: (Agent)   49

_____
Address   50

_____
City, State, Zip   51

_____
Phone   52

_____
E-mail Address

Buyer's Agent's Compensation. There are a variety of ways in which a buyer's agent may be compensated. The three most common are:

- a retainer,
- a seller-paid fee, and/or
- a buyer-paid fee.

A **retainer** is a fee paid up front before services are provided. Some buyer's agents collect a retainer when they enter into a buyer agency relationship, to ensure that their services won't go entirely uncompensated. The retainer is usually nonrefundable, but it will be credited against any fee or commission that the agent becomes entitled to.

In many cases, a buyer's agent is paid by the seller through a **commission split**. The commission split is based on a provision found in most MLS listing agreements, whereby any cooperating broker who procures a buyer is entitled to the selling broker's portion of the commission, regardless of which party that cooperating broker represents. Note that the source of the agent's commission does not determine the identity of his or her principal; accepting a seller-paid fee does not create agency duties toward the seller.

> **Example:** Helman lists his property with Broker Thurston and agrees to pay him 6% of the sales price. The listing agreement includes a clause that entitles any cooperating broker who procures a buyer to the selling broker's portion of the commission.
>
> Broker Adams has a buyer agency agreement with Gray. Gray offers $150,000 for Helman's house and Helman accepts the offer.
>
> When the transaction closes, Helman pays a $9,000 commission; $4,500 goes to Broker Thurston and $4,500 goes to Broker Adams.

Most buyer representation agreements also provide for payment by means of a commission split when the buyer purchases a home that is listed through a multiple listing service. However, a buyer representation agreement may provide for a **buyer-paid fee** instead. The buyer-paid fee might be based on an hourly rate, which essentially makes the agent a consultant. Alternatively, a buyer's agent may charge a percentage fee, so that the commission is a percentage of the purchase price. A third possibility is a flat fee—a specified sum that is payable if the buyer purchases a property found by the agent.

Some buyer agency agreements provide that the buyer's agent will accept a commission split if one is available, but the buyer will pay the fee if the purchased property was unlisted (for example, if it was for sale by owner).

Dual Agency. A dual agency relationship exists whenever a real estate agent represents both the seller and the buyer in the same transaction. Because the interests of the buyer and the seller usually conflict, it is difficult to represent them both without being disloyal to one or both.

> **Example:** Broker Davis represents both the buyer and the seller in a transaction. The seller informs Davis that she is in a big hurry to sell and will accept any reasonable offer. The buyer tells Davis that he is very interested in the house, and is willing to pay the full listing price. Should Davis tell the buyer of the seller's eagerness to sell? Should Davis tell the seller about the buyer's willingness to pay the full price?

In fact, it's really impossible for a dual agent to fully represent both parties. Thus, instead of the duty of loyalty, Washington law imposes on a dual agent the duty to refrain from acting to the detriment of either party. The dual agent must do his or her best to act impartially and treat both clients equally.

Each party to a dual agency should be informed that he or she will not receive full representation. Certain facts must necessarily be withheld from each party; the dual agent cannot divulge confidential information about one party to the other party. Returning to the previous example, the dual agent must not tell the buyer the seller's bottom line price, nor tell the seller how much the buyer is willing to pay.

Before acting as a dual agent, a licensee must have the informed written consent of both parties to the transaction. Acting as a dual agent without full disclosure and written consent is a violation of the real estate license law, and will lead to disciplinary action (see Chapter 17). Statutory agency disclosure requirements are discussed in the next section of this chapter.

In-house Transactions. Under the Real Estate Brokerage Relationships Act, dual agency occurs most often in in-house transactions. It's an in-house transaction when the listing salesperson and the selling salesperson both work for the same broker. In this situation, the listing salesperson represents only the seller, the selling salesperson represents only the buyer, and the broker is a dual agent, representing both parties.

> **Example:** Salesperson Winston, who works for Broker Roberts, has shown Buyer King several houses over the course of a few weeks. Finally, Winston shows King a house listed by Salesperson Vincent, who also works for Broker Roberts. King decides to make an offer on the house. In this transaction, Winston, the selling salesperson, is the buyer's agent; Vincent, the listing salesperson, is the seller's agent; and Roberts, the broker, is a dual agent.

Non-Agency. In some transactions, a real estate licensee might choose to act only as a facilitator and refuse to assume any agency duties at all. This is called non-agency, and it is legal under Washington's real estate agency law. However, a non-agent still owes general statutory duties to any party he or she works with. There is no way for a licensee to opt out of the duties of disclosure, reasonable skill and care, honesty and good faith, and so on.

Agency Disclosure Requirements

As we explained earlier, licensees must give anyone they render services to a pamphlet setting forth the provisions of the real estate agency law. In addition, Washington law requires licensees to disclose to all the parties in a transaction which party (or parties) they represent. A listing agent must inform both the buyer and the seller which of them he or she is representing in the transaction. The selling agent must do the same.

The agency disclosures must be made to the buyer before the buyer signs the offer to purchase, and to the seller before the seller signs the offer. The disclosures must be in writing in a separate paragraph in the purchase and sale agreement. The parties' signatures on the agreement indicate their acceptance and understanding of the stated agency relationships (see Chapter 9). Alternatively, the disclosures may be made in a separate disclosure document, which also must be signed by the parties. An example is shown in Figure 7.5.

Fig. 7.5 Agency disclosure form

NWMLS Form No. 42
Agency Disclosure
Rev. 1/97
Page 1 of 1

AGENCY DISCLOSURE

Washington State law requires real estate licensees to disclose to all parties to whom the licensee   1
renders real estate brokerage services whether the Licensee represents the Seller (or Lessor), the   2
Buyer (or Lessee), both the Seller/Lessor and Buyer/Lessee, or neither.   3

YOU ARE ADVISED THAT THE UNDERSIGNED IS THE AGENT OF THE BUYER/LESSEE (strike   4
one), UNLESS OTHERWISE STATED HERE: 5

THE UNDERSIGNED REPRESENTS: _____   6

THE UNDERSIGNED BUYER/LESSEE OR SELLER/LESSOR ACKNOWLEDGES RECEIPT   7
OF A COPY OF THE PAMPHLET ENTITLED "THE LAW OF REAL ESTATE AGENCY"   8

BUYER/LESSEE _____ DATE _____   9
                         (Signature)

BUYER/LESSEE _____ DATE _____   10
                         (Signature)

SELLER/LESSOR _____ DATE _____   11
                         (Signature)

SELLER/LESSOR _____ DATE _____   12
                         (Signature)

LICENSEE _____   13
                    (Print/Type)

LICENSEE'S SIGNATURE _____   14

COMPANY NAME AS LICENSED _____   15
                                  (Print/Type)

Dual Agency Disclosure. Before acting as a dual agent, a licensee must obtain the informed written consent of both parties. The dual agent must disclose to both parties that he or she will be acting as a dual agent. The terms of the dual agent's compensation must also be revealed. The parties will then sign the confirmation of the agency disclosure in the purchase and sale agreement.

Real estate licensees should be extra careful with their disclosures in the context of dual agency. Buyers and sellers, eager to get on with the business of buying and selling a home, may agree to a dual agency without really understanding what it means. They may accept the agent's explanation at face value and sign a disclosure form without question. Later, one party might feel that the licensee breached his agency duties. This kind of disappointment often leads to legal action.

The Broker/Salesperson Relationship

Finally, let's discuss the legal relationship between a real estate salesperson and the broker he or she works for. As you know, the salesperson works as an agent of the broker and as a subagent of the broker's client. The salesperson is not licensed to represent members of the public directly, and the broker is responsible for supervising the salesperson's actions.

For certain purposes, a real estate salesperson is classified either as the broker's **employee** or as an **independent contractor**. An independent contractor is hired to perform a particular job, and uses his or her own judgment to decide how the job should be completed. In contrast, an employee is hired to perform whatever tasks the employer requires, and is given instructions on how to accomplish each task. An employee is supervised and controlled much more closely than an independent contractor. Various employment and tax laws apply only when someone is hired as an employee, and not when someone is hired as an independent contractor.

A real estate broker is virtually always an independent contractor in relation to his or her principal (the buyer or the seller). When it comes to the relationship between a broker and a salesperson, however, the distinction between employee and independent contractor may be an issue.

Whether a salesperson is his or her broker's employee or an independent contractor depends on the degree of control the broker exercises over the salesperson. If the broker closely directs the activities of the salesperson and controls how the salesperson carries out his or her work, the salesperson may be considered an employee. For example, if the broker requires the salesperson to work on a set schedule, tells the salesperson when to go where, and decides what steps the salesperson should take in marketing each property, the salesperson is probably the broker's employee.

Most brokers exercise much less control over their salespersons' work than that. They generally focus on the end results—listings, closings, and satisfied clients—and not on the details of how the salesperson accomplishes those results. A broker usually isn't concerned with where the salesperson is or what he or she is doing at any given time. The salesperson is paid on the basis of results (by commission) rather than hours spent on the job. Thus, in most cases, a real estate salesperson is an independent contractor, not the broker's employee.

If a salesperson were an employee, the broker would be required to withhold money from the salesperson's compensation to pay certain federal and state taxes (income tax, social security, unemployment insurance, and industrial accident insurance). An independent contractor, on the other hand, is responsible for paying his or her own social security and income taxes.

The Internal Revenue Code provides that a real estate salesperson will be considered an independent contractor for federal income tax purposes if three conditions are met:

1. the individual is a licensed real estate salesperson;
2. substantially all of his or her compensation is based on commission rather than hours worked; and,
3. the services are performed under a written contract providing that the individual will not be treated as an employee for federal tax purposes.

Bear in mind that even when a real estate salesperson meets the criteria for independent contractor status, the license law makes the broker responsible for the salesperson's conduct.

Chapter Summary

1. In an agency relationship, the agent represents the principal in dealings with third parties. An agent may be a universal, general, or special agent, depending on the scope of authority granted.

2. Most agency relationships are created by express agreement (oral or written), but they can also be created by ratification, estoppel, or implication. Acts performed by an agent or an ostensible agent are binding on the principal if they fall within the scope of the agent's actual or apparent authority.

3. A real estate licensee who performs real estate brokerage services for a buyer automatically becomes the buyer's agent, unless there is a written agreement to the contrary.

4. A licensee owes several duties to any party to whom the licensee renders real estate services, whether or not there is an agency relationship. These duties include reasonable skill and care, honesty and good faith, presenting all written communications, disclosure of material facts, accounting, providing an agency law pamphlet, and making an agency disclosure.

5. When a licensee enters into an agency relationship, he or she owes certain additional duties to the principal, including loyalty, disclosure of conflicts of interest, confidentiality, advising the principal to seek expert advice, and a good faith and continuous effort to fulfill the terms of the agency agreement.

6. An agency relationship is terminated by mutual agreement; revocation; renunciation; expiration; fulfillment of purpose; the death, incapacity, or bankruptcy of either party; or extinction of the subject matter.

7. Under Washington law, a real estate licensee may act as the seller's agent, the buyer's agent, a dual agent, or a non-agent.

8. A seller agency is usually created with a listing agreement. A seller's agent owes agency duties to the seller and general licensee duties to the buyer. A listing agent must be careful to avoid any actions that might give rise to an agency relationship with the buyer.

9. A buyer agency relationship is created automatically, but the licensee and the buyer may also enter into a representation agreement. A buyer's agent may be paid by the seller (through a commission split) or by the buyer (with a commission, an hourly fee, or a flat rate).

10. A licensee is a dual agent when he or she represents both the seller and the buyer in the same transaction. Dual agency is unlawful without the full, informed, written consent of both parties. Dual agency most commonly arises in in-house transactions.

11. A licensee is required to disclose to each party which party he or she represents in the transaction. The disclosure must be made to each party before that party signs an offer to purchase (a purchase and sale agreement). The disclosure must be in writing; it may take the form of a provision included in the purchase and sale agreement, or it may be a separate document.

12. For the purposes of certain tax and employment laws, a real estate salesperson may be classified either as his or her broker's employee, or as an independent contractor. In most cases, a salesperson is considered to be an independent contractor, even though the broker has legal responsibility for the salesperson's conduct.

🔑 Key Terms

Principal—The person who authorizes an agent to act on his or her behalf.

Agent—A person authorized to represent another in dealings with third parties.

Third party—A person seeking to deal with the principal through the agent.

Fiduciary—Someone who holds a special position of trust and confidence in relation to another.

Ratification—When the principal gives approval to unauthorized actions after they are performed, creating an agency relationship after the fact.

Estoppel—When the principal allows a third party to believe an agency relationship exists, so that the principal is legally precluded (estopped) from denying the agency.

Actual authority—Authority the principal grants to the agent either expressly or by implication.

Apparent authority—Where no actual authority has been granted, but the principal allows it to appear that the agent is authorized, and therefore is estopped from denying the agency. Also called ostensible authority.

Material facts—Information that has a substantial negative impact on the value of the property or on a party's ability to perform, or would defeat the purpose of the transaction.

Confidential information—Information from or concerning a principal that was acquired during the course of an agency relationship, that the principal reasonably expects to be kept confidential, that the principal has not disclosed to third parties, that would operate to the detriment of the principal, and that the principal is not legally obligated to disclose to the other party.

Secret profit—Any profit an agent receives as a result of the agency relationship and does not disclose to the principal.

Listing agent—The agent that takes the listing on a property, and who may or may not be the agent who procures a buyer.

Selling agent—The agent who procures a buyer for a property, and who may or may not have taken the listing.

Subagent—An "agent of an agent." A salesperson is generally considered to be a subagent of his or her broker's principal.

In-house transaction—A sale in which the buyer and the seller are brought together by salespersons working for the same broker.

Employee—Someone who works under the direction and control of another.

Independent contractor—A person who contracts to do a job for another, but retains control over how he or she will carry out the task, rather than following detailed instructions.

Chapter Quiz

1. An agency relationship can be created in any of the following ways, except:

   a) written agreement
   b) oral agreement
   c) ratification
   d) verification

2. After an agency relationship terminates, the agent still owes the principal the duty of:

   a) loyalty
   b) confidentiality
   c) reasonable skill and care
   d) disclosure of material facts

3. Garcia acted on behalf of Hilton without her authorization. At a later date, Hilton gave her approval to Garcia's actions. This is an example of:

   a) express agreement
   b) ratification
   c) estoppel
   d) assumption of authority

4. A seller lists his home with a broker at $190,000; he asks for a quick sale. When the listing broker shows the home to a buyer, he says the seller is financially insolvent and will take $180,000. The buyer offers $180,000 and the seller accepts. The broker:

   a) did not violate his duties to the seller, because the seller accepted the offer
   b) did not violate his duties to the seller, since he fulfilled the purpose of his agency
   c) violated his duties to the seller by disclosing confidential information to the buyer
   d) was unethical, but did not violate his duties to the seller, since he did not receive a secret profit

5. Stark lists his property with Bell, a licensed broker. Bell shows the property to her cousin, who decides he would like to buy it. Which of the following is true?

   a) Bell can present her cousin's offer to Stark, as long as she tells Stark that the prospective buyer is one of her relatives
   b) Bell violated her duties to Stark by showing the property to one of her relatives
   c) It was not unethical for Bell to show the property to a relative, but it would be a violation of her duties if she presented her cousin's offer to Stark
   d) It is not necessary for Bell to tell Stark that the buyer is related to her, as long as he is offering the full listing price for the property

6. A principal can be held liable for harm caused by a real estate licensee if:

   a) the act resulting in harm was authorized by the principal
   b) the licensee has a reputation for unethical practices
   c) the licensee has many assets that could be awarded to the injured party
   d) the licensee assured the third party that the principal would be liable for any harm caused by the transaction

7. A real estate agent tells potential buyers: "This is a great old house. They just don't make them like they used to." This statement would be considered:

   a) a misrepresentation
   b) actual fraud
   c) self-dealing
   d) puffing

8. In most cases, a listing broker:

   a) is authorized to enter into contracts on behalf of the seller
   b) is considered a special agent
   c) Both of the above
   d) Neither of the above

9. Dual agency is:

   a) no longer legal in Washington State
   b) legal as long as both principals consent to the arrangement in writing
   c) legal as long as the agent receives equal compensation from both principals
   d) encouraged by many professional associations as the best way of representing a client's interests

10. Able listed Glover's property. Able:

    a) cannot give a buyer any information about Glover's property without being considered a dual agent
    b) may give a buyer information about Glover's property without owing agency duties to the buyer
    c) must sign a disclaimer of liability if he presents a buyer's offer to purchase to Glover
    d) is a non-agent

11. Salesperson Grant, who works for Broker Carter, is showing Buyer Manning a property listed by Salesperson Lee, who also works for Carter. Who is most likely to be acting as a dual agent?

    Grant

12. Salesperson Kelley works for Broker Forrest. A good friend wants Kelley to try to find a house for her. Kelley shows her a house listed by one of Forrest's other sales agents. Kelley:

    a) is in danger of becoming a dual agent
    b) is automatically acting as a buyer's agent in this situation
    c) should request special approval of the sale from the Real Estate Commission
    d) is the seller's agent, no matter how she behaves towards her friend

13. A buyer's agent:

    a) may not accept compensation paid by the seller
    b) must have a written buyer agency agreement in order to be compensated
    c) may be paid through a commission split
    d) may not receive compensation that is based on the property's sales price

14. Disclosure of and consent to a dual agency:

    a) must be in writing
    b) is required only in an in-house transaction
    c) should come after the parties sign the purchase and sale agreement
    d) must be given to the buyer only after presenting the written offer to purchase

15. A dual agent must:

    a) keep each party's negotiating position confidential
    b) disclose all material facts to both parties, no matter how confidential
    c) act only as a facilitator, with no agency duties to either party
    d) refer all conflicts of interest to the Board of Equalization

☞ Answer Key

1. d) An agency relationship may be created by express agreement (written or oral), ratification, estoppel, or implication.

2. b) After an agency relationship terminates, the agent still owes the principal the duties of confidentiality and accounting.

3. b) An agency relationship is created by ratification when the principal gives approval to unauthorized actions after the fact.

4. c) The broker was disloyal to his principal and violated his fiduciary duties by disclosing confidential information to a third party.

5. a) A seller's real estate agent is required to tell the seller if the prospective buyer is related to the agent.

6. a) A principal cannot be held liable for harm caused by a licensee unless the act that resulted in harm was authorized by the principal, or the principal benefited from the act and there is little chance that the third party will be able to recover damages from the licensee.

7. d) This is an example of puffing, an exaggerated statement that the buyers should realize they can't depend on.

8. b) A listing broker is usually a special agent, with limited authority to represent the principal in a particular transaction. A listing broker is ordinarily not authorized to sign contracts on behalf of the principal.

9. b) Dual agency is legal, but only if both the seller and the buyer are informed that the agent is representing both of them, and they both give their written consent to the arrangement.

10. b) A seller's agent can give a buyer information about the seller's property without becoming a dual agent.

11. b) Broker Carter would be considered a dual agent in this situation. Grant (the selling agent) is the buyer's agent. Lee (the listing agent) is the seller's agent.

12. b) Kelley is representing the buyer only, although Broker Forrest is considered a dual agent.

13. c) Buyer's agents often accept a share of the commission that the listing broker receives from the seller. This arrangement does not create an agency relationship between the buyer's agent and the seller.

14. a) Disclosure of a dual agency must be in writing, and the parties' consent must also be in writing.

15. a) A dual agent must not disclose confidential information about one party to the other party. This includes information on each party's negotiating position.

Listing Agreements

I. Earning a Commission
   A. Ready, willing, and able buyer
   B. Types of listing agreements
      1. open
      2. exclusive agency
      3. exclusive right to sell
II. Elements of a Listing Agreement
   A. Basic requirements
   B. Provisions of a typical listing form
      1. broker's authority
      2. listing period
      3. multiple listing provision
      4. access and keyboxes
      5. agency disclosure
      6. commission and extender clause
      7. rental or option by seller
      8. property description
      9. closing costs
     10. seller's warranties
     11. attorneys' fees
     12. seller disclosure statement
     13. signatures
     14. listing information
     15. receipt of copy
     16. receipt of agency pamphlet

Chapter Overview

A listing agreement is a written employment contract between a property owner and a real estate broker. The owner hires the broker to find a buyer or a tenant who is ready, willing, and able to buy or lease the property on the owner's terms. The listing agreement defines the rights and responsibilities of the owner and broker in their employment relationship. This chapter explains what a listing broker is required to do in order to earn a commission, the distinctions between the different types of listings, and the elements of a typical listing agreement.

Introduction

When a seller hires a real estate broker to help sell a piece of property, they enter into a contract called a **listing agreement**. Even though the listing agreement form is frequently filled out and signed by a salesperson working for the listing broker, the contract is between the seller and the broker (not the salesperson). Only a broker may directly contract with members of the public for brokerage services.

The listing agreement creates an agency relationship between the broker and the seller. As you saw in Chapter 7, agency carries with it a high level of responsibility. The broker/agent is a fiduciary, required to act in the best interests of the seller/principal in carrying out the agency.

Fiduciary duties are imposed on the broker by law; in addition, the parties agree to take on certain contractual duties via the listing agreement. The terms of the listing agreement determine what the broker is obligated to do, and under what circumstances the seller will be obligated to pay the broker a commission.

Earning a Commission

The standard form of payment for a real estate broker is the commission, also called a **brokerage fee**. The commission is usually computed as a percentage of the sales price (the price that the property is sold for), as opposed to the listing price.

A broker cannot sue a seller for compensation unless they had a written employment agreement and the broker was properly licensed at the time the brokerage services were provided. In addition, the broker must have fulfilled the terms of the employment agreement.

A listing agreement can make payment of the broker's commission depend on any conditions that are mutually acceptable to the broker and the seller. For example, the seller might ask to include a "no sale, no commission" provision in the agreement. This would make the broker's commission payable only if the transaction actually closes and the seller receives full payment from the buyer.

Unless otherwise agreed, however, certain standard rules are followed regarding payment of the broker's commission. These include the rules concerning a ready, willing, and able buyer, and those concerning the three types of listings.

Ready, Willing, and Able Buyer

As a general rule, a listing agreement obligates the seller to pay the listing broker a commission only if a **ready, willing, and able** buyer is found during the listing period.

An Acceptable Offer. A buyer is considered "ready and willing" if he or she makes an offer that meets the seller's stated terms. In the listing agreement, the seller sets forth the terms on which he or she wants to sell the property: price, closing date, financing arrangements, etc. If a buyer makes an offer that matches those terms, the broker is usually entitled to the commission—even if the seller decides not to accept that offer after all.

When a buyer makes an offer on terms other than those set forth in the listing agreement, the seller can turn down the offer without becoming liable for the broker's commission. But if the seller accepts an offer, he or she generally is required to pay the broker's commission even if the offer did not match the terms set forth in the listing agreement.

Able to Buy. A ready and willing buyer is considered "able" if he or she has the capacity to contract and the financial ability to complete the purchase. The buyer must have enough cash to buy the property on the agreed terms, or else be eligible for the necessary financing.

Commission Without Closing. Generally, once a ready, willing, and able buyer has been found, the broker has earned the commission, whether or not the sale is ever completed. When failure to close is the seller's fault, the broker is still entitled to the commission (although the broker might decide not to demand payment). For example, once the seller accepts an offer, he or she still owes the broker a commission if the sale fails to close for any of these reasons:

- the seller has a change of heart and decides not to sell;
- the seller does not have marketable title;
- the seller is unable to deliver possession of the property to the buyer; or
- the seller and the buyer mutually agree to terminate their contract.

Unless specifically required by the listing agreement, it is not even necessary for the buyer and seller to execute a written purchase and sale agreement in order for the broker to be entitled to a commission. It is enough if the buyer and seller have reached an agreement as to the essential terms of the sale: the price, downpayment, loan term, interest rate, and amortization. If the seller backs out before the agreement is put into writing, the broker could still claim the commission.

Sometimes the seller and the broker disagree as to whether the buyer located by the broker was in fact ready, willing, and able. In most states, a court will presume that the buyer was ready, willing, and able if a written purchase and sale agreement was signed. Since the seller accepted the buyer by entering into the contract, the seller has waived the right to claim that the buyer was unacceptable. This rule can be applied even if the buyer immediately defaulted because of financial inability to go through with the purchase.

On the other hand, if no contract has been signed and the agreement between the buyer and the seller is still at the unwritten stage when it falls through, the broker is not entitled to a commission unless he or she can prove that the buyer was financially able to perform the contract.

Types of Listing Agreements

The circumstances under which a seller is required to pay the broker's commission also depend on the type of listing agreement they have. The three basic types of listing agreements in current use are:

- the open listing,
- the exclusive agency listing, and
- the exclusive right to sell listing.

Open Listing. Under an open listing agreement, the seller is obligated to pay the broker a commission only if the broker was the **procuring cause** of the sale. The procuring cause is the person who was primarily responsible for bringing about the agreement between the parties. To be the procuring cause, a broker (or one of his or her salespersons) must have personally negotiated the offer from the ready, willing, and able buyer.

An open listing is also called a non-exclusive listing, because a seller is free to give open listings to any number of brokers. If a seller signs two open listing agreements with two different brokers, and one of the brokers sells the property, only the broker who made the sale is entitled to a commission. The other broker is not compensated for his or her efforts. Or if the seller sells the property directly, without the help of either broker, then the seller does not have to pay any commission at all. The sale of the property terminates all outstanding listings.

The open listing arrangement has obvious disadvantages. If two competing brokers both negotiate with the person who ends up buying the property, there may be a dispute over which broker was the procuring cause of the sale. Also, because a broker with an open listing agreement is not assured of a commission when the property sells, he or she may not put as much effort into marketing the property, so it may take longer to sell. For the most part, open listing agreements are used only when a seller is unwilling to execute an exclusive listing agreement.

Exclusive Agency Listing. In an exclusive agency listing, the seller agrees to list with only one broker, but retains the right to sell the property him or herself without being obligated to pay the broker a commission. The broker is entitled to a commission if anyone other than the seller finds a buyer for the property, but not if the seller finds the buyer without the help of an agent.

Exclusive Right to Sell Listing. Under an exclusive right to sell listing, the seller agrees to list with only one broker, and that broker is entitled to a commission if the property sells during the listing term, regardless of who finds the buyer. Even if the seller makes the sale directly, the broker is still entitled to the commission.

In spite of the designation "exclusive right to sell," this type of listing agreement does not actually authorize the broker to sell the property. As with the other types of listings, the broker is authorized only to submit offers to purchase to the seller.

The exclusive right to sell listing is preferred by most brokers, because it provides the most protection for the broker. It's the type of listing that is most commonly used.

Due Diligence. An important distinction between open and exclusive listings concerns the broker's contractual obligations. An open listing is considered to be a unilateral contract: the seller promises to pay the broker a commission if the broker finds a buyer, but the broker does not promise to make any effort to do so. If the broker does nothing at all, it is not a breach of contract.

On the other hand, an exclusive listing is considered to be a bilateral contract. In exchange for the seller's promise to pay a commission no matter who finds a buyer, the broker (by implication, if not expressly) promises to market the property and make a diligent effort to find a buyer. If the seller can prove that the listing broker did nothing to help sell the property, a court might not require the seller to pay the broker's commission.

Elements of a Listing Agreement

Although a broker and a seller can draw up their listing agreement from scratch, that is not a common practice today. Most brokers use one of several available listing agreement forms and make few—if any—modifications to it. If the broker belongs to a multiple listing service (discussed below), he or she is usually required to use the listing form provided by the MLS.

In this section of the chapter, we will first discuss the basic requirements for any listing agreement, and then look at the specific provisions of a typical listing agreement form.

Basic Requirements

Under Washington law, there are four requirements for an enforceable listing agreement. Every listing agreement must:

- identify the property to be sold (or leased),
- include a promise to compensate the broker,
- specify a fixed amount of compensation for the broker, and
- be in writing and signed by the seller.

A complete legal description of the property is not absolutely required by Washington law, as long as the agreement clearly identifies the property in question.

The broker's commission may be stated as a percentage of the sales price (which is the standard practice), or as a set dollar amount. But the compensation must be fixed in the listing agreement.

Because of this rule, **net listings** are not legal in Washington. In a net listing, the seller stipulates what net amount he or she will accept as the proceeds from the sale of the property. If the sales price exceeds that net figure, the agent is entitled to keep the excess as his or her compensation—no matter how much it may amount to. (Even in those states where net listings are legal, they are generally frowned upon; an unscrupulous broker can use them to take advantage of clients.)

So a slip of paper that says "I will pay Betty Diaz $1,000 for helping me to sell Claraway Farm" could be an enforceable listing agreement in Washington, as long as it is signed by a competent seller. Of course, it is much better to have a formal legal document that sets forth all of the terms of employment. All listing agreements should, at a minimum, contain the following provisions:

1. a description of the property, including a section describing the features of the property, such as the number of bedrooms and bathrooms;
2. an authorization of the broker to act as the seller's agent in marketing the property;
3. the seller's agreement to pay the broker a commission and the amount of the commission to be paid;
4. the terms of sale the seller will accept;
5. the conditions under which the commission will be payable;
6. the duration of the listing agreement; and
7. the seller's warranties as to the accuracy of the information given to the broker and included in the listing agreement.

The sixth item listed above—the duration of the listing—is especially important in an exclusive listing agreement. Since an exclusive listing effectively prevents the seller from hiring other agents, an ending date for the listing period should always be specified in the agreement.

However, unlike several other states, Washington has no law that requires a specific termination date for listing agreements. In Washington, a listing (exclusive or open) with no ending date will terminate after a reasonable time.

Provisions of a Typical Listing Agreement Form

In Washington and most other states, there is no single listing agreement form required by law. However, an organization called the Washington Information Network (WIN) has developed a uniform listing agreement that is used by many of the multiple listing services throughout the state. This form and various other listing agreement forms are available through multiple listing services, brokers' associations, and general publishers of legal forms. Although all listing forms tend to have many common elements, there may also be significant differences between them. A real estate salesperson should use only the forms chosen by his or her broker, and should become familiar with the provisions of those particular forms. We will present a general discussion of provisions likely to be encountered in a typical form, but any given form might omit some of these provisions and include others not discussed here.

Most residential listings are exclusive right to sell agreements with a multiple listing authorization. As an example, the WIN uniform listing agreement form is shown in Figure 8.1. A listing input form is shown in Figure 8.2.

Broker's Authority. The first lines in a listing agreement form usually identify the broker, establish the broker's agency authority, and specify the date on which the listing period will expire.

The clause in the listing agreement that gives the broker his or her authority usually says something like, "The agent shall have the sole and exclusive right to submit offers to purchase." Note that the agent is not given authority to sell the property. (To grant an agent the right to sell the property, the seller would have to execute and record a power of attorney.)

The agent is usually also given the authority to "receipt for deposits," to accept earnest money deposits from any prospective buyers on behalf of the

Fig. 8.1 Exclusive right to sell listing agreement

NWMLS Form No. 1A
W.A.R. Form No. L-102-R
Exclusive Sale
Rev. 12/96
Page 1 of 3 pages

EXCLUSIVE SALE AND LISTING AGREEMENT

© Copyright 1996
Washington Information Network
ALL RIGHTS RESERVED

The undersigned Seller ("Seller") hereby grants to _____ , ("Broker")   1

from date hereof until midnight of _____ , the sole and exclusive right to submit offers to purchase, and to receipt   2

for deposits in connection therewith, the real property ("the Property") commonly known as _____   3

in the City of _____ , County of _____ , State of Washington, Zip _____ ; and legally   4

described as: LOT _____ , BLOCK _____ , DIVISION _____ ,   5

_____ VOL _____ , PAGE _____   6

_____   7

1. **DEFINITIONS.** For purposes of this Agreement: (a) "MLS" means the Northwest Multiple Listing Service; and (b) "sell" includes a contract to sell; an exchange or   8
contract to exchange; an option to purchase; and/or a lease with option to purchase.   9

2. **AGENCY/DUAL AGENCY.** Seller authorizes Broker to appoint _____ to act as Seller's Listing Agent(s). It is understood and   10
agreed that this Agreement creates an agency relationship with Listing Agent(s) and Broker only, not with any other sales persons of Broker; provided, Seller   11
authorizes Broker to appoint other salespersons affiliated with Broker as subagents to act on Seller's behalf as and when needed, at Broker's discretion. Any   12
broker or salesperson, other than Broker or Listing Agent, who procures a prospective buyer for the Property will not be representing Seller and may represent the   13
Buyer. Accordingly, for the purposes of this Agreement, the term "Broker" means Listing Agent(s) including any subagents and Listing Agent's Broker, Designated   14
Broker or Branch Manager, unless expressly stated otherwise.   15
Seller agrees that if the Property is sold to a buyer represented by one of Broker's salespersons other than Listing Agent(s), then Seller consents to Broker acting   16
as a dual agent. Seller further agrees that if the Property is sold to a buyer who Listing Agent also represents, then Seller consents to Listing Agent(s) and Broker   17
acting as dual agents. Seller agrees that different sales persons affiliated with Broker may represent different sellers in competing transactions involving the   18
same buyer and that this shall not be considered action by Broker that is adverse or detrimental to the interests of either seller, nor shall it be considered a   19
conflict of interest on the part of Broker. Seller acknowledges receipt of the pamphlet entitled "The Law of Real Estate Agency."   20
If Broker acts as a dual agent, then Broker shall be entitled to the entire commission payable under this Agreement plus any additional compensation Broker   21
may have negotiated with the Buyer.   22

3. **COMMISSION.** If (a) Broker procures a Buyer on the terms in this Agreement, or on other terms acceptable to Seller; or (b) Seller directly or indirectly or through   23
any person or entity other than Broker, during the term hereof, sells the Property; then Seller will pay Broker a commission of (fill in one and strike the other)   24
_____ % of the sales price, or _____ . Further, if Seller shall, within six months after the expira-   25
tion of this Agreement, sell the Property to any person to whose attention it was brought through the signs, advertising or other action of Broker, or on information   26
secured directly or indirectly from or through Broker, during the term of this Agreement, then Seller will pay Broker the above commission. Provided, that if a   27
commission is paid to a member of MLS or a cooperating MLS in conjunction with a sale, the amount of commission payable to Broker shall be limited to the   28
amount of commission which would have been payable pursuant to this Agreement less any commission so paid to another member of MLS. Provided further,   29
that if Seller cancels this Agreement without legal cause, Seller may be liable for damages incurred by Broker as a result of cancellation, regardless of whether   30
Seller pays a commission to another MLS member.   31

4. **KEYBOX.** Broker is authorized to install a keybox on the Property. Such keybox may be opened by a master key held by all members of MLS and their sales-   32
people. A master key also may be held by affiliated third parties such as inspectors and appraisers who cannot have access to the Property without Broker's   33
prior approval which will not be given without Broker first making reasonable efforts to obtain Seller's approval.   34

5. **SELLER'S WARRANTIES AND REPRESENTATIONS.** Seller warrants that he/she has the right to sell the Property on the terms herein and that the Property   35
information on the additional pages to this Agreement is correct. Further, Seller represents that to the best of Seller's knowledge, there are no structures or   36
boundary indicators that either encroach on adjacent property or on this Property. Seller understands that Broker and other members of MLS will make   37
representations to prospective buyers based on the Property information on the additional pages to this Agreement. Seller agrees to indemnify and hold Broker   38
and other members of MLS harmless in the event the foregoing warranties and representations are incorrect.   39

6. **CLOSING COSTS.** Seller agrees to furnish and pay for a buyer's policy of title insurance showing marketable title to the Property. Seller agrees to pay real estate   40
excise tax and one-half of any escrow fees or such portion of escrow fees and any other fees or charges as provided by law in the case of FHA or VA financed sale.   41
Rent, taxes, interest, reserves, assumed encumbrances, homeowner fees and insurance are to be prorated between Seller and Buyer as of the date of closing.   42

7. **MULTIPLE LISTING.** Broker shall cause this listing to be published by MLS. Broker may refer this listing to any other cooperating multiple listing service at Bro-   43
ker's discretion. Broker shall cooperate with all other members of MLS, or of a multiple listing service to which this listing is referred, in working toward the sale of   44
the Property. Regardless of whether a cooperating MLS member is the agent of the Buyer, the Seller, neither or both, the member shall be entitled to receive the   45
selling office's share of the commission. SELLER UNDERSTANDS AND AGREES THAT THE PROPERTY INFORMATION ON THE ADDITIONAL PAGES OF   46
THIS AGREEMENT WILL BE GIVEN TO PROSPECTIVE BUYERS AND TO OTHER COOPERATING MEMBERS OF MLS WHO DO NOT REPRESENT THE SELLER   47
AND, IN SOME INSTANCES, MAY REPRESENT THE BUYER. IT IS UNDERSTOOD THAT MLS IS NOT A PARTY TO THIS AGREEMENT AND ITS SOLE   48
FUNCTION IS TO FURNISH THE DESCRIPTIVE INFORMATION ON THE ADDITIONAL PAGES OF THIS LISTING TO ITS MEMBERS, WITHOUT VERIFICATION   49
AND WITHOUT ASSUMING ANY RESPONSIBILITY FOR SUCH INFORMATION OR IN RESPECT TO THIS AGREEMENT.   50

8. **DISCLAIMER/SELLER'S INSURANCE.** Neither Broker, MLS, nor any members of MLS or of any multiple listing service to which this listing is referred shall be res-   51
ponsible for loss, theft, or damage of any nature or kind whatsoever to the Property and/or to any personal property therein, including entry by the master key to   52
keybox and/or at open houses. **Seller is advised to notify Seller's insurance company that the Property is listed for sale and ascertain that the Seller has**   53
adequate insurance coverage. If the Property is to be vacant during all or part of the term of this listing, Seller should request that a "vacancy clause" be   54
added to Seller's insurance policy.   55

9. **BROKER'S RIGHT TO MARKET THE PROPERTY** Seller shall not commit any act which materially impairs Broker's ability to market and sell the Property under the   56
terms of this Agreement. In the event of breach of the foregoing, Seller agrees to pay Broker a commission in the above amount, or at the above rate applied to   57
the listing price herein, whichever is applicable. Broker shall be entitled to show the Property at all reasonable times. Broker need not submit to Seller any offers   58
to lease, rent, execute an option to purchase, or enter into any agreement other than for immediate sale of the Property.   59

10. **REAL PROPERTY TRANSFER DISCLOSURE STATEMENT.** Unless Seller is exempt under RCW 64.06, Seller shall provide to Broker as soon as reasonably prac-   60
ticable a completed and signed "Real Property Transfer Disclosure Statement" (W.A.R. Form D-5 or NWMLS Form 17). Seller agrees to indemnify, defend and   61
hold Broker harmless from and against any and all claims that the information Seller provides on W.A.R. Form D-5 or NWMLS Form 17 is inaccurate.   62

11. **DAMAGES IN THE EVENT OF BUYER'S BREACH** In the event Seller retains earnest money as liquidated damages on Buyer's breach, any costs advanced or com-   63
mitted by Broker on Seller's behalf shall be paid therefrom and the balance divided equally between Seller and Broker.   64

12. **ATTORNEYS' FEES.** In the event either party employs an attorney to enforce any terms of this Agreement and is successful, the other party agrees to pay reason-   65
able attorneys' fees. In the event of trial, the successful party shall be entitled to an award of attorneys' fees and expenses; the amount of the attorneys' fees and   66
expenses shall be fixed by the court. The venue of any suit shall be the county in which the property is located.   67

DATED THIS _____ DAY OF _____ . Are the undersigned the sole owner(s)? ☐ YES ☐ NO   68

BROKER (COMPANY) _____ SELLER _____   69

BY _____ SELLER _____   70

Reprinted with permission, Northwest Multiple Listing Service. No endorsement implied.

Fig. 8.2 Listing input form

NWMLS Form 1 Rev. 7/02
Copyright 2002
Northwest Multiple Listing Service
All Rights Reserved

RESIDENTIAL Exclusive Listing Agreement (page 2 of 3)
LISTING INPUT SHEET
• Indicates Required information   ( ) Indicates Maximum Choice

PROPERTY TYPE **1**

LISTING #

• **COUNTY**

• **TAX ID#**

• **Listing Office ID#**   (Listing Office Name & Phone No. including area code)

• **LAG-Listing Agent ID#**   (Listing AgentName & Phone No. including area code)

Co Listing Office ID#   Co Agent - ID #

• **AREA**   • **Community/District**

• **Street # (HSN)   Modifier**

☐ E   ☐ NW   ☐ SW
☐ N   ☐ S   ☐ W
☐ NE   ☐ SE
Direction

• **Street Name**

☐ Av Ct ☐ Cir   ☐ Dr   ☐ Lp   ☐ St   ☐ Terr
☐ Av Pl ☐ Cr St ☐ Dr Ct ☐ Pkwy ☐ St Ct ☐ Wy
☐ Ave   ☐ Ct   ☐ Hwy   ☐ Place ☐ St Dr
☐ Blvd   ☐ Ct Av ☐ Lane ☐ Rd   ☐ St Pl
Suffix

☐ E   ☐ NE   ☐ SW
☐ N   ☐ NW   ☐ W
☐ KPN ☐ SE
☐ KPS ☐ SE
Post Direction

Unit #

• **CITY**

• **ZIP Code   + 4**

☐ Thomas   ☐ RR-Mason   ☐ Totem
☐ RR-Kitsap ☐ RR-Thurston ☐ Yellow
☐ RR-Jeff   ☐ RR-Lewis   ☐ Unknown
• **MAP BOOK**
Show Map Link (Y/N) ☐ (by default 'Yes')

• **Map Page**   • **Top Map** Coord.

• **Side Map** Coord.

• **Listing Price**

• **Internet Advertising** (Y/N) ☐ (by default 'Yes')

Show Address to Public (Y/N) ☐ (by default 'Yes')

• **Primary Photo By** (1) ☐ Agent/Office ☐ No Photo ☐ NWMLS Photographer

Photographer Instructions

• **SOC** (Selling Office Com.)   **Selling Office Commission Comments**

• **Number of Bedrooms**   • **Total Bathrooms**

ASF - Total   Lot Size   ☐ Square Feet ☐ Acres

• **Year Built**   • **Listing Date**   • **Expiration Date**

• **School District** (see Code List) ☐

• **Occupant Type** Owner/Presale/Tenant/Vacant ☐ (O/P/T/V)

• **Owner's Name**   • **Owner's Phone**

• **Occupant's Name**   • **Phone to Show**

• **Owner's City and State**

Marketing Remarks. CAUTION! The comments you make in the following lines are limited to descriptions of the land and improvements only. These remarks will appear in the client handouts and websites. (500)

Confidential Agent-Only Remarks. Comments in this category are for agent's use only. (250)

Legal Description. (100)

Driving Directions to Property (125)

LOCATION

Lot Number

Block

Plat/Subdivision/Building Name

• **Preliminary Title Ordered** (Y/N)

LISTING INFORMATION

• **Possession** (3)
☐ Closing   ☐ Closing + 3 Days
☐ Negotiable   ☐ Subject to Tenant's Rights
☐ See Remarks

• **Showing Information** (No Limit)
☐ Appointment   ☐ Call Listing Office
☐ Day Sleeper   ☐ Gate Code Needed
☐ MLS Keybox   ☐ Other Keybox
☐ Owner-Call First ☐ Pet in House
☐ Power Off   ☐ Renter - Call First
☐ Security System ☐ Vacant
☐ See Remarks

• **Form 17** (1)
☐ Provided   ☐ Not Provided
☐ Exempt

• **Tax Year**

• **Annual Taxes** $

• **Senior Exemption**   ☐ (Y/N)

Monthly Homeowner Dues $

Monthly Rent - if rented $

• **Potential Terms** (10)
☐ Assumable   ☐ Cash Out
☐ Conventional   ☐ Farm Home Loan
☐ FHA   ☐ Lease/Purchase
☐ Owner Financing ☐ Rehab Loan
☐ State Bond   ☐ VA
☐ Variable Price Listing ☐ See Remarks

NWMLS Form 1 Rev. 7/02
Copyright 2002
Northwest Multiple Listing Service
All Rights Reserved

RESIDENTIAL Exclusive Listing Agreement (page 3 of 3)
LISTING INPUT SHEET

Listing Address:

PROPERTY TYPE **1**

LAG #

SITE INFORMATION

Lot Dimensions

Waterfront Footage

Lot Topog./Veg.(4)
- ❑ Brush
- ❑ Equestrian
- ❑ Garden Space
- ❑ Partial Slope
- ❑ Rolling
- ❑ Steep Slope
- ❑ Wooded
- ❑ Dune
- ❑ Fruit Trees
- ❑ Level
- ❑ Pasture
- ❑ Sloped
- ❑ Terraces

View (4)
- ❑ Bay
- ❑ City
- ❑ Jetty
- ❑ Mountain
- ❑ Partial
- ❑ Sound
- ❑ See Remarks
- ❑ Canal
- ❑ Golf Course
- ❑ Lake
- ❑ Ocean
- ❑ River
- ❑ Territorial

Lot Details (4)
- ❑ Alley
- ❑ Cul-de-sac
- ❑ Dead End Street
- ❑ High Voltage Line
- ❑ Private
- ❑ Corner Lot
- ❑ Curbs
- ❑ Open Space
- ❑ Paved Street
- ❑ Sidewalk

Waterfront (4)
- ❑ Bank-High
- ❑ Bank-Medium
- ❑ Bulkhead
- ❑ Beach Rights
- ❑ Creek
- ❑ Lake
- ❑ River
- ❑ Bank-Low
- ❑ No Bank
- ❑ Bay
- ❑ Canal
- ❑ Jetty
- ❑ Ocean
- ❑ Sound

Site Features (10)
- ❑ Arena-Indoor
- ❑ Athletic Court
- ❑ Boat House
- ❑ Cable TV
- ❑ Disabled Access
- ❑ Dog Run
- ❑ Fenced-Partially
- ❑ Gated Entry
- ❑ Hot Tub/Spa
- ❑ Patio
- ❑ RV Parking
- ❑ Sprinkler System
- ❑ Arena-Outdoor
- ❑ Barn
- ❑ Cabana/Gazebo
- ❑ Deck
- ❑ Dock
- ❑ Fenced-Fully
- ❑ Gas Available
- ❑ Green House
- ❑ Outbuildings
- ❑ Propane
- ❑ Shop
- ❑ Stable

Pool (1)
- ❑ Above Ground
- ❑ Community
- ❑ Indoor
- ❑ In-Ground

BUILDING INFORMATION

• **Sewer** (2)
- ❑ Sewer Connected
- ❑ Septic
- ❑ Sewer Available

Basement (2)
- ❑ Daylight
- ❑ Partially Finished
- ❑ Unfinished
- ❑ Fully Finished
- ❑ Roughed In
- ❑ None

• **Parking Type** (4)
- ❑ Carport-Attached
- ❑ Garage-Attached
- ❑ None
- ❑ Carport-Detached
- ❑ Garage-Detached

• **Total Covered Parking**

Approved for # of Bedrooms (septic)

Builder

New Constructions   U=Under Construction, P=Presale, C=Completed

• **STYLE Code**

• **Building Information**
- ❑ Additional Dwelling
- ❑ PUD
- ❑ Stick Built On Lot
- ❑ Manufactured Home
- ❑ Stick Built Off Site
- ❑ Zero Lot Line

Manufactured Home Serial No.

Manufactured Home Manufacturer

Manufactured Home Model Name

Foundation (2)
- ❑ Concrete Block
- ❑ Post & Block
- ❑ Poured Concrete
- ❑ Tie Down
- ❑ Concrete Ribbon
- ❑ Post & Pillar
- ❑ Slab
- ❑ See Remarks

Building Condition (1)
- ❑ Average
- ❑ Fair
- ❑ Fixer
- ❑ Good
- ❑ Remodeled
- ❑ Restored
- ❑ Under Construction
- ❑ Very Good

• **Roof** (2)
- ❑ Built-up
- ❑ Composition
- ❑ Metal
- ❑ Torch Down
- ❑ Cedar Shake
- ❑ Flat
- ❑ Tile
- ❑ See Remarks

• **Exterior** (2)
- ❑ Brick
- ❑ Log
- ❑ Stone
- ❑ Wood
- ❑ See Remarks
- ❑ Cement/Concrete
- ❑ Metal/Vinyl
- ❑ Stucco
- ❑ Wood Products

Architecture (1)
- ❑ Cabin
- ❑ Cape Cod
- ❑ Colonial
- ❑ Contemporary
- ❑ Craftsman
- ❑ Spanish/SW
- ❑ Tudor
- ❑ Victorian
- ❑ See Remarks

INTERIOR FEATURES

(Approximate Square Footage Excluding Garage)

Finished   **Unfinished**

Square Footage Source

Leased Equipment

Water Heater (Type/Location)

• **Energy Source** (4)
- ❑ Electric
- ❑ Oil
- ❑ Propane
- ❑ See Remarks
- ❑ Natural Gas
- ❑ Pellet
- ❑ Wood

• **Heating/Cooling** (4)
- ❑ Baseboard
- ❑ Heat Pump
- ❑ Radiant
- ❑ Stove/Free Stdg
- ❑ Forced Air
- ❑ Insert
- ❑ Radiator
- ❑ Wall

Floor Covering (4)
- ❑ Ceramic Tile
- ❑ Fir/Softwood
- ❑ Slate
- ❑ Wall to Wall Carpet
- ❑ Concrete
- ❑ Hardwood
- ❑ Vinyl
- ❑ See Remarks

Interior Features (10)
- ❑ Bath Off Master
- ❑ Ceiling Fan(s)
- ❑ Disabled Access
- ❑ Fireplace in Master BR
- ❑ Hot Tub/Spa
- ❑ Jetted Tub
- ❑ Sauna
- ❑ Skylights
- ❑ Vaulted Ceilings
- ❑ Wet Bar
- ❑ 2nd Kitchen
- ❑ Built-in Vacuum
- ❑ Dining Room
- ❑ Dble Pane/Strm Wind
- ❑ High Tech Cabling
- ❑ Intercom
- ❑ Pantry
- ❑ Security System
- ❑ Solarium/Artrium
- ❑ Walk-in Closet
- ❑ Wired for Generator

Appliances That Stay (10)
- ❑ Dishwasher
- ❑ Dryer
- ❑ Microwave
- ❑ Refrigerator
- ❑ Washer
- ❑ Double Oven
- ❑ Garbage Disposal
- ❑ Range/Oven
- ❑ Trash Compactor
- ❑ See Remarks

Total Number of Fireplaces

No. of Full Bathrooms (1.0)

No. of ¾ Bathrooms (.75)

No. of ½ Bathrooms (.5)

ROOM LOCATION

Level (1) U for Upper M for Main L for Lower
S for Split G for Garage

Entry	U	M	L	S
Living Room	U	M	L	
Dining Room	U	M	L	
Kitchen w/Eating Space	U	M	L	
Kitchen	U	M	L	
Master Bedroom	U	M	L	
Bonus Room	U	M	L	
Den/Office	U	M	L	
Family Room	U	M	L	
Rec Room	U	M	L	
Extra Fin. Room	U	M	L	G

No. of Bedrooms   U___ M___ L___
No. of Full Baths   U___ M___ L___ G___
No. of ¾ Baths   U___ M___ L___ G___
No. of ½ Baths   U___ M___ L___ G___
No. of Fireplaces   U___ M___ L___
Utility Rooms   U___ M___ L___ G___
Approved Accessory Dwelling Unit   U___ M___ L___

UTILITY / SCHOOL

• **Water Source** (2)
- ❑ Community
- ❑ Private
- ❑ Shared Well
- ❑ See Remarks
- ❑ Individual Well
- ❑ Public
- ❑ Shares

Water Company

Power Company

Sewer Company

Elementary School

Junior High/Middle School

Senior High School

Bus Line Nearby Y/N ☐

INITIALS: _____ _____ _____
              Seller   Date   Seller   Date   Agent   Date

seller. As a result of this authorization, if the agent were to misappropriate the deposit, the seller rather than the buyer would suffer the loss. Without this authorization, the agent would be accepting the earnest money on behalf of the buyer, and any misappropriation would be the buyer's loss.

Listing Period. The listing agreement form usually provides that the listing period begins on the date that the agreement is executed and lasts until a specific termination date chosen by the parties. Many listing forms also provide that if the seller signs a purchase and sale agreement, the listing period is extended to the date set for closing the sale. There may also be an automatic extension for an additional period in case the sale fails to close by the established closing date.

Multiple Listing Provision. A multiple listing service (MLS) is a regional cooperative made up of licensed brokers who exchange information about their exclusive listings to increase exposure of the properties to the public. Listings are circulated (usually in a regular publication) to all members of the association. Any member may try to secure buyers for any of the listed properties. The listing agreement forms used by an MLS include a provision authorizing the broker to submit the listing to the MLS for publication.

The members of the listing broker's multiple listing service are typically considered "cooperating agents" and may act as the agent of the buyer, the agent of the seller, or in some other capacity as agreed to by the parties. The MLS provision in a listing agreement form generally includes a clause that makes this clear. In whatever capacity the cooperating broker is acting, he or she will ordinarily be entitled to receive the selling office's share of the commission. (See Chapter 7 for further discussion of cooperating agents.)

MLS forms include a disclaimer provision stating that the information given in the listing is not confidential and will be available to third parties, and that the MLS is not a party to the listing contract. An MLS assumes no responsibility with respect to particular transactions beyond gathering and circulating information about the properties. It assumes no responsibility for verifying that the information is accurate.

Agency Disclosure. Listing agreement forms often include an agency disclosure provision, as part of the broker's compliance with Washington's agency disclosure law. In this provision, the seller authorizes the broker to appoint the listing salesperson to act as a subagent of the seller. The provision also states that other salespersons affiliated with the broker do not represent the seller, and may represent the buyer. If another salesperson who works for the broker finds the buyer, then the broker will be a dual agent. By signing a listing agreement containing this provision, the seller consents to such a dual agency.

Access and Keyboxes. A listing form typically provides that the agent will have access to the property at reasonable times, so that he or she can show it to prospective buyers.

Multiple listing services often use keyboxes to facilitate access to listed properties when the owners are not home. MLS listing forms usually include a provision authorizing the installation of a keybox on the property and permitting MLS agents to enter and show the home. The form may also provide that a master key may be given to affiliated third parties, such as appraisers or inspectors. The form will also have a disclaimer of liability on the part of the MLS or the agents for any loss or damage to the seller's property—the listed home itself and personal property on the premises.

Commission. The percentage or amount of the broker's commission for a given transaction is set in the listing agreement, not by law. Commissions must be negotiable between the seller and the broker; it is a violation of antitrust laws for brokers to set uniform commission rates. (See Chapter 17 for a discussion of antitrust laws and how they affect licensees.) So an amount or percentage can't be preprinted on the listing agreement form; instead, there is a blank to be filled in when the form is executed for a particular transaction.

Beyond setting the commission amount or rate, the listing agreement should spell out how and when the broker earns the commission. An exclusive right to sell listing form typically provides that the broker will earn a commission if any of the following events occur:

1. During the listing period, the broker (or another agent in the MLS) secures a buyer who is willing to buy on the exact terms specified by the seller in the listing agreement or on other terms acceptable to the seller (i.e., a ready, willing, and able buyer).
2. The seller sells, exchanges, or enters into a contract to sell or exchange the property during the term of the listing agreement.
3. The seller sells the property within a certain period (e.g., six months) after the expiration date of the listing agreement, to anyone who first became aware of the property through any advertising or other marketing activities of the broker (or other agents in the MLS).

Extender Clause. The third condition listed above is an example of an extender clause (sometimes called a "safety" or "carryover" clause). It is intended to prevent the seller from delaying acceptance of a buyer's offer until after the listing expires in order to avoid paying a commission.

Most listing agreements contain an extender clause, but the specific terms differ. For example, sometimes the obligation to pay a commission after the listing has expired is only triggered when the property is sold to a buyer that the agent actually negotiated with during the listing period. Or the clause may be broader, obligating the seller to pay a commission if the property is sold within the extension period to anyone who first learned about it in any way that could be traced to the listing broker or an MLS agent. Under such a broad provision, the seller could become liable for a commission unwittingly, since it can be very difficult for a seller to know the names of all potential buyers who were exposed to the property during the listing period.

Sometimes if a property fails to sell during the listing period, the seller then lists it with a second broker. In that case, it's possible for the seller to become liable for a commission to two different brokers. If the sale occurs during the first listing's extension period and the buyer was exposed to the property during the first listing period, the first broker is entitled to a commission under the extender clause, and the second broker becomes entitled to a commission under the terms of the second listing. If both brokers are members of the same MLS, it is common (but not mandatory) for them to agree to split one commission rather than make the seller pay twice.

Often extender clauses include safeguards for the seller. The listing broker may be required to give the seller a list of the potential buyers he or she negotiated with during the listing period. Or the extender clause might state that a commission will not be due if the property is listed with another real estate broker during the extension period, protecting the seller from becoming liable for two commissions.

Rental or Option by the Seller. Under the terms of many listing forms, the seller agrees not to lease the property, grant an option, or enter into any other agreement that might interfere with the marketing or sale of the property. If the seller breaches this agreement, he or she will be liable to the broker for the full commission.

The form may also state that the listing agent is not obligated to submit any offers to the seller other than offers for immediate purchase, so that offers to lease the property or requests for an option to purchase need not be relayed to the seller.

Property Description. A listing agreement should include a full and accurate description of the property—preferably a correct legal description. The agent filling out the form might ask to see the seller's deed and copy the description from that document. If it is something more than a lot and block description, the agent should attach a separate sheet with the full description as an exhibit to the listing agreement, writing "See attached" or "See Exhibit A" in the space provided for a description on the form. When the description is long and complicated, it's often better to photocopy it rather than writing or typing it.

It is useful to include the property's street address on the listing form, but as a general rule the address alone is not a sufficient description for an enforceable listing agreement. Land descriptions are discussed in Chapter 1.

Closing Costs. The listing agreement form is likely to provide that the seller will pay for the buyer's title insurance policy and certain other closing costs, such as the excise tax and half of the escrow fee. Keep in mind that these provisions in the listing agreement do not create any obligation toward potential buyers. These are promises that the seller makes to his or her broker, and failure to fulfill them can lead only to liability for the broker's commission, not to liability toward a buyer.

Seller's Warranties. Most listing forms include some warranties by the seller, which allow the broker to rely on certain information the seller provides. Most fundamentally, the seller warrants that he or she has the right to sell the property on the stated terms. The seller also warrants the accuracy of the property information that is made part of the listing agreement (see the discussion of the listing input sheet, below).

The listing agreement form may include additional warranties; for example, the seller may warrant that there are no encroachments, or that the property conforms to applicable zoning regulations.

The listing agreement form usually states that the seller takes responsibility for the information given and will indemnify the broker against any losses caused by errors or omissions. This statement is called a "hold harmless agreement."

Seller Disclosure Statement. A listing form may include a provision concerning the seller disclosure statement (also called a transfer disclosure statement) that Washington law requires a seller in a residential transaction to give to the buyer upon the execution of a purchase and sale agreement (see Chapter 9). Such a provision in the listing usually states that the seller will give the listing agent a completed and signed disclosure statement, unless the transaction is exempt from the disclosure law.

Although the law doesn't require the seller to give the buyer a disclosure statement until a purchase and sale agreement is signed, this provision in the listing obligates the seller to fill out a disclosure statement and give it to the listing agent as soon as possible. This makes it possible for the listing agent to learn about any potential problems with the property early on in the selling process.

The listing provision typically also states that the seller will take full responsibility for the information given in the disclosure statement. The seller agrees to defend the broker against any claims based on any inaccuracies in the statement.

Attorneys' Fees. Many listing agreement forms provide that if either party has to resort to a lawsuit to enforce the contract and wins the suit, his or her attorneys' fees must be paid by the other party.

Signatures. The listing agreement form is signed by both parties, the listing broker and the seller. If the form is prepared by one of the broker's salespersons, the salesperson should write the broker's name on the line labeled "Broker (Company)," and then sign his or her own name on the "By" line underneath.

If the property is owned by more than one person, all co-owners should sign the listing agreement. If a seller is married, the seller's spouse should sign the document as well as the seller.

Listing Information. The listing forms used by multiple listing services include a page for information about the property, such as the NWMLS "Listing Input Sheet" shown in Figure 8.2. The purpose of a listing input sheet is to generate detailed information about the property and the listing that will be distributed in the MLS publications. Much of the information is coded to make computer input easier.

All of the following information is generally required on a listing input sheet:

- the property address,
- the location on a coded map,
- the architectural style of the home,
- the listing price,
- identification of the listing agent,
- the expiration date of the listing,
- the age of the home,
- the number of bedrooms,
- the number of baths,
- the county tax ID number,
- the commission split,
- the name of the occupant, and
- the name, address, and phone number of the owner.

The rest of the input sheet has spaces to fill in or boxes to check to describe a wide variety of property features and amenities. There is also a place for information about existing encumbrances and property taxes.

Receipt of Copy. Real estate licensees are required to give a copy of any document they prepare to the parties at the time of signature. So a listing agreement form may include the seller's acknowledgment of receipt of a copy of the agreement.

Receipt of Agency Pamphlet. When the parties enter into a listing agreement, the agent is legally obligated to provide the seller with a pamphlet on Washington's real estate agency law (see Chapter 7). Many listing agreements include a provision in which the seller acknowledges the receipt of this pamphlet.

Chapter Summary

1. The listing agreement is an employment contract between the seller and the real estate broker. The seller agrees to pay the broker a stated commission if a ready, willing, and able buyer is found during the listing period.

2. The three basic types of listing agreements are the open listing, the exclusive agency listing, and the exclusive right to sell listing. The type of listing determines the circumstances under which the broker is entitled to be paid a commission.

3. A written listing agreement is an enforceable contract if it adequately identifies the property to be sold, includes a promise to pay a fixed compensation to the broker, and is signed by the seller.

4. The listing agreement should also state the terms of sale the seller will accept, the conditions under which the commission would be paid, the duration of the contract, and the seller's warranties regarding the accuracy of the information provided about the property.

5. A multiple listing service is a cooperative association of licensed brokers who exchange information about their exclusive listings and help sell property listed by other members.

6. An extender clause provides that the seller will be liable for the broker's commission if the property is sold during a certain period after the listing expires to a buyer the broker dealt with during the listing period.

🔑 Key Terms

Open listing—A non-exclusive listing under which the broker earns a commission only if he or she is the procuring cause of the sale.

Procuring cause—The person who directly or indirectly brings about a sale.

Exclusive agency listing—A listing under which the broker is entitled to a commission if any agent sells the property, but the owner may sell the property directly without being obligated to pay a commission.

Exclusive right to sell listing—A listing under which the owner must pay the broker a commission on the sale of the property, no matter who was the procuring cause.

Multiple listing service—A regional cooperative of brokers who exchange listing information and help market the listings of other members.

Net listing—A listing in which the commission is any amount received from the sale over and above the "net" required by the seller. (Net listings are not enforceable in Washington.)

Extender clause—A provision in a listing agreement that obligates the seller to pay a commission if the property is sold within a certain period after the listing expires to someone the broker introduced to the property during the listing period. Also called a safety clause or carryover clause.

🔾🔾 Chapter Quiz

1. The type of listing that provides for payment of a commission to the listing broker regardless of who sells the property is:

    a) an open listing
    b) an exclusive agency listing
    c) an exclusive right to sell listing
    d) a net listing

2. The type of listing that provides for the payment of a commission to the listing broker only if he or she was the procuring cause of the sale is:

    a) an open listing
    b) an exclusive agency listing
    c) an exclusive right to sell listing
    d) a net listing

3. A type of listing that provides for the payment of a commission that consists of any proceeds from the sale over a specified amount is:

    a) an open listing
    b) an exclusive agency listing
    c) an exclusive right to sell listing
    d) a net listing

4. Net listings are:

    a) unenforceable in Washington
    b) legal, but discouraged in Washington
    c) valid and enforceable in Washington
    d) valid in Washington unless used in conjunction with an open listing

5. A type of listing that provides for the payment of a commission to the listing broker if anyone other than the seller finds the buyer is:

    a) an open listing
    b) an exclusive agency listing
    c) an exclusive right to sell listing
    d) a net listing

6. The listing broker has negotiated an offer from a ready, willing, and able buyer that matches the seller's terms of sale set forth in the listing agreement. Which of the following is true?

    a) The seller is required to accept the offer and pay the listing broker a commission
    b) The seller is required to accept the offer, but not required to pay the listing broker a commission
    c) The listing broker has earned the commission, whether or not the seller accepts the offer
    d) The listing broker has not earned the commission unless this is an exclusive agency listing

7. Which of these is a basic requirement for an enforceable listing agreement in Washington?

    a) A promise to compensate the broker
    b) A multiple listing provision
    c) An extender clause
    d) A warranty that the seller owns the property

8. An extender clause provides that:

    a) the broker is entitled to a commission whether or not the broker is the procuring cause
    b) the buyer must share the cost of the broker's commission
    c) the seller warrants the safety of the premises
    d) the broker is entitled to a commission if the property is sold after the listing expires to someone the broker previously showed the house to

9. Matthews, a property owner, entered into an exclusive right to sell listing agreement with Broker Ferris. Ferris negotiated a sale between Matthews and Buyer Swanson. Both Matthews and Swanson signed a purchase and sale agreement. Two weeks later, Matthews and Swanson mutually agreed to cancel the sale agreement. Under the circumstances:

a) Matthews must still pay Ferris the full sales commission
b) Matthews owes Ferris half of the sales commission
c) Swanson owes Ferris the full sales commission
d) Ferris is not entitled to a commission, because the sale did not close

10. Under an exclusive right to sell listing, the listing broker:

a) has the authority to accept an offer on the seller's behalf
b) is authorized to reject offers that do not meet the seller's stated terms
c) will earn the sales commission only if someone other than the owner procures a buyer
d) has the exclusive right to submit offers to purchase to the seller

11. A multiple listing provision in a listing agreement generally:

a) makes other members of the MLS cooperating agents
b) authorizes the listing broker to submit the listing to the MLS for publication
c) includes a disclaimer provision that states that the MLS is not a party to the listing agreement
d) All of the above

12. Which of these types of listings is considered to be a unilateral contract?

a) Open listing
b) Exclusive agency listing
c) Exclusive right to sell listing
d) Net listing

13. Under the terms of most listings, the seller will owe the broker the commission even if:

a) the seller turns down a reasonable offer for less than the listing price
b) the prospective buyer is not ready, willing, and able
c) the sale fails to close because the seller's title is not marketable
d) the broker terminates the agreement

14. Under the terms of an exclusive listing agreement, the broker is:

a) under no obligation to make an effort to find a buyer
b) required to find at least three ready, willing, and able buyers during the listing period
c) obligated to market the property and make a diligent effort to find a buyer
d) None of the above

15. In the listing agreement, the seller agrees to pay certain closing costs. This creates a legal obligation to:

a) the buyer only
b) the broker only
c) both the buyer and the broker
d) neither the buyer nor the broker

Answer Key

1. c) The exclusive right to sell obligates the seller to pay the listing broker a commission if the property sells during the listing period, regardless of who brings about the sale.

2. a) An open listing obligates the seller to pay a commission to the listing broker only if the broker was the procuring cause of the sale.

3. d) A net listing is a way of determining the amount of the commission, rather than the circumstances under which a commission is owed.

4. a) Net listings are unenforceable contracts in Washington.

5. b) An exclusive agency listing obligates the seller to pay the listing broker a commission if any agent (anyone other than the seller) sells the property.

6. c) When the broker presents an offer that matches the seller's terms of sale, the broker has earned the commission whether or not the seller accepts the offer. The seller is under no obligation to accept the offer.

7. a) In Washington, a listing agreement is not enforceable unless it includes a promise to pay the broker a fixed compensation, adequately identifies the property, and is signed by the seller.

8. d) An extender clause entitles the broker to a commission if the property is sold within a certain time after the listing expires to someone he or she introduced to the property or negotiated with during the listing period.

9. a) Because the parties voluntarily backed out of the transaction, Ferris is still legally entitled to collect a full commission from Matthews.

10. d) The listing broker under an exclusive right to sell listing has the exclusive right to submit offers to the seller.

11. d) A multiple listing provision typically makes all other MLS members cooperating agents, authorizes the listing broker to submit the listing to the MLS for publication, and states that the MLS is not a party to the contract.

12. a) An open listing is considered to be a unilateral contract, because only the seller promises performance.

13. c) The seller owes the broker a commission even when a transaction fails to close, if the failure was the seller's fault. This rule applies in the situation described in the question, where the seller's title turns out to be unmarketable.

14. c) Unlike an open listing, an exclusive listing obligates the broker to make a diligent effort to find a buyer for the property.

15. b) The listing agreement is a contract between the seller and the broker; it does not create any legal obligations to prospective buyers.

Purchase and Sale Agreements

Chapter Overview

Most real estate sales are initiated by a written contract between the buyer and the seller, who agree on a price and the other terms of sale. The contract between the buyer and the seller of real property is the purchase and sale agreement, which may also be called an earnest money agreement or a deposit receipt. This chapter will describe the purpose and effect of a purchase and sale agreement, preparation of the agreement, the elements required to make it a binding contract, and the operation of contingency clauses. The final section of the chapter covers laws requiring certain information to be disclosed when property is sold, including Washington's seller disclosure law and the federal law concerning lead-based paint.

Purpose and Effect of a Purchase and Sale Agreement

The contract between a buyer and a seller to purchase and sell real property is more than a preliminary agreement. If it contains the necessary elements and is properly executed, the parties are legally bound by all of the terms of the agreement. Neither may change or add any terms without the written consent of the other, and neither may withdraw from the transaction without legal consequences. In fact, the whole purpose of a purchase and sale agreement is to hold the buyer and the seller to the original terms of their agreement until the transaction is ready to close.

To be a valid and enforceable contract, the purchase and sale agreement must be created by offer and acceptance and supported by consideration (see Chapter 6). In most cases, the buyer is the offeror, offering to buy the seller's property on specific terms. The buyer usually makes an **earnest money deposit** at the same time the offer is submitted, to show the seller that he or she is in earnest about the purchase. The buyer's written offer is set forth on a purchase and sale agreement form, which the buyer signs before it is presented to the seller. The same form serves as the buyer's receipt for the deposit. If the seller decides to accept the buyer's offer, he or she also signs the form, and it becomes a binding contract. The mutual promises of the parties (the promise to buy and the promise to sell) are the consideration supporting the contract.

The basic requirements for a valid purchase and sale agreement are relatively simple. The agreement must identify the parties and the property, state the price and method of payment, and state the time for delivery of title and possession. Despite this basic simplicity, most purchase and sale agreements are quite detailed. It is important that the agreement between the parties be stated clearly and accurately; anything that isn't made absolutely clear at the outset can give rise to a dispute later on, and may prevent the transaction from closing.

In practical terms, the buyer and seller need a document that preserves their agreement while other matters are attended to that enable the sale to close. For instance, most buyers do not have the cash necessary to close the sale, so they have to arrange to borrow all or part of the money for the purchase. The buyer also needs to make sure that the seller actually owns the property (through a title search), and may want to arrange for a physical inspection of the property. There might be liens or other encumbrances that need to be dealt with, and the seller may be required to repair the property to satisfy the requirements of the buyer's lender.

All of these things cost time and money. And neither party wants to spend time or money without the assurance that the original agreement is still in effect. Since the purchase and sale agreement is a valid contract, it protects both parties by providing legal recourse if one fails to perform. Either party could file a lawsuit for specific performance, asking the court to order the other party to complete his or her side of the bargain. Alternatively, the court could award monetary damages, compensating one party for losses resulting from the other party's breach of contract.

Who May Prepare a Purchase and Sale Agreement

It is legal—though often unwise—for the parties to an agreement to write their own contract. But when someone who is not a party draws up a contract on behalf of the parties, that is considered to be the practice of law. As a general rule, only a licensed attorney at law is allowed to write a contract for others.

However, there is a limited exception to that rule for purchase and sale agreements. A real estate agent is allowed to prepare routine purchase and sale agreements using standard printed forms. The provisions of these contract forms were originally written and approved by attorneys with expertise in real estate law.

In the typical residential real estate transaction, the real estate agent fills in the blanks of a standard purchase and sale agreement form and obtains the signatures of the parties. In filling out the form, the agent is held to the same standard of care that is demanded of an attorney. An agent who prepared a purchase and sale agreement improperly could be held liable for any damages caused to either party.

Real estate agents run into trouble when they go beyond merely filling in the blanks. Sometimes an agent writes a special clause to insert into the preprinted form to meet an unusual situation. Or an agent might give the parties his or her opinion of the meaning or effect of provisions in the document. Actions like these go beyond what the law typically allows real estate agents to do and may constitute the unauthorized practice of law. The unauthorized practice of law is a criminal offense, and a real estate agent can be prosecuted even if he or she gave accurate legal advice. It is also grounds for suspension or revocation of the agent's real estate license (see Chapter 17).

A real estate agent may only fill out forms in connection with a transaction actually being handled by that agent. And an agent is not allowed to charge a separate fee (in addition to the brokerage commission) for completing the forms.

Example: Suppose Broker Dahl is involved in a complicated commercial real estate transaction. He is confused by some of the paperwork, so he gets Broker Merrick (a friend of his) to fill out the purchase and sale agreement. Merrick charges the client a separate fee for her work. This is the unauthorized practice of law, because Merrick filled out forms for a transaction that she was not handling and accepted separate compensation for her work.

Available Forms and Guidance

In Washington and most other states, there is no single purchase and sale agreement form that all real estate agents use. A variety of forms are available from multiple listing services, other professional organizations, and legal form publishers. A residential purchase and sale agreement form from the Northwest Multiple Listing Service (NWMLS) is shown in Figure 9.1 as an example.

The organizations that provide forms sometimes offer line-by-line guidance for filling in each provision. A real estate agent should read any explanatory materials provided and obtain advice for any aspects of the form that he or she does not understand. Relying on advice from professional sources helps ensure that the agent will meet the required standard of care.

Here are two basic precautions to take when filling out a purchase and sale agreement:

- A form must be used only for the purpose intended. For instance, the NWMLS purchase and sale agreement form shown here is intended for residential sales only. It shouldn't be used for anything else.

- Forms should always be filled in completely. If an entry is not applicable to a given transaction, the agent should write in "N/A," rather than leaving the space blank. All boxes should be checked where appropriate.

Elements of a Purchase and Sale Agreement

As explained in Chapter 6, the statute of frauds requires every real estate purchase and sale agreement to be in writing. An enforceable purchase and sale agreement generally must contain all of the following elements:

- identification of the parties,
- an adequate description of the property,
- the total price and method of payment,
- the closing date,
- the date of possession,
- the type of deed and condition of title,
- liens or other encumbrances the buyer will take title subject to, and
- any conditions or contingencies (such as a financing contingency).

We will look at several of these elements more closely, and then discuss contingency clauses in detail, since they play a crucial role in many real estate transactions.

The Parties

Of course, the parties to the purchase and sale agreement are the buyer and the seller. When preparing a purchase and sale agreement, there are two key questions to ask about the parties. First, does everyone who is signing have the capacity to contract? If any of the parties is underage or mentally incompetent, the purchase and sale agreement—like any contract—will be voidable or void. (See Chapter 6.)

Fig. 9.1 Purchase and sale agreement

NWMLS Form 21
Residential Purchase & Sale Agreement
Revised 03/03
Page 1 of 4

©Copyright 2003
Northwest Multiple Listing Service
ALL RIGHTS RESERVED

RESIDENTIAL REAL ESTATE PURCHASE AND SALE AGREEMENT
SPECIFIC TERMS

1. **Date:** _____ , _____   **MLS No.:** _____

2. **Buyer:** _____

3. **Seller:** _____

4. **Property:** Tax Parcel Nos.: _____ (_____ County)
    Street Address: _____ Washington _____
    Included Items: ☐ stove/range ☐ refrigerator ☐ washer ☐ dryer ☐ dishwasher ☐ hot tub ☐ fireplace insert
    ☐ wood stove ☐ satellite dish ☐ security system ☐ other _____
    Legal Description:

5. **Purchase Price:** _____

6. **Earnest Money:** (To be held by ☐ Selling Broker ☐ Closing Agent)
    Personal Check: _____
    Note: _____
    Other (_____): _____

7. **Default:** (check only one) ☐ Forfeiture of Earnest Money ☐ Seller's Election of Remedies

8. **Title Insurance Company:** _____

9. **Closing Agent:** ☐ a qualified closing agent of Buyer's choice ☐ _____

10. **Closing Date:** _____

11. **Possession Date:** ☐ on Closing ☐ _____ calendar days after Closing ☐ _____

12. **Offer Expiration Date:** _____

13. **Counteroffer Expiration Date:** _____

14. **Addenda:** _____

    Inspection Addendum: ☐ NWMLS 35A ☐ NWMLS 35B ☐ Other ☐ None

15. **Agency Disclosure:** Selling Licensee represents ☐ Buyer ☐ Seller ☐ both parties ☐ neither party
    Listing Agent represents ☐ Seller ☐ both parties

16. **Services of Closing Agent for Payment of Utilities:** ☐ Requested (Attach NWMLS Form 22K) ☐ Waived

Buyer's Signature Date	Seller's Signature Date
Buyer's Signature Date	Seller's Signature Date
Buyer's Address	Seller's Address
City, State, Zip	City, State, Zip
Phone Fax	Phone Fax
Buyer's E-mail Address	Seller's E-mail Address
Selling Broker MLS Office No.	Listing Broker MLS Office No.
Selling Licensee (Print)	Listing Agent (Print)
Phone Fax	Phone Fax

Reprinted with permission, Northwest Multiple Listing Service. No endorsement implied.

NWMLS Form 21
Residential Purchase & Sale Agreement
Revised 03/03
Page 2 of 4

RESIDENTIAL REAL ESTATE PURCHASE AND SALE AGREEMENT
GENERAL TERMS
(continued)

a. **Purchase Price.** Buyer agrees to pay to Seller the Purchase Price, including the Earnest Money, in cash at Closing, unless otherwise specified in this Agreement. Buyer represents that Buyer has sufficient funds to close this sale in accordance with this Agreement and is not relying on any contingent source of funds or gifts, except to the extent otherwise specified in this Agreement.

b. **Earnest Money.** Buyer agrees to deliver the Earnest Money within 2 days after mutual acceptance of this Agreement to Selling Licensee who will deposit any check to be held by Selling Broker, or deliver any Earnest Money to be held by Closing Agent, within 3 days of receipt or mutual acceptance, whichever occurs later. If the Earnest Money is held by Selling Broker and is over $10,000.00 it shall be deposited into an interest bearing trust account in Selling Broker's name provided that Buyer completes an IRS Form W-9. Interest, if any, after deduction of bank charges and fees, will be paid to Buyer. Buyer agrees to reimburse Selling Broker for bank charges and fees in excess of the interest earned, if any. If the Earnest Money held by Selling Broker is over $10,000.00 Buyer has the option to require Selling Broker to deposit the Earnest Money into the Housing Trust Fund Account, with the interest paid to the State Treasurer, if both Seller and Buyer so agree in writing. If the Buyer does not complete an IRS Form W-9 before Selling Broker must deposit the Earnest Money or the Earnest Money is $10,000.00 or less, the Earnest Money shall be deposited into the Housing Trust Fund Account. Selling Broker may transfer the Earnest Money to Closing Agent at Closing. If all or part of the Earnest Money is to be refunded to Buyer and any such costs remain unpaid, the Selling Broker or Closing Agent may deduct and pay them therefrom. The parties instruct Closing Agent to: (1) provide written verification of receipt of the Earnest Money and notice of dishonor of any check to the parties and licensees at the addresses and/or fax numbers provided herein; and (2) commence an interpleader action in the Superior Court for the county in which the Property is located within 30 days of a party's demand for the Earnest Money (and deduct up to $250.00 of the costs thereof) unless the parties agree otherwise in writing.

c. **Included Items.** Any of the following items located in or on the Property are included in the sale: built-in appliances; wall-to-wall carpeting; curtains, drapes and all other window treatments; window and door screens; awnings; storm doors and windows; installed television antennas; ventilating, air conditioning and heating fixtures; trash compactor; fireplace doors, gas logs and gas log lighters; irrigation fixtures; electric garage door openers; water heaters; installed electrical fixtures; lighting fixtures; shrubs, plants and trees planted in the ground; and all bathroom and other fixtures. However, items identified in Specific Term No. 4 are included only if the corresponding box is checked. If any of the above Included Items are leased or encumbered, Seller agrees to acquire and clear title at or before Closing.

d. **Condition of Title.** Buyer and Seller authorize Selling Licensee, Listing Agent or Closing Agent to insert, attach or correct the Legal Description of the Property. Unless otherwise specified in this Agreement, title to the Property shall be marketable at Closing. The following shall not cause the title to be unmarketable: rights, reservations, covenants, conditions and restrictions, presently of record and general to the area; easements and encroachments, not materially affecting the value of or unduly interfering with Buyer's reasonable use of the Property; and reserved oil and/or mining rights. Monetary encumbrances not assumed by Buyer shall be paid by Seller on or before Closing. Title shall be conveyed by a Statutory Warranty Deed. If this Agreement is for conveyance of a buyer's interest in a Real Estate Contract, the Statutory Warranty Deed shall include a buyer's assignment of the contract sufficient to convey after acquired title.

e. **Title Insurance.** Seller authorizes Buyer's lender or Closing Agent, at Seller's expense, to apply for a standard form owner's policy of title insurance, with homeowner's additional protection and inflation protection endorsements if available at no additional cost, from the Title Insurance Company. The Title Insurance Company is to send a copy of the preliminary commitment to both Listing Agent and Selling Licensee. The preliminary commitment, and the title policy to be issued, shall contain no exceptions other than the General Exclusions and Exceptions in said standard form and Special Exceptions consistent with the Condition of Title herein provided. If title cannot be made so insurable prior to the Closing Date, then as Buyer's sole and exclusive remedy, the Earnest Money shall, unless Buyer elects to waive such defects or encumbrances, be refunded to the Buyer, less any unpaid costs described in this Agreement, and this Agreement shall thereupon be terminated. Buyer shall have no right to specific performance or damages as a consequence of Seller's inability to provide insurable title.

f. **Closing.** This sale shall be closed by the Closing Agent on the Closing Date. If the Closing Date falls on a Saturday, Sunday, or legal holiday as defined in RCW 1.16.050, the Closing Agent shall close the transaction on the next day that is not a Saturday, Sunday, or legal holiday. "Closing" means the date on which all documents are recorded and the sale proceeds are available to Seller. Seller shall deliver keys to Buyer on the Closing Date or on the Possession Date, whichever occurs first.

Initials: BUYER: _____ DATE: _____ SELLER: _____ DATE: _____

BUYER: _____ DATE: _____ SELLER: _____ DATE: _____

NWMLS Form 21
Residential Purchase & Sale Agreement
Revised 03/03
Page 3 of 4

©Copyright 2003
Northwest Multiple Listing Service
ALL RIGHTS RESERVED

RESIDENTIAL REAL ESTATE PURCHASE AND SALE AGREEMENT
GENERAL TERMS
(continued)

g. Possession. Buyer shall be entitled to possession at 9:00 p.m. on the Possession Date. Seller agrees to maintain the 55
Property in its present condition, normal wear and tear excepted, until the Buyer is entitled to possession. 56

h. Closing Costs and Prorations. Seller and Buyer shall each pay one-half of the escrow fee unless this sale is FHA or 57
VA financed, in which case it shall be paid according to FHA or VA regulations. Taxes for the current year, rent, 58
interest, and lienable homeowner's association dues shall be prorated as of Closing. Buyer agrees to pay Buyer's loan 59
costs, including credit report, appraisal charge and lender's title insurance, unless provided otherwise in this 60
Agreement. If any payments are delinquent on encumbrances which will remain after Closing, Closing Agent is 61
instructed to pay them at Closing from money due, or to be paid by, Seller. Buyer agrees to pay for remaining fuel in 62
the fuel tank if, prior to Closing, Seller obtains a written statement as to the quantity and current price from the 63
supplier. Seller agrees to pay all utility charges, including unbilled charges. Unless waived in Specific Term No. 16, 64
Seller and Buyer request the services of Closing Agent in disbursing funds necessary to satisfy unpaid utility charges 65
in accordance with RCW 60.80 and Seller agrees to provide the names and addresses of all utilities providing service 66
to the Property and having lien rights (attach NWMLS Form 22K Identification of Utilities or equivalent). 67

i. Sale Information. The Listing Agent or Selling Licensee is authorized to report this Agreement (including price and 68
all terms) to the Multiple Listing Service that published it and to its members, financing institutions, appraisers, and 69
anyone else related to this sale. Buyer and Seller expressly authorize all lenders, financial institutions, Closing 70
Agents, appraisers, title insurance companies, and others related to this Sale, to furnish the Listing Agent and/or 71
Selling Licensee, on request, any and all information and copies of documents concerning the status, progress and 72
final disposition of financing, appraisal, Closing, title condition, and any other matter concerning this sale, including 73
buyer's credit report. In addition, Buyer shall provide any additional consent or authorization necessary to permit 74
Buyer's lender or financing institution to provide information concerning the status, progress and final disposition of 75
financing to the Listing Agent and/or Selling Licensee. 76

j. FIRPTA - Tax Withholding at Closing. The Closing Agent is instructed to prepare a certification (NWMLS Form 22E 77
or equivalent) that Seller is not a "foreign person" within the meaning of the Foreign Investment In Real Property Tax 78
Act. Seller agrees to sign this certification. If Seller is a foreign person, and this transaction is not otherwise exempt 79
from FIRPTA, Closing Agent is instructed to withhold and pay the required amount to the Internal Revenue Service. 80

k. Notices. Unless otherwise specified in this Agreement, any notice required or permitted in, or related to, this Agree- 81
ment (including revocations of offers or counteroffers) must be in writing. Notices to Seller must be signed by at least 82
one Buyer and shall be deemed given only when the notice is received by Seller, by Listing Agent or at the licensed 83
office of Listing Agent. Notices to Buyer must be signed by at least one Seller and shall be deemed given only when 84
the notice is received by Buyer, by Selling Licensee or at the licensed office of Selling Licensee. Receipt by Selling 85
Licensee of a Real Property Transfer Disclosure Statement, Disclosure of Information on Lead-Based Paint and 86
Lead-Based Paint Hazards, Public Offering Statement and/or Resale Certificate shall be deemed receipt by Buyer. 87
Selling Licensee and Listing Agent have no responsibility to advise of receipt of a notice beyond either phoning the 88
party or causing a copy of the notice to be delivered to the party's address shown on this Agreement. Buyer and 89
Seller must keep Selling Licensee and Listing Agent advised of their whereabouts in order to receive prompt 90
notification of receipt of a notice. 91

l. Computation of Time. Unless otherwise specified in this Agreement, any period of time stated in this Agreement shall 92
start on the day following the event commencing the period and shall expire at 9:00 p.m. of the last calendar day of the 93
specified period of time. Except for the Possession Date, if the last day is a Saturday, Sunday or legal holiday as 94
defined in RCW 1.16.050, the specified period of time shall expire on the next day that is not a Saturday, Sunday or 95
legal holiday. Any specified period of 5 days or less shall not include Saturdays, Sundays or legal holidays. Time is of 96
the essence of this Agreement. 97

m. Facsimile and E-mail Transmission. Facsimile transmission of any signed original document, and retransmission of 98
any signed facsimile transmission, shall be the same as delivery of an original. At the request of either party, or the 99
Closing Agent, the parties will confirm facsimile transmitted signatures by signing an original document. E-mail trans- 100
mission of any document or notice shall not be effective unless the parties to this Agreement otherwise agree in writing. 101

n. Integration. This Agreement constitutes the entire understanding between the parties and supersedes all prior or 102
contemporaneous understandings and representations. No modification of this Agreement shall be effective unless 103
agreed in writing and signed by Buyer and Seller. 104

Initials: BUYER: _____ DATE: _____ SELLER: _____ DATE: _____ 105

BUYER: _____ DATE: _____ SELLER: _____ DATE: _____ 106

NWMLS Form 21
Residential Purchase & Sale Agreement
Revised 03/03
Page 4 of 4

RESIDENTIAL REAL ESTATE PURCHASE AND SALE AGREEMENT
GENERAL TERMS
(continued)

o. Assignment. Buyer may not assign this Agreement, or Buyer's rights hereunder, without Seller's prior written consent, unless provided otherwise herein. 107 108

p. Default. In the event Buyer fails, without legal excuse, to complete the purchase of the Property, then the following provision, as identified in Specific Term No. 7, shall apply: 109 110

    i. Forfeiture of Earnest Money. That portion of the Earnest Money that does not exceed five percent (5%) of the Purchase Price shall be forfeited to the Seller as the sole and exclusive remedy available to Seller for such failure. 111 112

    ii. Seller's Election of Remedies. Seller may, at Seller's option, (a) keep the Earnest Money as liquidated damages as the sole and exclusive remedy available to Seller for such failure, (b) bring suit against Buyer for Seller's actual damages, (c) bring suit to specifically enforce this Agreement and recover any incidental damages, or (d) pursue any other rights or remedies available at law or equity. 113 114 115 116

q. Attorneys' Fees. If Buyer or Seller institutes suit against the other concerning this Agreement, the prevailing party is entitled to reasonable attorneys' fees and expenses. 117 118

r. Offer. Buyer agrees to purchase the Property under the terms and conditions of this Agreement. Seller shall have until 9:00 p.m. on the Offer Expiration Date to accept this offer, unless sooner withdrawn. Acceptance shall not be effective until a signed copy is actually received by Buyer, by Selling Licensee or at the licensed office of Selling Licensee. If this offer is not so accepted, it shall lapse and any Earnest Money shall be refunded to Buyer. 119 120 121 122

s. Counteroffer. Seller agrees to sell the Property under the terms and conditions of this Agreement. If Seller makes a counteroffer, Buyer shall have until 9:00 p.m. on the Counteroffer Expiration Date to accept the counteroffer, unless sooner withdrawn. Acceptance shall not be effective until a signed copy is actually received by Seller, by Listing Agent or at the licensed office of Listing Agent. If the counteroffer is not so accepted, it shall lapse and any Earnest Money shall be refunded to Buyer. If no expiration date is specified for a future counteroffer, the counteroffer shall expire at 9:00 p.m. on the second day after the counteroffer is signed by the last party making the counteroffer, unless sooner withdrawn. 123 124 125 126 127 128 129

t. Agency Disclosure. Selling Broker represents the same party that Selling Licensee represents. Listing Broker represents the same party that the Listing Agent represents. If Selling Licensee and Listing Agent are different salespersons affiliated with the same Broker, then both Buyer and Seller confirm their consent to that Broker representing both parties as a dual agent. If Selling Licensee and Listing Agent are the same salesperson representing both parties then both Buyer and Seller confirm their consent to that salesperson and his/her Broker representing both parties as dual agents. All parties acknowledge receipt of the pamphlet entitled "The Law of Real Estate Agency." 130 131 132 133 134 135 136

u. Commission. Seller and Buyer agree to pay a commission in accordance with any listing or commission agreement to which they are a party. The Listing Broker's commission shall be apportioned between Listing Broker and Selling Broker as specified in the listing. Seller and Buyer hereby consent to Listing Broker or Selling Broker receiving compensation from more than one party. Seller and Buyer hereby assign to Listing Broker and Selling Broker, as applicable, a portion of their funds in escrow equal to such commission(s) and irrevocably instruct the Closing Agent to disburse the commission(s) directly to the Broker(s). In any action by Listing or Selling Broker to enforce this paragraph, the prevailing party is entitled to court costs and reasonable attorneys' fees. 137 138 139 140 141 142 143

v. Cancellation Rights/Lead-Based Paint. If a residential dwelling was built on the Property prior to 1978, and Buyer receives a Disclosure of Information on Lead-Based Paint and Lead-Based Paint Hazards (NWMLS Form 22J) after mutual acceptance, Buyer may rescind this Agreement at any time up to 3 days thereafter. 144 145 146

w. Property Condition Disclaimer. Real estate brokers and salespersons do not guarantee the value, quality or condition of the Property. Some properties may contain building materials, including siding, roofing, ceiling, insulation, electrical, and plumbing materials, that have been the subject of lawsuits and/or governmental inquiry because of possible defects or health hazards. In addition, some properties may have other defects arising after construction, such as drainage, leakage, pest, rot and mold problems. Real estate licensees do not have the expertise to identify or assess defective products, materials, or conditions. Buyer is urged to retain inspectors qualified to identify the presence of defective materials and evaluate the condition of the Property. 147 148 149 150 151 152 153

Initials: BUYER: _____ DATE: _____ SELLER: _____ DATE: _____ 154

        BUYER: _____ DATE: _____ SELLER: _____ DATE: _____ 155

Second, is everyone with an ownership interest in the property signing the contract? If not, the buyer may only be able to force the sale of a partial interest in the property. In some cases, the buyer would not be able to enforce the contract at all.

Particular care should be taken with married parties. In Washington and other community property states, the law requires both husband and wife to join in any sale, encumbrance, purchase, or contract to purchase community property. Since a real estate agent is rarely in a position to know for certain whether the property is community property, the signatures of both spouses should be obtained in all transactions.

Associations as Parties. When a partnership is a party to a purchase and sale agreement, the names of all general partners (and their spouses) and the name of the partnership itself should be listed in the contract. For both partnerships and corporations, the company's address and the state in which it is organized or incorporated should also be shown.

For partnerships, corporations, and other types of business associations, the legal authority to enter into the transaction must be established. Before closing, the escrow agent (or other closing agent) will require documentation proving that the partner, corporate officer, or other representative who is signing on behalf of the association has the authority to do so. The documentation could take the form of a power of attorney or a resolution of the board of directors.

Note that even if the closing agent is specific about what documentation and signatures are required to close the transaction, that doesn't mean that those will, in fact, make the transaction legally valid. A closing agent does not give legal advice. So if there is any doubt about who needs to sign the documents, it is best to seek the advice of a lawyer.

Property Description

A purchase and sale agreement is not enforceable unless it includes an adequate description of the property, one that would be sufficient in a deed (see Chapter 1). A complete legal description should always be used. When there is insufficient space for it on the form, an exhibit containing the description should be attached to the agreement. There should be a reference to this exhibit in the space provided for the description of the property (for example, "See Exhibit A").

Price and Method of Payment

The full purchase price, including any mortgages or other liens that the buyer is assuming, should be stated in the agreement. For example, if the buyer is going to assume the seller's existing mortgage (which has a balance of $110,000) and also give the seller $25,000 in cash at closing, $135,000 should be filled in as the purchase price.

It's also important to set forth the method of payment in detail. Will the buyer be paying the full price at closing? Or will the buyer be assuming a mortgage and paying the rest of the price in cash? If so, the mortgage balance, interest rate, and monthly payment should be specified.

Or perhaps the seller will be financing all or part of the purchase, accepting a cash downpayment and a deed of trust or real estate contract for the remainder.

In that case, the interest rate and payment amount for the seller financing must be stated, and a copy of the financing document forms that the parties will be executing must be attached to the purchase and sale agreement. (For more information about financing arrangements, see Chapters 10 and 11.)

Included Items

An "Included Items" paragraph states that certain items are included in the sale unless otherwise noted in the agreement. The list usually includes carpeting, built-in appliances, window coverings, air conditioning equipment, shrubs, and so forth. Even without this provision in the agreement, many of the items listed would be considered fixtures or attachments and included in the sale (see Chapter 1), but the provision prevents disputes over this issue.

If there is an item on the list that the seller does not want to include in the sale, the real estate agent should be sure to attach an addendum to the agreement stating that the item is excluded. Similarly, if items that do not appear on the list will be included in the sale, those should be specified in an addendum.

Closing Date

The closing date is the date when the proceeds of the sale are disbursed to the seller, the deed is delivered to the buyer, and all the appropriate documents are recorded.

The purchase and sale agreement must provide a specific date for closing. A lender should be consulted and will recommend a suitable date. In setting a closing date, it is important to consider how long it will take to meet any conditions that have been set. The buyer may have to obtain a loan and sell his or her current home. The seller will have to obtain title insurance, clear any liens, and perhaps make some repairs. (These conditions are discussed in more detail later in this chapter.) The chosen closing date must allow the parties sufficient time for all these obligations and conditions to be met.

Example: The purchase and sale agreement is conditioned on the buyer obtaining a VA-guaranteed loan. A lender tells the real estate agent that it currently takes ten to twelve weeks to obtain VA loan approval, and the agent knows it normally takes four or five business days after loan approval and the satisfaction of any other conditions for the closing officer to finish the necessary work and close the transaction. Therefore, the agent should suggest a closing date no sooner than 90 days from the date the purchase and sale agreement is signed. If that date is acceptable to both parties, it should be included in the agreement.

If the closing date is approaching and an inspection report is not yet available, or it looks like some other contingency will not be satisfied in time, the parties may want to change the closing date by executing a written extension agreement. The purchase and sale agreement will terminate on the date set for closing, so it is important to get an extension agreement signed as soon as possible. Failure to extend the closing date may result in an unenforceable agreement. An extension agreement may be a special form, or simply an addendum to the purchase and sale agreement in which the parties agree to defer the closing to a later date.

Closing Agent and Closing Costs

It's a good idea for an escrow agent or other closing agent to be appointed in the purchase and sale agreement. Closing agents perform a wide variety of tasks connected with closing a real estate transaction, such as ordering inspections and title insurance, arranging for liens to be paid off and released, and preparing and recording documents on behalf of both the buyer and seller. They may also hold funds and documents in escrow for the parties, distributing them only when specified conditions have been fulfilled. (Escrow and the closing process are discussed in more detail in Chapter 13.)

The purchase and sale agreement should also state which party is responsible for paying the escrow agent's fees (typically, they are split between the parties) and various other closing costs (such as costs connected with the buyer's loan). In addition, the agreement should set forth how certain property expenses (taxes, homeowner's association dues, etc.) and income (rent from tenants) will be shared. These are ordinarily prorated as of the closing date, unless otherwise agreed (see Chapter 13).

A federal law, the Foreign Investment in Real Property Tax Act (FIRPTA), applies to some transactions in which the seller is not a U.S. citizen. FIRPTA requires the buyer or the closing agent to withhold a certain percentage of the price from the seller and then turn the money over to the Internal Revenue Service. The purchase and sale agreement may include a provision concerning compliance with this law. Note that many residential transactions are exempt from FIRPTA.

Possession

Unless the parties make other arrangements, possession of the property is usually transferred to the buyer at closing. If the buyer wants to take possession earlier, or if the seller wants a few extra days to vacate the property, that should be provided for in the purchase and sale agreement, and the parties should also execute a separate rental agreement.

The seller usually agrees that the property will be maintained in its present condition until the buyer takes possession.

Casualty Loss

Another issue that may be addressed in the purchase and sale agreement is casualty loss. For instance, what happens if the house burns down after the agreement is executed, but before closing? Unless the buyer has already taken possession of the property, the seller ordinarily bears the risk of loss until closing. So if the property is destroyed or substantially damaged before the transaction closes, the buyer is generally not required to go through with the purchase.

Seller's Representations

A purchase and sale agreement frequently contains representations or warranties from the seller concerning various aspects of the property. For example, there might be warranties concerning the property's connection to utilities and the condition of the well and septic system (if any). Many forms also contain a statement that the seller has no knowledge or notice of any violation of laws relating to the property, such as zoning or building code violations.

Conveyance and Title

Almost every purchase and sale agreement includes provisions pertaining to the conveyance of the property and the condition of title. The type of deed that the seller will execute in favor of the buyer (ordinarily a warranty deed) is specified. There is usually a clause in which the seller agrees to provide marketable title, free of undisclosed encumbrances, with a standard coverage title insurance policy. The seller also agrees to pay off at closing (if not before) any liens that the buyer is not assuming. Any unusual encumbrances that will remain after closing must be disclosed in the purchase and sale agreement.

Many agreements go into more detail about what will be considered marketable title. For example, an agreement might say that CC&Rs that apply to the entire neighborhood or subdivision will not make the title unmarketable, nor will easements that do not significantly interfere with the buyer's use of the property (an easement for underground wiring, for instance). There will be no problem if encumbrances of that type show up as exceptions on the preliminary title report. However, if the report reveals other undisclosed encumbrances (such as an access easement that would interfere with the buyer's use of the property) and the seller cannot remove them before closing, then the title will be considered unmarketable and the buyer can refuse to go through with the purchase.

Time is of the Essence

A purchase and sale agreement usually states that "Time is of the essence of this agreement." This phrase means more than that the parties hope the sale progresses as quickly as possible; it means they are legally required to meet all deadlines set in the agreement.

A contract in which time is of the essence is one in which performance on or before the exact dates specified (not just within a reasonable time thereafter) is considered one of the essential terms of the agreement. Failure to meet any of the deadlines is a breach of contract.

So when time is of the essence in a purchase and sale agreement, the closing must take place on or by the exact date set out in the agreement. It's possible for either party to waive this clause, allowing the other party to perform after the deadline. But as a general rule, meeting all deadlines is an essential part of fulfilling a purchase and sale agreement.

Default

Another issue that is addressed in a purchase and sale agreement is default. The agreement will cover the seller's remedies in the event that the buyer defaults, and what will happen to the earnest money deposit. (Usually the buyer's remedies are not specifically listed; they include the right to sue for damages or specific performance, as explained in Chapter 6.)

A purchase and sale agreement often provides that the earnest money will be treated as liquidated damages if the buyer defaults. In that case, the seller would be entitled to keep the earnest money without having to prove that he or she suffered a loss as a result of the buyer's default. But the seller would also give up the right to sue the buyer for any additional damages or for specific performance. Keeping the earnest money would be the seller's only remedy.

Under Washington law, no more than 5% of the property's sales price can be treated as liquidated damages in a purchase and sale agreement. So if the buyer's earnest money deposit was more than 5% of the price, the seller is required to return the excess to the buyer. In a residential transaction, a liquidated damages provision in the purchase and sale agreement must be initialed by the buyer and the seller, to show that they both were aware of the provision and specifically consented to it. Otherwise the provision is unenforceable, so that in the event of default the seller would be able to sue the buyer for additional damages.

Many purchase and sale agreements provide that the listing agent is entitled to half of any damages that the seller receives upon the buyer's default, up to the amount of the agreed brokerage fee. In practical terms, this usually means that the listing agent will get half of the forfeited earnest money.

A purchase and sale agreement also typically includes an attorneys' fees provision. If one of the parties must resort to a lawsuit to enforce the contract and wins the lawsuit, then the losing party is obligated to pay the winning party's attorneys' fees.

Agency Disclosure

Washington law requires a purchase and sale agreement to include an agency disclosure provision. In this provision, the real estate agents involved in the transaction specify which party each of them is representing. This information must be disclosed in writing to each party before he or she signs an offer, and the provision in the purchase and sale agreement fulfills this requirement. The parties' signatures on the agreement indicate their acceptance and understanding of the stated agency relationships.

Addenda

A paragraph that may be labeled "Addenda" or "Additional Provisions" indicates whether there are attachments to the agreement that contain additional contract provisions. There might be addenda concerning fixtures to be excluded from the sale, FHA/VA financing, inspections, and so on. In order to incorporate additional provisions into the agreement, the attachments should be listed in the space provided, and the parties must initial and date each page of the attachments.

Earnest Money Receipt

As explained earlier in the chapter, the purchase and sale agreement form also serves as the buyer's receipt for the earnest money. The agent that accepts the deposit from the buyer signs a provision in the agreement acknowledging receipt of the funds and explaining how they will be held. The agreement should also state what form the deposit takes: cash, check, or promissory note.

In most cases, the buyer gives the selling agent a check for the deposit, and the purchase and sale agreement provides that the selling agent will hold the check undeposited until the seller has accepted the buyer's offer. That makes it easy to return the deposit to the buyer if the seller rejects the offer.

If the seller accepts the offer, the selling agent may turn the check over to the closing agent for deposit in an escrow account, or else may deposit it in a broker's trust account. The procedures concerning brokers' trust accounts in Washington are explained in Chapter 17. Briefly, if the check is for $10,000 or less, it would have to be kept in a pooled trust account, with interest on the account paid to the state Housing Trust Fund. If the check is for more than $10,000, the parties may choose instead to have it deposited in a separate trust account, with the interest paid either to the buyer or to the seller, as agreed.

When a transaction falls through after the earnest money has been deposited into escrow or a broker's trust account, there may be a dispute over the earnest money; the buyer and seller may each feel entitled to it. In this situation, the escrow agent or broker who holds the funds in trust may file an **interpleader** action, turning the matter over to a court. The court will decide which party is the rightful owner of the funds.

The appropriate amount for an earnest money deposit varies according to local custom; it can be any amount that both parties agree on. Naturally, the buyer wants to make a small deposit, while the seller wants to receive a large deposit. The deposit is supposed to express the buyer's commitment to the purchase, and it should not be so small that forfeiting it would be painless. If the buyer goes through with the transaction, the deposit is ordinarily applied to the purchase price.

Signatures

Of course, space is provided at the end of the form for each party's signature. The buyer's signature turns the form into an offer to purchase, and the seller's signature turns it into a binding contract.

Offer and Acceptance. The purchase and sale agreement form provides space in which to set a deadline for acceptance of the offer; this clause often appears directly above the buyer's signature. The manner in which the seller is required to communicate acceptance may also be specified. For example, it might say the seller's acceptance is not effective until a copy of the agreement signed by the seller has been returned to the selling agent (the agent who presented the buyer's offer). If the seller fails to accept in the prescribed manner by the deadline, the offer terminates and the earnest money is returned to the buyer.

Brokerage Fee. Nearly all purchase and sale agreement forms also have a clause in which the seller agrees to pay the real estate brokers their commission. This is typically printed immediately above the space for the seller's signature. The clause is a safety net for the brokers, in case the seller never signed a listing agreement. It is a sufficient written employment contract to satisfy the statute of frauds, allowing the brokers to sue the seller for their commission.

Counteroffers

The purchase and sale agreement form may include a provision concerning counteroffers, in case the seller wants to modify the buyer's offer instead of accepting it outright. The provision may set a deadline for the buyer's acceptance of the counteroffer. Remember that a counteroffer is not an acceptance; the buyer isn't bound unless he or she accepts the seller's counteroffer.

When a seller wants to make a counteroffer, it's best to write it on another form or a separate attachment, rather than crossing out or writing over the terms on the original form. Printed counteroffer forms are available for this purpose.

Amendments

After the buyer and seller have signed the purchase and sale agreement, the terms of the contract can only be modified in writing. All parties who signed the original agreement must sign the amendment, or it will be unenforceable.

Don't confuse an amendment with an addendum. An amendment is a written modification that occurs after the parties have signed the purchase and sale agreement, while an addendum is an attachment added to the agreement prior to signature.

Contingency Clauses

Most of the time, the agreement between a buyer and a seller is conditional; in other words, it is legally binding only if certain conditions are fulfilled. These conditions are called "contingency clauses," or simply "contingencies." Most printed forms provide space for various kinds of contingencies. The most common type is a financing contingency, which makes the contract depend on the buyer's ability to obtain financing. Other common contingencies concern the sale of the buyer's present home, or the satisfactory completion of some type of inspection (e.g., structural, pest, septic tank).

If a contract contains a contingency clause, the contract will be enforceable if—and only if—that contingent event occurs. If it does not occur, the contract is terminated. When a contract terminates because a contingent event does not occur, the buyer is usually entitled to a refund of the earnest money deposit.

The parties are obligated to make a reasonable effort to fulfill the condition set forth in the contingency clause. For instance, the buyer must apply for financing, or the seller must order the required inspections. As with every contract, the parties to a purchase and sale agreement have an obligation to act in good faith; each must cooperate so that both can benefit from the contract. It is best to make this obligation of good faith explicit in the contingency clause.

A purchase and sale agreement cannot make fulfillment of a condition completely discretionary. If the buyer or the seller has complete discretion as to whether to fulfill a condition and make the contract binding, the purchase and sale agreement will be considered an "illusory contract." That is, it is not a contract at all, since one party is not obligated to perform any of his or her contractual duties.

Example: A provision in the purchase and sale agreement states that the sale of the home "is conditioned on Seller accepting a job in Portland." Since this clause gives the seller complete discretion to accept a job or not at will, the seller has control over whether a sale will take place. The buyer cannot make the seller accept a job. Any "rights" the buyer has under this agreement are, therefore, illusory.

The party who benefits from the contingency clause usually has the right to waive it. For example, a buyer could waive a pest inspection contingency. In that case the seller would be bound by the agreement whether or not the results of the pest inspection were satisfactory, or even if no pest inspection were performed.

If a real estate agent believes that fulfillment of a condition in a purchase and sale agreement may affect the date of closing, or the time that the buyer can take possession of the property, the agent should point that out to the parties.

All contingencies must be spelled out in the purchase and sale agreement or in an attached addendum that is incorporated into the agreement. If a printed form contains boxes to be checked for each of the different kinds of contingencies, the agent filling out the form must be sure that all appropriate boxes are checked.

Any contingency clause should include these four things:

1. a clear statement of exactly what the condition is and what has to be done to meet it;
2. the procedure for notifying the other party of either satisfaction or waiver of the condition;
3. a stated time by which the condition must be satisfied or waived; and
4. the rights of the parties in the event the condition is not satisfied or waived by the specified date.

As with the purchase and sale agreement itself, there are attorney-approved contingency forms that can be attached as addenda to the agreement. A real estate agent should use those forms instead of writing a complicated provision.

Financing Contingencies

Nearly all residential transactions are contingent on the buyer's ability to obtain financing. That's why it's particularly important to describe the financing arrangements in the purchase and sale agreement. The buyer is required to make a diligent, good faith effort to obtain financing on the terms stated in the agreement. But if, despite the buyer's best efforts, no lenders are willing to make a loan on those terms, then the buyer can terminate the agreement without forfeiting the deposit.

A financing contingency clause should contain enough information to clearly identify the type of loan that the buyer wants. It is not possible to include the details of all loan programs a buyer might qualify for, but the contingency clause should include the following basic information:

1. the principal amount of the loan;
2. the loan term;
3. the interest rate;
4. the amortization period (which may or may not be the same as the loan term); and
5. the party who is to pay the costs and fees associated with the loan application (normally the buyer).

FHA and VA Financing. Some transactions are contingent on whether the buyer is able to obtain FHA or VA financing. This type of contingency clause would include the requirement that the seller deliver a written appraisal of the

Fig. 9.2 Sample financing contingency clause

Necessary Financing. This offer is conditioned upon Buyer obtaining a conventional purchase loan of not less than $_____, payable over a term of not less than ____ years, with a fixed interest rate not to exceed ____% per annum.

Buyer agrees to make written application for such a loan within ____ days after the date of Seller's acceptance of this offer, to use reasonable diligence to obtain the loan, and to pay all costs associated with the loan application.

Buyer agrees to deliver to Seller a written firm commitment from a lender for such financing within ____ days after acceptance of this offer.

If Buyer fails to obtain financing as indicated by the stated date or to waive Buyer's rights under this clause, then either party may terminate this contract and Buyer's deposit will be returned.

property which values it at no less than the agreed sales price. If the appraisal shows that the property is worth less than the price, the buyer can either pay the difference in cash or rescind the contract.

The FHA/VA paragraph will also provide for inspections at the seller's expense to ensure that the property's physical condition complies with federal requirements. The paragraph also usually provides that if "work orders" are issued (that is, repairs are required), the seller may either pay for the repairs or terminate the contract.

Contract Conditioned on Sale of Buyer's Home

Purchase and sale agreements are often contingent on the buyer's ability to sell his or her current home. In fact, even when this is not an express condition, it may be a hidden one. Most buyers are planning to use part of the proceeds from the sale of the current home for a downpayment on the new home, and won't be able to qualify for the loan described in the financing contingency clause without selling the current home.

Under those circumstances, the sale of the current home should be an express condition in the purchase and sale agreement. Otherwise the seller may be misled into believing that the buyer has a much better chance of being able to complete the purchase than he or she actually has. It's generally a waste of time for the seller to accept a contingent offer from a buyer who is unlikely to be able to fulfill the condition.

The contract clause should specify what will fulfill a condition concerning sale of the current home. Is it fulfilled when the buyer accepts an offer on the current home? Or is it fulfilled only when the sale of the current home actually closes? The parties and the agent should carefully consider how much time is allowed for this contingency. There's a natural conflict between the desires of the buyer and the seller. The buyer wants as much time as possible in order to get the highest possible price for his or her current home. The seller wants the present transaction to close as soon as possible.

Fig. 9.3 Sample contingency clause concerning sale of buyer's home

> **Sale of Buyer's Home.** This agreement is contingent upon Buyer's accepting an offer to sell Buyer's present residence, located at _____. Buyer must notify Seller, in writing, within ____ days after the date of the Seller's signature on this agreement that Buyer has accepted a written offer to sell Buyer's home. The price and terms of that sale agreement must be such that Buyer will receive sufficient net proceeds to make completion of this transaction possible. If Buyer fails to provide Seller with such notice within said ____-day period, then this purchase and sale agreement shall become null and void and Buyer's earnest money deposit shall be refunded.
>
> This purchase and sale agreement is also conditioned upon the closing of and distribution of the proceeds from the sale of the Buyer's home on or before the closing date of this agreement. If the sale of Buyer's home fails to close by that date through no fault of Buyer, then this agreement becomes null and void and Buyer's earnest money shall be refunded.

Bump Clauses. To deal with these conflicting interests, the **bump clause** has evolved. A bump clause enables the seller to keep the property on the market pending fulfillment of a contingency. It's now common to include one in the purchase and sale agreement when the transaction depends on the sale of the buyer's current home. If the seller receives another offer before the buyer's home is sold, the seller can demand that the buyer waive the condition or rescind the contract. A bump clause can be used with any condition, and one is most likely to be used when there is a good chance that the contingency clause will not be fulfilled on time.

Time Frame. Although it is difficult, if not impossible, to predict how long it will take the buyer to sell his or her home, there is one practical detail to keep in mind. The agent must make sure that there isn't a conflict in the terms of the purchase and sale agreement. The buyer should not be given 60 days to find a buyer for his or her home if the original sale is supposed to close in 45 days.

Inspection Contingencies

Another kind of contingency clause concerns an expert inspection of the property. For example, a purchase and sale agreement might include provisions making the contract contingent upon a structural inspection, a geological inspection, or a pest control inspection. In fact, if an appraiser notes that pests might be a problem, then the buyer's lender may require a pest control inspection to be performed before the buyer's loan is approved.

There are some common problems in this area that a real estate agent should be aware of. Contingency clauses dealing with inspections sometimes simply state that they can be met only with "satisfactory" test results, leaving what is satisfactory to the buyer's discretion. However, the best clauses are written to include some objective standard, such as a determination that no immediate repairs are needed, or that necessary repairs can't exceed a set cost, such as

$1,000. Remember, a contract based on an illusory promise is not enforceable. An inspection contingency with no objective standards of fulfillment could make the whole contract illusory.

Yet the objective standards set in the inspection contingency clause should be ones that will satisfy the buyer's personal standards. For example, a particular buyer might not want to buy a house that has ever had a termite infestation. Even if there is no immediate need of repair, or if the damage is negligible, that buyer simply does not want a house that is subject to termite infestation. In that case, the clause should allow the buyer to withdraw from the transaction if the inspection reveals any past or present infestation.

An inspection contingency clause is often a separate page attached to the purchase and sale agreement as an addendum. It should establish:

- who is responsible for ordering and paying for the inspection;
- when and how the buyer must give the seller notice of disapproval of the inspection report;
- the seller's option to either perform repairs or terminate the purchase and sale agreement, refunding the buyer's earnest money; and
- a time limit for re-inspection by the buyer if the seller performs repairs.

The seller should be aware that if an inspection reveals building code violations or certain other problems, public authorities could order the seller to correct the violations, whether or not the transaction proceeds.

Second Buyer Contingencies

When it appears that a transaction might fail because a condition is not met, the seller may want to accept an offer from a second buyer. To allow this, a provision is usually included in the second purchase and sale agreement making it contingent on the failure of the first transaction, and on the first buyer's release of all claims. The best way to accomplish this is by asking the first buyer to execute a release of contract form in which the parties agree to rescind the first contract.

Property Disclosure Laws

A real property seller is required by law to make certain disclosures to the buyer about the property being transferred. In this section, we'll explain Washington's residential property seller disclosure law and a federal law concerning lead-based paint disclosures.

Seller Disclosure Law

Washington requires all sellers of residential property to give the buyer a disclosure statement when a purchase and sale agreement is signed. (For the purposes of the disclosure law, a residential transaction includes any residential dwelling with one to four units.) The purpose of the statement is to disclose the seller's knowledge regarding the condition of the property, including the condition of the buildings and utilities, the existence of any easements and encumbrances, and other material information. The statement is for disclosure purposes only, and is not a part of the sales agreement. A copy of the seller disclosure statement (formerly called the real property transfer disclosure statement) is shown in Figure 9.4.

The seller must give the buyer the disclosure statement within **five days** of the signing of a purchase and sale agreement, unless the parties agree in writing to another time frame or the buyer signs a written waiver of the right to receive the statement. Within **three business days** of receiving the statement, the buyer can either "approve and accept" the disclosure statement or rescind the purchase and sale agreement. The choice between acceptance and rescission is in the complete discretion of the buyer. There are no objective standards that can be applied to the disclosure statement to measure its adequacy. If the buyer does not like the information found in the disclosure statement for any reason, however trivial, the buyer can rescind the agreement.

If the buyer decides to rescind the agreement, he or she must notify the seller in writing within the three-day period. The buyer will then be entitled to a full refund of the earnest money deposit.

If the buyer accepts the disclosure statement, information may later come to light that makes the disclosure statement inaccurate.

> **Example:** The seller filled out the property disclosure statement and gave it to the buyer within the five-day time frame. The buyer examined the statement, was satisfied with it, and waived the right to rescind the agreement. Two weeks later, the seller realized that there was an encroachment on the property. The disclosure statement given to the buyer is no longer accurate.

When that happens, the seller may either give the buyer an amended disclosure statement, or else take corrective action so that the disclosure statement is made accurate once again. If no corrective action is taken prior to the closing date, the buyer can either accept the amended disclosure statement or rescind the purchase and sale agreement.

> **Example:** The seller in the previous example gives the buyer an amended disclosure statement. The buyer, who has had second thoughts about buying the property anyway, decides to rescind the sales agreement.

If new information comes to light after the sale closes, the buyer does not have the right to rescind the sale.

If the seller refuses to give the buyer a disclosure statement within the statutory time limit, the buyer has the right to rescind the purchase and sale agreement at any time until closing.

Washington's seller disclosure law specifically states that the information in the disclosure statement is based on the seller's actual knowledge of the property; it may not be regarded as representations made by the real estate agent. Furthermore, the statement is not a warranty from either the seller or the agent. Neither the seller nor the agent will be liable for any inaccuracies in the statement unless they had personal knowledge of the inaccuracies.

Lead-Based Paint Disclosure Law

Another type of property disclosure is now required by federal law. In transactions involving housing built before 1978, a seller must disclose information concerning lead-based paint to potential buyers. A landlord is also required

Figure 9.4 Seller disclosure form

NWMLS Form No. 17
W.A.R. Form No. D-5
Rev. 7/03
Page 1 of 5 Pages

SELLER DISCLOSURE STATEMENT †

© Copyright 2003
Northwest Multiple Listing Service
ALL RIGHTS RESERVED

SELLER: _____ 1

† To be used in transfers of residential real property, including multi-family dwellings up to four units; new construction; condominiums not subject   2
to a public offering statement, certain timeshares, and manufactured and mobile homes. See RCW Chapter 64.06 and Section 43.22.432 for   3
further explanations.   4

INSTRUCTIONS TO THE SELLER   5
Please complete the following form. Do not leave any spaces blank. If the question clearly does not apply to the property write "NA." If the   6
answer is "yes" to any asterisked (*) item(s), please explain on attached sheets. Please refer to the line number(s) of the question(s) when you   7
provide your explanation(s). For your protection you must date and initial each page of this disclosure statement and each attachment. Delivery of   8
the disclosure statement must occur not later than five (5) business days, unless otherwise agreed, after mutual acceptance of a written purchase   9
and sale agreement between Buyer and Seller.   10

NOTICE TO THE BUYER   11
THE FOLLOWING DISCLOSURES ARE MADE BY THE SELLER ABOUT THE CONDITION OF THE PROPERTY LOCATED AT   12
_____ ,   13

CITY _____ , COUNTY _____ ("THE PROPERTY") OR AS LEGALLY DESCRIBED ON THE   14
ATTACHED EXHIBIT A. SELLER MAKES THE FOLLOWING DISCLOSURES OF EXISTING MATERIAL FACTS OR MATERIAL   15
DEFECTS TO BUYER BASED ON SELLER'S ACTUAL KNOWLEDGE OF THE PROPERTY AT THE TIME SELLER COMPLETES   16
THIS DISCLOSURE STATEMENT. UNLESS YOU AND SELLER OTHERWISE AGREE IN WRITING, YOU HAVE THREE (3)   17
BUSINESS DAYS FROM THE DAY SELLER OR SELLER'S AGENT DELIVERS THIS DISCLOSURE STATEMENT TO YOU TO   18
RESCIND THE AGREEMENT BY DELIVERING A SEPARATELY SIGNED WRITTEN STATEMENT OF RESCISSION TO SELLER   19
OR SELLER'S AGENT. IF THE SELLER DOES NOT GIVE YOU A COMPLETED DISCLOSURE STATEMENT, THEN YOU MAY   20
WAIVE THE RIGHT TO RESCIND PRIOR TO OR AFTER THE TIME YOU ENTER INTO A PURCHASE AND SALE AGREEMENT.   21

THE FOLLOWING ARE DISCLOSURES MADE BY SELLER AND ARE NOT THE REPRESENTATIONS OF ANY REAL ESTATE   22
LICENSEE OR OTHER PARTY. THIS INFORMATION IS FOR DISCLOSURE ONLY AND IS NOT INTENDED TO BE A PART OF   23
ANY WRITTEN AGREEMENT BETWEEN BUYER AND SELLER.   24

FOR A MORE COMPREHENSIVE EXAMINATION OF THE SPECIFIC CONDITION OF THIS PROPERTY YOU ARE ADVISED   25
TO OBTAIN AND PAY FOR THE SERVICES OF QUALIFIED EXPERTS TO INSPECT THE PROPERTY, WHICH MAY INCLUDE,   26
WITHOUT LIMITATION, ARCHITECTS, ENGINEERS, LAND SURVEYORS, PLUMBERS, ELECTRICIANS, ROOFERS, BUILDING   27
INSPECTORS, ON-SITE WASTEWATER TREATMENT INSPECTORS, OR STRUCTURAL PEST INSPECTORS. THE PROSPECTIVE   28
BUYER AND SELLER MAY WISH TO OBTAIN PROFESSIONAL ADVICE OR INSPECTIONS OF THE PROPERTY OR TO   29
PROVIDE APPROPRIATE PROVISIONS IN A CONTRACT BETWEEN THEM WITH RESPECT TO ANY ADVICE, INSPECTION,   30
DEFECTS OR WARRANTIES.   31

Seller ☐ is/ ☐ is not occupying the property.   32

I. SELLER'S DISCLOSURES: 33
  * If you answer "Yes" to a question with an asterisk (*), please explain your answer and attach documents, if available and not otherwise   34
  publicly recorded. If necessary, use an attached sheet.   35

	YES	NO	DON'T KNOW	
1. TITLE				36
A. Do you have legal authority to sell the property? If not, please explain.	☐	☐	☐	37
*B. Is title to the property subject to any of the following?	☐	☐	☐	38
(1) First right of refusal	☐	☐	☐	39
(2) Option	☐	☐	☐	40
(3) Lease or rental agreement	☐	☐	☐	41
(4) Life estate	☐	☐	☐	42
*C. Are there any encroachments, boundary agreements, or boundary disputes?	☐	☐	☐	43
*D. Are there any rights of way, easements, or access limitations that may affect				44
Buyer's use of the property?	☐	☐	☐	45
*E. Are there any written agreements for joint maintenance of an easement or right of way?	☐	☐	☐	46
*F. Is there any study, survey project, or notice that would adversely affect the property?	☐	☐	☐	47
*G. Are there any pending or existing assessments against the property?	☐	☐	☐	48
*H. Are there any zoning violations, nonconforming uses, or any unusual restrictions				49
on the property that would affect future construction or remodeling?	☐	☐	☐	50
*I. Is there a boundary survey for the property?	☐	☐	☐	51
*J. Are there any covenants, conditions, or restrictions which affect the property?	☐	☐	☐	52

PLEASE NOTE: Covenants, conditions, and restrictions which purport to forbid or restrict the conveyance, encumbrance, occupancy, or lease of   53
real property to individuals based on race, creed, color, sex, national origin, familial status, or disability are void, unenforceable, and illegal. RCW   54
49.60.224.   55

SELLER'S INITIAL: _____ DATE: _____   SELLER'S INITIAL: _____ DATE: _____   56

1

Reprinted with permission, Northwest Multiple Listing Service. No endorsement implied.

NWMLS Form No. 17
W.A.R. Form No. D-5
Rev. 7/03
Page 2 of 5 Pages

SELLER DISCLOSURE STATEMENT

	YES	NO	DON'T KNOW	
2. WATER				57 58
A. Household Water				59
(1) The source of water for the property is: ☐ Private or publicly owned water system				60
☐ Private well serving only the subject property * ☐ Other water system				61
*If shared, are there any written agreements?	☐	☐	☐	62
*(2) Is there an easement (recorded or unrecorded) for access to and/or maintenance of the water source?	☐	☐	☐	63 64
*(3) Are there any known problems or repairs needed?	☐	☐	☐	65
(4) During your ownership, has the source provided an adequate year round supply of potable water?	☐	☐	☐	66 67
If no, please explain: _____				68
*(5) Are there any water treatment systems for the property?	☐	☐	☐	69
If yes, are they: ☐ Leased ☐ Owned				70
B. Irrigation				71
(1) Are there any water rights for the property, such as a water right, permit, certificate, or claim?	☐	☐	☐	72 73
*(a) If yes, have the water rights been used during the last five-years?	☐	☐	☐	74
*(b) If so, is the certificate available?	☐	☐	☐	75
C. Outdoor Sprinkler System				76
(1) Is there an outdoor sprinkler system for the property?	☐	☐	☐	77
*(2) If yes, are there any defects in the system?	☐	☐	☐	78
*(3) If yes, is the sprinkler system connected to irrigation water?	☐	☐	☐	79
3. SEWER/ON-SITE SEWAGE SYSTEM				80
A. The property is served by:				81
☐ Public sewer system ☐ On-site sewage system (including pipes, tanks, drainfields, and all other component parts)				82
☐ Other disposal system				83
Please describe: _____				84
B. If public sewer system service is available to the property, is the house connected to the sewer main?	☐	☐	☐	85 86
If no, please explain: _____				87
C. Is the property subject to any sewage system fees or charges in addition to those covered in your regularly billed sewer or on-site sewage system maintenance service?	☐	☐	☐	88 89
D. If the property is connected to an on-site sewage system:				90
*(1) Was a permit issued for its construction, and was it approved by the local health department or district following its construction?	☐	☐	☐	91 92
(2) When was it last pumped? _____	☐	☐	☐	93
*(3) Are there any defects in the operation of the on-site sewage system?	☐	☐	☐	94
(4) When was it last inspected? _____			☐	95
By whom: _____				96
(5) For how many bedrooms was the on-site sewage system approved? _____ bedrooms			☐	97
E. Are all plumbing fixtures, including laundry drain, connected to the sewer/on-site sewage system?	☐	☐	☐	98 99
If no, please explain: _____				100
*F. Have there been any changes or repairs to the on-site sewage system?	☐	☐	☐	101
G. Is the on-site sewage system, including the drainfield, located entirely within the boundaries of the property?	☐	☐	☐	102 103
If no, please explain: _____				104
H. Does the on-site sewage system require monitoring and maintenance services more frequently than once a year?	☐	☐	☐	105 106
If yes, please explain: _____				107

SELLER'S INITIAL: _____ DATE: _____   SELLER'S INITIAL: _____ DATE: _____ 108

2

NWMLS Form No. 17
W.A.R. Form No. D-5
Rev. 7/03
Page 3 of 5 Pages

SELLER DISCLOSURE STATEMENT

© Copyright 2003
Northwest Multiple Listing Service
ALL RIGHTS RESERVED

NOTICE: IF THIS SELLER DISCLOSURE STATEMENT IS BEING COMPLETED FOR NEW CONSTRUCTION WHICH 109
HAS NEVER BEEN OCCUPIED, SELLER IS NOT REQUIRED TO COMPLETE THE QUESTIONS LISTED IN ITEM 4 110
(STRUCTURAL) OR ITEM 5 (SYSTEMS AND FIXTURES). 111

	YES	NO	DON'T KNOW	

4. STRUCTURAL 113

	YES	NO	DON'T KNOW	
*A. Has the roof leaked?	☐	☐	☐	114
*B. Has the basement flooded or leaked?	☐	☐	☐	115
*C. Have there been any conversions, additions or remodeling?	☐	☐	☐	116
*(1) If yes, were all building permits obtained?	☐	☐	☐	117
*(2) If yes, were all final inspections obtained?	☐	☐	☐	118
*D. Do you know the age of the house?	☐	☐	☐	119

If yes, year of original construction: _____ 120

	YES	NO	DON'T KNOW	
*E. Has there been any settling, slippage, or sliding of the property or its improvements?	☐	☐	☐	121
*F. Are there any defects with the following: (If yes, please check applicable items and explain.)	☐	☐	☐	122

☐ Foundations	☐ Decks	☐ Exterior Walls	123
☐ Chimneys	☐ Interior Walls	☐ Fire Alarms	124
☐ Doors	☐ Windows	☐ Patios	125
☐ Ceilings	☐ Slab Floors	☐ Driveways	126
☐ Pools	☐ Hot Tub	☐ Sauna	127
☐ Sidewalks	☐ Outbuildings	☐ Fireplaces	128
☐ Garage Floors	☐ Walkways	☐ Wood Stoves	129
☐ Siding	☐ Other _____		130

	YES	NO	DON'T KNOW	
*G. Was a structural pest or "whole house" inspection done?	☐	☐	☐	131

If yes, when and by whom was the inspection completed? 132

_____ 133

	YES	NO	DON'T KNOW	
*H. During your ownership, has the property had any wood destroying organisms or pest infestations?	☐	☐	☐	134
I. Is the attic insulated?	☐	☐	☐	135
J. Is the basement insulated?	☐	☐	☐	136

5. SYSTEMS AND FIXTURES 137

*A. If any of the following systems or fixtures are included with the transfer, are there any defects? 138

If yes, please explain: _____ 139

	YES	NO	DON'T KNOW	
Electrical system, including wiring, switches, outlets, and service	☐	☐	☐	140
Plumbing system, including pipes, faucets, fixtures, and toilets	☐	☐	☐	141
Hot water tank	☐	☐	☐	142
Garbage disposal	☐	☐	☐	143
Appliances	☐	☐	☐	144
Sump pump	☐	☐	☐	145
Heating and cooling systems	☐	☐	☐	146
Security system ☐ Leased ☐ Owned	☐	☐	☐	147
Other _____	☐	☐	☐	148

*B. If any of the following fixtures or property is included with the transfer, are they leased? 149
(If yes, please attach copy of lease.) 150

	YES	NO	DON'T KNOW	
Security System	☐	☐	☐	151
Tanks (type): _____	☐	☐	☐	152
Satellite dish	☐	☐	☐	153
Other: _____	☐	☐	☐	154

SELLER'S INITIAL: _____ DATE: _____   SELLER'S INITIAL: _____ DATE: _____ 155

3

NWMLS Form No. 17
W.A.R. Form No. D-5
Rev. 7/03
Page 4 of 5 Pages

SELLER DISCLOSURE STATEMENT

	YES	NO	DON'T KNOW	

6. COMMON INTERESTS

A. Is there a Home Owners' Association? ☐ ☐ ☐ 156 157 158

Name of Association _____ 159

B. Are there regular periodic assessments? ☐ ☐ ☐ 160

_____ per ☐ month ☐ years 161

☐ Other _____ 162

*C. Are there any pending special assessments? ☐ ☐ ☐ 163

*D. Are there any shared "common areas" or any joint maintenance agreements (facilities such as walls, fences, landscaping, pools, tennis courts, walkways, or other areas co-owned in undivided interest with others)? ☐ ☐ ☐ 164 165 166

7. GENERAL 167

*A. Have there been any drainage problems on the property? ☐ ☐ ☐ 168

*B. Does the property contain fill material? ☐ ☐ ☐ 169

*C. Is there any material damage to the property from fire, wind, floods, beach movements, earthquake, expansive soils, or landslides? ☐ ☐ ☐ 170 171

D. Is the property in a designated flood plain? ☐ ☐ ☐ 172

E. Has the local (city or county) planning agency designated your property as a "frequently flooded area"? ☐ ☐ ☐ 173 174

*F. Are there any substances, materials, or products on the property that may be environmental concerns, such as asbestos, formaldehyde, radon gas, lead-based paint, fuel or chemical storage tanks, or contaminated soil or water? ☐ ☐ ☐ 175 176 177

*G. Are there any tanks or underground storage tanks (e.g., chemical, fuel, etc.) on the property? ☐ ☐ ☐ 178

*H. Has the property ever been used as an illegal drug manufacturing site? ☐ ☐ ☐ 179

*I. Are there any radio towers in the area that may cause interference with telephone reception? ☐ ☐ ☐ 180

8. LEAD BASED PAINT (Applicable if the house was built before 1978.) 181

A. Presence of lead-based paint and/or lead-based paint hazards (check one below): 182

☐ Known lead-based paint and/or lead-based paint hazards are present in the housing (explain). _____ 183 184

☐ Seller has no knowledge of lead-based paint and/or lead-based paint hazards in the housing. 185

B. Records and reports available to the Seller (check one below): 186

☐ Seller has provided the purchaser with all available records and reports pertaining to lead-based paint and/or lead-based paint hazards in the housing (list documents below). 187 188

_____ 189

☐ Seller has no reports or records pertaining to lead-based paint and/or lead-based paint hazards in the housing. 190

9. MANUFACTURED AND MOBILE HOMES 191

If the property includes a manufactured or mobile home, 192

*A. Did you make any alterations to the home? ☐ ☐ ☐ 193

If yes, please describe the alterations: _____ 194

*B. Did any previous owner make any alterations to the home? ☐ ☐ ☐ 195

If yes, please describe the alterations: _____ 196

*C. If alterations were made, were permits or variances for these alterations obtained? ☐ ☐ ☐ 197

10. FULL DISCLOSURE BY SELLERS 198

A. Other conditions or defects: 199

*Are there any other existing material defects affecting the property that a prospective buyer should know about? ☐ ☐ ☐ 200 201

SELLER'S INITIAL: _____ DATE: _____ SELLER'S INITIAL: _____ DATE: _____ 202

NWMLS Form No. 17
W.A.R. Form No. D-5
Rev. 7/03
Page 5 of 5 Pages

SELLER DISCLOSURE STATEMENT

B. Verification   203

The foregoing answers and attached explanations (if any) are complete and correct to the best of Seller's knowledge and Seller has   204
received a copy hereof. Seller agrees to defend, indemnify and hold real estate licensees harmless from and against any and all claims   205
that the above information is inaccurate. Seller authorizes real estate licensees, if any, to deliver a copy of this disclosure statement to   206
other real estate licensees and all prospective buyers of the Property.   207

Date: _____   Date: _____   208

Seller _____   Seller _____   209

II. BUYER'S ACKNOWLEDGEMENT   210

Buyer hereby acknowledges that: 211

A. Buyer has a duty to pay diligent attention to any material defects that are known to Buyer or can be known to Buyer by utilizing diligent   212
    attention and observation.   213

B. The disclosures set forth in this statement and in any amendments to this statement are made only by the Seller and not by any real   214
    estate licensee or other party.   215

C. Buyer acknowledges that, pursuant to RCW 64.06.050 (2), real estate licensees are not liable for inaccurate information provided by   216
    Seller, except to the extent that real estate licensees know of such inaccurate information.   217

D. This information is for disclosure only and is not intended to be a part of the written agreement between Buyer and Seller.   218

E. Buyer (which term includes all persons signing the "Buyer's acceptance" portion of this disclosure statement below) has received a copy   219
    of this Disclosure Statement (including attachments, if any) bearing Seller's signature(s).   220

F. If the house was built prior to 1978, Buyer acknowledges receipt of the pamphlet *Protect Your Family From Lead in Your Home.*   221

DISCLOSURES CONTAINED IN THIS DISCLOSURE STATEMENT ARE PROVIDED BY SELLER BASED ON SELLER'S ACTUAL   222
KNOWLEDGE OF THE PROPERTY AT THE TIME SELLER COMPLETES THIS DISCLOSURE. UNLESS BUYER AND SELLER   223
OTHERWISE AGREE IN WRITING, BUYER SHALL HAVE THREE (3) BUSINESS DAYS FROM THE DAY SELLER OR SELLER'S   224
AGENT DELIVERS THIS DISCLOSURE STATEMENT TO RESCIND THE AGREEMENT BY DELIVERING A SEPARATELY   225
SIGNED WRITTEN STATEMENT OF RESCISSION TO SELLER OR SELLER'S AGENT. IF SELLER DOES NOT GIVE YOU A   226
COMPLETED DISCLOSURE STATEMENT, THEN YOU MAY WAIVE THE RIGHT TO RESCIND PRIOR TO OR AFTER THE TIME   227
YOU ENTER INTO A SALE AGREEMENT.   228

BUYER HEREBY ACKNOWLEDGES RECEIPT OF A COPY OF THIS DISCLOSURE STATEMENT AND ACKNOWLEDGES THAT   229
THE DISCLOSURES MADE HEREIN ARE THOSE OF THE SELLER ONLY, AND NOT OF ANY REAL ESTATE LICENSEE OR   230
OTHER PARTY.   231

DATE: _____   DATE: _____   232

BUYER: _____   BUYER: _____   233

BUYER'S WAIVER OF RIGHT TO REVOKE OFFER   234

Buyer has read and reviewed the Seller's responses to this Seller Disclosure Statement. Buyer approves this statement and waives Buyer's right   235
to revoke Buyer's offer based on this disclosure.   236

DATE: _____   DATE: _____   237

BUYER: _____   BUYER: _____   238

BUYER'S WAIVER OF RIGHT TO RECEIVE COMPLETED SELLER DISCLOSURE STATEMENT   239

Buyer has been advised of Buyer's right to receive a completed Seller Disclosure Statement. Buyer waives that right.   240

DATE: _____   DATE: _____   241

BUYER: _____   BUYER: _____   242

If the answer is "Yes" to any asterisked (*) items, please explain below (use additional sheets if necessary). Please refer to the line number(s) of   243
the question(s).   244

_____   245
_____   246
_____   247
_____   248
_____   249
_____   250

SELLER'S INITIAL: _____ DATE: _____   SELLER'S INITIAL: _____ DATE: _____   251

5

to make these disclosures to potential tenants. About three-quarters of the homes built before 1978 contain some lead-based paint. The paint is usually not dangerous if properly maintained, but if it deteriorates, it may cause brain damage and organ damage in young children.

The law requires the seller or landlord of a dwelling built before 1978 to do all of the following:

- disclose the location of any lead-based paint that he or she is aware of in the home (in both the dwelling unit and the common areas, if applicable);
- provide a copy of any report concerning lead-based paint in the home, if it has been inspected; and
- give buyers or tenants a copy of a pamphlet on lead-based paint prepared by the U.S. Environmental Protection Agency.

In addition, buyers (but not tenants) must be offered at least a ten-day period in which to have the home tested for lead-based paint.

Specific warnings must be included in the purchase agreement or lease, along with signed statements from the parties acknowledging that the requirements of this law have been fulfilled. The signed acknowledgments must be kept for at least three years as proof of compliance.

Agent's Responsibilities. The law also imposes responsibilities on real estate agents in transactions involving pre-1978 housing. An agent is required to ensure that the seller or landlord knows his or her obligations under the disclosure law and fulfills those obligations. It is also the agent's responsibility to make sure that the purchase agreement or lease contains the required warnings, disclosures, and signatures.

Penalties. Sellers, landlords, or real estate agents who fail to fulfill their obligations under this law may be ordered to pay the buyer or tenant treble damages (three times the amount of any actual damages suffered by the buyer or tenant). Civil and criminal penalties may also be imposed. Although a real estate agent may be held liable for a seller or landlord's failure to comply with the law, the agent isn't responsible for information withheld by the seller or landlord.

Exemptions. Some transactions are exempt from the provisions of this rule, including transactions involving zero-bedroom units (such as efficiency apartments), leases for less than 100 days, housing for the elderly (unless children live there), housing for the handicapped (unless children live there), rental housing that has been inspected by a certified inspector and found to be free of lead-based paint, and foreclosure sales.

Chapter Summary

1. A properly executed purchase and sale agreement is a binding contract that holds the parties to the terms of their agreement until all conditions have been fulfilled and the transaction is ready to close.

2. A real estate agent may prepare a purchase and sale agreement form if the sale is a simple, routine transaction in which the agent is representing one of the parties. The agent is limited to filling in the blanks on standard forms that have been drafted by attorneys. No separate fee for completing the documents may be charged. The agent preparing the purchase and sale agreement will be held to the same standard of care as an attorney.

3. The parties to a purchase and sale agreement are the buyer and the seller, who must each have capacity to contract. Everyone with an interest in the property must sign the agreement. Signatures of both spouses should be obtained in a transaction involving married parties.

4. Every purchase and sale agreement must have an adequate description of the property, specify the total purchase price and method of payment, set a closing date and date of possession, and state by what type of deed and in what condition title will be conveyed.

5. Because a purchase and sale agreement typically contains a "time is of the essence" clause, the closing date is a material term of the contract. Closing must take place on or before the date stated in the agreement, unless the parties agree in writing to an extension.

6. In Washington, a purchase and sale agreement must include an agency disclosure paragraph, confirming that the agents involved in the transaction made the required disclosures (to both the buyer and the seller) concerning which party or parties they were representing.

7. The purchase and sale agreement form serves as the buyer's receipt for the earnest money deposit. The agent ordinarily holds the buyer's check undeposited until the seller has accepted the buyer's offer.

8. A purchase and sale agreement often has a provision that makes it contingent on whether one or more events occur. It is especially common for an agreement to be contingent on whether the buyer obtains financing, sells his or her current home, or both, or on a satisfactory inspection of the property. Contingency clauses must clearly state the condition to be fulfilled, notification procedures, time limits, and the rights of the parties if the conditions are not met.

9. In Washington, a home seller is required to give the buyer a seller disclosure statement, disclosing anything that would affect the value or desirability of the property. Based on the information in the disclosure statement, the buyer can rescind the purchase and sale agreement.

Key Terms

Purchase and sale agreement—A binding contract between a buyer and a seller of real property, and also a receipt for the earnest money deposit.

Earnest money—A sum the buyer gives to the seller when making an offer to purchase, as a sign of good faith; it is applied to the purchase price if the buyer goes through with the transaction, and forfeited to the seller if the buyer defaults.

Time is of the essence clause—A provision that imposes a legal duty to meet all the deadlines in the contract.

Closing—When all appropriate documents are recorded and the sale proceeds are available for disbursement to the seller.

Contingency clause—A contract clause which provides that unless some specified event occurs, the contract is null and void.

Bump clause—A clause that allows the seller to demand that the buyer waive the "sale of the buyer's home" contingency or rescind the contract.

Chapter Quiz

1. A purchase and sale agreement form serves as:

   a) the buyer's receipt for the earnest money deposit
   b) the buyer's offer to purchase
   c) a binding contract between the buyer and the seller
   d) All of the above

2. Which of the following may NOT fill out a purchase and sale agreement form?

   a) An attorney at law
   b) A real estate agent representing one of the parties
   c) A real estate agent who is not a party and is not representing either party
   d) The seller

3. A purchase and sale agreement should state:

   a) only the essential terms of the sale, leaving other details to be worked out in the final contract
   b) the listing price as well as the purchase price
   c) the total purchase price, the method of payment, and the basic financing terms
   d) the seller's reasons for selling the property

4. The purchase and sale agreement states that it will not be binding unless the buyer can obtain financing. This is:

   a) a contingency clause
   b) a defeasibility clause
   c) a bump clause
   d) an escrow clause

9. The purchase and sale agree... financing contingency. If ... lenders but cannot obta... specified terms:

   a) the seller is ... chase
   b) the b... fa...
   c)

   a) the contract provisions must be performed on or before the specified date(s)
   b) the seller is in a hurry to sell the property
   c) the buyer must obtain the necessary financing within 30 days
   d) the broker's commission must be paid before closing

7. The closing date specified in the purchase and sale agreement:

   a) is just an estimate, without real significance
   b) should allow time for all contingencies to be satisfied
   c) can be changed (if necessary) by the real estate agent without the parties' consent
   d) should be the same as the closing date set forth in the listing agreement

8. A bump clause:

   a) allows the closing to be delayed for 30 days at either party's option
   b) increases the purchase price at closing to reflect the inflation rate
   c) prevents the buyer from waiving any contingencies
   d) allows the seller to keep the property on the market after accepting the buyer's offer

...ent includes a
...the buyer applies to
...n financing on the

...required to finance the pur-

...uyer is required to accept less
...vorable terms
...the transaction is terminated, and the seller
will return the buyer's earnest money

d) the transaction is terminated, and the seller
is allowed to keep the earnest money

10. When a contract includes a contingency
clause:

a) the parties are required to make a good
faith effort to fulfill the condition
b) the contingency can be waived by the
party for whose benefit it was included
c) Both of the above
d) Neither of the above

11. If the seller is going to finance the purchase:

a) the financing section of the purchase and
sale agreement can be left blank
b) a copy of the financing documents the
parties will be using should be attached to
the purchase and sale agreement
c) the real estate agent should oversee the
finance arrangements
d) the purchase and sale agreement should
include a bump clause

12. Sam is purchasing a home from Hal and Rita,
a married couple. Hal assures Sam that title to
the property is in Hal's name alone, and that
Rita does not need to sign the purchase and
sale agreement.

a) Sam should insist that both Hal and Rita
sign the purchase and sale agreement
b) Only Hal needs to sign the purchase and
sale agreement
c) Sam should insist that both Hal and the
selling agent sign the purchase and sale
agreement
d) If only Hal signs the purchase and sale
agreement, Sam should purchase additional title insurance

13. If the seller rejects the buyer's offer and
presents the buyer with a counteroffer, the
agent's best course of action would be to:

a) cross out the old terms on the purchase
and sale agreement, fill in the new terms,
and have the buyer initial the changes
b) cross out the old terms on the purchase
and sale agreement, fill in the new terms,
and have the seller initial the changes
c) use a counteroffer form, signed by the
seller, to present the seller's counteroffer
to the buyer
d) relay the counteroffer to the buyer by
phone

14. An inspection contingency clause should
include all of the following, except:

a) who is responsible for paying for the
inspection
b) the method for notifying the seller of
disapproval of the inspection report
c) the amount of the penalty the buyer must
pay for rejecting the inspection report
d) the seller's option to perform the repairs
or terminate the contract

15. The brokerage fee:

   a) is typically provided for in a purchase and sale agreement, which satisfies the requirement for a written employment contract

   b) should never be included in a purchase and sale agreement, since the amount of the commission should not be disclosed to the buyer

   c) must be set out in the purchase and sale agreement in extra large type

   d) will be forfeited completely if the parties default on the purchase and sale agreement

👉 Answer Key

1. d) The purchase and sale agreement form is used to set forth the buyer's offer, and also serves as the receipt for the earnest money deposit. If the seller signs the form, it becomes a binding contract.

2. c) A real estate agent is not allowed to complete a purchase and sale agreement unless he or she is representing the buyer or the seller (or both parties).

3. c) A purchase and sale agreement should state all of the terms of sale, including the total purchase price, the method of payment, and the terms on which the buyer will finance the purchase.

4. a) A provision that makes the purchase and sale agreement contingent on the occurrence of a certain event is a contingency clause.

5. b) If the buyer defaults on the purchase and sale agreement, the seller often retains the earnest money deposit as liquidated damages.

6. a) "Time is of the essence" means that the parties must perform by or before the exact times specified; failure to meet a deadline in the agreement is a breach of contract.

7. b) The closing date should be far enough off so that all contingencies can be met. If a transaction does not close by the specified date, the contract becomes unenforceable.

8. d) A bump clause allows the seller to keep the property on the market until a contingency is satisfied or waived by the buyer. If a second buyer makes an offer, the seller can ask the first buyer to waive the contingency or terminate their agreement.

9. c) When a contingency in the purchase and sale agreement is not fulfilled, the contract terminates, and the buyer is usually entitled to have the earnest money refunded.

10. c) The parties are required to make a good faith effort to fulfill the conditions in their contract; one party can't deliberately avoid fulfilling a condition and then use that as an excuse for terminating the contract. A contingency clause can usually be waived by the party for whose benefit it was included in the contract.

11. b) It is extremely important to attach to the purchase and sale agreement copies of any financing documents that will be used in a seller-financed transaction.

12. a) When one of the parties to a purchase and sale agreement is married, his or her spouse should always sign the agreement, even if he or she insists that the spouse's signature isn't necessary.

13. c) When a counteroffer is presented, it is much less confusing to use a counteroffer form than to try to change the terms on the original purchase and sale agreement.

14. c) A buyer ordinarily does not have to pay a penalty for rejecting an inspection report.

15. a) A clause establishing the amount of the brokerage fee and the duty to pay it is often included in the purchase and sale agreement. This clause will satisfy the requirement for a written employment agreement, if the broker failed to get a signed listing agreement on the property.

Principles of
Real Estate Financing

Chapter Overview

Finance—lending and borrowing money—is essential to the real estate industry. If financing weren't available, buyers would have to pay cash for their property, and very few people could afford to do so. Thus, once a purchase and sale agreement has been signed, in most cases the next step is to arrange financing for the transaction. Real estate agents often help their clients and customers with this process, so they need a thorough understanding of real estate finance. This chapter starts with background information about real estate cycles, how the government influences real estate finance, and the secondary market. The chapter then goes on to explain how mortgages and other financing instruments work, the foreclosure process, and the various types of mortgage loans. The process of applying for a mortgage loan is covered in Chapter 11.

The Economics of Real Estate Finance

Nearly every buyer needs to borrow money in order to purchase real estate. Whether a particular buyer will be able to obtain a loan depends in part on his or her personal financial circumstances, and in part on national and local economic conditions. We're going to discuss real estate cycles and the government's role in the economy, to help you understand the economic factors that affect real estate lending.

From a lender's point of view, a loan is an investment. A lender loans money in the expectation of a return on the investment. The borrower will repay the money borrowed, plus interest; the interest is the lender's return.

As a general rule, investors demand a higher return on risky investments than they do on comparatively safe ones. That holds true for loan transactions; the greater the risk that the borrower won't repay the loan, the higher the interest rate charged. But the interest rate a lender charges on a particular loan also depends on market forces.

Real Estate Cycles

The real estate market is cyclical: it goes through active periods followed by slumps. These periodic shifts in the level of activity in the real estate market are called **real estate cycles**. Residential real estate cycles can be dramatic or moderate, and they can be local or regional. At any given time and place, there may be a buyer's market, where few people are buying and homes sit on the market for a long time, or there may be a seller's market, where many people are buying and homes sell rapidly.

These cycles obey the law of supply and demand. When demand for a product exceeds the supply (a seller's market), the price charged for the product tends to rise, and the price increase stimulates more production. As production increases, more of the demand is satisfied, until eventually the supply outstrips demand and a buyer's market is created. At that point, prices fall and production tapers off until demand catches up with supply, and the cycle begins again.

Real estate cycles are caused by changes in the supply of and demand for mortgage loan funds. The supply of mortgage funds depends on how much money investors have available and choose to invest in real estate loans. The demand for mortgage funds depends on how many people want to purchase real estate and can afford to borrow enough money to do so.

Interest rates represent the price of mortgage funds. They affect supply and demand, and they also fluctuate in response to changes in supply and demand. Interest is sometimes called the cost of money.

In a healthy economy, supply and demand are more or less in balance. This is the ideal; in reality, the forces affecting supply and demand are constantly changing, and so is the balance between them. But as long as supply and demand are reasonably close, the economy functions well. When supply far exceeds demand, or vice versa, the economy suffers.

Real estate cycles can be moderated, though not eliminated. Severe slumps can be prevented by factors that either help keep interest rates under control or directly affect the supply of mortgage funds. Federal economic policy plays a key role in moderating real estate cycles.

Interest Rates and Federal Policy

Economic stability is directly tied to the supply of and demand for money. If money is plentiful and can be borrowed cheaply (that is, interest rates are low), increased economic activity is usually the result. On the other hand, if funds are scarce or expensive to borrow, an economic slowdown will result.

Thus, manipulation of the availability and cost of money can do much to achieve economic balance. The federal government influences real estate finance, as well as the rest of the U.S. economy, through its **fiscal policy** and its **monetary policy**.

Fiscal Policy. Fiscal policy refers to the way in which the federal government manages its money. Congress and the President determine fiscal policy through tax legislation and the federal budget. The U.S. Treasury implements fiscal policy by managing tax revenues, expenditures, and the national debt.

When the federal government spends more money than it takes in, a shortfall called the **federal deficit** results. It is the Treasury's responsibility to borrow enough money to cover the deficit. It does this by issuing interest-bearing securities that are backed by the U.S. government and purchased by private investors. The securities can be issued for less than one year (Treasury bills), from one to five years (Treasury notes), or from five to ten years (Treasury certificates). Investors often prefer to invest in these government securities instead of other investments because they are comparatively low-risk.

When the government borrows money, it competes with private industry for available investment funds. Economists and politicians debate what impact this has on the economy. According to some, by draining the number of dollars in circulation, heavy government borrowing may lead to an economic slowdown. The greater the federal deficit, the more money the government has to borrow, and the greater the effect on the economy.

The government's taxation policies also affect the supply of and demand for money. As with the deficit, the effect of taxation on the economy is controversial. Basically, when taxes are low, taxpayers have more money to lend and invest. When taxes are high, taxpayers not only have less money to lend or invest, they also may be more likely to invest what money they do have in tax-exempt securities instead of taxable investments. Since real estate and real estate mortgages are taxable investments, this may have a significant impact on the real estate finance industry.

Monetary Policy. Monetary policy refers to the direct control the federal government exerts over the money supply and interest rates. The main goal of monetary policy is to keep the U.S. economy healthy.

Monetary policy is determined by the Federal Reserve, commonly called "the Fed." The Federal Reserve System, established in 1913, is the nation's central banking system. It is governed by the Federal Reserve Board and the board's chairman. It has twelve districts nationwide, with a Federal Reserve Bank in each district. Thousands of commercial banks across the country are members of the Federal Reserve.

The Fed is responsible for regulating commercial banks, and it also oversees implementation of the Truth in Lending Act (discussed in Chapter 11). But setting and implementing the government's monetary policy is perhaps the Fed's most important function.

The major objectives of monetary policy are high employment, economic growth, price stability, interest rate stability, and stability in financial and foreign exchange markets. Although these goals are interrelated, we are most concerned with the Federal Reserve policies that affect the availability and cost of borrowed money (interest rates), since those have the most direct impact on the real estate industry.

The Fed uses three tools to implement its monetary policy and influence the economy:

- key interest rates,
- reserve requirements, and
- open market operations.

Key Interest Rates. The Fed sets two interest rates, the federal funds rate and the discount rate. These are the interest rates charged when a bank borrows money, either from another bank or from a Federal Reserve Bank. When the Fed raises or lowers the interest rates that its member banks have to pay, the

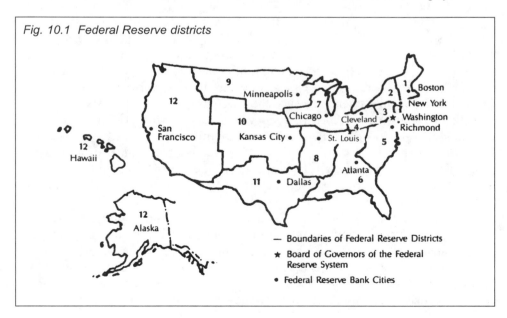

Fig. 10.1 Federal Reserve districts

— Boundaries of Federal Reserve Districts
★ Board of Governors of the Federal Reserve System
• Federal Reserve Bank Cities

banks then raise or lower the interest rates they charge their customers. Lower interest rates tend to stimulate the economy, and higher rates tend to slow it down. The Fed may judge that a slower pace is desirable to keep price inflation in check.

Reserve Requirements. A commercial bank's reserve requirements are the percentages of deposits that the bank is required to maintain on deposit at the Federal Reserve Bank. Reserve requirements help prevent financial panics (a "run on the bank") by assuring depositors that their funds are safe and accessible; the bank will always have enough money available to meet unusual customer demand.

Reserve requirements also give the Fed some control over the growth of credit. By increasing reserve requirements, the Fed can reduce the amount of money banks have available to lend. On the other hand, a reduction in reserve requirements frees more money for investment or lending. So an increase in reserve requirements tends to decrease available loan funds and increase interest rates. Conversely, a decrease in reserve requirements tends to increase available loan funds and decrease interest rates.

Open Market Operations. The Fed also buys and sells government securities; these transactions are called open market operations. They are the Fed's chief method of controlling the money supply, and with the money supply, inflation and interest rates. Only money in circulation is considered part of the money supply, so actions by the Fed that put money into circulation increase the money supply, and actions that take money out of circulation decrease it.

When the Fed buys government securities from an investor, it increases the money supply, because the money it uses to pay for the securities goes into circulation. When the Fed sells government securities, the money the buyer uses to pay for the securities is taken out of circulation, decreasing the money supply. Interest rates tend to fall with increases in the money supply, and to rise with decreases in the money supply.

Other Agencies that Affect Finance. Aside from the Federal Reserve, there are a number of other federal agencies and programs that have some influence on real estate finance.

Federal Home Loan Bank System. The Federal Home Loan Bank System (FHLB) serves many of the same functions in regard to savings and loans that the Federal Reserve System serves in regard to banks. It has much less impact on the national economy than the Federal Reserve, however, since commercial banks control a much greater volume of deposits than savings and loans. The FHLB is headed by the Federal Housing Finance Board.

Federal Deposit Insurance Corporation. The FDIC was created in 1933 to insure bank deposits against bank insolvency. It now includes two separate insurance funds, the Bank Insurance Fund and the Savings Association Insurance Fund. If a bank or savings and loan fails, the FDIC will step in to protect the institution's customers against the loss of their deposited funds, up to specified limits.

HUD. The Department of Housing and Urban Development (HUD) is a federal cabinet department. Among many other things, HUD's responsibilities include urban renewal projects, public housing, FHA-insured loan programs, and enforcement of the Federal Fair Housing Act (see Chapter 15). Ginnie Mae (discussed later in this chapter) and the Federal Housing Administration (discussed in Chapter 11) are both part of HUD.

Rural Housing Service. Formerly known as the Farmers Home Administration or FmHA, the Rural Housing Service is an agency within the Department of Agriculture. To help people living in rural areas purchase and improve their homes, the Rural Housing Service makes loans and grants and also guarantees loans made by lending institutions. In addition, it finances the construction of affordable housing in rural areas.

Farm Credit System. Originally developed by the federal government, the Farm Credit System is now a privately owned cooperative. It provides financial assistance to farmers, ranchers, and others in rural areas.

Real Estate Finance Markets

There are two "markets" that supply the funds available for real estate loans: the primary market and the secondary market. In addition to using monetary policy to control the money supply and interest rates, another way in which the federal government has helped moderate the severity and duration of real estate cycles is by establishing a strong, nationwide secondary market. The secondary market limits the adverse effects of local economic circumstances on real estate lending. We'll look first at the primary market, then at the secondary market.

Primary Market

The primary market is the local mortgage finance market, made up of the various lending institutions in a community. For example, if the Browns want to borrow money to finance the purchase of a home, they will seek a loan in the primary market, perhaps from a bank or a savings and loan.

The traditional source of funds for the primary market is the savings of individuals and businesses in the local area. For instance, a community savings and loan association is a typical lender in the primary market. It gets its funds from the savings deposits of members of the community. It will use the savings to make real estate loans to members of that same community.

The local economy has a significant effect on the amount of funds a local lender has available. When employment is high, consumers are more likely to borrow money for cars, vacations, or homes. Businesses expand and borrow to finance their growth. Banks and other lending institutions increase their lending activities to meet the demand, but at the same time, fewer people are saving. This decrease in deposits and corresponding increase in loan demand steadily depletes the funds available for lending. If local lenders could not attract money from other parts of the country to help meet the demand, their funds would be exhausted and the community's economy severely disrupted. The reverse is also true. When an area is in an economic slump, consumers are more inclined to save than to borrow. Businesses suspend plans for growth. The result is a drop in the demand for money, and the lending institutions' deposits grow.

From a lender's point of view, either too little or too much money on deposit is cause for concern. In the first case, with little money to lend, a lender's primary source of income is affected. In the second case, the lender is paying interest to its depositors, and if it is unable to reinvest the deposited funds quickly, it will lose money.

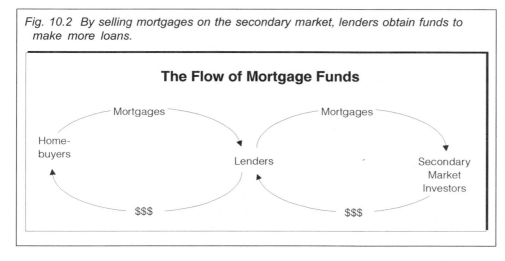

Fig. 10.2 By selling mortgages on the secondary market, lenders obtain funds to make more loans.

To get additional funds for real estate lending, a local lender may sell the mortgage loans it has already made. To do so, the lender will probably turn to the secondary market.

Secondary Market

The secondary market is a national market. It consists of private investors and government-sponsored agencies that buy and sell mortgages secured by real estate in all parts of the United States. Mortgage loans can be bought and sold just like other investments—stocks or bonds, for example. The value of a loan is influenced by the rate of return on the loan compared to the market rate of return, as well as the degree of risk associated with the loan (the likelihood of default). Investors generally buy mortgage loans at a discount, for less than their face value.

The availability of funds in the primary market (a local lender's ability to lend money to prospective borrowers) depends a great deal on the existence of the national secondary market. As explained above, a particular lender may have either too much or too little money to lend, depending on conditions in the local economy. It is the secondary market that provides balance by transferring funds from areas where there is an excess to areas where there is a shortage.

The secondary market has a stabilizing effect on local mortgage markets. Lenders are willing to commit themselves to long-term real estate loans even when local funds are scarce, because they can raise more funds by liquidating their loans on the secondary market.

Government-sponsored Agencies. The major players in the secondary market are three government-sponsored agencies:

- Fannie Mae,
- Freddie Mac, and
- Ginnie Mae.

Fannie Mae. The Federal National Mortgage Association (FNMA), often referred to as "Fannie Mae," started out as a federal agency in 1938. Its original purpose was to provide a secondary market for FHA-insured loans.

Fannie Mae has now been reorganized as a private corporation, but it is still chartered by the government and supervised by the Department of Housing and Urban Development (HUD). Fannie Mae now purchases conventional, FHA, and VA loans.

Freddie Mac. Congress created the Federal Home Loan Mortgage Corporation, nicknamed "Freddie Mac," in 1970. Its original purpose was to assist savings and loan associations (which had been hit particularly hard by a recession) by buying their conventional loans. Freddie Mac is now authorized to buy conventional, FHA, and VA loans from any type of lender. Like Fannie Mae, it is government-chartered and supervised by HUD.

Ginnie Mae. The Government National Mortgage Association, nicknamed "Ginnie Mae," is one of the federal agencies that make up HUD. Among many other things, Ginnie Mae provides secondary market funds for government-insured loans made through the FHA and VA loan programs. (FHA and VA loans are discussed in Chapter 11.)

Uniform Underwriting Standards. Investors are willing to buy mortgage loans on the secondary market, without ever meeting the borrowers or seeing the properties, because the secondary market agencies have established uniform underwriting standards. Underwriting standards are the criteria lenders use to evaluate a loan applicant and the property offered as security, to determine if the loan would be a good investment or would involve too great a risk of default. (This is discussed in more detail in Chapter 11.) A lender generally cannot sell a mortgage on the secondary market unless the loan conforms to the secondary market's underwriting standards. The uniform standards impose a kind of quality control, assuring investors that the loans they're buying are reasonably safe investments.

Real Estate Finance Documents

Now let's turn to the legal aspects of a real estate finance transaction. Once a buyer has found a lender willing to finance his or her purchase on acceptable terms, the buyer is required to sign the finance documents. The legal documents used in conjunction with most real estate loans are the promissory note and a security instrument, which is either a mortgage or a deed of trust.

We'll look first at promissory notes, then at security instruments and foreclosure procedures, and then at the land contract, a document used in some seller-financed transactions.

Promissory Notes

A promissory note is a written promise to repay a debt. One person loans another money, and the other signs a promissory note, promising to repay the loan (plus interest, in most cases). The borrower who signs the note is called the maker, and the lender is called the payee.

Basic Provisions. A promissory note states the loan amount (the principal), the amount of the payments, when and how the payments are to be made, and the maturity date—when the loan is to be repaid in full. The note also states the interest rate, and whether it is fixed or variable. (In some situations, the state

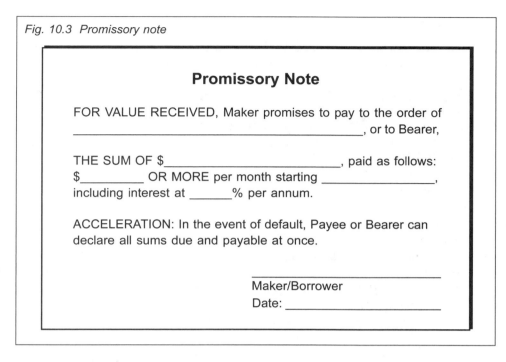

Fig. 10.3 Promissory note

Promissory Note

FOR VALUE RECEIVED, Maker promises to pay to the order of
_____, or to Bearer,

THE SUM OF $_____, paid as follows:
$_____ OR MORE per month starting _____,
including interest at _____% per annum.

ACCELERATION: In the event of default, Payee or Bearer can
declare all sums due and payable at once.

_____
Maker/Borrower
Date: _____

usury law may prohibit the interest rate charged from exceeding a specified maximum.)

A promissory note does not need to contain a legal description of the property, because the note concerns only the debt, not the property. The legal description is instead included in the security instrument.

The note usually explains the consequences of a failure to repay the loan as agreed. Real estate lenders often protect themselves with late charges, acceleration clauses, and similar provisions; these will be discussed later in this chapter.

Types of Notes. There are various types of promissory notes, classified according to the way the principal and interest is paid off. With a **straight note**, the periodic payments are interest only, and the full amount of the principal is due in a lump sum (called a balloon payment) when the loan term ends. With an **installment note**, the periodic payments include part of the principal as well as interest. If the installment note is **fully amortized**, the periodic payments are enough to pay off the entire loan, both principal and interest, by the end of the term. (Amortization is discussed in Chapter 11.)

Whether the payments are interest-only or amortized, the interest paid on a real estate loan is virtually always **simple interest**. In other words, it is computed annually on the remaining principal balance.

Negotiable Instrument. A promissory note is usually a negotiable instrument, which means that the payee (the lender) has the option of assigning the debt to someone else by endorsing the note. A note is endorsed to transfer the right to payment to another party in the same way that a check is endorsed. A check is another example of a negotiable instrument.

The payee transferring the note may state that the endorsement is "without recourse." This means that the issue of future payments is strictly between the maker (the borrower) and the purchaser of the note; the original payee will not be liable to the purchaser if the maker fails to pay as agreed.

Security Instruments

When someone borrows money to buy real estate, in addition to signing a promissory note in favor of the lender, he or she is also required to sign a security instrument. As we said earlier, the security instrument is either a mortgage or deed of trust.

Relationship between Note and Security Instrument. It's important to understand the relationship between the promissory note and the security instrument. The promissory note is the borrower's binding promise to repay the loan. The security instrument is a contract that makes the real property collateral for the loan; it secures the loan by creating a lien on the property. If the borrower doesn't repay the loan as agreed, the security instrument gives the lender the right to foreclose on the property.

A promissory note can be enforced even if it is not accompanied by a security instrument. If the borrower does not repay as agreed, then the lender can file a lawsuit and obtain a judgment against the defaulting borrower. But without a security instrument, the lender might have no way of collecting the judgment. For example, the borrower may have already sold all of his or her property, leaving nothing for the lender (now the judgment creditor) to obtain a lien against.

Title Theory vs. Lien Theory. To understand how security instruments work, it's useful to know how they developed. Historically, to protect the lender against default, a real estate borrower was required to transfer title to the property to the lender for the term of the loan. The borrower remained in possession of the property and had the full use of it, but the lender held title until the loan was paid off. If it wasn't paid off as agreed, the lender could take possession of the property.

This arrangement—in which title to property is given as collateral, but the borrower retains possession—is called **hypothecation**. When title is transferred only as collateral, unaccompanied by possessory rights, it is called legal title, bare title, or naked title. The property rights the borrower retains (without legal title) are referred to as equitable rights or equitable title.

In the United States today, the execution of a mortgage or a deed of trust is still regarded as a transfer of legal title to the lender in a handful of states. Those states are called "title theory" states. However, most states (including Washington) now follow "lien theory." According to lien theory, execution of a mortgage or a deed of trust only creates a lien against the property; it does not transfer title. The borrower retains full title to the property throughout the term of the loan, and the lender simply has the right to foreclose the lien if the borrower defaults.

There are actually not many differences between lending and foreclosure procedures in title theory and lien theory states now; the distinction is more theoretical than practical. Under either theory, the borrower will lose the property if the loan is not repaid.

Fig. 10.4 Purpose of a security instrument

Security Instrument
Mortgage or Deed of Trust

- Makes the borrower's property collateral for the loan
- Gives the lender the power to foreclose if the debt is not paid

Mortgage vs. Deed of Trust. Now let's consider the two types of security instruments, mortgages and deeds of trust. Both are contracts in which a property owner gives someone else a security interest in the property, usually as collateral for a loan. The most important difference between a mortgage and a deed of trust concerns the procedures for foreclosure if the borrower defaults. We will discuss the foreclosure process later in this chapter.

There are two parties to a mortgage: the **mortgagor** and the **mortgagee**. The mortgagor is the property owner and borrower. The mortgagee is the lender.

A deed of trust (sometimes called a trust deed) has three parties: the **trustor** or **grantor** (the borrower), the **beneficiary** (the lender), and the **trustee**. The trustee is a neutral third party who will handle the foreclosure process, if that proves necessary.

Foreclosure can be considerably easier with a deed of trust than with a mortgage, which makes deeds of trust popular with lenders. In Washington and a number of other states, deeds of trust are now much more widely used than mortgages.

The terminology used in a deed of trust has its roots in title theory. The document is called a "deed," and it purports to convey legal title to the trustee. The trustee holds the deed "in trust" pending repayment of the debt. When the loan has been repaid, the trustee "reconveys" title to the trustor. In spite of this language, in a lien theory state like Washington a deed of trust (just like a mortgage) only creates a lien against the property.

Recording. Whether it's a mortgage or a deed of trust, the lender should always record the security instrument immediately after the loan is made. The security instrument does not have to be recorded to create a valid lien on the property, but without recording only the lender and borrower would know the lien exists. Other parties who acquired an interest in the property without notice of the lender's security interest would not be subject to it, and subsequent liens would have priority over the lender's.

Security Instrument Provisions

There is no standard mortgage or deed of trust form, but any security instrument must contain certain provisions and should contain certain others. Most of the following provisions will be found in nearly every mortgage or deed of trust; some of them may also appear in the promissory note. In a few cases (noted below), there is a distinction between the type of provision found in a mortgage and the type found in a deed of trust.

Clause Pledging the Property. Every security instrument is required to include a statement expressing what the instrument is designed to do, indicating that the property is being pledged as security for the loan. This is sometimes called the mortgaging clause or (in a deed of trust) the granting clause. The clause may include the words "grant, bargain, sell, and convey," much like a deed, even if the transaction takes place in a lien theory state, where no actual transfer of title occurs.

Property Description. Like a deed or any other document that transfers an interest in real estate, the security instrument must contain a complete and unambiguous description of the collateral property.

Taxes and Insurance. Security instruments invariably require the borrower to pay general real estate taxes, special assessments, and hazard insurance premiums when due. If the borrower were to allow the taxes to become delinquent or the insurance to lapse, the value of the lender's security interest could be severely diminished—by tax lien foreclosure or a fire, for example.

Acceleration Clause. An acceleration clause states that if the borrower defaults, the lender has the option of declaring the entire loan balance (all the principal still owed) due and payable immediately. Sometimes this is referred to as "calling the note." If the borrower fails to pay the balance as demanded, the lender can sue on the note or foreclose the lien.

An acceleration clause is likely to appear in both the promissory note and in the security instrument. Acceleration can be triggered by failure to make loan payments as agreed in the note, or by breach of a provision in the security instrument, such as failure to keep the property insured.

Alienation Clause. An alienation clause is also called a **due-on-sale clause.** This provision gives the lender the right to accelerate the loan—demanding immediate payment of the entire loan balance, as described above—if the borrower sells the property or otherwise alienates an interest in it. (Alienation refers to any transfer of an interest in real estate. See Chapter 3.) An alienation clause does not prohibit the sale of the property, but it allows the lender to force the borrower to pay off the loan if the property is sold without the lender's approval.

Whether or not there is an alienation clause in the mortgage or deed of trust, sale of the property does not extinguish the lender's lien. If the loan is not paid off at closing, the purchaser can either assume the mortgage or deed of trust, or else take title subject to it.

In an **assumption**, the borrower sells the security property to a purchaser who agrees to "assume and pay the mortgage [or deed of trust] according to its terms." The purchaser becomes primarily liable to the lender for repayment of the loan, but the original borrower retains secondary liability in case the purchaser defaults.

By contrast, when a purchaser takes title **subject to** an existing mortgage or deed of trust (without assuming it), the original borrower remains fully liable for the debt. The purchaser is not personally liable to the lender, although in case of default the lender can still foreclose.

Even though the sale of the property doesn't extinguish the mortgage or deed of trust lien, lenders prefer to have the opportunity to approve or reject a prospective purchaser. Thus, most mortgages and deeds of trust include an alienation clause. When a lender evaluates a purchaser and concludes that he or she is creditworthy, the lender may agree to an assumption of the loan. The lender will usually charge an assumption fee, and may also raise the interest rate on the loan. In most cases, the lender will release the original borrower from any further liability; this is called a novation.

Late Payment Penalty. If the lender wants to impose penalties for late payments, the charges must be clearly defined in the finance documents. Late payment charges are not considered interest on the loan and so are not deductible on income tax statements. A court will refuse to enforce excessive late charges.

Lock-in Clause. A lock-in clause prohibits the borrower from prepaying the loan—paying it off early, before payment is due. The borrower is "locked in" to the loan for the full term or for a specified number of years, so that the lender will not be deprived of interest it expects to collect.

Prepayment Penalty. Some lenders do not impose any restrictions on prepayment. This is usually addressed in the promissory note; for example, a note might call for a payment of "$500.00 or more." The words "or more" indicate that prepayment is allowed.

In some notes, there is a provision that allows prepayment of a certain percentage of the principal each year, but imposes a penalty if the borrower prepays more than that percentage. For example, a note might state, "The borrower may prepay up to 15% of the original loan amount during any twelve-month period without penalty. If the borrower prepays more than 15%, a prepayment fee equal to six months' interest on the excess will be charged."

Most mortgages today do not have prepayment penalties. A mortgage without a prepayment penalty is sometimes referred to as an **open mortgage**.

Subordination Clause. Occasionally a security instrument includes a subordination clause, which states that the instrument will have lower lien priority than another mortgage or deed of trust to be executed in the future. The clause makes it possible for a later security instrument to assume a higher priority position—usually first lien position—even though this earlier security instrument was executed and recorded first.

Subordination clauses are common in mortgages and deeds of trust that secure purchase loans for unimproved land, when the borrower is planning to get a construction loan later on. The construction lender will demand first lien position for its loan. Lien priority is ordinarily determined by recording date ("first in time is first in right"), but the subordination clause in the earlier land loan allows the later construction loan to have first lien position.

Defeasance Clause. A defeasance clause states that the borrower will regain title and the security instrument will be canceled when the debt has been paid.

When a mortgage debt has been paid in full, a document called a **satisfaction of mortgage** (or a "satisfaction piece") is used to release the mortgage lien. The lender must deliver the satisfaction of mortgage to the borrower after the final loan payment has been made. The mortgage will be a cloud on the borrower's title until he or she has the satisfaction recorded.

Under a deed of trust, when the trustor has repaid the loan, the lien is removed by means of a **deed of reconveyance**, also called a reconveyance deed. Like a satisfaction of mortgage, the deed of reconveyance should be recorded to clear the title. Either a satisfaction of mortgage or a deed of reconveyance may be referred to as a **lien release**.

Foreclosure Procedures

If the borrower doesn't repay a secured loan as agreed, the lender may foreclose and collect the debt from the proceeds of a forced sale. Establishing the lender's right to foreclose is the basic purpose of a security instrument. There are different foreclosure procedures for mortgages and deeds of trust; in fact, that is the key difference between the two types of security instruments.

Mortgage Foreclosure. Mortgage foreclosures are sometimes called judicial foreclosures because they are carried out through the court system. Upon default, the lender files a lawsuit against the borrower in a court in the county where the collateral property is located. Any lienholders who have liens with lower priority than the mortgage (junior lienholders) are notified of the foreclosure action, so that they can take steps to protect their interests.

When the complaint is heard in court, in the absence of unusual circumstances the judge will order the property to be sold to satisfy the debt. The sale takes the form of an auction, and since it is usually the county sheriff's office that conducts the auction, it is referred to as a **sheriff's sale**. The property is sold to the highest bidder, who is given a **certificate of sale**.

Between the time the lawsuit is filed and the actual sale of the property, the borrower is entitled to redeem the property by paying off the mortgage debt in full, plus any costs incurred. This is referred to as the period of **equitable redemption**. After the sale, the borrower is given an additional period to redeem the property, which is called the **statutory redemption period**. In Washington, the statutory redemption period is one year, unless the lender has waived his or her rights to a deficiency judgment. In that case, the period of redemption is eight months. A **deficiency judgment** is a judgment against the borrower for the difference between the debt and the proceeds of the sheriff's sale, if the proceeds were not sufficient to pay off the debt in full.

In certain circumstances, a mortgagee is not entitled to a deficiency judgment. When a deficiency judgment is not allowed, the mortgage is referred to as a **non-recourse mortgage**.

During the statutory redemption period, the holder of the certificate of sale does not have title to the property. If the property is not redeemed, a **sheriff's deed** is provided to the holder of the certificate of sale when the redemption period expires. At that point, the debtor has no further claim to the property.

The redemption period makes bidding at a mortgage foreclosure unappealing to many investors; understandably, they do not want to wait so long to gain title to the property. For this reason, there are often no outside bidders at a judicial foreclosure sale, and the lender acquires the property by bidding the amount the debtor owes.

When there are outside bidders at the auction, if the proceeds from the sale exceed the amount necessary to satisfy all valid liens against the property, the surplus belongs to the foreclosed owner.

Deed of Trust Foreclosure. Every deed of trust has a **power of sale clause**. This is a provision that authorizes the trustee to sell the property if the trustor defaults, through a process known as non-judicial foreclosure. Without having to obtain a decree of foreclosure from a court, the trustee can conduct an auction called a **trustee's sale** and use the sale proceeds to pay off the debt owed to the beneficiary. As with a sheriff's sale, if the trustee's sale results in a surplus, the excess amount belongs to the foreclosed owner.

Non-judicial foreclosure must be conducted in accordance with procedures prescribed by statute. These procedures are designed to give the debtor an opportunity to **cure** the default and **reinstate** the loan. First, the trustee must give a notice of default to the borrower and to any junior lienholders who have requested one. A month after the notice of default, the trustee issues a notice of sale to the borrower and also records a notice of sale in the county where the property is located.

Fig. 10.5 Comparison of mortgages and deeds of trust

Security Instruments	
Mortgage	**Deed of Trust**
• Mortgagor and mortgagee • Judicial foreclosure • Equitable redemption before decree of foreclosure • Statutory redemption after sheriff's sale • Deficiency judgment allowed (subject to limitations)	• Trustor, beneficiary, and trustee • Non-judicial foreclosure • Reinstatement before trustee's sale • No post-sale redemption • No deficiency judgment

Until shortly before the sale, if the borrower pays the lender the delinquent amount plus late charges and costs incurred, the default is cured. The foreclosure is terminated and the loan is reinstated. This is very different from the right of equitable redemption in a judicial foreclosure, where the borrower has to pay off the entire debt (not just the delinquent amount) in order to prevent foreclosure.

Many lenders prefer a deed of trust to a mortgage because it enables them to bypass court proceedings, which are often slow. Also, the trustee's sale is final; there is no statutory redemption period afterward. The successful bidder at a trustee's sale is given a trustee's deed and takes title immediately. The disadvantage of a deed of trust from the lender's point of view is that after non-judicial foreclosure there is no right to a deficiency judgment. If the proceeds of the trustee's sale are insufficient to satisfy the debt, the lender takes a loss; the lender is not allowed to sue the borrower to make up the deficiency.

Deed in Lieu of Foreclosure. A defaulting borrower who doesn't have the resources to cure the default or redeem the foreclosed property may opt to give the lender a deed in lieu of foreclosure. The deed in lieu transfers title from the borrower to the lender; this satisfies the debt and stops foreclosure proceedings. A borrower might do this in order to protect his or her credit rating.

The lender takes title subject to any other liens that encumber the property. Thus, before accepting a deed in lieu, the lender will determine what other liens have attached to the property since the original loan was made.

Land Contracts

Most real estate buyers finance their purchases with loans from an institutional lender. But some transactions are financed by the seller; the seller extends credit to the buyer, accepting a downpayment and arranging to be paid over time, instead of requiring full payment at closing. In certain cases a seller offers more favorable terms than institutional lenders (such as an exceptionally low interest rate), in order to attract a wider range of potential buyers and obtain a higher price for the property.

In a seller-financed transaction, the seller may ask the buyer to execute a mortgage or a deed of trust, just like an institutional lender. Sellers also have the option of using a third type of security instrument: the **land contract**, also called a contract for deed, installment sales contract, real estate contract, or contract of sale.

The parties to a land contract are the **vendor** (the seller) and the **vendee** (the buyer). The vendee agrees to pay the purchase price (plus interest) in installments over a specified number of years. The vendee takes possession of the property right away, but the vendor retains legal title until the full price has been paid. In the meantime, the vendee has equitable title to the property. When the contract is finally paid off, the vendor delivers the deed to the vendee.

The vendee should have the contract recorded promptly after signing it, to protect his or her equitable interest. While the contract is being paid off, the vendee is usually required to pay the property taxes and keep the property insured. The vendor may use the legal title to the property for any purpose that does not impair the vendee's interest. The vendor is not allowed to encumber the property in any way that would prevent the transfer of clear title to the vendee as agreed.

Forfeiture. If a vendee defaults on a land contract, the vendor can foreclose judicially. Alternatively, the vendor may choose to declare a **forfeiture**, which is a remedy available only in connection with a land contract. In a forfeiture, the vendor terminates the contract without having to go to court, and without having to refund any of the payments the vendee has made. Washington law allows this only if there is a forfeiture clause in the contract (nearly all land contracts have one) and the contract is recorded. The law also includes provisions that give a vendee with substantial equity in the property some protection against forfeiture.

Types of Mortgage Loans

You will often hear "mortgage" or "deed of trust" coupled with an adjective that serves to describe the particular function of the security instrument or the circumstances in which it is used. For example, a "construction mortgage" is a mortgage used to secure a construction loan; a "blanket mortgage" is one that secures a loan with two or more parcels of property as collateral. Below are explanations of some of the most common of these terms. For the most part, we will use the term "mortgage" here, rather than the more cumbersome term "mortgage or deed of trust." In each case, however, a deed of trust could be (and today often would be) used instead of a mortgage.

First Mortgage. A first mortgage is simply any security instrument that holds first lien position; it has the highest lien priority. A second mortgage is one that holds second lien position, and so on.

Senior and Junior Mortgages. Any mortgage that has a higher lien position than another is called a senior mortgage in relation to that other one, which is called a junior mortgage. A first mortgage is senior to a second mortgage; a second mortgage is junior to a first mortgage, but senior to a third.

As was explained in Chapter 4, lien priority is important in the event of a foreclosure, because the sale proceeds are used to pay off the first lien first. If any money remains, the second lien is paid; then the third is paid, and so on, until the money is exhausted. Obviously, it is much better to be in first lien position than in third.

Purchase Money Mortgage. This term is used in two ways. Sometimes it means any mortgage loan used to finance the purchase of the property that is the collateral for the loan: a buyer borrows money to buy property and gives the lender a mortgage on that same property to secure the loan.

In other cases, "purchase money mortgage" is used more narrowly, to mean a mortgage that a buyer gives to a seller in a seller-financed transaction. Instead of paying the full price in cash at closing, the buyer gives the seller a mortgage on the property and pays the price off in installments.

> **Example:** The sales price is $180,000. The buyer makes a $20,000 downpayment and signs a note and purchase money mortgage in favor of the seller for the remaining $160,000. The buyer will pay the seller in monthly installments at 7% interest over the next 15 years.

In this narrower sense, a purchase money mortgage is sometimes called a **soft money mortgage**, because the borrower receives credit instead of actual cash. If a borrower gives a lender a mortgage and receives cash in return (as with a bank loan), it is called a **hard money mortgage**.

Budget Mortgage. The monthly payment on a budget mortgage includes not just principal and interest on the loan, but one-twelfth of the year's property taxes and hazard insurance premiums as well. Most residential loans are secured by budget mortgages. This is the safest and most practical way for lenders to make sure the property taxes and insurance premiums are paid on time.

Package Mortgage. When personal property is included in the sale of real estate and financed along with the real estate with one loan, the security instrument is called a package mortgage. For example, if a buyer bought ovens, freezers, and other equipment along with a restaurant building, the purchase might be financed with a package mortgage.

Construction Mortgage. A construction mortgage is simply a mortgage that secures a construction loan. A construction loan (sometimes called an **interim loan**) is a temporary loan used to finance the construction of improvements on the land. When the construction is completed, the construction loan is replaced by permanent financing, which is called a **take-out loan**.

Construction loans can be profitable, but they are considered quite risky. Accordingly, lenders charge high interest rates and loan fees on construction loans, and they supervise the progress of the construction. There is always a danger that the borrower will overspend on a construction project and exhaust the loan proceeds before construction is completed. If the borrower cannot afford to finish, the lender is left with a security interest in a partially completed project.

Lenders have devised a variety of plans for disbursement of construction loan proceeds that guard against overspending by the borrower. Perhaps the most common is the **fixed disbursement plan**. This calls for a series of predetermined disbursements, called obligatory advances, at various stages of construction. Interest begins to accrue with the first disbursement.

> **Example:** The construction loan agreement stipulates that the lender will release 10% of the proceeds when the project is 20% complete, and thereafter 20% draws will be available whenever construction has progressed another 20% toward completion.

The lender will often hold back 10% or more of the loan proceeds until the period for claiming construction liens has expired, to protect against unpaid liens that could affect the marketability of the property. The construction loan agreement usually states that if a valid construction lien is recorded, the lender may use the undisbursed portion of the loan to pay it off.

Blanket Mortgage. Sometimes a borrower mortgages several pieces of property as security for one loan. For example, a ten-acre parcel subdivided into twenty lots might be used to secure one loan made to the subdivider. Blanket mortgages usually have a **partial release clause** (also called a partial satisfaction clause, or in a blanket deed of trust, a partial reconveyance clause). This provision requires the lender to release certain parcels from the blanket lien when specified portions of the overall debt have been paid off.

> **Example:** A ten-acre parcel subdivided into twenty lots secures a $500,000 loan. After selling one lot for $50,000, the subdivider pays the lender $45,000 and receives a release for the lot that is being sold. The blanket mortgage is no longer a lien against that lot, so the subdivider can convey clear title to the lot buyer.

Participation Mortgage. A participation mortgage allows the lender to participate in the earnings generated by the mortgaged property, usually in addition to collecting interest payments on the principal. In some cases the lender participates by becoming a part-owner of the property. Participation loans are most common on large commercial projects where the lender is an insurance company or other large investor.

Shared Appreciation Mortgage. Real property usually appreciates (increases in value) over time. Appreciation usually benefits only the property owner, by adding to his or her equity. With a shared appreciation mortgage, however, the lender is entitled to a specified share of the increase in the property's value.

Wraparound Mortgage. A wraparound mortgage is a new mortgage that includes or "wraps around" an existing first mortgage on the property. Wraparounds are generally used only in seller-financed transactions.

> **Example:** A home is being sold for $100,000; there is an existing $40,000 mortgage on the property. Instead of assuming that mortgage, the buyer merely takes title subject to it. The buyer gives the seller a $20,000 downpayment and a second mortgage for the remaining $80,000 of the purchase price. The $80,000 second mortgage is a wraparound mortgage. Each month, the buyer makes a payment on the wraparound to the seller, and the seller uses part of that payment to make the monthly payment on the underlying $40,000 mortgage.

Wraparound financing works only if the underlying loan does not contain an alienation clause (see the discussion earlier in this chapter). Otherwise the lender would require the seller to pay off the underlying loan at the time of sale. A wraparound arrangement should always be designed so that the underlying loan will be paid off before the wraparound, to ensure that the buyer's title will not still be encumbered with the seller's debt after the buyer has paid the full purchase price.

Open-end Mortgage. An open-end mortgage sets a borrowing limit, but allows the borrower to reborrow, when needed, any part of the debt that has been repaid without having to negotiate a new mortgage. The interest rate on the loan is usually a variable rate that rises and falls with market interest rates. The open-end mortgage is often used as a business tool by builders and farmers.

Graduated Payment Mortgage. A graduated payment mortgage allows the borrower to make smaller payments at first and gradually step up to larger payments. For example, the payments might increase annually for the first three to five years of the loan, and then remain level for the rest of the loan term. This arrangement can benefit borrowers who expect their earnings to increase during the next few years.

Swing Loan. It often happens that buyers are ready to purchase a new home before they've succeeded in selling their current home. They need funds for their downpayment and closing costs right away, without waiting for the proceeds from the eventual sale of the current home. In this situation, the buyers may be able to obtain a swing loan. A swing loan is usually secured by equity in the property that is for sale, and it will be paid off when that sale closes. A swing loan is also called a **gap loan** or **bridge loan**.

Reverse Equity Mortgage. A reverse equity mortgage, sometimes called a reverse annuity mortgage, is designed to provide income to older homeowners. The owner borrows against the home's equity but will receive a monthly check from the lender, rather than making monthly payments. Typically, a reverse equity borrower must be over a certain age (for example, 62 or 65) and must own the home with little or no outstanding mortgage balance. The home usually must be sold when the owner dies in order to pay back the mortgage.

Chapter Summary

1. The federal government influences real estate finance directly and indirectly through its fiscal and monetary policy. The federal deficit may affect the availability of investment funds. The Federal Reserve Board uses reserve requirements, the discount rate, and open market operations to implement monetary policy, influencing the pace of economic growth and market interest rates.

2. The primary market is the local finance market, in which lenders make mortgage loans to borrowers. In the secondary market, mortgages are bought and sold by investors. The federal government created the major secondary market agencies, Fannie Mae, Freddie Mac, and Ginnie Mae, to help moderate local real estate cycles.

3. A promissory note is a written promise to repay a debt. For a real estate loan, the borrower is required to sign a negotiable promissory note along with a security instrument, which makes the borrower's property collateral for the loan.

4. The two main types of security instruments are mortgages and deeds of trust. The central difference between the two is that a deed of trust includes a power of sale clause, which allows the trustee to foreclose non-judicially in the event of default.

5. Most security instruments include an acceleration clause and an alienation clause; some also have a prepayment provision or a subordination clause. If there is no alienation clause, the loan can be assumed without the lender's consent.

6. A mortgage is foreclosed judicially. The borrower has an equitable right of redemption before the sheriff's sale and a statutory right of redemption for a certain period afterwards. The lender may be entitled to a deficiency judgment.

7. A deed of trust can be foreclosed non-judicially, by the trustee, which is usually much faster and less expensive than judicial foreclosure. Before the trustee's sale, the borrower has the right to cure the default and reinstate the loan. After the sale, the borrower has no right of redemption. The lender cannot obtain a deficiency judgment.

8. With a land contract, the buyer takes possession of the property and makes installment payments to the seller; the seller retains legal title until the contract is paid off. If the buyer breaches the contract, the seller may declare a forfeiture.

9. There are many different types of mortgage loans, including purchase money, budget, package, construction, blanket, participation, shared appreciation, wraparound, open-end, graduated payment, and reverse equity mortgages.

Key Terms

Federal Reserve Board—The body that regulates commercial banks and sets and implements the federal government's monetary policy; commonly called "the Fed."

Reserve requirements—The percentages of deposits commercial banks must keep on reserve with a Federal Reserve Bank.

Discount rate and federal funds rate—Two interest rates set by the Fed that have an effect on market interest rates.

Open market operations—The Fed's activities in buying and selling government securities.

Primary market—The local finance market, where individuals obtain loans (from mutual savings banks, savings and loans, etc.).

Secondary market—The national finance market, where mortgages are bought and sold as investments.

Promissory note—A written promise to repay a debt.

Mortgage—A two-party security instrument that gives the lender (mortgagee) the right to foreclose on the security property by judicial process if the borrower (mortgagor) defaults.

Deed of trust—A three-party security instrument that includes a power of sale clause, allowing the trustee to foreclose non-judicially if the borrower (trustor) fails to pay the lender (beneficiary) or otherwise defaults.

Acceleration clause—A provision in loan documents that gives the lender the right to demand immediate payment in full if the borrower defaults.

Alienation clause—A provision in a security instrument that gives the lender the right to accelerate the loan if the borrower transfers the property; also called a due-on-sale clause.

Assumption—When a borrower sells the security property to a buyer who agrees to take on personal liability for repayment of the existing mortgage or deed of trust.

Defeasance clause—A provision giving the borrower the right to regain title to the security property when the debt is repaid.

Satisfaction of mortgage—The document a mortgagee gives to the mortgagor when the mortgage debt is paid off, releasing the property from the lien. Also called a satisfaction piece.

Deed of reconveyance—The document a beneficiary gives the trustor when the debt secured by a deed of trust is paid off, releasing the property from the lien.

Land contract—A contract between a seller (vendor) and a buyer (vendee) of real estate, in which the seller retains legal title to the property while the buyer pays off the purchase price in installments.

Chapter Quiz

1. In a tight money market, when business is slow, a reduction in interest rates would be expected to cause:

    a) an increase in real estate sales
    b) more bank lending activity
    c) increased business activity
    d) All of the above

2. Which of the following actions by the Federal Reserve Board would tend to increase the money supply?

    a) Selling government securities on the open market
    b) Buying government securities on the open market
    c) Increasing the federal discount rate
    d) Increasing reserve requirements

3. Funds for single-family mortgage loans are supplied by:

    a) Fannie Mae
    b) savings and loan associations
    c) Both a) and b)
    d) Neither a) nor b)

4. With an installment note, the periodic payments:

    a) include both principal and interest
    b) are interest only
    c) are principal only
    d) are called balloon payments

5. A mortgage loan provision that permits the lender to declare the entire loan balance due upon default by the borrower is:

    a) an acceleration clause
    b) an escalator clause
    c) a forfeiture clause
    d) a subordination clause

6. A mortgage loan provision that permits the lender to declare the entire loan balance due if the property is sold is:

    a) an escalator clause
    b) a subordination clause
    c) an alienation clause
    d) a prepayment provision

7. After a sheriff's sale, the mortgagor has a specific period in which to redeem the property. This period is called the:

    a) lien period
    b) equitable redemption period
    c) statutory redemption period
    d) reinstatement period

8. After a trustee's sale, if there are any sale proceeds left over after paying off liens and foreclosure expenses, the money belongs to the:

    a) sheriff
    b) beneficiary
    c) trustee
    d) foreclosed owner

9. The document that a mortgagee gives a mortgagor after the debt has been completely paid off is called a:

    a) partial release
    b) satisfaction of mortgage
    c) deed of reconveyance
    d) sheriff's deed

10. In a non-judicial foreclosure, the borrower is entitled to:

    a) a statutory redemption period following the sheriff's sale
    b) a deficiency judgment
    c) a deed in lieu of foreclosure
    d) cure the default and reinstate the loan before the trustee's sale

11. When a buyer gives a mortgage to the seller rather than an institutional lender, it may be referred to as a:

   a) purchase money mortgage
   b) land contract
   c) shared appreciation mortgage
   d) reverse equity mortgage

12. A budget mortgage:

   a) is a loan made to a low-income borrower
   b) is a construction loan with a fixed disbursement plan
   c) is secured by personal property as well as real property
   d) has monthly payments that include taxes and insurance as well as principal and interest

13. The owner of five parcels of real property wants a loan. She offers all five parcels as security. She will be required to execute a:

   a) soft money mortgage
   b) participation mortgage
   c) package mortgage
   d) blanket mortgage

14. Victor is borrowing money to buy some land, and he plans to build a home on the property later on. To ensure that he will be able to get a construction loan when the time comes, Victor should make sure the mortgage he executes for the land loan includes:

   a) a lien waiver
   b) a subordination clause
   c) an acceleration clause
   d) a wraparound clause

15. Under a fixed disbursement plan for a construction loan, the contractor is entitled to his or her final draw when:

   a) the project has been satisfactorily completed
   b) 80% of the work has been completed
   c) the building department issues a certificate of occupancy
   d) the period for claiming construction liens expires

Answer Key

1. d) The Fed lowers interest rates in times of economic downturn in an attempt to stimulate the economy.

2. b) When the Fed buys government securities, it puts more money into circulation, which increases the money supply.

3. c) Mortgage money comes from the primary market (in the form of savings deposits) and from the secondary market (when investors like Fannie Mae buy mortgages).

4. a) An installment note involves periodic payments that include some of the principal as well as interest.

5. a) An acceleration clause gives the lender the right to declare the entire debt immediately due and payable if the borrower defaults.

6. c) An alienation clause allows the lender to accelerate the loan if the borrower transfers the security property without the lender's approval.

7. c) The statutory redemption period is the period of time after the sheriff's sale in which the borrower has the right to redeem the property by paying off the entire debt, plus costs.

8. d) Any excess proceeds from a foreclosure sale belong to the borrower—that is, to the foreclosed owner.

9. b) When the debt has been fully paid off, a mortgagee gives the mortgagor a satisfaction of mortgage, releasing the property from the lien.

10. d) In the non-judicial foreclosure of a deed of trust, the trustor is permitted to cure the default and reinstate the loan (as opposed to paying off the loan) before the trustee's sale is held.

11. a) A mortgage given by a buyer to a seller is sometimes called a purchase money mortgage.

12. d) A budget mortgage payment includes a share of the property taxes and hazard insurance as well as principal and interest.

13. d) A blanket mortgage has more than one parcel of property as collateral.

14. b) A subordination clause in the mortgage for the land loan would give it a lower priority than a mortgage executed later on for a construction loan. Lenders generally require first lien position for construction loans, because they are considered especially risky.

15. d) Construction lenders usually delay the final disbursement until no more construction liens can be filed.

Applying for a Residential Loan

Chapter Overview

When it's time to arrange financing, a home buyer must shop for a loan and choose a lender. Next, the buyer fills out a loan application and supplies supporting documentation. Then the lender evaluates the application and decides whether or not to approve the loan. The first part of this chapter describes the different types of lenders in the primary market, explains loan fees, and discusses the Truth in Lending Act, a law that helps prospective borrowers compare loans. The second part of the chapter covers the loan application form and the underwriting process. The last part of the chapter explains various features of a home purchase loan and provides an overview of the major residential finance programs: conventional loans, FHA-insured loans, and VA-guaranteed loans.

Choosing a Lender

Many home buyers look to their real estate agent for guidance in choosing a lender. Agents should be familiar with the lenders in their area and know how to help buyers compare the loans that different lenders are offering. We're going to discuss the various types of lenders that make home purchase loans, the fees that lenders charge, and the Truth in Lending Act.

Types of Mortgage Lenders

There are several major sources of residential financing in the primary market. Residential mortgage lenders include:

- savings and loans,
- commercial banks,
- savings banks,
- credit unions, and
- mortgage companies.

Savings and Loans. Savings and loan associations (S&Ls) are sometimes called "thrift institutions" or simply "thrifts." An S&L is chartered (authorized to do business) by either the federal government or a state government.

Savings and loans started out in the nineteenth century strictly as residential real estate lenders. Over the years they carried on their original function, investing the majority of their assets in purchase loans for single-family homes. By the mid-1950s, they dominated local residential mortgage markets, becoming the nation's largest single source of funds for financing homes.

Many factors contributed to the dominance of savings and loans; one of the most important was that home purchase loans had become long-term loans, usually having a 30-year term. Since most of the funds held by S&Ls were long-term deposits, S&Ls were comfortable making long-term home loans.

While savings and loans have branched out into different types of lending, they continue to focus on home mortgage loans. Yet S&Ls no longer dominate the residential finance market, because other types of lenders have become more involved in it.

Commercial Banks. A commercial bank is either a national bank, chartered by the federal government, or a state bank, chartered by a state government. Commercial banks are the largest source of investment funds in the United States. As their name implies, they were traditionally oriented toward commercial lending activities, supplying capital for business ventures and construction activities on a comparatively short-term basis.

In the past, residential mortgages were not a major part of commercial banks' business. That was partly because most of their deposits were demand deposits (checking accounts), and the government limited the amount of long-term investments the banks could make. But eventually banks began accepting more and more long-term deposits; demand deposits now represent a much smaller share of banks' total deposits than they once did.

While banks have continued to emphasize commercial loans, they have also diversified their lending, with a substantial increase in personal loans and home mortgages. They now have a significant share of the residential finance market.

Savings Banks. Savings banks started out in the nineteenth century offering financial services to small depositors, especially immigrants and members of the working class. They were called mutual savings banks (MSBs) because they were organized as mutual companies, owned by and operated for the benefit of their depositors (as opposed to stockholders).

Traditionally, MSBs were similar to savings and loans. They served their local communities. Their customers were individuals rather than businesses, and most of their deposits were savings deposits. Although the MSBs made many residential mortgage loans, they did not concentrate on them to the extent that S&Ls did. The MSBs were also involved in other types of lending, such as personal loans.

Today savings banks can be organized as mutual companies or stock companies. Residential mortgages continue to be an important part of their business.

Credit Unions. Credit unions are depository institutions, like banks and S&Ls. But unlike banks and S&Ls, credit unions usually serve only members of a particular group; for example, the members of a union or a professional association, or the employees of a large company.

Credit unions traditionally provided small personal loans to their members. In recent years, many credit unions have emphasized home equity loans, which are generally short-term. (A **home equity loan** is a mortgage on the borrower's equity in the home he or she already owns.) Some credit unions now make home purchase loans, and they're likely to expand that aspect of their business.

Mortgage Companies. Mortgage companies have been a rapidly growing force in residential lending. Unlike banks, S&Ls, and credit unions, mortgage companies are not depository institutions, so they don't lend out depositors' funds. Instead, they act as loan correspondents, intermediaries between large investors and home buyers applying for financing.

A loan correspondent lends an investor's money to buyers and then services the loans (collecting and processing the loan payments on behalf of the investor) in exchange for servicing fees. In some cases a bank or an S&L will act as a loan correspondent, but mortgage companies have specialized in this role.

Mortgage companies often act on behalf of large investors such as life insurance companies and pension funds. These investors control vast amounts of capital in the form of insurance premiums and employer contributions to employee pensions. This money generally isn't subject to sudden withdrawal, so it's well suited to investment in long-term mortgages. Since these large investors often operate on a national scale, they have neither the time nor the resources to understand the particular risks of local real estate markets or to deal with the day-to-day management of their loans. So they hire local loan correspondents.

Mortgage companies also borrow money from banks, use it to originate mortgages, then package the mortgages and sell them to the secondary market and other private investors. In many cases, insurance companies, pension funds, and other large investors now simply buy loans from mortgage companies instead of using them as loan correspondents.

Unlike banks and S&Ls, mortgage companies do not keep any of the loans they make. The loans are either made on behalf of an investor or else immediately sold to an investor.

Mortgage companies are sometimes called mortgage bankers. The term "mortgage banker" should not be confused with "mortgage broker." A mortgage broker simply negotiates loans, bringing borrowers together with lenders in exchange for a commission. Once the loan has been arranged, the mortgage broker's involvement ends. Mortgage bankers, on the other hand, originate loans on behalf of an investor and then service the loans to the end of their terms, in exchange for servicing fees. Although mortgage companies may act as mortgage brokers, for the most part they are mortgage bankers.

Private Lenders. Real estate limited partnerships, real estate investment trusts (see Chapter 2), and other types of private investment groups put a great deal of money into real estate. They often finance large residential developments and commercial ventures, such as shopping centers and office buildings. They do not offer loans to individual home buyers, however.

From the home buyer's point of view, the most important type of private lender is the home seller. Sometimes sellers provide all the financing for the purchase of their homes, and it's quite common for sellers to supplement the financing their buyers obtain from an institutional lender. Sellers are an especially important source of financing when institutional loans are hard to come by or market interest rates are high.

Comparing Types of Lenders. At one time, financial institutions in the United States were quite specialized. It was almost as if each type of institution had its own function—its own types of deposits, its own types of services, and its own types of loans. That is no longer true. To a great extent, all of the major depository institutions can now be regarded as "financial supermarkets," offering a wide range of services and loans.

There still are differences between the types of institutions, in terms of lending habits and government regulations, but these generally will not affect a loan applicant who wants to finance the purchase of a home.

Loan Costs

For the majority of buyers, the primary consideration in choosing a lender is how much the loan they need is going to cost. While the interest rate has the greatest impact, lenders impose other charges that can greatly affect the cost of a loan. Most important among these are origination fees and discount points. Both are often simply grouped together as "points;" the term "point" is short for "percentage point." A point is one percentage point (one percent) of the loan amount. For example, on a $90,000 loan, one point would be $900; six points would be $5,400.

Origination Fees. A loan origination fee is designed to pay administrative costs the lender incurs in processing a loan; it is sometimes called a service fee, an administrative charge, or simply a loan fee. An origination fee is charged in virtually every residential loan transaction. It is a closing cost, paid when the transaction closes, and it is usually paid by the buyer.

> **Example:** The buyer is borrowing $100,000, and the lender is charging 1.5 points (1.5% of the loan amount) as an origination fee. The buyer will pay this $1,500 fee to the lender at closing.

Discount Points. Discount points are used to increase the lender's yield, or profit, on the loan. By charging discount points, the lender not only gets interest throughout the loan term, it collects an additional sum of money up front, when the loan is funded. As a result, the lender is willing to make the loan at a lower interest rate than it would have without the discount points. In effect, the lender is paid a lump sum at closing so the borrower can avoid paying more interest later. A lower interest rate also translates into a lower monthly payment.

Discount points are not charged in all loan transactions, but they have become increasingly common. The number of discount points charged usually depends on how the loan's interest rate compares to market interest rates; typically, a lender that offers an especially low rate charges more points to make up for it.

As a rule of thumb, it generally takes about six discount points to increase the lender's yield on a 30-year loan by 1%. So a lender offering an interest rate 1% below market might charge six points to make up the difference. This rule of thumb gives only a rough estimate, however.

In some cases, the seller is willing to pay the discount points on the buyer's loan in order to help the buyer qualify for financing. Even when the lender is not charging discount points, the seller may offer to pay points to make the loan more affordable. This type of arrangement is called a **buydown**: the seller pays the lender points to "buy down" the interest rate on the buyer's loan.

Truth in Lending Act. An origination fee, discount points, and other charges may increase the cost of a mortgage loan significantly. They also make it more difficult to compare the cost of loans offered by different lenders. For example, suppose one lender charges 7% interest, a 1% origination fee, and no discount points, while another charges 6.75% interest, a 1% origination fee, and two discount points. It isn't easy to tell at a glance which of these loans will cost the borrower more in the long term. (The second loan is just slightly less expensive.)

The Truth in Lending Act (TILA) is a federal consumer protection law that addresses this problem of comparing loan costs. The act requires lenders to disclose the complete cost of credit to consumer loan applicants, and also regulates the advertisement of consumer loans. The Truth in Lending Act is implemented by **Regulation Z**, a regulation adopted by the Federal Reserve Board. TILA is enforced by the Federal Trade Commission.

Fig. 11.1 Truth in Lending Act disclosure form

BORROWER(S)

TRUTH-IN-LENDING DISCLOSURE STATEMENT
REQUIRED BY FEDERAL RESERVE REGULATIONS Z

DATE 19	LOAN NUMBER
TYPE OF LOAN	LOAN TERM YEARS
PROPERTY LOCATION	

ANNUAL PERCENTAGE RATE The cost of your credit as a yearly rate	FINANCE CHARGE The dollar amount your credit will cost you	AMOUNT FINANCED The amount of credit provided to you or on your behalf	TOTAL OF PAYMENTS The amount you will have paid after you have paid all payments as scheduled
%	$	$	$

Notice to Borrower(s):   In compliance with Truth-In-Lending Law you are receiving a Good Faith Estimate of Settlement Charges in lieu of an itemization statement.

Your Payment Schedule will be:	Number of Payments	Amount of Payments	When Payments Are Due	Number of Payments	Amount of Payments	When Payments Are Due
		$			$	
Monthly Beginning		$			$	
		$			$	
Date		$			$	

☐ This loan has a **Demand Feature.**

☐ Your loan contains a **Variable Rate Feature.** Disclosures about the Variable Rate have been provided to you earlier. Your ARM Loan ☐ has ☐ does not have a **Conversion Feature.** (The option to convert your ARM loan to a Fixed Rate Mortgage loan.) If choose to convert to a Fixed Rate mortgage loan, your new interest rate will not be higher than _____ %, which is the Maximum Rate.

☐ **Variable Rate not applicable.**

☐ **Insurance:** The following insurance is required: ☐ Property Insurance ☐ Flood Insurance
You may obtain insurance from an agent of your choice, provided they are acceptable to this lender.
  ☐ Property Insurance is available through the lender at a cost of $_____ for a one year term.
  ☐ Flood Insurance is available through the lender at a cost of $_____ for a one year term.
  ☐ Credit Life Insurance or Disability Insurance are not required.
  ☐ Credit Life Insurance and/or Disability Insurance are not provided.
  ☐ Credit Life Insurance and/or Disability Insurance are not available through this lender.
  ☐ Credit Life is available at a cost of $_____ for a _____ term. (X _____)
  ☐ Disability Insurance is available at a cost of $_____ for a _____ term. (X _____)

Security: You are giving a Security Interest ☐ in the property being purchased ☐ other accounts you have with us other (describe) _____

Late Charge: If your payment is _____ days late, you will be required to pay a Penalty charge of _____% of your payment.

Prepayment: If you pay this loan early, you ☐ will ☐ will not have to pay a penalty and you ☐ may ☐ will not be entitled to a refund of a part of the finance charge.

Assumption: Someone buying your property ☐ may, subject to conditions ☐ may not assume the remainder of your loan on the Original terms.

☐ This is an assumption of an existing loan. The interest rate for the term of the loan will not exceed _____%, which is the maximum rate.

☐ Filing Fees $_____

☐ This is an **Early Disclosure** and all dates and numerical disclosures are estimates except for late payment disclosures.

☐ This is your **Final Disclosure**

NOTE: See your contract documents for any additional information about nonpayment. default, any required repayment in full before the scheduled date and prepayment refunds and penalties.

(e) means an-estimate _____

I/we acknowledge receipt of a completed copy of this disclosure statement.

X _____ Date _____ 19 ___ X _____
  Borrower   *Co-Borrower*

Loans Covered by TILA. A loan is a **consumer loan** if it is used for personal, family, or household purposes. A consumer loan is covered by the Truth in Lending Act if it is to be repaid in more than four installments, or is subject to finance charges, and is either:

- for $25,000 or less, or
- secured by real property.

Thus, any mortgage loan is covered by the Truth in Lending Act as long as the proceeds are used for personal, family, or household purposes (such as buying a home or sending children to college).

Loans Exempt from TILA. The Truth in Lending Act applies only to loans made to natural persons, so loans made to corporations or organizations aren't covered. Loans for business, commercial, or agricultural purposes are also exempt. So are loans in excess of $25,000, unless the loan is secured by real property. (Real estate loans for personal, family, or household purposes are covered regardless of the loan amount.) Most seller financing is exempt, because extending credit isn't in the seller's ordinary course of business.

Disclosure Requirements. The primary disclosures that the Truth in Lending Act requires a lender or credit arranger to make to a loan applicant are the total finance charge and the annual percentage rate.

The **total finance charge** is the sum of all fees and charges the borrower pays in connection with the loan. In addition to the interest on the loan, all of the following would be included in the total finance charge: origination fee, discount points paid by the borrower, finder's fees, service fees, and mortgage insurance premiums.

In real estate loan transactions, appraisal fees, credit report charges, and points paid by the seller are not included in the total finance charge.

The **annual percentage rate** (APR) expresses the total cost of the loan as an annual percentage of the loan amount. This key figure enables a prospective borrower to compare loans much more accurately than the interest rate alone.

In a residential mortgage transaction, the lender or credit arranger must give the loan applicant a **disclosure statement** listing good faith estimates of the finance charges within three days after receiving the written application.

Home Equity Loans. The Truth in Lending Act has a special rule for home equity loans. When the security property is the borrower's existing principal residence, the act gives the borrower a right of rescission: he or she may rescind the loan agreement up until three days after signing it, receiving the disclosure statement, or receiving notice of the right of rescission, whichever comes latest. If the borrower never receives the statement or the notice, the right of rescission does not expire for three years. (Remember that this right applies only to home equity loans. There is no right of rescission for a loan financing the purchase or construction of the borrower's principal residence.)

Advertising Under TILA. The Truth in Lending Act strictly controls advertising of credit terms. Its advertising rules apply to anyone who advertises consumer credit, not just lenders and credit arrangers. For example, a real estate broker advertising financing terms for a listed home has to comply with TILA and Regulation Z.

It is always legal to state the cash price or the annual percentage rate in an ad. But if any other particular loan terms (such as the downpayment or the interest rate) are stated in the ad, then all the rest of the terms must also be included. For example, if an ad says, "Assume VA loan at 9% interest," it will violate the Truth in Lending Act if it does not go on to reveal the APR, the downpayment, and all the terms of repayment. However, general statements such as "low downpayment," "easy terms," or "affordable interest rate" do not trigger the full disclosure requirement.

Rate Lock-ins. There's one other issue concerning loan costs that we should mention. A prospective borrower may want to have the interest rate quoted by the lender "locked in" for a specified period. Unless the interest rate is locked in, the lender can change it at any time until the transaction closes. If market interest rates are rising, the lender is likely to increase the interest rate on the loan. That could cost the borrower a lot of money over the long term, or else actually price the borrower out of the transaction altogether.

Locking in the interest rate is generally not desirable when market interest rates are expected to go down. A lender will typically charge the borrower the locked-in rate even if market rates drop in the period before closing.

Most lenders charge the borrower a fee to lock in the interest rate. The fee is typically applied to the borrower's closing costs if the transaction closes. If the lender rejects the borrower's application, the fee is refunded; it will be forfeited to the lender, though, if the borrower withdraws from the transaction.

The Loan Application Process

Once a buyer has compared loan costs and selected a lender, the next step is applying for the loan. The buyer fills out a loan application form and provides the lender with supporting documentation. The application is then submitted to the lender's underwriting department, which evaluates the application and ultimately approves or rejects the proposed loan.

Preapproval

Traditionally, a buyer would first find the house he or she wanted, then apply for a loan. In recent years, however, getting **preapproved** for a loan has become a common practice. To get preapproved, a prospective buyer submits a loan application to a lender before starting to house-hunt. If the lender approves the application, the buyer is preapproved for a specified maximum loan amount.

Preapproval lets the buyer know in advance, before shopping, just how expensive a house he or she can afford. If a house meets the lender's standards and is in the established price range, the buyer will be able to buy it. This spares the buyer the disappointment of initially choosing a house that turns out to be too expensive and having the loan request turned down. Preapproval also helps streamline the closing process once the buyer has found the right house.

The Application Form

A mortgage loan application form asks the prospective borrower for detailed information about his or her finances. The lender requires this information because it wants its loans to be profitable investments. A loan is unlikely to be profitable if the borrower doesn't have the financial resources to make the payments reliably, or if the borrower has a habit of defaulting on debts. The application helps the lender identify and turn down potential borrowers who are likely to create collection problems.

Most mortgage lenders use a standard residential loan application form developed by Fannie Mae and Freddie Mac. The form requires all of the following information.

Personal Information. In addition to basic information such as address and social security number, loan applicants must also supply certain personal information that has some bearing on their financial condition. This includes the applicant's age, education, marital status, and number of dependents.

Housing Expense. The applicant is asked how much he or she currently spends on housing. This will be the applicant's monthly rent or monthly house payment. In addition to principal and interest, the house payment would include property taxes, homeowner's insurance, any mortgage insurance, and any homeowner's association dues.

Employment. The application form asks the name of the applicant's current employer, what type of business it is, the applicant's position and title, and how many years the applicant has spent at that job and in that line of work. If the applicant has been with his or her current employer for less than two years, information about previous employment is required.

Income. A loan applicant should list all of his or her sources of income. In regard to employment income, this includes not only the applicant's salary or wages, but also overtime, bonuses, and commissions. Dividends, interest, pension payments, and income from any other sources should be listed as well. The lender will verify the applicant's employment income by contacting the employer, and will require the applicant to submit documentation of other income sources along with the application.

Assets and Liabilities. The loan application form calls for a list of the applicant's assets, which may include money in bank accounts, stocks and bonds, life insurance, real estate, retirement funds, automobiles, and other personal property. The applicant must also list liabilities, which may include credit card debts, car loans, real estate loans, alimony or child support payments, and unpaid taxes. The lender will verify the applicant's asset and liability information (for example, by sending a verification form to the financial institutions where the applicant has accounts).

Underwriting the Loan

Once a loan application has been submitted and the information has been verified, the loan is ready for underwriting. **Loan underwriting** is the process of evaluating both the applicant and the property he or she wants to buy to determine whether they meet the lender's minimum standards. The person who conducts the evaluation is called a loan underwriter or credit underwriter.

In theory, a lender is free to set its own underwriting standards, taking virtually any risks it likes. In practice, however, most lenders apply standards set by the major secondary market agencies (or in the case of an FHA or VA loan, standards set by the FHA or VA).

Qualifying the Buyer. In evaluating a loan applicant's financial situation, an underwriter must consider many factors. These factors fall into three main groups: income, net worth, and credit history.

Income. A primary consideration for the underwriter is whether the loan applicant's monthly income is enough to cover the proposed monthly mortgage payment in addition to all of the applicant's other expenses. So the underwriter needs to determine how much income the applicant has.

Not all income is equal in an underwriter's eyes, however. To be taken into account in deciding whether the applicant qualifies for the loan, his or her income must meet standards of quality and durability. In other words, it must be from a dependable source, such as an established business, and it must be likely to continue for some time. Income that meets the tests of quality and durability is generally referred to as the loan applicant's **stable monthly income**.

Once the underwriter has calculated the loan applicant's stable monthly income, the next step is to measure its adequacy: Is the stable monthly income enough so that the applicant can afford the proposed monthly mortgage payment? To answer this question, underwriters use **income ratios**. The rationale behind the ratios is that if a borrower's expenses exceed a certain percentage of his or her monthly income, the borrower may have a difficult time making the payments on the loan.

There are two types of income ratios:

- A **housing expense to income ratio** measures the proposed monthly mortgage payment against the applicant's stable monthly income.

- A **debt to income ratio** measures all of the applicant's monthly obligations (the proposed mortgage payment, plus car payments, child support payments, etc.) against the stable monthly income.

For these calculations, the monthly mortgage payment includes principal, interest, taxes, and insurance (often abbreviated PITI). Each ratio is expressed as a percentage; for example, a loan applicant's housing expense to income ratio would be 29% if her proposed mortgage payment represented 29% of her stable monthly income. Whether that ratio would be considered too high would depend on the lender and on the type of loan applied for. As we'll discuss later in the chapter, each of the major loan programs (conventional, FHA-insured, or VA-guaranteed) has its own income ratio limits.

Net Worth. An individual's net worth is determined by subtracting total personal liabilities from total personal assets. According to Fannie Mae, "accumulation of net worth is a strong indication of creditworthiness." A loan applicant who has built up a significant net worth from earnings, savings, and other investments clearly has the ability to manage financial affairs.

Getting an idea of the loan applicant's financial skills is not the only reason for investigating his or her net worth, however. The underwriter needs to make sure the applicant has sufficient funds to cover the downpayment, the closing costs, and other expenses incidental to the purchase of the property.

In addition, a loan applicant is often required to have cash reserves left over after closing. This provides some assurance that the applicant would be able to handle financial emergencies, such as unexpected bills or a temporary interruption of income, without defaulting on the mortgage.

Credit History. In addition to evaluating a loan applicant's income and net worth, the underwriter also analyzes the applicant's credit history, using a credit report obtained from a credit reporting agency. The credit report indicates how reliably the applicant has paid bills and other debts, and whether there have been any severe problems such as bankruptcy or foreclosure.

Many underwriters use **credit scores** to help assess how likely it is that a loan applicant will default on the proposed loan. A credit reporting agency calculates an individual's credit score using the credit report and a statistical model that correlates different types of negative credit information with actual loan defaults.

Credit problems can be an indication of financial irresponsibility, but in some cases they result from a personal crisis such as loss of a job, divorce, or hospitalization. A loan applicant with a poor credit history should explain any extenuating circumstances to the lender.

Qualifying the Property. In addition to deciding whether the buyer is a good risk, the underwriter also has to consider whether the property that the buyer wants to purchase is a good risk. Is the property worth enough to serve as collateral for the loan amount in question? In other words, if foreclosure became necessary, would the property sell for enough money to pay off the loan? To answer these questions, the underwriter relies on an appraisal report commissioned by the lender. The appraisal provides an expert's estimate of the property's value. (Appraisal is discussed in Chapter 12.)

Basic Loan Features

In this section, we'll look at the basic features of a home mortgage loan. These include the loan term; the amortization; the loan-to-value ratio; a secondary financing arrangement (in some cases); and a fixed or adjustable interest rate. A lender is likely to present a home buyer with a number of options concerning these various loan features. For example, the buyer may be offered a choice between a 30-year loan and a 15-year loan, and between a fixed-rate loan and an adjustable-rate loan. Each of these choices has an impact on how large a loan the buyer will qualify for, and ultimately on how expensive a home the buyer can purchase.

Loan Term

A mortgage loan's term (also known as the repayment period) has a significant impact on both the monthly mortgage payment and the total amount of interest paid over the life of the loan. The longer the term, the lower the monthly payment, and the more interest paid.

Since the 1930s, the standard term for a mortgage loan has been 30 years. This long repayment period makes the monthly payments affordable, which reduces the risk of default.

Although 30-year loans continue to predominate, 15-year loans have also become popular. A 15-year loan has higher monthly payments than a comparable 30-year loan, but the 15-year loan offers substantial savings for the borrower in the long run. Lenders frequently offer lower interest rates on 15-year loans, because the shorter term means less risk for the lender. And the borrower will save thousands of dollars in total interest charges over the life of the loan (see

Fig. 11.2 A 15-year loan offers substantial savings over a 30-year loan.

Figure 11.2). A 15-year loan also offers free and clear ownership of the property in half the time.

However, the monthly payments are significantly higher for a 15-year loan, and in some cases a much larger downpayment would be necessary to reduce the monthly payments to a level the borrower can afford.

Example: Bob has a choice between a 30-year loan at 7.5% and a 15-year loan at 7%. Based on his stable monthly income, he can afford to make monthly principal and interest payments of $1,000. This is enough to amortize a $143,000 loan at 7.5% over 30 years, but it will amortize only about $111,250 at 7% over 15 years. In other words, Bob could qualify for a $143,000 loan under the 30-year plan, but will qualify for only $111,250 if he chooses the 15-year option. The difference between the two loan amounts would have to be made up with a larger downpayment.

Amortization

Almost all institutional loans are **fully amortized**. A fully amortized loan is repaid within a certain period of time by means of regular payments that include a portion for principal and a portion for interest. As each payment is made, the appropriate amount of principal is deducted from the debt and the remainder of the payment, which represents the interest, is retained by the lender as earnings or profit. With each payment, the amount of the debt is reduced and the interest due with the next payment is recalculated based on the lower balance. The total payment remains the same throughout the term of the loan, but every month the interest portion of the payment is reduced and the principal portion is increased. (See Figure 11.3.) The final payment pays off the loan completely; the principal balance is zero and no further interest is owed.

Example: A $190,000 loan at 7.25% interest can be fully amortized over a 30-year term with monthly principal and interest payments of $1,296.13. If the borrower pays $1,296.13 each month, then the loan will be fully repaid (with interest) after 30 years.

There are two alternatives to the fully amortized loan. A **partially amortized** loan requires regular payments of both interest and principal, but those payments are not enough to repay all of the principal; the borrower is required to make a large balloon payment (the remaining principal balance) at the end of the loan term.

Example: Betty takes back a $190,000 mortgage at 7.25% interest on the sale of her home to Bob. The mortgage calls for regular monthly payments of $1,296.13 for principal and interest, with a loan term of five years. Because the monthly payments are more than enough to cover the interest on the loan, some of the principal will be repaid during the five-year term. But since it would take 30 years to fully repay the loan at this rate, a substantial amount of principal (roughly $179,000) will still be unpaid after only five years. This amount will be due as a balloon payment, which Bob will have to either refinance or pay in cash.

With an **interest-only** loan, the borrower pays only the interest during the loan term, and all of the principal—the entire amount originally borrowed—is due at the end of the term.

Example: Suppose Betty (from the previous example) had given Bob an interest-only loan for $190,000 at 7.25% interest. In that case, the monthly payments would be only $1,147.92, the amount needed to cover the monthly interest on the loan. At the end of the five-year term, Bob would owe the full $190,000 of principal to Betty.

Partial amortization and interest-only loans are fairly common in seller financing arrangements, but institutional lenders do not use them for residential mortgage loans very often.

Loan-to-Value Ratios

The loan-to-value ratio (LTV) for a particular transaction expresses the relationship between the loan amount and the value of the property. The lower the LTV, the smaller the loan amount and the bigger the downpayment.

Example: If a lender makes an $80,000 loan secured by a home appraised at $100,000, the loan-to-value ratio is 80%. The loan amount is 80% of the property's value, and the buyer makes a 20% downpayment. If the lender loaned $75,000 secured by the same property, the LTV would be 75% and the downpayment would be 25%.

Fig. 11.3 Payments for a fully amortized loan

Example: $190,000 loan @ 7.25%, 30-year term, monthly payments

Payment No.	Beginning Balance	Total Payment	Interest Portion	Principal Portion	Ending Balance
1	$190,000.00	$1,296.13	$1,147.92	$148.22	$189,851.78
2	$189,851.78	$1,296.13	$1,147.02	$149.11	$189,702.67
3	$189,702.67	$1,296.13	$1,146.12	$150.01	$189,552.65
4	$189,552.65	$1,296.13	$1,145.21	$150.92	$189,401.73
5	$189,401.73	$1,296.13	$1,144.30	$151.83	$189,249.90

The loan-to-value ratio affects the degree of risk involved in the loan—both the risk of default and the risk of loss in the event of default. A borrower who has a substantial investment in the property will try harder to avoid foreclosure; and when foreclosure is necessary, the lender is more likely to recover the entire debt if the LTV is relatively low.

The higher the LTV, the greater the lender's risk. So lenders use loan-to-value ratios to set maximum loan amounts.

> **Example:** If a lender's maximum LTV for a certain type of loan is 75%, and the property's appraised value is $100,000, then $75,000 would be the maximum loan amount.

Lenders actually base the maximum loan amount on the sales price or the appraised value, whichever is less. Thus, if the $100,000 property in the example above was selling for $95,000, the maximum loan amount would be $71,250 (75% of $95,000).

Many lenders have special rules for high-LTV loans because of the extra risk they pose. We'll discuss these rules later in the chapter.

Secondary Financing

Sometimes a buyer obtains two mortgage loans at once: a primary loan to pay for most of the purchase price, and a second loan to pay part of the downpayment or closing costs required for the first loan. This supplementary second loan is called **secondary financing**. Secondary financing may come from an institutional lender, the seller, or a private third party.

In most cases, the primary lender will allow secondary financing only if it complies with certain requirements. For example, the borrower must be able to qualify for the combined payment on the first and second loans. The borrower is usually required to make a minimum downpayment out of his or her own funds. And the second loan must be payable at any time, without a prepayment penalty.

Fixed and Adjustable Interest Rates

A fixed-rate loan is repaid over its term at an unchanging rate of interest. For example, the interest rate is set at 6.75% when the loan is made, and the borrower pays 6.75% interest on the unpaid principal throughout the loan term.

When market interest rates are relatively low and stable, fixed-rate loans work well for borrowers and lenders. But in periods when market rates are high and volatile, neither borrowers nor lenders are comfortable with fixed-rate loans. High interest rates price many borrowers out of the market. And if market rates are fluctuating rapidly, lenders prefer not to tie up their funds for long periods at a set interest rate.

A type of loan that addresses both of these issues is the **adjustable-rate mortgage** (ARM). An ARM permits the lender to periodically adjust the loan's interest rate so that it accurately reflects changes in the cost of money. With an ARM, it is the borrower who is affected by interest rate fluctuations. If rates climb, the borrower's monthly payment goes up; if they decline, the payment goes down. Because the ARM shifts this risk to the borrower, lenders usually charge a lower rate for an ARM than for a fixed-rate loan.

How an ARM Works. With an ARM, the borrower's interest rate is determined initially by the cost of money at the time the loan is made. Once the rate has been set, it's tied to one of several widely recognized indexes, and future interest adjustments are based on the upward and downward movements of the index.

Index and Margin. An **index** is a published statistical rate that is a reliable indicator of changes in the cost of money. Examples include the one-year Treasury bill index and the Eleventh District cost of funds index. At the time a loan is made, the lender selects the index it prefers, and thereafter the loan's interest rate will rise and fall with the rates reported for the index.

Since the index is a reflection of the lender's cost of money, it is necessary to add a **margin** to the index to ensure sufficient income for administrative expenses and profit. The lender's margin is usually 2% or 3%, or somewhere in between. The index plus the margin equals the interest rate charged to the borrower.

Example:

5.25%	Current index value
+ 2.00%	Margin
7.25%	Borrower's interest rate

It is the index that fluctuates during the loan term and causes the borrower's interest rate to increase and decrease; the lender's margin remains constant.

Adjustment Periods. The borrower's interest rate is not adjusted every time the index changes. Each ARM has a rate adjustment period, which determines how often its interest rate is adjusted. A rate adjustment period of one year is the most common.

An ARM also has a payment adjustment period, which determines how often the borrower's monthly mortgage payment is increased or decreased (reflecting changes in the interest rate). For most ARMs, payment adjustments are made at the same intervals as rate adjustments.

Caps. One problem associated with ARMs is a phenomenon known as "payment shock." If market interest rates rise rapidly, so will an ARM's index, which could lead to a sharp increase in the interest rate the lender charges the borrower. Of course, a higher interest rate translates into a higher monthly payment. If the payment increases so dramatically that the borrower can no longer afford it, it's called payment shock.

To protect borrowers from payment shock and themselves from default, lenders impose caps on their ARMs. An interest rate cap limits how much the lender can raise the interest rate on the loan, even if the index goes way up. A mortgage payment cap limits how much the lender can increase the monthly payment.

Negative Amortization. If an ARM has certain features, payment increases may not keep up with increases in the loan's interest rate, so that the monthly payments do not cover all the interest owed. The lender usually handles this by adding the unpaid interest to the loan's principal balance; this is called **negative amortization**. Ordinarily, a loan's principal balance declines steadily, although gradually. But negative amortization causes the principal balance to go up instead of down. The borrower may owe the lender more money than he or she originally borrowed. Today, lenders generally structure their ARMs to avoid negative amortization.

Residential Financing Programs

Residential financing programs can be divided into two main groups: conventional loans and government-sponsored loans. In this section, we'll look first at conventional loans, and then at the most important loan programs sponsored by the federal government: the FHA-insured loan program and the VA-guaranteed loan program. As you'll see, each program has its own qualifying standards and its own rules concerning the downpayment and other aspects of the loan.

Conventional Loans

A conventional loan is simply any institutional loan that is not insured or guaranteed by a government agency. For example, FHA-insured and VA-guaranteed loans are not conventional loans, because they are backed by a government agency.

The rules for conventional loans presented here reflect the criteria established by the secondary market agencies that purchase conventional loans, Fannie Mae and Freddie Mac (see Chapter 10). When a loan does not meet secondary market criteria it is considered **nonconforming** and cannot be sold to the major secondary market agencies. Today, most lenders want to be able to sell their loans on the secondary market, so they tailor their standards for conventional loans to match those set by Fannie Mae or Freddie Mac.

Conventional LTVs. For decades, the standard conventional loan-to-value ratio has been 80% of the appraised value or sales price of the home, whichever is less. Lenders feel confident that a borrower who makes a 20% downpayment with his or her own funds is unlikely to default; the borrower has too much to lose. And even if the borrower were to default, a foreclosure sale would be likely to generate at least 80% of the purchase price.

While 80% is the standard LTV for a conventional loan, it is not the maximum. Lenders make conventional loans with loan-to-value ratios up to 95%. The loans are classified as 80%, 90%, or 95% loans, and different rules apply to each category. A loan is classified as an 80% loan if the LTV is 80% or less, as a 90% loan if the LTV is over 80% but not more than 90%, and as a 95% loan if the LTV is over 90% but not more than 95%.

> **Example:** A home has been appraised at $100,000, which is also the sales price. The buyers have $18,000 to use as a downpayment, and the lender has agreed to loan them $82,000, the balance of the price. The LTV for this loan is 82%. Since the LTV is over 80% but not more than 90%, the loan will be treated as a 90% loan.

Because the lender's risk is greater when the borrower's downpayment is smaller, lenders require borrowers to obtain private mortgage insurance for 90% and 95% loans, although it is not required for 80% loans. (Private mortgage insurance is discussed below.) Some lenders also charge higher interest rates and larger loan fees for 90% and 95% loans than for 80% loans.

The rules for 95% loans tend to be especially strict. Most lenders require a 95% loan to have a fixed interest rate, because there's a greater risk of default with an adjustable-rate mortgage. And the underwriting standards for 95% loans are more stringent, so that it's harder for a buyer to qualify for a loan with such a low downpayment.

Owner-Occupancy. Unless the borrower is making an unusually large down-payment—well over the standard 20%—owner-occupancy is usually required for a conventional loan. That is, the borrower must intend to occupy the home purchased with the loan, as opposed to renting it out to tenants. Owner-occupants are considered less likely to default than non-occupant borrowers.

Private Mortgage Insurance. Private mortgage insurance (PMI) is designed to protect lenders from the greater risk of high LTV loans; PMI makes up for the reduced borrower equity. PMI is usually required on conventional loans with downpayments of less than 20%.

When insuring a loan, the mortgage insurance company actually assumes only a portion of the risk of default. It does not insure the entire loan amount, but rather the upper portion of the loan. The amount of coverage varies; typically it is 20% to 25% of the loan amount.

Example: 20% coverage

$100,000	Sales price
× 90%	LTV
$90,000	90% loan
× 20%	Amount of coverage
$18,000	Amount of policy

In the event of default and foreclosure, the lender, at the insurer's option, will either sell the property and make a claim for reimbursement of actual losses (if any) up to the amount of the policy, or relinquish the property to the insurer and make a claim for actual losses up to the policy amount. Losses incurred by the lender take the form of unpaid interest, property taxes and hazard insurance, attorney's fees, and the cost of preserving the property during the period of foreclosure and resale, as well as the expense of selling the property itself.

Conventional Qualifying Standards. Fannie Mae and Freddie Mac's underwriting standards include detailed guidelines for evaluation of a conventional loan applicant's income, net worth, and credit history. To determine whether the applicant's stable monthly income is sufficient, an underwriter often calculates both a housing expense to income ratio and a total debt to income ratio.

Example: Suppose the lender's maximum housing expense to income ratio is 28% and maximum debt to income ratio is 36%. If a loan applicant's housing expense to income ratio is 27% (under the lender's limit), but her debt to income ratio is 38% (over the lender's limit), then the lender probably won't approve the loan.

In some cases, however, the underwriter will consider only the total debt to income ratio. Because the debt to income ratio takes all of the applicant's monthly obligations into account, it is considered a more reliable indicator of creditworthiness than the housing expense to income ratio.

Note that many lenders have lower maximum income ratios for 95% loans, to make up for the greater risk posed by a high-LTV loan.

As a general rule, an applicant for a conventional loan must have the equivalent of two months' mortgage payments in reserve after making the downpayment and paying all their closing costs. For 95% loans, some lenders require three months' mortgage payments in reserve.

Assumption. Most conventional loan agreements include an alienation clause, so the borrower can't sell the property and arrange for the buyer to assume the loan without the lender's permission. Typically, the lender will evaluate the buyer with the same qualifying standards that it applies in a new loan transaction. If the lender approves the assumption, it will charge an assumption fee, and it may also adjust the interest rate to the prevailing rates at that time.

FHA-Insured Loans

The Federal Housing Administration (FHA) was created by Congress in 1934 as part of the National Housing Act. The purpose of the act, and of the FHA, was to generate new jobs through increased construction activity, to exert a stabilizing influence on the mortgage market, and to promote the financing, repair, improvement, and sale of real estate nationwide.

Today the FHA is part of the Department of Housing and Urban Development (HUD). Its primary function is insuring mortgage loans; the FHA compensates lenders who make loans through its programs for losses that result from borrower default. The FHA does not build homes or make loans.

In effect, the FHA serves as a giant mortgage insurance agency. Its insurance program, known as the **Mutual Mortgage Insurance Plan**, is funded with premiums paid by FHA borrowers.

Under the plan, lenders who have been approved by the FHA to make insured loans either submit applications from prospective borrowers to the local FHA office for approval or, if authorized by the FHA to do so, perform the underwriting functions themselves. (Note that prospective borrowers always apply to an FHA-approved lender, not to the FHA itself.) Lenders who are authorized to underwrite their own FHA loan applications are called direct endorsers.

Lenders who don't underwrite their own FHA loans forward applications to the local FHA office for underwriting and approval. The FHA does not accept applications directly from borrowers; they must begin with a lender such as a bank or a mortgage company.

As the insurer, the FHA is liable to the lender for the full amount of any losses resulting from default and foreclosure. In exchange for insuring a loan, the FHA regulates many of the terms and conditions on which the loan is made.

Characteristics of FHA Loans. The typical FHA-insured loan has a 30-year term, although the borrower may have the option of a shorter term (as short as 15 years). The property purchased with an FHA loan must be the borrower's primary residence.

A lender must charge a 1% origination fee on an FHA loan, and may also charge discount points. The discount points can be paid either by the borrower or by the seller.

FHA loans have a number of features that distinguish them from conventional loans. Here are the most significant differences:

1. **Less stringent qualifying standards.** It is easier to qualify for an FHA loan than for a conventional loan.

2. **Low downpayments.** The downpayment required for an FHA loan is often considerably less than it would be for a comparable conventional loan.

3. **Minimum cash investment.** The FHA requires the borrower to make a minimum cash investment of at least 3% of the property's sales price. But most closing costs paid by the borrower, as well as the borrower's downpayment, count toward meeting this requirement. (Note, however, that discount points paid by the borrower do not count.)

4. **Mortgage insurance is required on all loans.** Regardless of the size of the downpayment, mortgage insurance is required on all FHA-insured loans.

FHA Loan Amounts. FHA programs are primarily intended to help low- and middle-income home buyers. So HUD sets maximum loan amounts, limiting the size of loans that can be insured under a particular program. Maximum loan amounts vary from one place to another because they are based on median housing costs in each area. An area where housing is expensive has a higher maximum loan amount than a low-cost area.

The size of an FHA loan is limited not only by the maximum loan amount for the area, but also by the FHA's loan-to-value rules. The LTV limit that applies to a particular transaction depends on the appraised value or sales price of the home being purchased. For most transactions, the LTV can be over 97%; in some, it can be over 98%. As a result, the amount of cash an FHA borrower needs at closing can be much less than a conventional borrower would need for the same purchase.

FHA Qualifying Standards. As with any institutional loan, the underwriting for an FHA-insured loan involves the analysis of the applicant's income, net worth, and credit history. But the FHA's underwriting standards are not as strict as the Fannie Mae/Freddie Mac standards used for conventional loans. The FHA standards make it easier for low- and middle-income home buyers to qualify for a mortgage.

Income. Just as with a conventional loan, an underwriter evaluating an application for an FHA loan will apply two ratios to determine the adequacy of the applicant's income. However, the FHA's maximum income ratios are higher than the ones typically set for conventional loans. This means that an FHA borrower's mortgage payment and other monthly obligations can be a larger percentage of his or her income than a conventional borrower's.

Although the FHA loan program is targeted toward low- and middle-income buyers, there is no maximum income level. A person with a high income could qualify for an FHA loan, so long as the requested loan didn't exceed the maximum loan amount for the area.

Funds for Closing. At closing an FHA borrower must have sufficient funds to cover the minimum cash investment, any discount points he or she has agreed to pay, and certain other closing costs. An FHA borrower is usually not required to have reserves after closing.

FHA Insurance Premiums. Mortgage insurance premiums for FHA loans are commonly referred to as the **MIP**. For most programs, an FHA borrower pays both a one-time premium and annual premiums. The one-time premium may be paid at closing, or else financed along with the loan amount and paid off over the loan term.

Assumption of FHA Loans. FHA loans made before 1990 can be assumed without the lender's approval, if the seller does not need a release of liability. Loans made since then can be assumed only by a buyer who meets FHA underwriting standards. The buyer must intend to occupy the home as his or her primary residence.

VA-Guaranteed Loans

The VA-guaranteed home loan program was established to help veterans finance the purchase of their homes with affordable loans. VA financing offers many advantages over conventional financing and has few disadvantages.

Eligibility for VA Loans. Eligibility for a VA home loan is based on length of continuous active service in the U.S. armed forces. The minimum requirement varies from **90 days** to **24 months**, depending on when the veteran served. (Longer periods are required for peacetime service.) Eligibility may also be based on longtime service in the national guard or reserves. Military personnel who receive a dishonorable discharge are not eligible for VA loans.

A veteran's surviving spouse may be eligible for a VA loan if he or she has not remarried and the veteran was killed in action or died of service-related injuries. A veteran's spouse may also be eligible if the veteran is listed as missing in action or is a prisoner of war.

Application Process. An eligible veteran will be issued a **Certificate of Eligibility** by the Department of Veterans Affairs (VA). To apply for a VA loan, the applicant must present the certificate to an institutional lender. The lender will process the veteran's loan application and forward it to the VA. Note that the Certificate of Eligibility is not a guarantee that the veteran will qualify for a loan.

The property that the veteran wants to purchase must be appraised in accordance with VA guidelines. The appraised value is set forth in a document called a **Certificate of Reasonable Value** (CRV).

When a lender approves a VA loan, the loan is guaranteed by the federal government. If the borrower defaults, the VA will reimburse the lender for part or all of its loss. The loan guaranty works essentially like mortgage insurance—it protects the lender against a large loss if the borrower fails to repay the loan.

Characteristics of VA Loans. A VA loan can be used to finance the purchase or construction of a single-family residence or a multifamily residence with up to four units. The veteran must intend to occupy the home. (In the case of a multifamily property, the veteran must occupy one of the units.)

VA-guaranteed loans are attractive to borrowers for several reasons, including the following:

- Unlike most loans, a typical VA loan does not require a downpayment. The loan amount can be as large as the sales price or appraised value, whichever is less. In other words, the loan-to-value ratio can be 100%.
- There is no maximum loan amount, nor are there income restrictions. (VA loans are not limited to low- or middle-income buyers.)
- VA underwriting standards are less stringent than either conventional or FHA qualifying standards.
- VA loans do not require mortgage insurance.

Interest Rate. Traditionally, the interest rate for VA loans was set by the VA, but that's no longer the case. The interest rate for a VA loan is now negotiated between the lender and the borrower in the usual way. It's typically a fixed rate, but in some cases an adjustable rate is an option.

Discount Points. A lender may charge discount points on a VA loan. At one time, VA borrowers were not allowed to pay discount points themselves, so any points charged had to be paid by the seller or a third party. That rule no longer applies; the borrower may pay the points.

VA Guaranty. One of the most important characteristics of VA loans is that they are guaranteed by the U.S. government. The VA guaranty reduces the lender's risk of loss in case of default. Without the guaranty, a lender would be reluctant to make a no-downpayment loan.

Like private mortgage insurance, the VA guaranty covers only part of the loan amount, up to a maximum set by the government. The maximum guaranty amount is increased periodically. The amount of the guaranty available to a particular veteran is sometimes called the vet's "entitlement."

Because the guaranty amount is limited, a large loan amount presents some risk for the lender. Many lenders require the VA borrower to make at least a small downpayment if the loan amount exceeds a certain limit. This is a limit set by the lender, however, not by the VA.

Reinstatement. If a veteran sells property he or she financed with a VA loan and repays the loan in full from the proceeds of the sale, the veteran is entitled to a full reinstatement of guaranty rights for future use. However, because of the owner-occupancy requirement, the vet must demonstrate a need for new housing in order to obtain a new VA loan.

Substitution of Entitlement. If the home is sold and the loan is assumed instead of repaid, the veteran's entitlement can be restored under certain circumstances. The buyer who assumes the loan must be an eligible veteran and agree to substitute his or her entitlement for the seller's. The loan payments must be current, and the buyer must be an acceptable credit risk. If these conditions are met, the vet can formally request a substitution of entitlement from the VA.

Note that a VA loan can be assumed by a non-veteran who meets the VA's standards of creditworthiness. But the entitlement of the veteran seller will not be restored if the buyer assuming the loan is not a veteran.

Qualifying Standards. Lenders must follow guidelines established by the VA to evaluate a VA loan applicant's creditworthiness. The VA's rules for income analysis are quite different from those used for conventional or FHA loans.

Instead of using both a housing expense to income ratio and a total debt to income ratio, the VA uses only a total debt to income ratio. The VA's maximum debt to income ratio is considerably higher than the conventional maximum.

In addition to the total debt to income ratio, the underwriter will also consider the veteran's **residual income**. This is calculated by subtracting the proposed mortgage payment, all other recurring obligations, and certain taxes from the veteran's gross monthly income. The veteran's residual income must meet the VA's minimum requirements, which vary based on the region of the country where the veteran lives, family size, and the size of the proposed loan.

Overall, the VA's qualifying standards are much more liberal than conventional standards. A buyer who'd be considered marginal for a conventional loan might easily qualify for a VA loan—as long as he or she is an eligible veteran.

📖 Chapter Summary

1. Real estate lenders in the primary market include savings and loan associations, commercial banks, savings banks, mortgage companies, credit unions, and private lenders.

2. Lenders charge an origination fee to cover their administrative costs, and sometimes charge discount points to increase the yield on the loan. One point is 1% of the loan amount.

3. The Truth in Lending Act applies to any consumer loan that is secured by real property. It requires lenders and credit arrangers to give loan applicants a disclosure statement about loan costs. It also regulates how financing information is presented in advertising.

4. In qualifying a buyer for a real estate loan, an underwriter examines the buyer's income, net worth, and credit history to determine if he or she can be expected to make the proposed monthly mortgage payments.

5. An underwriter evaluates the quantity, quality, and durability of the loan applicant's income. Income that meets the tests of quality and durability is counted as part of the applicant's stable monthly income. Income ratios measure the adequacy of the stable monthly income—whether the applicant can afford the proposed mortgage payment.

6. The traditional loan term for a mortgage loan is 30 years, but 15-year loans are also available. A 15-year loan requires higher payments than a comparable 30-year loan, but it saves the borrower thousands of dollars in interest.

7. Nearly all institutional mortgage loans are fully amortized. Partially amortized loans and interest-only loans are sometimes used in seller financing arrangements.

8. The loan-to-value ratio for a particular transaction expresses the relationship between the loan amount and the property's appraised value or sales price, whichever is less. The higher the loan-to-value ratio, the greater the lender's risk.

9. Secondary financing may be used to cover part of the downpayment and closing costs required for the primary loan. A secondary financing arrangement must comply with rules set by the primary lender.

10. The interest rate on a mortgage loan may be either fixed or adjustable. An ARM's interest rate is tied to an index, and it is adjusted at specified intervals to reflect changes in the index.

11. A conventional loan is an institutional loan that is not insured or guaranteed by the government. A conventional loan that conforms to the standards set by Fannie Mae and Freddie Mac can be sold to the major secondary market agencies.

12. A conventional loan is classified as an 80%, 90%, or 95% loan, depending on the loan-to-value ratio; owner-occupancy is generally required. Private mortgage insurance is required for loans with LTVs over 80%.

13. FHA-insured loans are distinguished from conventional loans by less stringent qualifying standards, lower downpayments, and less cash needed for closing.

14. A home purchased with an FHA loan must be an owner-occupied primary residence. The maximum loan amount available for an FHA loan depends on housing costs in the area where the property is located. FHA mortgage insurance is required on all FHA loans.

15. Eligible veterans may obtain a VA-guaranteed home loan. No downpayment is required for a VA loan. There is no maximum loan amount, although there is a maximum guaranty amount.

16. The qualifying standards for a VA loan are considerably less stringent than the standards for conventional or FHA loans.

Key Terms

Mortgage company—A type of lender that is not a depository institution and that makes and services loans on behalf of large investors. Sometimes called a mortgage banker.

Mortgage broker—An individual or company that arranges loans between borrowers and investors, but does not service the loans.

Point—One percent of the amount of a loan.

Origination fee—A fee that a lender charges to cover the administrative costs of processing a loan.

Discount points—A fee that a lender may charge to increase the yield on the loan, over and above the interest rate.

Truth in Lending Act (TILA)—A federal consumer protection law that requires disclosure of financing costs to consumer loan applicants and in advertising.

Regulation Z—The Federal Reserve Board's regulation that implements the Truth in Lending Act.

APR—Annual percentage rate; the relationship of the total finance charge to the loan amount, expressed as an annual percentage.

Loan underwriting—Evaluating the creditworthiness of the buyer and the value of the property to determine if a loan should be approved.

Stable monthly income—Income that satisfies the lender's standards of quality and durability.

Income ratios—Percentages used to determine whether a loan applicant's stable monthly income is sufficient.

Housing expense to income ratio—A percentage that measures a loan applicant's proposed monthly mortgage payment against the applicant's stable monthly income.

Debt to income ratio—A percentage that measures all of a loan applicant's monthly obligations (including the proposed mortgage payment) against the stable monthly income. Also called total debt service to income ratio.

Net worth—Total personal assets less total personal liabilities.

Fully amortized loan—A loan that is repaid by the end of its term by means of regular principal and interest payments.

Loan-to-value ratio—The relationship between the loan amount and the property's appraised value or sales price, whichever is less.

Secondary financing—A second loan to help pay the downpayment or closing costs associated with the primary loan.

Fixed-rate loan—A loan repaid over its term at an unchanging rate of interest.

Adjustable-rate mortgage—A loan that allows the lender to periodically adjust the loan's interest rate to reflect changes in the cost of money.

Index—A published rate that is a reliable indicator of the current cost of money.

Margin—The difference between the index value on an ARM and the interest rate the borrower is charged.

Negative amortization—When unpaid interest is added to the loan balance.

Conventional loan—Any institutional loan that is not insured or guaranteed by a government agency.

Nonconforming loan—A loan that does not meet the underwriting standards of the major secondary market agencies.

PMI—Private mortgage insurance; insurance designed to protect lenders from the greater risks of high-LTV conventional loans.

MIP—The mortgage insurance premiums required for FHA-insured loans.

Certificate of Eligibility—The document that establishes a veteran's eligibility to apply for a VA home loan.

Certificate of Reasonable Value—The document issued when a home is appraised in connection with the underwriting of a VA loan.

Residual income—The amount of monthly income a VA borrower has left over after deducting monthly expenses and taxes.

Chapter Quiz

1. A mortgage company:

   a) arranges loans but does not service them
   b) services loans but does not make them
   c) is the same as a mortgage broker
   d) is sometimes called a mortgage banker

2. To increase its yield on the loan, the lender is charging 2% of the loan amount, to be paid at closing. This charge is called:

   a) the origination fee
   b) PMI
   c) the index
   d) discount points

3. The Truth in Lending Act and Regulation Z:

   a) place restrictions on how much a lender can charge for a consumer loan
   b) require lenders to give loan applicants a disclosure statement concerning loan costs
   c) prohibit lenders from advertising specific financing terms
   d) All of the above

4. A loan's APR expresses the relationship between:

   a) the total finance charge and the loan amount
   b) the interest rate on the loan and the discount rate
   c) the downpayment and the total finance charge
   d) the monthly payment and the interest rate

5. After determining the quantity of the loan applicant's stable monthly income, the underwriter measures the adequacy of the income using:

   a) the consumer price index
   b) income ratios
   c) credit scoring
   d) federal income tax tables

6. Fifteen-year mortgages typically have all of the following disadvantages, except:

   a) a higher interest rate
   b) higher monthly payments
   c) a larger downpayment
   d) All of these are disadvantages of a 15-year mortgage

7. The house was appraised for $193,000 and the sales price is $190,000. If the loan-to-value ratio is 90%, how much is the loan amount?

   a) $154,400
   b) $171,000
   c) $173,700
   d) $214,400

8. With an adjustable-rate mortgage, the interest rate:

   a) is adjusted at specified intervals, and so is the payment amount
   b) is adjusted monthly, and so is the payment amount
   c) increases and decreases, but the payment amount remains the same
   d) may increase periodically, but does not decrease

9. Unpaid interest added to the loan balance is referred to as:

   a) payment shock
   b) partial amortization
   c) negative amortization
   d) participation interest

10. For conventional loans, private mortgage insurance is required when the loan-to-value ratio is:

    a) 75% or higher
    b) 90% or higher
    c) over 95%
    d) over 80%

11. To qualify for a conventional loan, the borrower is typically required to have:

   a) at least two months' mortgage payments in reserve
   b) secondary financing for the downpayment
   c) residual income that meets minimum requirements
   d) a 3% margin to provide for emergencies

12. The FHA:

   a) makes loans
   b) insures loans
   c) buys and sells loans
   d) All of the above

13. All of the following statements about FHA loans are true, except:

   a) No downpayment is required
   b) The borrower is usually not required to have reserves after closing
   c) Mortgage insurance is required on all loans
   d) The borrower must occupy the property as his or her primary residence

14. A VA loan can be assumed:

   a) only by an eligible veteran
   b) only by an eligible veteran who agrees to a substitution of entitlement
   c) by any buyer who passes the credit check
   d) by any buyer, without regard to creditworthiness

15. A veteran may obtain a VA-guaranteed loan on a:

   a) single-family residence only
   b) four-plex, as long as all of the units are rented out
   c) residence with up to two units, as long as the veteran occupies one unit
   d) one- to four-unit residence, as long as the veteran occupies one unit

Answer Key

1. d) A mortgage com
       mortgage ban
       loans and
       invest

2. d)

...pany is sometimes called a ...ker. Mortgage companies make ...lso service loans on behalf of ...rs.

Discount points are a percentage of the loan amount paid at closing to increase the lender's yield on the loan.

3. b) TILA and Regulation Z require lenders to disclose loan costs to loan applicants, but they do not restrict how much a lender can charge in connection with a loan. And while these laws regulate how financing terms are presented in advertising, they do not prohibit advertisement of financing terms.

4. a) The APR is the annual percentage rate, which indicates the relationship between the total finance charge and the loan amount.

5. b) Income ratios are used to measure the adequacy or sufficiency of a loan applicant's stable monthly income.

6. a) Fifteen-year mortgages usually have lower interest rates than 30-year mortgages.

7. b) The loan amount is $171,000, because the loan-to-value ratio is based on the appraised value or the sales price, whichever is less. $190,000 × 90% = $171,000.

8. a) Both the interest rate and the payment amount for an ARM are adjusted at specified intervals. The rate and the payment amount may increase or decrease to reflect changes in the index.

9. c) Negative amortization is unpaid interest that is added to the loan balance.

10. d) When the LTV of a conventional loan is more than 80%, PMI is required.

11. a) To qualify for a conventional loan, the borrower is typically required to have at least two months' mortgage payments in reserve.

12. b) The FHA only insures loans made by institutional lenders. It does not make loans itself, nor does it buy and sell loans on the secondary market.

13. a) A downpayment is required for an FHA loan.

14. c) A VA loan can be assumed by any buyer, whether or not he or she is an eligible veteran. The buyer is required to pass a credit check, however.

15. d) An eligible veteran can get a VA loan on a one- to four-unit residence, as long as he or she occupies one of the units.

Real Estate Appraisal

Chapter Overview

The foundation of each real estate transaction is the value placed on the property in question. The value of a home affects its selling price, its financing terms, its rental rate, its income tax consequences, its property tax assessment, and its insurance coverage. It is important to know what the property is worth aside from any emotional or subjective value placed on it by the buyer or seller. An estimate or opinion of value is called an appraisal. This chapter examines what is meant by the term "value," and explains the various methods appraisers use to estimate value.

Introduction to Appraisal

An **appraisal** is an estimate or an opinion of value. It usually takes the form of a written statement, called an **appraisal report**, setting forth the appraiser's opinion of the value of a piece of property as of a given date. A synonym for appraisal is **valuation**.

An appraiser may be asked to help a seller decide on a fair asking price, or a buyer may seek an opinion as to how much to pay for the property. Most often, an appraisal is requested by a mortgage lender, when a buyer has applied for a loan. The lender uses the appraisal to decide whether the property the buyer has chosen is suitable security for a loan, and if so, what the maximum loan amount should be.

In addition to helping to determine a fair price or a maximum loan amount, an appraiser's services are regularly required in order to:

- identify raw land's highest and best use;
- estimate a property's value for purposes of taxation;
- establish rental rates;
- estimate the relative values of properties being exchanged;
- determine the amount of hazard insurance coverage necessary;
- estimate remodeling costs or their contribution to value;
- help establish just compensation in a condemnation proceeding; or
- estimate the value of properties involved in the liquidation of estates, corporate mergers and acquisitions, or bankruptcies.

Regardless of the situation, whoever employs the appraiser is the client. The appraiser is the client's agent. A principal/agent relationship exists and the laws of agency apply (see Chapter 7).

An appraiser's fee is determined in advance, based on the expected difficulty of the appraisal and the amount of time it is likely to take. The fee cannot be calculated as a percentage of the appraised value of the property, nor can it be based on the client's satisfaction with the appraiser's findings.

Washington State certifies appraisers. Although the state does not require all appraisers to be certified, under federal law only appraisals prepared by state-licensed or certified appraisers in accordance with the Uniform Standards of Professional Appraisal Practice can be used in "federally related" loan transactions. The Uniform Standards are guidelines adopted by the Appraisal Foundation, a non-profit organization. The majority of real estate loans are federally related, since the category includes loans made by any bank or savings and loan association that is regulated or insured by the federal government. Transactions for $250,000 or less are exempt from this certified appraisal requirement, however.

Value

Value is a term with many meanings. One common definition is "the present worth of future benefits." Value is usually measured in terms of money. For appraisal purposes, value falls into two general classifications: **value in use** and **value in exchange**. Value in use is the subjective value placed on a property by a particular person, while value in exchange is the objective value of a property as viewed by the average person. Value in use and value in exchange may be quite different, depending on the circumstances.

> **Example:** A large, expensive, one-bedroom home, designed, built, and occupied by its owner, would undoubtedly be worth more to the owner than to the average buyer. Most buyers would look at the property objectively and expect more than one bedroom for the price.

Market Value

Value in exchange, more commonly called market value, is the more significant of the two types of value. Estimating a property's market value is the purpose of most appraisals.

For a thing to have market value, four elements are required: utility, scarcity, transferability, and demand. This holds true for real property as well as other commodities.

Here is the most widely accepted definition of market value, taken from the Uniform Standards of Professional Appraisal Practice:

> *The most probable price which a property should bring in a competitive and open market under all conditions requisite to a fair sale, the buyer and seller each acting prudently and knowledgeably, and assuming the price is not affected by undue stimulus.*

Notice that according to this definition, market value is the *most probable* price (not "the highest price") that the property *should bring* (not "will bring"). Appraisal is a matter of estimation and likelihood, not certainty.

The Federal Housing Administration offers this succinct explanation of market value: "The price which typical buyers would be warranted in paying for the property for long-term use or investment, if they were well informed and acted intelligently, voluntarily, and without necessity."

Market Value vs. Market Price. There is an important distinction between market value and market price. Market price is the price actually paid for a property, regardless of whether the parties to the transaction were informed and acting free of unusual pressure. Market value is what should be paid if a property is purchased and sold under all the conditions requisite to a fair sale.

These conditions include an open and competitive market, prudent and informed parties, and no undue stimulus (that is, no unusual pressure to sell or buy immediately). A sale made under those conditions is called an **arm's length transaction**.

Principles of Value

Of the major forces that influence our attitudes and behavior, three interact to create, support, or erode property values:

- social ideals and standards,
- economic fluctuations, and
- government regulations.

A change in attitudes regarding family size and the emergence of the two-car family are examples of social forces that affect the value of homes (in this case, homes with too many bedrooms or one-car garages). Economic forces include employment levels, interest rates, and any other factors that affect the community's purchasing power. Government regulations, such as zoning ordinances, serve to promote, stabilize, or discourage the demand for property.

Over the years, appraisers have developed a reliable body of principles, referred to as the **principles of value**, that take these factors into account and guide appraisers in making decisions in the valuation process.

Principle of Highest and Best Use. Highest and best use refers to the most profitable use of a piece of property, the use that will provide the greatest net return over a period of time. Net return usually refers to net income, but it cannot always be measured in terms of money. With residential properties, for example, net return might manifest itself in the form of amenities—the pleasure and satisfaction derived from living on the property.

Determining the highest and best use may be a simple matter of confirming that deed restrictions or an existing zoning ordinance limit the property to its present use. Often the present use of a property is its highest and best use. But change is constant, and a warehouse site that was once profitable might now generate a greater net return as a parking lot.

Fig. 12.1 Principle of highest and best use

Highest and Best Use (Alternative Use Considerations)		
	Annual Income	**Estimated Value**
Present Use: Warehouse	$19,280 (actual)	$175,000
Alternative Use 1: Parking lot	$16,800 (estimated)	$151,000
Alternative Use 2: Gas station	$20,500 (estimated)	$184,000
Alternative Use 3: Triplex	$14,300 (estimated)	$132,000

Principle of Change. The principle of change holds that real estate values are constantly in flux, moving up and down in response to changes in the various social, economic, and governmental forces that affect value. A property's value also changes as the property itself improves or deteriorates. A property that was worth $100,000 last year may be worth $120,000 today, and its value is likely to change in the coming year as well. Because value is always subject to change, an estimate of value must be tied to a specific point in time, called the **effective date** of the appraisal.

Related to the principle of change is the idea that property has a four-phase life cycle: **integration**, **equilibrium**, **disintegration**, and **rejuvenation**. Integration (also called development) is the early stage, when the property is being developed. Equilibrium is a period of stability, when the property undergoes little, if any, change. Disintegration is a period of decline, when the property's economic usefulness is near an end and constant upkeep is necessary. And rejuvenation (also known as revitalization) is a period of renewal, when the property is reborn, usually with a different highest and best use.

Every property has both a physical and an economic life cycle. It is invariably the economic life—the period when the land and its improvements are profitable—that ends first. The appraiser must recognize and take into account which stage of the life cycle a property is in when estimating its present worth.

Principle of Anticipation. It is the future, not the past, that is important to appraisers. Knowing that property values change, an appraiser asks: What is happening to this property? What is its future? How do prospective buyers view its potential? The appraiser must be aware of the social, economic, and governmental factors that will affect the future value of the property.

Value is created by the anticipated future benefits of owning a property. It is future benefits, not past benefits, that arouse a desire to own.

Anticipation can help or hurt value, depending on what informed buyers and sellers expect to happen to the property in the future. They usually expect property values to increase, but in certain situations they anticipate that values will decline, as when the community is experiencing a severe recession.

Principle of Supply and Demand. The principle of supply and demand affects almost every commodity, including real estate. Values tend to rise as demand increases and supply decreases, and diminish when the reverse is true. It is not so much the demand for or supply of real estate in general that affects values, but the demand for or supply of a particular type of property. For instance, a generally depressed community may have one or two very attractive, sought-after neighborhoods. The value of these homes remains high, no matter what the general trend is for the rest of the community.

Principle of Substitution. This principle states that no one will pay more for a property than they would have to pay for an equally desirable substitute property, provided there would be no unreasonable delay in acquiring that substitute. Explained another way, the principle of substitution holds that if two properties for sale are alike in every respect, the least expensive will be in greater demand.

Principle of Conformity. The maximum value of land is achieved when there is an acceptable degree of social and economic conformity in the area. Conformity should be reasonable, not carried to an extreme.

In a residential appraisal, one aspect of conformity the appraiser considers is similarity in the size, age, and quality of the homes in the neighborhood. Nonconformity can work to the benefit or to the detriment of the nonconforming home. The value of a home of much lower quality than those around it is increased by its association with the higher quality homes; this is the principle of **progression.**

> **Example:** A small, unkempt home surrounded by large, attractive homes will be worth more in this neighborhood than it would be if it were situated in a neighborhood of other small homes in poor condition.

Conversely, the value of a large, expensive home in a neighborhood of small, inexpensive homes will suffer because of its surroundings; this is the principle of **regression**.

Principle of Contribution. Contribution refers to the value an improvement adds to the overall value of the property. Some improvements will add more value than the expense of making them; others will cost more than they contribute to value.

A remodeled basement ordinarily will not contribute its cost to the value of the home. On the other hand, the addition of a second bathroom may increase a home's value by more than the cost of installing it.

Principle of Competition. Competition may have a dramatic impact on the value of property, especially income property. For example, if one convenience store in a neighborhood is extremely profitable, its success is very likely to bring a competing convenience store into the area. This competition will probably mean lower profits for the first store (as some of its customers begin doing business with the second store), and lower profits will reduce the property's value.

The Appraisal Process

Properly done, the appraisal process is orderly and systematic. While there is no official procedure, appraisers generally carry out the appraisal process in the following manner.

1. **Define the problem.** Each client wants an appraiser to solve a specific problem: to estimate the value of a particular property as of a particular date and for a particular purpose. The first step in the appraisal process is to define the problem to be solved. This involves identifying the subject property—what property and which aspect(s) of it are to be appraised—and establishing the function of the appraisal and how the client intends to use it. Unless instructed to do otherwise, the appraiser will estimate the property's value as of the date the appraisal is performed.
2. **Determine what data is needed and where it can be found.** The data that the value estimate will be based on is divided into two categories: general and specific.

Fig. 12.2 The appraisal process

Steps in the Appraisal Process

1. Define the problem
2. Determine data needed
3. Gather and verify general data
4. Gather and verify specific data
5. Select and apply valuation methods
    • Sales comparison approach
    • Cost approach
    • Income approach
6. Reconciliation and final estimate
7. Issue appraisal report

General data concerns matters outside the subject property that affect its value. It includes population trends, prevailing economic circumstances, zoning, and proximity of amenities (such as shopping, schools, and transportation), as well as the condition and quality of the neighborhood. Specific data concerns the subject property itself. The appraiser will gather information about the title, the buildings, and the site. (General and specific data will be discussed in more detail in the next section of the chapter.)

3. **Gather and verify the general data.**
4. **Gather and verify the specific data.**
5. **Select and apply the valuation method(s).** In some cases, the appraiser will approach the problem of estimating value three different ways: with the sales comparison approach, the cost approach, and the income approach. In other cases, he or she will use only the method that seems most appropriate for the problem to be solved. Whether one, two, or three approaches are used is a matter of judgment.

    Sometimes a particular method cannot be used. Raw land, for example, cannot be appraised using the cost approach. A public library, on the other hand, must be appraised by the cost method because it does not generate income and no market exists for it.
6. **Reconcile value indicators for the final value estimate.** The figures yielded by each of the three approaches are called value indicators; they give indications of what the property is worth, but are not final estimates themselves.

    The appraiser will take into consideration the purpose of the appraisal, the type of property being appraised, and the reliability of the data gathered for each of the three approaches. He or she will place the greatest emphasis on the approach that seems to be the most reliable indication of value.
7. **Issue appraisal report.** The formal presentation of the value estimate and an explanation of what went into its determination are made in the form of an appraisal report.

Gathering Data

Once the appraiser knows what property he or she is to appraise and what the purpose of the appraisal is, the appraiser begins to gather the necessary data. As mentioned above, data is broken down into general data (about the neighborhood and other external influences) and specific data (about the subject property itself).

General Data

General data includes both general economic data about the community and information about the subject property's neighborhood.

Economic Trends. The appraiser examines economic trends for hints as to the direction the property's value might take in the future. Economic trends can take shape at the local, regional, national, or international level, although local trends have the most significant impact on a property's value. Generally, prosperous conditions tend to have a positive effect on property values; economic declines have the opposite effect.

Economic forces include population growth shifts, employment and wage levels (purchasing power), price levels, building cycles, personal tax and property tax rates, building costs, and interest rates.

Neighborhood Analysis. A property's value is inevitably tied to its surrounding neighborhood. A neighborhood is a residential, commercial, industrial, or agricultural area that contains similar types of properties. Its boundaries are determined by physical barriers (such as highways and bodies of water), land use patterns, the age or value of homes or other buildings, and the economic status of the residents.

Neighborhoods are continually changing and, like the individual properties that make them up, they have a four-phase life cycle of integration, equilibrium, disintegration, and rejuvenation. When evaluating the future of a neighborhood, the appraiser must consider its physical, social, and economic characteristics, and also governmental influences.

Here are some of the specific factors appraisers look at when gathering data about a residential neighborhood:

1. **Percentage of home ownership.** Is there a high degree of owner-occupancy or do rental properties predominate? Owner-occupied neighborhoods are generally better maintained and less susceptible to deterioration.
2. **Vacant homes and lots.** An unusual number of vacant homes or lots suggests a low level of interest in the area, which has a negative effect on property values. On the other hand, significant construction activity in a neighborhood signals strong interest in the area.
3. **Conformity.** The homes in a neighborhood should be reasonably similar to one another in style, age, size, and quality. Strictly enforced zoning and private restrictions promote conformity and protect property values.
4. **Changing land use.** Is the neighborhood in the midst of a transition from residential use to some other type of use? If so, the properties may be losing their value.

Fig. 12.3 Neighborhood data form

NEIGHBORHOOD DATA FORM

Property adjacent to:

NORTH _____ *Plum Boulevard, garden apartments* _____
SOUTH _____ *Cherry Boulevard, single-family residences* _____
EAST _____ *14th Avenue, single-family residences* _____
WEST _____ *12th Avenue, single-family residences* _____

Population: ☐ increasing ☐ decreasing ☑ stable

Stage of Life Cycle: ☐ integration ☑ equilibrium ☐ disintegration ☐ rebirth

Tax Rate: ☐ higher   ☐ lower   ☑ same as competing areas

Services: ☑ police   ☑ fire   ☑ garbage   ☐ other

Average family size: _____ *3.5* _____
Predominant occupations: _____ *white collar, skilled tradesman* _____

Distance from:
Commercial areas _____ *3 miles* _____
Primary schools _____ *6 blocks* _____
Secondary schools _____ *1 mile* _____
Recreational areas _____ *2 miles* _____
Cultural areas _____ *3 miles* _____
Places of worship _____ *Methodist, Catholic, Baptist* _____
Public transportation _____ *Bus stops nearby, excellent service* _____
Freeways/highways _____ *10 blocks* _____

Typical Properties	%	Age	Price Range	% Owner-Occupied
vacant lots	0			
single-family residences	80%	10 years	$180,000-195,000	93%
2- to 4-unit apartments	15%	15 years		
over 4-unit apartments	5%	5 years		
non-residential	0			

Nuisances in neighborhood (odors, noise, etc.) _____ *none* _____
Hazards in neighborhood (chemical storage, pollution, etc.) _____ *none* _____

5. **Contour of the land.** Mildly rolling topography is preferred to terrain that is either monotonously flat or excessively hilly.
6. **Streets.** Wide, gently curving streets are more appealing than narrow or straight ones. Streets should be hard surfaced and well maintained.
7. **Utilities.** Is the neighborhood adequately serviced by electricity, water, gas, sewers, telephones, and cable TV?
8. **Nuisances.** Nuisances in or near a neighborhood (odors, eyesores, industrial noises or pollutants, or exposure to unusual winds, smog, or fog) hurt property values.
9. **Prestige.** Is the neighborhood considered prestigious, in comparison to others in the community? If so, that will increase property values.
10. **Proximity.** How far is it to traffic arterials and to important points such as downtown, employment centers, and shopping centers?
11. **Schools.** What schools serve the neighborhood? Are they highly regarded? Are they within walking distance? The quality of a school or school district can make a major difference in property values in a residential neighborhood.
12. **Public services.** Is the neighborhood properly serviced by public transportation, police, and fire units?
13. **Government influences.** Does zoning in and around the neighborhood promote residential use and insulate the property owner from nuisances? How do the property tax rates compare with those of other neighborhoods nearby?

Specific Data

Specific data has to do with the property itself. Often the appraiser will evaluate the site (the land and utilities) and the improvements to the site separately. For example, where properties are being assessed for tax purposes, most states require the assessments to show the distribution of value between land and its improvements. Another reason for appraising the land separately is to see if it is worth too much or too little compared to the value of the improvements. Where an imbalance exists, the land is not serving its highest and best use. The primary purpose of site analysis is to determine highest and best use.

Site Analysis. A thorough site analysis calls for accumulation of a good deal of data concerning the property's physical characteristics, as well as factors that affect its use or the title. A site's physical characteristics include all of the following:

1. **Width.** This refers to the lot's measurements from one side boundary to the other. Width can vary from front to back, as in the case of a pie-shaped lot on a cul-de-sac.
2. **Frontage.** Frontage is the length of the front boundary of the lot, the boundary that abuts a street or a body of water. The amount of frontage is often a more important consideration than width because it measures the property's accessibility, or its access to something desirable.
3. **Area.** Area is the size of the site, usually measured in square feet or acres. Comparisons between lots often focus on the features of frontage and area.

Commercial land is usually valued in terms of frontage; that is, it is worth a certain number of dollars per front foot. Industrial land, on the other hand, tends to be valued in terms of square feet or acreage. Residential lots are measured both ways: by square feet or by acreage in most instances, but by front foot when the property abuts a lake or river, or some other desirable feature.

4. **Depth.** Depth is the distance between the site's front boundary and its rear boundary. Greater depth (more than the norm) can mean greater value, but it doesn't always. For example, suppose Lot 1 and Lot 2 have the same amount of frontage along a lake, but Lot 2 is deeper; Lot 2 is not necessarily more valuable than Lot 1. The additional square footage of Lot 2 might simply be considered **excess land**. Each situation must be analyzed individually to determine whether more depth translates into greater value.

   Under certain circumstances, combining two or more adjoining lots to achieve greater width, depth, or area will make the larger parcel more valuable than the sum of the values of its component parcels. The increment of value that results when two or more lots are combined to produce greater value is called **plottage**. The process of assembling lots to increase their value is most frequently part of industrial or commercial land development.

5. **Shape.** Lots with uniform width and depth (such as rectangular lots) are almost always more useful than irregularly shaped lots. This is true for any kind of lot—residential, commercial, or industrial.

6. **Topography.** A site is generally more valuable if it is aesthetically appealing. Rolling terrain is preferable to flat, monotonous land. On the other hand, if the site would be costly to develop because it sits well above or below the street or is excessively hilly, then that lessens its value.

7. **Utilities.** Site analysis includes an investigation into the availability and cost of utility connections. Remote parcels lose value because the cost of bringing utility lines to the site is high or even prohibitive.

Fig. 12.4 Site data form

SITE DATA FORM

Address: _10157 - 13th Avenue_

Legal Description: _see attached description_

Size _50' x 200'_   Shape _Rectangular_

Square Feet _10,000_   Street Paving _Asphalt_

Landscaping _professional_ Topsoil _good_

Drainage _good_   Frontage _good_
                           ☐ corner lot   ☑ inside lot

Utilities: ☑ water ☑ telephone   **Improvements:** ☑ sidewalks
☑ gas ☑ sewers ☑ electricity   ☑ curb ☑ alleys ☑ driveway
☑ storm drains

8. **Site in relation to area.** How a lot is situated in relation to the surrounding area influences its value. For instance, a retail store is often worth more if it is located on a corner, because it enjoys more exposure and its customers have access from two different streets. The effect the corner location has on the value of a business site is called corner influence.

   By contrast, a corner location has a negative effect on the value of a residential property. A corner lot is more exposed to through traffic than a lot in the middle of the block.

Building Analysis. The improvements to the site must also be analyzed. Here are some of the primary considerations in a residential appraisal:

1. **Construction quality.** Is the quality of the materials and workmanship good, average, or poor?
2. **Age/condition.** How old is the home? Is its overall condition good, average, or poor?
3. **Size of house (square footage).** This includes the improved living area, excluding the garage, basement, and porches.
4. **Basement.** A functional basement, especially a finished basement, contributes to value. (As we mentioned earlier, however, the amount a finished basement contributes to value is often not enough to recover the cost of the finish work.)
5. **Interior layout.** Is the floor plan functional and convenient? It should not be necessary to pass through a public room (such as the living room) to reach other rooms, or to pass through one of the bedrooms to reach another.
6. **Number of rooms.** The appraiser will add up the total number of rooms in the house, excluding bathrooms and (usually) basement rooms.
7. **Number of bedrooms.** The number of bedrooms has a major impact on value. For instance, if all else is equal, a two-bedroom home is worth considerably less than a three-bedroom home.
8. **Number of bathrooms.** A full bath is a lavatory (wash basin), toilet, and bathtub, with or without a shower; a three-quarters bath is a lavatory, toilet, and shower (no tub); a half bath is a lavatory and toilet only. The number of bathrooms can have a noticeable effect on value.
9. **Air conditioning.** The presence or absence of an air conditioning system is important in hot regions.
10. **Energy efficiency.** With spiraling energy costs, an energy-efficient home is more valuable than a comparable one that is not. Energy-efficient features such as double-paned windows, good insulation, and weather stripping increase value.
11. **Garage/carport.** As a general rule, an enclosed garage is considered better than a carport. How many cars can the garage accommodate? Is there work or storage space in addition to parking space? Is it possible to enter the home directly from the garage or carport, protected from the weather?

Fig. 12.5 Building data form

BUILDING DATA FORM

Address: _____ 10157 - 13th Avenue _____

Age: __ 7 yrs. ____ Square feet: ____ 1,350 ___

Number of rooms: __7__ Quality of construction: __ excellent __

Style: __ ranch ____

	Good	Bad	Fair
Exterior (general condition)	✔		
Foundation (slab/bsmt./(crawl sp.))	✔		
Exterior (brick/(frame)/veneer/stucco/aluminum)	✔		
Garage ((attached)/detached/single/double)	✔		
(Patio)/porch/shed/other	✔		
Interior (general condition)	✔		
Walls ((drywall)/wood/plaster)	✔		
Ceilings	✔		
Floor (wood/tile/(carpet)/concrete)	✔		
Electrical wiring	✔		
Heating ((electrical)/gas/oil/other)	✔		
Air conditioning	✔		
Fireplace(s) one	✔		
Kitchen	✔		
Bathroom(s) two	✔		
Bedroom(s) three	✔		

Additional amenities _____ none _____

Design advantages _____ convenient, sunny kitchen _____

Design flaws _____ none _____

Energy efficiency _____ insulation, weather-stripping, storm windows, heat pump _____

	Living Rm.	Dining Rm.	Ktchn.	Bdrm.	Bath	Family Rm.
Basement						
1st Floor	✔	✔	✔	✔	✔	
2nd Floor						
Attic						

Depreciation:

   Deferred Maintenance _____ normal wear _____

   Functional Obsolescence _____ none _____

   External Obsolescence _____ none _____

Methods of Appraisal

Once the appraiser has accumulated the necessary general and specific data, he or she will begin applying one or more of the three methods of appraising property:

- the sales comparison approach,
- the cost approach, and
- the income approach.

Different types of properties lend themselves to different appraisal methods. For example, appraisers rely most on the sales comparison method in valuing older residential properties. Churches and public buildings, such as libraries or courthouses, aren't sold on the open market, nor do they generate income, so the cost approach is invariably used. On the other hand, the income approach is usually the most reliable method for appraising an apartment complex.

Sales Comparison Approach to Value

The sales comparison approach (also known as the market data approach) is the best method for appraising residential property, and the only reliable method for appraising raw land. It involves comparing the subject property to similar properties that have recently sold, referred to as **comparable sales** or **comparables**. The appraiser gathers pertinent information about comparables and makes feature-by-feature comparisons with the subject property. The appraiser then translates his or her findings into an estimate of the market value of the subject property. Appraisers use this method whenever possible because the sales prices of comparables—which reflect the actions of informed buyers and sellers in the marketplace—are excellent indicators of market value.

An appraiser needs at least three reliable comparable sales to have enough data to evaluate a residential property. It is usually possible to find three good comparables, but when it isn't, the appraiser will turn to the alternative appraisal methods—the cost approach and the income approach.

Elements of Comparison. To determine whether a particular sale can legitimately be used as a comparable, the appraiser will check the following aspects of the transaction, which are known as the primary elements of comparison.

Date of Comparable Sale. The sale should be recent, within the past six months if possible. Recent sales give a more accurate indication of what is happening in the marketplace today. If the market has been inactive and there are not three legitimate comparable sales from the past six months, the appraiser can go back further. (Comparable sales over one year old are generally not acceptable, however.) When using a comparable more than six months old, it is necessary to make adjustments for the time factor, allowing for inflationary or deflationary trends or any other forces that have affected prices in the area.

> **Example:** A comparable residential property sold ten months ago for $180,000. Local property values have risen by 5% over the past ten months. The comparable property, then, should be worth approximately 5% more than it was ten months ago.
>
> | | |
> |---|---|
> | $180,000 | Value ten months ago |
> | × 105% | Inflation factor |
> | $189,000 | Approximate present value |

Location of Comparable Sale. Whenever possible, comparables should be selected from the neighborhood where the subject property is located. In the absence of any legitimate comparables in the neighborhood, the appraiser can look elsewhere, but the properties selected should at least come from comparable neighborhoods.

If a comparable selected from an inferior neighborhood is structurally identical to the subject property, it is probably less valuable; conversely, a structurally identical comparable in a superior neighborhood is probably more valuable than the subject property. It is generally conceded that location contributes more to the value of real estate than any other characteristic. A high-quality property cannot overcome the adverse effects on value that a low-quality neighborhood causes. On the other hand, the value of a relatively weak property is enhanced by a stable and desirable neighborhood.

Physical Characteristics. To qualify as a comparable, a property should have physical characteristics (construction quality, design, amenities, etc.) that are similar to those of the subject property. When a comparable has a feature that the subject property lacks, or lacks a feature that the subject property has, the appraiser will adjust the comparable's price.

Example: One of the comparables the appraiser is using is quite similar to the subject property overall, but there are several significant differences. The subject property has a two-car garage, while the comparable has only a one-car garage. Based on experience, the appraiser estimates that space for a second car adds approximately $2,000 to the value of a home in this area. The comparable actually sold for $122,500. The appraiser will add $2,000 to that price, to estimate what the comparable would have been worth with a two-car garage.

On the other hand, the comparable has a fireplace and the subject property does not. The appraiser estimates that a fireplace adds approximately $800 to the value of a home. She will subtract $800 from the comparable's price, to estimate what the comparable would have sold for without a fireplace.

After adjusting the comparable's price up or down for each difference in this way, the appraiser can identify what the comparable would have sold for if it had been identical to the subject property. When the appraiser repeats this process for each comparable, the value of the subject property becomes evident.

Terms of Sale. The terms of sale can affect the price a buyer will pay for a property. Attractive financing concessions (such as seller-paid discount points or seller financing with an especially low interest rate) can make a buyer willing to pay a higher price than he or she would otherwise be willing to pay.

An appraiser has to take into account the influence the terms of sale may have had on the price paid for a comparable property. If the seller offered the property on very favorable terms, there is an excellent chance the sales price did not represent the true market value of the comparable.

Under the Uniform Standards of Professional Appraisal Practice, an appraiser giving an estimate of market value must state whether it's the most probable price:

1. in terms of cash;
2. in terms of financial arrangements equivalent to cash; or
3. in other precisely defined terms.

If the estimate is based on financing with special conditions or incentives, those terms must be clearly set forth, and the appraiser must estimate their effect on the property's value. Market data supporting the value estimate (comparable sales) must be explained in the same way.

Arm's Length Transaction. Last but not least, a comparable sale can be relied on as an indication of what the subject property is worth only if it was an arm's length transaction. That is, both the buyer and seller were informed of the property's attributes and deficiencies; both were acting free of unusual pressure; and the property was offered for sale on the open market for a reasonable length of time.

Thus, the appraiser must investigate the circumstances of each comparable sale to determine whether the price paid was influenced by a condition that would render it unreliable as an indication of value. For example, if the property sold only days before a scheduled foreclosure sale, the sales price may have reflected the pressure under which the seller was acting. Or if the buyer and seller were relatives, it's possible that the price was less than it would have been between two strangers. Or if the home sold the same day it was listed, it may have been underpriced. In each of these cases, there is reason to suspect that the sales price did not reflect the property's true value, so the appraiser would not use the transaction as a comparable sale.

Comparing Properties and Making Adjustments. A proper comparison between the subject property and each comparable is essential to an accurate estimate of value. The more similar the properties, the easier the comparison. A comparable property that is the same design and in the same condition as the subject property, on a very similar site in the same neighborhood, which sold under typical financing terms the previous month, will give an excellent indication of the market value of the subject property. However, except perhaps in a new subdivision where the houses are nearly identical, the appraiser usually cannot find such ideal comparables. There are likely to be at least some significant differences between the comparables and the subject property. So, as you've seen, the appraiser has to make adjustments, taking into account differences in time, location, physical characteristics, and terms of sale, in order to arrive at an **adjusted selling price** for each comparable.

It stands to reason that the more adjustments an appraiser has to make, the less reliable the resulting estimate of value will be. These adjustments are an inevitable part of the sales comparison approach, but appraisers try to keep them to a minimum by selecting the best comparables available.

The appraiser bases his or her estimate of the subject property's value on the adjusted prices of the comparables, but the value estimate is never merely an average of those prices; careful analysis is required. Also note that the original cost of the subject property (how much the current owners paid for it) is irrelevant to the appraisal process.

Use of Listings. When comparable sales are scarce (as when the market is just emerging from a dormant period), the appraiser may compare the subject property to properties that are presently listed for sale. The appraiser must keep in mind, however, that listing prices tend to be high and frequently represent the ceiling of the market value range. The appraiser might also use prices offered by buyers, though these can be difficult to confirm, since records of offers aren't always kept. Offers are usually at the low end of the market value range. Actual market value is typically somewhere between offers and listing prices.

Fig. 12.6 Comparable sales comparison chart

Comparable Sales Comparison Chart

	Subject Property	Comparables			
		1	2	3	4
Sales price		$191,750	$196,500	$187,000	$188,500
Location	quiet street				
Age	7 yrs.				
Lot size	50'x200'				
Construction	frame			+6,000	
Style	ranch				
Number of Rooms	7		−5,000		
Number of Bedrooms	3				
Number of Baths	2	+3,500		+3,500	+3,500
Square feet	1,350				
Exterior	good				
Interior	good				
Garage	1 car attached				
Other improvements		−4,000			
Financing					
Date of sale		−3,000	−3,000		
Net Adjustments		−3,500	−8,000	+9,500	+3,500
Adjusted Price		$188,250	$188,500	$196,500	$192,000

Cost Approach to Value

The cost approach is based on the premise that the value of a property is limited by the cost of replacing it. (This is the principle of substitution: if the asking price for a home was more than it would cost to build a new one just like it, no one would buy it.)

This approach involves estimating how much it would cost to replace the subject property's existing buildings, then adding to that the estimated value of the site on which they rest. Because the cost approach involves estimating the value of land and buildings separately, then adding the estimates together, it is sometimes called the summation method.

There are three steps to the cost approach:

1. Estimate the cost of replacing the improvements.
2. Estimate and deduct any accrued depreciation.
3. Add the value of the lot to the depreciated value of the improvements.

It is important to distinguish between replacement cost and reproduction cost. **Reproduction cost** is the cost of constructing an exact duplicate—a replica—of the subject building, at current prices. **Replacement cost**, on the other hand, is the current cost of constructing a building with a utility equivalent to the subject—that is, a building that can be used in the same way. Reproduction cost and replacement cost may be the same if the subject property is a new home. But if the structure is older, and was built with the detailed workmanship and expensive materials of earlier times, then the reproduction cost and the replacement cost will be quite different. So the appraiser must base his or her estimate of value on the replacement cost. The reproduction cost would be prohibitive, and it would not represent the current market value of the improvements.

Estimating Replacement Cost. The replacement cost of a building can be estimated in three different ways:

1. the square foot method,
2. the unit-in-place method, and
3. the quantity survey method.

Square Foot. The simplest way to estimate replacement cost is the square foot method (also known as the comparative cost method). By analyzing the average cost per square foot of construction for recently built comparable homes, the appraiser can calculate what the square foot cost of replacing the subject home would be. The number of square feet in a home is determined by measuring the outside dimensions of each floor of the structure.

To calculate the cost of replacing the subject property's improvements, the appraiser multiplies the estimated cost per square foot by the number of square feet in the subject.

Example: The subject property is a ranch-style house with a wooden exterior, containing 1,600 square feet. Based on an analysis of the construction costs of three recently built homes of comparable size and quality, the appraiser estimates that it would cost $59.38 per square foot to replace the home.

1,600	Square feet
× 59.38	Cost per square foot
$95,008	Estimated cost of replacing improvements

Of course, a comparable structure (or "benchmark" building) is unlikely to be exactly the same as the subject property. Variations in design, shape, and grade of construction will affect the square-foot cost, either moderately or substantially. When recently built comparable homes are not available, then the appraiser relies on

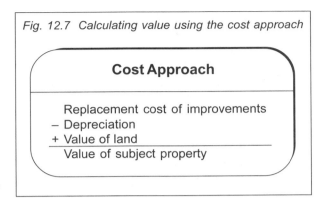

Fig. 12.7 Calculating value using the cost approach

Cost Approach

Replacement cost of improvements
– Depreciation
+ Value of land
Value of subject property

current cost manuals to estimate the basic construction costs.

Unit-in-Place. The unit-in-place method involves estimating the cost of replacing specific components of the building, such as the floors, roof, plumbing, and foundation. For example, one of the estimates might be a certain number of dollars per one hundred square feet of roofing. Another component estimate would be a certain amount per cubic yard of concrete for an installed foundation. Then the appraiser adds all the estimates together to determine the replacement cost of the structure itself.

Quantity Survey. The quantity survey method involves a detailed estimate of the quantities and prices of construction materials and labor, which are added to the indirect costs (building permit, survey, etc.) for what is generally regarded as the most accurate replacement cost estimate. Because it's complex and time consuming, this method is generally used only by experienced contractors and price estimators.

Estimating Depreciation. When the property being appraised is a used home, the presumption is that it is not as valuable as a comparable new home; it has depreciated in value. So, after estimating replacement cost—which indicates what the improvements would be worth if they were new—the appraiser's next step is to estimate the depreciation.

Depreciation is a loss in value due to any cause. Value can be lost as a result of physical wear and tear (**deferred maintenance**); functional inadequacies, often caused by age or poor design (**functional obsolescence**); and factors outside the property, such as a deteriorating neighborhood or poor access to important areas like downtown and employment centers (**external obsolescence**).

Deferred Maintenance. This includes any type of physical deterioration (wear and tear, decay, cracks, etc.) and structural defects. Deferred maintenance is measured in terms of how much it would cost to correct it. It is the easiest form of depreciation to spot, and also the easiest to estimate.

Functional Obsolescence. This is a loss in value due to functional inadequacies such as a poor floor plan, unappealing design, outdated fixtures, or too few bathrooms in relation to the number of bedrooms.

Deferred maintenance and functional obsolescence may be either **curable** or **incurable**. Depreciation is considered curable if the cost of correcting it could be recovered in the sales price when the property is sold. Depreciation is incurable if it is impossible to correct, or if it would cost so much to correct that it would be impractical to do so.

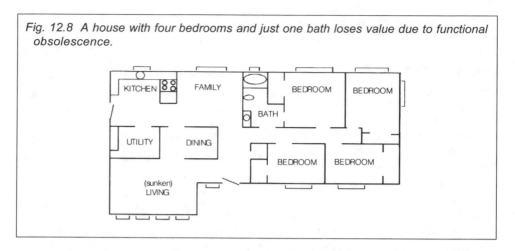

Fig. 12.8 *A house with four bedrooms and just one bath loses value due to functional obsolescence.*

External Obsolescence. External obsolescence (also referred to as economic obsolescence) is caused by conditions outside the property itself, such as zoning changes, neighborhood deterioration, traffic problems, or exposure to nuisances, like noise from airport flight patterns. Identifying external obsolescence is the primary purpose of an appraiser's neighborhood analysis. Since external obsolescence is beyond a property owner's control, it is virtually always incurable.

Estimating depreciation accurately is the most difficult phase of the replacement cost method of appraisal. In many cases, depreciation estimates are highly subjective, and they are never any more reliable than the judgment and skill of the appraiser who is making them.

Adding Land Value. The last step in the replacement cost process is to add the value of the land to the depreciated value of the improvements. The value of the land is estimated by the sales comparison method. Prices recently paid for lots similar to the subject lot are compared and used as indications of what the subject lot is worth.

Keep in mind that the value of the land is not depreciated. An appraiser regards land as indestructible; it does not lose value.

Income Approach to Value

The income method of appraisal (also known as the capitalization method) is based on the idea that there is a relationship between the income a property generates and its market value to an investor. In effect, the income method seeks to determine the present value of a property's future income.

Gross Income. When using the income method, the appraiser first finds the property's gross income. He or she does this by estimating the rent the property would bring if it were presently available for lease on the open market. What it would earn on the open market is called the **economic rent**, as distinguished from what it is actually earning now, which is called the **contract rent** or **historical rent**. Contract rent can be used to gauge the property's earnings potential. A pattern of rent increases or decreases is a strong indication of whether the contract rent is above or below the economic rent.

The economic rent is the property's **potential gross income**, what it could earn if it were fully occupied and all rents owed were collected. But it is unrealistic to expect a rental property to be fully occupied throughout its productive life; vacancies must be expected. Also, there are going to be tenants who do not pay their rent. So the appraiser must make a deduction from potential gross income to allow for occasional vacancies and unpaid rents. Called a **bad debt and vacancy factor**, this deduction is expressed as a percentage of the potential gross income. For example, the appraiser might deduct 5% from potential gross income as a bad debt and vacancy factor. Once the bad debt and vacancy factor is deducted, the appraiser is left with a more reliable income figure, called **effective gross income**.

Operating Expenses. From the effective gross income, the appraiser deducts the expenses connected with operating the building. They fall into three classifications: fixed expenses, maintenance expenses, and reserves for replacement.

- **Fixed expenses:** Real estate taxes and hazard insurance.
- **Maintenance expenses:** Services for tenants, utilities, supplies, cleaning, administration costs, building employee wages, and repairs.
- **Reserves for replacement:** Regular allowances set aside to replace structures and equipment that are expected to wear out, such as roofs, heating equipment, air conditioners, and (in a residential building) kitchen ranges and refrigerators.

The income that is left when operating expenses are deducted from effective gross income is called **net income**. It is net income that is capitalized to determine the property's value.

Some expenses, such as the owner's income taxes, depreciation reserves, and mortgage payments (called **debt service**) are not deducted from the effective gross income to arrive at the net income. These are not considered operating expenses from an appraisal standpoint.

Capitalization. The process of converting net income into a meaningful value is called capitalization. The mathematical procedure is expressed in this formula:

$$\text{Annual Net Income} \div \text{Capitalization Rate} = \text{Value}$$

Example: The property's net income is $25,700 and the capitalization rate is 11%. According to the capitalization formula, the property's value is $233,636.

$$\$25,700 \div 0.11 = \$233,636$$

The capitalization rate is the rate of return an investor (a potential purchaser) would want to receive on the money he or she invests in the property (the purchase price). When the investor chooses the rate of return, it is plugged into the formula shown above. By dividing the net income by the desired rate of return, the investor can determine how much he or she can pay for the property and still realize that desired return.

Example: The property's annual net income is $10,000 and the investor's desired return is 12%.

$$\$10,000 \div 12\% = \$83,333$$

The investor can pay up to $83,333 for a property earning $10,000 net income and realize her desired yield of 12%.

Selecting a Capitalization Rate. To appraise property using the income approach, the appraiser must be familiar with the rate of return that investors generally demand for similar properties.

There are a number of ways for an appraiser to determine a property's capitalization rate. For instance, the appraiser could analyze recent sales of comparable income properties and assume that the subject property would have a capitalization rate similar to theirs. This is known as the **direct comparison method**.

Regardless of the method used for selecting the capitalization rate, two very important considerations are the quality and durability of the investment property's income. Quality (how reliable the tenants are) and durability (how long the income can be expected to last) influence the risk factor. The greater the risk, the higher the capitalization rate and the lower the property's value. On the other hand, the smaller the risk, the lower the capitalization rate and the higher the value.

Gross Multipliers. Residences generally aren't thought of as income-producing properties, so traditional income analysis techniques do not apply. If a residential appraiser uses an income method at all, he or she will use a simplified version called the **gross multiplier method**. As a rule, this method is applied only when appraising residential rental properties.

In the gross multiplier method, the appraiser looks at the relationship between a rental property's income and the price paid for the property.

Example:

Sales price: $126,000
Monthly rent: $835
Conclusion: The monthly rent is equal to 0.66% of the sales price; the sales price is approximately 150 times the monthly rent.

Monthly rents may run about 1% of selling prices in one market, and more or less in another. A market exists where specific rental properties compete with each other for tenants. For competitive reasons, rents charged for similar properties tend to be much alike within the same market. As a result, if one rental property has a monthly income that is 1% of its sales price, comparable properties will have similar income-to-price ratios.

A monthly multiplier (called the gross rent multiplier or GRM) is established by dividing the sales price by the monthly rental income. An annual multiplier (called the gross income multiplier or GIM) is calculated by dividing the sales price by the annual rental income.

Example:

Sales Price		Monthly Rent		Gross Rent Multiplier
$126,000	÷	$835	=	150.90
Sales Price		Annual Rent		Gross Income Multiplier
$126,000	÷	$10,020	=	12.57

After locating at least four comparable residential rental properties, the appraiser can determine their gross rent or gross income multipliers (either is acceptable—it's a matter of the appraiser's preference) by dividing the rents into their respective selling prices. In this example, we will use gross rent multipliers, the monthly figure.

Example:

Comp No.	Sales Price	Monthly Rent	Gross Rent Multiplier
1	$117,500	$800	146.88
2	$125,000	$825	151.52
3	$132,600	$895	148.16
4	$137,800	$950	145.05

The appraiser uses the multipliers of the comparables to determine an appropriate multiplier for the subject property, taking into account the similarities and differences between the properties. Then the appraiser multiplies the rent that the subject property is generating by the chosen gross rent multiplier for a rough estimate of its value as income-producing property.

The principal weakness of the gross multiplier method is that it is based on gross income figures and does not take into account vacancies or operating expenses. If two rental homes have the same rental income, the gross multiplier method would indicate they are worth the same amount; but if one is older and has higher maintenance costs, the net return to the owner would be less, and so would be the value of the property.

If possible, the appraiser should use the subject property's economic rent as opposed to the contract rent (the rent the owner is actually receiving) in calculating the gross multiplier.

Example: The owner leased the home two years ago for $850 a month, and the lease contract has another year to go. Market rents have risen sharply over the past two years, so that the property could now command a much higher rent—probably about $1,075 a month. If the appraiser were to use the $850 contract rent in the gross rent multiplier method instead of the $1,075 economic rent, it would distort the estimate of value.

Reconciliation and Final Estimate of Value

Throughout the appraisal process, the appraiser is gathering facts on which he or she will base the ultimate conclusion, the final estimate of the property's value. In many cases, the facts require nothing beyond simple verification; their meaning is self-evident. In other instances, they require expert interpretation. Appraisers refer to the assembly and interpretation of all the facts that influence a property's value as **reconciliation**. Nowhere in the appraisal process does the appraiser's experience and judgment play a more critical role.

The final value estimate is not simply the average of the results yielded by the three appraisal methods—sales comparison, cost, and income. Rather, it is the figure that represents the appraiser's expert opinion of the subject property's value after all the data have been assembled and analyzed.

Once the appraiser has determined the final estimate of value, he or she presents it to the client in an appraisal report. The two most common types of reports are the narrative report and the form report. A **narrative report** is a thorough, detailed, written presentation of the facts and reasoning behind the appraiser's estimate of value. A **form report** is a brief, standard form used by lending institutions and government agencies (e.g., the FHA and VA), presenting only the key data and the appraiser's conclusions. This is the most common type of appraisal report; a copy of the standard form report for residential appraisals is shown in Figure 12.9.

Fig. 12.9 Uniform Residential Appraisal Report form

Property Description X X

UNIFORM RESIDENTIAL APPRAISAL REPORT   File No.

SUBJECT

Property Address		City		State	Zip Code
Legal Description			County		
Assessor's Parcel No.		Tax Year	R.E. Taxes $	Special Assessments $	
Borrower	Current Owner		Occupant	Owner	Tenant	Vacant

Property rights appraised ☐ Fee Simple ☐ Leasehold   Project Type ☐ PUD ☐ Condominium (HUD/VA only)   HOA$ _____ /Mo.

Neighborhood or Project Name _____ Map Reference _____ Census Tract _____

Sales Price $ _____ Date of Sale _____ Description and $ amount of loan charges/concessions to be paid by seller _____

Lender/Client _____ Address _____

Appraiser _____ Address _____

NEIGHBORHOOD

Location	☐ Urban	☐ Suburban	☐ Rural	**Predominant occupancy**	**Single family housing** PRICE $ (000) AGE (yrs)	**Present land use %**	**Land use change**
Built up	☐ Over 75%	☐ 25-75%	☐ Under 25%			One family _____	☐ Not likely ☐ Likely
Growth rate	☐ Rapid	☐ Stable	☐ Slow	☐ Owner Low		2-4 family _____	☐ In process
Property values	☐ Increasing	☐ Stable	☐ Declining	☐ Tenant High		Multi-family _____	To: _____
Demand/supply	☐ Shortage	☐ In balance	☐ Over supply	☐ Vacant (0-5%) ▨▨ Predominant ▨▨		Commercial _____	
Marketing time	☐ Under 3 mos.	☐ 3-6 mos.	☐ Over 6 mos.	☐ Vacant (over 5%)		( ) _____	

Note: Race and the racial composition of the neighborhood are not appraisal factors.

Neighborhood boundaries and characteristics: _____

Factors that affect the marketability of the properties in the neighborhood (proximity to employment and amenities, employment stability, appeal to market, etc.): _____

Market conditions in the subject neighborhood (including support for the above conclusions related to the trend of property values, demand/supply, and marketing time - - such as data on competitive properties for sale in the neighborhood, description of the prevalence of sales and financing concessions, etc.): _____

PUD

Project Information for PUDs (If applicable) - - is the developer/builder in control of the Home Owners' Association (HOA)?   ☐ Yes   ☐ No

Approximate total number of units in the subject project _____ . Approximate total number of units for sale in the subject project _____ .

Describe common elements and recreational facilities: _____

SITE

Dimensions _____	Topography _____
Site area _____ Corner Lot ☐ Yes ☐ No	Size _____
Specific zoning classification and description _____	Shape _____
Zoning compliance ☐ Legal ☐ Legal nonconforming (Grandfathered use) ☐ Illegal ☐ No zoning	Drainage _____
Highest & best use as improved ☐ Present use ☐ Other use (explain)	View _____

Utilities	Public	Other	Off-site Improvements	Type	Public	Private	
Electricity	☐		Street	_____	☐	☐	Landscaping _____
Gas	☐		Curb/gutter	_____	☐	☐	Driveway Surface _____
Water	☐		Sidewalk	_____	☐	☐	Apparent easements _____
Sanitary sewer	☐		Street lights	_____	☐	☐	FEMA Special Flood Hazard Area ☐ Yes ☐ No
Storm sewer	☐		Alley	_____	☐	☐	FEMA Zone _____ Map Date _____
							FEMA Map No. _____

Comments (apparent adverse easements, encroachments, special assessments, slide areas, illegal or legal nonconforming zoning use, etc.): _____

DESCRIPTION OF IMPROVEMENTS

GENERAL DESCRIPTION	EXTERIOR DESCRIPTION	FOUNDATION	BASEMENT	INSULATION
No. of Units _____	Foundation _____	Slab _____	Area Sq. Ft. _____	Roof ☐
No. of Stories _____	Exterior Walls _____	Crawl Space _____	% Finished _____	Ceiling ☐
Type (Det./Att.) _____	Roof Surface _____	Basement _____	Ceiling _____	Walls ☐
Design (Style) _____	Gutters & Dwnspts. _____	Sump Pump _____	Walls _____	Floor ☐
Existing/Proposed _____	Window Type _____	Dampness _____	Floor _____	None ☐
Age (Yrs.) _____	Storm/Screens _____	Settlement _____	Outside Entry _____	Unknown ☐
Effective Age (Yrs.) _____	Manufactured House _____	Infestation _____		

ROOMS	Foyer	Living	Dining	Kitchen	Den	Family Rm.	Rec. Rm.	Bedrooms	# Baths	Laundry	Other	Area Sq. Ft.
Basement												
Level 1												
Level 2												

Finished area **above** grade contains: _____ Rooms; _____ Bedroom(s); _____ Bath(s); _____ Square Feet of Gross Living Area

INTERIOR	Materials/Condition	HEATING		KITCHEN EQUIP.		ATTIC		AMENITIES		CAR STORAGE:	
Floors	_____	Type	_____	Refrigerator	☐	None		Fireplace(s) # _____		None ☐	
Walls	_____	Fuel	_____	Range/Oven	☐	Stairs	☐	Patio		Garage	# of cars
Trim/Finish	_____	Condition	_____	Disposal	☐	Drop Stair	☐	Deck		Attached _____	
Bath Floor	_____	COOLING		Dishwasher	☐	Scuttle	☐	Porch		Detached _____	
Bath Wainscot	_____	Central	_____	Fan/Hood	☐	Floor	☐	Fence		Built-In _____	
Doors	_____	Other	_____	Microwave	☐	Heated	☐	Pool		Carport _____	
		Condition	_____	Washer/Dryer	☐	Finished	☐			Driveway _____	

COMMENTS

Additional features (special energy efficient items, etc.): _____

Condition of the improvements, depreciation (physical, functional, and external), repairs needed, quality of construction, remodeling/additions, etc.: _____

Adverse environmental conditions (such as, but not limited to, hazardous wastes, toxic substances, etc.) present in the improvements, on the site, or in the immediate vicinity of the subject property: _____

Valuation Section

UNIFORM RESIDENTIAL APPRAISAL REPORT   File No. _____

COST APPROACH	
ESTIMATED SITE VALUE. = $ _____	Comments on Cost Approach (such as, source of cost estimate, site value, square foot calculation and, for HUD, VA and FmHA, the estimated remaining economic life of the property): _____
ESTIMATED REPRODUCTION COST-NEW OF IMPROVEMENTS:	
Dwelling _____ Sq. Ft @ $ _____ = $ _____	
_____ Sq. Ft @ $ _____ = _____	
_____ = _____	
Garage/Carport _____ Sq. Ft @ $ _____ = _____	
Total Estimated Cost-New . . . . = $ _____	
Less Physical	Functional	External	
Depreciation _____ = $ _____	
Depreciated Value of Improvements . . . . = $ _____	
"As-is" Value of Site Improvements . . . . = $ _____	
INDICATED VALUE BY COST APPROACH . . . . = $ _____	

ITEM	SUBJECT	COMPARABLE NO. 1	COMPARABLE NO. 2	COMPARABLE NO. 3
Address				
Proximity to Subject				
Sales Price	$	$	$	$
Price/Gross Liv. Area	$	$	$	$
Data and/or Verification Sources				

VALUE ADJUSTMENTS	DESCRIPTION	DESCRIPTION	+ (−) $ Adjustment	DESCRIPTION	+ (−) $ Adjustment	DESCRIPTION	+ (−) $ Adjustment
Sales or Financing Concessions							
Date of Sale/Time							
Location							
Leasehold/Fee Simple							
Site							
View							
Design and Appeal							
Quality of Construction							
Age							
Condition							
Above Grade Room Count	Total Bdrms Baths	Total Bdrms Baths		Total Bdrms Baths		Total Bdrms Baths	
Gross Living Area	Sq. Ft.	Sq. Ft.		Sq. Ft.		Sq. Ft.	
Basement & Finished Rooms Below Grade							
Functional Utility							
Heating/Cooling							
Energy Efficient Items							
Garage/Carport							
Porch, Patio, Deck, Fireplace(s), etc.							
Fence, Pool, etc.							
Net Adj. (total)		+ ☐ − ☐ $		+ ☐ − ☐ $		+ ☐ − ☐ $	
Adjusted Sales Price of Comparable		$		$		$	

Comments on Sales Comparison (including the subject property's compatibility to the neighborhood, etc.): _____

ITEM	SUBJECT	COMPARABLE NO. 1	COMPARABLE NO. 2	COMPARABLE NO. 3
Date, Price and Data Source for prior sales within year of appraisal				

Analysis of any current agreement of sale, option, or listing of the subject property and analysis of any prior sales of subject and comparables within one year of the date of appraisal: _____

INDICATED VALUE BY SALES COMPARISON APPROACH . . . . $ _____

INDICATED VALUE BY INCOME APPROACH (If Applicable) Estimated Market Rent $ _____ /Mo. x Gross Rent Multiplier _____ = $ _____

This appraisal is made ☐ "as is" ☐ subject to the repairs, alterations, inspections, or conditions listed below ☐ subject to completion per plans and specifications.

Conditions of Appraisal: _____

Final Reconciliation: _____

The purpose of this appraisal is to estimate the market value of the real property that is the subject of this report, based on the above conditions and the certification, contingent and limiting conditions, and market value definition that are stated in the attached Freddie Mac Form 439/Fannie Mae Form 1004B (Revised _____).

I (WE) ESTIMATE THE MARKET VALUE, AS DEFINED, OF THE REAL PROPERTY THAT IS THE SUBJECT OF THIS REPORT, AS OF _____ (WHICH IS THE DATE OF INSPECTION AND THE EFFECTIVE DATE OF THIS REPORT) TO BE $ _____

APPRAISER:	SUPERVISORY APPRAISER (ONLY IF REQUIRED):	☐ Did ☐ Did Not
Signature _____	Signature _____	Inspect Property
Name _____	Name _____	
Date Report Signed _____	Date Report Signed _____	
State Certification # _____ State	State Certification # _____ State	
Or State License # _____ State	Or State License # _____ State	

Freddie Mac Form 70 6–93   10 CH.   PAGE 2 OF 2   Fannie Mae Form 1004 6–93

Chapter Summary

1. An appraisal is an estimate or an opinion of value. Most real estate appraisals concern a property's market value, the price it is likely to bring on the open market in an arm's length transaction.

2. Appraisers have developed many "principles of value" that guide them in the valuation process. These include the principles of highest and best use, change, supply and demand, substitution, conformity, contribution, anticipation, and competition.

3. The steps in the appraisal process include defining the problem, determining what data is needed and where it can be found, gathering and verifying general and specific data, selecting and applying the valuation methods, reconciling the value indicators, and issuing the appraisal report.

4. General data concerns factors outside the subject property itself that influence the property's value; the appraiser gathers general data by evaluating economic and social trends and by performing a neighborhood analysis. Specific data (about the subject property itself) is gathered through site analysis and building analysis.

5. In the sales comparison approach to value (which is the most important method of appraisal for residential properties), the appraiser compares the subject property to comparable properties that were sold recently, and uses the adjusted selling prices of the comparables to estimate the value of the subject property.

6. In the cost approach, the appraiser estimates the cost of replacing the improvements, deducts any depreciation, and adds the estimated value of the land to arrive at an estimate of the value of the whole property. Depreciation takes the form of deferred maintenance, functional obsolescence, and external obsolescence.

7. In the income approach to value, the appraiser divides the property's net income by a capitalization rate to estimate its value to an investor. The appraiser first estimates the property's potential gross income (economic rent), then deducts a bad debt and vacancy factor to determine the effective gross income, then deducts operating expenses to determine net income. The gross multiplier method is a simplified version of the income approach that is sometimes used in appraising residential rental properties.

🔑 Key Terms

Market value—The most probable price that a property should bring in a competitive and open market under all conditions requisite to a fair sale, the buyer and seller each acting prudently and knowledgeably, and assuming the price is not affected by undue stimulus.

Arm's length transaction—A transaction in which both parties have full knowledge of the property's merits and shortcomings, neither party is acting under unusual pressure, and the property has been exposed on the open market for a reasonable length of time.

Highest and best use—The most profitable use of the property; the one that provides the greatest net return over time.

Principle of change—Real property is in a constant state of change; it goes through a four-phase life cycle of integration, equilibrium, disintegration, and rejuvenation.

Principle of substitution—No one will pay more for a piece of property than they would have to pay for an equally desirable substitute.

Sales comparison approach—The method of appraisal in which the appraiser compares the subject property to recently sold comparable properties.

Cost approach—The method of appraisal in which the appraiser estimates the replacement cost of the building, deducts depreciation, and adds the value of the site.

Depreciation—Loss in value due to any cause.

Deferred maintenance—Depreciation caused by wear and tear; physical deterioration.

Functional obsolescence—Depreciation caused by functional inadequacies or outmoded design.

External obsolescence—Depreciation caused by forces outside the property, such as neighborhood decline or proximity to nuisances; also called economic obsolescence.

Income approach—The method of appraising property in which net income is converted into value by use of a capitalization rate.

Effective gross income—Potential gross income less a bad debt and vacancy factor.

Net income—Effective gross income less operating expenses.

Capitalization rate—The rate of return an investor wants on his or her investment in the property.

Economic rent—The rent that a property would earn on the open market if it were currently available for rent, as distinguished from the rent it is actually earning now (the contract rent).

Chapter Quiz

1. An appraisal is:

   a) a scientific determination of a property's value

   b) a property's average value, as indicated by general and specific data

   c) an estimate of a property's value as of a specific date

   d) a mathematical analysis of a property's value

2. The focus of most appraisals is the subject property's:

   a) market value

   b) market price

   c) sales price

   d) value in use

3. A property's highest and best use is:

   a) the use that will generate the greatest net return

   b) the best use it could be put to if there were no zoning or other restrictions

   c) the use that best promotes the public health, safety, and welfare

   d) the use that is best suited to the present owner's plans

4. The earliest phase of a property's life cycle, when it is being developed, is called:

   a) substitution

   b) regression

   c) integration

   d) disintegration

5. Developers have announced plans to build a multi-million dollar shopping center next door to a vacant commercial lot you own. Property values in the area will tend to increase as a result of this announcement. This is an example of the principle of:

   a) highest and best use

   b) supply and demand

   c) substitution

   d) anticipation

6. The owner of an apartment building has asked an appraiser to determine if it would make financial sense to put in a swimming pool for the tenants' use. The appraiser will be most concerned with the principle of:

   a) regression

   b) substitution

   c) conformity

   d) contribution

7. If someone were to build a high-quality home costing $450,000 in a neighborhood where all of the other homes were valued at around $175,000, the expensive home would suffer a loss in value. This illustrates the principle of:

   a) regression

   b) supply and demand

   c) progression

   d) aversion

8. An appraiser gathers general data in a:

   a) site analysis

   b) building analysis

   c) neighborhood analysis

   d) None of the above

9. The sales comparison approach would almost certainly be much more important than the other two methods (the cost approach and the income approach) in the appraisal of:

   a) a six-unit apartment building
   b) an industrial building
   c) a shopping center
   d) a single-family home

10. A residential appraiser looking for good comparables is most likely to consider homes that:

   a) have not changed hands within the past three years
   b) are currently listed for sale
   c) were sold within the past six months
   d) were listed for less than they eventually sold for

11. In which of the following situations would the sales comparison method of appraisal be least reliable?

   a) When all the comparables are in the same price range
   b) In an inactive real estate market
   c) When some of the comparables are located in another neighborhood
   d) When the subject property is in better condition than the comparables

12. When applying the sales comparison method to appraise a single-family home, an appraiser would never use as a comparable a similar home that:

   a) sold over six months age
   b) sold recently but is located in another neighborhood
   c) was sold by owners who were forced to sell because of financial difficulties
   d) is situated on a corner lot

13. When using the replacement cost approach, which of the following would be least important?

   a) Current construction cost per square foot
   b) Rental cost per square foot
   c) Depreciation
   d) Estimated land value

14. An appraiser is applying the cost approach in valuing an elegant building that was built in 1894. Which of the following is most likely to be true?

   a) The building's replacement cost is the same as its reproduction cost
   b) The building's replacement cost is a better indicator of its market value than its reproduction cost
   c) The building's reproduction cost is a better indicator of its market value than its replacement cost
   d) The building's replacement cost is much greater than its reproduction cost

15. In the income approach to value, which of the following is not considered to be one of the property's operating expenses?

   a) General real estate taxes
   b) Maintenance expenses
   c) Reserves for replacement
   d) Mortgage payments

Answer Key

1. c) An appraisal is only an estimate or opinion of value, and it is valid only in regard to a specified date.

2. a) An appraiser is usually asked to determine the subject property's market value (or value in exchange).

3. a) The highest and best use is the use that would produce the greatest net return over time, given the current zoning and other restrictions on use.

4. c) Integration is the period during which the property is being developed.

5. d) This is an example of the principle of anticipation, which holds that value is created by the expectation of future benefits to be derived from owning a property.

6. d) The appraiser will be concerned with the principle of contribution. Will the proposed improvement—the swimming pool—contribute enough to the property's value (in the form of higher rents from tenants, and, ultimately, net income to the owner) to justify the expense of installing it?

7. a) The principle of regression holds that association with properties of much lower quality reduces a property's value.

8. c) General data is data concerning factors outside the subject property itself that affect the property's value. A neighborhood analysis involves collection of general data, whereas the site and building analysis involve collection of specific data about the subject property itself.

9. d) In the appraisal of single-family homes, the sales comparison approach is given the most weight.

10. c) A sales comparison appraisal of residential property is usually based on the sales prices of homes that sold within the past six months.

11. b) There is little data available in an inactive market. (However, the appraiser can use comparable sales that took place up to one year earlier, if he or she determines the rate of appreciation or depreciation and adjusts the prices accordingly.)

12. c) Forced sales are never used as comparables for appraisal purposes. Comparable sales must be arm's length transactions, where neither party was acting under unusual pressure.

13. b) The cost method involves estimating the current cost of construction, subtracting the amount of accrued depreciation, then adding back in the estimated value of the land. How much the property rents for is irrelevant to the cost approach.

14. b) The cost of producing a replica of an old building at current prices (reproduction cost) is invariably much higher than the cost of constructing a building with the equivalent utility using modern materials (replacement cost). Reproduction cost is not a good indicator of an old building's market value.

15. d) The mortgage payments—referred to as the property's debt service—are not considered operating expenses for the purposes of the income approach.

Closing Real Estate Transactions

⬛ Chapter Overview

The real estate agent's job doesn't end when the parties sign the purchase and sale agreement. Many matters must be taken care of before the sale can be finalized, and the service provided by the real estate agent during the closing process is just as important as the agent's marketing efforts before the sale. Guiding the parties through closing prevents unnecessary delays and earns the agent a reputation for professionalism. Every real estate agent should be familiar with escrow procedures and the allocation of closing costs. This chapter explains the purpose of escrow, the steps involved in closing, and Washington's Escrow Agent Registration Act. It also discusses how settlement statements work, how closing costs are allocated and prorated, income tax aspects of closing, and the requirements of the federal Real Estate Settlement Procedures Act.

Introduction

Once a purchase and sale agreement has been signed and all the contingencies (such as arranging financing) have been satisfied, preparations are made to finalize the transaction. Finalizing a real estate transaction is called **closing** or **settlement**.

The closing process varies considerably from one state to another. In some states, all of the parties involved in the transaction get together to sign and exchange documents and transfer funds. In many other states (including Washington), the closing process is handled by a neutral third party, through the creation of an escrow.

Escrow

Escrow is an arrangement in which money and documents are held by a neutral third party (the **escrow agent**) on behalf of the buyer and the seller. The parties usually give the escrow agent written **escrow instructions**, which determine under what conditions and at what time the agent will distribute the money and documents to the proper parties. The escrow agent is a dual agent, representing both the buyer and the seller, with fiduciary duties to both parties (see Chapter 7).

The purpose of escrow is to ensure that the seller receives the purchase price, the buyer receives clear title to the property, and the lender's security interest in the property is perfected. Escrow protects each party from the other's change of mind. For example, if the seller suddenly doesn't want to sell the property as agreed, he or she can't just refuse to deliver the deed to the buyer. Once a deed has been given to an escrow agent, if the buyer fulfills all the conditions specified in the escrow instructions and deposits the purchase price into escrow, the escrow agent is required to deliver the deed to the buyer. An added advantage of escrow is convenience: the parties do not have to be present to close the transaction.

Escrow agents perform a wide variety of services to prepare a transaction for closing. Most escrow closings involve all of the following steps:

- gathering the information necessary to prepare escrow instructions;
- obtaining a preliminary title report from the title insurance company;
- paying off existing loans secured by the property;
- preparing documents, such as the deed;
- depositing funds from the buyer (and seller if necessary);
- prorating expenses and allocating closing costs;
- preparing a Uniform Settlement Statement;
- obtaining title insurance policies;
- recording documents; and
- disbursing funds and delivering documents.

Escrow Agent Registration Act

Washington's Escrow Agent Registration Act requires escrow agents to be licensed and registered with the Department of Financial Institutions. A company that is licensed to engage in the escrow business under the Registration Act is called a **certified escrow agent**. Before the company is certified, its sole proprietor, partner, or corporate officer must have passed a state examination, paid a fee, and submitted three affidavits of good character, a commercial credit report reflecting good credit, and a fidelity bond. A certified escrow agent may employ **escrow officers**, who also must take a state exam and be properly licensed.

A certified escrow agent is responsible for keeping adequate records of all transactions. When an escrow agent handles funds on behalf of buyers or sellers, they must be placed in a trust account maintained in a recognized Washington depository.

The Director of the Department of Licensing may investigate the actions of any certified escrow agent or escrow officer. The Director can temporarily suspend or permanently revoke the license of an escrow agent or officer who is guilty of converting trust funds to personal use, or who has committed any other dishonest or prohibited acts.

Exemptions. There are several significant exemptions from the Escrow Agent Registration Act's registration and licensing requirements. Attorneys, title companies, banks, savings and loans, credit unions, insurance companies, and federally approved lenders are allowed to perform escrow services without being licensed or registered under the act; so are those acting under the supervision of a court, such as receivers, trustees in bankruptcy, guardians, executors, and probate administrators. Real estate brokers handling escrow for their own transactions (those in which they are providing brokerage services) are also exempt, provided that they do not charge an additional fee for their escrow services.

Throughout this chapter, we'll be referring to the person who handles the closing process for a transaction as the escrow agent. Keep in mind, however, that the closing agent is not necessarily a certified escrow agent or a licensed escrow officer. In some transactions, the closing agent is the real estate broker or one of the other parties that are exempt from the Registration Act.

Closing Costs and Settlement Statements

Most real estate transactions involve a wide variety of costs in addition to the purchase price: inspection fees, title insurance charges, loan fees, and so on. These are known as **closing costs**. Some of these closing costs are paid by the buyer, and some are paid by the seller. Some are paid by one party to the other; for example, the buyer may have to reimburse the seller for property taxes the seller already paid. Other closing costs are paid by one of the parties to a third party; the seller may be required to pay a pest inspector's fee, for instance.

There are also other payments to be made in connection with closing. For example, the seller often has to pay off an existing mortgage or other liens. Who is required to pay how much to whom at closing can be a complicated matter.

So for each transaction, the escrow agent prepares a **settlement statement**. A settlement statement (also known as a closing statement) sets forth all the financial aspects of the transaction in detail. It shows exactly how much the buyer will have to pay at closing, and exactly how much the seller will take away from closing. A simplified example of a settlement statement is shown in Figure 13.1.

Preparing a Settlement Statement

The items listed on the settlement statement are either **debits** or **credits**. A debit is a charge payable by a particular party; the purchase price is a debit to the buyer, for example, and the sales commission is a debit to the seller. Credits are items payable to a party; the buyer is credited for his or her new loan, and the seller for the purchase price.

Preparing a settlement statement involves little more than determining what charges and credits apply to a given transaction and making sure each one is allocated to the right party. When allocating expenses, an escrow agent is generally guided by the terms of the purchase and sale agreement or the escrow instructions. The allocation can also be determined by custom (local or general), provided the custom doesn't conflict with the terms of the parties' contract. For example, in most places the buyer usually pays the cost of an appraisal, so that cost would ordinarily be charged to the buyer at closing. But if the seller agreed in the purchase and sale agreement to pay the appraisal fee, custom would be disregarded and the expense would be a debit to the seller at closing.

Of course, neither custom nor the agreement between the parties can be followed if they are contrary to local, state, or federal law.

Although a real estate agent will not necessarily ever be called upon to prepare a formal settlement statement, every agent should know what closing costs are likely to be involved in a transaction and how they are customarily allocated. The buyer and the seller may want to negotiate about the allocation of particular costs, and in any case they are entitled to know the full extent of their costs before signing a contract. A real estate agent should be able to prepare a good estimate of closing costs for each party.

Guide to Settlement Statements

The double entry accounting method is used for settlement statements, so each party has a credit column and a debit column. The sum of the buyer's credits must equal the sum of his or her debits. This is also true of the seller's

Fig. 13.1 Simplified settlement statement

	Buyer		Seller	
	Debits	**Credits**	**Debits**	**Credits**
Purchase price	175,000.00			175,000.00
Deposit		8,750.00		
Excise tax			2,240.00	
Sales commission			12,250.00	
Payoff of seller's loan			92,950.00	
Assumption of seller's loan				
New loan		140,000.00		
Seller financing				
Owner's title insurance			120.00	
Lender's title insurance	456.00			
Origination/assumption fee	2,100.00			
Discount points				
Property taxes				
In arrears				
Paid in advance	684.50			684.50
Hazard insurance				
Assumption of policy				
New policy	260.00			
Interest				
Payoff of seller's loan			382.86	
Assumption				
New loan (prepaid)	161.08			
Reserve account				
Payoff of seller's loan				286.05
Assumption				
Credit report	40.00			
Appraisal	275.00			
Survey				
Pest inspection and repairs			150.00	
Personal property				
Recording fees	50.00		25.00	
Escrow fee	147.00		147.00	
Balance due from buyer		30,423.58		
Balance due to seller			67,705.69	
TOTALS	179,173.58	179,173.58	175,970.55	175,970.55

credits and debits. Think of the settlement statement as a check register for a bank account. Debits are like checks written against the account, and credits are the equivalent of deposits into the account. When the transaction closes, the balance in each party's account should be zero.

When an item is payable by one party to the other, it will appear on the settlement statement as a debit to the paying party and as a credit to the party paid. An obvious example is the purchase price, which is debited to the buyer and credited to the seller.

If an item is paid by one of the parties to a third party, it appears on the settlement statement in the paying party's debit column, and it does not appear in the other party's columns at all. For example, the seller is customarily charged for the state excise tax, which is paid to the county treasurer. The tax is a debit to the seller, but it is not a credit to the buyer.

Similarly, certain items are shown as a credit to one party, but not as a debit to the other. The seller's reserve balance is a case in point. If the sale calls for the payoff of the seller's existing mortgage, any property tax and insurance reserves held by the seller's lender are refunded. They are a credit to the seller, but not a debit to the buyer.

Settlement Charges. Here is a list of the items that appear on the settlement statements for most standard transactions.

Purchase Price. Paid by the buyer to the seller, the purchase price is listed as a debit to the buyer and a credit to the seller.

Earnest Money Deposit. In most transactions, the buyer gives the seller an earnest money deposit when the purchase and sale agreement is signed. If the transaction closes, the earnest money is applied to the purchase price. Since the buyer has already paid the earnest money, it appears on the settlement statement as a credit to the buyer. And since the full purchase price has already been debited to the buyer and credited to the seller, no entry is made on the seller's side of the statement.

Sales Commission. The real estate broker's commission is normally paid by the seller, so it is entered as a debit to the seller.

New Loan. If the buyer secures a new loan to finance part or all of the sale, the loan amount is listed as a credit to the buyer. Like the deposit, the buyer's loan is part of the purchase price already credited to the seller, so no entry is made on the seller's side of the statement.

Assumed Loan. If the buyer assumes the seller's existing loan, it is part of the money used to finance the transaction, so (like a new loan) it is credited to the buyer. The assumed loan balance is a debit to the seller.

Seller Financing. If the seller accepts a mortgage or deed of trust from the buyer for part of the purchase price, that shows up in the buyer's credit column, just like an institutional loan. At the same time, a seller financing arrangement reduces the amount of cash the seller will receive at closing, so it is listed as a debit to the seller.

If the property is sold under a land contract, the contract price (less the downpayment) is credit extended by the seller. It reduces the seller's net at closing and is used by the buyer to finance the purchase, so it is a debit to the seller and a credit to the buyer.

Payoff of Seller's Loan. If the seller pays off an existing mortgage loan, his or her net is reduced by that amount. The payoff is a debit to the seller. No entry is made on the buyer's side of the statement.

Prepayment Penalty. A prepayment penalty is a charge the seller's lender may impose on the seller for paying the loan off before the end of its term. It would be a debit to the seller on the settlement statement.

Seller's Reserve Account. As was mentioned earlier, the seller often has reserves on deposit with his or her lender to cover property taxes and hazard insurance premiums. When the seller's loan is paid off, the unused balance in the reserve account is refunded to the seller. It appears as a credit on the seller's side of the settlement statement. If the buyer is assuming the loan and the reserve account, the reserves would appear as a credit to the seller and a debit to the buyer.

Appraisal Fee. The appraisal is usually required by the buyer's lender, so the fee is ordinarily a debit to the buyer.

Credit Report. The buyer's lender charges the buyer for the credit investigation, so this is also a debit to the buyer.

Survey. Sometimes a lender requires a survey as a condition for making the loan. Unless otherwise agreed, the cost of the survey is a debit to the buyer.

Origination Fee. This is the lender's one-time charge to the borrower for setting up the loan (see Chapter 11). It's a debit to the buyer.

Discount Points. The discount points are a debit to the buyer, unless the seller has agreed to pay for a buydown (see Chapter 11). In that case, the points are a debit to the seller.

Assumption Fee. A lender charges an assumption fee when the buyer is assuming the seller's existing loan. The assumption fee is a debit to the buyer.

Owner's Title Insurance Premium. The premium for the owner's title insurance policy (which protects the buyer) is customarily paid by the seller. So this is a debit to the seller, unless otherwise agreed.

Lender's Title Insurance Premium. The lender requires the buyer to provide an extended coverage policy to protect the lender's lien priority. The premium for this policy is a debit to the buyer, unless otherwise agreed.

Sale of Personal Property. If the seller is selling the buyer some personal property along with the real property, the price of these items should be credited to the seller and debited to the buyer. (The seller should sign a bill of sale to be delivered to the buyer at closing along with the deed.)

Inspection Fees. The cost of an inspection is allocated by agreement between the parties. For example, the buyer might agree to pay for the cost of a pest inspection, while the seller agrees to pay for repairs if the inspection shows that any are necessary.

Hazard Insurance Policy. The lender generally requires the buyer to pay for one to three years of hazard insurance coverage in advance. This is a debit to the buyer.

Excise Tax. This is a tax imposed on every sale of real property in Washington (see Chapter 5). It is customarily paid by the seller, so it would usually be listed in the seller's debit column.

Attorney's Fees. A buyer or seller who is represented by an attorney in the transaction is responsible for his or her own attorney's fees. On the settlement statement, the fees will show up as a debit to the appropriate party.

Recording Fees. The fees for recording the various documents involved in the transaction are usually charged to the party who benefits from the recording. For example, the fees for recording the deed and the new mortgage or deed of trust are debits to the buyer; the fee for recording a satisfaction of the old mortgage is a debit to the seller.

Escrow Fee. Also called a settlement fee or closing fee, the escrow fee is the escrow agent's charge for his or her services. The buyer and the seller commonly agree to split the escrow fee; in that case, half the fee will be debited to each party.

Prorations. There are, of course, certain recurring expenses connected with ownership of real estate, including property taxes, hazard insurance premiums, and mortgage interest payments. As a general rule, the seller is responsible for these expenses during his or her period of ownership, but not beyond. In preparing a settlement statement, the escrow agent checks to see whether the seller will be current, in arrears, or paid in advance with respect to these expenses on the closing date. The escrow agent then **prorates** the expenses, determining what share of them the seller is responsible for. To prorate an expense is to divide and allocate it proportionately, according to time, interest, or benefit.

If, in regard to a particular expense, the seller will be in arrears on the closing date, the amount that he or she owes is entered as a debit on the settlement statement. If the seller has paid in advance, he or she is entitled to a partial refund, which appears as a credit on the statement. If the expense is one that will continue after closing (as in the case of property taxes), the buyer is responsible for it once his or her period of ownership begins. That will show up on the buyer's side of the settlement statement as a credit (if the seller is in arrears) or as a debit (if the seller has paid in advance).

The first step in prorating an expense is to divide it by the number of days it covers to determine the **per diem** (daily) rate. So an annual expense would be divided by 365 days (366 in a leap year); the per diem rate would be $^1/_{365}$ of the annual amount. A monthly expense would be divided by the number of days in the month in question (28, 29, 30, or 31).*

The next step is to determine the number of days during which a particular party is responsible for the expense. The final step is to multiply that number of days by the per diem rate, to arrive at the share of the expense that party is responsible for. Examples appear below. (See Chapter 18 for further discussion of proration calculations.)

Property Taxes. The seller is responsible for property taxes up to the day of closing; the buyer is responsible for them on the day of closing and thereafter. If the seller has already paid the property taxes for the year, he or she is entitled to a prorated refund at closing. On the settlement statement, this will appear as a credit to the seller and a debit to the buyer.

> **Example:** Sharon is selling her house to Ben. The transaction will close July 14. This year the property taxes on the house are $1,200.85. The escrow agent calculates the per diem rate by dividing the property tax figure by 365, the number of days in the year.
>
> $$\$1,200.85 \div 365 = \$3.29 \text{ per diem}$$

---

* It was once a common practice to simplify proration calculations by using a 360-day year and 30-day months (regardless of how many days there actually were in a particular month or year). But now that calculators are so widely available, most closing agents use the exact number of days in the year or month in question. Also note that in order for the result of a proration to be completely accurate, the per diem rate must be calculated to an accuracy of at least 4 decimal places for monthly amounts, and 5 decimal places for annual amounts. Here again, calculators make this a painless process.

Sharon, the seller, is responsible for the property taxes through July 13—in other words, for the first 194 days of the year. The buyer, Ben, is responsible for the taxes from July 14 forward—the remaining 171 days in the year.

Sharon has already paid the full year's taxes, so at closing she'll be entitled to a credit for the share that is Ben's responsibility. The escrow agent multiplies the number of days for which Ben is responsible by the per diem rate to determine the amount Ben will owe Sharon at closing.

$$171 \text{ days} \times \$3.29 = \$562.59$$

This $562.59 will appear as a credit on the seller's side of the settlement statement, and as a debit on the buyer's side of the statement.

If the taxes are in arrears, the amount the seller should have paid for the period before closing will be a debit to the seller on the settlement statement.

Hazard Insurance. Hazard insurance is usually paid for well in advance. At closing, the seller is entitled to a refund for the unused portion of the policy. For example, if the seller has paid the premium for the year, and there are three months left in the year, the seller is entitled to a refund of one-fourth of the premium. This would show up as a credit to the seller on the settlement statement. If the buyer is going to assume the policy, the seller will be credited and the buyer will be debited for the appropriate amount.

Interest on Seller's Loan. Interest on a real estate loan is almost always paid in arrears. In other words, the interest accruing during a given month is paid as part of the next month's payment. For instance, a loan payment due on September 1 includes the interest that accrued during August. If a transaction closes in the middle of the payment period, the seller owes the lender some interest.

Example: The closing date is August 15. Although the seller made a payment on her loan on August 1, that payment did not include any of the interest that is accruing during August. At closing, the seller will owe the lender interest for the period from August 1 through August 15. The escrow agent prorates the interest, charging the seller only for those days, rather than the whole month's interest. The prorated amount is entered on the settlement statement as a debit to the seller.

If the buyer assumes the loan, his first payment will be due September 1, and it will pay all of the interest for August. The seller will be debited for the interest owed up to August 15, and the buyer will be credited for the same amount.

Prepaid Interest on Buyer's Loan. Another expense that the escrow agent prorates (one that does not concern the seller) is the interest on the buyer's new mortgage loan. As a general rule, the first payment date of a new loan is not the first day of the month immediately following closing, but rather the first day of the next month after that.

Example: The buyer is financing the purchase with a new institutional loan. Closing takes place on January 23. The buyer is not required to make a payment on the new loan on February 1. Instead, the first payment is not due until March 1.

Even though the first payment isn't due for an extra month, interest begins accruing on the loan on the closing date. As was explained above, the first regular payment will cover the interest for the preceding month. So if the transaction closes on January 23, the first payment will be due on March 1, and that payment will cover the interest accrued in February. However, it will not cover the interest accrued between January 23 and January 31. Instead, the lender requires the buyer to pay the interest for those nine days in January at closing. This is called prepaid interest or interim interest. It will appear as a debit to the buyer on the settlement statement.

Example: The buyer is borrowing $230,000 at 7% interest to finance the purchase. The annual interest on the loan during the first year will be $16,100 ($230,000 × 7% = $16,100). The escrow agent divides that annual figure by 365 to determine the per diem interest rate.

$$\$16,100 \div 365 = \$44.11 \text{ per diem}$$

There are nine days between the closing date (January 23) and the first day of the following month, so the lender will expect the buyer to prepay nine days' worth of interest at closing.

$$\$44.11 \times 9 \text{ days} = \$396.99 \text{ prepaid interest}$$

The escrow agent will enter $396.99 as a debit to the buyer on the settlement statement.

Rent. So far we've only discussed prorated expenses. In some transactions, there is also income to be prorated at closing. If the property generates rental income and the tenants have paid for some period beyond the closing date, the seller is debited and the buyer credited for the rent paid in advance. If the rent is paid in arrears, the seller will be credited for the amount due up to closing, and the buyer will be debited for the same amount.

Note that tenants' security deposits are not prorated. The seller must transfer all of the deposits to the buyer, since the leases will continue after closing.

Cash at Closing. As we said earlier, on a settlement statement the sum of one party's credits should equal the sum of that party's debits, so that the final balance in each party's "account" is zero. In order for the statement to work this way, it must list the amount of cash that the buyer will have to bring to closing, and also the amount of cash the seller will take away from closing.

Balance Due from Buyer. Add up all of the buyer's credits, then add up all of the buyer's debits. Subtract the buyer's credits from the buyer's debits to find the balance due, which is the amount of cash the buyer will have to pay at closing. Enter this amount as a credit for the buyer. Now the buyer's credits column should add up to exactly the same amount as the buyer's debits column.

Balance Due to Seller. Add up all of the seller's credits, then add up all of the seller's debits. Subtract the seller's debits from the seller's credits. The result is the amount of cash the seller will receive at closing (if any). Enter this amount as a debit if credits exceed debits, but as a credit if debits exceed credits. Now the seller's credits column should add up to exactly the same amount as the seller's debits column.

Income Tax Aspects of Closing

Nearly all real estate transactions have tax implications for the parties (see Chapter 14) and, naturally, it is up to each party to fulfill his or her own tax obligations. However, escrow agents must meet certain reporting requirements.

Real estate agents need to be familiar with these requirements because, if an escrow agent fails to comply with them, the real estate agents involved in the transaction may be liable.

1099 Reporting

Escrow agents must report every sale of real property to the Internal Revenue Service. Form 1099-S is used to report the seller's name and social security number and the gross proceeds from the sale. The escrow agent may not charge an extra fee for filling out the 1099-S.

If the escrow agent fails to report the sale to the IRS, the mortgage lender is required to do so. If the mortgage lender also fails to report the sale, it becomes the real estate broker's responsibility to do so.

FIRPTA

The Foreign Investment in Real Property Tax Act (FIRPTA) was passed in 1980 to help prevent foreign investors from evading their tax liability on income generated from the sale of real estate. FIRPTA requires escrow agents to determine whether the property seller is a U.S. citizen. If the seller is not a citizen, the escrow agent must withhold 10% of the net proceeds of the sale and forward that amount to the IRS. Payment must be made within ten days after the transfer date. (Many residential transactions are exempt from FIRPTA.)

If the escrow agent fails to comply with this rule, anyone involved in the sale, including the real estate agents, can be required to pay the money to the IRS.

Real Estate Settlement Procedures Act

The Real Estate Settlement Procedures Act (**RESPA**), a federal law, was passed in 1974. It affects how closing is handled in most residential transactions financed with institutional loans. The law has two main goals:

- to provide borrowers with information about their closing costs; and
- to eliminate kickbacks and referral fees that unnecessarily increase the costs of settlement.

Transactions Covered by RESPA

RESPA applies to "federally related" loan transactions. A loan is federally related if:

1. it will be secured by a mortgage or deed of trust against:
    - property on which there is (or on which the loan proceeds will be used to build) a dwelling with four or fewer units;
    - a condominium unit or a cooperative apartment;
    - a lot with (or on which the loan proceeds will be used to place) a mobile home; and
2. the lender is federally regulated, has federally insured accounts, is assisted by the federal government, makes loans in connection with a federal program, sells loans to Fannie Mae, Ginnie Mae, or Freddie Mac, or makes real estate loans totaling more than $1,000,000 per year.

In short, the act applies to almost all institutional lenders and to most residential loans.

Exemptions. RESPA does not apply to the following loan transactions:

- a loan used to purchase 25 acres or more;
- a loan primarily for a business, commercial, or agricultural purpose;
- a loan used to purchase vacant land, unless there will be a one- to four-unit dwelling built on it or a mobile home placed on it;
- temporary financing, such as a construction loan;
- an assumption for which the lender's approval is neither required nor obtained.

Note that RESPA also does not apply to seller-financed transactions, since they are not federally regulated.

RESPA Requirements

RESPA has these requirements for federally related loan transactions:

1. Within three days after receiving a written loan application, the lender must give all loan applicants:
   - a copy of a **booklet about settlement procedures**, prepared by HUD, which explains RESPA, closing costs, and the settlement statement;
   - a **good faith estimate of closing costs** (see Figure 13.2), which must also include information about any provider of settlement services (such as a particular title insurance company or escrow agent) that the lender requires the borrower to use; and
   - a **mortgage servicing disclosure statement**, which discloses whether the lender intends to service the loan or transfer it to another lender.
2. The closing agent (whoever handles closing, whether it's an escrow agent, an employee of the lender, a real estate broker, a lawyer, etc.) must itemize all loan settlement charges on a **Uniform Settlement Statement** form (discussed below).
3. If the borrower will have to make deposits into an escrow account (impound account) to cover taxes, insurance, and other recurring costs, the lender cannot require excessive deposits (more than necessary to cover the expenses when they come due).
4. A lender or a provider of settlement services (such as a title company) may not:
   - pay kickbacks or referral fees to anyone for referring customers;
   - accept unearned fees—that is, fees for settlement services that were not actually provided; or
   - charge a fee for the preparation of the Uniform Settlement Statement, an escrow account statement, or the disclosure statement required by the Truth in Lending Act.
5. The seller may not require the buyer to use a particular title company.

Fig. 13.2 Good faith estimate of closing costs

GOOD FAITH ESTIMATE

Date: _____

Borrower: _____

Property Address: _____

This gives an **ESTIMATE** of most of the charges you will have to pay at the settlement of your loan. The figures shown **AS ESTIMATES**, are subject to change. The figures are computed on an estimated value of $_____, a loan amount of $ _____ an interest rate of _____%, a term of _____ and a LTV of _____%.

_____ owner occupied _____ non-owner occupied   Loan Type _____

Unless otherwise discussed rates and fees are not locked in.

ESTIMATED CLOSING COSTS

801 Loan Origination Fee _____% _____
802 Discount _____ _____
803 Appraisal Fee _____
804 Borrower Credit Report(s) _____
808 Document Preparation Fee/Underwriting Fee _____
810 Tax Registration _____
812 Processing Fee _____
1101 Escrow Fee _____
1106 Flood Determination Letter/Courier/Fed. Express _____
1108 Title Insurance Premium _____
1201 Recording Fees _____
   Total Closing Costs $ _____

PREPAID ITEMS AND RESERVES

901 Interim Interest _____ Days @ $ _____ _____
902 Mortgage Insurance Premium _____
902 Hazard Insurance Premium (12 months to be prepaid) _____
1001 Hazard Insurance Reserve _____ mos. @ $_____ _____
1002 Mortgage Insurance Reserve _____ mos. @ $_____ _____
1004 Property Tax Reserve for _____mos. @ $_____ _____
   Total Prepaids and Reserves to be paid at closing $ _____

ESTIMATED MONTHLY PAYMENT

Principal & Interest $_____
Property Tax $_____
Hazard Insurance $_____
Mortgage Insurance $_____
Total Estimated Monthly Payment $_____

ESTIMATED CASH REQUIRED AT CLOSING

Sales Price/Cost to Build/Payoff $_____
Closing Costs $_____
Prepaid Items & Reserves $_____
Sub-Total $_____
Less Earnest Money $_____
Less Good Faith Deposit $_____
Less Standby Takeout Fee $_____
Less Seller Contributions $_____
Less Loan Amount $_____
Est. Cash Req. at Closing $_____

The above is for information only and is not a loan commitment.

The information provided below reflects estimates of the charges which you are likely to incur at the settlement of your loan. The fees listed are estimate - the actual charges may be more or less. Your transaction may not involve a fee for every item listed. The numbers listed beside the estimates generally correspond to the numbered lines contained in the HUD-1 settlement statement which you will be receiving at settlement. The HUD-1 settlement statement will show you the actual cost for items paid at settlement.

An applicant, by signing this Good Faith Estimate, acknowledges receipt of HUD Booklet outlining settlement costs.

An applicant for an Adjustable Rate Mortgage, by signing this Good Faith Estimate, acknowledges receipt of the booklet entitled, "Consumer Handbook on Adjustable Rate Mortgages".

_____ _____ DATE
_____ _____ DATE
Prepared by: _____ _____ DATE

Uniform Settlement Statement

The closing agent must provide completed Uniform Settlement Statement forms to the borrower, the seller, and the lender on or before the closing date. (The borrower may sign a written waiver of the right to receive the form by closing, in which case it must be provided to the parties as soon as practicable after closing.) If the borrower requests it, the closing agent must allow the borrower to inspect the statement one business day before closing.

A copy of the Uniform Settlement Statement form is shown in Figure 13.3. It does not have the same format as the simplified settlement statement shown earlier in this chapter (with buyer's credit and debit columns and seller's credit and debit columns side by side), but it presents the same information.

On the Uniform Statement, each party's closing costs are itemized on the back of the form (that is, on the second page shown here), with the buyer's costs in the left column and the seller's costs in the right column. Each party's costs are added up, and the total is transferred to the front of the form. The buyer's total costs are entered on line 103, and the seller's total costs are entered on line 502.

On the front of the Uniform Settlement Statement form, lines 101 through 120 correspond to the "Buyer's Debits" column on the simplified version. Lines 201 through 301 correspond to the "Buyer's Credits" column. Lines 401 through 420 are the equivalent of the "Seller's Credits" column, and lines 501 through 601 represent the "Seller's Debits" column. The amount of cash the buyer must bring to closing is shown on line 303, and the amount of cash the seller will receive at closing is shown on line 603.

Fig. 13.3 Uniform Settlement Statement

A. **Settlement Statement**   **U.S. Department of Housing and Urban Development**   OMB Approval No. 2502-0265

B. Type of Loan

| 1. ☐ FHA 2. ☐ FmHA 3. ☐ Conv. Unins. | 6. File Number: | 7. Loan Number: | 8. Mortgage Insurance Case Number: |
| 4. ☐ VA 5. ☐ Conv. Ins. | | | |

C. Note: This form is furnished to give you a statement of actual settlement costs. Amounts paid to and by the settlement agent are shown. Items marked "(p.o.c.)" were paid outside the closing; they are shown here for informational purposes and are not included in the totals.

D. Name & Address of Borrower:	E. Name & Address of Seller:	F. Name & Address of Lender:

| G. Property Location: | H. Settlement Agent: | |
| | Place of Settlement: | I. Settlement Date: |

J. Summary of Borrower's Transaction		**K. Summary of Seller's Transaction**	
100. Gross Amount Due From Borrower		**400. Gross Amount Due To Seller**	
101. Contract sales price		401. Contract sales price	
102. Personal property		402. Personal property	
103. Settlement charges to borrower (line 1400)		403.	
104.		404.	
105.		405.	
Adjustments for items paid by seller in advance		**Adjustments for items paid by seller in advance**	
106. City/town taxes to		406. City/town taxes to	
107. County taxes to		407. County taxes to	
108. Assessments to		408. Assessments to	
109.		409.	
110.		410.	
111.		411.	
112.		412.	
120. Gross Amount Due From Borrower		**420. Gross Amount Due To Seller**	
200. Amounts Paid By Or In Behalf Of Borrower		**500. Reductions In Amount Due To Seller**	
201. Deposit or earnest money		501. Excess deposit (see instructions)	
202. Principal amount of new loan(s)		502. Settlement charges to seller (line 1400)	
203. Existing loan(s) taken subject to		503. Existing loan(s) taken subject to	
204.		504. Payoff of first mortgage loan	
205.		505. Payoff of second mortgage loan	
206.		506.	
207.		507.	
208.		508.	
209.		509.	
Adjustments for items unpaid by seller		**Adjustments for items unpaid by seller**	
210. City/town taxes to		510. City/town taxes to	
211. County taxes to		511. County taxes to	
212. Assessments to		512. Assessments to	
213.		513.	
214.		514.	
215.		515.	
216.		516.	
217.		517.	
218.		518.	
219.		519.	
220. Total Paid By/For Borrower		**520. Total Reduction Amount Due Seller**	
300. Cash At Settlement From/To Borrower		**600. Cash At Settlement To/From Seller**	
301. Gross Amount due from borrower (line 120)		601. Gross amount due to seller (line 420)	
302. Less amounts paid by/for borrower (line 220)	( )	602. Less reductions in amt. due seller (line 520)	( )
303. Cash ☐ From ☐ To Borrower		**603. Cash** ☐ To ☐ From Seller	

Section 5 of the Real Estate Settlement Procedures Act (RESPA) requires the following: • HUD must develop a Special Information Booklet to help persons borrowing money to finance the purchase of residential real estate to better understand the nature and costs of real estate settlement services; • Each lender must provide the booklet to all applicants from whom it receives or for whom it prepares a written application to borrow money to finance the purchase of residential real estate; • Lenders must prepare and distribute with the Booklet a Good Faith Estimate of the settlement costs that the borrower is likely to incur in connection with the settlement. These disclosures are manadatory.

Section 4(a) of RESPA mandates that HUD develop and prescribe this standard form to be used at the time of loan settlement to provide full disclosure of all charges imposed upon the borrower and seller. These are third party disclosures that are designed to provide the borrower with pertinent information during the settlement process in order to be a better shopper.

The Public Reporting Burden for this collection of information is estimated to average one hour per response, including the time for reviewing instructions, searching existing data sources, gathering and maintaining the data needed, and completing and reviewing the collection of information.

This agency may not collect this information, and you are not required to complete this form, unless it displays a currently valid OMB control number.

The information requested does not lend itself to confidentiality.

Previous editions are obsolete   Page 1 of 2   form **HUD-1** (3/86) ref Handbook 4305.2

L. Settlement Charges

700.	Total Sales/Broker's Commission based on price $	@	% =	Paid From Borrowers Funds at Settlement	Paid From Seller's Funds at Settlement
	Division of Commission (line 700) as follows:				
701.	$	to			
702.	$	to			
703.	Commission paid at Settlement				
704.					
800.	**Items Payable In Connection With Loan**				
801.	Loan Origination Fee	%			
802.	Loan Discount	%			
803.	Appraisal Fee	to			
804.	Credit Report	to			
805.	Lender's Inspection Fee				
806.	Mortgage Insurance Application Fee to				
807.	Assumption Fee				
808.					
809.					
810.					
811.					
900.	**Items Required By Lender To Be Paid In Advance**				
901.	Interest from to	@$	/day		
902.	Mortgage Insurance Premium for		months to		
903.	Hazard Insurance Premium for		years to		
904.			years to		
905.					
1000.	**Reserves Deposited With Lender**				
1001.	Hazard insurance	months@$	per month		
1002.	Mortgage insurance	months@$	per month		
1003.	City property taxes	months@$	per month		
1004.	County property taxes	months@$	per month		
1005.	Annual assessments	months@$	per month		
1006.		months@$	per month		
1007.		months@$	per month		
1008.		months@$	per month		
1100.	**Title Charges**				
1101.	Settlement or closing fee	to			
1102.	Abstract or title search	to			
1103.	Title examination	to			
1104.	Title insurance binder	to			
1105.	Document preparation	to			
1106.	Notary fees	to			
1107.	Attorney's fees	to			
	(includes above items numbers:		)		
1108.	Title insurance	to			
	(includes above items numbers:		)		
1109.	Lender's coverage	$			
1110.	Owner's coverage	$			
1111.					
1112.					
1113.					
1200.	**Government Recording and Transfer Charges**				
1201.	Recording fees: Deed $; Mortgage $; Releases $				
1202.	City/county tax/stamps: Deed $; Mortgage $				
1203.	State tax/stamps: Deed $; Mortgage $				
1204.					
1205.					
1300.	**Additional Settlement Charges**				
1301.	Survey to				
1302.	Pest inspection to				
1303.					
1304.					
1305.					
1400.	**Total Settlement Charges (enter on lines 103, Section J and 502, Section K)**				

Chapter Summary

1. After a purchase and sale agreement has been signed, the next stage of the transaction is the closing process. Closing is often handled through escrow, an arrangement in which money and documents are held by a neutral third party (the escrow agent) on behalf of the buyer and the seller, and distributed when all of the conditions in the escrow instructions have been fulfilled.

2. In Washington, escrow agents and escrow officers must be licensed and registered, but many groups (including lawyers, title companies, and lenders) are exempt from those requirements. A real estate broker is exempt while handling escrow for a transaction in which he or she is also providing brokerage services, as long as no special fee is charged.

3. The escrow agent prepares a settlement statement, detailing all the charges payable by (debits) and payable to (credits) each of the parties at closing. Who pays which closing costs may be determined by agreement or by local custom. Certain expenses must be prorated as of the closing date.

4. Real estate agents must be aware of the closing agent's obligation to comply with 1099 reporting and FIRPTA requirements. If the closing agent does not fulfill those requirements, the real estate agent may be held liable.

5. RESPA applies to almost all residential purchase loan transactions involving institutional lenders. It requires a lender to give a loan applicant a good faith estimate of closing costs within three days after a written loan application is submitted. RESPA also requires the lender to complete a Uniform Settlement Statement and have it available to the buyer one day before closing, if the buyer asks to see it in advance.

🔑 Key Terms

Closing—The final stage of a real estate transaction, in which documents are signed and delivered and funds are transferred.

Escrow—An arrangement in which money and documents are held by a neutral third party on behalf of the buyer and the seller.

Escrow agent—A neutral third party who holds money and documents in trust and carries out the closing process. Also called a closing agent.

Certified escrow agent—A business that is licensed to provide escrow services under Washington's Escrow Agent Registration Act.

Licensed escrow officer—An individual who is licensed under the Escrow Agent Registration Act to perform escrow services as an employee of a certified escrow agent.

Escrow instructions—A written document that tells the escrow agent how to proceed and states the conditions each party must fulfill before the transaction can close.

Settlement statement—A statement that sets forth all the financial aspects of a real estate transaction in detail and indicates how much cash each party will be required to pay or will receive at closing.

Debit—A charge payable by a party.

Credit—A charge payable to a party.

Reserve account—Funds on deposit with a lender to pay the property taxes and insurance premiums when due.

Prorate—To divide and allocate an expense proportionately, according to time, interest, or benefit, determining what share of it a particular party is responsible for.

Prepaid interest—Interest on the buyer's new mortgage loan that the lender requires to be paid at closing, covering the period from the closing date through the last day of the month.

Uniform Settlement Statement—The settlement statement form that closing agents are required to use in transactions covered by the Real Estate Settlement Procedures Act.

Chapter Quiz

1. The Henrys listed their property with Louise, a licensed real estate broker, who found them a buyer. Now Louise is handling the closing for this transaction. She is exempt from the licensing and registration requirements of the Washington Escrow Agent Registration Act only if:

   a) this is a residential transaction
   b) the sales price is $100,000 or less
   c) she does not charge a separate fee for her escrow services
   d) the escrow fee she charges does not exceed the limits set by the Registration Act

2. Every debit on the buyer's side of the settlement statement is a charge that:

   a) will be paid to the buyer at closing
   b) must be paid by the buyer at closing
   c) the buyer must pay to the seller at closing
   d) the seller must pay to the buyer at closing

3. On a settlement statement, the purchase price will be listed as:

   a) a debit to the buyer
   b) a debit to the seller
   c) Both of the above
   d) Neither of the above

4. The transaction is closing on September 16. The seller has already paid the annual premium for hazard insurance, and the buyer will not be assuming the policy. On the settlement statement, part of the insurance premium will be listed as:

   a) a debit to the buyer and a credit to the seller
   b) a debit to the seller and a credit to the buyer
   c) a credit to the buyer
   d) a credit to the seller

5. How does the buyer's earnest money deposit show up on a settlement statement?

   a) It is listed as a debit on the buyer's side of the statement, and as a credit on the seller's side of the statement
   b) It is listed as a credit on the buyer's side of the statement, but it is not listed on the seller's side because it is included in the purchase price
   c) It is listed as a credit on the seller's side of the statement, but it is not listed on the buyer's side because it will be refunded at closing
   d) It is listed as a debit on both the buyer's side and the seller's side of the statement

6. When a buyer assumes a mortgage, how does the mortgage balance appear on the settlement statement?

   a) Only as a credit to the seller
   b) Only as a debit on the seller's side of the statement
   c) As a credit to the buyer and a debit to the seller
   d) As a credit to the seller and a debit to buyer

7. Which of the following is ordinarily one of the seller's closing costs?

   a) Sales commission
   b) Credit report fee
   c) Appraisal fee
   d) Origination fee

8. Which of the following is ordinarily one of the buyer's closing costs?

   a) Sales commission
   b) Lender's title insurance premium
   c) Excise tax
   d) None of the above

9. On a settlement statement, prepaid interest would usually appear as a:

   a) seller's debit
   b) buyer's credit
   c) seller's credit
   d) buyer's debit

10. The Matsons are selling their home. They are current on their mortgage payments, having made their most recent payment on May 1. They will be paying off their mortgage when the sale closes on May 17. At closing, the Matsons will probably be:

    a) entitled to a refund of the mortgage interest accruing in May
    b) required to pay the mortgage interest accruing in May
    c) entitled to a refund of the prepayment penalty
    d) required to pay part of the mortgage interest that accrued in April

11. A settlement statement:

    a) is given only to the buyer
    b) sets out the items to be paid by each party
    c) is given to the lender
    d) None of the above

12. When an item is prorated it means that:

    a) it is deleted from the cost of the sale
    b) it is calculated on the basis of a particular time period
    c) it is not paid until closing
    d) the escrow agent must pay the fee

13. Under RESPA, a loan is considered federally related if:

    a) it will be used to finance the purchase of real property
    b) it is secured by a first or second mortgage
    c) the lender is federally regulated
    d) All of the above

14. Under FIRPTA:

    a) a foreign investor can never buy or sell property without special authorization
    b) if a seller is not a U.S. citizen, the escrow agent will have to deduct 10% of the sale proceeds and send it to the IRS
    c) escrow agents must notify the real estate broker if the buyer is a foreigner investor
    d) a foreign investor purchasing property in the U.S. must pay an additional 10% over and above the purchase price and submit it to the IRS

15. Tim, a real estate agent, has a friend who is purchasing a property through another agent. The purchase price is $95,000. Tim offers to act as escrow agent for the transaction for a small fee. Tim:

    a) is exempt from the Escrow Agent Registration Act because he is a real estate agent
    b) must comply with the Escrow Agent Registration Act because he is not acting as an agent in the transaction
    c) is exempt from the Escrow Agent Registration Act because he is acting for a personal acquaintance
    d) is exempt from the Escrow Agent Registration Act because the sales price is less than $100,000

👉 **Answer Key**

1. c) A real estate broker is exempt from the Escrow Agent Registration Act when handling closing for a transaction in which he or she is providing brokerage services, as long as the broker does not charge a separate fee for escrow services.

2. b) A debit on the buyer's side of the statement is a charge that the buyer must pay. In some cases, it is a charge that the buyer must pay to the seller (a refund for taxes paid in advance, for example), but in other cases the buyer owes it to a third party (the loan fee paid to the lender, for example).

3. a) The purchase price is a debit to the buyer and a credit to the seller.

4. d) The seller is entitled to a refund for the insurance he or she paid in advance, and this will show up as a credit on the seller's side of the settlement statement. Since the buyer is not assuming the policy, the seller's insurance is not listed on the buyer's side of the statement.

5. b) The earnest money deposit is a credit to the buyer, since it has already been paid. It does not appear on the seller's side of the statement, because the full purchase price is listed as a credit to the seller, and the deposit is included in the price.

6. c) A loan the buyer uses to finance the transaction is listed as a credit to the buyer, whatever its source. When the financing comes through the seller—either through an assumption of the seller's loan, or through seller financing—it is a debit to the seller as well as a credit to the buyer.

7. a) The seller almost always pays the real estate broker's commission. The other expenses listed relate to the buyer's loan, and they are ordinarily paid by the buyer.

8. b) The buyer is usually required to pay the premium for the lender's extended coverage title insurance policy.

9. d) Prepaid interest—interest on a new loan to cover the period from the closing date through the last day of the month—is one of the buyer's debits.

10. b) Because mortgage interest is paid in arrears—the month after it accrues—at closing the sellers will be required to pay the interest that has accrued during May. (Their May 1 mortgage payment included the interest that accrued in April.)

11. b) A settlement statement sets forth the charges that must be paid by each party.

12. b) Prorating an expense is calculating it on the basis of a particular time period, such as number of days.

13. d) All of these are elements of a federally related loan under RESPA.

14. b) FIRPTA requires the escrow agent to deduct 10% of the sales price and send it to the IRS when the seller is a foreign investor.

15. b) A real estate agent must comply with the Escrow Agent Registration Act if he or she is not acting as an agent for that transaction.

Federal Income Taxation and Real Estate

Chapter Overview

Almost every business transaction has tax consequences, and real estate transactions are no exception. Not only are there taxes that arise at the time of sale (such as the real estate excise tax discussed in Chapter 5), there are also income tax ramifications for the parties involved. This chapter provides an overview of how federal income taxation affects the transfer and ownership of real estate. It explains some income tax terminology, discusses certain types of transactions that receive special treatment, and also covers tax deductions available to real estate owners.

Basic Taxation Concepts

As you almost certainly know, in the United States the federal government taxes the income of individuals and businesses on an annual basis. Before discussing how the transfer or acquisition of real estate can affect the federal income taxes a seller or buyer is required to pay, we need to explain some basic terms and concepts.

Progressive Tax

A tax may be "proportional," "regressive," or "progressive," depending on how its burden is distributed among taxpayers. A tax is proportional if the same tax rate is applied to all levels of income. A tax is regressive if the rate applied to higher levels of income is lower than the rate applied to lower levels. Our federal income tax is a **progressive** tax. This means that the more a taxpayer earns in a given tax year, the higher his or her tax rate will be. In other words, someone who earns a large income is generally required not just to pay more taxes than someone who earns a small income, but to pay a greater percentage of his or her income in taxes.

Tax rates increase in uneven steps called **tax brackets**. An additional dollar earned by a given taxpayer may be taxed at a higher rate than the dollar earned just before it, because it crosses the line into a higher bracket. But the additional dollar earned will not increase the tax the taxpayer is required to pay on dollars previously earned.

Income

When asked about their income, many people tend to think only in terms of the wages or salary they earn at a job. The Internal Revenue Service (IRS) takes a much broader view of income, however. It regards any economic benefit realized by a taxpayer as part of his or her income, unless it is a type of benefit specifically excluded from income by the tax code. (The concept of realization is discussed below.)

Deductions and Tax Credits

The tax code authorizes certain expenses to be deducted from income. For example, if a business loses money in a particular tax year, the owner may be allowed to deduct the loss. A taxpayer who is entitled to a deduction can subtract a specified amount from his or her income before it is taxed. By reducing the amount of income that is taxed, the deduction also reduces the amount of tax the taxpayer owes.

In contrast to deductions, tax credits are subtracted directly from the amount of tax owed. The taxpayer's income is added up, the tax rate is applied, and then any applicable tax credits are subtracted to determine how much the taxpayer will actually have to pay.

The government often uses deductions and tax credits to implement social and economic policy. For example, allowing homeowners to deduct mortgage interest from their taxable income helps make homeownership more affordable. (The mortgage interest deduction is explained later in this chapter.)

Gains and Losses

The sale or exchange of an asset (such as real estate) nearly always results in either a gain or a loss. Gains are treated as income, so any gain is taxable unless the tax code specifically says otherwise. On the other hand, a loss may be deducted from income only if the deduction is specifically authorized by the tax code. Most deductible losses are losses incurred in a trade or business or in transactions entered into for profit. A business entity (such as a corporation) can deduct all of its losses. An individual taxpayer can deduct a loss only if it was incurred in connection with:

1. the taxpayer's trade or business,
2. a transaction entered into for profit, or
3. a casualty loss or theft of the taxpayer's property.

No deduction is allowed for a loss suffered on the sale of the taxpayer's principal residence or other real property owned for personal use.

A gain or loss on the sale of an asset held for personal use or as an investment is considered a **capital gain** or a **capital loss**. Capital gains and losses are netted against each other. If there is a net gain, it is taxed as a capital gain. (The maximum tax rate applied to most capital gains is considerably lower than the rate for other income.) If there is a net loss, it may be deducted, but there is an annual limit on how much may be deducted. Losses in excess of the limit may be carried forward and deducted in future years.

Basis

For income tax purposes, a property owner's **basis** in the property is his or her investment in it. If a taxpayer sells an asset, the basis is the maximum amount that he or she can receive in payment for the asset without realizing a gain. To determine gains and losses, it is necessary to know the taxpayer's basis in the property in question.

In most cases, a taxpayer's initial basis is equal to the actual amount of his or her investment—that is, how much it cost to acquire the property. A person who paid $180,000 for a rental house plus $9,000 in closing costs has an initial basis of $189,000 in the property. He or she could turn around and sell the house for $189,000 without having to report a gain to the IRS.

Adjusted Basis

The initial basis may be increased or decreased to arrive at an **adjusted basis**, which reflects capital expenditures and any allowable depreciation or cost recovery deductions. **Capital expenditures** are expenditures made to improve the property, such as money a homeowner spends on adding a new room or remodeling the kitchen. Capital expenditures increase the value of the property or significantly extend its useful life. They are added to the initial basis in calculating the adjusted basis.

> **Example:** Greene buys a duplex as a rental property for $345,000 plus $11,000 in closing costs. Four years later, she spends $45,000 on improvements to the property, remodeling the bathrooms and the kitchen in both units. Her adjusted basis in the property is now $401,000.

Maintenance expenses, such as repainting or replacing a broken window, are not capital expenditures. Maintenance expenses do not affect basis.

For certain types of property, a taxpayer's initial basis is also adjusted to take into account depreciation or cost recovery deductions, which will be discussed later in this chapter. These deductions are subtracted from the initial basis in calculating the adjusted basis.

```
   Initial basis
 + Capital expenditures
 − Depreciation/Cost recovery deductions
   Adjusted basis
```

Realization

Not every gain is immediately taxable. A gain is not considered taxable income until it is **realized**. Ownership of an asset involves gain if the asset is appreciating in value. But for tax purposes, a gain is realized only when a sale or exchange occurs; the gain is then separated from the asset.

> **Example:** Referring back to the example given above, suppose that during Greene's six years of ownership property values have been increasing steadily. Her improved duplex (which she bought for $356,000 and invested another $45,000 in) now has a market value of $489,000. She has enjoyed an economic gain or benefit: she now owns property that is worth $88,000 more than what she put into it. However, that $88,000 is not realized—and therefore is not treated as income subject to taxation—until she sells the duplex.

The gain or loss realized on a transaction is the difference between the net sales price (referred to as the **amount realized**) and the adjusted basis of the property:

```
   Amount realized (net sales price)
 − Adjusted basis
   Gain or loss
```

In calculating the amount realized, the sales price includes money or other property received in exchange for the property, plus the amount of any mortgage debt that is eliminated. This means that if the buyer takes the property subject to the seller's mortgage or assumes it, the amount of that debt is treated as part of the sales price for tax purposes.

The sales price is reduced by selling expenses (such as the brokerage commission and the seller's other closing costs) to arrive at the amount realized.

> Money received
> + Market value of other property received
> + Mortgage debt disposed of
> − Selling expenses
> _____
> Amount realized (net sales price)

Recognition and Deferral

A gain is said to be **recognized** in the year it is taxed. A gain will be recognized in the year it is realized, unless there is a specific exception in the tax code that allows the taxpayer to defer payment of taxes on the gain until a later tax year or a later transaction, or exclude payment of taxes altogether. For example, the tax code permits an individual selling his or her rental property on an installment basis to defer taxation of part of the gain to the year in which it is actually received (rather than the year the sales takes place). The tax code provisions that allow recognition of a gain to be deferred are called "nonrecognition provisions."

Nonrecognition provisions that apply to real estate transactions (including the rule already mentioned concerning installment sales) and exclusion provisions are discussed in detail later in this chapter.

Classifications of Real Property

Whether a particular type of real estate transaction qualifies for special tax treatment depends on the type of property involved. The tax code divides real property into the following classes:

1. principal residence property,
2. personal use property,
3. unimproved investment property,
4. property held for the production of income,
5. property used in a trade or business, and
6. dealer property.

Principal Residence Property. This is the home the taxpayer owns and occupies as his or her primary dwelling. It may be a single-family home, a duplex, a condominium unit, a cooperative apartment, or a mobile home. If the taxpayer owns two homes and lives in both of them, the one in which he or she lives most of the time is the principal residence. A taxpayer cannot have two principal residences at the same time.

Personal Use Property. Real property that a taxpayer owns for personal use, other than the principal residence, is classified as personal use property. A second home or a vacation cabin would belong in this category.

Unimproved Investment Property. Unimproved investment property is vacant land that produces no rental income. The land is held simply as an investment, in the expectation that it will appreciate in value.

Property Held for Production of Income. Property held for the production of income includes residential, commercial, and industrial property that is used to generate rental income for the owner.

Property Used in a Trade or Business. This category includes land and buildings that the taxpayer owns and uses in his or her trade or business, such as a factory owned by the manufacturer, or a small building the owner uses for his or her own retail business.

Dealer Property. This is property held primarily for sale to customers rather than for long-term investment. If a developer subdivides land for sale to the public, the lots will usually be included in this classification until they are sold.

Nonrecognition Transactions

As was explained earlier, when a nonrecognition provision in the tax code applies to a particular transaction, the taxpayer is not required to pay taxes on a gain in the year it is realized. The real estate transactions that are covered by nonrecognition provisions include all of the following:

- installment sales,
- involuntary conversions,
- sales of low-income housing, and
- "tax-free" exchanges.

Keep in mind that nonrecognition provisions do not completely exclude the gain from taxation, but merely defer the tax consequences to a later tax year. These are not really "tax-free" transactions. The realized gain is simply recognized and taxed in a subsequent year.

Installment Sales

The tax code considers a sale to be an installment sale if less than 100% of the sales price is received in the year of sale. Nearly all seller-financed transactions are installment sales. Installment sale reporting allows the taxpayer/seller to defer recognition of part of the gain to the year(s) in which it is actually received. In effect, taxes are paid only on the portion of the profit received each year. Installment sale reporting is permitted for all classes of property, except that dealer property is eligible only under special conditions.

In installment sales, the gain recognized in any given year is calculated based on the ratio of gross profit to the contract price. The **gross profit** is the difference between the sales price and the adjusted basis.

Fig.14.1 Eligibility for installment sale reporting

Installment Sale Reporting

1. Less than 100% of sales price received in year of sale

2. All classifications of real property eligible except dealer property

To calculate the gross profit, take the seller's adjusted basis at the time of sale, add the amount of the commission and other selling expenses, and subtract this sum from the sales price.

> **Example:** Once again, we'll use Greene as an example. Her basis in her duplex was $401,000. She sold the property for $489,000. She had to pay a $29,000 commission and $8,200 in other selling expenses.

$489,000	Sales price

$401,000	Seller's basis
+ 37,200	Commission and selling expenses
$438,200	Adjusted basis

$489,000	Sales price
− 438,200	Adjusted basis
$50,800	Gross profit

The next step is to compare the gross profit to the contract price to arrive at the gross profit ratio. The contract price is the total amount of all principal payments the buyer will pay the seller. In most cases, unless the buyer assumes an existing loan, the contract price is the same as the sales price.

> **Example:**
>
> | Gross Profit | ÷ | Contract Price | = | Gross Profit Ratio |
> |---|---|---|---|---|
> | $50,800 | ÷ | $489,000 | = | 10% |

The gross profit ratio is applied to the principal payments received in each year to determine how much of the principal is gain to be taxed that year. Note that the gross profit ratio is not applied to the interest the buyer pays the seller; all of the interest payments are treated as taxable income in the year received.

If the seller in the example above received a $48,900 downpayment, $2,500 in principal installment payments, and $30,500 in interest the first year, the taxable income would be calculated as follows:

$48,900	Downpayment
+ 2,500	Installment principal payments
$51,400	Total principal payments

$51,400	Total principal payments
× 10%	Gross profit ratio
$5,140	Recognized gain
+ 30,500	Interest income
$35,640	Total taxable income

If the buyer assumes or takes subject to a mortgage that is larger than the seller's basis in the property, the excess is treated as payment received from the buyer. If the property is subject to recapture provisions because of depreciation or cost recovery deductions (discussed later in this chapter), the amount recaptured is also treated as a payment received in the year of sale.

Involuntary Conversions

An involuntary conversion occurs when an asset is turned into cash without the voluntary action of the owner, as when an asset is condemned, destroyed, stolen, or lost, and the owner receives a condemnation award or insurance proceeds. Since the award or proceeds usually represent the property's replacement cost or market value, the owner often realizes a gain on an involuntary conversion.

However, recognition of a gain on an involuntary conversion can be deferred if the taxpayer uses the money received to replace the property within the replacement period set by the IRS. Generally, the replacement period lasts for two years after the end of the tax year in which the gain was realized; for business or income property, the period is three years. Recognition of the gain is deferred only to the extent that the condemnation award or insurance proceeds are reinvested in the replacement property. Any part of the gain used for purposes other than purchase of replacement property will be taxed as income.

Sales of Low-Income Housing

A taxpayer who owns certain qualified low-income housing may sell it and reinvest the proceeds in similar housing within one year without recognizing a gain on the sale. Gain that is not reinvested in similar property is recognized in the year of the sale.

"Tax-Free" Exchanges

A "tax-free" exchange is really just a tax-deferred exchange. If unimproved investment property, income property, or property used in a trade or business is exchanged for **like-kind** property, recognition of any realized gain will be deferred. A principal residence, personal use property, and dealer property are not eligible for this type of deferral.

Tax-free exchanges are used to reduce or eliminate current tax expenses. And a taxpayer may be able to acquire property in an exchange that it would have been impossible to buy with the after-tax proceeds from the sale of the old property.

The property the taxpayer receives in the exchange must be like-kind—that is, the same kind as the property given. This requirement refers to the general nature of the properties rather than their quality. Most real estate is considered to be of like kind for the purposes of the exchange deferral, without regard to whether it is improved, unimproved, residential, commercial, or industrial. For example, if a taxpayer exchanges a strip shopping center for an apartment complex, the transaction can qualify as a tax-free exchange. Both of the

Fig. 14.2 Eligibility for tax-free exchanges

"Tax-Free" Exchanges

1. Only property held for production of income, property used in a trade or business, or unimproved investment property is eligible.
2. Must be exchanged for like-kind property.
3. Any boot is taxed in the year it is received.

exchanged properties must be located in the United States to be considered like-kind property.

If nothing other than like-kind property is received in the exchange, no gain or loss is recognized in the year of the exchange. However, anything other than like-kind property that the taxpayer receives is called **boot** and recognized in the year of the exchange. In a real estate exchange, boot might be cash, stock, other types of personal property, or the difference between mortgage balances.

> **Example:** A taxpayer trades a property with a mortgage debt of $120,000 for a property with a mortgage debt of $100,000. The taxpayer has received $20,000 in boot because of the reduction in debt (regardless of whether or not there has been a formal assumption of the loan). The taxpayer will have to pay taxes on a gain of $20,000, just as if she had received $20,000 in cash along with the real property.

The taxpayer's basis in the property exchanged is transferred to the property he or she receives. If nothing other than like-kind property is exchanged, no adjustments are necessary. But if the exchange involved boot, the basis must be adjusted for any boot that was paid or received, and for any gain or loss that was recognized because of the boot.

Exclusion of Gain from the Sale of a Principal Residence

We will discuss only one exclusion from capital gains taxation, the one that will be of greatest interest to most homeowners: the exclusion of gain on the sale of a principal residence.

Until May 1997, an individual who sold his or her principal residence was often eligible for the "rollover" deferral of taxation. The seller was allowed to defer taxation of the gain if the sale proceeds were used within two years to buy another residence. And a seller who was 55 or older could take advantage of a one-time exclusion of gain from the sale of the principal residence, even if the gain was not invested in a new residence. The 1997 tax bill replaced both of these tax benefits with a single, less complicated exclusion from taxation.

Amount of Gain Excluded. Under current law, a taxpayer may exclude the entire gain on the sale of his or her principal residence, up to $250,000 if the taxpayer is filing a single return, or $500,000 if the taxpayer is married and filing a joint return.

Example:

$275,000	Amount realized (after selling costs)
− 80,000	Seller's basis in home
$195,000	Gain realized

Whether filing singly or jointly, the seller will be able to exclude the entire amount of gain—$195,000—from taxation.

If the amount of the gain on the sale of the home exceeds the $250,000 or $500,000 limit, the amount in excess of the limit will be taxed at the capital gains rate.

Example:

$375,000	Amount realized (after selling costs)
– 70,000	Seller's basis in home
$305,000	Gain realized

If the seller is filing a single return, only $250,000 of the $305,000 gain will be excluded from taxation. The seller will have to pay capital gains taxes on the $55,000 that exceeded the exclusion limit.

Eligibility. To qualify for this exclusion, the seller must have both owned and used the property as a principal residence for at least two years during the previous five-year period. Because of this rule, this exclusion is available only once every two years.

Note that if the sellers are married and filing a joint return, only one spouse has to meet the ownership test, but both spouses must meet the use test. If only one spouse meets both the ownership test and the use test, the maximum exclusion the married couple can claim is $250,000, even if they file a joint return.

If the seller owned and used the property as a principal residence for less than two years because of special circumstances (for example, if he or she sold the home after only a year because of a change in health or employment), the seller may be able to claim a reduced exclusion.

Deductions Available to Property Owners

As was explained earlier, a deduction is subtracted from a taxpayer's income before the tax rate is applied. The income tax deductions allowed to real property owners are a significant benefit of ownership. There are deductions for:

- depreciation and cost recovery,
- repairs,
- real property taxes,
- mortgage interest, and
- passive losses.

Depreciation and Cost Recovery Deductions

What used to be called depreciation deductions in the tax code are now called cost recovery deductions, but they are essentially the same thing. They permit a taxpayer to recover the cost of an asset used for the production of income or used in a trade or business. They cannot be taken in connection with a principal residence, personal use property, unimproved investment property, or dealer property.

Depreciable Property. In general, only property that wears out and will eventually have to be replaced is **depreciable**—that is, eligible for depreciation or cost recovery deductions. For example, apartment buildings, business or factory equipment, and commercial fruit orchards all have to be replaced, so they are depreciable. But land does not wear out, so it is not depreciable.

Time Frame. The entire expense of acquiring an asset cannot be deducted in the year it is incurred (although that is permitted with many other business expenses, such as wages, supplies, and utilities). However, the expense can be deducted over a number of years; for most real estate, the recovery period is between 15 and 31½ years. The length of the recovery period is a reflection of legislative policy and has little, if any, relationship to the actual length of time that the property will be economically useful. The whole field of depreciation and cost recovery deductions has been subject to frequent modification by Congress.

Effect on Basis. As we said in the discussion of basis at the beginning of the chapter, any allowable depreciation or cost recovery deductions reduce the taxpayer's adjusted basis in the property. Note that this reduction occurs whether or not the taxpayer actually takes the deduction. If the deduction was allowable—that is, the taxpayer was entitled to take it—the basis will be reduced. By reducing the basis, these deductions affect the taxpayer's eventual gain or loss on resale of the property.

Repair Deductions

For most real estate other than principal residences and personal use property, expenditures for repairs are deductible in the year paid. A repair expense is one incurred to keep the property in ordinary, efficient, operating condition.

Repair expenses should not be confused with capital expenditures. As explained earlier, capital expenditures add to the value of the property and frequently prolong its economic life. Capital expenditures are not deductible in the year made, but rather are added to the taxpayer's basis. The resulting increase in the basis will affect the gain or loss on the eventual sale of the property. It will also increase the allowable depreciation or cost recovery deductions if the property is eligible for those.

Fig. 14.3 Tax-deferred transactions

Eligibility for Favorable Income Tax Treatment			
	Installment Sale	"Tax-Free" Exchange	Depreciation Deductions
Principal Residence	Yes	No	No
Personal Use	Yes	No	No
Unimproved Investment	Yes	Yes	No
Trade or Business	Yes	Yes	Yes
Income	Yes	Yes	Yes
Dealer	No	No	No

Property Tax Deductions

General real estate taxes are deductible. Special assessments for repairs or maintenance are deductible, but those for improvements (such as new sidewalks) are not.

Mortgage Interest Deductions

For most property, interest paid on a mortgage or deed of trust is usually completely deductible. However, there are some limitations on interest deductions for personal residences (which are the only allowable consumer interest deductions).

A taxpayer may deduct interest payments on mortgage debt of up to $1,000,000 used to buy, build, or improve a first or second residence. In addition, interest on a home equity loan of up to $100,000 can be deducted without regard to the purpose of the loan. When the loan amount exceeds these limits, the interest on the excess is not deductible.

Chapter Summary

1. Any economic benefit realized by a taxpayer is treated as part of his or her income, unless there is a specific provision of the tax code that excludes it from income. The tax code provides for certain deductions from income before the tax rate is applied, and also for tax credits, which are subtracted from the amount of tax owed.

2. A gain or a loss is realized when an asset is sold. A gain is recognized (taxed) in the year it is realized, unless a nonrecognition or exclusion provision in the tax code applies.

3. A taxpayer's initial basis in property is the amount he or she originally invested in it. To determine the adjusted basis, capital expenditures are added to the initial basis, and allowable cost recovery deductions are subtracted from it. The taxpayer's gain or loss is the difference between the amount realized and the adjusted basis.

4. In the tax code, real property is classified as principal residence property, personal use property, unimproved investment property, property held for the production of income, property used in a trade or business, or dealer property.

5. The tax code's nonrecognition provisions for real property transactions allow taxation of gain to be deferred in installment sales, involuntary conversions, sales of certain low-income housing, and "tax-free" exchanges. There is also an exclusion of up to $250,000 (or $500,000 if filing jointly) of gain allowed on the sale of a principal residence.

6. The tax deductions available to property owners include cost recovery deductions (only for income property and property used in a trade or business); repair deductions (not for principal residences or personal use property); deduction of property taxes; and deduction of mortgage interest. There are some limits on the mortgage interest deduction for personal residences.

🔑 Key Terms

Income—Any economic benefit realized by a taxpayer that is not excluded from income by the tax code.

Deduction—An expense that can be used to reduce taxable income.

Initial basis—The amount of the taxpayer's original investment in the property; what it cost to acquire the property.

Adjusted basis—The initial basis plus capital expenditures and minus allowable depreciation or cost recovery deductions.

Realization—A gain or a loss is realized when it is separated from the asset; this separation generally occurs when the asset is sold.

Recognition—A gain is said to be recognized when it is taxable; it is recognized in the year it is realized unless recognition is deferred by the tax code.

Installment sale—A sale in which less than 100% of the sales price is received in the year of sale.

Involuntary conversion—When property is converted to cash without the voluntary action of the owner, as when it is condemned, destroyed, stolen, or lost.

Cost recovery deductions—Deductions from the taxpayer's income to allow the cost of an asset to be recovered; allowed only for depreciable property that is held for the production of income or used in a trade or business. Also called depreciation deductions.

Repair expenses—Money spent on repairs to keep property in ordinary, efficient operating condition.

Capital expenditures—Money spent on improvements to property, which add to its value or prolong its economic life.

"Tax-free" exchange—When like-kind property is exchanged, allowing taxation of the gain to be deferred.

Like-kind property—In a tax-free exchange, property received that is of the same kind as the property transferred; any two pieces of real estate are considered to be of like kind.

Boot—Something given or received in a tax-free exchange that is not like-kind property, such as cash.

Chapter Quiz

1. A homeowner's basis would be adjusted to reflect:

   a) cost recovery deductions
   b) expenses incurred to keep the property in good repair
   c) mortgage interest paid
   d) the cost of installing a deck

2. A married couple bought a home for $150,000. After living in the home for three years, they sold it for only $146,000. How much of this loss can they deduct on their federal income tax return?

   a) The full $4,000 loss
   b) Only $3,000
   c) Only $2,000
   d) None of it

3. Which of the following could the owner of unimproved investment property deduct on his or her federal income tax return?

   a) A loss on the sale of the property
   b) The depreciation of the land
   c) Cost recovery deductions
   d) Any of the above

4. Which of the following exchanges could not qualify as a "tax-free" exchange?

   a) An office building for a hotel
   b) An apartment house for a warehouse
   c) Timber land for farm equipment
   d) A city lot for a ranch

5. Under the federal income tax code, income is always taxed in the year it is:

   a) realized
   b) recognized
   c) recovered
   d) deferred

6. Munson just sold his principal residence. After deducting his selling costs, the amount of gain realized was $163,000. Munson will be allowed to exclude the entire amount of the gain from taxation only if:

   a) he is married and is filing a joint return
   b) he has never claimed this exclusion before, since it can only be used once in a lifetime
   c) the gain is not considered capital gain
   d) he owned and occupied the property as his principal residence for two of the previous five years

7. Torino owns a triplex. She paid $450,000 for it, including her closing costs. The allowable cost recovery deductions for the property have amounted to $20,000, Torino has spent $50,000 on capital improvements, and the market value of the property has risen by 15%. What is Torino's adjusted basis?

   a) $537,500
   b) $500,000
   c) $480,000
   d) $430,000

8. Gillespie is buying a home that will be his principal residence. He is financing the purchase with a $200,000 mortgage loan. How much of the interest that he pays on the loan can he deduct from his income?

   a) All of it
   b) Up to $100,000 in interest
   c) 50%
   d) None of it

9. The Byrnes are selling some property on a five-year contract. Their gross profit ratio on the sale is 15%. This year, they will receive $4,775 in interest and $1,675 in principal. With installment sale reporting, approximately how much of that will be recognized and included in the Byrnes' taxable income for this year?

   a) $251
   b) $967
   c) $2,391
   d) $5,026

10. Sherrick is selling a lot for $72,000. Her adjusted basis in the property is $56,000. In addition to the 6% commission she'll be paying her real estate broker, she will also have to pay $2,500 in closing costs. For federal income tax purposes, what is the gain Sherrick will realize in this transaction?

   a) $6,820
   b) $9,180
   c) $16,000
   d) $22,820

👉 Answer Key

1. d) The cost of installing a deck is a capital expenditure, which would be added to the taxpayer's basis. Remember that personal residences do not qualify for depreciation or cost recovery deductions.

2. d) A loss on the sale of a personal residence is never deductible.

3. a) If the owner loses money on the sale of the property, he or she may be able to deduct that loss. Depreciation and cost recovery deductions are not allowed for unimproved investment property, because land is not depreciable.

4. c) The like-kind property requirement means that real estate must be exchanged for other real estate.

5. b) Income is taxed when it is recognized. It is often recognized in the same year it is realized, but that is not true if a nonrecognition provision applies.

6. d) To qualify for the exclusion from taxation, the taxpayer must have both owned and used the property as a principal residence for two of the previous five years.

7. c) The initial basis, plus the capital expenditures, less the allowable cost recovery deductions, equals an adjusted basis of $480,000.

   $450,000 + $50,000 - $20,000 = $480,000$

   (Ignore the increase in market value; it does not affect the taxpayer's basis.)

8. a) A taxpayer can deduct all of the interest paid on a loan of up to $1,000,000 used to purchase a first or second personal residence.

9. d) Multiply the principal payments by the gross profit ratio to determine the amount of principal that will be recognized this year. Then add that to the entire amount of interest received (all of the interest is taxable).

   $1,675 \times 15\% = $251.25 + $4,775 = $5,026.25$

10. b) Sherrick will realize a $9,180 gain in the transaction. First subtract her selling expenses (the commission and closing costs) from the sales price to determine the amount realized; then subtract her adjusted basis from the amount realized to determine the gain.

    $72,000 \times 6\% = $4,320 \text{ commission}$

    $4,320 + $2,500 \text{ costs} = $6,820$

    $72,000 - $6,820 = $65,180 \text{ (amount realized)}$

    $65,180 - $56,000 = $9,180 \text{ (gain realized)}$

Civil Rights and Fair Housing

Chapter Overview

Unfair discrimination is prohibited in almost all real estate transactions by federal and state law. With limited exceptions, it is illegal for either property owners or real estate professionals to discriminate. In this chapter, we will cover several federal antidiscrimination laws, including the Civil Rights Act of 1866, the Federal Fair Housing Act, and the Americans with Disabilities Act. We will also discuss various state laws that prohibit discrimination in housing as well as in other real estate transactions.

Introduction

Over the years, various civil rights laws have been enacted to achieve one major goal: the freedom of choice. In the context of real estate, freedom of choice means that all types of people with similar financial resources should have equal access to the same types of housing. Anyone with the requisite income, net worth, and credit history should be able to choose a home or apartment in any affordable neighborhood, regardless of race, national origin, gender, or other similar characteristics.

Today, civil rights laws are an integral part of the real estate profession. The importance of the right to equal housing is well established, and real estate professionals must be familiar with both federal and state laws that prohibit discrimination.

The Civil Rights Act of 1866

This law states that "all citizens of the United States shall have the same right, in every state and territory as is enjoyed by white citizens thereof to inherit, purchase, lease, sell, hold and convey real and personal property." The act prohibits any discrimination based on race or ancestry.

Enacted immediately after the Civil War, the act was largely ignored for almost a century. In the 1960s, during the civil rights movement, the act was challenged as an unconstitutional interference with private property rights. But the U.S. Supreme Court upheld the act in the landmark case of *Jones v. Mayer*, decided in 1968. The court ruled that the 1866 Act "prohibits all racial discrimination, private or public, in the sale and rental of property," and that it is constitutional based on the 13th Amendment to the U.S. Constitution, which prohibits slavery.

Someone who has been discriminated against in violation of the Civil Rights Act of 1866 can sue in federal court. The court could issue an injunction ordering the defendant to stop discriminating. The court could also order the defendant to pay the plaintiff both compensatory damages (to compensate for losses and suffering caused by the discrimination) and punitive damages (an additional sum to punish the defendant for wrongdoing).

The Civil Rights Act of 1964

The Civil Rights Act of 1964 was one of the first attempts made by the federal government to implement fair housing ideals. The act prohibited discrimination based on race, color, religion, or national origin in many programs and activities for which the federal government offered financial assistance. Unfortunately, the effect of the act was extremely limited, because most FHA and VA loans were not covered. In fact, it is estimated that less than 1% of all houses purchased were covered by the act. It was not until the Civil Rights Act of 1968 that major progress was made towards fair housing.

The Federal Fair Housing Act

Contained in Title VIII of the Civil Rights Act of 1968, this law goes much further than either the 1866 Act or the 1964 Act, making it illegal to discriminate on the basis of **race, color, religion, sex, national origin, disability**, or **familial status** in the sale or lease of residential property or in the sale or lease of vacant land for the construction of residential buildings. The law also prohibits discrimination in advertising, lending, real estate brokerage, and other services in connection with residential real estate transactions. However, unlike the 1866 Act, the Fair Housing Act does not apply to nonresidential transactions, such as those involving commercial or industrial properties.

Exemptions

While the Fair Housing Act applies to the majority of residential real estate transactions, there are four types of transactions that are exempt from it.

1. The law does not apply to the sale or rental of a single-family home by its owner, provided that:
    - the owner does not own more than three such homes;
    - no real estate broker or agent is employed in the transaction; and
    - no discriminatory advertising is used.

    If the owner isn't the most recent occupant of the home, he or she may use this exemption only once every 24 months.

2. The law does not apply to the rental of a unit or a room in a dwelling with up to four units, provided that:
    - the owner occupies one of the units as his or her residence;
    - no real estate broker or agent is employed; and
    - no discriminatory advertising is used.

    (This is sometimes called the **Mrs. Murphy exemption**.)

3. In dealing with their own property in noncommercial transactions, religious organizations or societies or affiliated nonprofit organizations may limit occupancy to or give preference to their own members, provided that membership isn't restricted on the basis of race, color, or national origin.

4. Private clubs with lodgings that aren't open to the public and that aren't operated for a commercial purpose may limit occupancy to or give preference to their own members.

Fig.15.1 Fair housing poster

U.S. Department of Housing and Urban Development

EQUAL HOUSING OPPORTUNITY

We Do Business in Accordance With the Federal Fair Housing Law

(The Fair Housing Amendments Act of 1988)

It Is Illegal To Discriminate Against Any Person Because of Race, Color, Religion, Sex, Handicap, Familial Status, or National Origin

- In the sale or rental of housing or residential lots
- In advertising the sale or rental of housing
- In the financing of housing

- In the provision of real estate brokerage services
- In the appraisal of housing
- Blockbusting is also illegal

Anyone who feels he or she has been discriminated against may file a complaint of housing discrimination with the:

U.S. Department of Housing and Urban Development Assistant Secretary for Fair Housing and Equal Opportunity Washington, D.C. 20410

Previous editions are obsolete   form HUD-928.1 (3-89)

These limited exemptions apply very rarely. Remember, the 1866 Civil Rights Act prohibits discrimination based on race or ancestry in any property transaction regardless of any exemptions available under the Fair Housing Act. In addition, there is no exemption for any transaction involving a real estate licensee. And for Washington residents, these exemptions don't really exist. Washington law governing discrimination in real estate transactions contains only narrow exemptions that will be discussed later in the chapter.

Prohibited Acts

The Fair Housing Act prohibits any of the following acts if they are done on the basis of race, color, religion, sex, national origin, handicap, or familial status:

- refusing to rent or sell residential property after receiving a bona fide offer;
- refusing to negotiate for the sale or rental of residential property, or otherwise making it unavailable;
- changing the terms of sale or lease for different potential buyers or tenants;
- using advertising that indicates a preference or intent to discriminate;
- representing that property is not available for inspection, sale, or rent when it is in fact available;
- using discriminatory criteria when making a housing loan;
- limiting participation in a multiple listing service or similar service;
- coercing, intimidating, threatening, or interfering with anyone on account of his or her enjoyment, attempt to enjoy, or encouragement or assistance to others in enjoying the rights granted by the Fair Housing Act.

Also prohibited are the discriminatory practices known as blockbusting, steering, and redlining.

- **Blockbusting** occurs when someone tries to induce homeowners to list or sell their properties by predicting that members of another race (or disabled people, people of a particular ethnic background, etc.) will be moving into the neighborhood, and that this will have undesirable consequences such as lower property values. The blockbuster then profits by purchasing the homes at reduced prices or (in the case of a real estate agent) by collecting commissions on the induced sales. Blockbusting is also known as **panic selling**.

    Example: An African-American family recently moved into an all-white neighborhood. XYZ Realty immediately began calling all the homeowners in the neighborhood. XYZ's salespeople warned the homeowners of the following: several African-American families were planning on moving into the neighborhood, city police predicted a significant increase in crime in the neighborhood, property values would drop dramatically, and within months homeowners would find it difficult to sell their properties to anyone at any price. Because of these "facts" made up by XYZ agents, several homeowners immediately listed their homes with XYZ Realty. XYZ Realty is guilty of blockbusting.

- **Steering** refers to channeling prospective buyers or tenants toward or away from specific neighborhoods based on their race (or religion, national origin, etc.) in order to maintain or change the character of those neighborhoods.

  Example: The salespeople at PQR Realty are "encouraged" to show Hispanic buyers only properties in the city's predominantly Hispanic neighborhood. Non-Hispanic buyers aren't shown properties there, except by specific request. This is done on the principle that Hispanic buyers would be more "comfortable" living in the Hispanic neighborhood and non-Hispanic buyers would be "uncomfortable" there. PQR Realty is guilty of steering.

- **Redlining** is the refusal to make a loan because of the racial or ethnic composition of the neighborhood in which the security property is located.

  Example: Buyer Jones applies to Community Savings for a loan to purchase a home located in the Cherrywood neighborhood. Cherrywood is a predominantly minority neighborhood. Community Savings rejects the loan, because it fears that property values in Cherrywood may suffer in the future because of possible racial tension. Community Savings is guilty of redlining.

The prohibition against redlining is enforced by the **Home Mortgage Disclosure Act of 1975**, which requires large institutional lenders to file an annual report of all mortgage loans made. The loans are categorized according to the locations of the properties, which makes it easier to discover cases of redlining.

Handicap and Familial Status

Originally, the Fair Housing Act did not prohibit discrimination based on handicap or familial status; these classifications were added to the law in 1988.

Handicap. Under the Fair Housing Act, it is illegal to discriminate against someone because he or she has a physical disability or mental impairment that substantially limits one or more major life activities. This includes people suffering from chronic alcoholism, mental illness, or AIDS. But the act does not protect those who are a direct threat to the health or safety of others, or who are currently using controlled substances.

A residential landlord must allow a disabled tenant to make reasonable modifications to the property at the tenant's expense, so long as the modifications are necessary for the tenant's full use and enjoyment of the premises. (The tenant can be required to restore the premises to their original condition at the end of the tenancy, however.) Landlords must also make reasonable exceptions to their rules to accommodate disabled tenants. For example, even if they don't allow pets, they can't refuse to rent to someone with a guide dog.

There are special wheelchair accessibility rules that apply to newer residential construction with four or more units.

Familial Status. Discrimination on the basis of familial status refers to discrimination against a person because he or she has a child (under 18 years old) living with him or her. Parents, legal guardians, pregnant women, and those in the process of obtaining custody of a child are protected against discrimination on the basis of their familial status.

While the Federal Fair Housing Act does not override local laws limiting the number of occupants permitted in a dwelling, it is unlawful for anyone to discriminate in selling, renting, or lending money to buy residential property because the applicant is pregnant or lives with a child. "Adults only" apartment or condominium complexes are forbidden, and so are complexes divided into "adult" and "family" areas.

However, the law includes an exemption for properties that qualify as "housing for older persons." Children can be excluded from properties that fit into one of the following categories:

1. properties developed under a government program to assist the elderly;
2. properties intended for and solely occupied by persons 62 years old or older; or
3. properties intended for older persons and designed to meet their physical and social needs, if at least 80% of the units are occupied by at least one person who is 55 years old or older.

Enforcement

The Fair Housing Act is enforced by the Department of Housing and Urban Development (HUD), through its Office of Fair Housing and Equal Opportunity. An aggrieved person may file a complaint with HUD or may file a lawsuit in federal or state court. If a complaint is filed with HUD, the agency will investigate the complaint and attempt to confer with the parties in order to reconcile their differences and persuade them to abide by the law.

If this doesn't resolve the dispute and the claims are found to have merit, an administrative hearing will be held, unless either party chooses to have the case decided in federal court instead. In an administrative hearing, HUD attorneys litigate the case on behalf of the complainant. If the case goes from HUD to federal court, the U.S. Attorney General's office litigates for the complainant.

When someone is held to have violated the Fair Housing Act, the administrative law judge or the court may issue an injunction ordering the violator to stop certain discriminatory conduct. The violator may also be ordered to pay compensatory damages and attorneys' fees to the complainant. A federal court can order the violator to pay punitive damages to the complainant. An administrative law judge can't impose punitive damages, but can impose a civil penalty (ranging from a maximum of $10,000 for a first offense, to $50,000 for the third offense within seven years), which the violator must pay to the government.

In states such as Washington, where the state fair housing laws are very similar to the federal law, HUD may refer complaints to the equivalent state agency (e.g., the Washington Human Rights Commission).

Fair Lending Laws

Real estate agents and sellers are not the only ones who must avoid discriminatory activities. There are federal laws designed to eliminate discrimination in lending. They include:

- the Federal Fair Housing Act (discussed above),
- the Equal Credit Opportunity Act, and
- the Home Mortgage Disclosure Act.

The Fair Housing Act prohibits discrimination in home loans and other aspects of residential financing. It does not apply to any other credit transactions.

The **Equal Credit Opportunity Act** (ECOA) applies to all consumer credit, including residential real estate loans. Consumer credit is credit that is extended to an individual (not a corporation or business) for personal, family, or household purposes. The act prohibits lenders from discriminating based on race, color, religion, national origin, sex, marital status, age (as long as the applicant is of legal age), or because the applicant's income is derived partly or wholly from public assistance.

The **Home Mortgage Disclosure Act** is a way of learning whether lenders are fulfilling their obligation to serve the housing needs of the communities where they are located. The act facilitates the enforcement of federal laws against redlining.

Under the Home Mortgage Disclosure Act, institutional lenders in metropolitan areas with assets of over $28 million must make annual reports on residential mortgage loans (both purchase and improvement loans) that were originated or purchased during the fiscal year. The information is categorized as to number and dollar amount, type of loan (FHA, VA, other), and geographic location by census tract or county (for small counties with no established census tracts). The reports disclose areas where few or no home loans have been made and alert investigators to potential redlining.

Equal Access to Facilities

The **Americans with Disabilities Act** (ADA), which became effective in January of 1992, is a federal law that was passed to ensure that disabled persons have equal access to public facilities. The ADA requires any business or other facility open to the public to be accessible to the disabled.

Under the ADA, no one can be discriminated against on the basis of disability in any place of public accommodation. A **public accommodation** is defined as any private entity with facilities open to the public, as long as the operation of the facility affects commerce. A **disability** is defined as any physical or mental impairment that substantially limits one or more of the individual's major life activities.

Real estate offices are considered to be public accommodations, along with hotels, restaurants, retail stores, shopping centers, banks, and the offices of attorneys, accountants, and doctors.

To ensure the accessibility of public accommodations, the ADA requires each of the following to be accomplished, as long as it is "readily achievable":

- Both architectural and communication barriers must be removed so that goods and services are accessible to the disabled.
- Auxiliary aids and services must be provided so that no disabled person is excluded, denied services, segregated, or otherwise treated differently than other individuals.
- New commercial construction must be accessible to the disabled, unless structurally impractical.

For example, the owner of a commercial building with no elevator may have to install automatic entry doors and a buzzer at street level so that customers of a second-floor business can ask for assistance. A commercial building owner might also be required to alter the height of a pay phone to make it accessible to someone in a wheelchair, add grab bars to restroom stalls, and take a variety of other steps to make the building's facilities accessible.

Washington Antidiscrimination Legislation

Not only must real estate agents, sellers, and landlords comply with the federal laws we've covered, they must also comply with state laws that prohibit discrimination. The Washington Law Against Discrimination, the Fair Lending Act, and the Washington Real Estate License Law all include provisions designed to promote fairness in real estate transactions.

Washington Law Against Discrimination

The Washington Law Against Discrimination declares that discrimination is a matter of state concern because it threatens the rights and privileges of state inhabitants and the foundations of a free democratic society. In fact, the Washington Law Against Discrimination is stricter than any of the federal laws we've discussed, both as to the types of activities covered and the classes of persons protected from discrimination.

Washington law prohibits discrimination based on **race**, **creed**, **color**, **national origin**, **sex**, **marital status**, **familial status**, or **sensory**, **physical**, **or mental disability**, or the **use of a trained guide dog or service dog**. Note that those infected or perceived to be infected with **HIV** are protected from discrimination in the same manner as those suffering from any other sensory, physical, or mental disability.

To further the purposes of the Washington Law Against Discrimination, the Human Rights Commission was created and given the mission of eliminating and preventing discrimination in this state.

Prohibited Practices. The Washington Law Against Discrimination is not just a fair housing law. It prohibits a wide range of discriminatory practices in employment, insurance and credit transactions, places of public accommodation and amusement (such as restaurants, movie theaters, hotels, beauty shops, and most other commercial enterprises), and in regard to all types of real property.

Discrimination is prohibited in any real estate transaction, including the sale, appraisal, brokering, exchange, purchase, rental, or lease of real property; transacting or applying for a real estate loan; and the provision of brokerage services.

If based on discrimination against a protected class (race, creed, color, national origin, sex, marital status, familial status, or sensory, physical, or mental disability, or the use of a trained guide dog or service dog), it is against the law to:

- refuse to engage in a real estate transaction;
- discriminate in the terms or conditions of a transaction;

- discriminate in providing services or facilities in connection with a real estate transaction;
- refuse to receive or fail to transmit a bona fide offer;
- refuse to negotiate;
- represent that property is not available for inspection, sale, rental, or lease when it is in fact available;
- fail to advise a prospect about a property listing or refuse to allow him or her to inspect the property;
- publish any advertisement, notice, or sign which indicates, directly or indirectly, an intent to discriminate;
- use any application form or make any record or inquiry which indicates, directly or indirectly, an intent to discriminate;
- offer, solicit, accept, or retain a listing with the understanding that a person may be discriminated against;
- expel a person from occupancy;
- discriminate in negotiating, executing, or financing a real estate transaction;
- discriminate in negotiating or executing any service or item in connection with a real estate transaction (such as title insurance or mortgage insurance);
- induce or attempt to induce, for profit, anyone to sell or rent by making representations regarding entry into the neighborhood of a person of a protected class (blockbusting);
- insert in a written instrument relating to real property, or honor or attempt to honor, any condition, restriction, or prohibition based on a protected class (any such provision in a deed or any other conveyance or instrument relating to real property is void); or
- discriminate in any credit transaction (whether or not it is real estate related) in denying credit, increasing fees, requiring collateral, or in any other terms or conditions.

In short, just about every form of discrimination in real estate transactions or any services associated with real estate transactions is unlawful if it is because the person is a member of any of the protected classes.

It is important for real estate agents, property sellers, and landlords to remember that, unlike the Federal Fair Housing Act, the Washington law has no exemptions for individual owners. A person who owns only one home is still prohibited from discriminating in selling or renting that home. People are also prohibited from discriminating when renting rooms in their own homes. However, based on the right of privacy, including the right to choose the sex of persons with whom one lives, the Human Rights Commission has ruled that it will not hear cases involving discrimination based on sex in the rental of rooms where the parties are to share living space. This ruling was prompted by an inquiry from a woman who wanted to let a room in her home only if she could rent it to another woman.

Exemptions. The Washington law has very few exemptions. Educational institutions may discriminate based on sex or marital status in student housing, and private clubs and certain cemeteries and mausoleums operated by religious or sectarian institutions are also exempt as to religious preference. There are no exemptions for a seller or lessor of real property in an ordinary transaction, and certainly none for a real estate broker or salesperson engaged in professional activity.

Enforcement. An injured party may file a complaint with the Human Rights Commission within six months after the alleged discrimination took place. The Commission will then conduct an investigation. If the investigation reveals a reasonable basis for a belief that discrimination occurred, the Commission will act on the complaint. First, the Commission will try to eliminate the unlawful discrimination by conference, conciliation, and persuasion.

If that is unsuccessful, the Commission may schedule a hearing before an administrative law judge. If the judge finds unlawful discrimination, a cease and desist order may be issued. The judge may also require affirmative relief, payment of actual damages to the victim, and payment of a civil penalty to the government. As with violations of the Fair Housing Act, the civil penalty can range from $10,000 for a first offense up to $50,000 for the third offense within seven years.

The alleged discriminator may appeal the outcome of the administrative hearing to the superior court by filing an appeal within 30 days after being served with the final order.

As an alternative to an administrative hearing, the injured party may choose to have the attorney general enforce the law by bringing a civil action against the alleged discriminator.

Washington Fairness in Lending Act

The Washington Fairness in Lending Act prohibits redlining. Under this act, financial institutions may not deny single-family home loan applications solely because the home is located in a particular geographic area. They also may not vary the terms of the loan (such as by requiring a higher downpayment, higher interest rate, or shorter amortization term, or by deliberately under-appraising the value of the property).

The act does not prevent a lending institution from using sound underwriting practices (including considering the borrower's creditworthiness and the market value of the property), but it outlaws the use of lending standards that have no financial basis.

Fig.15.2 Antidiscrimination legislation

Legislation	Prohibits Discrimination
Civil Rights Act of 1866	Based on race
Civil Rights Act of 1964	In some federal programs
Federal Fair Housing Act	In sale, lease, or financing of housing
Americans with Disabilities Act	Based on disability
Washington Law Against Discrimination	In sale, lease, or financing of property

Washington Real Estate License Law

In addition to complying with the federal and state laws already discussed, real estate licensees must also adhere to the provisions of the state license law and regulations.

According to the license law, violating any fair housing or civil rights laws or regulations is grounds for disciplinary action. If a broker or salesperson discriminates in sales or hiring activity on the basis of a protected class, his or her license could be suspended or revoked. Furthermore, the licensee could face a fine of up to $5,000 for each offense, and/or be required to complete an educational course in civil rights laws and nondiscriminatory real estate practices. Violations of the license law are also punishable as gross misdemeanors.

📖 Chapter Summary

1. Discrimination in real estate transactions is prohibited by the Civil Rights Act of 1866, the Federal Fair Housing Act, and Washington antidiscrimination statutes.

2. The Civil Rights Act of 1866 prohibits all discrimination based on race or ancestry in the sale and rental of property. The Civil Rights Act of 1964 prohibits discrimination in programs and services for which the federal government provided financial assistance.

3. The Federal Fair Housing Act goes farther than the Civil Rights Acts of 1866 and 1964 by prohibiting discrimination based on race, color, religion, sex, national origin, handicap, or familial status. However, it applies only to transactions involving residential property.

4. Three specifically prohibited acts under the Federal Fair Housing Act are blockbusting, steering, and redlining. Blockbusting is attempting to obtain listings or arrange sales by predicting the entry of minorities into the neighborhood and implying that this will cause a decline in the neighborhood. Steering is the channeling of buyers or renters to specific neighborhoods based on race or other protected characteristics. Redlining is the refusal to make loans on properties located in particular areas for discriminatory reasons.

5. Several federal laws prohibit discrimination in credit transactions: the Federal Fair Housing Act, the Equal Credit Opportunity Act, and the Home Mortgage Disclosure Act.

6. The Americans with Disabilities Act guarantees equal access to public accommodations regardless of physical or mental disability.

7. Washington state law prohibits discrimination not just in housing, but also in employment, insurance and credit transactions, places of public accommodation, and all types of real property transactions. There are only limited exemptions.

🔑 Key Terms

Blockbusting—Attempting to induce homeowners to list or sell their homes by predicting that members of another race or ethnic group, or people suffering from some disability, will be moving into the neighborhood.

Steering—Channeling prospective buyers or tenants toward or away from particular neighborhoods based on their race, religion, or national origin, in order to maintain or change the character of the neighborhoods.

Redlining—Refusing to make a loan because of the racial or ethnic composition of the neighborhood in which the security property is located.

Familial status—A category including persons who have children (under 18 years old) living with them. It also includes someone who is pregnant or is in the process of securing custody of a child.

Disability—A physical disability or mental impairment that substantially limits one or more major life activities.

Chapter Quiz

1. When a real estate agent channels prospective buyers away from a particular neighborhood because of their race, it is called:

   a) blockbusting
   b) steering
   c) redlining
   d) clipping

2. Rental of a room in an owner-occupied dwelling is exempt from the Federal Fair Housing Act if the dwelling contains:

   a) two or more units
   b) three units or less
   c) less than five units
   d) six units or more

3. A real estate broker is helping the Jacksons sell their single-family home. Can this transaction be exempt from the Federal Fair Housing Act?

   a) Yes, as long as the Jacksons own no more than three single-family homes
   b) Yes, as long as no discriminatory advertising is used
   c) No, because a real estate agent is involved
   d) No, the act applies to all residential sales transactions, without exception

4. The Gardenia Village condominium has a "no kids" rule. This is not a violation of the Federal Fair Housing Act:

   a) if the condo qualifies as "housing for older persons" under the terms of the law
   b) if no discriminatory advertising is used
   c) because age discrimination is not prohibited by the law
   d) because condominiums aren't covered by the law

5. Title VIII of the Civil Rights Act of 1968 precludes:

   a) discrimination in housing
   b) discrimination in lending
   c) Both a) and b)
   d) Neither a) nor b)

6. Blockbusting is an acceptable practice:

   a) only under the supervision of real estate licensees
   b) only when approved by either HUD or the Justice Department
   c) under no circumstances
   d) only if the seller and buyer mutually agree

7. Under the Washington Law Against Discrimination, complaints should be filed with the:

   a) Department of Fair Employment and Housing
   b) Washington Human Rights Commission
   c) Washington Housing Council
   d) Washington Association of Realtors

8. The Home Mortgage Disclosure Act helps to enforce the prohibition against:

   a) redlining
   b) steering
   c) blockbusting
   d) None of the above

9. A landlord who is subject to the provisions of the Federal Fair Housing Act must:

   a) permit a disabled tenant to make reasonable modifications to the property at the tenant's expense
   b) make reasonable exceptions to the landlord's rules to accommodate disabled tenants
   c) Both a) and b)
   d) Neither a) nor b)

10. Under Washington law, it would be permissible for a landlord to refuse to rent to a prospective tenant because she:

   a) has a child
   b) was born in Germany
   c) has a low income
   d) None of the above

11. Washington laws against discrimination:

   a) are broader in application, with fewer exemptions, than the federal laws
   b) are narrower in scope than federal laws
   c) provide exactly the same coverage as federal legislation
   d) are enforceable only by federal equal housing agencies

12. Which of the following is not covered by the Federal Fair Housing Act?

   a) A commercial property
   b) An eight-unit multifamily dwelling
   c) A triplex listed for sale with a real estate broker
   d) A vacant lot intended for residential construction

13. A developer who intended to rent housing in a particular development only to persons 45 years of age or over would be in violation of the:

   a) Civil Rights Act of 1866
   b) Civil Rights Act of 1964
   c) Federal Fair Housing Act
   d) Americans with Disabilities Act

14. Under the Americans with Disabilities Act:

   a) real estate firms are exempt
   b) real estate firms may discriminate against the disabled when taking listings, if appropriate
   c) real estate firms must be accessible to the disabled
   d) only individual real estate agents are prohibited from discriminating against the disabled

15. The Washington Fairness in Lending Act prohibits:

   a) redlining
   b) steering
   c) blockbusting
   d) panic selling

👉 Answer Key

1. b) Channeling prospective buyers or tenants away from (or toward) certain neighborhoods based on their race, religion, or national origin is called steering. It is a violation of the Federal Fair Housing Act.

2. c) The Fair Housing Act exemption for rentals applies to owner-occupied dwellings with up to four units.

3. c) No residential transaction in which a real estate agent is employed is exempt from the Federal Fair Housing Act.

4. a) The Federal Fair Housing Act does not allow apartment houses and condominiums to discriminate on the basis of familial status unless the complex qualifies as "housing for older persons."

5. c) Title VIII of the 1968 Civil Rights Act (better known as the Federal Fair Housing Act) prohibits discriminatory practices when selling, renting, advertising, or financing housing.

6. c) Blockbusting is a discriminatory practice entirely prohibited by the Federal Fair Housing Act.

7. b) The Washington Human Rights Commission is charged with enforcing the Washington Law Against Discrimination.

8. a) The Home Mortgage Disclosure Act helps to enforce the prohibition against redlining by requiring large institutional lenders to file an annual report of all mortgage loans made during that year. Loans are categorized according to location, alerting investigators to areas of possible redlining.

9. c) The Fair Housing Act requires a residential landlord to allow a disabled tenant to make reasonable modifications to the property. The landlord must also make reasonable exceptions to the rules to accommodate a disabled tenant.

10. c) A landlord may (and should) base his or her rental decision on whether the tenant can afford the rent. However, the landlord cannot take into account the prospective tenant's national origin or familial status.

11. a) Washington laws provide more protection against discrimination and have fewer exemptions than federal laws.

12. a) The Federal Fair Housing Act applies to residential properties, not commercial or industrial properties.

13. c) The developer's age limit would violate the Federal Fair Housing Act. Senior housing is okay, but 45 is not the cutoff age.

14. c) Under the provisions of the ADA, real estate firms must take reasonable actions necessary to make their accommodations accessible to the disabled.

15. a) The Washington Fairness in Lending Act prohibits redlining, among other discriminatory lending practices.

Property Management

⌂⌂⌂ Chapter Overview

Many brokerage offices engage in property management to some degree, so all real estate agents should have a basic knowledge of property management principles. This chapter gives the reader an overview of the property management profession. The first section of the chapter discusses the basics of investing in real estate. The next section describes some of the differences between types of managed properties. After that, we'll discuss the management agreement, the management plan, and the various functions of a property manager. The final section of the chapter will look at the laws that govern landlord/tenant relationships.

Introduction to Property Management

Property management refers to a situation in which a person other than the owner supervises the operation of income property in exchange for a fee. Prior to the 1930s, real estate owners usually managed their own properties, although sometimes they hired assistants to collect rents. Then in the 1930s, during the Great Depression, countless borrowers defaulted on their mortgages and many properties ended up in the hands of lenders. These lenders were saddled with management responsibilities for extensive property holdings, but they had little property management experience. Of necessity, some formed their own property management departments, and others came to depend on the real estate industry to provide the necessary expertise. Although the lenders eventually resold the properties they acquired during the Depression, the value of efficient property management had been discovered, and increasing numbers of property owners began to use the services of property managers.

In the years following World War II, property management became even more important as construction and business practices changed. Apartment and office buildings became larger as elevators and steel framing allowed the construction of multistory structures. Shopping centers replaced the corner store and flourishing commercial activity led to the creation of industrial parks. It became increasingly difficult for property owners to manage all of their holdings, and professional, efficient, and effective outside management became a necessity rather than a luxury.

Investing in Real Estate

A property manager's job begins after someone has decided to invest in income-producing property, such as an apartment building, office building, or shopping center. As you will learn later, the primary function of a property manager is to help the property owner achieve his or her investment goals. So before discussing the nuts and bolts of property management, let's take a brief look at general investment principles and at real estate as an investment. (A word of caution: Real estate agents should not act as investment counselors; they should always refer clients to an accountant, attorney, or investment specialist for investment advice.)

An investment is an asset that is expected to generate a **return** (a profit). A return on an investment can take various forms, including interest, dividends, or appreciation in value. An asset appreciates in value because of inflation, and may also appreciate because of a rising demand for the asset. For example, a parcel of prime vacant land appreciates in value as developable land becomes increasingly scarce.

Types of Investments

Investments can be divided into two general categories: ownership investments and debt investments. With **ownership investments**, the investor takes an ownership interest in the asset. Real estate and stocks are examples of ownership investments. The return on ownership investments usually takes the form of dividends or appreciation (or both in some cases).

A **debt investment** is essentially a loan that an investor makes to an entity. For example, a bond is a debt owed to an investor by a government entity or corporation. The investor lends the entity money for a set period of time, and in return the entity promises to repay the money at a specific date (the maturity date) along with a certain amount of interest.

Investors often choose to diversify their investments—that is, they choose to invest in a variety of different types of investments. The mix of investments owned by an individual or company is referred to as a **portfolio**.

Note that for tax purposes, investment income (such as interest, dividends, or rent) is sometimes distinguished from earned income (salaries, wages, or self-employment income).

Investment Characteristics

An investor considers any investment in terms of three potential advantages: liquidity, safety, and total return on the investment (sometimes called **yield**). These three characteristics are interrelated. For example, liquidity and safety generally go together. On the other hand, for a high return an investor often sacrifices safety or liquidity, or both.

A **liquid asset** is one that can be converted into cash quickly. Money in a bank account is extremely liquid: to convert it into cash, the investor need only present the bank with a withdrawal slip or check. Mutual funds, stocks, and bonds are less liquid—they take a little longer (perhaps a week or so) to convert into cash. Other items, such as jewelry or coin collections, are not considered liquid at all, because an investor might have to wait months to exchange those assets for cash. Real estate is not considered a liquid asset.

Liquid investments do not offer very high returns. In general, the more liquid the asset, the lower the return. For example, the money in your wallet is the most liquid asset you can have, but it earns no return (interest) at all. Money in a savings account is a little less liquid—you have to go to the bank to withdraw it—but it offers a modest return in the form of a low rate of interest. By contrast, real estate can offer a very high rate of return, but it is not at all liquid.

The most liquid investments are generally considered the safest. With liquid assets, there is little risk of losing the asset itself. Money in the bank is both liquid and safe. Since your deposit is insured by the federal government (up to $100,000), there is little chance of losing your investment. Other, less liquid types of investments, such as gold or real estate, are not as safe. For example, if a property owner must sell when real estate values are low, the owner may lose a good portion of his or her original investment in the property.

Investments that are both safe and liquid offer the lowest returns. In a sense, investors "pay" for safety and liquidity with a low return. Savings accounts and certificates of deposits, both safe investments, offer relatively low returns. Mutual funds, gold, and real estate can generate high returns, but at a considerable risk to the investor. For some types of assets, such as real estate, the safety of the investment will increase if the investor can afford to keep the investment for a long period of time. For example, if an investor does not need to cash out his or her investment in real estate for ten or fifteen years, chances are good that the investor will reap a high return. This is true because the investor will have more control over when to sell the asset, and will be able to take full advantage of healthy market conditions.

> **Example:** Jeanne and Harold both invest $20,000 in rental homes in the same year. One year later, Jeanne desperately needs some cash and is forced to sell her rental home at a loss. She ends up with only $17,000 of her original $20,000 investment.
>
> Harold, on the other hand, keeps his rental home for twelve years. He's in no hurry to sell his property, so he can wait for optimal market conditions. He sells at the peak of a real estate cycle, when property values are high. Because Harold could afford to choose when he sold the property, he walked away from the transaction with $60,000, a very healthy return on his original $20,000 investment.

Advantages of Investing in Real Estate

People invest in real estate for many reasons. The advantages of investing in real estate can be broken down into three general categories:

- appreciation,
- leverage, and
- cash flow.

Appreciation. Appreciation refers to an increase in a property's value due to changes in the economy or other outside factors. Although real estate values may fluctuate, over a period of several years real estate usually increases in value at a rate equal to or higher than the rate of inflation. Thus, real estate is considered an effective hedge against inflation. And when buildable property becomes scarce, the value of properties in prime locations increases even more rapidly.

Appreciation causes a property owner's equity to increase. **Equity** is the difference between the value of the property and the liens against it, so an increase in the property's value increases the owner's equity in the property. Also, each monthly mortgage payment increases the owner's equity, in proportion to the reduction of the principal amount of the loan. Equity adds to the investor's net worth and can also be used to secure a home equity loan. So even though real estate is not considered a liquid asset, equity in real estate can be used to generate cash funds.

Fig. 16.1 Investing in real estate

Advantages of Real Estate Investment

- Appreciation
- Leverage
- Cash flow

Leverage. Real estate investors can take advantage of leverage, which is defined as using borrowed money to invest in an asset. If the asset appreciates, then the investor earns money on the money borrowed as well as the money he or she invested.

Example: Martin purchases a rental home for $215,000. He makes a $43,000 downpayment and borrows the rest of the purchase price. The rent generated by the property covers all the expenses of operating the property, plus the mortgage payment and income taxes. The property appreciates at 3% per year for five years. At the end of the five years, Martin sells the property for $249,000. He's made a $34,000 profit over five years on his $43,000 investment. This represents a 79% return over the five-year period. The property appreciated at 3% per year, but because he only invested 20% of the purchase price, Martin was able to generate a 79% return on his investment.

Cash Flow. Many real estate investments generate a positive cash flow, as well as appreciate in value. Cash flow is defined as spendable income—the amount of money left after all the property's expenses have been paid, including operating costs, mortgage payments, and taxes. When a real estate investment generates a positive cash flow, the investor's monthly income increases. Thus, a real estate investment can increase both the investor's net worth (through appreciation) and his or her income (through positive cash flow).

Another way in which a property can generate cash flow is through a **sale-leaseback** arrangement. In a sale-leaseback, the owner of a building (typically a commercial property) sells the building to an investor, but then leases the property back from the investor and continues to use it. The money generated by the sale can be used for expansion, acquiring inventory, or investment else-where. At the same time, the seller can deduct the rent paid to lease the property from his or her income taxes as a business expense. Sometimes a sale-leaseback arrangement also includes a **buyback** agreement, in which it's agreed that the seller will buy the property back for its fair market value after a certain number of years.

Investors sometimes use the term "cash on cash," which refers to a property's first year cash flow divided by the initial investment. It pinpoints the ratio between cash invested (equity) and cash received.

Types of Managed Properties

Now let's consider the different types of properties that a property manager may be called upon to manage. There are four basic types of income-producing properties:

1. residential rental property,
2. office buildings,
3. retail property, and
4. industrial property.

Each type of property has its own unique characteristics and management needs. Because each type of property demands a different kind of expertise, property managers often specialize in one particular type of property. The following are a few examples of the differences between property types.

Apartment buildings, which typically offer six-month or one-year leases, have a much higher turnover rate than industrial property, where leases often run for ten years or more. As a result, residential property managers tend to spend more of their time marketing and leasing out space. Residential property managers also must fulfill the legal responsibilities imposed by the landlord-tenant laws, which are designed to protect the health and well-being of residential tenants.

Fig. 16.2 Income-producing properties

Types of Income Properties

Residential
(rental homes, apartments, condos)
Office
(office buildings and office parks)
Retail
(stores and shopping centers)
Industrial
(industrial parks)

Office buildings have very different housekeeping requirements than residential buildings: they endure much heavier foot traffic; they have facilities that get continuous use (such as washrooms and elevators) and thus need frequent cleaning; and management is often responsible for cleaning the tenants' spaces as well as the common areas. Lease negotiations are also very different for office buildings than for residential space: rent is based on a price per square foot (rather than per unit); the leases are for longer periods of time and usually include some type of escalation clause (to provide for automatic increases in rent); and landlords commonly offer major concessions to attract tenants, such as free rent for a limited period or extensive remodeling.

Leasing space to an appropriate tenant is a concern with any type of property, but it is especially important when managing a shopping center. The success of each tenant in a shopping center depends in part on the customers that each of the other tenants attract, so it is vital to lease to strong tenants. Also, a portion of the rent is often based on the tenant's income, so the owner has a vested interest in the financial success of each tenant. The tenant mix must appeal to the widest variety of potential shoppers, while avoiding direct competition within the shopping center itself.

These are only a few of the ways in which property types differ. Even from such a small sampling, however, it is easy to see that different management plans are required for each type of property. The benefits of specializing in one or two property types are evident.

Our discussion will focus mainly on managing residential properties, but most of the principles and practices we'll be describing apply to the management of any type of property.

The Management Agreement

The first step in the management process is entering into a management agreement. The management agreement establishes the working relationship between the property manager and the property owner. In the same way that a listing agreement creates an agency relationship between a broker and a seller, the management agreement creates an agency relationship between the manager and the owner.

The management agreement must be in writing and signed by both parties. It is very important that the written document contain all the terms and conditions of the agreement. It is especially important that the exact duties and powers of the manager be explicitly stated. What kinds of decisions can the manager freely make, and what kinds must be referred to the owner? For example, suppose several units in an apartment building needed new carpets. Could the manager replace the carpets without consulting the owner, or is this a decision that the owner wants to make? Other areas in which questions might arise include the authority to execute leases, make major repairs, choose an insurance company and policy for the property, or embark on a major advertising campaign.

At a minimum, the following points should be included in the management agreement:

- the term of the agreement;
- the manager's compensation (a percentage of gross income, a commission on new rentals, a fixed fee, or a combination of all of these);
- the type of property;
- the legal description of the property;
- the number of units or square footage;
- whether the manager is authorized to collect and disburse funds, and if so, for what purposes;
- whether the manager is authorized to hold and disburse tenant security deposits; and
- provisions concerning the manager's reports to the owner, specifying the frequency and level of detail of the reports.

In most cases, these additional provisions should also be included in the management agreement:

- a description of other management responsibilities (duties should be stated, exceptions noted);
- a statement of the owner's goals (for example, to maximize income, or to increase the capital value of the property);
- the extent of the manager's authority (for example, fixing rental rates, hiring and firing, authorizing repairs);
- allocation of costs (which expenses the manager will pay and which expenses the owner will pay—such as office help, advertising, or telephone expenses).

The property manager must bear in mind that after the management agreement is signed, an agency relationship exists between the manager and the owner, and thus the manager is bound by all the duties and responsibilities of an agent (see Chapter 7).

The Management Plan

Once a manager has entered into a management agreement, the actual business of managing begins. The first (and often most important) step in managing a property is drawing up a management plan. A management plan outlines the manager's strategy for financial management and physical upkeep, and focuses on achieving the owner's goals.

The management plan should implement the owner's goals in the most effective manner possible. It is important to remember that there are many different reasons for investing in income property—different property owners have different management goals. For instance, one property owner may simply want a steady, reliable stream of income. Another owner may want a tax shelter. Another may want to increase the property's value in order to reap a bigger profit in later years. An owner's goals can also change over the period of ownership.

> **Example:** When he's in his early forties, Greg decides to purchase a small apartment building. He has other sources of income, so he is most interested in the long-term investment and tax shelter aspects of real estate ownership. However, as the years pass, Greg's needs change. When he retires, he is suddenly more interested in receiving a steady cash flow from his property.

Preliminary Study

A management plan can be created only after a comprehensive study of all of the facets of the property, including its location, its physical characteristics, its financial status, and its policies of operation. This preliminary study includes a regional analysis, a neighborhood analysis, a property analysis, and a market analysis.

Regional Analysis. Preparing a management plan begins with a study of the region (city or metropolitan area) in which the property is located. The manager analyzes the general economic conditions, physical attributes, and population growth and distribution. Among the most significant considerations are trends in occupancy rates, market rental rates, employment levels, and (for residential property) family size and lifestyle.

Occupancy Rates. According to the law of supply and demand, when the demand for an item is greater than the supply, the price or value of the item increases. And when the supply exceeds the demand, the price or value of the item decreases. This basic rule applies to rental properties just as it applies to other commodities.

From a property manager's point of view, the supply of rental units is the total number of units available for occupancy in the area where the managed property is located. The demand for rental units is the total number of potential tenants in that area who are able to pay the rent for those units. When demand exceeds supply, rental rates go up; when supply exceeds demand, rental rates go down.

There is a **technical oversupply** of property when there are more units than potential tenants. There is an **economic oversupply** when there are enough potential tenants, but they are unable to pay the current rent. Likewise, there may be a **technical shortage** (when there are more potential tenants than units) or an **economic shortage** (when there are more able-to-pay tenants than units).

To set rental rates for a managed property, a property manager must determine the occupancy trend for the area. If the trend is toward higher occupancy levels, the value of the units will increase because space is becoming more scarce. It is during these times that managers raise rents and reduce services. On the other hand, if there is a trend toward higher vacancy rates, a unit's value will decrease. In periods of high vacancy, tenants are likely to resist rent increases or make more demands for services or repairs when leases are renewed.

Occupancy levels are constantly fluctuating. The direction and speed in which they are moving will have a significant impact on the property manager's operating and marketing policies.

Market Rental Rates. In addition to evaluating occupancy trends, a property manager should keep track of market rental rates, the rates currently being charged for comparable rental units. The manager should set rental rates for the managed units at a level that will enable them to compete in the current market.

There are published reports that provide information about rental rates, such as the Bureau of Labor's statistics on rents paid for residential units. A property manager may also evaluate the properties that he or she is managing to determine the average monthly rent per unit or square foot. Statistics kept by an individual property manager can be combined with statistics kept by other managers in the area to get a broader perspective. Rental rates stated in classified ads can also be considered. These methods, while not precise, can give a manager a basic picture of market trends.

Employment Levels. The property manager should be aware of local employment trends, since employment levels affect how many potential tenants can afford to rent. A property manager should also know whether earnings are increasing or decreasing, and about savings rates in the community. Clearly, if potential tenants cannot afford a particular rental unit or would rather save than spend, the property manager's product is not going to be sold.

Family Size and Lifestyle. Family size has a great deal to do with the value of particular residential units. If the average family size were three (two parents and one child), five-bedroom units would have little appeal and two-bedroom units would be very attractive. Thus, the two-bedroom units will command a higher price per square foot than the five-bedroom units. A property manager needs to be aware of the national trend toward smaller and even single-person households, and also any local trends in family size and lifestyle.

Neighborhood Analysis. After the regional analysis, the next step in the preliminary study is to analyze the specific neighborhood where the property is located. The definition of a neighborhood varies considerably from one place to another. In rural areas, a neighborhood may consist of many square miles. In an urban area, a neighborhood may be only a few blocks.

The qualities of the neighborhood have a significant bearing on the property's value and use. Important neighborhood characteristics include:

- the level of maintenance (Are the buildings and grounds well cared for, or in poor condition?);
- a growth or decline in population; and
- the economic status of the residents.

A property manager should discover the reasons behind any neighborhood trends. Is the population density increasing because of further development or because single-family homes are changing into rooming houses? Development is a sign of economic prosperity, rooming house tenancies are not.

A neighborhood analysis helps a property manager factor location into the management plan. No matter how effectively a property is operated, its profitability will be strongly affected by its location. Once the characteristics of the location have been determined, realistic management goals can be set.

Property Analysis. Of course, to develop a management plan the manager must become very familiar with the physical characteristics of the property itself. He or she will inspect the property, noting its architectural design, physical condition, facilities, and general layout.

The following characteristics are particularly important:

- the number and size of the living units, or the number of rentable square feet;
- the appearance of the property and the rental spaces (age, architectural style, layout, view, fixtures, etc.);
- the physical condition of the building (roof, elevators, windows, etc.);
- the physical condition of the rental spaces (floor coverings, stairways, shades or blinds, walls, entryways);
- the amenities provided (laundry room, recreational facilities, etc.);
- the services provided (janitorial services, repair services, or security);
- the relationship of the land to the building (Is the land used efficiently? Is there adequate parking?);
- the current occupancy rate and tenant composition; and
- the size and efficiency of the current staff.

Market Analysis. The last step in the preliminary study for a management plan is the market analysis, which provides information on competing properties. To do a market analysis, the manager must first define the pertinent market. The major divisions of the real estate market are residential, commercial, retail, and industrial. Each of these can be broken down into subcategories. For instance, the residential market can be divided into single-family rental homes, duplexes, townhouses, walk-up apartments, small multistory apartments, and large apartment complexes.

Once the manager has identified the market that the managed property competes in, there are several characteristics that must be examined:

- the number of units available in the area;
- the average age and character of the buildings in which the units are located;
- the quality of the average unit in the market (size, condition, layout, facilities, etc.);
- the number of potential tenants in the area;
- the current price for the average unit; and
- the occupancy rate for the average unit.

The property manager compares the managed property to comparable properties in the neighborhood. In this way, the manager can evaluate what the property has to offer and what its disadvantages are. Armed with this information, the manager can establish an effective management strategy.

The Management Proposal

After completing the preliminary study, the property manager develops a management proposal and submits it to the property owner for approval. The manager's proposal will include a rental schedule, income and expense projections, a schedule of day-to-day operations, and perhaps suggestions for physical changes to the property itself.

Rental Schedule. A rental schedule is a list of all the rental rates assigned to the different types of units. For example, an apartment building may consist of studio apartments, one-bedroom apartments, and two-bedroom apartments. Some apartments may have views, others may not. A rental schedule lists the various types of units and their rental rates.

Rental schedules are based on all the data collected during the regional, neighborhood, property, and market analyses. This information helps the manager determine the optimum rent that can be charged while maintaining the optimum occupancy level. To set the rate for a particular type of unit, the manager can adjust the market rental rate for the average comparable unit up or down to reflect the differences between the comparable and the type of unit in question. Because this method of setting rates depends on market conditions, the rental schedule should be reexamined periodically to see if it is current. Either an unusually high vacancy rate or an unusually low vacancy rate is an indication that the property's rental rates are out of line with the community. If the vacancy rate is too high, the rent may be too expensive; if the vacancy rate is unusually low, the rent may be below the norm.

Budgets. The property manager also sets up a budget of income and operating expenses (see Figure 16.3). The manager lists the total value of all rentable space at the scheduled rental rates, then subtracts a figure for delinquent rental payments and vacancies (sometimes called a bad debt and vacancy factor). Any other income sources, such as laundry facilities, vending machines, or parking, should also be listed.

Next, the estimated operating expenses—both fixed expenses and variable expenses—are listed. **Fixed expenses** include such items as property taxes, insurance premiums, and employee salaries. **Variable expenses** include utilities, maintenance, and repairs. Finally, the manager deducts projected operating expenses from projected revenues to arrive at a cash flow figure.

Day-to-Day Operations. In addition to long-range financial planning, the management proposal should include the manager's plans for the day-to-day operations of the property. This means that the manager has to decide how much (if any) staffing will be required and what the employment policies and procedures will be.

Physical Alterations. In some cases, the property manager's proposal will include recommendations for remodeling, rehabilitation, or other physical alterations to the property. For instance, after a thorough examination of the property, the customer base, and the market, a manager might decide that the property would be worth much more to the owner if the building were altered to match current family size and lifestyle trends.

> **Example:** An older building is made up of four- and five-bedroom units in a neighborhood predominantly made up of one- and two-person households. If the apartments were converted to smaller units, the owner's profits would probably increase significantly.

Owner's Approval. Once completed, the management proposal is presented to the property owner. When the proposal is approved, it becomes the management plan: the blueprint for managing the property.

Fig. 16.3 Operating budget

	Jan	Feb	Mar	Apr	May	June	July	Aug	Sept	Oct	Nov	Dec	Annual
Income													
Scheduled Rents													
Less:													
Vacancies													
Rent Loss													
Effective Rent													
Miscellaneous Income													
Total Income													
Expenses													
Administrative													
Management Costs													
Other Adm. Costs													
Operating													
Payroll													
Supplies													
Heating													
Electricity													
Water and Sewer													
Gas													
Maintenance													
Grounds													
Maint. and Repairs													
Painting, Decorating													
Taxes and Insurance													
Real Estate Taxes													
Other Taxes, Fees													
Insurance													
Contract Service													
Total Expenses													
Net Operating Income													
Less Reserves													
Net Income													
Less Debt Service													
Cash Flow													

Management Functions

Property managers must possess the skills necessary to perform a variety of management functions. They must be able to market the property, negotiate leases, and handle tenant relations. They must be able to keep and understand detailed financial records and report to the property owner on a regular basis. They must also be able to arrange for the maintenance and repairs that will preserve the value of the property.

Leasing and Tenant Relations

The property manager's tasks involved in leasing and tenant relations include marketing the rental spaces, negotiating leases, addressing tenants' complaints, and collecting rents.

Marketing. The more people who view a rental space, the more likely it is to be rented out. So property managers generally use advertising to bring potential tenants to their properties.

Different types of properties require different types and amounts of advertising. For some properties, advertising is necessary only when there is a vacancy to fill. If the property is in a prominent location and attractive to potential tenants, advertising may not be necessary at all. On the other hand, if the property is in an isolated location, continuous advertising may be required to generate enough interest to fill vacancies when they occur.

Successful advertising brings in a good number of potential tenants in the least amount of time for the lowest cost. Property managers often evaluate the effectiveness of their advertising in terms of the number of potential tenants for the advertising dollars spent. For example, based on experience, a property manager might have a general rule of thumb that the cost of advertising should not exceed $25 to $35 per prospect. Thus, newspaper advertising that costs $300 should bring in 9 to 12 prospective tenants to the property.

To reach the greatest number of potential tenants for the lowest possible cost, the property manager must be familiar with the various types of advertising and know which will be most effective for the property in question. The manager may consider using signs, newspaper ads, radio or television spots, direct mail, or some combination of these tools.

Signs. Small, tasteful signs are often used, whether there is a vacancy or not, to inform passersby of the name of the manager and how to acquire rental information. The use of signs is most successful for office buildings, large apartment complexes, and shopping centers.

Newspaper Advertising. Newspaper advertising includes classified ads and display ads. Classified ads (inexpensive line-type advertising that appears in the "classified" section of the newspaper) are the most popular way to advertise residential rental space. Display ads are larger and more expensive than classified ads. A display ad often includes a photograph of the property, and it may appear in any section of the newspaper. Display advertising is generally an effective way to advertise space in a new office building, industrial park, or shopping center.

Radio and Television. Property managers occasionally use radio and television ads for large commercial and residential properties. Although broadcast advertising reaches a large audience, there usually aren't many potential tenants in the audience. Since broadcast advertising (especially television advertising) is quite expensive, it generally isn't cost-effective for most rental properties.

Direct Mail. To be effective, direct mail advertising must be received by potential tenants, not just the general public. So a property manager who wants to use direct mail must compile or purchase a mailing list. With a good mailing list and a brochure designed to appeal to prospective tenants, direct mail can be an effective means of advertising. Also, the same brochure can be handed out to those who visit the property.

Fig.16.4 Types of advertising and their uses

Types of Advertising	
Type	**Most Effective Use**
Signs	Tell prospects how to get rental information
Classified ads	Fill residential vacancies
Display ads	Fill vacancies in larger properties
Radio and TV	Not cost-effective for most properties
Direct mail	Effective if mailing list is good

Leasing. A prospect has seen an advertisement and come to look at the available rental space. Now it is the property manager's job to convince the prospect that the rental space is desirable. They will usually tour the property together, and during the tour the manager will emphasize all of the property's positive qualities and all of its amenities. The manager will point out traffic patterns and access to public transportation, the characteristics of the other tenants, the exterior and interior condition of the property, and its overall cleanliness. If it's commercial property, the manager and the prospect may discuss how the space could be altered to suit the prospect's needs.

After the tour, if the prospect is still interested in the property, it is the property manager's responsibility to make sure that the prospect is qualified to lease it. Although financial stability is a key consideration, it's not the only one. The manager must also decide whether the prospect is likely to be a responsible and cooperative tenant. At a minimum, this will involve checking the prospect's references and contacting the previous landlord. The manager can also use his or her own judgment, but must be very careful to avoid violating antidiscrimination laws (see Chapter 15).

If the manager decides in favor of the prospect, the next step is to execute a rental agreement or lease. The requirements for a valid lease are explained later in this chapter, in the discussion of landlord/tenant law.

Lease Renewal. Unless the tenant has caused problems, a property manager would much rather renew an existing lease than find a new tenant. Renewal avoids a vacancy between the time one tenant moves out and another moves in. A building has greater stability with long-term tenants, and it is usually easier and less expensive to satisfy the requirements of an existing tenant than improve the space for a new tenant.

A property manager should always be aware of which tenants are nearing the end of their lease terms and notify them that their leases are about to expire. Then the manager should follow up on the notices, by phone or in person, to inquire whether the tenant wants to renew. If the tenant is going to renew the lease, the terms of the new lease must be negotiated.

Some leases contain an **automatic renewal clause**, which provides that the lease will be automatically renewed on the same terms unless one party notifies the other of his or her intent to terminate the lease.

Tenant Complaints. Of course, keeping tenants happy is an important part of the property manager's job. Making sure that the property is kept clean and in good repair is essential, and so is responding promptly and professionally to requests and complaints.

Rent Collection. Rental property cannot be profitable unless the rents are collected when due. Careful selection of tenants in the first place is one of the most effective ways of avoiding delinquent rents. A high occupancy rate doesn't benefit the property owner unless the tenants are likely to meet their financial obligations.

The amount of the rent, the time and place of rent payment, and any penalties imposed for late payment should be clearly stated in the lease. The manager should consistently follow a collection plan that includes adequate recordkeeping and immediate notification of late payments. When all collection attempts fail, the manager must be prepared to take legal action to evict the tenant in accordance with the owner's policies.

Recordkeeping and Manager/Owner Relations

A property manager must account to the owner for all money received and disbursed. It is up to the owner to decide how frequent and detailed operating reports should be. This often depends on how involved the owner wants to be in the management of the property. For example, an owner with extensive property holdings who is also engaged in another full-time occupation may not want to be bothered with detailed, time-consuming reports. But a retired person with only one or two income-producing properties may want to be very involved in their management.

Statement of Operations. In many cases, the property manager's report to the owner takes the form of a monthly statement of operations. A statement of operations typically includes the following sections: a summary of operations, the rent roll, a statement of disbursements, and a narrative report of operations.

The **summary of operations** is a brief description of the property's income and expenses that makes it easier for the owner to evaluate the property's monthly financial performance. The summary is supported by the accompanying information in the rest of the statement of operations.

The **rent roll** is a report on rent collection. Both occupied and vacant units are listed in the rent roll, as well as the total of rental income earned, both collected and uncollected. (The combined rental values of the leased and the vacant space should equal the total rental value of the building.) The rent roll breaks down rental figures into the previous balance, current rent, total amount received, and balance due.

The information in the rent roll is obtained from the individual ledger sheets kept on each tenant and rental space. A ledger sheet typically shows the tenant's name, unit, phone number, regular rent, other recurring charges, security deposit information, move-in date, lease term, payments made, and balances owed.

Fig. 16.5 Rent roll

Rent Roll

Property _Magnolia Heights_   **Period** _April_

Owner _S.T Jones_   **Prepared by** _M. Smith_

Unit Number	Occupant	Previous Balance	Current Rent	Date Received	Other Amounts	Description	Total Received	Balance Due
101	G. Tsui	0	900	4/1			900	0
102	F. Brown	700	700	4/9			1400	0
103	K. Plane	0	700	4/2	100	Parking	800	0
104	C. Flynn	0	850	4/1			850	0
105	P. Sneed	850	850	4/15			850	850
106	L. Hurt	0	850	4/1	100	Parking	950	0
107	E. Winn	0	700	4/2			700	0

The **statement of disbursements** lists all of the expenses paid during the pertinent time period. A written order should be prepared for every purchase and payment so that an accurate account can be made of all expenditures and the purpose of each one. Disbursements are usually classified according to type, which makes analysis easier. For example, all maintenance expenses should be listed together, and so should all tax and insurance expenses, all administrative expenses, and so on.

In addition to the numerical accounts given to the owner, it is often helpful to include a **narrative report of operations** in the statement of operations. This is simply a letter explaining the information set forth in the other sections of the statement. The narrative report adds a personal touch, and it is especially important if the income was lower or the expenses were higher than expected. If there is a deviation from the normal cash flow, the owner will want a clear explanation. If the reason for a drop in cash flow is not explained, the owner may doubt the competence or integrity of the property manager.

Keeping in Touch. In addition to sending various reports and statements to the owner, the manager should contact the owner in person from time to time. A telephone call or an appointment to explain a particular proposal or problem or to ask a question is much more effective than a letter. A formal meeting is a good idea if the monthly report is especially unusual.

Maintenance

In addition to leasing, tenant relations, recordkeeping, and reporting to the owner, a property manager is responsible for the supervision of property maintenance. There are four basic categories of maintenance activities:

1. **Preventive maintenance:** This preserves the physical integrity of the premises and reduces corrective maintenance costs. (Cleaning the gutters is an example of preventive maintenance.)

2. **Corrective maintenance:** Actual repairs that keep equipment, utilities, and amenities functioning in a proper manner. (Fixing a leaking faucet is an example of corrective maintenance.)
3. **Housekeeping:** Cleaning the common areas and grounds on a regular basis (for example, vacuuming hallways and cleaning elevators).
4. **New construction:** This includes tenant alterations made at the beginning of the tenancy and when the lease is renewed, as well as cosmetic changes designed to make the building more attractive (for example, remodeling the lobby).

When managing commercial or industrial property, a property manager is often required to alter the interior of the building to meet the needs of a new tenant. These alterations can range from a simple repainting job to completely redesigning or rebuilding the space. (If the property is new construction, the interior is often left incomplete so that it can be built to fit the needs of the individual tenants.) Property managers dealing with remodeling or new construction must be aware of federal laws requiring public accommodations to be accessible to the disabled. (See the discussion of the ADA in Chapter 15.)

Property managers are not required to know how to fix the building's plumbing or electrical wiring themselves. Most maintenance activities are handled by building maintenance employees or by outside maintenance services. However, a property manager must be able to recognize the maintenance needs of the property and see that they are fulfilled.

The property manager should direct the activities of the maintenance staff or independent contractors with a schedule of inspection and maintenance. First, the manager should inventory the building's equipment and physical elements (plumbing, furnace, roof, walls, etc.). Then a schedule of regular inspections, cleaning, and repairs should be set. For instance, walls and roofs should be scheduled for periodic inspection, painting, and repairs. Elevators should be serviced on a regular basis.

Fig. 16.6 Property maintenance record

Property Maintenance Record

Property *Magnolia Heights*

Date	Action	Location	by Whom	Time	Cost
4/12	inspect elevator	lobby	Elevator Express	1.5 hr.	contract
4/22	clean roof	roof	Johnson	5 hr.	contract
4/23	fix drain	Unit 104	Top Plumbing	1 hr.	55.00

The property manager should keep accurate and up-to-date records on when the various elements were inspected, serviced, replaced, or repaired. These routine inspections and maintenance activities will help preserve the capital value of the building and prevent major repair expenses.

Landlord/Tenant Law

A property manager needs to understand the rules that govern the relationship between landlord and tenant. The landlord-tenant relationship is defined both by law and by the terms of the lease contract itself. We'll start with the requirements for a valid lease, and then consider various landlord/tenant issues that are often addressed in a lease.

Requirements for a Valid Lease

A **lease**, or rental agreement, is a contract between a property owner (the landlord) and a tenant that gives the tenant possession of the property for a period of time, in exchange for rent. The lease must meet all of the requirements for a valid contract (see Chapter 6), and it must include an accurate description of the property.

In Washington, a lease for any fixed term must be in writing and signed by the landlord. If the term is over one year, the landlord's signature must be acknowledged (notarized).

However, the rental agreement for a periodic tenancy, such as a month-to-month tenancy, need not be put into writing. (The only exception to this rule is when the rental period is more than one year.) A lease that should be in writing, but is not, creates a periodic tenancy instead of a lease for a fixed term. (See Chapter 2 for a discussion of the different types of leasehold estates.)

A lease may be valid even if the tenant doesn't sign it; the tenant's acceptance of the lease is implied by occupancy and payment of rent. Even so, to protect both parties, it's better to have both landlord and tenant sign the lease.

In many cases, the management agreement authorizes the property manager to sign leases as the landlord's agent. Without such a specific authorization, the property manager's signature will not create a valid lease.

Lease Provisions

The following issues are commonly addressed by the provisions of a lease. As you'll see, the law also has a bearing on many of these issues. Some legal rules apply only when the lease doesn't address a particular issue; others override any contradictory provisions in the lease. The legal rules are especially likely to control in residential tenancies, which are governed by Washington's Residential Landlord-Tenant Act.

Payment of Rent. The consideration that the tenant gives the landlord for the lease is the promise to pay rent. Most leases spell out when the rent is to be paid, and they usually require payment at the beginning of the rental period. If a lease does not specify when the rent is to be paid, however, it is not due until the end of the rental period.

Use of Premises. Not surprisingly, the law restricts a tenant's use of the leased property to legal uses. Many leases place additional restrictions on the use of the property; for example, a commercial lease might have a provision restricting the rented space to retail use. The restricting language must be clear. At a minimum, the lease should state that the premises are to be used only for the specified purpose and for no other. If there is no limitation in the lease, or if the language is not clearly restrictive, the tenant may use the premises for any legal purpose.

Security Deposit. Most property managers require a **security deposit** from the tenant when the tenant signs the lease, especially in residential tenancies. The deposit gives the landlord some protection against tenant default.

In Washington, a residential landlord (or the property manager) is required to put the security deposit in a trust account and give the tenant a receipt for the funds. At the end of the tenancy, the landlord must return the security deposit to the tenant within 14 days after the lease terminates, or else inform the tenant of the specific reasons why all or part of the deposit is being retained.

The landlord is allowed to keep the deposit to cover unpaid rent, to pay for cleaning the premises, or to pay for repairing any damage to the property. But no portion of the deposit may be kept on account of reasonable wear and tear. Any nonrefundable fees (such as a nonrefundable cleaning fee) must be designated "nonrefundable" in the lease.

Entry and Inspection. A lease typically provides for inspection of the leased premises by the landlord during the lease term, under specified conditions. In Washington, a residential tenant may not unreasonably refuse the landlord's legitimate requests to enter the unit to inspect it, perform repairs, provide other agreed-upon services, or show the unit to prospective buyers or tenants. Except in an emergency, the landlord must give the tenant notice before entering the unit. Two days' notice is usually required, but only one day's notice is necessary if the landlord wants to show the unit.

Option to Renew. A lease may contain a provision that gives the tenant an option to renew the lease at the end of its term. Most options require the tenant to give notice of his or her intention to exercise the option on or before a specific date.

Maintenance. The tenant must return the premises to the landlord in the same condition in which they were received, with allowances for normal wear and tear. The landlord is usually responsible for making necessary repairs to common areas, such as the stairs, hallways, or elevators.

Transferring Leasehold Estates

A landlord can sell the leased property during the term of the lease, but the buyer takes title subject to the lease. This means the buyer must honor the lease for the remainder of its term.

The tenant can also transfer his or her leasehold estate to another party, through assignment, subleasing, or novation. The tenant has the right to assign or sublease without the landlord's consent, unless the lease provides otherwise. A novation always requires the landlord's consent.

In an **assignment**, the tenant transfers the leasehold estate for the entire remainder of the lease term.

> **Example:** Landlord leases property to Tenant for a period starting January 1, 2002, and ending June 30, 2005. On July 1, 2002, Tenant transfers possession of the property to XYZ Corporation for a term starting July 1, 2002 and ending June 30, 2005. The agreement between Tenant and XYZ is an assignment because the transfer is for the balance of the unexpired term.

The assignee (the new tenant) becomes liable to the landlord for the rent, and the original tenant becomes secondarily liable for the rent. The assignee has the primary responsibility for paying the rent, but the original tenant is not fully released from the duty to pay it.

A **sublease** is a transfer of the leasehold estate for a period shorter than the unexpired term. The original tenant retains part of the leasehold.

> **Example:** Landlord leases property to Tenant for a period starting January 1, 2002 and ending June 30, 2005. On July 1, 2002, Tenant transfers possession of the property to XYZ Corporation for a period starting July 1, 2002, and ending June 30, 2004, reserving the last year for himself. This agreement is a sublease because the tenant has transferred less than the full balance of the lease term.

The sublessee (the new tenant) is liable for the rent to the original tenant, rather than to the landlord, and the original tenant is still liable to the landlord. This situation is sometimes referred to as a **sandwich lease**, since the original tenant is in the middle, sandwiched between the landlord and the sublessee.

A **novation** is an alternative to an assignment or a sublease. In a novation, a new contract is created and the old contract is extinguished. A landlord might agree to accept a new tenant in place of the original tenant, creating a new lease. The purpose of a novation is to terminate the liability of the tenant under the terms of the original lease.

Terminating a Leasehold Interest

As was discussed in Chapter 2, how a lease terminates depends on the type of tenancy in question. A month-to-month tenancy or other periodic tenancy ends when either party gives the other proper notice of termination. A lease for a fixed term terminates automatically at the end of its term, but it also may be terminated prior to the end of its term in any of the following ways.

Surrender. A landlord and a tenant may mutually agree to terminate a lease. This is known as surrender.

Breach of the Implied Covenant of Quiet Enjoyment. Every lease carries an implied covenant of quiet enjoyment, even if it is not actually stated in the lease. This covenant is the landlord's implied promise that the tenant's possession of the property will not be disturbed, either by the landlord or by a third party with a lawful claim to the property. The tenant is guaranteed exclusive possession and quiet enjoyment of his or her leasehold estate.

The covenant of quiet enjoyment is breached when the tenant is wrongfully evicted from the leased property. There are two types of eviction: actual and constructive.

Actual eviction occurs when the landlord actually expels the tenant from the property. **Constructive eviction** occurs when the landlord causes or permits a substantial interference with the tenant's possession of the property. For example, a landlord's failure to provide heat in the wintertime has been found to result in constructive eviction.

Breach of the Implied Warranty of Habitability. By law, all residential leases carry the landlord's implied guarantee that the premises meet all building and housing code regulations that affect health and safety. If the premises do not meet these criteria, then the tenant must notify the landlord of the defective condition and the landlord must correct it within a certain time period prescribed by statute. If the landlord takes legal action to evict the tenant for nonpayment of rent, the tenant can use the poor condition of the premises as a defense in court.

Failure to Pay Rent. The tenant has a duty to pay rent as required by the terms of the lease. However, if the tenant fails to pay the rent, there is not an automatic termination of the leasehold estate. The landlord is required by statute to give notice to the tenant of the nonpayment. After receiving notice, if the tenant still fails to pay, the landlord may file an **unlawful detainer action**, asking the court to evict the tenant.

If the court finds the tenant in default, it may issue a **writ of possession**, which requires the tenant to move out peaceably or be forcibly removed by the county sheriff.

Although unlawful detainer actions are given priority on the court's docket, the legal process of eviction is often slow. However, landlords and property managers should not take matters into their own hands. A landlord or manager who tries "self-help" eviction (forcing the tenant out with threats, or by cutting off the utilities) instead of the legal process may end up defending a costly lawsuit.

Illegal or Unauthorized Use. If a tenant uses the leased premises in an illegal manner (for example, in violation of the zoning code), the landlord may demand that the tenant cease the illegal activity or leave the premises. Similarly, if a tenant uses the premises in a manner that is not authorized by the lease, then the tenant has violated the lease and the landlord has the right to terminate the tenancy before the end of the term.

Destruction of the Premises. Destruction of the leased premises by a fire or other natural disaster may terminate a lease, but it doesn't necessarily. If the lease is for only a part of a building, such as an office, apartment, or commercial space, the destruction of the building frustrates the entire purpose of the lease, so the tenant will be released from his or her duty to pay the rent. On the other hand, if the lease agreement is for the use of a building and the land it rests on, the destruction of the building does not terminate the lease, because the purpose of the lease is not entirely frustrated. The tenant is not relieved from the duty to pay the rent to the end of the rental period.

Condemnation. Condemnation of property by a government entity can also result in the premature termination of a lease. (See Chapter 5 for a discussion of condemnation.)

Types of Leases

There are five major types of leases: fixed leases, graduated leases, percentage leases, net leases, and ground leases.

Sometimes called a flat, straight, or gross lease, a **fixed lease** provides for a fixed rental amount. The tenant is obligated to pay a fixed sum of money and the landlord is obligated to pay all utilities, maintenance costs, taxes, and insurance. This type of lease is most commonly found in residential apartment rentals.

A **graduated lease** is similar to a fixed lease, but it provides for periodic increases in the rent, usually set at specific future dates and often based on the Consumer Price Index or some other measure of inflation. These increases are made possible by the inclusion of an **escalation clause**. This type of lease is also called a step-up lease or an index lease.

A **net lease** requires the tenant to pay the landlord a fixed rent, plus some or all of the operating expenses. Commercial leases are often net leases.

Many retail businesses have **percentage leases**, especially in shopping centers. The rent is based on a percentage of the gross or net income from the tenant's business. Typically, the lease provides for a minimum rent plus a percentage of the tenant's business income above the stated minimum.

When a tenant leases land and agrees to construct a building on that land, it is called a **ground lease**. Ground leases are common in metropolitan areas; they are usually long-term, in order to make the construction of the building worth the tenant's while.

Chapter Summary

1. An investment is an asset that is expected to generate a return for the investor. Three basic characteristics of an investment are the liquidity, safety, and yield. The advantages of real estate investment include appreciation, leverage, and cash flow.

2. There are four main types of income-producing properties: residential, office, retail, and industrial. Property managers often specialize in one or two types.

3. A property manager must have a written management agreement with the property owner. The agreement should include all of the terms and conditions of the management arrangement, including compensation, the type of property, the manager's duties and authority, allocation of costs, and provisions for reporting to the owner.

4. Before preparing a management plan, the manager should conduct a regional analysis, a neighborhood analysis, a property analysis, and a market analysis. The information gathered during this preliminary study will help the manager set a rental schedule, prepare a budget, and plan the day-to-day operations.

5. The functions of a property manager include marketing the property, leasing, handling tenant complaints, rent collection, recordkeeping, preparing reports for the owner, and arranging for the maintenance of the property.

6. A landlord/tenant relationship is governed by the terms of the lease and by landlord/tenant law. Unless otherwise agreed in the lease, assignment and subleasing are allowed without the landlord's consent, although the original tenant will not be released from liability.

7. A lease may terminate before the end of its term as a result of surrender, breach of the implied covenant of quiet enjoyment, breach of the implied warranty of habitability, failure to pay rent, illegal or unauthorized use of the premises, or the destruction or condemnation of the property.

8. The various types of leases include the fixed lease, graduated payment lease, net lease, percentage lease, and ground lease.

O—⚿ Key Terms

Investment—An asset that is expected to generate a return (a profit).

Portfolio—The mix of investments owned by an individual or company.

Liquidity—An asset's ability to be converted into cash quickly.

Appreciation—An increase in the value of an asset; generally due either to inflation or to an increasing scarcity of or demand for the asset.

Equity—The difference between a property's value and the liens against it.

Leverage—Using borrowed money to invest in an asset. If the asset appreciates, the investor earns money on the money borrowed as well as the money invested.

Cash flow—Spendable income; the amount of money left after all of the property's expenses (operating costs, mortgage payments, and taxes) have been paid.

Property management—When someone other than the property owner supervises the property's operation.

Rental schedule—A list of the rental rates for units in a given building.

Fixed expense—A property management expense that does not vary (for example, property taxes).

Variable expense—A property management expense that varies depending on current management needs (for example, repair expenses).

Lease—A contract for possession of real estate in return for payment of rent.

Automatic renewal clause—A lease provision that ensures automatic renewal of the lease unless the tenant or the landlord gives the other party notice of termination.

Statement of operations—A periodic report showing the total money received and disbursed and the overall condition of the property during a given period.

Rent roll—A report on rent collections; a list of the total amount of rent earned, both collected and uncollected.

Statement of disbursements—A listing of all of a property's expenses incurred during a specific operating period.

Preventive maintenance—A program of regular inspection and care to prevent problems or provide for their immediate repair.

Corrective maintenance—Ongoing repairs that are made to a building and its equipment to restore it to good operating condition.

Assignment—When the original tenant transfers his or her entire remaining leasehold estate to another.

Sublease—When a tenant grants someone else the right to possess leased property for part of the remainder of the lease term.

Novation—The substitution of a new lease obligation for an old one, or a new party for the original party.

Eviction—The expulsion of someone from real property, which may be actual or constructive.

Unlawful detainer—A lawsuit filed by a landlord to evict a defaulting tenant.

Chapter Quiz

1. The main disadvantage of investing in real estate is:

   a) the use of leverage to increase returns
   b) lack of liquidity
   c) uniformly low returns
   d) a constantly increasing supply, which decreases values

2. The difference between the value of real property and the liens against it is called:

   a) equity
   b) leverage
   c) portfolio
   d) cash flow

3. When population decreases, which type of oversupply results?

   a) Technical
   b) Economic
   c) Operational
   d) Constructive

4. The property manager's main purpose must be to fulfill:

   a) his or her career goals
   b) the owner's objectives
   c) the government's affordable housing goals
   d) his or her office's cash flow goals

5. If a regional analysis shows that the typical family size is four, with two parents and two children, which of the following apartment units would be the most marketable?

   a) Studio
   b) Five-bedroom
   c) Three-bedroom
   d) It is unlikely that one type of unit would be preferred over any another

6. The type of property that ordinarily demands the most marketing is:

   a) residential
   b) office
   c) retail
   d) industrial

7. A property management agreement should always include the:

   a) manager's regional analysis
   b) manager's compensation
   c) owner's future plans for the property
   d) statement of operations

8. By completing a market analysis, a property manager discovers that the average rental rate for comparable residential units is $950. For the subject property, the property manager should set a rental rate of:

   a) $850 per unit, to undercut the competition
   b) $1,025 per unit, because tenants are not very well informed and will probably pay a higher-than-average price
   c) $950 per unit, to remain competitive
   d) None of the above; a fixed rental rate should not be set, so the property manager can maintain flexibility when renting units

9. The most expensive form of advertising is usually:

   a) television
   b) direct mail
   c) classified advertising
   d) handing out full-color brochures

10. Insurance premiums would be considered a:

    a) variable expense
    b) daily expense
    c) fixed expense
    d) pro rata expense

11. A brief description of the property's income and expenses is called a:

a) statement of operations
b) summary of operations
c) statement of disbursements
d) rent roll

12. If a property owner wants to know which tenants are behind in their rent, he or she should examine the:

a) rent schedule
b) statement of disbursements
c) narrative report of operations
d) rent roll

13. The most effective way to reduce expensive repair bills is to:

a) emphasize preventive maintenance
b) put off repairs for as long as possible
c) institute a policy of tenant-paid repairs
d) find cheap repair companies

14. Repairs that keep equipment functioning in a proper manner are called:

a) preventive maintenance
b) corrective maintenance
c) general housekeeping
d) remodeling

15. A property manager wants to begin managing a new building. All of the following should be accomplished prior to actual management of the property, except:

a) execution of a property management agreement
b) preparation of a property management proposal
c) preparation of a statement of operations
d) completion of a market analysis

👉 Answer Key

1. b) The lack of liquidity is the main disadvantage of investing in real estate.

2. a) The difference between the value of real estate and the liens against it is the owner's equity.

3. a) A technical oversupply occurs when there are not enough potential tenants for the supply of a certain type of property.

4. b) A property manager must try to achieve the property owner's objectives.

5. c) The typical family would be more likely to rent a three-bedroom unit than either a studio or a five-bedroom apartment.

6. a) Because residential lease terms are relatively short, managing residential property tends to involve more marketing than managing other types of property.

7. b) A property management agreement should always include a provision that describes the manager's compensation.

8. c) Rental rates should not be much lower or much higher than the rates for competitive properties.

9. a) Television is usually the most expensive form of advertising. Property managers do not use it as often as other forms of advertising.

10. c) Fixed expenses remain the same, regardless of rental income. Insurance premiums are fixed expenses.

11. b) A summary of operations is a brief summary of the detailed information in the other sections of the statement of operations.

12. d) A rent roll is a report on the collection of rent.

13. a) Preventive maintenance preserves the physical integrity of the property and reduces the need for corrective maintenance.

14. b) Repairs are classified as corrective maintenance.

15. c) A property manager cannot perform any management functions until he or she has a written management agreement. The market analysis and the management proposal should also be completed before the manager begins managing the property.

Washington Real Estate License Law

Chapter Overview

Every state licenses real estate agents and regulates their activities. Real estate license laws are based on the police power—the government's power to regulate for the protection of the public welfare—and their purpose is to protect real estate buyers and sellers. This chapter first explains who administers Washington's license law, when a real estate license is required, and the qualifications for licensure. It then explains how the license law regulates the business practices of real estate professionals, controlling how brokers form agency relationships, how they run their offices, how they supervise their sales agents, and how they handle client funds. The final section of the chapter discusses how antitrust laws affect real estate agents.

Administration of the License Law

The Washington State Department of Licensing is responsible for administration of the real estate license law. The Director of the Department of Licensing is in charge of all of the divisions within the department, including the Real Estate Division. The Director and all Real Estate Division staff are employees of the State of Washington. They are not allowed to own any interest in a real estate firm.

The Director

The Director of the Department of Licensing is appointed by the Governor. The Director is charged with enforcing all laws, rules, and regulations relating to the licensing of real estate brokers and salespersons. He or she has the authority to grant or deny licenses, and to hold disciplinary hearings and impose penalties for violations of the license law. And with the advice and approval of the Real Estate Commission, the Director also issues rules and regulations to govern the activities and practices of real estate licensees.

In fact, the term "real estate license law" is commonly used to refer not only to the statutory provisions adopted by the state legislature, but to the regulations issued by the Director as well. All real estate licensees are required to obtain a copy of the Director's regulations (available from the Department of Licensing) and to keep informed of changes in the regulations.

The Real Estate Commission

The Real Estate Commission is made up of the Director and six commissioners. The commissioners are appointed by the Governor to advise the Director on the real estate industry and profession.

The commissioners are generally required to have at least five years of real estate experience; they are usually real estate brokers. Each commissioner serves on a part-time basis for a six-year term. The commissioners are paid a per diem stipend, plus travel expenses, for the days they spend holding public hearings, meeting with the Director, and conducting other Commission business.

The Commission prepares and conducts the real estate license examinations. It is also authorized to hold educational conferences for the benefit of the real estate industry. The Commission has created a Real Estate Research Center to study statewide real estate concerns such as affordable housing. The Real Estate Research Center is funded through a surcharge imposed on real estate license renewals.

The Attorney General

The state Attorney General is the Director's legal advisor on matters relating to the license law. The Attorney General also acts as the attorney for the Director in any legal proceedings involving the Real Estate Division.

Real Estate Licenses

By requiring real estate agents to be licensed, the state ensures that they have at least a minimum level of competence in handling real estate transactions. The license also serves as a tool for enforcement of real estate regulations; if an agent fails to comply with the law, his or her license can be suspended or taken away altogether.

When a License is Required

It is unlawful to act as a real estate broker or salesperson without first obtaining the appropriate license.

The license law defines a real estate **broker** as follows:

"Real estate broker," or "broker," means a person, while acting for another for commissions or other compensation or the promise thereof, or a licensee...while acting in his or her own behalf, who:

a) Sells or offers for sale, lists or offers to list, buys or offers to buy real estate or business opportunities, or any interest therein, for others;

b) Negotiates or offers to negotiate, either directly or indirectly, the purchase, sale, exchange, lease, or rental of real estate or business opportunities, or any interest therein, for others;

c) Negotiates or offers to negotiate, either directly or indirectly, the purchase, sale, or exchange of a manufactured or mobile home in conjunction with the purchase, sale, exchange, rental, or lease of the land on which the manufactured or mobile home is or will be located;

d) Advertises or holds himself or herself out to the public by any oral or printed solicitation or representation that he or she is so engaged; or

e) Engages, directs, or assists in procuring prospects or in negotiating or closing any transaction which results in or is calculated to result in any of these acts.

Under the law, a real estate **salesperson** is someone who is employed by or represents a real estate broker in the performance of any of the activities listed in the definition of broker given above.

The main thrust of this definition is that it applies to anyone engaged in any of the listed activities: 1) on behalf of another person, and 2) for compensation. However, the law states that the definition also applies to "a licensee...while acting in his or her own behalf." Thus, real estate agents are required to comply with the license law even when they are buying, selling, or leasing property for themselves, not just when they are representing others.

Note that the definition of broker covers business opportunities as well as real estate. Someone who represents another in the purchase, sale, exchange, or lease of a business, a business opportunity, or the goodwill of a business is required to have a real estate license if the transaction involves real estate.

Also note that the definition of a broker may include a person who sells a manufactured home before it is attached to real property.

Exemptions from Licensing Requirements

The following people are exempt from the real estate licensing requirement. They are not required to have a license, even when their activities fall within the definition of broker or salesperson.

1. Anyone buying or leasing property for him or herself, or on behalf of a group to which he or she belongs, or disposing of property he or she owns or co-owns.
2. An authorized attorney in fact acting without compensation.
3. An attorney at law, in the performance of his or her duties.
4. A receiver, trustee in bankruptcy, executor, administrator, or guardian, when acting in that capacity, or any person acting under court order, or a trustee selling under a deed of trust.
5. A secretary, bookkeeper, accountant, or other office personnel performing purely clerical duties.
6. The owner of a rental property, or a member of the owner's family, engaged in transactions relating to that property.
7. The resident manager of a residential apartment complex, in the performance of his or her duties related to that property.
8. Anyone who manages residential property (whether or not he or she lives on the property) on an incidental basis and not as his or her principal source of income, as long as he or she does not advertise or hold him or herself out as a property manager.
9. The owner or manager of a rental self-storage facility, when renting units in the facility.

As we said, the license law defines a broker as someone who acts on behalf of another and for compensation. Thus, someone who acts on his or her own behalf in a real estate transaction is exempt from the licensing requirement; this is the first exemption on the list above.

> **Example:** Matilda Thorn owns several pieces of property: three single-family homes, a duplex, an apartment building, and two vacant lots. If she decides to sell one of these properties, she can do so without having to obtain a real estate license.

In addition, someone acting on behalf of another but *without compensation* is also exempt; this is the second exemption on the list, the one for an authorized attorney in fact. An **attorney in fact** is not necessarily a lawyer—it is anyone a principal appoints to act as his or her agent in a power of attorney. As long as the attorney in fact is not compensated for services rendered, he or she is allowed to engage in the activities of a real estate broker without a license.

Example: Suppose Matilda from the previous example is old and unwell. She gives her niece, Trudy, a power of attorney that is duly recorded. The power of attorney authorizes Trudy to sell Matilda's property for her. As long as Trudy is acting without compensation, she doesn't need a real estate license to sell the property.

Out-of-State Licensees. A real estate broker licensed in another state may handle transactions concerning commercial real estate in Washington without obtaining a Washington license. However, the out-of-state broker must have a written agreement with and work in cooperation with a broker who is licensed in Washington. The Washington broker's name must be included on all advertising, and the Washington broker must have custody of the records for the out-of-state broker's Washington transactions. For the purposes of this rule, commercial real estate is any property other than residential property with up to four dwelling units.

A real estate salesperson licensed in another state can handle commercial real estate transactions here without a Washington license, as long as he or she is affiliated with an out-of-state broker who is working in cooperation with a Washington broker, as described above.

Types of Licenses

There are three basic types of real estate licenses in Washington: broker, associate broker, and salesperson.

Broker. A broker's license may be issued to an individual, or to a business entity such as a corporation or a partnership. The license authorizes the broker to operate a brokerage business and represent clients in real estate transactions.

A broker is also authorized to employ associate brokers and salespersons. Associate brokers and salespersons are sometimes referred to in the license law as their broker's **affiliated licensees**. The law defines affiliated licensees as "the natural persons licensed as salespersons, associate brokers, and/or branch managers employed by a real estate broker and who are licensed to represent a broker in the performance of any of the acts" for which a real estate license is required.

Only a broker may be paid a commission or other compensation by clients or by other brokers. Associate brokers and salespersons may only be paid by or through their own broker.

Fig. 17.1 Types of licensees

Real Estate Broker	
• Individual or business entity • Authorized to operate a brokerage and represent clients	
Affiliated Licensees	
Associate Broker	**Salesperson**
• Works for and represents broker • May manage a branch office	• Works for and represents broker • Can't manage a branch office

The Director may issue a **temporary broker's permit** to the senior qualified salesperson or another qualified representative in the event of the death or incapacitation of a broker. The permit can be valid for no more than four months.

Associate Broker. An associate broker's license may be issued to an individual or to a one-person corporation. The licensee is authorized to work with and represent his or her broker, and to manage a branch office of the brokerage.

An associate broker has satisfied all of the requirements for a broker's license (see below). So if he or she chooses to do so, the associate broker can terminate affiliation with the broker, have his or her license reissued as a broker's license, and operate a brokerage on his or her own.

Salesperson. A salesperson's license may only be issued to an individual. The license authorizes the salesperson to work with and represent his or her broker. A salesperson is not authorized to manage a branch office.

Business Entities. As mentioned above, a broker's license may be issued to a business entity. This may be a corporation, a partnership, a limited liability company, or a limited partnership. The license names the firm as the broker and one member of the firm, such as a corporate officer or a general partner, as its **designated broker**. The designated broker, who is authorized to act as a broker on behalf of the business, must satisfy all of the ordinary requirements for a broker's license. (The firm and the designated broker are only required to pay a single license fee, however.) All other members of the firm who act as brokers or salespersons for the firm must be individually licensed.

Licensing Qualifications and Applications

Applicants for real estate licenses must satisfy specified age and educational requirements and pass an examination. In addition, applicants for a broker's license are required to satisfy experience requirements. All education and experience requirements must be met before applying for the exam.

Broker and Salesperson Qualifications. The qualifications for the broker's license and the salesperson's license are as follows.

Broker. The qualifications required for a broker's license and for an associate broker's license are the same. The applicant must:

1. be at least 18 years old;
2. have a high school diploma or the equivalent;
3. have at least two years of experience within the last five years as a full-time real estate salesperson in this state or another state with similar licensing requirements;
4. have successfully completed 120 clock hours of approved real estate education courses within the previous five years, including one 30-hour course in real estate law, one 30-hour course in brokerage management, and one 30-hour course in business management; and
5. pass the broker's examination.

An applicant may satisfy the experience requirement (number 3 above) by showing either that he or she was engaged in licensed real estate activities for a minimum of 40 hours per week for two years, or that licensed real estate activities were a major source of income, continuously, during the two-year period.

An applicant who lacks two years' experience as a salesperson may be allowed to take the broker's exam if the Director of the Department of Licensing determines that the applicant has other education or experience that is a satisfactory substitute. Examples of experience that may qualify include:

- post-secondary education with an emphasis on real estate studies, together with one year of experience as a real estate salesperson or one year of experience from the other professional activities below;
- at least one year of experience as an attorney specializing in real estate transactions;
- five years' experience in closing real estate transactions for escrow companies or mortgage companies;
- five years' experience as an officer of a commercial bank, savings and loan association, title company, or mortgage company, involving all phases of a real estate transaction;
- five years' experience as a real estate appraiser;
- five years' experience in all phases of land development, construction, financing, selling and leasing residential or commercial buildings; or
- five years' experience in real estate investment, property management, or investment analysis.

If a broker applicant receives a waiver from the experience requirement but fails the license exam, the waiver is forfeited. The broker applicant must satisfy the experience requirement before retaking the exam.

The 120 clock hours of approved courses required for the broker's license (number 4 on the list above) are in addition to any courses the Department required the applicant to take for other reasons. For example, if the applicant had to take a 30-hour course to fulfill the continuing education requirement and to renew his or her salesperson's license, those 30 hours cannot be counted as part of the 120 hours required for the broker's license.

The Director may waive the 120 clock-hour requirement if the Director feels that the applicant has completed the equivalent educational course work in any institution of higher learning or degree-granting institution.

Salesperson. An applicant for a salesperson's license must:

1. be at least 18 years old;
2. have successfully completed a 60 clock-hour course in real estate fundamentals; and
3. pass the salesperson's examination.

The Director may waive the 60 clock-hour requirement if the Director feels that the applicant has completed the equivalent educational course work in any institution of higher learning or degree-granting institution.

Note that a high school diploma isn't required for a salesperson's license.

Real Estate Examination. The license law and regulations set forth the requirements for applying for and passing the real estate examination.

Exam Reservations. A person who fulfills the age, education, and experience requirements may make a reservation to take the examination. All examinations are by reservation only; there are no walk-in examinations. A reservation must be made at least three days in advance of the desired test date. Salesperson candidates must bring a candidate examination document, stamped and signed by the real estate school representative indicating completion of the required prelicense clock hours. Broker candidates must have their candidate examination document signed and stamped by the Department of Licensing.

If an applicant does not show up for the exam, he or she forfeits the exam fee. Anyone who fails either the salesperson's exam or the broker's exam may retake it (more than once, if necessary), but he or she must reapply and pay the fee again.

License applicants who have questions about the examination should contact the Department of Licensing for more information about the license application process.

Scope of the Examination. The real estate exam tests each applicant for:

- appropriate knowledge of the English language and arithmetic;
- an understanding of the principles of real estate conveyancing and the general purposes and legal effect of deeds, mortgages, land contracts, exchanges, rental and option agreements, and leases;
- an understanding of the principles of land economics and appraisal;
- an understanding of the obligations between principal and agent;
- an understanding of the principles of real estate practice and the canons of business ethics; and
- an understanding of real estate license laws.

The real estate examination consists of two portions:

1. a national portion consisting of questions that test knowledge of general real estate brokerage practices, and
2. a state portion consisting of questions that test knowledge of Washington license laws and regulations.

The state portion of the broker's exam also includes a section on the settlement process.

To pass the exam, a real estate salesperson must get a score of at least 70% on each portion of the exam. A broker must get a score of at least 75% on each portion of the exam. When an applicant passes one portion of the exam but fails the other, the passing score is valid for six months. If the applicant retakes and passes the other portion of the exam within that six-month period, he or she can then apply for a license.

Licensees from Other Jurisdictions. A license applicant who is actively licensed in the same or greater capacity in another jurisdiction is automatically

Fig. 17.2 Topics on the real estate exam

The Real Estate Exam

- Real estate conveyancing:
  - deeds
  - mortgages
  - land contracts
  - exchanges
  - rental and option agreements
  - leases
- Land economics and appraisal
- Agency law
- Real estate practices and business ethics
- Real estate license laws

Other basic requirements: English language; arithmetic

eligible to take the Washington state portion of the exam. The applicant must submit an exam application to the Department along with evidence of licensure in another jurisdiction. Once the evidence of licensure has been verified by the Department, the applicant may take the exam. The additional requirements for licensure (education, experience, and passage of the national portion of the exam) are waived.

Obtaining a License. After taking the exam, the next step is obtaining the real estate license.

Application for License. After passing the exam, it's necessary to apply for the license itself. Examination results are only valid for one year. If someone passes the exam, but does not become licensed within one year after the exam date, he or she will be required to pass the exam again before a license can be issued.

An application for a salesperson's or associate broker's license must be signed by the broker or designated broker that the applicant is going to work for. The license will be issued to that broker.

Anyone who has been convicted of a crime within ten years before applying for a license must submit fingerprint identification on a form provided by the Department.

Interim License. An applicant for a salesperson's license who has been notified that he or she passed the exam may begin working on the date he or she mails or hand delivers the signed, dated, and completed application form and license fee to the Department. The completed form serves as an interim license for up to 45 days after the postmark or hand delivery date.

There are no interim licenses for broker's or associate broker's license applicants.

License Expiration and Renewal

An individual's initial real estate license expires on his or her second birthday following issuance of the license. The licensee must apply for renewal and pay a renewal fee. Thereafter, the license must be renewed **every two years** on or before the licensee's birthday. If the renewal application is late, the licensee must pay a penalty (in addition to the renewal fee).

Licenses issued to corporations, partnerships, and other business entities also must be renewed every two years. The renewal date for this type of license is the date on which the license was issued. A single renewal fee covers the firm and the designated broker.

Continuing Education Requirement. To renew their licenses, all brokers and salespersons must submit proof that they have successfully completed a total of **30 clock hours** of approved continuing education courses.

Beginning June 1, 2004, licensees must also complete a three-hour **core curriculum course** as part of their 30 hours. The core curriculum course presents practical information on contemporary real estate issues. The three core curriculum hours may be taken as an independent course, or they may be incorporated into a longer course.

A licensee can use a course to fulfill the continuing education requirement only if he or she began the course after issuance of his or her initial license. The licensee must have completed at least 15 of the 30 clock hours (including the three core curriculum hours) within 24 months before the renewal date. The remaining 15 hours can be completed up to 36 months before the renewal date. If the licensee exceeds the 30-hour requirement, up to 15 hours can be carried forward for credit in the next two-year renewal period.

A course the licensee used to fulfill pre-license requirements for either a salesperson's or a broker's license, or to fulfill the requirements for reinstatement (see below), cannot also be used for the continuing education requirement.

Fig. 17.3 Education requirements for renewal

License Renewal (every two years)

First renewal for salesperson:
- 30 clock-hour course in real estate practices, and
- 30 clock hours of continuing education

Subsequent renewals:
- 30 clock hours of continuing education

Salesperson's First Renewal. When renewing for the first time, a salesperson must submit proof of completion of an approved 30 clock-hour course in real estate practices, in addition to the 30 hours of continuing education courses described above.

Cancellation and Reinstatement. If a license isn't renewed within one year after it expires, the license is canceled. A license can be reinstated within two years after cancellation if the licensee:

- successfully completes 60 clock hours of approved real estate courses (including a 30-hour real estate law course) within one year before applying for reinstatement;
- pays all back renewal fees, plus penalties; and
- pays a reinstatement penalty.

Alternatively, the license will be reinstated if the licensee follows the procedures and satisfies the qualifications for initial licensure. That will mean passing the license exam again. And if more than five years have elapsed since the licensee took the real estate courses required for licensure, he or she will have to take them over again before retaking the exam. (In some cases, starting over in this way would be less expensive than paying the back fees and penalties.)

If it has been more than two years since the license was canceled, the former licensee cannot be reinstated unless he or she satisfies the qualifications for initial licensure again.

Inactive Licenses. An inactive license is a license that has been turned over to the Director temporarily. (This may occur for a variety of reasons; some of these reasons are discussed later in this chapter.) The holder of an inactive license is generally deemed to be unlicensed. He or she is not permitted to engage in activities requiring a license, but is still subject to disciplinary action for violations of the license law.

Although an inactive license must be renewed on its renewal date, the holder is usually not required to comply with the continuing education requirement for renewal. (A licensee is not allowed to use inactive status simply as a means of avoiding the continuing education requirement, however.) Failure to renew an inactive license results in cancellation, just as with an active license.

To reactivate a license that has been inactive for more than three years, the holder must complete a 30 clock-hour real estate course. A salesperson may use the 30-hour real estate practices course to both activate an inactive license and satisfy the requirements for first renewal of an active license.

A licensee may not reactivate an inactive license if proceedings to suspend or revoke his or her license have begun.

Change in Mailing Address or Name. While licensed—whether the license is active or inactive—a broker or salesperson is required to notify the Director if his or her mailing address changes. The Director should also be notified of a name change. For example, if a licensee marries and takes her husband's last name, she should notify the Director of her new name. (It isn't necessary to give notice of a change in marital status if there is no name change, however.)

License Fees. Fees collected for licensing (application fees, renewal fees, etc.) are placed in the Real Estate Education Account in the state treasury.

Regulation of Business Practices

Many provisions of the license law, as well as other state and federal laws, govern the day-to-day business practices of brokers and salespersons. There are rules concerning:
- the relationship between licensees and their clients and customers;
- the relationship between a broker and his or her affiliated licensees;
- broker's offices, trust accounts, and business records; and
- how real estate transactions are handled.

Agency Relationships

One of a licensee's most important responsibilities is to comply with Washington's real estate agency law. This law determines when and how an agency relationship is formed, the licensee's duties to clients and customers, when an agency relationship terminates, and liability for harm caused while acting as an agent. (For a more detailed discussion of the agency law, see Chapter 7.)

Creating Agency Relationships. The agency law describes how agency relationships are created. A seller's agent forms an agency relationship with his or her client when a listing agreement is signed. A buyer's agent enters into an agency relationship as soon as he or she performs any real estate brokerage services for a buyer, unless there is a written agreement to the contrary. If the seller's agent and the buyer's agent in a transaction are employed by the same broker, that broker is a dual agent. A dual agency arrangement is unlawful without the written consent of both parties.

Agency relationships are not affected by the payment of compensation. For instance, a buyer's agent may receive compensation from the seller without breaching any duty to the buyer.

Duties Owed by Licensee. Washington's agency law sets forth the duties a licensee owes to any party, and the special duties a licensee owes to a party he or she represents.

Duties Owed to Any Party. Any licensee owes a number of duties to any party when rendering real estate brokerage services, whether the licensee is acting as a buyer's agent, seller's agent, dual agent, or non-agent. The licensee must:

- exercise reasonable skill and care;
- deal honestly and in good faith;
- present all written communications to and from either party in a timely manner;
- disclose all material facts known by the licensee and not readily apparent to a party;
- account in a timely manner for money or property received from or on behalf of either party;
- provide a pamphlet on real estate agency law to all parties; and
- disclose in writing to all parties to whom the licensee renders services whether the licensee represents the buyer, seller, both, or neither.

The agency disclosure must be made before the party signs an offer in a transaction handled by the licensee. It must be either a separate paragraph entitled "Agency Disclosure" in the purchase and sale agreement, or a separate document entitled "Agency Disclosure."

An agent does not owe anyone the duty of independent inspection of the property, independent investigation of either party's financial condition, or independent verification of the accuracy of any statement reasonably believed to be reliable.

Duties Owed to a Principal. In addition to the duties owed to any party, a licensee owes certain duties only to the party he or she represents. The licensee must:

- be loyal to the client, by taking no action that is detrimental to the client's interest;
- disclose any conflicts of interest;
- advise the client to seek expert advice on matters outside the agent's knowledge;
- refrain from disclosing confidential information from or about the client; and
- make a good faith and continuous effort to complete the transaction.

Duties Owed by a Dual Agent. A dual agent owes the duties just listed to both clients, with one key exception. Since a dual agent cannot be completely loyal to both parties, he or she must instead refrain from taking action that is detrimental to either party's interest in the transaction. A dual agent owes the duty of good faith and continuous effort in both finding a buyer for the seller's property and finding a property for the buyer.

Terminating Agency Relationships. All of the duties owed by the licensee continue until the agency relationship terminates. This occurs upon:

- full performance by the licensee,
- expiration of the agreed-upon term,
- termination by mutual agreement, or
- termination by unilateral action.

The duties of confidentiality and accounting, however, do not expire upon the termination of the agency relationship.

Vicarious Liability. Under Washington's real estate agency law, a principal is not liable for harm caused by any act or omission of an agent or subagent. The two exceptions are: 1) when the principal participated in or authorized the wrongful act, or 2) when the principal benefited from the act and a court determines that the claimant could not enforce a judgment against the agent.

Imputed Knowledge. A principal is not held to have notice of any facts known by an agent or subagent that are not actually known by the principal, unless the principal and agent have agreed otherwise in writing. For instance, suppose a property was due to be condemned to build a new freeway on-ramp. The seller did not know about the likely condemnation, but the listing agent did and kept silent about it. If the buyer sued, the seller would not be found liable for the buyer's financial losses caused by the condemnation, although the listing agent might be.

Broker's Supervisory Responsibilities

A broker is responsible for the proper supervision of all of his or her affiliated licensees (salespersons, associate brokers, and branch managers), whether they are independent contractors or employees. For branch offices, both the branch office manager and the broker are responsible for associate brokers and salespersons working at the branch.

A **fee broker** is a licensed broker who does not own or manage a brokerage, but allows another person to operate a brokerage using his or her name and license, usually for a fee. This arrangement is a violation of the license law, even if the broker does not receive any compensation. A broker must actively manage and supervise the brokerage, and he or she cannot avoid those responsibilities through any contract, agreement, or understanding with another person.

Liability for Violations of Affiliated Licensees. A broker who fails to supervise his or her salespersons and associate brokers properly may be held responsible for their actions. If an affiliated licensee violates the license law, in addition to other possible consequences for the broker, the Director may suspend or revoke the broker's license.

However, the license law provides that the broker will not be held responsible for inadequate supervision if:

1. the affiliated licensee's violation contravened the supervising broker's specific written policies or instructions;
2. the broker had established reasonable procedures to verify that there was adequate supervision;
3. the broker attempted to mitigate any damage caused by the violation as soon as he or she learned of it;
4. the broker did not participate in or ratify the affiliated licensee's conduct; and
5. the broker did not try to avoid learning of the violation.

A broker whose procedures and conduct met all of these requirements would not be subject to disciplinary action by the Director. However, if the affiliated licensee's actions caused harm to a client or customer, the broker could still be sued by the injured party (see Chapter 7).

Affiliations and Termination

A licensed salesperson or associate broker must be affiliated with a broker in order for his or her license to be active. A salesperson or associate broker is not allowed to engage in real estate activities except under the supervision of and as a representative of a broker. The broker has custody of the licenses of his or her affiliated licensees.

The relationship between a broker and an affiliated licensee may be terminated at any time by either party. When an affiliation is terminated, the broker must notify the Director and surrender the salesperson's or associate broker's license without delay. (It is not necessary to notify the Real Estate Commission of the termination.)

To give notice of termination, the broker signs the license and mails or hand delivers it to the Department of Licensing, or the affiliated licensee surrenders the license him or herself. The termination date is the postmark date or the date the license is hand-delivered to the Department. The license is inactive until the salesperson or associate broker has found a new broker to work for and a new license is issued.

The broker has an absolute duty to surrender the license, so that the salesperson or associate broker can go to work for someone else. Failure to surrender a license promptly is grounds for disciplinary action against the broker. The broker cannot place any conditions on its surrender. For example, if a terminated salesperson owes the broker money, the broker can't refuse to surrender the license unless the money is repaid. If the broker places conditions on surrender of the license, the salesperson or associate broker should notify the Department of Licensing in writing. The Department will process the license transfer, and the broker's conduct will be investigated.

If the license has been lost, the broker and the salesperson or associate broker must submit an affidavit of lost license on a form provided by the Department.

When a salesperson or associate broker has been terminated because of conduct that would be grounds for disciplinary action under the license law, the broker must send the Director a written statement of the facts surrounding the termination.

The Broker's Office

A broker licensed in Washington is required to maintain an office in this state. The office must be open to the public and clearly identified by a sign (visible to the public) that includes the broker's name as it appears on his or her license.

The broker's license must be prominently displayed at the office, along with the licenses of all of the broker's affiliated licensees. If the broker has more than one office, his or her license is displayed in the main office, and the licenses of affiliated licensees are displayed in the office where they work (which should be the address shown on the license).

If the location of a broker's office changes, the broker must promptly submit a change of address application to the Director, return all licenses (the broker's and those of any affiliated licensees), and pay a fee. The Department will issue licenses for the new address.

Two Businesses in the Same Office. It is not unusual for a broker to be involved in other business activities that are related to, or at least not in conflict with, real estate brokerage. For example, in many areas it is common for real estate brokers to also act as property managers. A broker is allowed to operate two businesses out of the same office if:

- the other business is compatible with real estate brokerage activity; and,
- the brokerage business is carried out separate and apart from other business activities, with its records kept completely separate.

Brokerages Sharing an Office. Two or more separate brokerage businesses may share an office with a single entrance and mailing address, as long as the public is not deceived as to the separate identities of the brokerages. The brokerages must be physically separated inside the office facility, and each must be clearly identified by a sign visible to the public.

Branch Offices. There is no limit on the number of branch offices a broker can have, but every branch office must be licensed. Every branch office is also required to have a branch manager, who must be an associate broker.

A broker may establish branch offices under the same name as the main office or, with the permission of the Director, under different names. (One broker is not allowed to have branch offices under more than three names, however.) A branch office's sign must identify it as a branch of the main office, stating the names of both offices. The names of both the branch office and the main office must also appear in the firm's letterhead and advertisements.

A separate license is not required for a branch office where sales activity concerns only a particular subdivision or tract. This applies only if the subdivision is within 35 miles of a licensed office.

Dual State Brokers. Brokers who are actively licensed in another state as well as in Washington and have a full-time office in that other state are not required to have their own office here. However, they must maintain a trust account in a Washington depository and keep records of their Washington transactions at a registered location in this state.

The broker must notify the Department of Licensing of the location of the records and allow representatives of the Department access to them. The broker is also required to give the parties involved in a transaction access to the records. The broker's license should be displayed at the same place that the records are kept.

Advertising

Advertising by real estate licensees must be truthful and not misleading, and it must include the broker's name as licensed. An ad without the broker's name, which is called a **blind ad**, violates the license law. There is one exception to this rule: if a licensee is advertising his or her own property for sale or lease, the broker's name does not have to appear in the ad. The ad must disclose that the seller or landlord holds a real estate license, however.

The requirement to use the broker's name applies to franchise advertising. A broker using the name of a franchise service (such as a national brokerage organization) must include his or her own name as it appears on the Washington license on all signs and in all advertisements, in addition to the franchise name.

With the Director's written consent, a broker, associate broker, or salesperson can do business under a name other than the name on his or her license, as long as there is no intent to mislead or defraud the public. A broker may not use a name that is deceptively similar to that of another licensee, nor one that creates the impression that the firm is a nonprofit organization, a research organization, or a public group.

Advertising and the Internet. The Real Estate Commission has adopted guidelines to help licensees use the Internet to increase their sales while avoiding violations of advertising rules and regulations.

According to these guidelines, a licensee should be careful to fully disclose his or her licensed status in all Internet communications. To meet the requirement for full disclosure, a licensee should disclose:

- the licensee's name, the name of the firm with which the licensee is affiliated, the city and state in which the licensee's office is located, and the states in which the licensee holds a real estate license; and
- the firm's name as registered with the Department of Licensing, the city and state in which the firm is located, and the states in which the firm is licensed.

The guidelines include suggestions on how to meet the requirement of full disclosure for each of the following types of Internet communications:

- **Website:** Each viewable page should include or link to (via a single click) a full disclosure.
- **Email, newsgroups, discussion lists, bulletin boards:** Each should include a full disclosure at the beginning or end of each message, except when the licensee is communicating with a member of the public and the licensee's initial communication contained a full disclosure.
- **Instant messages:** Full disclosure is not necessary in this format if the licensee provided full disclosure in another format before providing or offering to provide real estate services.
- **Chat:** Full disclosure should be given before providing or offering to provide real estate services during the chat session, or it should appear in text visible on the same web page that contains the chat session if the licensee controls the website hosting the chat session.
- **Banner ads:** Each ad should link to (via a single click) a website that has a full disclosure, unless the banner ad itself has a full disclosure.

The Commission's guidelines also offer the following advice on prospecting over the Internet:

- If listings are maintained on a website, they should be removed in a timely manner when they have expired.
- If a licensee submits listing information to a third-party site, he or she should provide written communication of any change of listing status to the publisher in a timely manner.
- Licensees should not advertise the listings of other licensees without their written permission. If permission is given, licensees should not alter the online display or any informational part of the listing without the written permission of the listing broker.

- Metatags are descriptive words hidden in a website's code that search engines use to index the website. Occasionally, a website owner will insert the name of his or her competitor into the metatags, so that when a potential customer searches for the competitor's site, the owner's site will also come up as a match. Licensees should avoid this practice, as courts have ruled that it may constitute trademark infringement.
- Licensees should periodically review the advertising and marketing information on their website to make sure that it is current and not misleading.

Trust Accounts

Every broker must maintain one or more trust accounts (also called escrow accounts) for funds held on behalf of clients and customers. The accounts must be in a recognized financial institution in Washington State. Trust accounts must be separate from the broker's general business and personal accounts, so that trust funds will not be commingled with the broker's own money. The trust accounts should be opened in the name of the broker as licensed, and specifically designated as trust accounts.

All funds the broker is given to hold until a transaction closes (such as earnest money) or until paid to a client (such as rents collected) must be deposited in a trust account no later than the **first banking day after receipt**, unless otherwise specified in the license law. For the purposes of this rule, Saturday is not considered a banking day.

Interest-Bearing Accounts. With the exception of property management trust accounts, brokers' trust accounts are required to be interest-bearing accounts that allow the broker to make withdrawals without delay (other than any minimum notice period required by banking regulations).

The broker is required to put all deposits of **$10,000 or less** into a pooled account. (The license law refers to deposits of $10,000 or less as "nominal deposits.") The interest that accrues on this account, after deducting reasonable bank charges, must be paid to the state Treasurer. It will be divided between the Washington Housing Trust Fund (which will receive 75%) and the Real Estate Education Account (25%).

For deposits **over $10,000**, the client or customer who is turning the funds over to the broker has a choice. With the

Fig. 17.4 Rules for handling trust funds

Trust Accounts

- Trust funds must be deposited by the first banking day after receipt
- Accounts must be interest-bearing
- Deposits of $10,000 or less:
  - must be placed in pooled account
  - interest is paid to State
- Deposits over $10,000:
  Customer or client chooses to put funds in:
  - pooled account with interest paid to State, or
  - separate account with interest paid to customer or client

written consent of the parties, the funds can be deposited in the pooled account, in which case the interest will be paid to the state. Or the broker can establish a separate trust account for the deposit, with the interest to be paid to the client or customer to whom the funds belong. The broker must inform the client or customer of these alternatives in writing.

Property Management Trust Accounts. The rules just outlined do not apply to trust funds that a broker handles in property management transactions (such as rents or tenant security deposits). Property management trust accounts don't have to be interest-bearing accounts, and property management trust funds do not have to be placed in the broker's pooled account. A property management account can be interest-bearing, however, if the broker's written management agreement with the property owner provides for that, and if the broker follows certain special rules in the license law. If any commissions or property management fees are to be paid out of the trust account directly to the broker, they must be removed from the trust account at least once a month.

Trust Account Procedures. The broker must establish a system of records and procedures that provides an audit trail for all funds received and disbursed, identified to each client. The broker can either follow the procedures set forth in the Director's regulations, or submit an alternative system to the Department for approval. The system can be either manual or computerized.

Only trust funds may be maintained in the trust account. No funds belonging to the broker should be in the account—not even money to open the account, pay bank charges, or maintain a minimum balance to keep the account open. If a client or customer has assigned the interest on a trust account to the broker (in writing), the broker must make arrangements with the financial institution to credit the interest to his or her general account.

Trust Account Disbursements. As a general rule, a broker may not make any disbursements from a trust account before closing, or before a condition in the purchase and sale agreement has been fulfilled. There are three important exceptions to that rule, however. The broker may disburse funds:

1. with the written consent of all parties to the transaction;
2. when the transaction fails to close, if the purchase and sale agreement provides for disbursement without a written release in case of failure to close; or
3. to the closing agent named in the agreement far enough in advance so that the checks will clear by the closing date.

A broker may not pay his or her own business expenses directly out of a trust account. If the client owes the broker money, the funds must first be transferred from the trust account to the broker's general business account before the broker can use them for business expenses.

Commissions Paid from Trust Accounts. Commissions payable to the broker and to other cooperating brokers may be paid directly from the trust account. The broker must draw a separate check for each commission after the transaction closes.

Commissions the broker owes to his or her affiliated licensees *may not be paid* directly out of the trust account. These commissions are handled the same way as the broker's business expenses. Funds must first be transferred to the broker's general business account, and then the broker can pay the associate brokers or salespersons with checks drawn on that account.

Records

The license law requires real estate brokers to keep adequate records of the transactions they handle for at least **three years** after closing. (It's wise to keep records for even longer than this minimum requirement, since the statute of limitations for some claims against a broker may not run out for several more years.)

Although a broker may delegate recordkeeping duties to someone else, the broker is still responsible for the custody and accuracy of the required records. The broker must make the records available to auditors from the Department of Licensing, and provide copies to the Director upon demand.

For each transaction, the broker must have a **transaction folder** that includes all of the following that apply:

- the listing agreement,
- the purchase and sale agreement,
- the lease or rental agreement,
- any modifications or addenda to those agreements,
- the settlement statement, and
- all other agreements or documents relevant to the transaction.

In addition, the broker is required to keep all of the following **trust account records**:

- a duplicate receipt book or cash receipts journal showing all receipts;
- prenumbered trust account checks with a check register, cash disbursements journal, or check stubs;
- validated duplicate bank deposit slips;
- a client's ledger summarizing all receipts and disbursements for each transaction, property management account, or contract or mortgage collection account;
- separate ledger sheets for each tenant, lessee, vendee, or mortgagor;
- a ledger for the interest on the broker's pooled Housing Trust Fund account; and
- reconciled bank statements and canceled checks, including voided checks. (Trust account checks must be prenumbered, so even voided checks must be kept to show that all checks are accounted for.)

A broker is supposed to keep all records at the main office or a branch office. Property managers who employ resident managers may keep the original leases or rental agreements at the property site, as long as the broker (the property manager) has a source document with the tenant information and lease terms at his or her office.

Commissions

A valid real estate license is a prerequisite to collecting a commission (or any form of compensation) for brokerage services. A licensee cannot sue for a commission unless there is proof that he or she was properly licensed before he or she:

- offered to perform any act or service that requires licensure, or
- procured a promise or contract for the payment of compensation for such an act or service.

This rule applies to lawsuits brought by one licensee against another (a salesperson's suit against his or her broker, for example), as well as to lawsuits brought by a broker against a client.

A broker may share a commission with or pay compensation to any broker who is licensed in the United States, in a U.S. possession, or in Canada, and to his or her own affiliated licensees. This includes a transaction with a licensed manufactured or mobile home dealer, where the purchase or lease of land is part of the transaction.

A broker may not pay any compensation directly to an associate broker or salesperson licensed with another broker. Payment must be made to the other broker, who then pays the associate broker or salesperson.

Salespersons and associate brokers may receive compensation only from their broker. They cannot collect a commission directly from a client or from another broker. They also are not allowed to share their compensation with other licensees. If two salespersons are going to split a commission, the split must be handled by their broker or brokers.

Handling Transactions

The Director's regulations include several rules governing how licensees serve their clients and customers in a real estate transaction, from the negotiation of the purchase and sale agreement through closing.

Negotiating Purchase and Sale Agreements. When involved in negotiations between a buyer and a seller, a licensee must present all written communications (including offers and counteroffers) from one party to the other.

A licensee is responsible for providing clients and customers with copies of any documents they sign (the listing agreement, escrow instructions, etc.) at the time they sign them. The license law specifies that the parties to a purchase and sale agreement should be given copies at certain stages in the negotiations. The buyer should be given a copy of the offer immediately after he or she signs it. If the seller decides to accept the offer and signs it, the licensee should give the seller a copy of the agreement immediately. The licensee is also required to deliver a copy of the signed agreement to the buyer, as proof of the seller's acceptance. This completes the process of contract formation: offer, acceptance, and notification of acceptance.

Each broker who participates in a transaction (the listing broker, the selling broker, and any other cooperating brokers) must keep a copy of the purchase and sale agreement in his or her transaction records.

Earnest Money Deposits. It is a standard practice for buyers to make an earnest money deposit by writing a check payable to the broker as licensed, so that the broker can deposit it in a trust account. As explained earlier in the chapter, the broker is ordinarily required to deposit the check by the end of the first banking day after receipt. But the broker is allowed to hold the earnest money check without depositing it for a specific length of time or until a particular event occurs (e.g., the seller accepts or rejects the offer) if that is what the purchase and sale agreement directs the broker to do.

In some transactions, the agreement provides for someone other than the broker to hold the earnest money deposit until closing; the designated person is usually an escrow agent, but in some cases it is the seller. Unless the parties give the broker other instructions in writing, the broker is required to deliver the check to the designated person within one banking day after the agreement is signed. The broker should obtain a dated receipt to include in the transaction file.

When there is more than one broker involved in a transaction (as in typical multiple listing transactions), the broker who first receives the earnest money deposit is the one who is responsible for handling the funds in compliance with the license law. This is usually the selling broker, who takes the earnest money check when the buyer makes an offer.

It is a violation of the license law to accept an earnest money deposit in the form of a promissory note (or some other form that is not considered the equivalent of cash) unless the licensee discloses that fact to the seller before the seller accepts the offer, and the purchase and sale agreement also states the form of the earnest money.

Expeditious Performance. When a purchase and sale agreement or other contract obligates a licensee to perform certain acts (for example, ordering an inspection), they must be performed as expeditiously as possible. Under the license law, a licensee's intentional or negligent delay is considered to be "conduct...that demonstrates bad faith, dishonesty, untrustworthiness or incompetency," and is therefore grounds for disciplinary action.

Closings. The broker is responsible for ensuring that the parties to every transaction receive a complete, detailed settlement statement at closing. The broker is not required to prepare the statement (most are prepared by escrow agents—see Chapter 13), but making sure the parties receive it is one of the broker's duties under the license law. The broker also has to keep a copy of the settlement statement in the transaction folder, even if it was prepared by someone else.

The license law allows a broker to close a transaction in which he or she is already representing the buyer or the seller (or both), if the broker is designated as the closing agent in the purchase and sale agreement. Unless the broker is a certified escrow agent, however, he or she cannot charge either party any fee (beyond the sales commission) for closing services. Only certified escrow agents and attorneys can charge a fee for closing real estate transactions. (See Chapter 13 for information about the Washington Escrow Agent Registration Act.)

Property Management Agreements. A broker must have a written property management agreement with the owner or owners of each property he or she manages. The license law requires the agreement to state (at least) all of the following:

- the broker's compensation;
- the type of property (e.g., apartment, industrial, office space);
- the number of units or square footage;
- whether the broker is authorized to collect and disburse funds, and if so, for what purposes;
- whether the broker is authorized to hold and disburse tenant security deposits, and if so, how; and
- how often the broker is to provide summary statements to the owner.

Note that the broker is not required to describe the property's physical condition in the agreement.

A **summary statement** is a brief report showing the property's financial status over a certain period of time, such as one month or one quarter. A broker must provide a summary statement to the owner or owners for each property managed as often as the management agreement requires. The broker also keeps a copy of each statement. A summary statement shows:

- the balance carried forward from the last statement;
- the total rent receipts;
- other itemized receipts (e.g., from laundry or vending machines);
- contributions from the owner;
- itemized expenditures;
- the ending balance; and
- the number of units or square footage rented.

The broker must have a copy of the management agreement and all summary statements for his or her records. The management agreement can only be modified in writing, and the modification must be signed by both the broker and the owner. For all rental properties managed by the broker, the leases or rental agreements must be in writing.

The broker may provide other services to the owner of property he or she manages, such as janitorial and repair services, with the owner's consent. The broker must make a full written disclosure of his or her relationship with the firm providing the services, and state what fees are charged. (Property management is discussed in detail in Chapter 16.)

Discrimination

The license law prohibits licensees from doing any of the following in real estate transactions, if the action involves discrimination on the basis of race, color, creed, sex, marital status, familial status, age, national origin, or the presence of any sensory, mental, or physical handicap:

- refusing to communicate offers for discriminatory reasons;
- refusing to negotiate for discriminatory reasons;
- discriminating in the terms or conditions of sale or rental;
- using discriminatory advertising;
- representing that property is not available when it is in fact available; and
- blockbusting.

In addition, the license law prohibits discrimination on the basis of race, color, creed, or national origin in hiring practices or sales activity. And any violation of a state or federal antidiscrimination law (see Chapter 15) is also a violation of the license law.

Disciplinary Action

The Director has the authority to investigate the actions of any real estate licensee and impose sanctions (including license suspension or revocation) for violations of the license law. This is true regardless of whether the licensee was acting on behalf of another or for his or her own account, and regardless of whether his or her license is active or inactive.

Grounds for Disciplinary Action

A licensee or license applicant may be subject to disciplinary action either for engaging in unprofessional conduct or for engaging in one of the activities specifically listed in the license law as being grounds for disciplinary action.

Unprofessional conduct is defined by law to include any of the following conduct, acts, or conditions:

1. the commission of any act involving moral turpitude, dishonesty, or corruption relating to real estate activities, regardless of whether the act constitutes a crime;
2. misrepresentation or concealment of a material fact in obtaining or reinstating a license;
3. false, deceptive, or misleading advertising;
4. incompetence, negligence, or malpractice that harms or may harm a consumer;
5. having any business or professional license suspended, revoked, or restricted by any government entity;
6. failure to cooperate with the Director of the Department of Licensing in the course of an investigation, audit, or inspection;
7. failure to comply with an order issued by the Director;
8. violating any lawful rule made by the Director;
9. aiding or abetting an unlicensed person to perform real estate activities that require a license;
10. practice or operation of a business or profession beyond the scope of practice or operation as defined by law;
11. any type of misrepresentation in the conduct of real estate activities;
12. failure to adequately supervise or oversee staff, whether employees or independent contractors, to the extent that consumers may be harmed or damaged;
13. being convicted of any gross misdemeanor or felony relating to real estate activities; or
14. interference with an investigation or disciplinary action by willfully misrepresenting facts, or by threatening, harassing, or bribing customers or witnesses to prevent them from providing evidence.

Further grounds for disciplinary action are included in the license law. One of the first items on this list is "Violating any provisions of [the real estate license law statute] or any lawful regulations made by the director pursuant thereto..." In other words, any violation of the license law is grounds for disciplinary action. So a broker or salesperson who failed to comply with any of the rules explained in this chapter could lose his or her license as a result.

Here is a brief summary of the items listed in the license law that have not been mentioned elsewhere in this chapter. A licensee is subject to disciplinary action for:

*   being convicted of forgery, embezzlement, extortion, fraud, or similar offenses;
*   making or authorizing statements that he or she knew (or could have known by the exercise of reasonable care) were false;

- converting trust funds to his or her own use;
- failing to disclose information or to produce records for inspection upon request by the Director;
- selling real estate according to a plan that endangers the public interest, after the Director has objected in writing;
- accepting money from more than one party in a transaction without first disclosing this to all interested parties in writing;
- accepting a profit on expenditures made for a principal without disclosing it to the principal;
- accepting compensation for an appraisal contingent on reporting a predetermined value;
- issuing an appraisal for property in which he or she has an interest without disclosing that interest in the appraisal report;
- falsely claiming to be a member of a state or national real estate association;
- directing a client or customer to a lending institution or escrow company in expectation of a kickback, without disclosing that expectation to the party he or she is representing;
- buying, selling, or leasing property (directly or through a third party) without disclosing that he or she holds a real estate license;
- any conduct in a real estate transaction which demonstrates bad faith, dishonesty, untrustworthiness, or incompetency.

The Director is also given the power to suspend the license of any real estate licensee who has been certified by a lending agency for nonpayment or default on a federal or state guaranteed education loan or service-conditioned scholarship. The same applies to any licensee who is not in compliance with a child support or visitation order, as certified by the Department of Social and Health Services. License reinstatement is automatic upon repayment or compliance.

Disciplinary Procedures

The procedures for disciplinary action are designed to give the licensee notice of the charges and an opportunity to present a defense. The usual procedures include an investigation, a hearing, and, depending on the outcome of the hearing, either no action or some form of sanctions against the licensee. Either party (the licensee or the Department of Licensing) may appeal the result.

Statement of Charges. If, after investigation, the Director decides there is reason to believe there has been a violation of the license law, the licensee will be served with a statement of charges. The statement of charges must be accompanied by a notice informing the licensee that he or she may request a hearing to contest the charges. The licensee must file a request for a hearing within 20 days after receiving the statement of charges. If the licensee fails to request a hearing, the licensee will be considered in default and the Director may enter a decision based on the facts available at that time.

Hearing. Once a hearing has been requested, the Director will fix the time for the hearing. The time must be as soon as is convenient, but at least 30 days after the statement of charges was served on the licensee. The only exception to this rule is if the Director issued a summary (or immediate) suspension or restriction, in which case the hearing may be held sooner.

The hearing may be conducted by the Director, but in most cases the hearing officer is an administrative law judge. The licensee and the Department of Licensing may each be represented by attorneys in the hearing. The Department and the licensee will each have an opportunity to present evidence and testimony, to cross-examine witnesses for the other side, and to present arguments to the hearing officer. A court reporter makes a transcript of the proceedings, just as in a trial.

If the accusation is not proved by a preponderance of the evidence, no action is taken against the licensee and the case is dismissed. If the accusation is proved, the Director may impose any of the sanctions permitted by law (discussed below). An order imposing the sanctions will be filed with the Director's office and immediately mailed to the licensee. The sanctions called for in the order take effect as soon as the order is received by the licensee.

Appeal. A licensee who is dissatisfied with the outcome of a disciplinary hearing may file an appeal in superior court. The appeal must be filed within 30 days after the date of the Director's decision and order. The licensee will be required to post a $500 appeal bond to cover court costs—in case the judge decides against the licensee—and must also pay for a copy of the transcript of the hearing. Filing an appeal does not automatically stay the Director's order. In other words, if the Director suspended the licensee's license, it will remain suspended during the appeal process. However, the Director may choose to stay the sanctions during the appeal process, if it is appropriate to do so and any conditions necessary to protect the public are imposed.

Sanctions for License Law Violations

After a disciplinary hearing, if the licensee (or license applicant) is held to have violated the license law, the Director may impose any or all of the following sanctions:

- revocation of the license;
- suspension of the license for a fixed or indefinite term;
- restriction or limitation of real estate activities;
- satisfactory completion of a specific program of remedial education or treatment;
- monitoring of real estate activities according to the Director's order;
- censure or reprimand;
- compliance with conditions of probation for a designated period of time;
- payment of a fine for each violation found by the Director, of up to $5,000 per violation;
- denial of an initial or renewal license application; or
- other corrective action.

When one of a broker's affiliated licensees has been found guilty of a violation, the Director may also suspend or revoke the broker's authority to be that person's broker. All fines collected are placed in the Real Estate Education Account, to be used for education for the benefit of licensees.

A **cease and desist order** is issued to stop a licensee (or an unlicensed person) from violating the law. After a disciplinary hearing, the Director might issue a cease and desist order to prevent continuation of an illegal activity. In special circumstances, the Director is also authorized to issue a temporary cease and desist order even before a hearing is held. The Director is only allowed to do this when a delay in issuing the order would result in irreparable harm to the public. The temporary order must advise the licensee that he or she has a right to a hearing to determine if the order should be canceled, modified, or made permanent. If the licensee requests a hearing, the Director must hold one within 30 days (unless the licensee requests more time).

Fig. 17.5 *Penalties after disciplinary action*

Penalties for Violation of the License Law

- License suspension, revocation, or denial
- Restriction and/or monitoring of real estate activities
- Relevant real estate education
- Censure or reprimand
- Probation
- Fines (up to $5,000 per violation)
- Other

Alternatively, the Director can ask a court to issue an injunction ordering a licensee or an unlicensed person to stop an ongoing violation. The Director can also ask the court to appoint a receiver to take over or close a real estate office operating in violation of the law until a hearing can be held.

Criminal Prosecution. Violations of the license law are gross misdemeanors. If the Director decides that criminal charges should be filed against a licensee, the prosecution would ordinarily be handled by the prosecuting attorney in the county where the violation is alleged to have occurred. If the prosecutor fails to act, the Director can ask the state Attorney General to prosecute instead.

Civil Liability. Anyone who has been injured by a licensee's actions or failure to act can file a civil lawsuit for damages. (See the discussion of tort suits in Chapter 7.) Note, however, that the Director of the Department of Licensing does not have the power to award damages to the victims of real estate fraud or other wrongful actions. Compensation for injured parties is handled through the court system, not by the Department of Licensing.

Notifying Department of Legal Action. A licensee is required to notify the Department of Licensing within 20 days after learning of:

- any criminal complaint, information, indictment, or conviction in which the licensee is named as a defendant; or
- any civil court order, verdict, or judgment entered against the licensee if the case involves any of his or her real estate or business activities.

Antitrust Laws and Their Effect on Licensees

In addition to the real estate license law, federal antitrust laws impose certain restrictions on a real estate agent's behavior towards clients, customers, and other agents.

Federal antitrust laws are not new: the **Sherman Act** was passed in 1890, over a century ago. The Sherman Act prohibits any agreement that has the effect of restraining trade, including conspiracies. A **conspiracy** occurs when two or more business entities participate in a common scheme, the effect of which is the restraint of trade.

At the foundation of antitrust laws is the notion that free enterprise is a part of our democratic society, and that competition is good for both the economy and society as a whole. While many people associate antitrust laws with big steel mills and telephone companies, in 1950 antitrust laws were held to apply to the real estate industry. In a landmark case, the United States Supreme Court held that mandatory fee schedules, established and enforced by a real estate board, violated the Sherman Act (*U.S. v. National Association of Real Estate Boards*).

If a real estate agent violates antitrust laws, he or she may be subject to both civil and criminal actions. If an individual is found guilty of violating the Sherman Act, he or she can be fined up to $350,000 and/or sentenced to three years' imprisonment. If a corporation is found guilty of violating the Sherman Act, it can be fined up to ten million dollars.

The activities that are prohibited by antitrust laws can be grouped into three main categories:

- price fixing (fixing commission rates),
- group boycotts, and
- tie-in arrangements.

Price Fixing. Price fixing is defined as the cooperative setting of prices or price ranges by competing firms. To avoid the appearance of price fixing, two agents from different brokerages should never discuss their commission rates. It is a discussion between competing agents that is dangerous—a broker can discuss commission rates with his or her own salespeople. One exception to this general prohibition is that two competing brokers may discuss a commission split in a cooperative sale (the split between the listing broker and the selling broker).

Even a casual announcement that a broker is planning on raising his or her commission rates could lead to antitrust problems.

> **Example:** Broker Wood goes to a dinner given by his local MLS. He is called on to discuss current market conditions and, in the middle of his speech, he announces that he is going to raise his commission rate, no matter what anyone else does. This statement could be viewed as an invitation to conspire to fix prices. If any other MLS members raise their rates in response to his announcement, they can be held to have accepted Wood's invitation to conspire.

Brokers must understand that they do not have to actually consult with each other to be charged with conspiring to fix commission rates. The kind of scenario described in the example is enough to lead to an antitrust lawsuit.

Publications that appear to fix prices are prohibited as well. Any MLS or other association that tries to publish "recommended" or "going" rates for commissions could be sued.

Group Boycotts. A group boycott is an agreement between two or more real estate brokers to exclude other brokers from fair participation in real estate activities.

Example: Becker and Jordan are both brokers. They have lunch together and begin discussing the business practices of a third broker, Harley. Becker says that Harley is just a "discount broker" and is dishonest and lazy. Becker states that he will never do business with him. Jordan laughs and agrees. She says that she never returns any of Harley's calls when he is inquiring about a listed property. She suggests that Becker do the same. Becker and Jordan could be found guilty of a conspiracy to boycott.

If a broker feels another broker is dishonest or unethical, he or she may choose not to do business with him or her. However, that broker cannot tell other brokers to do the same.

The purpose of group boycotts is to hurt or destroy a competitor, and they are automatically unlawful under antitrust laws.

Tie-in Arrangements. A tie-in arrangement is defined as "an agreement to sell one product, only on the condition that the buyer also purchases a different (or tied) product..."

Example: Brown is a subdivision developer. Tyson, a builder, wants to buy a lot. Brown tells Tyson that he will sell him a lot only if Tyson agrees that after Tyson builds a house on the lot, he will list the improved property with Brown. (This is called a "list-back" agreement.)

Tie-in arrangements are automatically violations of the antitrust laws. Note that list-back agreements only violate antitrust laws if they are a required condition of the sale. Two parties may mutually agree on a list-back agreement without violating antitrust laws.

Avoiding Antitrust Violations. There are several ways to prevent possible antitrust violations. Brokers should:

- always establish their fees and other listing policies independently, without consulting competing firms;
- never use listing forms that contain preprinted commission rates;
- never imply to a client that the commission rate is fixed or non-negotiable, or refer to a competitor's commission policies when discussing commission rates;
- never discuss their business plans with competitors;
- never tell clients or competitors that they won't do business with a competing firm, or tell them not to work with that firm because of doubts about its competence or integrity; and
- train their licensees to be aware of what may constitute an antitrust law violation.

Chapter Summary

1. Washington's real estate license law is administered by the Director of the Department of Licensing and the Real Estate Commission.

2. It is unlawful to act as a real estate broker or salesperson without a license. There are several important exemptions from the licensing requirement, however, including someone buying or selling on his or her own behalf, and an uncompensated attorney in fact.

3. There are three types of real estate licenses: broker, associate broker, and salesperson. Only a broker is authorized to operate a brokerage business and represent clients. Associate brokers and salespersons may only work for and represent a broker. An associate broker is also authorized to manage a branch office.

4. Any license applicant must be at least 18 years old, have completed certain real estate courses, and pass an examination. An applicant for a broker's license must also have a high school diploma and two years of experience as a salesperson. The qualifications for an associate broker's license are the same as those for a broker's license.

5. Licenses must be renewed every two years. For renewal, the licensee must complete 30 clock hours of approved continuing education courses. For a first renewal, a salesperson must have also completed a 30 clock-hour course in real estate practices.

6. An agency relationship is formed when a licensee begins performing brokerage services for a client. An agent owes a number of duties to a principal, in addition to the duties any licensee owes to all parties in a transaction. An agency relationship can be terminated through full performance, expiration of the term, mutual agreement, or unilateral action.

7. A broker is responsible for the supervision of all of his or her affiliated licensees. A fee brokerage arrangement violates the license law. When an affiliation is terminated, the salesperson's or associate broker's license is returned to the Director; it is inactive until reissued for affiliation with another broker.

8. A broker is required to maintain an office in Washington that is open to the public, and may have one or more branch offices. Each branch office must be licensed and must be managed by an associate broker. Each license must be displayed in the office where the licensee works.

9. Advertising by real estate licensees must include the broker's name as licensed; blind ads are not allowed. An ad for the licensee's own property does not have to state the broker's name, but it must disclose the licensed status of the seller.

10. Trust funds must be placed in an interest-bearing trust account no later than the first banking day after receipt; deposits of $10,000 or less are placed in a pooled account, with interest paid to the state. (Property management trust accounts do not have to be interest-bearing accounts.) A broker may not pay business expenses or an affiliated licensee's share of a commission directly out of a trust account.

11. A broker is required to keep records (including a transaction folder and trust account records) for at least three years after a transaction closes.

12. A valid real estate license is a prerequisite to payment of a commission or other compensation for brokerage services.

13. In handling a real estate transaction, a licensee is required to provide copies to the parties after documents are signed; to make an agency disclosure; to perform expeditiously any acts he or she is obligated to perform by the purchase and sale agreement; and to make sure that the parties receive settlement statements.

14. The license law specifically prohibits certain forms of discrimination by licensees, and any violation of a state or federal antidiscrimination law is also a violation of the license law.

15. When a licensee is accused of violating the license law, there is an investigation and then a disciplinary hearing. The possible sanctions include license suspension, revocation, or denial; fines; relevant coursework; restrictions on or monitoring of real estate activities; censure or reprimand; probation; or other corrective action. Violation of the license law is a gross misdemeanor and may lead to criminal prosecution.

16. Antitrust laws prohibit price fixing, group boycotts, and tie-in arrangements. Real estate brokers must be especially careful to avoid discussing commission rates with competing brokers.

🔑 Key Terms

License law—The state statute that governs the licensing and business practices of real estate agents, along with the regulations issued by the Director of the Department of Licensing to implement that statute.

Real Estate Commission—A commission made up of the Director of the Department of Licensing and six commissioners who advise the Director.

Real estate broker—A person who is licensed to represent others in real estate transactions for compensation.

Real estate salesperson—A person who is licensed to work for and represent a broker in real estate transactions.

Associate broker—A person who has qualified as a broker, but is affiliated with another broker.

Affiliated licensee—A salesperson or associate broker who is licensed under a particular broker.

Designated broker—A corporate officer or general partner who is authorized to act as the broker for a licensed corporation or partnership.

Business opportunity—A business that is for sale, including inventory and goodwill.

Interim license—The completed application form for a salesperson's license, which serves as a temporary license until the permanent license is issued.

Inactive license—A license in the possession of the Director of the Department of Licensing.

Vicarious liability—The liability of a principal for a harm caused by the act or omission of an agent or subagent.

Imputed knowledge—The assumption that a principal has notice of facts known to an agent or subagent.

Fee broker—A broker who allows another person to use his or her license to operate a brokerage (which is a violation of the license law).

Blind ad—An advertisement placed by a real estate licensee that does not state the name of the broker as licensed (which is a violation of the license law).

Trust account—A specially designated bank account in a broker's name for funds held by the broker on behalf of clients, to keep those funds segregated from the broker's own money.

Transaction folder—Part of the records a broker is required to keep; the contracts and other documents connected with a particular transaction.

Cease and desist order—An order issued by the Director of the Department of Licensing in a disciplinary action, to stop a violation of the license law.

Chapter Quiz

1. The members of the Washington Real Estate Commission are appointed by:

   a) the Governor
   b) the Real Estate Program Manager
   c) the Director of the Department of Licensing
   d) the President of the Washington Association of Realtors

2. The Morenos want to sell their house. They gave their friend Jessica Norwood a power of attorney, authorizing her to represent them in the transaction. Norwood does not have a real estate license. It is legal for Norwood to represent the Morenos:

   a) only if she is licensed to practice law
   b) only if she will not be compensated for her services
   c) as long as she obtains a real estate license before the transaction closes
   d) None of the above; it is not legal for Norwood to represent the Morenos

3. Mark Cutler does not have a real estate license. Cutler's father owns an apartment building, and Cutler routinely shows the apartments to prospective tenants and negotiates rental agreements. This is legal:

   a) only if Cutler is the resident manager of the building
   b) only if Cutler has a power of attorney from his father
   c) only if the building has five units or less
   d) because Cutler is a member of the owner's family

4. Unlike a salesperson, an associate broker:

   a) must have a high school diploma or the equivalent
   b) can accept compensation directly from a seller
   c) does not have to be licensed under a broker
   d) All of the above

5. Real estate licenses must be renewed:

   a) annually
   b) every two years
   c) every three years
   d) every five years

6. Paul Doren's real estate license expired last month, and now he wants to renew it. In order to do so, Doren will be required to:

   a) complete an additional 60 clock hours of approved real estate courses
   b) pass the license exam again
   c) pay a penalty in addition to the renewal fee
   d) All of the above

7. To renew a real estate license, a broker must show that he or she has taken a certain number of clock hours of approved continuing education courses. The required total is:

   a) 30 hours commenced within 12 months preceding the licensee's renewal date
   b) 30 hours; at least 15 commenced within 24 months preceding the licensee's renewal date, and the remainder commenced within 36 months preceding the renewal date
   c) 20 hours completed within 24 months preceding the licensee's renewal date
   d) 20 hours completed within 36 months preceding the licensee's renewal date

8. For their first renewal, real estate salespersons must:

   a) complete 30 clock hours of continuing education
   b) complete a 30 clock-hour course in real estate practices
   c) Both a) and b)
   d) Neither a) nor b)

9. Harrison is a resident manager of a small apartment building. He collects rents and completes minor repairs in exchange for a reduction in rent. Harrison:

   a) must have a real estate license
   b) need not be licensed
   c) must have a property management license
   d) need not be licensed, as long as he is supervised by a licensed broker

10. Jenkins, who lives in Portland, has a valid Oregon real estate license. She decides that she needs a Washington real estate license so she can show some of her Portland customers properties in Vancouver, Washington. Jenkins:

   a) must fulfill all the normal broker licensure requirements, just as if she were not already licensed in Oregon
   b) can apply for a Washington real estate license without taking the license exam
   c) only has to take the Washington portion of the real estate exam
   d) can get a special dispensation from the Director and receive a license upon completion of a 30-hour brokerage management course

11. Peterson hires an assistant to help him with his real estate business. His assistant answers phones, sets up appointments, and fills out paperwork. Peterson's assistant:

   a) need not be licensed
   b) must have a real estate license
   c) need not be licensed as long as Peterson has written authorization from his broker to hire an assistant
   d) must have a special real estate assistant license

12. Cortez has one year of experience as a real estate salesperson. He wants to become a real estate broker. He may get the two-year experience requirement waived if he can show:

   a) post-secondary education with an emphasis on real estate studies
   b) six months' experience as an attorney specializing in real estate transactions
   c) three years' experience closing real estate transactions for an escrow company
   d) All of the above

13. Harper had her experience requirement waived and took the real estate broker exam. Harper failed the exam. She:

   a) may retake the exam immediately
   b) must wait six months before retaking the exam
   c) must now fulfill the two-year experience requirement before retaking the exam
   d) may not retake the exam

14. To pass the real estate broker's exam, the applicant must score at least:

   a) 70%
   b) 75%
   c) 80%
   d) 85%

15. Which of the following may receive an interim license?

   a) A salesperson applicant who passed the exam
   b) A designated broker applicant who passed the exam
   c) An associate broker applicant who passed the exam
   d) All of the above

16. A dual agent may not:

   a) disclose a material fact that one party knows and wants to remain confidential
   b) disclose one party's intended negotiating position to the other party
   c) advise an inexperienced client to seek outside legal advice
   d) make his agency disclosure before either party has signed an offer in a transaction

17. A seller is not liable to the buyer for the cost of undisclosed damage to the foundation of the house if:

   a) the seller gave the broker the option of not mentioning the damage to the foundation
   b) the broker fled the country and the court has no jurisdiction over him
   c) the seller substantially profited from the deal, but the broker has since gone bankrupt
   d) the broker discovered the foundation damage and did not say anything about it to the seller

18. Ellen Kendrick is a licensed salesperson. She was not getting along with her broker, so they decided to terminate their affiliation, and the broker sent Kendrick's license back to the Department of Licensing. Which of the following is true?

   a) Kendrick's license is inactive
   b) Kendrick may continue with real estate transactions that were in progress at the time of her termination
   c) Kendrick will be required to take the license exam again in order to reinstate her license
   d) All of the above

19. One of Larry Sanborn's affiliated licensees violated the license law. Sanborn will be subject to disciplinary action as a result, unless he can show that:

   a) he was only a fee broker
   b) he provided adequate supervision
   c) the licensee was an independent contractor rather than an employee
   d) the licensee worked at a branch office

20. The license of a salesperson who works at a branch office is:

   a) kept at his or her home address
   b) displayed at the broker's main office
   c) displayed at the branch office where he or she works
   d) kept at the Department of Licensing in Olympia

21. Trust funds a licensee receives in a sales transaction must be placed in:

   a) an account that does not bear interest, by the third banking day after receipt
   b) an interest-bearing account, by the third banking day after receipt
   c) an account that does not bear interest, by the first banking day after receipt
   d) an interest-bearing account, by the first banking day after receipt

22. The license law requires a broker to keep transaction records for:

   a) six months
   b) one year
   c) three years
   d) five years

23. The listing was submitted to a multiple listing service, and the property was sold by a salesperson who does not work for the listing broker. How will that salesperson be paid a share of the commission?

   a) The listing broker must pay the salesperson's broker, who will then pay the salesperson
   b) The listing broker must pay the MLS, which will then pay the salesperson directly
   c) The listing broker may either pay the salesperson's broker or pay the salesperson directly
   d) The listing broker should pay the salesperson directly

24. Susan Kurosawa, a licensed salesperson, is advertising her own house for sale. The license law requires the ad to state:

   a) that the seller is a licensed real estate agent
   b) the name of Kurosawa's broker, as licensed
   c) Both of the above
   d) None of the above

25. A salesperson may manage a branch office for his or her broker:

   a) if the salesperson has at least two years of experience
   b) if the salesperson has taken an approved course in brokerage management
   c) if the office is in the salesperson's residence
   d) under no circumstances

26. A broker who is representing a seller is negotiating with a prospective buyer. Before the buyer signs an offer, the broker must:

   a) obtain the seller's written consent
   b) disclose to the buyer in writing that he is representing the seller
   c) explain to the buyer that he is acting as a dual agent
   d) have the buyer sign a buyer representation agreement

27. If a licensee accused of violating the license law does not request a hearing within 20 days after receiving the statement of charges:

   a) his or her license is automatically revoked
   b) the Director may enter a decision based on the available facts
   c) a hearing will automatically be scheduled for the licensee
   d) the Director will issue a cease and desist order

28. Howard Gray, a licensed salesperson, was involved in a traffic accident. The other driver (who was injured) sued Gray for compensation, and a judgment has just been entered against Gray. He is:

   a) required to notify the Department of Licensing within five days
   b) required to notify the Department of Licensing within 30 days
   c) not required to notify the Department of Licensing, because this was not a criminal charge
   d) not required to notify the Department of Licensing, because the lawsuit did not involve Gray's real estate or business activities

19 correct
9 Incorrect

29. A broker who is managing property must:

    a) have a written property management agreement with the owner
    b) keep a copy of all summary statements for the property in his or her records
    c) provide other services, such as repair services, to the property owner only after making a full written disclosure of his or her relationship with the firm providing the services
    d) All of the above

30. Barton, a real estate licensee, helps negotiate a sale. The purchase and sale agreement is contingent on a pest inspection, and Barton tells the parties he will arrange for an inspection to be done by August 19. But he forgets to request the inspection before taking his family on a planned vacation. When he gets back into town on August 18, he finally remembers to call the pest inspector. The inspector says she's very busy and won't be able to inspect the home until August 29.

    a) Since the pest inspection was not an important term in the purchase agreement, Barton has not done anything wrong
    b) Even though Barton was negligent in failing to perform his duty, he has not violated the license law
    c) The closing agent will cancel escrow immediately and terminate the sale
    d) Barton has failed to perform expeditiously, and may be subject to disciplinary action

31. Alberts is representing the seller in a transaction. She discloses this in writing to both the seller and the buyer. Later, Alberts decides that she can adequately represent both parties, and begins acting as a dual agent. Alberts:

    a) has done nothing wrong, as long as she acts in the best interests of both parties
    b) violated the agency disclosure requirement because she did not act in accordance with her disclosed agency status
    c) has done nothing wrong, because dual agency is not unlawful in Washington
    d) Both a) and c)

32. Broker Lee is licensed in both Washington and Oregon. He maintains his office in Oregon. Lee is representing the buyer, Morely, in a Washington transaction. Two weeks after the purchase and sale agreement is signed, Morely becomes very upset with Lee. She claims that Lee has not told her everything she needs to know about the sale and demands to see his records regarding the transaction.

    a) Since Lee must keep his records in a safe deposit box in a Washington financial institution, Morely has no right to view them
    b) Lee may show Morely the records only with the written authorization of a Real Estate Commissioner
    c) Lee is obligated to show Morely the records, since she's a party to the transaction
    d) Lee's records are confidential business papers and he can refuse to show them to Morely

33. Federal antitrust laws apply:

   a) only to franchised firms, because of their ability to conspire to restrain trade
   b) only to large real estate firms that could actually affect the real estate market
   c) only to individual agents, not to real estate companies
   d) to all members of the real estate industry

34. Great County MLS publishes a monthly list of the commission rates charged by all member firms. The multiple listing association:

   a) could be found guilty of price fixing
   b) is not guilty of price fixing, because it is simply reporting newsworthy information
   c) is not guilty of price fixing, because no two competing firms are discussing rates
   d) is not guilty of price fixing, because only real estate brokers can be guilty of price fixing, not multiple listing associations

35. A broker conducts a sales meeting once a week for her salespeople. At one meeting, she discusses commission rates at length. She is:

   a) guilty of price fixing
   b) guilty of a tie-in arrangement
   c) guilty of a group boycott
   d) not guilty of any antitrust violation

👉 Answer Key

1. a)   The Governor appoints the members of the Real Estate Commission, which includes six commissioners and the Director of the Department of Licensing.

2. b)   It is legal for an unlicensed person to represent another in a real estate transaction if authorized to do so by a power of attorney, as long as he or she is not acting for compensation.

3. d)   The owner of a rental property or a member of his or her family is not required to have a real estate license in transactions related to that property.

4. a)   The required qualifications for an associate broker's license are the same as those for a broker's license, and they include a high school diploma. (A salesperson is not required to be a high school graduate.) Just like a salesperson, an associate broker must be licensed under a broker and cannot accept compensation from anyone other than the broker.

5. b)   Real estate licenses must be renewed every two years.

6. c)   A real estate license can be renewed within one year after it expires if the licensee simply pays a penalty in addition to the renewal fee. After one year, the license is canceled, and there are several requirements for reinstatement.

7. b)   Renewal requires a total of 30 clock hours of continuing education courses. At least 15 of the 30 hours must have been commenced within 24 months preceding the licensee's renewal date. The remaining hours must have been commenced within 36 months preceding the renewal date.

8. c)   Salespeople must complete both a 30 clock-hour practices course and 30 clock hours of continuing education for their first renewal.

9. b)   A resident manager does not have to be licensed, as long as he or she is simply performing duties related to that property.

10. c)   Those licensed in other jurisdictions must take the Washington portion of the license exam to obtain an equivalent Washington license.

11. a)   Assistants need not be licensed, as long as they perform only clerical tasks. If an assistant were to engage in listing or selling activities, the assistant would have to obtain a license.

12. a)   One year of experience plus post-secondary education in real estate studies may be sufficient to merit a waiver of the two-year experience requirement.

13. c)   If an applicant fails the exam, the experience waiver no longer applies. The applicant must then fulfill the two-year experience requirement.

14. b)   75% is a passing score for the real estate broker's exam. (70% is a passing score for the real estate salesperson's exam.)

15. a)   Only salespersons receive an interim license; brokers and associate brokers may not.

16. b)   A dual agent must not take any action that is detrimental to either party's interest in a transaction.

17. d) Facts known by a real estate agent or subagent that are not known by the principal are not imputed to the principal.

18. a) When a salesperson's license is surrendered to the Director, it is inactive until the salesperson finds another broker to work for and the license is reissued. In the meantime, it is not legal for the salesperson to continue any activities for which a license is required.

19. b) A broker is responsible for supervising all of his or her affiliated licensees, whether they work as independent contractors or employees, and whether they work in the main office or a branch office. (In a branch office, the branch manager is also responsible for supervision.) If an affiliated licensee violates the license law, the broker will not be subject to disciplinary action if there was adequate supervision and the broker took action to mitigate the harm caused by the violation.

20. c) A real estate license is required to be prominently displayed in the office where the licensee works.

21. d) Trust funds must be placed in a trust account by the first banking day after receipt, unless the parties have instructed the broker in writing to handle the funds differently. Trust funds received in a sales transaction (or any trust funds other than property management trust funds) must be placed in an interest-bearing account.

22. c) Transaction records and trust account records must be kept for at least three years after a transaction closes (or is otherwise terminated).

23. a) A salesperson can only receive compensation through his or her broker. The listing broker will have to pay the salesperson's broker, who will then pay the salesperson.

24. a) When advertising their own properties, licensees are required to disclose their licensed status, but the broker's name does not have to be given. (The broker's name as licensed is required in ads for properties a licensee is advertising on behalf of someone else, however.)

25. d) A salesperson cannot manage a branch office; a branch office manager must have an associate broker's license.

26. b) Before the buyer signs an offer, the selling agent must disclose to the buyer in writing which party he or she is representing. The agency disclosure may be a separate paragraph in the purchase and sale agreement, or it may be a separate document.

27. b) If the licensee fails to request a hearing within 20 days, the licensee will be considered in default and the Director may enter a decision based on the available facts.

28. d) A licensee is only required to notify the Department of Licensing (within 20 days) of a judgment in a civil lawsuit if the case involves his or her real estate activities or other business activities. (With criminal charges, the Department of Licensing must be notified whether or not the charges involve real estate or business activities.)

29. d) A property manager must have a written
        management agreement with the owner,
        keep summary statements in his or her
        records, and fully disclose any interest in
        businesses that provide ancillary services.

30. d) Real estate licensees must perform their
        duties as agreed, in a timely manner.
        Failure to do so may result in disciplinary
        action.

31. b) Once a licensee discloses his or her agency
        status, that licensee must act in accordance
        with the disclosure. A new disclosure is
        required if the agent's representation in the
        transaction changes.

32. c) Parties to a transaction have the right to
        see the licensee's records regarding that
        transaction.

33. d) Federal antitrust laws were extended to the
        real estate industry in 1950.

34. a) Even publishing a list of the "going rates"
        for commissions may be considered price
        fixing.

35. d) A broker may discuss commission rates
        with his or her own affiliated salespeople
        without violating antitrust laws.

Real Estate Math

🏠 Chapter Overview

Real estate agents use math constantly: to calculate their commissions, to determine the square footage of homes they are listing or selling, to prorate closing costs, and so on. Electronic calculators make all of these tasks much easier than they once were, but it is still necessary to have a basic grasp of the math involved. This chapter provides step-by-step instructions for solving a wide variety of real estate math problems.

Solving Math Problems

We're going to begin our discussion of real estate math with a simple approach to solving math problems. Master this four-step process, and you'll be able to solve most math problems you are likely to encounter.

1. Read the question

The most important step is to thoroughly read and understand the question. You must know what you are looking for before you can successfully solve any math problem. Once you know what you want to find out (for example, the area, the commission amount, or the total profit), you'll be able to decide which formula to use.

2. Write down the formula

Write down the correct formula for the problem you need to solve. For example, the area formula is *Area = Length × Width*, which is abbreviated $A = L \times W$. Formulas for each type of problem are presented throughout this chapter, and there is a complete list at the end of the chapter.

3. Substitute

Substitute the relevant numbers from the problem into the formula. Sometimes there are numbers in the problem that you will not use. It's not unusual for a math problem to contain unnecessary information, which is why it is very important to read the question first and determine what you are looking for. The formula will help you distinguish between the relevant and irrelevant information given in the problem.

In some problems you will be able to substitute numbers into the formula without any additional steps, but in other problems one or more preliminary steps will be necessary. For instance, you may have to convert fractions to decimals.

4. Calculate

Once you have substituted the numbers into the formula, you are ready to perform the calculations to find the unknown—the component of the formula that was not given in the problem. Most of the formulas have the same basic form: $A = L \times W$. The problem will give you two of the three numbers (or information to enable you to find two of the numbers) and then you will either have to divide or multiply to find the third number, which is the solution to the problem.

Whether you'll multiply or divide is determined by which component in the formula is the unknown. For example, the formula $A = L \times W$ may be converted into two other formulas. All three formulas are equivalent, but they are put into different forms depending on the element to be discovered.

▸ If the quantity A (the area) is unknown, then the following formula is used.

$$\frac{Length}{\times\ Width}\ \ \text{or}\ \ A = L \times W$$
$$Area$$

The number L is **multiplied** by W. The product of L multiplied by W is A.

▸ If the quantity L (the length) is unknown, the following formula is used.

$$Width\overline{)\,\underset{}{\overset{Length}{Area}}}\ \ \text{or}\ \ L = A \div W$$

The number A is **divided** by W. The quotient of A divided by W is L.

▸ If the quantity W (the width) is unknown, the following formula is used.

$$Length\overline{)\,\underset{}{\overset{Width}{Area}}}\ \ \text{or}\ \ W = A \div L$$

The number A is **divided** by L. The quotient of A divided by L is W.

Thus, the formula $A = L \times W$ may be used three different ways depending on which quantity is unknown. For the examples below assume the area of a rectangle is 800 square feet, the length is 40 feet and the width is 20 feet.

$A = L \times W$	$L = A \div W$	$W = A \div L$
$A = 40' \times 20'$	$L = 800\ Sq.\ Ft. \div 20'$	$W = 800\ Sq.\ Ft. \div 40'$
$\begin{array}{r}40'\\ \times\ 20'\\ \hline 800\end{array}$ Sq. Ft.	$20'\overline{)\overset{40'}{800}}$ Sq. Ft.	$40'\overline{)\overset{20'}{800}}$ Sq. Ft.

After you've substituted the numbers given in the problem into the formula, you might have trouble deciding whether you're supposed to multiply or divide. It may help to compare your equation to the very familiar calculation $2 \times 3 = 6$. If the unknown component of your equation is in the same position as the 6 in $2 \times 3 = 6$, then you need to multiply the two given numbers to find the unknown.

If the unknown component is in the 2 position or the 3 position, you need to divide. You'll divide the given number in the 6 position by the other given number to find the unknown.

$? \times 3 = 6\ \ becomes\ \ 3\overline{)\overset{2}{6}}$ $2 \times ? = 6\ \ becomes\ \ 2\overline{)\overset{3}{6}}$

Now let's apply the four-step approach to an example. Suppose a room is 10 feet wide and 15 feet long. How many square feet does it contain?

1. **Read the question**. This problem asks you to find the square footage or area of a rectangular room. So you'll need the area formula for a rectangle.

2. **Write down the formula**. *Area = Length × Width*

3. **Substitute**. Substitute the numbers given in the problem into the formula. The length of the rectangle measures 15 feet, and the width measures 10 feet. *A = 15′ × 10′*

4. **Calculate**. Multiply *Length* times *Width* to get the answer.

$$\begin{array}{r} 15' \\ \times 10' \\ \hline 150 \text{ Sq. Ft.} \end{array}$$

Thus, *A = 150*. The area of the room is 150 square feet.

Suppose the problem gave you different pieces of information about the same room: the area is 150 square feet and it's 10 feet wide. How long is the room? Again, follow the four-step approach.

1. **Read the question**. You're asked to find the length or width of a rectangle. You'll need the area formula again.

2. **Write down the formula**. *Area = Length × Width*

3. **Substitute**. Substitute the numbers given in the problem into the formula. *150 = L × 10*

4. **Calculate**. The length of the rectangle is the unknown. Thus, the basic area formula is converted into a division problem to find the quantity *L*.

$$10'\overline{)150}\text{ Sq. Ft.}^{15'}$$

The quotient of 150 divided by 10 is 15. The length of the rectangle, or of the room, is therefore 15 feet.

Decimal Numbers

To carry out a calculation, it's easier to work with decimal numbers than with fractions or percentages. So if a problem presents you with fractions or percentages, you'll usually convert them into decimal numbers.

Converting Fractions. To convert a fraction into decimal form, divide the top number of the fraction (the numerator) by the bottom number of the fraction (the denominator).

Example: To change ¾ into a decimal, divide the top number, 3, by the bottom number, 4.

$$4\overline{)3.00}^{.75}$$

Example: To convert ²/₃ into a decimal, divide the top number, 2, by the bottom number, 3.

$$3)\overline{2.00}\quad\begin{array}{c}.66667\end{array}$$

If you don't already know them, it's useful to memorize the decimal equivalents of the most common fractions:

¼ = .25

½ = .5

¾ = .75

Converting Percentages. To solve a problem involving a percentage, you'll first convert the percentage into a decimal number, then convert the decimal answer back into percentage form.

To convert a percentage to a decimal, remove the percent sign and move the decimal point two places to the left. It may be necessary to add a zero.

Example:

98% becomes .98

5% becomes .05

32.5% becomes .325

17.5% becomes .175

To convert a decimal into a percentage, do just the opposite. Move the decimal point two places to the right and add a percent sign.

Example:

.15 becomes 15%

.08 becomes 08%

.095 becomes 09.5%

The percent key on a calculator performs the conversion of a percentage to a decimal number automatically. On most calculators, you can key in the digits and press the percent key, and the calculator will display the percentage in decimal form.

Decimal Calculations. Calculators handle decimal numbers in exactly the same way as whole numbers. If you enter a decimal number into the calculator with the decimal point in the correct place, the calculator will do the rest. But if you're working without a calculator, you'll need to apply the following rules.

To add or subtract decimals, put the numbers in a column with their decimal points lined up.

Example: To add 3.75, 14.62, 1.245, 679, 1,412.8, and 1.9, put the numbers in a column with the decimal points lined up as shown below, then add them together.

$$
\begin{array}{r}
3.75 \\
14.62 \\
1.245 \\
679.0 \\
1,412.8 \\
+\ \ \ 1.9 \\
\hline
2,113.315
\end{array}
$$

To multiply decimal numbers, first do the multiplication without worrying about the decimal points. Then put a decimal point into the answer in the correct place. The answer should have as many decimal places (that is, numbers to the right of its decimal point) as the total number of decimal places in the numbers that were multiplied. So count the decimal places in the numbers you are multiplying and put the decimal point the same number of places to the left in the answer.

Example: Multiply 24.6 times 16.7. The two numbers contain a total of two decimal places.

$$
\begin{array}{r}
24.6 \\
\times\ 16.7 \\
\hline
410.82
\end{array}
$$

In some cases, it will be necessary to include one or more zeros in the answer to have the correct number of decimal places.

Example: Multiply .2 times .4. There is a total of two decimal places.

$$
\begin{array}{r}
.2 \\
\times\ .4 \\
\hline
.08
\end{array}
$$

A zero has to be included in the answer in order to move the decimal point two places left.

To divide by a decimal number, move the decimal point in the denominator (the number you're dividing the other number by) all the way to the right. Then move the decimal point in the numerator (the number that you're dividing) the same number of places to the right. (In some cases it will be necessary to add one or more zeros to the numerator in order to move the decimal point the correct number of places.)

Example: Divide 26.145 by 1.5. First move the decimal point in 1.5 all the way to the right (in this case, that's only one place). Then move the decimal point in 26.145 the same number of places to the right.

$$26.145 \div 1.5 \text{ becomes } 261.45 \div 15$$

Now divide.

$$
\begin{array}{r}
17.43 \\
15\overline{)261.45}
\end{array}
$$

Remember, these steps are unnecessary if you're using a calculator. If the numbers are keyed in correctly, the calculator will automatically give you an answer with the decimal point in the correct place.

Area Problems

A real estate agent often needs to calculate the area of a lot, a building, or a room. Area is usually stated in square feet or square yards. The formula to be used for the calculation depends on the shape of the area in question. It may be a square, a rectangle, a triangle, or some combination of those shapes.

Squares and Rectangles

As stated earlier, the formula for finding the area of a square or a rectangle is $A = L \times W$.

Example: If a rectangular room measures 15 feet along one wall and 12 feet along the adjoining wall, how many square feet of carpet would be required to cover the floor?

1. **Read the question.** You're being asked to find the area (the square footage) of a rectangle.

2. **Write down the formula.** $A = L \times W$

3. **Substitute.** $A = 15' \times 12'$

4. **Calculate.** Since the quantity A is unknown, multiply L times W for the answer.

$$\begin{array}{r} 15' \\ \times 12' \\ \hline 180 \ Sq. \ Ft. \end{array}$$

180 square feet of carpet are needed to cover the floor.

Now take the problem one step further. If carpet is on sale for $12 per square yard, how much would it cost to carpet the room?

1. **Read the question.** You're first being asked to determine how many square feet there are in a square yard, and then to determine how many square yards there are in 180 square feet. A square yard is a square that measures one yard on each side. There are three feet in a yard.

2. **Write down the formula.** $A = L \times W$

3. **Substitute.** $A = 3' \times 3'$

4. **Calculate.** Since the quantity A is the unknown, multiply L times W.

$$\begin{array}{r} 3' \\ \times 3' \\ \hline 9 \ Sq. \ Ft. \end{array}$$

So there are 9 square feet in a square yard. Now divide 180 by 9 to see how many square yards there are in 180 square feet.

$$\begin{array}{r} 20 \ \textit{Sq.Yd.} \\ 9\overline{)180} \ \textit{Sq.Ft.} \end{array}$$

Now multiply the number of square yards (20) by the cost per square yard ($12).

$$\begin{array}{r} 20 \ \textit{Square yards} \\ \times \ \$12 \ \textit{Per yard} \\ \hline \$240 \ \textit{Cost to carpet room} \end{array}$$

Triangles

The formula for finding the area of a triangle is:

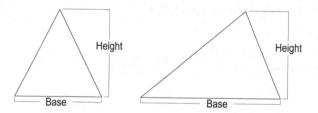

$$\begin{array}{r} \textit{Height} \\ \times \ \textit{½ Base} \\ \hline \textit{Area} \end{array} \quad \text{or} \quad \textit{Area = ½ Base × Height}$$

Example: If commercial building lots in a certain neighborhood are selling for approximately $5 per square foot, approximately how much should the lot pictured below sell for?

1. **Write down the formula.** $A = ½ B \times H$

2. **Substitute.** Area = 55′ (½ of 110) × 75′

3. **Calculate.**

$$\begin{array}{r} 75′ \\ \times \ 55′ \\ \hline 4,125 \ \textit{Sq. Ft.} \end{array}$$

The order of multiplication doesn't matter. You can multiply 110 times 75 and then divide it in half. Or you can divide 110 by 2 and then multiply the result by 75. Or you can divide 75 by 2 and then multiply the result by 110. Whichever way you do it, the answer will be the same.

	Step 1	**Step 2**	**Answer**
a)	$\begin{array}{r} 110 \\ \times\ 75 \\ \hline 8,250 \end{array}$	$\begin{array}{r} 4,125 \\ \overline{2\smash{)}8,250} \end{array}$	*4,125 Sq. Ft.*
b)	$\begin{array}{r} 55 \\ \overline{2\smash{)}110} \end{array}$	$\begin{array}{r} 55 \\ \times\ 75 \\ \hline 4,125 \end{array}$	*4,125 Sq. Ft.*
c)	$\begin{array}{r} 37.75 \\ \overline{2\smash{)}75} \end{array}$	$\begin{array}{r} 37.5 \\ \times\ 110 \\ \hline 4,125 \end{array}$	*4,125 Sq. Ft.*

The lot contains 4,125 square feet. If similar lots are selling for about $5 per square foot, this lot should sell for about $20,625.

$$\begin{array}{r} 4,125 \quad \textit{Square feet} \\ \times\ \$5 \quad \textit{Per square foot} \\ \hline \$20,625 \quad \textit{Selling price} \end{array}$$

Odd Shapes

The best approach to finding the area of an odd-shaped figure is to divide it up into squares, rectangles, and triangles. Find the areas of those figures and add them all up to arrive at the area of the odd-shaped lot, room, or building in question.

Example: If the lot pictured below is leased on a 50-year lease for $3 per square foot per year, with rental payments made monthly, how much would the monthly rent be?

First, divide the lot up into rectangles and triangles.

The next step is to find the area of each of the following figures. The height of the triangle is determined by adding together the 70 foot border of the small rectangle and the 40 foot border of the large rectangle, as shown above.

First, find the area of the triangle.

1. **Write down the formula**. *A = ½ Base × Height*

2. **Substitute**. *A = 32.5′ (½ of 65′) × 110′*

3. **Calculate**.

$$
\begin{array}{r}
32.5′ \\
\times\ 110′ \\
\hline
3{,}575\ \text{Sq. Ft.}
\end{array}
$$

Then, find the area of the large rectangle.

1. **Write down the formula**. *A = Length × Width*

2. **Substitute**. *A = 110′ × 60′*

3. **Calculate**.

$$
\begin{array}{r}
110′ \\
\times\ 60′ \\
\hline
6{,}600\ \text{Sq. Ft.}
\end{array}
$$

Next, find the area of the small rectangle.

1. **Write down the formula**. *A = Length × Width*

2. **Substitute**. *A = 70′ × 50′*

3. **Calculate**.

$$
\begin{array}{r}
50′ \\
\times\ 70′ \\
\hline
3{,}500\ \text{Sq. Ft.}
\end{array}
$$

Finally, add the three areas together to find the area of the entire lot.

$$\begin{array}{r} 3,575 \\ 6,600 \\ +\ 3,500 \\ \hline 13,675 \end{array} \text{ Total square feet}$$

The lot contains 13,675 square feet. At $3 per square foot per year, the annual rent would be $41,025.

$$\begin{array}{rl} 13,675 & \textit{Square feet} \\ \times\ \$3 & \textit{Rent per square foot} \\ \hline \$41,025 & \textit{Annual rent} \end{array}$$

The monthly rental payment would be one-twelfth of the annual rent.

$$\begin{array}{r} \$3,418.75 \\ \hline 12\,)\,\$41,025 \end{array}$$

Thus, the monthly rental payment for this odd-shaped lot is $3,418.75.

Volume Problems

Occasionally you may need to calculate the volume of a three-dimensional space. Volume is usually stated in cubic feet or cubic yards. A formula for calculating volume can be stated as: *Volume = Length × Width × Height*, or $V = L \times W \times H$. It's the same as the area formula, except it has one added element: H, the height of the space being measured.

Example: The floor of a storage unit measures 13 feet 6 inches by 20 feet, and it has a 12-foot ceiling. What is the volume of the unit in cubic yards?

1. **Write down the formula**. $V = L \times W \times H$

2. **Substitute**. $V = 20' \times 13.5' \times 12'$

3. **Calculate**.

<u>Step 1</u>	<u>Step 2</u>
$\begin{array}{rl} 20' & \\ \times\ 13.5' & \\ \hline 270 & \textit{Square feet} \end{array}$	$\begin{array}{rl} 270 & \textit{Square feet} \\ \times\ 12' & \\ \hline 3,240 & \textit{Cubic feet} \end{array}$

4. **Now convert the cubic feet into cubic yards.** As you saw earlier, a square yard measures 3 feet by 3 feet, or 9 square feet. A cubic yard measures 3 feet by 3 feet by 3 feet, or 27 cubic feet. Divide the volume of the storage area in cubic feet by 27 to find the volume in cubic yards.

$$\begin{array}{rl} 120 & \textit{Cubic yards} \\ \hline 27\,)\,3,240 & \textit{Cubic feet} \end{array}$$

The volume of the storage space is 120 cubic yards.

Percentage Problems

Many real estate math problems involve percentages. This includes problems about brokerage commissions, interest on mortgage loans, property appreciation or depreciation, and capitalization.

Solving Percentage Problems

To solve percentage problems, you'll usually convert the percentage into a decimal number, calculate, and then convert the answer back into percentage form. As explained earlier, a percentage is converted into a decimal number by removing the percent sign and moving the decimal point two places to the left. If the percentage is a single digit (for example, 7%), it will be necessary to add a zero (.07). To convert a decimal number into a percentage, you reverse those steps: move the decimal point two places to the right and add the percent sign.

In a math problem, whenever something is expressed as a percentage "of" another number, that indicates that you should multiply that other number by the percentage. For instance, what is 75% of $40,000?

<u>**Step 1**</u>   <u>**Step 2**</u>

75% becomes .75 $40,000
                            $\times$ .75
                            ——————
                            $30,000

Percentage problems basically ask you to find a part of a whole. The whole is a larger figure, such as a property's sales price. The part is a smaller figure, such as a broker's commission. The general formula might be stated thus: *A percentage of the whole equals the part.* This can be written as an equation.

$$\frac{Whole \times Percentage}{Part} \quad \text{or} \quad Part = Whole \times Percentage$$

Example: A house is listed for sale at a price of $172,000, with an agreement to pay the broker a commission of 6% of the sales price. The property sells for $170,000. How much is the commission?

1. **Write down the formula.** $P = W \times \%$

2. **Substitute**. Change the percentage into a decimal number: 6% becomes .06. $P = \$170,000 \times .06$

3. **Calculate**.

   $170,000 *Sales price*
   $\times$ .06 *Commission rate*
   ——————
   $10,200 *Commission*

The broker's commission is $10,200.

In some percentage problems, the part is given and you're asked to calculate either the whole or the percentage. For those problems, you'll need to rearrange the percentage formula into a division problem. If the whole is the unknown, divide the part by the percentage.

$$\text{Percentage}\overline{)\begin{array}{c}\textit{Whole}\\ \textit{Part}\end{array}}\qquad\text{or}\qquad \textit{Whole} = \textit{Part} \div \textit{Percentage}$$

If the percentage is the unknown, divide the part by the whole:

$$\text{Whole}\overline{)\begin{array}{c}\textit{Percentage}\\ \textit{Part}\end{array}}\qquad\text{or}\qquad \textit{Percentage} = \textit{Part} \div \textit{Whole}$$

Notice that in either case, you'll be dividing the value of the part by either the whole (to determine the percentage) or by the percentage (to determine the whole).

Commission Problems

Like the example above, most commission problems can be solved with the general percentage formula.

$$\begin{array}{c}\textit{Whole}\\ \underline{\times\ \textit{Percentage}}\\ \textit{Part}\end{array}\qquad\text{or}\qquad \textit{Part} = \textit{Whole} \times \textit{Percentage}$$

The percentage is the commission rate, and the whole is the amount that the commission is based on. In most problems, this will be the sales price of a piece of property. The part is the amount of the commission.

Example: A listing agreement provides for a commission of 7% of the sales price to be paid to the broker. If the broker has agreed to pay the salesperson 60% of the commission, how much will the salesperson receive if the property sells for $145,000?

1. **Write down the formula.** $P = W \times \%$

2. **Substitute**. Change the percentage to a decimal number: 7% becomes .07.
   $P = \$145,000 \times .07$

3. **Calculate.** The part is the unknown quantity, so the percentage is multiplied by the whole.

   $$\begin{array}{rl}\$145,000 & \textit{Sales price}\\ \underline{\times\ .07} & \textit{Commission rate}\\ \$10,150 & \textit{Total commission}\end{array}$$

The total commission is $10,150. The salesperson is entitled to 60% of the total commission. Apply the percentage formula again to determine the amount of the salesperson's share.

1. **Write down the formula.** $P = W \times \%$

2. **Substitute.** Convert the percentage to a decimal number: 60% becomes .60.
   $P = \$10,150 \times .60$

3. **Calculate.**

$10,150   *Total commission*
×.60   *Salesperson's percentage*
$6,090   *Saleperson's share*

The following example illustrates another form that commission problems can take.

Example: A listing agreement provided for a two-tiered commission based on the property's sales price. The commission would be 7% of the first $100,000 and 5% of any amount over $100,000. If the commission was $8,250, what was the sales price?

1. **Read the question.** You're given the commission rates and the amount of the commission, and then asked to find the sales price. Your first step in the process is to find out how much of the commission amount is attributable to the first $100,000 of the sales price.

2. **Write down the formula.** $P = W \times \%$

3. **Substitute**, converting the percentage to a decimal. $P = \$100,000 \times .07$

4. **Calculate**.

$100,000
× .07
$7,000

So $7,000 of the commission is based on the first $100,000 of the sales price. Next, subtract to find the amount of the rest of the commission.

$8,250   *Total commission*
− 7,000   *Commission from first $100,000*
$1,250

Now you know that out of the total commission, $1,250 is attributable to the part of the sales price in excess of $100,000. You can use that figure along with the second-tier commission rate (5% of the amount over $100,000) to determine by how much the sales price exceeded $100,000.

1. **Write down the formula.** $P = W \times \%$

2. **Substitute**, converting the percentage to a decimal. $\$1,250 = W \times .05$

3. **Calculate**. The quantity W (the whole) is the unknown. To isolate the unknown, the basic formula must be turned into a division problem. The part divided by the percentage equals the whole.

$$.05\overline{)\,\$1,250\,}^{\$25,000}$$

This shows that the portion of the sales price in excess of $100,000 amounted to $25,000. Thus, the total sales price is $100,000 plus $25,000, or $125,000.

Loan Problems

Loan problems include interest problems and principal balance problems. These can be solved using the general percentage formula, *Part = Whole × Percentage*. Here, the part is the amount of the interest, the whole is the loan amount or principal balance, and the percentage is the interest rate.

Example: Henry borrows $5,000 for one year and agrees to pay 7% interest. How much interest will he be required to pay?

1. **Write down the formula.** $P = W \times \%$

2. **Substitute.** $P = \$5,000 \times .07$

3. **Calculate.**

   5000 *Loan amount*
   $\times .07$ *Interest rate*
   $\overline{\$350}$ *Interest*

Henry will pay $350 in interest.

Interest rates are expressed as annual rates—a certain percentage per year. Some problems present you with monthly, quarterly, or semi-annual interest payments instead of the annual amount. In that case, you'll need to multiply the payment amount stated in the problem to determine the annual amount before you substitute the numbers into the formula.

Example: If $450 in interest accrues on a $7,200 interest-only loan in six months, what is the annual interest rate?

1. **Read the question.** You're asked to find the annual interest rate, but the interest amount given in the problem ($450) accrued in only six months. The annual interest amount would be double that, or $900.

2. **Write down the formula.** $P = W \times \%$

3. **Substitute.** For the part (the interest amount), be sure to use the annual figure, $900. $\$900 = \$7,000 \times Percentage$

4. **Calculate.** Rearrange the formula to isolate the unknown (in this case, the percentage). The part is divided by the whole to determine the percentage.

$$\frac{.125}{\$7,200)\overline{\$900}}$$

Convert the decimal number back into a percentage: .125 becomes 12.5%. Thus, the annual interest rate is 12½%.

Some loan problems ask you to determine a loan's current principal balance at a certain point in the loan term.

Example: A home loan has monthly payments of $625, which include principal and 9% interest and $47.50 per month for tax and insurance reserves. If $27.75

of the June 1 payment was applied to the principal, what was the outstanding principal balance during the month of May? (Mortgage interest is paid in arrears, so the June payment includes the interest that accrued during May.)

1. **Write down the formula**. $P = W \times \%$. Once again, in this context the part is the amount of interest, the whole is the loan balance, and the percentage is the interest rate.

2. **Substitute**. First, find the interest portion of the payment by subtracting the reserves and the principal portion.

$$
\begin{array}{rl}
\$625.00 & \text{Total June payment} \\
47.50 & \text{Reserves} \\
-\ 27.75 & \text{Principal} \\
\hline
\$549.75 & \text{Interest portion of payment}
\end{array}
$$

Next, multiply the interest portion by 12 to determine the annual interest amount.

$$
\begin{array}{r}
\$549.75 \\
\times\ 12 \\
\hline
\$6,597
\end{array}
$$

Now substitute the annual interest amount and rate into the formula. $\$6,597 = W \times .09$

3. **Calculate**. Rearrange the formula to isolate the unknown, W. This is a divison problem.

$$
.09 \overline{)\ \$6,597} = \$73,300
$$

The outstanding principal balance for May was $73,300.

Profit or Loss Problems

Profit or loss problems ask you to compare the cost or value of a piece of property at an earlier point in time with its cost or value at a later point. They can be solved using a variation on the percentage formula. Instead of *Part = Whole × Percentage*, the formula is stated like this:

$$
\begin{array}{c}
Then \\
\times\ Percentage \\
\hline
Now
\end{array}
\qquad \text{or} \qquad Now = Then \times Percentage
$$

The Then spot in the formula is for the value or cost of the property at an earlier time specified in the problem. The Now spot is for the value or cost at a later time. The percentage is 100% plus the percentage of profit or minus the percentage of loss.

The idea is to express the value of the property after a profit or loss (Now) as a percentage of the property's value before the profit or loss (Then). If there is no profit or loss, the Now value is exactly 100% of the Then value, because the value has not changed. If there is a profit, the Now value will be greater than 100% of the Then value, since the value has increased. If there is a loss, the Now value will be less than 100% of the Then value.

Example: Bonnie bought a house five years ago for $150,000 and sold it this year for 30% more than she paid for it. What did she sell it for?

1. **Write down the formula.** *Now = Then × %*

2. **Substitute.** To get the percentage, you must add the percentage of profit to or subtract the percentage of loss from 100%. In this case there is a profit, so you add 30% to 100%, then convert it to a decimal number. 130% becomes 1.30. *Now = $150,000 × 1.30*

3. **Calculate.**

$$\begin{array}{r} \$150,000 \\ \times\ \ 1.30 \\ \hline \$195,000 \end{array}$$

Bonnie sold her house for $195,000.

Example: Paul sold his house this year for $210,000. He paid $262,500 for it two years ago. What was the percentage of loss?

1. **Write down the formula.** *Now = Then × %*

2. **Substitute.** *$210,000 = $262,500 × %*

3. **Calculate.** The percentage is the unknown quantity; thus, the formula is rearranged to isolate the percentage.

$$\$262,500 \overline{)\,\$210,000} \quad .80\ or\ 80\%$$

The Now value is approximately 80% of the Then value. Subtract 80% from 100% to find the percentage of loss.

$$\begin{array}{r} 100\% \\ -\ \ 80\% \\ \hline 20\%\ \ Loss \end{array}$$

Paul took a 20% loss on the sale of his house.

Lets look at another example, except this time there is a profit instead of a loss.

Example: Martha bought her home six years ago for $125,800. She sold it recently for $140,900. What was her percentage of profit?

1. **Write down the formula.** *Now = Then × %*

2. **Substitute.** *$140,900 = $125,800 × %*

3. **Calculate.** Once again, the percentage is the unknown quantity; thus, the formula is rearranged to isolate the percentage.

$$\$125,800 \overline{)\,\$140,900} \quad 1.12\ or\ 112\%$$

The Now value is approximately 112% of the Then value. Subtract 100% from 112%, and you determine Martha received 100% of what she paid for it, plus a 12% profit.

Let's try to solve one last variation of this type of problem.

Example: Ken sold his duplex for $280,000, which represents a 16% profit over what he paid for it five years ago. What did Ken originally pay for the property?

1. **Write down the formula.** *Now = Then × %*

2. **Substitute.** *$280,000 = Then × 116%*

3. **Calculate.** In this instance, the unknown is the price Ken originally paid for the duplex; so you isolate the Then part of the equation.

$$1.16 \overline{) \begin{array}{c} \$241,379.31 \\ \$280,000 \end{array}}$$

The price paid by Ken was $241,380.31.

Some profit or loss problems involve appreciation or depreciation that has accrued at an annual rate over a specified number of years. You solve this type of problem by applying the Then and Now formula one year at a time.

Example: A property that is currently worth $174,000 has depreciated 3% per year for the past four years. How much was it worth four years ago?

1. **Write down the formula.** *Now = Then × %*

2. **Substitute.** Because the property is worth 3% less than it was one year ago, the percentage is 97% (100% − 3% = 97%). *$174,000 = Then × .97*

3. **Calculate.** Rearrange the formula to isolate the unknown, the Then value.

$$.97 \overline{) \begin{array}{c} \$179,381.44 \\ \$174,000 \end{array}}$$

The property was worth $179,381.44 one year ago. Apply the formula to $179,381.44 to determine the property's value two years ago. Repeat the process twice more to find the value four years ago.

$$\$179,381.44 \div .97 = \$184,929.31$$
$$\$184,929.31 \div .97 = \$190,648.77$$
$$\$190,648.77 \div .97 = \$196,545.12$$

The property was worth about $196,545 four years ago.

Capitalization Problems

Capitalization problems involve the capitalization approach to value, a method of real estate appraisal that is discussed in detail in Chapter 12.

The capitalization formula is another variation on the percentage formula. Instead of *Part = Whole × Percentage*, the formula is stated like this:

$$\frac{Value \times Capitalization\ Rate}{Income} \quad \text{or} \quad Income = Value \times Capitalization\ Rate$$

The value here is an investment property's value, or the purchase price an investor should be willing to pay for the property in order to obtain a specified rate of return.

The specified rate of return is the capitalization rate. This is the percentage of return the investor desires on the investment. The desired rate of return varies according to many factors. A higher desired rate of return will mean a higher capitalization rate and a lower value for the property.

The income in the capitalization formula is the annual net income produced by the investment property.

Example: A property produces an annual net income of $26,000. If an investor desires an 11% rate of return, what should he pay for the property?

1. **Write down the formula.** $I = V \times \%$

2. **Substitute.** $\$26,000 = V \times .11$

3. **Calculate.** Rearrange the formula to isolate the unknown, V.

$$.11\overline{)\ \$26,000}^{\ \$236,363.64}$$

The investor should be willing to pay approximately $236,364 for the property.

Example: If a property is valued at $100,000 using an 8% capitalization rate, what would its value be using a 10% capitalization rate? First, apply the capitalization formula to determine the property's annual net income.

1. **Write down the formula.** $I = V \times \%$

2. **Substitute.** $I = \$100,000 \times .08$

3. **Calculate.**

$$
\begin{array}{rl}
\$100,000 & Value \\
\times\ .08 & Capitalization\ rate \\
\hline
\$8,000 & Annual\ net\ income
\end{array}
$$

The net income is $8,000 annually. Now substitute that figure into the formula to find the value at a 10% capitalization rate.

4. **Substitute.** $\$8,000 = V \times .10$

5. **Calculate.** Rearrange the formula to isolate the unknown quantity, V.

$$.10\overline{)\ \$8,000}^{\ \$80,000}$$

So the value of the same property using a 10% capitalization rate is $80,000, compared to $100,000 at the 8% rate. As you can see, a higher capitalization rate applied to the same net income results in a lower value for the property.

In some problems, it's necessary to deduct a bad debt/vacancy factor and operating expenses from gross income to arrive at the net income.

Example: A ten-unit apartment building has six units that rent for $800 per month and four units that rent for $850 per month. Allow 5% for vacancies and uncollected rent. Operating expenses include: annual property taxes of $7,200, monthly utilities of $2,475, and maintenance expenses of approximately $13,600 per year. The owner has an outstanding mortgage balance of $257,000 at 8% interest, with monthly payments of $2,150. If an investor requires a 7.5% rate of return, how much should she offer for the property?

1. **Write down the formula.** $I = V \times \%$

2. **Substitute**. Remember that the income referred to in the capitalization formula is annual net income. Thus, it's necessary to calculate the annual net income before substituting. The first step in that process is calculating the annual gross income.

$$\$800 \times 12 \ months = \ \$9,600/year \times 6 \ units = \$57,600$$
$$\$850 \times 12 \ months = \$10,200/year \times 4 \ units = \underline{\$40,800}$$
$$\$98,400$$

The gross income is $98,400 per year.

Next, calculate the bad debt/vacancy factor and deduct it from the gross income to find the effective gross income. The bad debt/vacancy factor is 5% of the gross income.

$$\begin{array}{rl} \$98,400 & Gross \ income \\ \underline{\times \ \ .05} & \\ \$4,920 & Bad \ debts \ and \ vacancies \end{array}$$

Thus, the loss to be expected from uncollected rents and vacancies is $4,920 per year.

$$\begin{array}{rl} \$98,400 & Gross \ income \\ \underline{- \ \ 4,920} & Bad \ debts \ and \ vacancies \\ \$93,480 & Effective \ gross \ income \end{array}$$

The operating expenses must be deducted from the effective gross income to arrive at the net income. Remember, since you are trying to find annual net income, all the expenses must be annual also. The operating expenses add up as follows:

$$\begin{array}{rl} \$7,200 & Property \ taxes \\ \$29,700 & Utilities \ (at \ \$2,475 \ per \ month) \\ \underline{+ \ \$13,600} & Maintenance \\ \$50,500 & Annual \ operating \ expenses \end{array}$$

The annual operating expenses are $50,500. (The mortgage payments are not treated as operating expenses. See Chapter 12.) Subtract the operating expenses from the effective gross income to determine the annual net income.

$93,480   *Effective gross income*
$-\ 50,500$ *Annual operating expenses*
$\overline{\$42,980}$ *Annual net income*

Now, substitute the net income and the cap rate into the formula $I = V \times \%$.
$\$42,980 = V \times .075$

3. **Calculate**. Rearrange the formula to isolate the unknown quantity, V.

$$.075\overline{)\ \$42,980} \quad \$573,067$$

The investor should be willing to pay approximately $573,067 for the property.

Example: Continuing with the previous example, if an investor paid $750,000 for the apartment building, what capitalization rate was used? (Assume that the property's income and operating expenses were the same.)

1. **Write down the formula**. $V \times \% = I$

2. **Substitute**. You already know the net income from the preceding problem.
$\$42,980 = \$750,000 \times \%$

3. **Calculate**. Isolate the unknown quantity, the capitalization rate.

$$\$750,000\overline{)\ \$42,980} \quad .0573\ or\ 5.73\%$$

The investor used a capitalization rate of approximately 5.7%.

A capitalization problem may give you the property's **operating expense ratio** (O.E.R.). The O.E.R. is the percentage of the gross income that is used to pay the annual operating expenses. The remainder is the annual net income.

Example: The property's annual gross income is $480,000, and its O.E.R. is 79%. If an investor wants a 10½% return, how much is the property worth to her?

1. **Write down the formula**. $I = V \times \%$

2. **Substitute**. Calculate the annual operating expenses using the operating expense ratio. Then subtract the operating expenses from the gross income to arrive at the annual net income.

$\$480,000 \times .79 = \$379,200$ *Annual operating expenses*
$\$480,000 - \$379,200 = \$100,800$ *Annual net income*

Now substitute the income and the cap rate into the formula. $\$100,800 = V \times .105$

3. **Calculate**. Rearrange the formula to isolate the unknown, V.

$$.105\overline{)\ \$100,800} \quad \$960,000\ Value$$

The investor should be willing to pay $960,000 for the property.

Tax Assessment Problems

Many tax assessment problems can be solved using this formula: *Tax = Assessed Value × Tax Rate*. You may first have to determine the assessed value before you can carry out the rest of the calculations. Assessed value is a property's value for taxation purposes.

Example: According to the tax assessor, the property's market value is $292,300. The applicable assessment ratio is 85%. If the tax rate is 3%, how much is the annual tax amount?

1. **Multiply** the market value by the assessment ratio to determine the assessed value of the property. *$292,300 × 85% = $248,455 Assessed value*

2. **Substitute** the assessed value and the tax rate into the formula. *Tax = $248,455 × .03*

3. **Calculate**.

   $248,455   *Assessed value*
   × .03   *Tax rate*
   ──────────
   $7,453.65   *Annual taxes*

The annual taxes for this property are $7,453.65.

In some problems, the tax rate is not stated as a percentage of the assessed value. Instead, it is expressed as a dollar amount per hundred or per thousand dollars of assessed value.

Example: A property with an assessed value of $173,000 is taxed at a rate of $2.35 per hundred dollars of assessed value. How much is the annual tax amount?

1. **Divide** $173,000 by 100 to determine how many hundred dollar increments there are in the assessed value:

   $$100\overline{)\,173,000\,} \quad 1,730 \;\; \$100 \; increments$$

2. **Multiply** the number of hundred dollar increments by the tax rate to calculate the annual tax amount.

   1,730   *$100 increments*
   × $2.35   *Tax rate*
   ──────────
   $4,065.50   *Annual taxes*

The annual tax is $4,065.50.

In other problems, the tax rate is expressed as a specified number of mills per dollar of assessed value. A mill is one-tenth of one cent (.001). Ten mills equals one cent, and 100 mills equals 10 cents.

Example: The property's market value is $310,000 and the assessment ratio is 70%. The tax rate is 21 mills per dollar of assessed value. How much is the annual tax amount?

1. **Multiply** the market value by the assessment ratio to find the assessed value.

$310,000   Market value
   × .70   Assessment ratio
$217,000   Assessed value

2. **Multiply** the assessed value by the tax rate to determine the tax. In decimal form, 21 mills is .021.

$217,000   Assessed value
   × .021   Tax rate
  $4,557   Annual tax

The annual tax is $4,557.

Seller's Net Problems

In a seller's net problem, you're told that a seller wants to take away a specified net amount from closing, after paying the broker's commission and other closing costs. You're then asked to calculate how much the property will have to sell for if the seller is to receive the desired net.

Example: The seller wants to net $50,000 from the sale of her home. She will have to pay off her mortgage balance, which is approximately $126,500, and pay $1,560 for repairs, $2,015 for other closing costs, and a 7% broker's commission. What's the minimum sales price that will net the seller $50,000?

1. **Add** the seller's desired net to the costs of sale, excluding the commission.

$50,000   Seller's net
126,500   Mortgage
  1,560   Repairs
+ 2,015   Closing costs
$180,075   Total

$180,075 is the amount that must be left to the seller after the commision has been paid, if she is to be able to pay all of the listed expenses and still have $50,000 left over.

2. **Subtract** the commission rate from 100%. *100% – 7% = 93%*

3. **Divide** the total from step one by the percentage from step two. Since the commission rate will be 7% of the sales price, the seller's net plus the other costs will have to equal 93% of the sales price.

$193,629   Selling price
.93)$180,075

The property will have to sell for approximately $193,629 for the seller to net $50,000.

Proration Problems

Proration is the allocation of an expense between two or more parties. As was explained in Chapter 13, prorations are required in real estate closings, where a variety of expenses are prorated based on the closing date.

There are basically three steps in the proration process:

1. Calculate the per diem (daily) rate of the expense.
2. Determine the number of days for which one person is responsible for the expense.
3. Multiply the per diem rate by the number of days to determine the share of the expense that one party is responsible for.

$$\begin{array}{r} Day \\ \times\ Rate \\ \hline Share \end{array} \quad \text{or} \quad Share = Rate \times Days$$

To determine the per diem rate of an annual expense, divide the amount of the expense by 365 days, or 366 in a leap year. Some problems will instruct you to divide by 360 days instead, to simplify the calculation. (A 360-day year is sometimes referred to as a banker's year, as opposed to a calendar year.)

To determine the per diem rate of a monthly expense when you are prorating on the basis of a calendar year, divide the amount of the expense by the number of days in that particular month. Alternatively, to simplify the calculation, you may be instructed to base your prorations on a banker's year, which means that every month has 30 days, including February.

We'll present you with a series of examples concerning the proration of various expenses: property taxes, hazard insurance, rent, and mortgage interest. See Chapter 13 for more information about these expenses.

Property Tax Prorations

Property taxes are an annual expense. At closing, the taxes may or may not have been paid yet. If they've already been paid, the buyer will owe the seller a share of the taxes. If they haven't been paid, the seller will owe the buyer a share. Either way, the proration process is essentially the same.

Example: The closing date is August 3, and the seller has already paid the annual property taxes, which were $2,045. At closing, the seller is entitled to a credit for the tax amount covering the period from August 3 through December 31. The same amount will be a debit for the buyer. How much will the buyer owe the seller for the property taxes? Use a 360-day year with 30-day months for your calculations.

1. **Calculate the per diem rate** for the property taxes, using a 360-day year.

$$\begin{array}{r} \$5.68\ Per\ diem \\ 360\overline{)\$2,045} \end{array}$$

2. **Count the number of days** that the buyer is responsible for, using 30-day months.

    28 days   August 3 through 30
    30 days   September
    30 days   October
    30 days   November
    + 30 days   December
    _____
    148 days

3. **Substitute** the rate and number of days into the formula ($S = R \times D$), then calculate.

    148   Days
    × $5.68   Per diem
    _____
    $840.64   Credit to seller

At closing, the buyer will be debited $840.64 and the seller will be credited $840.64 for the property taxes from August 3 through the end of the year.

In the following example, the taxes haven't been paid yet. You're given the seller's share of the taxes and asked to calculate the annual tax amount.

Example: The seller hasn't paid any portion of the annual taxes. The closing is scheduled for March 21. At closing, the seller will owe the buyer $663.60 for the taxes. How much was the annual tax bill? This time, use a 365-day year and exact-day months in your calculations. The buyer's responsibility for the taxes begins on the day of closing.

1. **Write down the formula.** $S = R \times D$

2. **Substitute**. First add up the number of days that the seller is responsible for.

    31 days   January
    28 days   February
    + 20 days   March
    _____
    79 days

    Substitute the seller's share and the number of days into the formula. *$663.60 = R × 79*

3. **Calculate**. Rearrange the formula to isolate the unknown, *R*.

    $8.40   Per diem
    _____
    79)$663.60

    The per diem rate is $8.40. Multiply that by 365 to arrive at the annual tax amount.

    365   Days
    × $8.40   Per diem
    _____
    $3,066   Annual taxes

The annual taxes were $3,066.

Insurance Prorations

A seller is entitled to a refund from the hazard insurance company for any prepaid insurance coverage extending beyond the closing date.

Example: The Morgans are selling their house, and the transaction is closing on May 12. They paid an annual hazard insurance premium of $810 that provides coverage through the end of October. If the insurance company does not charge the sellers for the day of closing, how much of the premium will be refunded to them? Base your calculations on a 360-day year.

1. **Calculate the per diem rate** for the insurance, using a 360-day year.

$$\frac{\$2.25\ Per\ diem}{360\overline{)\$180}}$$

2. **Add up the number of days** the sellers are owed a refund for, using 30-day months.

$$
\begin{array}{rl}
19\ days & May \\
30\ days & June \\
30\ days & July \\
30\ days & August \\
30\ days & September \\
+\ 30\ days & October \\
\hline
169\ days &
\end{array}
$$

3. **Substitute** the rate and number of days into the formula ($S = R \times D$), then calculate.

$$
\begin{array}{rl}
169 & Days \\
\times\ \$2.25 & Per\ diem \\
\hline
\$380.25 & Credit\ to\ seller
\end{array}
$$

The insurance company will refund $380.25 to the sellers.

Rent Prorations

If the property being sold is rental property, the seller will owe the buyer a prorated share of any rent that has been paid in advance.

Example: A ten-unit apartment building is being sold, with the closing scheduled for April 23. Four of the units rent for $1,500 per month, and the other six rent for $1,200 per month. All of the tenants paid their April rent on time. What share of the prepaid rents will the seller owe the buyer at closing?

1. **Determine the total amount** of rent owed for April.

$$\$1,500 \times 4 = \$6,000$$
$$\$1,200 \times 6 = \$7,200$$
$$\$6,000 + \$7,200 = \$13,200$$

2. **Calculate the per diem rate** for the month of April.

$$\frac{\$440\ Per\ diem}{30\overline{)\$13,200}}$$

3. **Determine the number of days** of rent the buyer is entitled to, beginning on the closing date. April 23 through April 30 is eight days.

4. **Substitute** and **calculate**.

$$
\begin{array}{rl}
440 & \text{Per diem} \\
\times\ 8 & \text{Days} \\
\hline
\$3,520 & \text{Prorated rent}
\end{array}
$$

The seller will owe the buyer $3,520 in prepaid rents at closing.

Mortgage Interest Prorations

Two different types of mortgage interest prorations are necessary in most transactions, one for the seller and one for the buyer. The seller typically owes a final interest payment on the loan he is paying off.

Example: The remaining balance on the seller's mortgage is $317,550, and the interest rate is 8%. The closing date is set for July 6. Because mortgage interest is paid in arrears, the mortgage payment that the seller paid on July 1 covers the interest that accrued during June. At closing, the seller owes the lender interest covering July 1 through the closing date. How much will that interest payment be? Base your calculations on a calendar year.

1. First calculate the annual interest, using the percentage formula.

    a) **Write down the formula.** *Payment = Loan balance × Interest*

    b) **Substitute.** *P = $317,550 × .08*

    c) **Calculate.**

$$
\begin{array}{rl}
\$317,550 & \text{Loan amount} \\
\times\ .08 & \text{Interest rate} \\
\hline
\$25,404 & \text{Annual interest}
\end{array}
$$

2. Next, find the per diem rate of the expense. Divide the annual rate by 365.

$$
\begin{array}{r}
\$69.60\ \text{Per diem} \\
\hline
365\overline{)\$25,404}
\end{array}
$$

3. Determine the number of days the seller owes interest for. The lender will charge the seller interest for the day of closing. Thus, the seller owes interest for six days, from July 1 through July 6.

4. Finally, substitute the numbers into the proration formula ($S = R \times D$) and calculate.

$$
\begin{array}{rl}
\$69.60 & \text{Per diem} \\
\times\ 6 & \text{Days} \\
\hline
\$417.60 & \text{Final interest payment}
\end{array}
$$

At closing, the seller will be required to make a final interest payment of $417.60.

The buyer also owes some mortgage interest at closing. This is prepaid interest (interim interest) on the buyer's new loan. Prepaid interest covers the closing date through the last day of the month in which closing takes place.

Example: The principal amount of the buyer's new loan is $230,680. The interest rate is 8%. The transaction closes on June 22. How much prepaid interest will the buyer's lender require the buyer to pay at closing? Base your calculations on a 365-day year.

1. Use the percentage formula to calculate the annual amount of interest.

   a) **Write down the formula**. *Payment = Loan Balance × Interest rate*

   b) **Substitute**. *P = $230,680 × 8%*

   c) **Calculate**.

   $$\begin{array}{r} \$230,689 \\ \times\ .08 \\ \hline \$18,454.40 \end{array}$$

2. Find the per diem rate of the expense. Divide the annual rate by 365.

   $$365\overline{)\$18,454.40} \quad \$50.56 \text{ Per diem}$$

3. Determine the number of days the buyer is responsible for. In prepaid interest prorations, the buyer pays for the day of closing. There are nine days: June 22, 23, 24, 25, 26, 27, 28, 29, and 30.

4. Substitute the daily rate and number of days into the proration formula *(S = R × D)* and calculate.

   $$\begin{array}{r} \$50.56 \text{ Per diem} \\ \times\ 9 \text{ Days} \\ \hline \$455.04 \text{ Prepaid interest} \end{array}$$

The buyer's interest charge would be $455.04.

Chapter Summary

Converting fractions to decimals:
Divide numerator (top number) by denominator (bottom number).

Converting percentages to decimals:
Move decimal point two places to the left and drop the percent sign.

Converting decimals to percentages:
Move decimal point two places to the right and add a percent sign.

Area formula for squares and rectangles:
Area = Length × Width
A = L × W

Area formula for triangles:
Area = ½ Base × Height
A = ½ B × H

Volume formula:
Volume = Length × Width × Height
V = L × W × H

Percentage formula:
Part = Whole × Percentage
P = W × %

Profit or loss formula:
Now = Then × %

Capitalization formula:
Income = Rate × Value
I = V × %

Proration formula:
Share = Daily Rate × Number of Days
S = R × D

1. Find annual or monthly amount;

2. Find daily rate;

3. Determine number of days; and

4. Substitute and calculate.

Chapter Quiz

1. Christine and Tom bought a house one year ago for $168,500. If property values in their neighborhood are increasing at an annual rate of 7%, what is the current market value of their house?

   a) $180,295
   b) $184,270
   c) $195,980
   d) $198,893

2. A home just sold for $183,500. The listing broker charged the seller a 6½% commission. The listing broker will pay 50% of that amount to the selling broker, and 25% to the listing salesperson. How much will the listing salesperson's share of the commission be?

   a) $11,927
   b) $5,963
   c) $3,642
   d) $2,982

3. A rectangular lot that has a 45-foot frontage and contains 1,080 square yards has a depth of:

   a) 63 feet
   b) 216 feet
   c) 188 feet
   d) 97 feet

4. An acre contains 43,560 square feet. What is the maximum number of lots measuring 50 feet by 100 feet that can be created from a one-acre parcel?

   a) Six
   b) Seven
   c) Eight
   d) Nine

5. Felicia sold a client's building for $80,000 and received a commission of $5,600. What was her commission rate?

   a) 6.5%
   b) 7%
   c) 7.5%
   d) 8%

6. Jake bought a lot for $5,000 and later sold it for $8,000. What was his percentage of profit?

   a) 60%
   b) 75%
   c) 80%
   d) 85%

7. Diane wants to purchase an income property that has an annual net income of $16,000. If she wants at least an 8% return on her investment, what is the most she should pay for the property?

   a) $150,000
   b) $175,000
   c) $195,000
   d) $200,000

8. George purchases a building for $85,000. The building generates a yearly net income of $5,100. What is his rate of return?

   a) 5.5%
   b) 6%
   c) 6.5%
   d) 7%

9. How many square yards are there in a rectangle that measures 75 × 30 feet?

   a) 6,750
   b) 2,250
   c) 750
   d) 250

10. Mike is purchasing an apartment building. The closing date is September 15, and the seller has already collected the monthly rents in the amount of $13,960 for September. At closing, the seller will have to pay Mike a prorated share of the September rents, which will amount to approximately:

   a) $612
   b) $931
   c) $7,445
   d) $9,035

11. A triangular lot has a 40-foot base and a 30-foot height. What is the area of the lot?

   a) 500 square feet
   b) 600 square feet
   c) 750 square feet
   d) 650 square feet

12. What is the decimal equivalent of five-eighths (5/8)?

   a) .625
   b) .0825
   c) 1.58
   d) 1.60

13. Kay has obtained a $112,000 loan at 8.5% interest to finance the purchase of a home. At closing, the lender will require her to prepay interest for April 26 through April 30. Assuming that the closing agent uses a 365-day year for the proration, how much will that prepaid interest amount to?

   a) $64.35
   b) $104.32
   c) $130.40
   d) $1,403.84

14. The Binghams are selling their house and paying off the mortgage at closing. The remaining principal balance on the mortgage at closing will be $168,301.50. They will also have to pay interest that accrued over the 7-day period between their last mortgage payment and the closing date. If the annual interest rate on the Binghams' mortgage was 10%, how much will they have to pay in interest at closing? (Use a 365-day year for the proration.)

   a) $85.21
   b) $322.77
   c) $409.86
   d) $694.41

15. Carol has just paid $460,000 for a building that will bring her a 9.75% return on her investment. What is the building's annual net income?

   a) $34,965
   b) $36,750
   c) $41,220
   d) $44,850

👉 Answer Key

1. a)   The current market value of Christine and Tom's house is approximately $180,295. The question asks you to determine the current value of the house based on its earlier value, so the applicable formula is *Then × % = Now*. Here, the value has increased by 7%, so the appropriate percentage is 107% (100% + 7%), or 1.07 (as a decimal). *$168,500 × 1.07 = $180,295.*

2. d)   The listing salesperson will get $2,982. This is a percentage question with two parts. First multiply the sales price by the broker's commission rate to determine the full commission. *$183,500 × .065 = $11,927.50.* Then multiply that number by 25% to determine the listing salesperson's share: *$11,927.50 × .25 = $2,981.88*

3. b)   The depth of the lot is 216 feet. The question asks you to determine the length of one of the sides of a rectangle, so the applicable formula is *Area = Length × Width, A = L × W.*

First convert the area from square yards to square feet, so that it is in the same unit of measurement as the frontage. A square yard is a square that measures 3 feet on each side, or 9 square feet (3 × 3 = 9). Thus, 1,080 square yards is 9,720 square feet (*1,080 × 9 = 9,720*).

Now substitute the numbers you have into the formula. *9,720 = 45 × L.* Isolate the unknown quantity, H, by changing to another version of the same formula: *L = 9,720 ÷ 45.*

Divide the area, 9,720 square feet, by the width, 45 feet, to determine the length of the rectangle: *9,720 ÷ 45 = 216 feet.*

4. c)   There are eight 50' × 100' lots in an acre, with one somewhat smaller lot left over. Use the area formula to determine the area of a 50' × 100' lot. *A = 50 × 100 = 5,000 square feet.* Thus, each lot will have an area of 5,000 square feet. Now divide the total number of square feet in the acre by the area of each lot: *43,560 ÷ 5,000 = 8.71.*

5. b)   Felicia's commission rate was 7%. Use the percentage formula, *Part = Whole × Percentage, P = W × %.* You know the part ($5,600) and the total ($80,000), so switch the formula to isolate the percentage, then substitute and calculate.

P ÷ W = %

$5,600 ÷ $80,000 = %

$5,600 ÷ $80,000 = .07. Thus, the commission rate was 7%.

6. a)   Jake's profit on the sale of the lot was 60%. The question asks you to determine what percentage of the original price (the Then value) the sales price (the Now value) represents. So use the formula *Now = Then × %*, switching it around to isolate the unknown quantity, the percentage:

Now ÷ Then = %

$8,000 ÷ $5,000 = 1.60 = 160%

The Now value is 160% of the Then value—in other words, 60% more than the Then value. Thus, Jake's profit on the sale was 60%.

7. d) Diane could pay $200,000 for the property and get an 8% return on that investment. This is a capitalization problem, so use the capitalization formula, *Income = Rate × Value, I = R × V.* You know the net income ($16,000) and the capitalization rate (8%), so switch the formula to isolate the unknown quantity, V:

$I \div R = V$

$16,000 \div .08 = \$200,000$

8. b) George has a 6% return on his investment. This problem calls for the capitalization formula again, but this time it's the rate that is unknown. Switch the formula to isolate the rate, R:

$I \div V = R$

$5,100 \div \$85,000 = .06 = 6\%$

9. d) There are 250 square yards in a 75' × 30' rectangle. The area formula, A = B × H, will give you the area in square feet: *75 × 30 = 2,250 square feet.* Then you must convert that figure to square yards. There are 9 square feet in a square yard, so divide 2,250 by 9: *2,250 ÷ 9 = 250 square yards.*

10. c) Mike, the buyer, is entitled to approximately $7,445 in rent for the period from the closing date through September 30. The proration formula is *Share = daily Rate × number of Days, S = R × D.* First determine the per diem rate for the rents by dividing the total amount by the number of days in the month: *$13,960 ÷ 30 = $465.33.* Next, determine the number of days for which the buyer is entitled to the rent: September 15 through 30 is 16 days. Finally, multiply the rate by the number of days to find the buyer's share: *$465.33 × 16 = $7,445.*

11. b) The area of the lot is 600 square feet. Since the lot is triangular, the appropriate area formula is Area = ½ Base × Height, A = ½ B × H. Here, the base is 40 feet, so ½ the base is 20 feet. 20 feet × 30 feet = 600 square feet.

12. a) The decimal equivalent of 5/8 is .625. To determine this, divide the numerator of the fraction (the top number, 5) by the denominator (the bottom number, 8). *5 ÷ 8 = .625.*

13. c) The prepaid interest will be $130.40. First determine the annual interest, using the percentage formula: *Part = Whole × Percentage, P = W × %.* The principal (the whole) is $112,000 and the rate (the percentage) is 8.5%. *$112,000 × .085 = $9,520.* Next, divide the annual interest by 365 to determine the per diem rate. *$9,520 ÷ 365 = $26.08.* Multiply the per diem rate by the number of days for which Kay is responsible for this expense—five days. *$26.08 × 5 = $130.40.*

14. b) The Binghams will have to pay $322.77 in interest at closing. To find the annual interest amount, use the percentage formula, *P = W × %. $168,301.50 × .10 = $16,830.15.* Divide that figure by 365 to determine the per diem rate: *$16,830.15 ÷ 365 = $46.11.* Finally, multiply the per diem rate by the number of days: *$46.11 × 7 days = $322.77.*

15. d) The building's annual net income is $44,850. Use the capitalization formula, *Income = Rate × Value; .0975 × $460,000 = $44,850.*

The definitions given here explain how the listed terms are used in the real estate field. Some of the terms have additional meanings, which can be found in a standard dictionary.

Abandonment—Failure to occupy and use property, which may result in a loss of rights.

Abrogate—To repeal, annul, nullify, abolish, or otherwise bring to an end by official or formal action.

Absolute Fee—See: Fee Simple.

Abstract of Judgment—A document summarizing the essential provisions of a court judgment which, when recorded, creates a lien on the judgment debtor's real property.

Abstract of Title—See: Title, Abstract of.

Abut—To touch, border on, be adjacent to, or share a common boundary with.

Acceleration Clause—A provision in a promissory note or security instrument allowing the lender to declare the entire debt due immediately if the borrower breaches one or more provisions of the loan agreement. Also referred to as a call provision.

Acceptance—1. Agreeing to the terms of an offer to enter into a contract, thereby creating a binding contract. 2. Taking delivery of a deed from the grantor.

Acceptance, Qualified—See: Counteroffer.

Accession—The acquisition of title to additional property by its annexation to real estate already owned. This can be the result of human actions (as in the case of fixtures) or natural processes (such as accretion and reliction).

Accord and Satisfaction—An agreement to accept something different than (and usually less than) what the contract originally called for.

Accretion—A gradual addition to dry land by the forces of nature, as when waterborne sediment is deposited on waterfront property.

Accrued Items of Expense—Expenses that have been incurred but are not yet due or payable; in a settlement statement, the seller's accrued expenses are credited to the buyer.

Acknowledgment—When a person who has signed a document formally declares to an authorized official (usually a notary public) that he or she signed voluntarily. The official can then attest that the signature is voluntary and genuine.

Acquisition Cost—The amount of money a buyer was required to expend in order to acquire title to a piece of property; in addition to the purchase price, this might include closing costs, legal fees, and other expenses.

Acre—An area of land equal to 43,560 square feet, or 4,840 square yards, or 160 square rods.

Actual Age—See: Age, Actual.

Actual Authority—See: Authority, Actual.

Actual Eviction—See: Eviction, Actual.

Actual Notice—See: Notice, Actual.

ADA—Americans with Disabilities Act

Addendum—An attachment to a purchase and sale agreement or other contract that contains additional provisions that apply to that transaction.

Adjacent—Nearby, next to, bordering, or neighboring; may or may not be in actual contact.

Adjustable-Rate Mortgage—See: Mortgage, Adjustable-Rate.

Adjusted Basis—For income tax purposes, the initial basis plus capital expenditures, less any depreciation deductions.

Adjustment Period—The interval at which an adjustable-rate mortgage borrower's interest rate or monthly payment is changed.

Administrator—A person appointed by the probate court to manage and distribute the estate of a deceased person, when no executor is named in the will or there is no will.

Ad Valorem—A Latin phrase that means "according to value," used to refer to taxes that are assessed on the value of property.

Adverse Possession—Acquiring title to real property that belongs to someone else by taking possession of it without permission, in the manner and for the length of time prescribed by statute.

Affiant—One who makes an affidavit.

Affidavit—A sworn statement made before a notary public (or other official authorized to administer an oath) that has been written down and acknowledged.

Affiliated Licensee—A salesperson or associate broker who is licensed under a particular broker.

Affirm—1. To confirm or ratify. 2. To make a solemn declaration that is not under oath.

After-Acquired Title—See: Title, After-Acquired.

Age, Actual—The age of a structure from a chronological standpoint (as opposed to its effective age); how many years it has actually been in existence.

Age, Effective—The age of a structure indicated by its condition and remaining usefulness (as opposed to its actual age). Good maintenance may increase a building's effective age, and poor maintenance may decrease it; for example, a 50-year-old home that has been well maintained might have an effective age of 15 years, meaning that its remaining usefulness is equivalent to that of a 15-year-old home.

Age of Majority—See: Majority, Age of.

Agency—A relationship of trust created when one person (the principal) grants another (the agent) authority to represent the principal in dealings with third parties.

Agency, Apparent—When third parties are given the impression that someone who has not been authorized to represent another is that person's agent, or else given the impression that an agent has been authorized to perform acts which are in fact beyond the scope of his or her authority. Also called ostensible agency.

Agency, Dual—When an agent represents both parties to a transaction, as when a broker represents both the buyer and the seller.

Agency, Exclusive—See: Listing, Exclusive.

Agency, Ostensible—See: Agency, Apparent.

Agency Coupled with an Interest—When an agent has a claim against the property that is the subject of the agency, so that the principal cannot revoke the agent's authority.

Agent—A person authorized to represent another (the principal) in dealings with third parties.

Agent, Dual—See: Agency, Dual.

Agent, General—An agent authorized to handle all of the principal's affairs in one area or in specified areas.

Agent, Gratuitous—An agent who does not have a legal right to claim compensation for his or her services (such as a broker who does not have a written employment contract with the seller).

Agent, Special—An agent with limited authority to do a specific thing or conduct a specific transaction.

Agent, Universal—An agent authorized to do everything that can be lawfully delegated to a representative.

Agreement—See: Contract.

Air Lot—A parcel of property above the surface of the earth, not containing any land; for example, a condominium unit on the third floor.

Air Rights—The right to undisturbed use and control of the airspace over a parcel of land; may be transferred separately from the land.

Alienation—The transfer of ownership or an interest in property from one person to another, by any means.

Alienation, Involuntary—Transfer of an interest in property against the will of the owner, or without action by the owner, occurring through operation of law, natural processes, or adverse possession.

Alienation, Voluntary—When an owner voluntarily transfers an interest to someone else.

Alienation Clause—A provision in a security instrument that gives the lender the right to declare the entire loan balance due immediately if the borrower sells or otherwise transfers the security property. Also called a due-on-sale clause.

All-Inclusive Trust Deed—See: Mortgage, Wraparound.

Alluvion—The solid material deposited along a river bank or shore by accretion. Also called alluvium.

Amendment—A written modification to a contract that occurs after both parties have signed the document.

Amenities—Features of a property that contribute to the pleasure or convenience of owning it, such as a fireplace, a beautiful view, or its proximity to a good school.

Americans with Disabilities Act—A federal law requiring facilities that are open to the public to ensure accessibility to disabled persons, even if that accessibility requires making architectural modifications.

Amortization, Negative—When unpaid interest on a loan is added to the principal balance, increasing the amount owed.

Amortize—To gradually pay off a debt with installment payments that include both principal and interest. See also: Loan, Amortized.

Annexation—Attaching personal property to real property, so that it becomes part of the real property (a fixture) in the eyes of the law.

Annexation, Actual—When personal property is physically attached to real property, so that it becomes part of the real property.

Annexation, Constructive—When personal property becomes associated with real property in such a way that the law treats it as a fixture, even though it is not physically attached; for example, a house key is constructively annexed to the house.

Annual Percentage Rate (APR)—All of the charges that the borrower will pay for the loan (including the interest, loan fee, discount points, and mortgage insurance costs), expressed as an annual percentage of the loan amount.

Annuity—A sum of money received in a series of payments at regular intervals (often annually) over a period of time.

Anticipation, Principle of—An appraisal principle which holds that value is created by the expectation of benefits to be received in the future.

Anticipatory Repudiation—When one party to a contract informs the other before the time set for performance that he or she does not intend to fulfill the contract.

Antitrust Laws—Laws that prohibit any agreement that has the effect of restraining trade, including conspiracies.

Appeal—When one of the parties to a lawsuit asks a higher court to review the judgment or verdict reached in a lower court.

Appellant—The party who files an appeal because he or she is dissatisfied with the lower court's decision. Also called the petitioner.

Appellee—In an appeal, the party who did not file the appeal. Also called the respondent.

Apportionment—A division of property (as among tenants in common when the property is sold or partitioned) or liability (as when responsibility for closing costs is allocated between the buyer and seller) into proportionate, but not necessarily equal, parts.

Appraisal—An estimate or opinion of the value of a piece of property as of a particular date. Also called valuation.

Appraiser—One who estimates the value of property, especially an expert qualified to do so by training and experience.

Appreciation—An increase in value; the opposite of depreciation.

Appropriation—Taking property or reducing it to personal possession, to the exclusion of others.

Appropriation, Prior—A system of allocating water rights, under which a person who wants to use water from a certain lake or river is required to apply for a permit; a permit has priority over other permits that are issued later. Compare: Riparian Rights.

Appropriative Rights—The water rights of a person who holds a prior appropriation permit.

Appurtenances—Rights that go along with ownership of a particular piece of property, such as air rights or mineral rights; they are ordinarily transferred with the property, but may, in some cases, be sold separately.

Appurtenances, Intangible—Rights that go with ownership of a piece of property that do not involve physical objects or substances; for example, an access easement (as opposed to mineral rights).

Appurtenant Easement—See: Easement Appurtenant.

APR—See: Annual Percentage Rate.

Area—1. Locale or region. 2. The size of a surface, usually in square units of measure, such as square feet or square miles.

ARM—See: Mortgage, Adjustable-Rate.

Arm's Length Transaction—1. A transaction in which both parties are informed of the property's merits and shortcomings, neither is acting under unusual pressure, and the property has been exposed on the open market for a reasonable length of time. 2. A transaction in which there is no pre-existing family or business relationship between the parties.

Artificial Person—A legal entity such as a corporation, which the law treats as an individual with legal rights and responsibilities; as distinguished from a natural person, a human being. Sometimes called a legal person.

Assemblage—Combining two or more adjoining properties into one tract. Also called assembly.

Assessment—The valuation of property for purposes of taxation.

Assessor—An official who determines the value of property for taxation.

Asset—Anything of value that a person owns.

Assets, Liquid—Cash and other assets that can be readily turned into cash (liquidated), such as stock.

Assets, Section 1231—Properties used in a trade or business or held for the production of income (a reference to Section 1231 in the federal income tax code).

Assign—To transfer rights (especially contract rights) or interests to another.

Assignee—One to whom rights or interests have been assigned.

Assignment—1. A transfer of contract rights from one person to another. 2. In the case of a lease, when the original tenant transfers his or her entire leasehold estate to another. Compare: Sublease.

Assignment of Contract and Deed—The instrument used to substitute a new vendor for the original vendor in a land contract.

Assignor—One who has assigned his or her rights or interest to another.

Assumption—When a buyer takes on personal liability for paying off the seller's existing mortgage or deed of trust.

Assumption Fee—A fee paid to the lender, usually by the buyer, when a mortgage or deed of trust is assumed.

Attachment—Court-ordered seizure of property belonging to a defendant in a lawsuit, so that it will be available to satisfy a judgment if the plaintiff wins. In the case of real property, attachment creates a lien.

Attachments, Manmade—See: Fixture.

Attachments, Natural—Plants growing on a piece of land, such as trees, shrubs, or crops.

Attorney General—The principal legal advisor for state agencies and employees, including the Department of Licensing.

Attorney in Fact—Any person authorized to represent another by a power of attorney; not necessarily a lawyer (an attorney at law).

Attractive Nuisance—A property feature that is dangerous and inviting to children, and a potential source of liability to the property owner.

Auditing—Verification and examination of records, particularly the financial accounts of a business or other organization.

Authority, Actual—Authority actually given to an agent by the principal, either expressly or by implication.

Authority, Apparent—Authority to represent another that someone appears to have and that the principal is estopped from denying, although no actual authority has been granted.

Authority, Implied—An agent's authority to do everything reasonably necessary to carry out the principal's express orders.

Automatic Renewal Clause—A lease provision that ensures automatic renewal of the lease unless the tenant or the landlord gives the other party notice of an intent to terminate.

Avulsion—1. When land is suddenly (not gradually) torn away by the action of water. 2. A sudden shift in a watercourse.

Bad Debt/Vacancy Factor—A percentage deducted from a property's potential gross income to determine the effective gross income, estimating the income that will probably be lost because of vacancies and tenants who don't pay.

Balance, Principle of—An appraisal principle which holds that the maximum value of real estate is achieved when the agents in production (labor, coordination, capital, and land) are in proper balance with each other.

Balance Sheet—See: Financial Statement.

Balloon Payment—A payment on a loan (usually the final payment) that is significantly larger than the regular installment payments.

Bankruptcy—1. When the liabilities of an individual, corporation, or firm exceed the assets. 2. When a court declares an individual, corporation, or firm to be insolvent, so that the assets and debts will be administered under bankruptcy laws.

Base Line—In the rectangular survey system, a main east-west line from which township lines are established. Each principal meridian has one base line associated with it.

Basis—A figure used in calculating a gain on the sale of real estate for federal income tax purposes. Also called cost basis.

Basis, Adjusted—The owner's initial basis in the property, plus capital expenditures for improvements, and minus any allowable depreciation or cost recovery deductions.

Basis, Initial—The amount of the owner's original investment in the property; what it cost to acquire the property, which may include closing costs and certain other expenses, as well as the purchase price.

Bearer—Whoever has possession of a negotiable instrument. See: Endorsement in Blank.

Bench Mark—A surveyor's mark on a stationary object at a known point of elevation, used as a reference point in calculating other elevations in a surveyed area; often a metal disk set into cement or rock.

Beneficiary—1. One for whom a trust is created and on whose behalf the trustee administers the trust. 2. The lender in a deed of trust transaction. 3. One entitled to receive real or personal property under a will; a legatee or devisee.

Bequeath—To transfer personal property to another by will.

Bequest—Personal property (including money) that is transferred by will.

Betterment—An improvement to real property that is more extensive than ordinary repair or replacement and that increases the value of the property.

Bilateral Contract—See: Contract, Bilateral.

Bill of Sale—A document used to transfer title to personal property from one person to another.

Binder—1. An instrument providing immediate insurance coverage until the regular policy is issued. 2. Any payment or preliminary written statement intended to make an agreement legally binding until a formal contract has been drawn up.

Blind Ad—An advertisement placed by a real estate licensee that does not include the broker's name.

Block—In a subdivision, a group of lots surrounded by streets or unimproved land.

Blockbusting—Attempting to induce owners to list or sell their homes by predicting that members of another race or ethnic group, or people suffering from some disability, will be moving into the neighborhood; this violates anti-discrimination laws. Also called panic selling.

Blue Laws—Statutes or ordinances restricting the transaction of business or other activities on Sundays and certain holidays.

Board of Directors—The body responsible for governing a corporation on behalf of the share holders, which oversees the corporate management.

Bona Fide—In good faith; genuine; not fraudulent.

Bond—1. A written obligation, usually interest-bearing, to pay a certain sum at a specified time. 2. Money put up as a surety, protecting someone against failure to perform, negligent performance, or fraud.

Bond, Completion—A bond posted by a contractor to guarantee that a project will be completed satisfactorily and free of liens. Also called a performance bond.

Bonus—An extra payment, over and above what is strictly due.

Boot—In a tax-free exchange, something given or received that is not like-kind property; for example, in an exchange of real property, if one party gives the other cash in addition to real property, the cash is boot.

Boundary—The perimeter or border of a parcel of land; the dividing line between one piece of property and another.

Bounds—Boundaries. See: Metes and Bounds.

Branch Manager—An associate broker designated by a firm's primary broker to manage the operations of a branch office.

Breach—Violation of an obligation, duty, or law; especially an unexcused failure to perform a contractual obligation.

Broker—One who is licensed to represent members of the public in real estate transactions for compensation; may be an individual, a corporation, or a partnership.

Broker, Associate—A person who has qualified as a broker, but is affiliated with another broker.

Broker, Designated—A corporate officer or general partner who is authorized to act as the broker for a licensed corporation or partnership.

Broker, Fee—A real estate broker who allows another person to use his or her license to operate a brokerage, in violation of the license law.

Brokerage—A real estate broker's business.

Brokerage Fee—The commission or other compensation charged for a real estate broker's services.

Buffer—An undeveloped area of land that separates two areas zoned for incompatible uses.

Building Codes—Regulations that set minimum standards for construction methods and materials.

Building Restrictions—Rules concerning building size, placement, or type; they may be public restrictions (in a zoning ordinance, for example) or private restrictions (CC&Rs, for example).

Bump Clause—A provision in a purchase and sale agreement that allows the seller to keep the property on the market while waiting for a contingency clause to be fulfilled; if the seller receives another good offer in the meantime, he or she can require the buyer to either waive the contingency clause or terminate the contract.

Bundle of Rights—The rights inherent in ownership of property, including the right to use, lease, enjoy, encumber, will, sell, or do nothing with the property.

Business Opportunity—A business that is for sale.

Buydown—When discount points are paid to a lender to reduce (buy down) the interest rate charged to the borrower; especially when a seller pays discount points to help the buyer/borrower qualify for financing.

Call—In a metes and bounds description, a specification that describes a segment of the boundary; for example, "south 15° west 120 feet" is a call.

Call Provision—See: Acceleration Clause.

Cancellation—1. Termination of a contract without undoing acts that have been already performed under the contract. Compare: Rescission. 2. Termination of a license that has not been renewed in the year following its expiration date.

Capacity—The legal ability or competency to perform some act, such as enter into a contract or execute a deed or will.

Capital—Money (or other forms of wealth) available for use in the production of more money.

Capital Assets—Assets held by a taxpayer other than: 1) property held for sale to customers in the ordinary course of the taxpayer's business; and 2) depreciable property or real property used in the taxpayer's trade or business. Thus, real property is a capital asset if it is owned for personal use or for profit.

Capital Expenditures—Money spent on improvements and alterations that add to the value of the property and/or prolong its life.

Capital Gain—Profit realized from the sale of a capital asset. If the asset was held for more than one year, it is a long-term capital gain; if the asset was held for one year or less, it is a short-term capital gain.

Capital Improvement—Any improvement that is designed to become a permanent part of the real property or that will have the effect of significantly prolonging the property's life.

Capitalization—A method of appraising real property by converting the anticipated net income from the property into the present value. Also called the income approach to value.

Capitalization Rate—A percentage used in capitalization (Net Income = Capitalization Rate × Value). It is the rate believed to represent the proper relationship between the value of the property and the income it produces; the rate that would be a reasonable return on an investment of the type in question, or the yield necessary to attract investment of capital in property like the subject property.

Capitalize—1. To provide with cash, or capital. 2. To determine the present value of an asset using capitalization.

Capital Loss—A loss resulting from the sale of a capital asset; it may be long-term or short-term, depending on whether the asset was held for more than one year or for one year or less.

Capture, Rule of—A legal rule that grants a landowner the right to all oil and gas produced from wells on his or her land, even if it migrated from underneath land belonging to someone else.

Carryback Loan—See: Loan, Purchase Money.

Carryover Clause—See: Extender Clause.

Cash Flow—The residual income after deducting from gross income all operating expenses and debt service. Also called spendable income.

Cash on Cash—The ratio between the cash flow received from an investment in the first year and amount of the cash initially invested.

Caveat Emptor—A Latin phrase meaning "Let the buyer beware"; it expresses the idea that a buyer is expected to examine property carefully before buying, instead of relying on the seller to disclose problems. This was once a firm rule of law, but it has lost most of its force, especially in residential real estate transactions.

CC&Rs—A declaration of covenants, conditions, and restrictions; usually recorded by a developer to place restrictions on all lots within a new subdivision.

Cease and Desist Order—An order issued by the Director of the Department of Licensing in a disciplinary action, to stop a violation of the license law.

CERCLA—The Comprehensive Environmental Response, Compensation and Liability Act; a federal law concerning liability for cleanup of contaminated property.

Certificate of Eligibility—A document issued by the Veterans Administration as evidence of a veteran's eligibility for a VA-guaranteed loan.

Certificate of Occupancy—A statement issued by a local government agency (such as the building department) verifying that a newly constructed building is in compliance with all codes and may be occupied.

Certificate of Reasonable Value—A document issued by the Veterans Administration, setting forth the current market value of a property, based on a VA-approved appraisal.

Certificate of Sale—The document given to the purchaser at a mortgage foreclosure sale, instead of a deed; replaced with a sheriff's deed only after the redemption period expires.

Chain of Title—See: Title, Chain of.

Change, Principle of—An appraisal principle which holds that property values are in a state of flux, increasing and decreasing in response to social, economic, and governmental forces.

Charter—A written instrument granting a power or a right of franchise.

Chattel—An article of personal property.

Chattel Mortgage—See: Mortgage, Chattel.

Chattel Real—Personal property that is closely associated with real property; the primary example is a lease.

Civil Law—The body of law concerned with the rights and liabilities of one individual in relation to another; includes contract law, tort law, and property law. Compare: Criminal Law.

Civil Rights—Fundamental rights guaranteed to individuals by the law. The term is primarily used in reference to constitutional and statutory protections against discrimination or government interference.

Civil Rights Act of 1866—A federal law guaranteeing all citizens the right to purchase, lease, sell, convey and inherit property, regardless of race or ancestry.

Civil Rights Act of 1964—A federal law prohibiting discrimination on the basis of race, color, national origin, or religion in many programs for which the government provides financial assistance.

Civil Suit—A lawsuit in which one private party sues another private party (as opposed to a criminal suit, in which an individual is sued—prosecuted—by the government).

Civil Wrong—See: Tort.

Client—One who employs a broker, lawyer, or appraiser. A real estate broker's client can be the seller, the buyer, or both, but is usually the seller.

Closing—The final stage in a real estate transaction, when the seller receives the purchase money, the buyer receives the deed, and title is transferred. Also called settlement.

Closing Costs—Expenses incurred in the transfer of real estate in addition to the purchase price; for example, the appraisal fee, title insurance premium, broker's commission, and excise tax.

Closing Date—The date on which all the terms of a purchase and sale agreement must be met, or the contract is terminated.

Closing Statement—See: Settlement Statement.

Cloud on Title—A claim, encumbrance, or apparent defect that makes the title to a property unmarketable. See: Title, Marketable.

Code of Ethics—A body of rules setting forth accepted standards of conduct, reflecting principles of fairness and morality; especially one that the members of an organization are expected to follow.

Codicil—An addition to or revision of a will.

Collateral—Anything of value used as security for a debt or obligation.

Collusion—An agreement between two or more persons to defraud another.

Color of Title—See: Title, Color of.

Commercial Acre—The remainder of an acre of newly subdivided land after deducting the amount of land dedicated for streets and sidewalks.

Commercial Bank—A type of financial institution that has traditionally emphasized commercial lending (loans to businesses), but which also makes many residential mortgage loans.

Commercial Paper—Negotiable instruments, such as promissory notes, sold to meet the short-term capital needs of a business.

Commercial Property—Property zoned and used for business purposes, such as a restaurant or an office building; as distinguished from residential, industrial, or agricultural property.

Commingled Funds—Funds from different sources that are deposited in the same account and thereby lose their separate character; for example, if a spouse deposits cash that is his or her separate property in an account with funds that are community property, the entire amount may be treated as community property.

Commingling—Illegally mixing trust funds held on behalf of a client with personal funds.

Commission—1. The compensation paid to a broker for services in connection with a real estate transaction (usually a percentage of the sales price). 2. A group of people organized for a particular purpose or function; usually a governmental body, such as the Real Estate Commission.

Commitment—In real estate finance, a lender's promise to make a loan. A loan commitment may be "firm" or "conditional"; a conditional commitment is contingent on something, such as a satisfactory credit report on the borrower.

Common Areas—1. The land and improvements in a condominium, planned unit development, or other housing development that are owned and used collectively by all of the residents, such as parking lots, hallways, and recreational facilities available for common use. Also called common elements. 2. In a building with leased units or spaces, the areas that are available for use by all of the tenants.

Common Elements, Limited—In a condominium, areas outside of the units (such as balconies or assigned parking spaces) that are designated for the use of particular unit owners, rather than all of the residents.

Common Law—1. Early English law. 2. Long-established rules of law based on early English law. 3. Rules of law developed through court decisions, as opposed to statutory law.

Community Property—Property owned jointly by a married couple in Washington and other community property states, as distinguished from each spouse's separate property; generally, any property acquired through the labor or skill of either spouse during marriage.

Co-Mortgagor—Someone (usually a family member) who accepts responsibility for the repayment of a mortgage loan along with the primary borrower, to help the borrower qualify for the loan.

Comparable—A recently sold and similarly situated property that is used as a point of comparison by an appraiser using the sales comparison approach.

Competent—1. Of sound mind, for the purposes of entering a contract or executing an instrument. 2. Both of sound mind and having reached the age of majority.

Competition, Principle of—An appraisal principle which holds that profits tend to encourage competition, and excess profits tend to result in ruinous competition.

Competitive Market Analysis—A comparison of homes that are similar in location, style, and amenities to the subject property, in order to set a realistic listing price. Similar to the sales comparison approach to value.

Completion Bond—See: Bond, Completion.

Compliance Inspection—A building inspection to determine, for the benefit of a lender, whether building codes, specifications, or conditions established after a prior inspection have been met before a loan is made.

Comprehensive Environmental Response, Compensation and Liability Act—See: CERCLA.

Comprehensive Plan—See: General Plan.

Concurrent Ownership—See: Ownership, Concurrent.

Condemnation—1. Taking private property for public use through the government's power of eminent domain. 2. A declaration that a structure is unfit for occupancy and must be closed or demolished.

Condemnation Appraisal—An estimate of the value of condemned property to determine the just compensation to be paid to the owner.

Condition—1. A provision in a contract that makes the parties' rights and obligations depend on the occurrence (or nonoccurrence) of a particular event. Also called a contingency clause. 2. A provision in a deed that makes title depend on compliance with a particular restriction.

Conditional Commitment—See: Commitment.

Conditional Fee—See: Fee, Qualified.

Conditional Use Permit—A permit that allows a special use, such as a school or hospital, to operate in a neighborhood where it would otherwise be prohibited by the zoning. Also called a special exception permit.

Condition Precedent—An event that must occur before a right or interest will be gained.

Condition Subsequent—An event that will cause a right or interest to be lost if it occurs.

Condominium—Property developed for concurrent ownership, where each co-owner has a separate interest in an individual unit, combined with an undivided interest in the common areas of the property.

Confidential Information—Information from or concerning a principal that was acquired during the course of an agency relationship, that the principal reasonably expects to be kept confidential, that the principal has not disclosed to third parties, that would operate to the detriment of the principal, and that the principal would not be legally obligated to disclose to the other party.

Confirmation of Sale—Court approval of a sale of property by an executor, administrator, or guardian.

Conforming Loan—See: Loan, Conforming.

Conformity, Principle of—An appraisal principle which holds that the maximum value of property is realized when there is a reasonable degree of social and economic homogeneity in the neighborhood.

Conservation—1. Preservation of structures or neighborhoods in a sound condition. 2. Preservation or controlled use of natural resources for long-term benefits.

Conservator—A person appointed by a court to take care of the property of another who is incapable of taking care of it on his or her own.

Consideration—Anything of value given to induce another to enter into a contract, such as money, goods, services, or a promise. Sometimes called valuable consideration.

Conspiracy—An agreement or plan between two or more persons to perform an unlawful act.

Construction Lien—See: Lien, Construction.

Constructive—Held to be so in the eyes of the law, even if not so in fact. See: Annexation, Constructive; Eviction, Constructive; Notice, Constructive; Severance, Constructive.

Consumer Price Index—An index that tracks changes in the cost of goods and services for a typical consumer. Formerly called the cost of living index.

Consummate—To complete.

Contiguous—Adjacent, abutting, or in close proximity.

Contingency Clause—See: Condition.

Contour—The shape or configuration of a surface. A contour map depicts the topography of a piece of land by means of lines (contour lines) that connect points of equal elevation.

Contract—An agreement between two or more persons to do or not do a certain thing, for consideration.

Contract, Bilateral—A contract in which each party has made a binding promise to perform (as distinguished from a unilateral contract).

Contract, Broker and Salesperson—An employment contract between a broker and an affiliated salesperson, outlining their mutual obligations.

Contract, Conditional Sales—See: Contract, Land.

Contract, Executed—A contract in which both parties have completely performed their contractual obligations.

Contract, Executory—A contract in which one or both parties have not yet completed performance of their obligations.

Contract, Express—A contract that has been put into words, either spoken or written.

Contract, Implied—A contract that has not been put into words, but is implied by the actions of the parties.

Contract, Installment Sales—See: Contract, Land.

Contract, Land—A contract for the sale of real property in which the buyer (the vendee) pays in installments; the buyer takes possession of the property immediately, but the seller (the vendor) retains legal title until the full price has been paid. Also called a conditional sales contract, installment sales contract, real estate contract, or contract for deed.

Contract, Oral—A spoken agreement that has not been written down. Also called a parol contract.

Contract, Parol—See: Contract, Oral.

Contract, Real Estate—1. Any contract pertaining to real estate. 2. A land contract.

Contract, Sales—See: Purchase and Sale Agreement.

Contract, Unenforceable—An agreement that a court would refuse to enforce; for example, because its contents can't be proven or the statute of limitations has run out.

Contract, Unilateral—A contract that is accepted by performance; the offeror has promised to perform his or her side of the bargain if the other party performs, but the other party has not promised to do so. Compare: Contract, Bilateral.

Contract, Valid—A binding, legally enforceable contract.

Contract, Void—An agreement that is not an enforceable contract, because it lacks a required element (such as consideration) or is defective in some other respect.

Contract, Voidable—A contract that one of the parties can disaffirm without liability, because of lack of capacity or a negative factor such as fraud or duress.

Contract for Deed—See: Contract, Land.

Contract of Adhesion—A contract that is one-sided and unfair to one of the parties; a "take it or leave it" contract, in which the offeror had much greater bargaining power than the offeree.

Contract of Sale—See: Purchase and Sale Agreement.

Contract Rent—See: Rent, Contract.

Contractor—One who contracts to perform labor or supply materials for a construction project, or to do other work for a specified price.

Contractor, Independent—See: Independent Contractor.

Contribution, Principle of—An appraisal principle which holds that the value of real property is greatest when the improvements produce the highest return commensurate with their cost (the investment).

Conventional Financing—See: Loan, Conventional.

Conversion—1. Misappropriating property or funds belonging to another; for example, converting trust funds to one's own use. 2. The process of changing an apartment complex into a condominium or cooperative.

Conveyance—The transfer of title to real property from one person to another by means of a written document, especially a deed.

Cooperating Agent—A member of a multiple listing service who attempts to find a buyer for a listing.

Cooperative—A building owned by a corporation, where the residents are shareholders in the corporation; each shareholder receives a proprietary lease on an individual unit and the right to use the common areas.

Cooperative Sale—A sale in which the buyer and the seller are brought together by salespeople working for different brokers.

Co-Ownership—See: Ownership, Concurrent.

Corner Influence—The increase in a property's value that results from its location on or near a corner, with access and exposure on two streets.

Corporation—An association organized according to certain laws, in which individuals may purchase ownership shares; treated by the law as an artificial person, separate from the individual shareholders.

Corporation, Domestic—A corporation doing business in the state where it was created (incorporated).

Corporation, Foreign—A corporation doing business in one state, but created (incorporated) in another state, or in another country.

Correction Lines—In the rectangular survey system, adjustment lines used to compensate for the curvature of the earth; they occur at 24-mile intervals (every fourth township line), where the distance between range lines is corrected to six miles.

Corrective Maintenance—Ongoing repairs that are made to a building and its equipment in order to restore it to good operating condition.

Correlation—See: Reconciliation.

Cost—The amount paid for anything in money, goods, or services.

Cost, Replacement—In appraisal, the current cost of constructing a building with the same utility as the subject property using modern materials and construction methods.

Cost, Reproduction—In appraisal, the cost of constructing a replica (an exact duplicate) of the subject property, using the same materials and construction methods that were originally used, but at current prices.

Cost Approach to Value—One of the three main methods of appraisal, in which an estimate of the subject property's value is arrived at by estimating the cost of replacing (or reproducing) the improvements, then deducting the estimated accrued depreciation and adding the estimated market value of the land.

Cost Basis—See: Basis.

Cost of Living Index—See: Consumer Price Index.

Cost Recovery Deductions—See: Depreciation Deductions.

Co-Tenancy—See: Ownership, Concurrent.

Counteroffer—A response to a contract offer, changing some of the terms of the original offer; it operates as a rejection of the original offer (not as an acceptance). Also called qualified acceptance.

County—An administrative subdivision of the State, created by the State and deriving all of its powers from the State.

Course—In a metes and bounds description, a direction, stated in terms of a compass bearing.

Covenant—1. A contract. 2. A promise. 3. A guarantee (express or implied) in a document such as a deed or lease. 4. A restrictive covenant.

Covenant, Restrictive—A promise to do or not do an act relating to real property, especially a promise that runs with the land; usually an owner's promise to not use property in a specified manner.

Covenant Against Encumbrances—In a warranty deed, a promise that the property is not burdened by any encumbrances other than those that are disclosed in the deed.

Covenant of Quiet Enjoyment—A promise that a buyer or tenant's possession will not be disturbed by the previous owner, the lessor, or anyone else making a lawful claim against the property.

Covenant of Right to Convey—In a warranty deed, a promise that the grantor has the legal ability to make a valid conveyance.

Covenant of Seisin—In a warranty deed, a promise that the grantor actually owns the interest he or she is conveying to the grantee.

Covenant of Warranty—In a warranty deed, a promise that the grantor will defend the grantee's title against claims superior to the grantor's that exist when the conveyance is made.

CPM—Certified Property Manager; a property manager who has satisfied the requirements set by the Institute of Real Estate Management of the National Association of Realtors.

Credit—A payment receivable (owed to you), as opposed to a debit, which is a payment due (owed by you).

Credit History—An applicant's record of accruing debts and repaying loans, usually expressed in the form of a personal credit report.

Creditor—One who is owed a debt.

Creditor, Secured—A creditor with a security interest in or a lien against specific property; if the debt is not repaid, the creditor can repossess the property or (in the case of real estate) foreclose on the property and collect the debt from the sale proceeds.

Credit Union—A depository institution that serves only members of a particular group or profession, emphasizing small, short-term loans.

Criminal Law—The body of law under which the government can prosecute an individual for crimes, wrongs against society. Compare: Civil Law.

CRV—See: Certificate of Reasonable Value.

Customer—From the point of view of a real estate agent, a prospective property buyer.

Damage Deposit—See: Security Deposit.

Damages—In a civil lawsuit, an amount of money the defendant is ordered to pay the plaintiff.

Damages, Compensatory—Damages awarded to a plaintiff as compensation for injuries (personal injuries, property damage, or financial losses) caused by the defendant's act or failure to act.

Damages, Liquidated—A sum that the parties to a contract agree in advance (at the time the contract is made) will serve as full compensation in the event of a breach.

Damages, Punitive—In a civil lawsuit, an award added to compensatory damages, to punish the defendant for outrageous or malicious conduct and discourage others from similar conduct.

Datum—An artificial horizontal plane of elevation, established in reference to sea level, used by surveyors as a reference point in determining elevation.

Dealer—One who regularly buys and sells real estate in the ordinary course of business.

Dealer Property—Property held for sale to customers rather than long-term investment; a developer's inventory of subdivision lots, for example.

Debit—A charge or debt owed to another.

Debtor—One who owes money to another.

Debt Service—The amount of money required to make the periodic payments of principal and interest on an amortized debt, such as a mortgage.

Decedent—A person who has died.

Declaration of Abandonment—A document recorded by an owner that voluntarily releases a property from homestead protection.

Declaration of Homestead—A recorded document that establishes homestead protection for a property that would not otherwise receive it.

Declaration of Restrictions—See: CC&Rs.

Decrement—A decrease in value; the opposite of increment.

Dedication—A voluntary or involuntary gift of private property for public use; may transfer ownership or simply create an easement.

Dedication, Common Law—Involuntary dedication, resulting from a property owner's acquiescence to public use of his or her property over a long period. Also called implied dedication.

Dedication, Statutory—A dedication required by law; for example, dedication of property for streets and sidewalks as a prerequisite to subdivision approval.

Deduction—An amount a taxpayer is allowed to subtract from his or her income before the tax on the income is calculated (as distinguished from a tax credit, which is deducted from the tax owed).

Deed—An instrument which, when properly executed and delivered, conveys title to real property from the grantor to the grantee.

Deed, Administrator's—A deed used by the administrator of an estate to convey property owned by the deceased person to the heirs.

Deed, Bargain and Sale—See: Deed, Special Warranty.

Deed, Correction—A deed used to correct minor mistakes in an earlier deed, such as misspelled names or typographical errors in the legal description. Also called a deed of confirmation or reformation deed.

Deed, General Warranty—A deed in which the grantor warrants the title against defects that might have arisen before or during his or her period of ownership.

Deed, Gift—A deed that is not supported by valuable consideration; often lists "love and affection" as the consideration.

Deed, Grant—A deed that uses the word "grant" in its words of conveyance and carries certain implied warranties; rarely used in Washington.

Deed, Quitclaim—A deed that conveys any interest in a property that the grantor has at the time the deed is executed, without warranties.

Deed, Reformation—See: Deed, Correction.

Deed, Sheriff's—A deed delivered, on court order, to the holder of a certificate of sale when the redemption period after a mortgage foreclosure has expired.

Deed, Special Warranty—A deed in which the grantor warrants title only against defects that may have arisen during his or her period of ownership.

Deed, Statutory Warranty—A short form of the general warranty deed, in which the covenants are implied (by the use of language specified in the state statute) rather than spelled out.

Deed, Tax—A deed given to a purchaser of property at a tax foreclosure sale.

Deed, Trust—See: Deed of Trust.

Deed, Trustee's—A deed given to a purchaser of property at a trustee's sale.

Deed, Warranty—1. A general warranty deed. 2. Any type of deed that carries warranties.

Deed, Wild—A deed that won't be discovered in a standard title search, because of a break in the chain of title.

Deed Executed Under Court Order—A deed that is the result of a court action, such as judicial foreclosure or partition.

Deed in Lieu of Foreclosure—A deed given by a borrower to the lender, relinquishing ownership of the security property, to satisfy the debt and avoid foreclosure.

Deed of Confirmation—See: Deed, Correction.

Deed of Partition—Deed used by co-owners (such as tenants in common or joint tenants) to divide up the co-owned property so that each can own a portion in severalty.

Deed of Reconveyance—The instrument used to release the security property from the lien created by a deed of trust when the debt has been repaid.

Deed of Trust—An instrument that creates a voluntary lien on real property to secure the repayment of a debt, and which includes a power of sale clause permitting nonjudicial foreclosure; the parties are the grantor or trustor (borrower), the beneficiary (the lender), and the trustee (a neutral third party).

Deed Release Provision—See: Release Clause.

Deed Restrictions—Provisions in a deed that restrict use of the property, and which may be either covenants or conditions.

Default—Failure to fulfill an obligation, duty, or promise, as when a borrower fails to make payments, or a tenant fails to pay rent.

Default Judgment—See: Judgment, Default.

Defeasance Clause—A clause in a mortgage, deed of trust, or lease that cancels or defeats a certain right upon the occurrence of a particular event.

Defeasible Fee—See: Fee, Defeasible.

Defendant—1. The person being sued in a civil lawsuit. 2. The accused person in a criminal lawsuit.

Deferred Maintenance—Depreciation resulting from maintenance or repairs that were postponed, causing physical deterioration of the building.

Deficiency Judgment—See: Judgment, Deficiency.

Degree—In surveying, a unit of circular measurement equal to $^1/_{360}$ of one complete rotation around a point in a plane.

Delivery—The legal transfer of a deed from the grantor to the grantee, which results in the transfer of title.

Demand—Desire to own coupled with ability to afford; this is one of the four elements of value, along with scarcity, utility, and transferability.

Demise—The transfer of an estate or interest in property to another for years, for life, or at will.

Density—In a land use law, the number of buildings or occupants per unit of land.

Department of Licensing—The state agency in charge of administering the real estate license law in Washington

Deposit—Money offered as an indication of commitment or as a protection, and which may be refunded under certain circumstances, such as an earnest money deposit or a tenant's security deposit.

Deposition—The formal, out-of-court testimony of a witness in a lawsuit, taken before trial for possible use later, during the trial; either as part of the discovery process, to determine the facts of the case, or when the witness will not be available during the trial.

Deposit Receipt—See: Purchase and Sale Agreement.

Depreciable Property—In the federal income tax code, property that is eligible for cost recovery deductions, because it will wear out and have to be replaced.

Depreciation—1. A loss in value (caused by deferred maintenance, functional obsolescence, or external obsolescence). 2. For the purposes of income tax deductions, apportioning the cost of an asset over a period of time.

Depreciation, Accrued—Depreciation that has built up or accumulated over a period of time.

Depreciation, Curable—Deferred maintenance and functional obsolescence that would ordinarily be corrected by a prudent owner, because the correction cost could be recovered in the sales price.

Depreciation, Incurable—Deferred maintenance, functional obsolescence, or external obsolescence that is either impossible to correct, or not economically feasible to correct, because the cost could not be recovered in the sales price.

Depreciation Deductions—Under the federal income tax code, deductions from a taxpayer's income to permit the cost of an asset to be recovered; allowed only for depreciable property that is held for the production of income or used in a trade or business. Also called cost recovery deductions.

Dereliction—See: Reliction.

Descent—Acquiring property transferred by intestate succession. A person who receives property by intestate succession is said to receive it by descent.

Designated Broker—See: Broker, Designated.

Detached Residence—A home physically separated from the neighboring home(s), not connected by a common wall.

Developed Land—Land with manmade improvements, such as buildings or roads.

Developer—One who subdivides or improves land to achieve a profitable use.

Development—1. Any development project, such as a new office park. 2. A housing subdivision. 3. In reference to a property's life cycle, the earliest stage, also called integration.

Devise—1. (noun) A gift of real property through a will. 2. (verb) To transfer real property by will. Compare: Bequest; Bequeath; Legacy.

Devisee—Someone who receives title to real property through a will. Compare: Beneficiary; Legatee.

Devisor—A testator who devises real property in his or her will.

Directional Growth—The direction in which a city's residential neighborhoods are expanding or expected to expand.

Disability—According to the Americans with Disabilities Act and Fair Housing Act, a physical or mental impairment that substantially limits a person in one or more major life activities.

Disaffirm—To ask a court to terminate a voidable contract.

Disbursements—Money paid out or expended.

Disclaimer—A denial of legal responsibility.

Discount—1. (verb) To sell a promissory note at less than its face value. 2. (noun) An amount withheld from the loan amount by the lender when the loan is originated; discount points.

Discount Points—A percentage of the principal amount of a loan, collected by the lender at the time a loan is originated, to give the lender an additional yield.

Discount Rate—The interest rate charged when a member bank borrows money from the Federal Reserve Bank.

Discrimination—Treating people unequally because of their race, religion, sex, national origin, age, or some other characteristic.

Disintegration—In a property's life cycle, the period of decline when the property's present economic usefulness is near an end and constant upkeep is necessary.

Disintermediation—When depositors withdraw their savings deposits from financial institutions (such as savings and loan associations and commercial banks) in order to invest the funds directly.

Dispossess—To force someone out of possession of real property through legal procedures, as in an eviction.

Domicile—The state where a person has his or her permanent home.

Double-entry Bookkeeping—An accounting technique in which an item is entered in the ledger twice, once as a credit and once as a debit; used for settlement statements.

Downpayment—The part of the purchase price of property that the buyer is paying in cash; the difference between the purchase price and the financing.

Downzoning—Rezoning land for a more limited use.

Drainage—A system to draw water off land, either artificially (e.g., with pipes) or naturally (e.g., with a slope).

Dual Agency—See: Agency, Dual.

Due-on-Sale Clause—See: Alienation Clause.

Duplex—A structure that contains two separate housing units, with separate entrances, living areas, baths, and kitchens.

Duress—Unlawful force or constraint used to compel someone to do something (such as sign a contract) against his or her will.

Dwelling—A building or a part of a building used or intended to be used as living quarters.

Earnest Money—A deposit that a prospective buyer gives the seller as evidence of his or her good faith intent to complete the transaction.

Earnest Money Agreement—See: Purchase and Sale Agreement.

Easement—An irrevocable right to use some part of another person's real property for a particular purpose.

Easement, Access—An easement that enables the easement holder to reach and/or leave his or her property (the dominant tenement) by crossing the servient tenement. Also called an easement for ingress and egress.

Easement, Aviation—An easement by which a property owner allows aircraft to fly through the airspace over his or her property (above a specified height).

Easement, Implied—See: Easement by Implication.

Easement, Negative—An easement that prevents the servient tenant from using his or her own land in a certain way (instead of allowing the dominant tenant to use it); essentially the same thing as a restrictive covenant that runs with the land.

Easement, Positive—An easement that allows the dominant tenant to use the servient tenement in a particular way. This is the standard type of easement (see the first definition of Easement, above); the term "positive easement" is generally only used when contrasting a standard easement with a negative easement.

Easement, Prescriptive—An easement acquired by prescription; that is, by using the property openly and without the owner's permission for the period prescribed by statute.

Easement Appurtenant—An easement that benefits a piece of property, the dominant tenement. Compare: Easement in Gross.

Easement by Express Grant—An easement granted to another in a deed or other document.

Easement by Express Reservation—An easement created in a deed when a landowner is dividing the property, transferring the servient tenement but retaining the dominant tenement; an easement that the grantor reserves for his or her own use.

Easement by Implication—An easement created by law when a parcel of land is divided, if there has been long-standing, apparent prior use, and it is reasonably necessary for the enjoyment of the dominant tenement.

Easement by Necessity—A special type of easement by implication, created by law even when there has been no prior use, if the dominant tenement would be entirely useless without an easement.

Easement in Gross—An easement that benefits a person instead of a piece of land; there is a dominant tenant, but no dominant tenement. Compare: Easement Appurtenant.

Economic Life—The period during which improved property will yield a return over and above the rent due to the land itself; also called the useful life.

Economic Obsolescence—See: Obsolescence, External.

Economic Rent—See: Rent, Economic.

Effective Age—See: Age, Effective.

Egress—A means of exiting, a way to leave a property; the opposite of ingress. The terms ingress and egress are most commonly used in reference to an access easement.

EIS—Environmental Impact Statement.

Ejectment—A legal action to recover possession of real property from someone who is not legally entitled to possession of it; an eviction.

Elements of Comparison—In the sales comparison approach to appraisal, considerations taken into account in selecting comparables and comparing comparables to the subject property; they include date of sale, location, physical characteristics, and terms of sale.

Emblements—Crops that are produced annually through the labor of the cultivator, such as wheat.

Emblements, Doctrine of—The legal rule that gives an agricultural tenant the right to enter the land to harvest crops after the lease ends.

Eminent Domain—The government's constitutional power to take (condemn) private property for public use, as long as the owner is paid just compensation.

Employee—Someone who works under the direction and control of another. Compare: Independent Contractor.

Encroachment—A physical intrusion onto neighboring property, usually due to a mistake regarding the location of the boundary.

Encumber—To place a lien or other encumbrance against the title to a property.

Encumbrance—A nonpossessory interest in real property; a right or interest held by someone other than the property owner, which may be a lien, an easement, a profit, or a restrictive covenant.

Encumbrance, Financial—A lien.

Encumbrance, Non-Financial—An easement, a profit, or a restrictive covenant.

Endorsement—When the payee on a negotiable instrument (such as a check or promissory note) assigns the right to payment to another, by signing the back of the instrument.

Endorsement, Special—An endorsement to a specific person (as opposed to an endorsement in blank).

Endorsement in Blank—An endorsement that does not specify a particular holder, so that the bearer—whoever has possession of the instrument—is entitled to payment.

Enjoin—To prohibit an act, or command performance of an act, by court order; to issue an injunction.

EPA—Environmental Protection Agency.

Equal Credit Opportunity Act—A federal law prohibiting providers of consumer credit from discriminating based on race, color, religion, national origin, sex, marital status, age, or because the applicant receives public assistance.

Equilibrium—In the life cycle of a property, a period of stability, during which the property undergoes little, if any, change.

Equitable Interest or Title—See: Title, Equitable.

Equitable Redemption Period—The period between the initial complaint and the sale of a foreclosed property, during which time a borrower may redeem the property by paying the amount of the debt plus costs.

Equitable Remedy—In a civil lawsuit, a judgment granted to the plaintiff that is something other than an award of money (damages); an injunction, rescission, and specific performance are examples.

Equity—1. An owner's unencumbered interest in his or her property; the difference between the value of the property and the liens against it. 2. A judge's power to soften or set aside strict legal rules, to bring about a fair and just result in a particular case.

Erosion—Gradual loss of soil due to the action of water or wind.

Escalation Clause—A clause in a contract or mortgage that provides for payment or interest adjustments (usually increases) if specified events occur, such as a change in the property taxes or in the prime interest rate. Also called an escalator clause.

Escheat—When property reverts to the state after a person dies intestate and no heirs can be located.

Escrow—An arrangement in which something of value (such as money or a deed) is held on behalf of the parties to a transaction by a disinterested third party (an escrow agent) until specified conditions have been fulfilled.

Escrow Agent—1. A neutral third party who holds money and documents in trust and carries out the closing process. 2. A company (not a natural person) that is licensed to engage in the escrow business.

Escrow Instructions—A written document that tells the escrow agent how to proceed and states the conditions each party must fulfill before the transaction can close.

Escrow Officer—A person licensed to work for an escrow agent.

Estate—1. An interest in real property that is or may become possessory; either a freehold or a leasehold. 2. The property left by someone who has died.

Estate, Fee Simple—See: Fee Simple.

Estate, Periodic—See: Tenancy, Periodic.

Estate at Sufferance—See: Tenancy at Sufferance.

Estate at Will—See: Tenancy at Will.

Estate for Life—A freehold estate that lasts only as long as a specified person lives; that person is referred to as the measuring life. Commonly called a life estate.

Estate for Years—A leasehold estate set to last for a definite period (one week, three years, etc.), after which it terminates automatically. Also called a tenancy for years or term tenancy.

Estate of Inheritance—An estate that can pass to the holder's heirs; especially a fee simple.

Estoppel—A legal doctrine that prevents a person from asserting rights or facts that are inconsistent with his or her earlier actions or statements.

Estoppel Certificate—A document that prevents a person who signs it from later asserting facts different from those stated in the document; a certificate of no defense is one example. Also called an estoppel letter.

Et Al.—Abbreviation for the Latin phrase "et alius" or "et alii," meaning "and another" or "and others."

Ethics—A system of accepted principles or standards of moral conduct. See: Code of Ethics.

Et Ux.—Abbreviation for the Latin phrase "et uxor," meaning "and wife."

Eviction—Dispossession or expulsion of someone from real property.

Eviction, Actual—Physically forcing someone off of real property (or preventing them from re-entering), or using the legal process to make them leave. Compare: Eviction, Constructive.

Eviction, Constructive—When a landlord's act (or failure to act) interferes with the tenant's quiet enjoyment of the property, or makes the property unfit for its intended use, to such an extent that the tenant is forced to move out.

Eviction, Self-Help—When a landlord uses physical force, a lock-out, or a utility shut-off to evict a tenant, instead of the legal process. This is generally illegal.

Excess Land—That portion of a parcel of land that does not add to its value. For example, where the value of a property lies primarily in its frontage, additional depth beyond the normal lot size would not increase the property's value.

Exchange—See: Tax-free Exchange.

Excise Tax—See: Tax, Excise.

Exclusive Listing—See: Listing, Exclusive.

Exculpatory Clause—A clause in a contract that relieves one party of liability for certain defaults or problems; such provisions are not always enforceable.

Execute—1. To sign an instrument and take any other steps (such as acknowledgment) that may be necessary to its validity. 2. To perform or complete. See: Contract, Executed.

Execution—The legal process in which a court orders an official (such as the sheriff) to seize and sell the property of a judgment debtor to satisfy a lien.

Executor—A person named in a will to carry out its provisions. If it is a woman, she may be referred to as the executrix, but that term is passing out of use.

Exemption—A provision holding that a law or rule does not apply to a particular person or group; for example, a person entitled to a tax exemption is not required to pay the tax.

Expenses, Fixed—Recurring property expenses, such as general real estate taxes and hazard insurance.

Expenses, Maintenance—Cleaning, supplies, utilities, tenant services, and administrative costs for income-producing property.

Expenses, Operating—For income-producing property, the fixed expenses, maintenance expenses, and reserves for replacement; does not include debt service.

Expenses, Variable—Expenses incurred in connection with property that do not occur on a set schedule, such as the cost of repairing a roof damaged in a storm.

Express—Stated in words, whether spoken or written. Compare: Implied.

Extender Clause—A clause in a listing agreement providing that for a specified period after the listing expires, the broker will still be entitled to a commission if the property is sold to someone the broker dealt with during the listing term. Also called a safety clause or carryover clause.

External Obsolescence—See: Obsolescence, External.

Failure of Purpose—When the intended purpose of an agreement or arrangement can no longer be achieved; in most cases, this releases the parties from their obligations.

Fair Housing Act—A federal law prohibiting discrimination in the sale or lease of residential property on the basis of race, color, religion, sex, national origin, handicap, or familial status.

Fairness in Lending Act—A Washington state law that prohibits redlining.

Fannie Mae—Popular name for the Federal National Mortgage Association (FNMA).

Feasibility Study—A cost-benefit analysis of a proposed project, often required by lenders before they make a loan commitment.

Fed—The Federal Reserve.

Federal Reserve System—The government body that regulates commercial banks, and that implements monetary policy in an attempt to control the national economy.

Fee—See: Fee Simple.

Fee, Defeasible—See: Fee, Qualified.

Fee, Qualified—A fee simple estate that is subject to termination if a certain condition is not met or if a specified event occurs. It may be a fee simple determinable or a fee simple subject to condition subsequent. Also called a conditional fee or defeasible fee.

Fee Broker—See: Broker, Fee.

Fee Simple—The highest and most complete form of ownership, which is of potentially infinite duration. Also called a fee or a fee simple absolute.

Fee Simple Determinable—A qualified fee that ends automatically, without legal action by the grantor, if the condition is violated or the terminating event occurs.

Fee Simple Subject to a Condition Subsequent—A qualified fee that terminates only if the grantor takes legal action to terminate it after the specified condition has come to pass.

FHA—Federal Housing Administration. See also: Loan, FHA.

Fidelity Bond—A bond to cover losses resulting from the dishonesty of an employee.

Fiduciary Relationship—A relationship of trust and confidence, where one party owes the other (or both parties owe each other) loyalty and a higher standard of good faith than is owed to third parties. For example, an agent is a fiduciary in relation to the principal; husband and wife are fiduciaries in relation to one another.

Finance Charge—Any charge a borrower is assessed, directly or indirectly, in connection with a loan. See also: Total Finance Charge.

Financial Statement—A summary of facts showing the financial condition of an individual or a business, including a detailed list of assets and liabilities. Also called a balance sheet.

Financing Statement—A brief instrument that is recorded to perfect and give constructive notice of a creditor's security interest in an article of personal property.

Finder's Fee—A referral fee paid to someone for directing a buyer or a seller to a real estate agent.

Firm Commitment—See: Commitment.

FIRPTA—The Foreign Investment in Real Property Tax Act; this federal law requires an escrow agent to withhold funds from the sale of real property when the seller is not a U.S. citizen, in order to prevent tax evasion.

First Lien Position—The position held by a mortgage or deed of trust that has higher lien priority than any other mortgage or deed of trust against the property.

First Refusal, Right of—See: Right of First Refusal.

Fiscal Policy—The federal government's actions in raising revenue (through taxation), spending money, and managing its debt.

Fiscal Year—Any twelve-month period used as a business year for accounting, tax, and other financial purposes, as opposed to a calendar year.

Fixed Disbursement Plan—A construction financing arrangement that calls for the loan proceeds to be disbursed in a series of predetermined installments at various stages of the construction.

Fixed Expense—A property management expense that remains the same, regardless of rental income.

Fixed-Rate Loan—See: Loan, Fixed-Rate.

Fixed Term—A period of time that has a definite beginning and ending.

Fixture—An item that used to be personal property but has been attached to or closely associated with real property in such a way that it has legally become part of the real property. See: Annexation, Actual; Annexation, Constructive.

Floor Area Ratio—A zoning requirement that controls the ratio between a building's floor space and the percentage of the lot it occupies.

FmHA—Farmer's Home Administration.

Foreclosure—When a lienholder causes property to be sold against the owner's wishes, so that the unpaid lien can be satisfied from the sale proceeds.

Foreclosure, Judicial—1. The sale of property pursuant to court order to satisfy a lien. 2. A lawsuit filed by a mortgagee or deed of trust beneficiary to foreclose on the security property when the borrower has defaulted.

Foreclosure, Nonjudicial—Foreclosure by a trustee under the power of sale clause in a deed of trust.

Foreign Investment in Real Property Tax Act—See: FIRPTA.

Forfeiture—Loss of a right or something else of value as a result of failure to perform an obligation or fulfill a condition.

For Sale by Owner—A property that is being sold by the owner without the help of a real estate agent. Also called a FSBO.

Franchise—A right or privilege granted by a government to conduct a certain business, or a right granted by a private business to use its trade name in conducting business.

Fraud—An intentional or negligent misrepresentation or concealment of a material fact, which is relied upon by another, who is induced to enter a transaction and harmed as a result.

Fraud, Actual—Deceit or misrepresentation with the intention of cheating or defrauding another.

Fraud, Constructive—A breach of duty that misleads the person the duty was owed to, without an intention to deceive; for example, if a seller gives a buyer inaccurate information about the property without realizing that it is false, that may be constructive fraud.

Freddie Mac—Popular name for the Federal Home Loan Mortgage Corporation (FHLMC).

Free and Clear—Ownership of real property completely free of any liens.

Freehold—A possessory interest in real property that has an indeterminable duration; it can be either a fee simple or an estate for life. Someone who has a freehold estate has title to the property (as opposed to someone with a leasehold estate, who is only a tenant).

Frontage—The distance a property extends along a street or a body of water; the distance between the two side boundaries at the front of the lot.

Front Foot—A measurement of property for sale or valuation, with each foot of frontage presumed to extend the entire depth of the lot.

Front Money—The cash required to get a project or venture under way; includes initial expenses such as attorney's fees, feasibility studies, loan charges, and a downpayment.

Functional Obsolescence—See: Obsolescence, Functional.

Gain—Under the federal income tax code, that portion of the proceeds from the sale of a capital asset, such as real estate, that is recognized as taxable profit.

Garnishment—A legal process by which a creditor gains access to the personal property or funds of a debtor that are in the hands of a third party. For example, if the debtor's wages are garnished, the employer is required to turn over part of each paycheck to the creditor.

General Agent—See: Agent, General.

General Lien—See: Lien, General.

General Plan—A comprehensive, long-term plan of development for a community, which is implemented by zoning and other laws. Also called a comprehensive plan or master plan.

Gift Funds—Money that a relative (or other third party) gives to a buyer who otherwise would not have enough cash to close the transaction.

Ginnie Mae—The Government National Mortgage Association, GNMA.

Good Faith Improver—See: Innocent Improver.

Good Will—An intangible asset of a business resulting from a good reputation with the public, serving as an indication of future return business.

Government Lot—In the rectangular survey system, a parcel of land that is not a regular section (one mile square), because of the convergence of range lines, or because of a body of water or some other obstacle; assigned a government lot number.

Government Survey System—See: Rectangular Survey System.

Grant—To transfer or convey an interest in real property by means of a written instrument.

Grantee—One who receives a grant of real property.

Granting Clause—Words in a deed that indicate the grantor's intent to transfer an interest in property.

Grantor—One who grants an interest in real property to another.

Gross Income Multiplier—A figure which is multiplied by a rental property's annual gross income to arrive at an estimate of the property's value.

Gross Multiplier Method—A method of appraising residential property by reference to its rental value.

Gross Rent Multiplier—A figure which is multiplied by a rental property's monthly gross income to arrive at an estimate of the property's value.

Group Boycott—An agreement between two or more real estate brokers to exclude other brokers from equal participation in real estate activities.

Growth Management Act—A Washington state law aimed at limiting sprawl and concentrating growth in existing urban areas.

Guardian—A person appointed by a court to administer the affairs of a minor or an incompetent person.

Guide Meridians—See: Meridians, Guide.

Habendum Clause—A clause included after the granting clause in many deeds; it begins "to have and to hold" and describes the type of estate the grantee will hold.

Habitability, Implied Warranty of—A warranty implied by law in every residential lease, that the property is fit for habitation.

Heir—Someone entitled to inherit another's property under the laws of intestate succession.

Heirs and Assigns—A phrase used in legal documents to cover all successors to a person's interest in property; assigns are successors who acquire title in some manner other than inheritance, such as by deed.

Highest and Best Use—The use which, at the time of appraisal, is most likely to produce the greatest net return from the property over a given period of time.

Historical Rent—See: Rent, Contract.

Holder in Due Course—A person who obtains a negotiable instrument for value, in good faith, without notice that it is overdue or notice of any defenses against it.

Home Mortgage Disclosure Act—A federal law requiring institutional lenders to make annual disclosures of all mortgage loans made, as a means of enforcing prohibitions against redlining.

Homeowners Association—A nonprofit association made up of homeowners in a subdivision, responsible for enforcing the CC&Rs and managing other community affairs.

Homestead—An owner-occupied dwelling, together with any appurtenant outbuildings and land.

Homestead Law—A state law that provides limited protection against creditors' claims for homestead property.

HUD—The U.S. Department of Housing and Urban Development.

Hypothecate—To make property security for an obligation without giving up possession of it (as opposed to pledging, which involves surrender of possession).

Implied—Not expressed in words, but understood from actions or circumstances. Compare: Express.

Impound Account—A bank account maintained by a lender for payment of property taxes and insurance premiums on the security property; the lender requires the borrower to make regular deposits, and pays the expenses out of the account. Also called a reserve account.

Improvements—Manmade additions to real property.

Improvements, Misplaced—Improvements that do not fit the most profitable use of the site; they can be overimprovements or underimprovements.

Imputed Knowledge—A legal doctrine stating that a principal is considered to have notice of information that the agent has, even if the agent never passed that information on to the principal.

Inchoate—Partial, incomplete, unfinished; begun but not completed, as in the case of a contract that has not been executed by all the parties.

Inchoate Interest—A future interest in real estate, such as an interest a minor will receive when he or she comes of age.

Income, Disposable—Income remaining after income taxes have been paid.

Income, Effective Gross—A measure of a rental property's capacity to generate income; calculated by subtracting a bad debt/vacancy factor from the economic rent (potential gross income).

Income, Gross—A property's total income before making any deductions (for bad debts, vacancies, operating expenses, etc.).

Income, Net—The income that is capitalized to estimate the property's value; calculated by subtracting the property's operating expenses (fixed expenses, maintenance expenses, and reserves for replacement) from the effective gross income.

Income, Potential Gross—A property's economic rent; the income it could earn if it were available for lease in the current market.

Income, Residual—The amount of income that an applicant for a VA loan has left over after taxes, recurring obligations, and the proposed housing expense have been deducted from his or her gross monthly income.

Income, Spendable—The income that remains after deducting operating expenses, debt service, and income taxes from a property's gross income. Also called net spendable income or cash flow.

Income Approach to Value—One of the three main methods of appraisal, in which an estimate of the subject property's value is based on the net income it produces; also called the capitalization method or investor's method of appraisal.

Income Property—Property that generates rent or other income for the owner, such as an apartment building. In the federal income tax code, it is referred to as property held for the production of income.

Income Ratio—A standard used in qualifying a buyer for a loan, to determine whether he or she has sufficient income; the buyer's debts and proposed housing expense should not exceed a specified percentage of his or her income.

Incompetent—Not legally competent; not of sound mind.

Increment—An increase in value; the opposite of decrement.

Independent Contractor—A person who contracts to do a job for another, but retains control over how he or she will carry out the task, rather than following detailed instructions. Compare: Employee.

Index—A published statistical report that indicates changes in the cost of money; used as the basis for interest rate adjustments in an ARM.

Index, Tract—An index of recorded documents in which all documents that carry a particular legal description are grouped together.

Indexes, Grantor/Grantee—Indexes of recorded documents maintained by the recorder, with each document listed in alphabetical order according to the last name of the grantor (in the grantor index) and grantee (in the grantee index); the indexes list the recording number of each document, so that it can be located in the public record.

Ingress—A means of entering a property; the opposite of egress. The terms ingress and egress are most commonly used in reference to an access easement.

In-House Sale—A sale in which the buyer and the seller are brought together by salespeople working for the same broker.

Injunction—A court order prohibiting someone from performing an act, or commanding performance of an act.

Innocent Improver—Someone who makes an improvement on land in the mistaken belief that he or she owns the land. Also called a good faith improver.

Installment Note—See: Note, Installment.

Installment Sale—Under the federal income tax code, a sale in which less than 100% of the sales price is received in the year the sale takes place.

Instrument—A legal document, usually one that transfers title (such as a deed), creates a lien (such as a mortgage), or establishes a right to payment (such as a promissory note or contract).

Insurance, Hazard—Insurance against damage to real property caused by fire, flood, theft, or other mishap. Also called casualty insurance.

Insurance, Homeowner's—Insurance against damage to the real property and the homeowner's personal property.

Insurance, Mortgage—Insurance that protects a lender against losses resulting from the borrower's default.

Insurance, Mutual Mortgage—The mortgage insurance provided by the FHA to lenders who make loans through FHA programs.

Insurance, Private Mortgage (PMI)—Insurance provided by private companies to conventional lenders for loans with loan-to-value ratios over 80%.

Insurance, Title—Insurance that protects against losses resulting from undiscovered title defects. An owner's policy protects the buyer, while a mortgagee's policy protects the lien position of the buyer's lender.

Insurance, Title, Extended Coverage—Title insurance that covers problems that should be discovered by an inspection of the property (such as encroachments and adverse possession), in addition to the problems covered by standard coverage policies. An extended coverage policy is sometimes referred to as an ALTA (American Land Title Association) policy.

Insurance, Title, Standard Coverage—Title insurance that protects against latent title defects (such as forged deeds) and undiscovered recorded encumbrances, but does not protect against problems that would only be discovered by an inspection of the property.

Integration—In a property's life cycle, the earliest stage, when the property is being developed. Also called development.

Interest—1. A right or share in something (such as a piece of real estate). 2. A charge a borrower pays to a lender for the use of the lender's money.

Interest, Compound—Interest computed both on the principal and its accrued interest. Compare: Interest, Simple.

Interest, Future—An interest in property that will or may become possessory at some point in the future, such as a remainder or reversion.

Interest, Interim—See: Interest, Prepaid.

Interest, Prepaid—Interest on a new loan that must be paid at the time of closing; covers the interest due for the first month of the loan term. Also called interim interest.

Interest, Simple—Interest that is computed on the principal amount of the loan only, which is the type of interest charged in connection with real estate loans. Compare: Interest, Compound.

Interest, Undivided—A co-owner's interest, giving him or her the right to possession of the whole property, rather than to a particular section of it.

Interpleader—A court action filed by someone who is holding funds that two or more people are claiming. The holder turns the funds over to the court; the court resolves the dispute and delivers the money to the party who is entitled to it.

Interstate Land Sales Full Disclosure Act—A federal law requiring subdivision developers to make certain disclosures concerning the property to potential buyers.

Intestate—Without a valid will.

Intestate Succession—Distribution of the property of a person who died intestate to his or her heirs.

Invalid—Not legally binding or legally effective; not valid.

Inventory—A detailed list of the stock-in-trade of a business.

Inverse Condemnation Action—A court action by a private landowner against the government, seeking compensation for damage to property caused by government action.

Investment Property—Unimproved property held as an investment in the expectation that it will appreciate in value.

Inverted Pyramid—A way of visualizing ownership of real property; in theory, a property owner owns all the earth, water, and air enclosed by a pyramid that has its tip at the center of the earth and extends up through the property boundaries out into the sky.

Involuntary Conversion—For income tax purposes, when an asset is converted into cash without the voluntary action of the owner, such as through a condemnation award or insurance proceeds.

Involuntary Lien—See: Lien, Involuntary.

Joint Venture—Two or more individuals or companies joining together for one project or a related series of projects, but not as an ongoing business. Compare: Partnership.

Judgment—1. A court's binding determination of the rights and duties of the parties in a lawsuit. 2. A court order requiring one party to pay the other damages.

Judgment, Default—A court judgment in favor of the plaintiff due to the defendant's failure to answer the complaint or appear at a hearing.

Judgment, Deficiency—A personal judgment entered against a borrower in favor of the lender if the proceeds from a foreclosure sale of the security property are not enough to pay off the debt.

Judgment Creditor—A person who is owed money as a result of a judgment in a lawsuit.

Judgment Debtor—A person who owes money as a result of a judgment in a lawsuit.

Judgment Lien—See: Lien, Judgment.

Judicial Foreclosure—See: Foreclosure, Judicial.

Just Compensation—The compensation that the Constitution requires the government to pay a property owner when the property is taken under the power of eminent domain.

Laches, Doctrine of—A legal principle holding that the law will refuse to protect those who fail to assert their legal rights within the time period prescribed by the statute of limitations, or (if there is no applicable statute of limitations) within a reasonable time.

Land—In the legal sense, it is the solid part of the surface of the earth, everything affixed to it by nature or by man, or anything on it or in it, such as minerals and water; real property.

Land Contract—See: Contract, Land.

Landlocked Property—A parcel of land without access to a road or highway.

Landlord—A landowner who has leased his or her property to another. Also called a lessor.

Landmark—A monument, natural or artificial, set up on the boundary between two adjacent properties, to show where the boundary is.

Land Residual Process—A method of appraising vacant land.

Latent Defects—Defects that are not visible or apparent (as opposed to patent defects).

Lateral Support—See: Support, Lateral.

Lawful Object—An objective or purpose of a contract that does not violate the law or a judicial determination of public policy.

Lease—A conveyance of a leasehold estate from the fee owner to a tenant; a contract in which one party pays the other rent in exchange for the possession of real estate. Also called a rental agreement.

Lease, Fixed—A lease in which the rent is set at a fixed amount, and the landlord pays most or all of the operating expenses (such as utilities, taxes, insurance, and maintenance costs). Also called a flat lease, gross lease, or straight lease.

Lease, Graduated—A lease in which it is agreed that the rental payments will increase at intervals by a specified amount or according to a specified formula.

Lease, Gross—See: Lease, Fixed.

Lease, Ground—A lease of the land only, usually for a long term, to a tenant who intends to construct a building on the property.

Lease, Net—A lease requiring the tenant to pay all the costs of maintaining the property (such as taxes, insurance, and repairs), in addition to the rent paid to the landlord.

Lease, Percentage—A lease in which the rent is based on a percentage of the tenant's monthly or annual gross sales.

Lease, Sandwich—A leasehold interest lying between the property owner's interest and the interest of the tenant in possession; for example, when the tenant in a ground lease constructs a building and rents out space in the building, he or she is sandwiched between the landowner's interest and the interest of his or her building tenant.

Lease, Straight—See: Lease, Fixed.

Leaseback—See: Sale-Leaseback.

Leasehold—A possessory interest in real property that has a limited duration, such as an estate for years or a periodic tenancy. Also called a less-than-freehold estate.

Legacy—A gift of personal property by will. Also called a bequest.

Legal Description—A precise description of a parcel of real property; may be a lot and block description, a metes and bounds description, or a government survey description.

Legal Person—See: Artificial Person.

Legatee—Someone who receives personal property (a legacy) under a will.

Lender, Institutional—A bank, savings and loan, or similar organization that invests other people's funds in loans; as opposed to an individual or private lender, which invests its own funds.

Lessee—One who leases property from another; a tenant.

Lessor—One who leases property to another; a landlord.

Less-than-freehold—See: Leasehold.

Leverage—The effective use of borrowed money to finance an investment such as real estate.

Levy—To impose a tax.

Liability—1. A debt or obligation. 2. Legal responsibility.

Liability, Joint and Several—A form of liability in which two or more persons are responsible for a debt both individually and as a group.

Liability, Limited—When a business investor is not personally liable for the debts of the business, as in the case of a limited partner or a corporate shareholder.

Liability, Vicarious—A legal doctrine stating that a principal can be held liable for harm to third parties resulting from an agent's actions.

Liable—Legally responsible.

License—1. Official permission to do a particular thing that the law does not allow everyone to do. 2. Revocable, non-assignable permission to use another person's land for a particular purpose. Compare: Easement.

License, Inactive—Any real estate license that has been turned over to the Director temporarily. The holder of an inactive license is not permitted to engage in activities requiring a license.

LID—Local Improvement District.

Lien—A nonpossessory interest in real property, giving the lienholder the right to foreclose if the owner doesn't pay a debt owed to the lienholder; a financial encumbrance on the owner's title.

Lien, Attachment—A lien intended to prevent transfer of the property pending the outcome of litigation.

Lien, Construction—A lien on property in favor of someone who provided labor or materials to improve it. Also called a mechanic's lien or materialman's lien.

Lien, Equitable—A lien arising as a matter of fairness, rather than by agreement or by operation of law.

Lien, General—A lien against all the property of a debtor, rather than a particular piece of his or her property. Compare: Lien, Specific.

Lien, Involuntary—A lien that arises by operation of law, without the consent of the property owner. Also called a statutory lien.

Lien, Judgment—A general lien against a judgment debtor's property, which the judgment creditor creates by recording an abstract of judgment in the county where the property is located.

Lien, Materialman's—A construction lien in favor of someone who supplied materials for a project (as opposed to labor).

Lien, Mechanic's—See: Lien, Construction.

Lien, Property Tax—A specific lien on property to secure payment of property taxes.

Lien, Specific—A lien that attaches only to a particular piece of property (as opposed to a general lien, which attaches to all of the debtor's property).

Lien, Statutory—See: Lien, Involuntary.

Lien, Tax—A lien on property to secure the payment of taxes.

Lien, Voluntary—A lien placed against property with the consent of the owner; a deed of trust or a mortgage.

Lienholder, Junior—A secured creditor whose lien is lower in priority than another's lien.

Lien Priority—The order in which liens are paid off out of the proceeds of a foreclosure sale.

Lien Theory—The theory holding that a mortgage or deed of trust does not involve a transfer of title to the lender, but merely creates a lien against the property in the lender's favor. Compare: Title Theory.

Life Estate—A freehold estate that lasts only as long as a specified person lives. That person is referred to as the measuring life.

Life Tenant—Someone who owns a life estate; the person entitled to possession of the property during the measuring life.

Like-Kind Exchange—See: Tax-Free Exchange.

Limited Liability—See: Liability, Limited.

Limited Liability Company—A form of business entity that offers both limited liability for its owners and certain tax benefits.

Limited Partnership—See: Partnership, Limited

Liquidated Damages—See: Damages, Liquidated.

Liquidity—The ability to convert an asset into cash quickly.

Lis Pendens—A recorded notice stating that there is a lawsuit pending that may affect title to the defendant's real estate.

Listing—A written agency contract between a seller and a real estate broker, stipulating that the broker will be paid a commission for finding (or attempting to find) a buyer for the seller's property. Also called a listing agreement.

Listing Broker—The broker who takes a listing, and thus represents the seller.

Listing, Exclusive—Either an exclusive agency listing or an exclusive right to sell listing.

Listing, Exclusive Agency—A listing agreement that entitles the broker to a commission if anyone other than the seller finds a buyer for the property during the listing term.

Listing, Exclusive Right to Sell—A listing agreement that entitles the broker to a commission if anyone—including the seller—finds a buyer for the property during the listing term.

Listing, Multiple—A listing (usually an exclusive right to sell listing) that includes a provision allowing the broker to submit the listing to his or her multiple listing service for dissemination to cooperating brokers.

Listing, Net—A listing agreement in which the seller sets a net amount he or she is willing to accept for the property; if the actual selling price exceeds that amount, the broker is entitled to keep the excess as his or her commission. This is not legal in Washington.

Listing, Open—A nonexclusive listing, given by a seller to as many brokers as he or she chooses. If the property is sold, a broker is only entitled to a commission if he or she was the procuring cause of the sale.

Littoral Land—Land that borders on a stationary body of water (such as a lake, as opposed to a river or stream). Compare: Riparian Land.

Littoral Rights—The water rights of an owner of littoral land, in regard to use of the water in the lake.

Loan, Amortized—A loan that requires regular installment payments of both principal and interest (as opposed to an interest-only loan). It is fully amortized if the installment payments will pay off the full amount of the principal and all of the interest by the end of the repayment period. It is partially amortized if the installment payments will cover only part of the principal, so that a balloon payment of the remaining principal balance is required at the end of the repayment period.

Loan, Called—A loan that has been accelerated by the lender. See: Acceleration Clause.

Loan, Carryback—See: Loan, Purchase Money.

Loan, Conforming—A loan made in accordance with the standardized underwriting criteria of the major secondary market agencies, Fannie Mae and Freddie Mac, and which therefore can be sold to those agencies.

Loan, Construction—A loan to finance the cost of constructing a building, usually providing that the loan funds will be advanced in installments as the work progresses. Also called an interim loan.

Loan, Conventional—An institutional loan that is not insured or guaranteed by a government agency.

Loan, FHA—A loan made by an institutional lender and insured by the Federal Housing Administration, so that the FHA will reimburse the lender for losses that result if the borrower defaults.

Loan, Fixed-rate—A loan on which the interest rate will remain the same throughout the entire loan term. Compare: Mortgage, Adjustable-rate.

Loan, G.I.—See: Loan, VA-Guaranteed.

Loan, Guaranteed—A loan in which a third party has agreed to reimburse the lender for losses that result if the borrower defaults.

Loan, Home Equity—A loan secured by the borrower's equity in the home he or she already owns. Compare: Loan, Purchase Money.

Loan, Interest-only—A loan that requires the borrower to pay only the interest during the loan term, with the principal due at the end of the term.

Loan, Interim—See: Loan, Construction.

Loan, Participation—A loan in which the lender receives some yield on the loan in addition to the interest, such as a percentage of the income generated by the property, or a share in the borrower's equity.

Loan, Permanent—See: Loan, Take-out.

Loan, Rollover—A loan in which the interest rate is renegotiated at specified intervals.

Loan, Seasoned—A loan with an established record of timely payment by the borrower.

Loan, Take-out—Long-term financing used to replace a construction loan (an interim loan) when construction has been completed. Also called a permanent loan.

Loan, VA-Guaranteed—A home loan made by an institutional lender to an eligible veteran, where the Veterans Administration will reimburse the lender for losses if the veteran borrower defaults.

Loan Correspondent—An intermediary who arranges loans of an investor's money to borrowers, and then services the loans.

Loan Fee—A loan origination fee, an assumption fee, or discount points.

Loan Term—The length of time over which a mortgage will be repaid.

Loan-to-Value Ratio (LTV)—The relationship between the loan amount and either the sales price or the appraised value of the property (whichever is less), expressed as a percentage.

Local Market—See: Primary Mortgage Market.

Lock-in Clause—A clause in a promissory note or land contract that prohibits prepayment before a specified date, or prohibits it altogether.

Lot—A parcel of land; especially, a parcel in a subdivision.

Lot and Block Description—The type of legal description used for platted property; it states the property's lot number and block number and the name of the subdivision, referring to the plat map recorded in the county where the property is located. Sometimes called a maps and plats description.

Love and Affection—The consideration often listed on a deed when real estate is conveyed between family members with no money exchanged. The law recognizes love and affection as good consideration (as distinguished from valuable consideration, which is money, goods, or services).

LTV—See: Loan-to-Value Ratio.

Majority, Age of—The age at which a person becomes legally competent; in Washington, 18 years old. See: Minor.

Maker—The person who signs a promissory note, promising to repay a debt. Compare: Payee.

Maps and Plats—See: Lot and Block Description.

Margin—In an adjustable-rate mortgage, the difference between the index rate and the interest rate charged to the borrower.

Marginal Land—Land that is of little economic value and barely repays the cost of working it.

Marketable Title—See: Title, Marketable

Market Data Approach—See: Sales Comparison Approach.

Market Price—1. The current price generally being charged for something in the marketplace. 2. The price actually paid for a property. Compare: Value, Market.

Market Value—See: Value, Market.

Master Plan—See: General Plan.

Master/Servant Relationship—A legal term for a standard employer/employee relationship.

Material Fact—Information that has a substantial negative impact on the value of the property, on a party's ability to perform, or on the purpose of the transaction.

Maturity Date—The date by which a loan is supposed to be paid off in full.

Measuring Life—See: Life Estate.

Meeting of Minds—See: Mutual Consent.

Merger—1. Uniting two or more separate properties by transferring ownership of all of them to one person. 2. When the owner of one parcel acquires title to one or more adjacent parcels.

Meridian—An imaginary line running north and south, passing through the earth's poles. Also called a longitude line.

Meridian, Principal—In the rectangular survey system, the main north-south line in a particular grid, used as the starting point in numbering the ranges.

Meridians, Guide—In the rectangular survey system, lines running north-south (parallel to the principal meridian) at 24-mile intervals.

Metes—Measurements.

Metes and Bounds Description—A legal description that starts at an identifiable point of beginning, then describes the property's boundaries in terms of courses (compass directions) and distances, ultimately returning to the point of beginning.

Mill—One-tenth of one cent; a measure used to state property tax rates in some cases. For example, a tax rate of one mill on the dollar is the same as a rate of one-tenth of one percent of the assessed value of the property.

Mineral Rights—Rights to the minerals located beneath the surface of a piece of property.

Minimum Property Requirements (MPRs)—A lender's requirements concerning the physical condition of a building, which must be met before a loan can be approved.

Minor—A person who has not yet reached the age of majority; in Washington, a person under 18.

MIP—Mortgage insurance premium; especially a premium charged in connection with an FHA-insured loan.

Misrepresentation—A false or misleading statement. See: Fraud.

MLS—Multiple Listing Service.

Monopoly—When a single entity or group has exclusive control over the production or sale of a product or service.

Monetary Policy—The Federal Reserve Board's effort to control the supply and cost of money in the United States.

Monument—A visible marker (natural or artificial) used in a survey or a metes and bounds description to establish the boundaries of a piece of property.

Mortgage—1. An instrument that creates a voluntary lien on real property to secure repayment of a debt, and which (unlike a deed of trust) does not include a power of sale, so it can only be foreclosed judicially; the parties are the mortgagor (borrower) and mortgagee (lender). 2. The term is often used more generally, to refer to either a mortgage or a deed of trust. Note: If you do not find the specific term you are looking for here under "Mortgage," check the entries under "Loan."

Mortgage, Adjustable-Rate (ARM)—A loan in which the interest rate is periodically increased or decreased to reflect changes in the cost of money. Compare: Loan, Fixed-Rate.

Mortgage, Balloon—A partially amortized mortgage loan that requires a large balloon payment at the end of the loan term.

Mortgage, Blanket—A mortgage that covers more than one parcel of property.

Mortgage, Budget—A loan in which the monthly payments include a share of the property taxes and insurance, in addition to principal and interest; the lender places the money for taxes and insurance in an impound account.

Mortgage, Chattel—An instrument that makes personal property (chattels) security for a loan. In states that have adopted the Uniform Commercial Code (including Washington), the chattel mortgage has been replaced by the security agreement.

Mortgage, Closed—A loan that cannot be paid off early.

Mortgage, Closed End—A loan that does not allow the borrower to increase the balance owed; the opposite of an open-end mortgage.

Mortgage, Direct Reduction—A loan that requires a fixed amount of principal to be paid in each payment; the total payment becomes steadily smaller, because the interest portion becomes smaller with each payment as the principal balance decreases.

Mortgage, First—The mortgage on a property that has first lien position; the one with higher lien priority than any other mortgage against the property.

Mortgage, Graduated Payment—A loan in which the payments are increased periodically during the first years of the loan term, usually according to a fixed schedule.

Mortgage, Hard Money—A mortgage given to a lender in exchange for cash, as opposed to one given in exchange for credit.

Mortgage, Junior—A mortgage that has lower lien priority than another mortgage against the same property. Sometimes called a secondary mortgage.

Mortgage, Level Payment—An amortized loan with payments that are the same amount each month, although the portion of the payment that is applied to principal steadily increases and the portion of the payment applied to interest steadily decreases. See: Loan, Amortized.

Mortgage, Open—A mortgage without a prepayment penalty.

Mortgage, Open-End—A loan that permits the borrower to reborrow the money he or she has repaid on the principal, usually up to the original loan amount, without executing a new loan agreement.

Mortgage, Package—A mortgage that is secured by certain items of personal property (such as appliances or carpeting) in addition to the real property.

Mortgage, Participation—A loan made in exchange for a share of the borrower's equity in the property, and/or a share in the earnings of the property.

Mortgage, Purchase Money—1. When a seller extends credit to a buyer to finance the purchase of the property, accepting a deed of trust or mortgage instead of cash. Sometimes called a carryback loan. 2. In a more general sense, any loan the borrower uses to buy the security property (as opposed to a loan secured by property the borrower already owns).

Mortgage, Reverse Equity—An arrangement in which a homeowner mortgages the home to a lender in exchange for a monthly check from the lender.

Mortgage, Satisfaction of—The document a mortgagee gives the mortgagor when the mortgage debt has been paid in full, acknowledging that the debt has been paid and the mortgage is no longer a lien against the property.

Mortgage, Secondary—See: Mortgage, Junior.

Mortgage, Senior—A mortgage that has higher lien priority than another mortgage against the same property; the opposite of a junior mortgage.

Mortgage, Shared Appreciation—A mortgage in which a lender is entitled to a share of the increase in the value of the property.

Mortgage, Wraparound—A purchase money loan arrangement in which the seller uses part of the buyer's payments to make the payments on an existing loan (called the underlying loan); the buyer takes title subject to the underlying loan, but does not assume it. When the security instrument used for wraparound financing is a deed of trust instead of a mortgage, it may be referred to as an all-inclusive trust deed.

Mortgage Banker—An intermediary who originates and services real estate loans on behalf of investors.

Mortgage Broker—An intermediary who brings real estate lenders and borrowers together and negotiates loan agreements between them.

Mortgage Company—A type of real estate lender that originates and services loans on behalf of large investors (acting as a mortgage banker) or for resale on the secondary mortgage market.

Mortgagee—A lender who accepts a mortgage as security for repayment of the loan.

Mortgage Loan—Any loan secured by real property, whether the actual security instrument used is a mortgage or a deed of trust.

Mortgaging Clause—A clause in a mortgage that describes the security interest given to the mortgagee.

Mortgagor—A property owner (usually a borrower) who gives a mortgage to another (usually a lender) as security for payment of an obligation.

Multiple Listing Service (MLS)—An organization of brokers who share their exclusive listings.

Mutual Consent—When all parties freely agree to the terms of a contract, without fraud, undue influence, duress, menace, or mistake. Mutual consent is achieved through offer and acceptance; it is sometimes referred to as a "meeting of the minds."

NAR—National Association of Realtors

Narrative Report—A thorough appraisal report in which the appraiser summarizes the data and the appraisal methods used, to convince the reader of the soundness of the estimate; a more comprehensive presentation than a form report or an opinion letter.

National Environmental Policy Act—See: NEPA.

National Market—See: Secondary Mortgage Market.

Natural Person—A human being, an individual (as opposed to an artificial person, such as a corporation).

Navigable Waters—A body of water large enough so that watercraft can travel on it in the course of commerce.

Negligence—Conduct that falls below the standard of care that a reasonable person would exercise under the circumstances; carelessness or recklessness.

Negotiable Instrument—An instrument containing an unconditional promise to pay a certain sum of money, to order or to bearer, on demand or at a particular time. It can be a check, promissory note, bond, draft, or stock.

Neighborhood Analysis—The gathering of data on home sizes and styles, topography, features, and amenities in a neighborhood, as part of the appraisal or property management process.

NEPA—The National Environmental Policy Act; a federal law requiring the preparation of an environmental impact statement before any governmental action that would have a significant effect on the environment.

Net Income—See: Income, Net.

Net Listing—See: Listing, Net.

Net Spendable—See: Income, Spendable.

Net Worth—An individual's personal financial assets, minus his or her personal liabilities.

Nominal Interest Rate—The interest rate stated in a promissory note. Also called the note rate or coupon rate. Compare: Annual Percentage Rate.

Non-agency—An arrangement in which a real estate licensee acts as a facilitator in a real estate transaction without assuming any agency duties.

Nonconforming Loan—See: Loan, Conforming.

Nonconforming Use—A property use that does not conform to current zoning requirements, but is allowed because the property was being used in that way before the present zoning ordinance was enacted.

Nonpossessory Interest—An interest in property that does not include the right to possess and occupy the property; an encumbrance, such as a lien or an easement.

Nonrecognition Transaction—A transaction for which a taxpayer is not required to pay taxes in the year the gain is realized.

Notarize—To have a document certified by a notary public.

Notary Public—Someone who is officially authorized to witness and certify the acknowledgment made by someone signing a legal document.

Note—See: Note, Promissory.

Note, Demand—A promissory note that is due whenever the holder of the note demands payment.

Note, Installment—A promissory note that calls for regular payments of principal and interest until the debt is fully paid.

Note, Joint—A promissory note signed by two or more persons with equal liability for payment.

Note, Promissory—A written promise to repay a debt; it may or may not be a negotiable instrument.

Note, Straight—A promissory note that calls for regular payments of interest only, so that the entire principal amount is due in one lump sum at the end of the loan term.

Notice, Actual—Actual knowledge of a fact, as opposed to knowledge imputed by law (constructive notice).

Notice, Constructive—Knowledge of a fact imputed to a person by law. A person is held to have constructive notice of something when he or she should have known it (because he or she could have learned it through reasonable diligence or an inspection of the public record), even if he or she did not actually know it.

Notice of Cessation—A notice recorded when work on a construction project has ceased (although the project is unfinished), to limit the time allowed for recording construction liens.

Notice of Completion—A notice recorded when a construction project has been completed, to limit the time allowed for recording construction liens.

Notice of Default—A notice sent by a secured creditor to the debtor, informing the debtor that he or she has breached the loan agreement.

Notice of Non-Responsibility—A notice that a property owner may record and post on the property to protect his or her title against construction liens, when someone other than the owner (such as a tenant) has ordered work on the property.

Notice of Sale—A notice stating that foreclosure proceedings have been commenced against a property.

Notice to Quit—A notice to a tenant, demanding that he or she vacate the leased property.

Notice to the World—Constructive notice of the contents of a document provided to the general public by recording the document.

Novation—1. When one party to a contract withdraws and a new party is substituted, relieving the withdrawing party of liability. 2. The substitution of a new obligation for an old one.

Nuisance—A use of property that is offensive or annoying to neighboring landowners or to the community.

Obligatory Advances—Disbursements of construction loan funds that the lender is obligated to make (by prior agreement with the borrower) when the borrower has completed certain phases of construction.

Obsolescence—Any loss in value (depreciation) due to reduced desirability and usefulness.

Obsolescence, External—Loss in value resulting from factors outside the property itself, such as proximity to an airport. Also called economic obsolescence or external inadequacy.

Obsolescence, Functional—Loss in value due to inadequate or outmoded equipment, or as a result of a poor or outmoded design.

Offer—When one person (the offeror) proposes a contract to another (the offeree); if the offeree accepts the offer, a binding contract is formed.

Offer, Illusory—An offer that is not a valid contract offer, because it requires something more than simple acceptance in order to create a contract.

Offer, Tender—See: Tender.

Offeree—One to whom a contract offer is made.

Offeror—One who makes a contract offer.

Officer—In a corporation, an executive authorized by the board of directors to manage the business of the corporation.

Off-Site Improvements—Improvements that add to the usefulness of a site but are not located directly on it, such as curbs, street lights, and sidewalks.

One-Party Listing—A listing agreement that is only effective in regards to one particular buyer.

Open House—Showing a listed home to the public for a specified period of time.

Open Listing—See: Listing, Open.

Open Market Operations—The Federal Reserve's manipulation of the money supply through the purchase and sale of government securities.

Option—A contract giving one party the right to do something, without obligating him or her to do it.

Optionee—The person to whom an option is given.

Optionor—The person who gives an option.

Option to Purchase—An option giving the optionee the right to buy property owned by the optionor at an agreed price during a specified period.

Ordinance—A law passed by a local legislative body, such as a city council. Compare: Statute.

Orientation—The placement of a house on its lot, with regard to its exposure to the sun and wind, privacy from the street, and protection from outside noise.

Origination Fee—A fee a lender charges a borrower upon making a new loan, intended to cover the administrative costs of making the loan. Also called a loan fee.

"Or More"—A provision in a promissory note that allows the borrower to prepay the debt.

Outlawed—Barred by the statute of limitations.

Overimprovement—An improvement that is more expensive than justified by the value of the land.

Overlying Right—A landowner's right to use percolating or diffused ground water.

Oversupply, Economic—A situation where there are more units available in a rental market than potential tenants who are able to pay the rent.

Oversupply, Technical—A situation where there are more units available in a rental market than potential tenants.

Ownership—Title to property, dominion over property; the rights of possession and control.

Ownership, Concurrent—When two or more individuals share ownership of one piece of property, each owning an undivided interest in the property (as in a tenancy in common or joint tenancy, or with community property). Also called co-ownership or co-tenancy.

Ownership in Severalty—Ownership by a single individual.

Panic Selling—See: Blockbusting.

Par—1. The accepted standard of comparison; the average or typical rate or amount. 2. Face value; for example, a mortgage sold at the secondary market level for 97% of par has been sold for 3% less than its face value.

Parcel—A lot or piece of real estate, especially a specified part of a larger tract.

Parallels—Imaginary lines running east and west, parallel to the equator. Also called latitude lines.

Partial Reconveyance—The instrument given to the borrower when part of the security property is released from a blanket deed of trust under a partial release clause.

Partial Release Clause—See: Release Clause.

Partial Satisfaction—The instrument given to the borrower when part of the security property is released from a blanket mortgage under a partial release clause.

Partition—The division of a property among its co-owners, so that each owns part of it in severalty; this may occur by agreement of all the co-owners (voluntary partition), or by court order (judicial partition).

Partner, General—A partner who has the authority to manage and contract for a general or limited partnership, and who is personally liable for the partnership's debts.

Partner, Limited—A partner in a limited partnership who is primarily an investor and does not participate in the management of the business, and who is not personally liable for the partnership's debts.

Partnership—An association of two or more persons to carry on a business for profit. The law regards a partnership as a group of individuals, not as an entity separate from its owners. Compare: Corporation.

Partnership, General—A partnership in which each member has an equal right to manage the business and share in the profits, as well as equal responsibility for the partnership's debts.

Partnership, Limited—A partnership made up of one or more general partners and one or more limited partners.

Partnership Property—All property that partners bring into their business at the outset or later acquire for their business; property owned as tenants in partnership. See: Tenancy in Partnership.

Party Wall—A wall located on the boundary line between two adjoining parcels of land that is used by the owners of both properties.

Patent—The instrument used to convey government land to a private individual.

Patent Defect—A problem that is readily observable in an ordinary inspection of the property. Compare: Latent Defect.

Payee—In a promissory note, the party who is entitled to be paid; the lender. Compare: Maker.

Payment Cap—A limit on the amount an ARM's payments can be increased, either during a given year, or over the entire life of the loan.

Percolation Test—A test to determine the ability of the ground to absorb or drain water; used to determine whether a site is suitable for construction, particularly for installation of a septic tank system.

Per Diem—Daily.

Periodic Tenancy—See: Tenancy, Periodic.

Personal Property—Any property that is not real property; movable property not affixed to land. Also called chattels or personalty.

Personalty—Personal property.

Personal Use Property—Property that a taxpayer owns for his or her own use (or family use), as opposed to income property, investment property, dealer property, or property used in a trade or business.

Physical Deterioration—Loss in value (depreciation) resulting from wear and tear or deferred maintenance.

Physical Life—An estimate of the time a building will remain structurally sound and capable of being used. Compare: Economic Life.

Plaintiff—The party who brings or starts a civil lawsuit; the one who sues.

Planned Unit Development (PUD)—A development (usually residential) with small, clustered lots designed to leave more open space than traditional subdivisions have.

Planning Commission—A local government agency responsible for preparing the community's general plan for development.

Plat—A detailed survey map of a subdivision, recorded in the county where the land is located. Subdivided property is often called platted property.

Plat Book—A large book containing subdivision plats, kept at the county recorder's office.

Pledge—When a debtor transfers possession of property to the creditor as security for repayment of the debt. Compare: Hypothecate.

Plot Plan—A plan showing lot dimensions and the layout of improvements (such as buildings and landscaping) on a property site.

Plottage—The increment of value that results when two or more lots are combined to produce greater value. Also called the plottage increment.

PMI—See: Insurance, Private Mortgage.

Point—One percent of the principal amount of a loan.

Point of Beginning (POB)—The starting point in a metes and bounds description; a monument or a point described by reference to a monument.

Points—See: Discount Points.

Police Power—The constitutional power of state and local governments to enact and enforce laws for the protection of the public's health, safety, morals, and general welfare.

Portfolio—The mix of investments owned by an individual or company.

Possession—1. The holding and enjoyment of property. 2. Actual physical occupation of real property.

Possessory Interest—An interest in property that includes the right to possess and occupy the property. The term includes all estates (leasehold as well as freehold), but does not include encumbrances.

Potable Water—Water that is safe to drink.

Power of Attorney—An instrument authorizing one person (the attorney in fact) to act as another's agent, to the extent stated in the instrument.

Power of Sale Clause—A clause in a deed of trust giving the trustee the right to foreclose nonjudicially (sell the debtor's property without a court action) if the borrower defaults.

Preapproval—A process that allows a prospective borrower to submit a loan application to a lender and get approved for a loan before beginning the home-buying process.

Prepayment—Paying off part or all of a loan before payment is due.

Prepayment Penalty—A penalty charged to a borrower who prepays.

Prepayment Privilege—A provision in a promissory note allowing the borrower to prepay.

Prescription—Acquiring an interest in real property (usually an easement) by using it openly and without the owner's permission for the period prescribed by statute.

Preventive Maintenance—A program of regular inspection and care of a property and its fixtures, allowing the prevention of potential problems or their immediate repair.

Price Fixing—The cooperative setting of prices by competing firms; price fixing is an automatic violation of antitrust laws.

Prima Facie—At first sight; on the face of it.

Primary Mortgage Market—The market in which mortgage loans are originated, where lenders make loans to borrowers. Also called the local market. Compare: Secondary Mortgage Market.

Prime Rate—The interest rate a bank charges its largest and most desirable customers.

Principal—1. One who grants another person (an agent) authority to represent him or her in dealings with third parties. 2. One of the parties to a transaction (such as a buyer or seller), as opposed to those who are involved as agents or employees (such as a broker or escrow agent). 3. In regard to a loan, the amount originally borrowed, as opposed to the interest.

Principal Meridian—See: Meridian, Principal.

Principal Residence Property—Real property that is the owner's home, his or her main dwelling. Under the federal income tax laws, a person can only have one principal residence at a time.

Prior Appropriation—See: Appropriation, Prior.

Private Mortgage Insurance—See: Insurance, Private Mortgage.

Privity—The relationship between two persons who have simultaneous or successive interests in a contract or a property. For example, in an easement agreement, the dominant and servient tenants are in privity to one another; so are the seller and buyer of a property.

Probate—A judicial proceeding in which the validity of a will is established and the executor is authorized to distribute the estate property; or, when there is no valid will, in which an administrator is appointed to distribute the estate to the heirs.

Probate Court—A court that oversees the distribution of property under a will or intestate succession.

Procuring Cause—The real estate agent who is primarily responsible for bringing about a sale; for example, by negotiating the agreement between the buyer and seller.

Profit—A nonpossessory interest; the right to enter another person's land and take something (such as timber or minerals) away from it.

Progression, Principle of—An appraisal principle which holds that a property of lesser value tends to be worth more when it is located in an area with properties of greater value than it would be if located elsewhere. The opposite of the principle of regression.

Promisee—Someone who has been promised something; someone who is supposed to receive the benefit of a contractual promise.

Promisor—Someone who has made a contractual promise to another.

Promissory Note—See: Note, Promissory.

Property—1. The rights of ownership in a thing, such as the right to use, possess, transfer, or encumber it. 2. Something that is owned.

Property Held for Production of Income—See: Income Property.

Property Management Agreement—A document that creates an agency relationship between a property owner and property manager and establishes the terms and conditions of the relationship.

Property Management Plan—An outline for a property manager's strategy in meeting the owner's financial goals.

Property Manager—A person hired by a property owner to administer, merchandise, and maintain property, especially rental property.

Property Tax—See: Tax, Property.

Property Used in a Trade or Business—Property such as business sites and factories used in a taxpayer's trade or business.

Proprietorship, Individual or Sole—A business owned and operated by one person.

Proration—The process of dividing or allocating something (especially a sum of money or an expense) proportionately, according to time, interest, or benefit.

Public Record—The official collection of legal documents that individuals have filed with the county recorder in order to make the information contained in them public.

Public Use—A use that benefits the public. For a condemnation action to be constitutional, it must be for a public use.

Puffing—Superlative statements about the quality of a property that should not be considered assertions of fact.

Purchase and Sale Agreement—A contract in which a seller promises to convey title to real property to a buyer in exchange for the purchase price. Also called an earnest money agreement, deposit receipt, sales contract, or contract of sale.

Purchaser's Assignment of Contract and Deed—The instrument used to assign the vendee's equitable interest in a contract to another.

Qualified Acceptance—See: Counteroffer.

Qualifying Standards—The standards a lender requires a loan applicant to meet before a loan will be approved. Also called underwriting standards.

Quantity Survey Method—In appraisal, a method of estimating the replacement cost of a structure; it involves a detailed estimate of the quantities and cost of materials and labor, and overhead expenses such as insurance and contractor's profit.

Quiet Enjoyment—Use and possession of real property without interference from the previous owner, the lessor, or anyone else claiming title. See: Covenant of Quiet Enjoyment.

Quiet Title Action—A lawsuit to determine who has title to a piece of property, or to remove a cloud from the title.

Quitclaim Deed— See: Deed, Quitclaim.

Range—In the rectangular survey system, a strip of land six miles wide, running north and south.

Range Lines—In the rectangular survey system, the north-south lines (meridians) located six miles apart.

Ratify—To confirm or approve after the fact an act that was not authorized when it was performed.

Ready, Willing, and Able—A buyer is ready, willing, and able if he makes an offer that meets the seller's stated terms, and has the contractual capacity and financial resources to complete the transaction.

Real Estate—See: Real Property.

Real Estate Brokerage—A real estate broker's business; the business of bringing a buyer and seller together and negotiating a sales contract between the two parties.

Real Estate Brokerage Relationships Act—A Washington state law that significantly changes traditional agency law in regards to real estate transactions. It governs when and how real estate agency relationships are created and terminated, the duties owed by real estate licensees to the parties to a real estate transaction, and when and how agency disclosures are to be made.

Real Estate Commission—A commission appointed by the Governor, consisting of the Director of the Department of Licensing and six commissioners; responsible for preparing and conducting the real estate licensing examinations.

Real Estate Contract—1. A purchase and sale agreement. 2. A land contract. 3. Any contract having to do with real property.

Real Estate Investment Trust (REIT)—A real estate investment business with at least 100 investors, organized as a trust.

Real Estate Salesperson—A person who is licensed to work for and represent a broker in real estate transactions.

Real Estate Settlement Procedures Act—See: RESPA.

Realization—For income tax purposes, when a gain is separated from an asset, and therefore becomes taxable.

Real Property—Land and everything attached to or appurtenant to it. Also called realty or real estate. Compare: Personal Property.

Real Property Transfer Disclosure Statement—See: Seller Disclosure Statement.

Realtor—A real estate agent who is an active member of a state and local real estate board that is affiliated with the National Association of Realtors.

Realty—See: Real Property.

Reasonable Use Doctrine—A limitation of water rights, holding that there is no right to waste water.

Recapture—An investor's recovery of money invested in real estate.

Recapture Clause—1. A provision in a percentage lease that allows the landlord to terminate the lease and regain the premises if a certain minimum volume of business is not maintained. 2. A provision in a ground lease that allows the tenant to purchase the property after a specified period of time.

Receiver—A person appointed by a court to manage and look after property or funds involved in litigation.

Reconciliation—The final step in an appraisal, when the appraiser assembles and interprets the data in order to arrive at a final value estimate. Also called correlation.

Reconveyance—Releasing the security property from the lien created by a deed of trust, by recording a deed of reconveyance.

Recording—Filing a document at the county recorder's office, so that it will be placed in the public record.

Recording Numbers—The numbers stamped on documents when they're recorded, used to identify and locate the documents in the public record.

Rectangular Survey System—A system of grids, made up of range and township lines that divide the land into townships, which are further subdivided into sections; a particular property is identified by its location within a particular section, township, and range. Also called the government survey system.

Redemption—1. When a defaulting borrower prevents foreclosure by paying the full amount of the debt, plus costs. 2. When a mortgagor regains the property after foreclosure by paying whatever the foreclosure sale purchaser paid for it, plus interest and expenses.

Redemption, Equitable Right of—The right of a mortgagor to redeem property prior to the foreclosure sale.

Redemption, Statutory Right of—The right of a mortgagor to get his or her property back after a foreclosure sale.

Redlining—When a lender refuses to make loans secured by property in a certain neighborhood because of the racial or ethnic composition of the neighborhood.

Reformation—A legal action to correct a mistake, such as a typographical error, in a deed or other document. The court will order the execution of a correction deed.

Regression, Principle of—An appraisal principle which holds that a valuable property surrounded by properties of lesser value will tend to be worth less than it would be in a different location; the opposite of the principle of progression.

Regulation Z—The Federal Reserve Board's regulation that implements the Truth in Lending Act.

Reinstate—To prevent foreclosure by curing the default.

Release—1. To give up a legal right. 2. A document in which a legal right is given up.

Release, Lien—A document removing a lien, given to the borrower by the lender, once a mortgage or deed of trust has been paid off in full.

Release Clause—1. A clause in a blanket mortgage or deed of trust which allows the borrower to get part of the security property released from the lien when a certain portion of the debt has been paid or other conditions are fulfilled. Often called a partial release clause. 2. A clause in a land contract providing for a deed to a portion of the land to be delivered when a certain portion of the contract price has been paid. Also known as a deed release provision.

Reliction—When a body of water gradually recedes, exposing land that was previously under water. Also called dereliction.

Remainder—A future interest that becomes possessory when a life estate terminates, and that is held by someone other than the grantor of the life estate; as opposed to a reversion, which is a future interest held by the grantor.

Remainderman—The person who has an estate in remainder.

Remaining Economic Life—See: Economic Life.

Remise—To give up; a term used in quitclaim deeds.

Rent—Compensation paid by a tenant to the landlord in exchange for the possession and use of the property.

Rent, Contract—The rent that is actually being paid on property that is currently leased.

Rent, Economic—The rent that a property would be earning if it were available for lease in the current market.

Rent, Ground—The earnings of improved property attributed to the land itself, after allowance is made for the earnings attributable to the improvement.

Rent Roll—A report on rent collections; a list of the total amount of rent earned, both collected and uncollected.

Rental Schedule—A list of rental rates for the units in a given building.

Replacement Cost—See: Cost, Replacement.

Reproduction Cost—See: Cost, Reproduction.

Rescission—When a contract is terminated and each party gives anything acquired under the contract back to the other party. (The verb form is rescind.) Compare: Cancellation.

Reservation—A right retained by a grantor when conveying property; for example, mineral rights, an easement, or a life estate can be reserved in the deed.

Reserve Account—See: Impound Account.

Reserve Requirements—The percentage of deposits commercial banks must keep on reserve with the Federal Reserve Bank.

Reserves for Replacement—For income-producing property, regular allowances set aside to pay for the replacement of structures and equipment that are expected to wear out.

Resident Manager—A salaried manager of a single apartment building or complex, who resides on the property; unlike a property manager, a resident manager is not required to have a real estate license.

Residual—The property value remaining after the economic life of the improvements has been exhausted.

Residual Income—See: Income, Residual.

Residuals—Commissions in the form of delayed payments (when a part of the commission is paid with each installment on an installment sales contract, for example).

RESPA—The Real Estate Settlement Procedures Act; a federal law that requires lenders to disclose certain information about closing costs to loan applicants.

Restitution—Restoring something (especially money) that a person was unjustly deprived of.

Restriction—A limitation on the use of real property.

Restriction, Deed—A restrictive covenant in a deed.

Restriction, Private—A restriction imposed on property by a previous owner, a neighbor, or the subdivision developer; a restrictive covenant or a condition in a deed.

Restriction, Public—A law or regulation limiting or regulating the use of real property.

Restrictive Covenant—See: Covenant, Restrictive.

Retainer—A fee paid up front to a licensee when entering into an real estate agency (usually a buyer agency) relationship.

Return—A profit from an investment.

Reversion—A future interest that becomes possessory when a temporary estate (such as a life estate) terminates, and that is held by the grantor (or his or her successors in interest). Compare: Remainder.

Rezone—An amendment to a zoning ordinance, usually changing the uses allowed in a particular zone. Also called a zoning amendment.

Right of First Refusal—A right that gives the holder the first opportunity to purchase or lease a particular parcel of real property, should the owner decide to sell or lease it.

Right of Way—An easement that gives the holder the right to cross another person's land.

Riparian Land—Land that is adjacent to or crossed by a body of water. Compare: Littoral Land.

Riparian Rights—The water rights of a landowner whose property is adjacent to or crossed by a body of water. Compare: Appropriation, Prior.

Risk Analysis—See: Underwriting.

Rule of Capture—See: Capture, Rule of.

Running with the Land—Binding or benefiting the successive owners of a piece of property, rather than terminating when a particular owner transfers his or her interest. Usually said in reference to an easement or a restrictive covenant.

Safety Clause—See: Extender Clause.

Sale-Leaseback—A form of real estate financing in which the owner of industrial or commercial property sells the property and leases it back from the buyer; in addition to certain tax advantages, the seller/lessee obtains more cash through the sale than would normally be possible by borrowing and mortgaging the property, since lenders will not often lend 100% of the value.

Sales Comparison Approach—One of the three main methods of appraisal, in which the sales prices of comparable properties are used to estimate the value of the subject property. Also called the market data approach.

Salesperson—See: Real Estate Salesperson.

Sandwich Lease—See: Sublease.

Satisfaction of Mortgage—See: Mortgage, Satisfaction of.

Savings and Loan Association—A type of financial institution that emphasizes home mortgage loans.

Savings Bank—A type of financial institution that emphasizes consumer loans and home mortgages.

Scarcity—A limited or inadequate supply of something; one of the four elements of value (along with utility, demand, and transferability).

Secondary Financing—Money borrowed to pay part of the required downpayment or closing costs for a first loan, when the second loan is secured by the same property that secures the first loan.

Secondary Mortgage Market—The market in which investors (including Fannie Mae, Freddie Mac, and Ginnie Mae) purchase real estate loans from lenders; also called the national market.

Secret Profit—A financial benefit that an agent takes from a transaction without informing the principal.

Section—In the rectangular survey system, a section is one mile square and contains 640 acres. There are 36 sections in a township.

Securities—Investment instruments, such as stocks and bonds.

Security Agreement—Under the Uniform Commercial Code, a document that creates a lien on personal property being used to secure a loan.

Security Deposit—Money a tenant gives a landlord at the beginning of the tenancy to protect the landlord in case the tenant defaults; the landlord may retain all or part of the deposit to cover unpaid rent or repair costs at the end of the tenancy.

Security Instrument—A document that creates a voluntary lien, to secure repayment of a loan; for debts secured by real property, it is either a mortgage or a deed of trust.

Security Interest—The interest a creditor may acquire in the debtor's property to ensure that the debt will be paid.

Security Property—The property that a borrower gives a lender a voluntary lien against, so that the lender can foreclose if the borrower defaults.

Seisin—Actual possession of a freehold estate; ownership.

Seller Disclosure Statement—A form that state law requires a residential seller to give the buyer, disclosing problems with the property. Formerly called a transfer disclosure statement.

Selling Broker—The broker responsible for procuring a buyer for real estate; may represent either the seller or the buyer.

SEPA—The State Environmental Policy Act; a Washington state law analogous to NEPA that requires environmental impact statements before government actions that would have a significant effect on the environment.

Separate Property—Property owned by a married person that is not community property; includes property acquired before marriage or by gift or inheritance after marriage.

Servant—See: Master/Servant Relationship.

Setback Requirements—Provisions in a zoning ordinance that do not allow structures to be built within a certain distance of the property line.

Settlement—1. An agreement between the parties to a civil lawsuit, in which the plaintiff agrees to drop the suit in exchange for money or the defendant's promise to do or refrain from doing something. 2. Closing.

Settlement Statement—A document that presents a final, detailed accounting for a real estate transaction, listing each party's debits and credits and the amount each will receive or be required to pay at closing. Also called a closing statement.

Severalty—See: Ownership in Severalty.

Severance—1. Termination of a joint tenancy. 2. The permanent removal of a natural attachment, fixture, or appurtenance from real property, which transforms the item into personal property.

Severance, Constructive—When a landowner enters into a contract to sell an appurtenance or natural attachment, the contract constructively severs the item from the land—making it the personal property of the buyer—even before the buyer has actually taken it off the land.

Shareholder—An individual who holds ownership shares (shares of stock) in a corporation, and has limited liability in regard to the corporation's debts. Also called a stockholder.

Sheriff's Deed—See: Deed, Sheriff's.

Sheriff's Sale—A foreclosure sale held after a judicial foreclosure. Sometimes called an execution sale.

Sherman Act—A federal antitrust law prohibiting any agreement that has the effect of a restraint on trade, such as price fixing and tie-in arrangements.

Shoreline Management Act—A Washington state law regulating development within 200 feet of coastal shores.

Shortage, Economic—A situation where there are more potential tenants who are financially able to rent than there are available units in a rental market.

Shortage, Technical—A situation where there are more potential tenants than units available in a rental market.

Short Plat—The subdivision of a parcel of land into four or fewer lots.

Site Analysis—The gathering of data about the physical characteristics of a property and other factors affecting its use or title, as part of the appraisal process.

Special Agent—See: Agent, Special.

Special Assessment—A tax levied only against the properties that have benefited from a public improvement (such as a sewer or a street light), to cover the cost of the improvement; creates a special assessment lien.

Special Exception Permit—See: Conditional Use Permit.

Specific Lien—See: Lien, Specific.

Specific Performance—A legal remedy in which a court orders someone who has breached to actually perform the contract as agreed, rather than simply paying money damages.

Special Warranty Deed—See: Deed, Special Warranty.

Square Foot Method—In appraisal, a method of estimating replacement cost by calculating the square foot cost of replacing the subject home.

Stable Monthly Income—A loan applicant's gross monthly income that meets the lender's tests of quality and durability.

State Environmental Policy Act—See: SEPA.

Statement of Disbursements—A list of all of a property's expenses incurred during a specific operating period.

Statement of Operations—A periodic report showing the total money received and disbursed during, and the overall condition of the property for a given period.

Statute—A law enacted by a state legislature or the U.S. Congress. Compare: Ordinance.

Statute of Frauds—A law that requires certain types of contracts to be in writing and signed in order to be enforceable.

Statute of Limitations—A law requiring a particular type of lawsuit to be filed within a specified time after the event giving rise to the suit occurred.

Statutory Redemption Period—The period required by law (one year in Washington) following a sheriff's sale in which a foreclosed borrower may redeem a property.

Steering—Channeling prospective buyers or tenants to or away from particular neighborhoods based on their race, religion, national origin, or ancestry.

Stockholder—See: Shareholder.

Straight Note—See: Note, Straight.

Subagent—A person that an agent has delegated authority to, so that the subagent can assist in carrying out the principal's orders; the agent of an agent.

Subcontractor—A contractor who, at the request of the general contractor, provides a specific service, such as plumbing or drywalling, in connection with the overall construction project.

Subdivision—1. A piece of land divided into two or more parcels. 2. A residential development.

Subdivision Plat—See: Plat.

Subdivision Regulations—State and local laws that must be complied with before land can be subdivided.

Subjacent Support—See: Support, Subjacent.

Subject to—When a purchaser takes property subject to a trust deed or mortgage, he or she is not personally liable for paying off the loan; in case of default, however, the property can still be foreclosed on.

Sublease—When a tenant grants someone else the right to possession of the leased property for part of the remainder of the lease term; as opposed to an assignment, where the tenant gives up possession for the entire remainder of the lease term. Also called a sandwich lease.

Subordination Clause—A provision in a mortgage or deed of trust that permits a later mortgage or deed of trust to have higher lien priority than the one containing the clause.

Subrogation—The substitution of one person in the place of another with reference to a lawful claim or right. For instance, a title company that pays a claim on behalf of its insured, the property owner, is subrogated to any claim the owner successfully undertakes against the former owner.

Substitution, Principle of—A principle of appraisal holding that the maximum value of a property is set by how much it would cost to obtain another property that is equally desirable, assuming that there would not be a long delay or significant incidental expenses involved in obtaining the substitute.

Substitution of Liability—A buyer wishing to assume an existing loan may apply for the lender's approval; once approved, the buyer assumes liability for repayment of the loan, and the original borrower (the seller) is released from liability.

Succession—Acquiring property by will or inheritance.

Sufferance—Acquiescence, implied permission, or passive consent through a failure to act, as opposed to express permission.

Summary of Operations—The key portion of a property manager's statement of operations, which summarizes income and expenses.

Supply and Demand, Principle of—A principle holding that value varies directly with demand and inversely with supply; that is, the greater the demand the greater the value, and the greater the supply the lower the value.

Support, Lateral—The support that piece of land receives from the land adjacent to it.

Support, Subjacent—The support that the surface of a piece of land receives from the land beneath it.

Support Rights—The right to have one's land supported by the land adjacent to it and beneath it.

Surrender—Giving up an estate (such as a life estate or leasehold) before it has expired.

Survey—The process of precisely measuring the boundaries and determining the area of a parcel of land.

Survivorship, Right of—A characteristic of joint tenancy; surviving joint tenants automatically acquire a deceased joint tenant's interest in the property.

Syndicate—An association formed to operate an investment business. A syndicate is not a recognized legal entity; it can be organized as a corporation, partnership, or trust.

Tacking—When successive periods of use or possession by more than one person are added together to make up the period required for prescription or adverse possession.

Taking—When the government acquires private property for public use by condemnation, it's called "a taking." The term is also used in inverse condemnation lawsuits, when a government action has made private property useless.

Tax, Ad Valorem—A tax assessed on the value of property.

Tax, Excise—A state tax levied on every sale of real estate, to be paid by the seller.

Tax, General Real Estate—An annual ad valorem tax levied on real property.

Tax, Improvement—See: Special Assessment.

Tax, Progressive—A tax, such as the federal income tax, that imposes a higher tax rate on a taxpayer who earns a higher income.

Tax, Property—1. The general real estate tax. 2. Any ad valorem tax levied on real or personal property.

Tax Credit—A credit that is subtracted directly from the amount of tax owed. Compare: Deduction.

Tax Deed—See: Deed, Tax.

Tax-Free Exchange—A transaction in which one piece of property is traded for a piece of like-kind property; if the property involved is held for investment or the production of income, or used in a trade or business, tax on the gain may be deferred.

Tax Sale—Sale of property after foreclosure of a tax lien.

Tenancy—Lawful possession of real property; an estate.

Tenancy, Joint—A form of concurrent ownership in which the co-owners have unity of time, title, interest, and possession and the right of survivorship.

Tenancy, Periodic—A leasehold estate that continues for successive periods of equal length (such as from week to week or month to month), until terminated by proper notice from either party. Also called a month-to-month (or week-to-week, etc.) tenancy. Compare: Estate for Years.

Tenancy, Term—See: Estate for Years.

Tenancy at Sufferance—When a tenant (who entered into possession of the property lawfully) stays on after the lease ends without the landlord's permission.

Tenancy at Will—When a tenant is in possession with the owner's permission, but there's no definite lease term; as when a landlord allows a holdover tenant to remain on the premises until another tenant is found.

Tenancy by the Entireties—A form of joint ownership of property by husband and wife (in some states that don't use a community property system).

Tenancy for Years—See: Estate for Years.

Tenancy in Common—A form of concurrent ownership in which two or more persons each have an undivided interest in the entire property, but no right of survivorship. Compare: Tenancy, Joint.

Tenancy in Partnership—The form of concurrent ownership in which general partners own partnership property, whether or not title to the property is in the partnership's name. Each partner has an equal undivided interest, but no right to transfer the interest to someone outside the partnership.

Tenant—Someone in lawful possession of real property; especially, someone who has leased property from the owner.

Tenant, Dominant—A person who has easement rights on another's property; either the owner of a dominant tenement, or someone who has an easement in gross.

Tenant, Holdover—A lessee who remains in possession of the property after the lease term has expired.

Tenant, Life—Someone who owns a life estate. See: Estate for Life.

Tenant, Servient—The owner of a servient tenement—that is, someone whose property is burdened by an easement.

Tender—An unconditional offer by one of parties to a contract to perform his or her part of the agreement; made when the offeror believes the other party is breaching, it establishes the offeror's right to sue if the other party doesn't accept it. Also called a tender offer.

Tenements—Everything of a permanent nature associated with a piece of land that is ordinarily transferred with the land. Tenements are both tangible (buildings, for example) and intangible (air rights, for example).

Tenement, Dominant—Property that receives the benefit of an easement appurtenant.

Tenement, Servient—Property burdened by an easement. In other words, the owner of the servient tenement (the servient tenant) must allow someone who has an easement (the dominant tenant) to use the property.

Tenure—The period of time during which a person holds certain rights with respect to a piece of real property.

Term—A prescribed period of time; especially, the length of time a borrower has to pay off a loan, or the duration of a lease.

Testament—See: Will.

Testate—Refers to someone who has died and left a will. Compare: Intestate.

Testator—A person who makes a will. (If it is a woman, she may be referred to as a testatrix.)

Third Party—1. A person seeking to deal with a principal through an agent. 2. In a transaction, someone who is not one of the principals.

Tie-in Arrangements—An agreement to sell one product, only on the condition that the buyer also purchases a different product.

Tight Money Market—When loan funds are scarce, leading lenders to charge high interest rates and discount points.

TILA—Truth in Lending Act.

Time is of the Essence—A clause in a contract that means performance on the exact dates specified is an essential element of the contract; failure to perform on time is a material breach.

Title—Lawful ownership of real property. Also, the deed or other document that is evidence of that ownership.

Title, Abstract of—A brief, chronological summary of the recorded documents affecting title to a particular piece of real property.

Title, After-Acquired—Title acquired by a grantor after he or she attempted to convey property he or she didn't own.

Title, Chain of—1. The chain of deeds (and other documents) transferring title to a piece of property from one owner to the next, as disclosed in the public record. 2. A listing of all recorded documents affecting title to a particular property; more complete than an abstract.

Title, Clear—A good title to property, free from encumbrances or defects; marketable title.

Title, Color of—Title that appears to be good title, but which in fact is not; commonly based on a defective instrument, such as an invalid deed.

Title, Equitable—The vendee's interest in property under a land contract. Also called an equitable interest.

Title, Legal—The vendor's interest in property under a land contract.

Title, Marketable—Title free and clear of objectionable liens, encumbrances, or defects, so that a reasonably prudent person with full knowledge of the facts would not hesitate to purchase the property.

Title, Slander of—Disparaging or inaccurate statements, written or oral, concerning a person's title to property.

Title Company—A title insurance company.

Title Insurance—See: Insurance, Title.

Title Plant—A duplicate (usually microfilmed) of a county's public record, maintained by a title company at its offices for use in title searches.

Title Report, Preliminary—A report issued by a title company, disclosing the condition of the title to a specific piece of property, before the actual title insurance policy is issued.

Title Search—An inspection of the public record to determine all rights and encumbrances affecting title to a piece of property.

Title Theory—The theory holding that a mortgage or deed of trust gives the lender legal title to the security property while the debt is being repaid. Compare: Lien Theory.

Topography—The contours of the surface of the land (level, hilly, steep, etc.).

Tort—A breach of a duty imposed by law (as opposed to a duty voluntarily taken on in a contract) that causes harm to another person, giving the injured person the right to sue the one who breached the duty. Also called a civil wrong (in contrast to a criminal wrong, a crime).

Total Finance Charge—Under the Truth in Lending Act, the total finance charge on a loan includes interest, any discount points paid by the borrower, the loan origination fee, and mortgage insurance costs.

Township—In the rectangular survey system, a parcel of land 6 miles square, containing 36 sections; the intersection of a range and a township tier.

Township Lines—Lines running east-west, spaced six miles apart, in the rectangular survey system.

Township Tier—In the rectangular survey system, a strip of land running east-west, six miles wide and bounded on the north and south by township lines.

Tract—1. A piece of land of undefined size. 2. In the rectangular survey system, an area made up of 16 townships; 24 miles on each side.

Trade Fixtures—Articles of personal property annexed to real property by a tenant for use in his or her trade or business, which the tenant is allowed to remove at the end of the lease.

Transaction Folder—A record of all documents associated with a particular transaction, such as the listing agreement, the purchase and sale agreement, the settlement statement, and any modifications or addenda.

Transferability—If an object is transferable, then ownership and possession of that object can be conveyed from one person to another. Transferability is one of the four elements of value, along with utility, scarcity, and demand.

Trespass—An unlawful physical invasion of property owned by another.

Trust—A legal arrangement in which title to property (or funds) is vested in one or more trustees, who manage the property on behalf of the trust's beneficiaries, in accordance with instructions set forth in the document establishing the trust.

Trust Account—A bank account, separate from a real estate broker's personal and business accounts, used to segregate trust funds from the broker's own funds.

Trust Deed—See: Deed of Trust.

Trustee—1. A person appointed to manage a trust on behalf of the beneficiaries. 2. A neutral third party appointed in a deed of trust to handle the nonjudicial foreclosure process in case of default.

Trustee in Bankruptcy—An individual appointed by the court to handle the assets of a person in bankruptcy.

Trustee's Sale—A nonjudicial foreclosure sale under a deed of trust.

Trust Funds—Money or things of value received by an agent, not belonging to the agent but being held for the benefit of others.

Trustor—The borrower in a deed of trust. Also called the grantor.

Truth in Lending Act—A federal law that requires lenders and credit arrangers to make disclosures concerning loan costs (including the total finance charge and the annual percentage rate) to consumer loan applicants.

Underimprovement—An improvement which, because of deficiency in cost or size, is not the most profitable use of the land; not the highest and best use.

Underwriting—In real estate lending, the process of evaluating a loan application to determine the probability that the applicant would repay the loan, and matching the risk to an appropriate rate of return. Sometimes called risk analysis.

Undivided Interest—See: Interest, Undivided.

Undue Influence—Exerting excessive pressure on someone so as to overpower the person's free will and prevent him or her from making a rational or prudent decision; often involves abusing a relationship of trust.

Unenforceable—See: Contract, Unenforceable.

Uniform Settlement Statement—A settlement statement required for any transaction involving a loan that is subject to the Real Estate Settlement Procedures Act (RESPA).

Uniform Standards of Professional Appraisal Practice—Guidelines for appraisers adopted by the Appraisal Foundation, a nonprofit organization of professional appraiser associations.

Unilateral Contract—See: Contract, Unilateral.

Unit-in-Place Method—In appraisal, a method of estimating replacement cost by estimating the cost of each component (foundation, roof, etc.), then adding the costs of all components together.

Unity of Interest—In reference to concurrent ownership, when each co-owner has an equal interest (equal share of ownership) in the property. A requirement for joint tenancy.

Unity of Possession—When property is owned concurrently by two or more individuals, each co-owner is equally entitled to possession of the entire property, because their interests are undivided. This is a requirement for joint tenancy, but it is also a characteristic of all concurrent ownership.

Unity of Time—In reference to concurrent ownership, when each co-owner acquired title at the same time. A requirement for joint tenancy.

Unity of Title—In reference to concurrent ownership, when each co-owner acquired title through the same instrument (deed, will, or court order). A requirement for joint tenancy.

Universal Agent—See: Agent, Universal.

Unjust Enrichment—An undeserved benefit; a court generally will not allow a remedy (such as forfeiture of a land contract) if it would result in the unjust enrichment of one of the parties.

Unlawful Detainer—A summary legal action to regain possession of real property; especially, a suit filed by a landlord to evict a defaulting tenant.

Useful Life—See: Economic Life.

Use Value—See: Value, Use.

Usury—Charging an interest rate that exceeds legal limits.

Utility—The ability of an object to satisfy some need and/or arouse a desire for possession; one of the four elements of value, along with scarcity, demand, and transferability.

VA—Department of Veterans Affairs.

Vacancy Factor—See: Bad Debt/Vacancy Factor.

VA Entitlement—The guaranty amount that a particular veteran is entitled to.

Valid—The legal classification of a contract that is binding and enforceable in a court of law.

Valuable Consideration—See: Consideration.

Valuation—See: Appraisal.

Value—The present worth of future benefits.

Value, Assessed—The value placed on property by the taxing authority (the county assessor, for example) for the purposes of taxation.

Value, Face—The value of an instrument, such as a promissory note or a security, that is indicated on the face of the instrument itself.

Value, Market—The most probable price which a property should bring in a competitive and open market under all conditions requisite to a fair sale, the buyer and seller each acting prudently and knowledgeably, and assuming the price is not affected by undue stimulus. (This is the definition from the Uniform Standards of Professional Appraisal Practice.) Market value is also called fair market value, value in exchange, or objective value. Compare: Market Price.

Value, Subjective—The value of a property in the eyes of a particular person, as opposed to its market value (objective value).

Value, Utility—The value of a property to its owner or to a user. (A form of subjective value.) Also called value in use.

Value in Exchange—See: Value, Market.

Value in Use—See: Value, Utility.

Variable Expense—A property management expense that varies depending on current management needs (e.g., repair expenses).

Variable Interest Rate—A loan interest rate that can be adjusted periodically during the loan term, as in the case of an adjustable-rate mortgage.

Variance—Permission (from the local zoning authority) to use property or build a structure in a way that violates the strict terms of the zoning ordinance.

Vendee—A buyer or purchaser; particularly, someone buying property under a land contract.

Vendor—A seller; particularly, someone selling property by means of a land contract.

Verify—1. To confirm or substantiate. 2. To confirm under oath.

Vested—A person who has a present, fixed right or interest in property has a vested right or interest, even though he or she may not have the right to possession until sometime in the future. For example, a remainderman's interest in the property vests when it is granted (not when the life estate ends).

Vicarious Liability—See: Liability, Vicarious.

Void—Having no legal force or effect.

Voidable—See: Contract, Voidable.

Voluntary Lien—See: Lien, Voluntary.

Voucher System—In construction lending, a system in which the general contractor gives subcontractors vouchers (instead of cash) for services rendered. The vouchers, which are statements attesting to the sum owed, are then presented to the construction lender for payment.

Waiver—The voluntary relinquishment or surrender of a right.

Warrant System—In construction lending, a system in which bills are presented to the lender for direct payment to the supplier or laborer.

Warranty, Implied—In a sale or lease of property, a guarantee created by operation of law, whether or not the seller or landlord intended to offer it.

Warranty Deed—See: Deed, Warranty.

Warranty of Habitability—See: Habitability, Implied Warranty of.

Washington Human Rights Commission—The state agency that enforces the Law Against Discrimination.

Washington Land Development Act—A Washington state consumer protection law that requires a subdivision developer to provide a Public Offering Statement (which contains information about the development) to prospective purchasers.

Washington Law Against Discrimination—A state law that is stricter than the Fair Housing Act in its prohibition against discrimination in housing and other transactions on the basis of race, creed, color, national origin, sex, marital status, familial status, disability, or use of a service animal.

Waste—Destruction, damage, or material alteration of property by someone in possession who holds less than a fee estate (such as a life tenant or lessee), or by a co-owner.

Water Rights—The right to use water from a body of water. See: Appropriation, Prior; Littoral Rights; Riparian Rights.

Water Table—The level at which water may be found, either at the surface or underground.

Wild Deed—See: Deed, Wild.

Will—A person's stipulation regarding how his or her estate should be disposed of after he or she dies. Also called a testament.

Will, Formal—A will that meets the statutory requirements for validity; it must be in writing and signed in the presence of at least two competent witnesses.

Will, Holographic—A will written entirely in the testator's handwriting, which may be valid even if it was not witnessed. Not recognized in Washington.

Will, Nuncupative—An oral will made on the testator's deathbed; valid only as to bequests of personal property worth under $1,000.

Without Recourse—A qualified or conditional endorsement on a negotiable instrument, which relieves the endorser of liability under the instrument.

Wraparound Financing—See: Mortgage, Wraparound.

Writ of Attachment—See: Attachment.

Writ of Execution—A court order directing a public officer (usually the sheriff) to seize and sell property to satisfy a debt.

Writ of Possession—A court order issued after an unlawful detainer action, informing the tenant that he or she must vacate the landlord's property within a specified period or be forcibly removed by the sheriff.

Yield—The return of profit to an investor on an investment, stated as a percentage of the amount invested.

Zone—An area of land set off for a particular use or uses, subject to certain restrictions.

Zoning—Government regulation of the uses of property within specified areas.

Zoning Amendment—See: Rezone.